THE
unofficial GUIDE®
TO California
with Kids

5TH EDITION

THE *unofficial* GUIDE®

TO California with Kids

5TH EDITION

COLLEEN DUNN BATES *and*
SUSAN LATEMPA

WILEY

Please note that prices fluctuate in the course of time and that travel information changes under the impact of many factors that influence the travel industry. We therefore suggest that you write or call ahead for confirmation when making your travel plans. Every effort has been made to ensure the accuracy of information throughout this book, and the contents of this publication are believed to be correct at the time of printing. Nevertheless, the publishers cannot accept responsibility for errors or omissions, for changes in details given in this guide, or for the consequences of any reliance on the information provided by the same. Assessments of attractions and so forth are based upon the authors' own experiences; therefore, descriptions given in this guide necessarily contain an element of subjective opinion, which may not reflect the publisher's opinion or dictate a reader's own experience on another occasion. Readers are invited to write the publisher with ideas, comments, and suggestions for future editions.

Published by:
John Wiley & Sons, Inc.
111 River Street
Hoboken, NJ 07030-5774

Produced by Menasha Ridge Press

Cover design by Michael J. Freeland

Interior design by Vertigo Design

For information on our other products and services or to obtain technical support, please contact our Customer Care Department within the United States at 800-762-2974, outside the United States at 317-572-3993, or by fax at 317-572-4002.

John Wiley & Sons, Inc., also publishes its books in a variety of electronic formats. Some content that appears in print may not be available in electronic formats.

ISBN 0-471-79031-1

Manufactured in the United States of America

5 4 3 2 1

CONTENTS

LIST *of* MAPS

ACKNOWLEDGMENTS

THANKS TO LITERARY AGENT Betsy Amster for bringing us a project that has been so rewarding for our entire families. Thanks to Pam Brandon, author of *The Unofficial Guide to Florida with Kids*, who provided long-distance counsel, perspective, and laughs. Thanks to the publications that have sent us traveling with our families, especially *Westways, Journey*, the *Los Angeles Times, Travel & Leisure, Food & Wine, Working Mother, Parenting, FamilyFun*, and the *San Jose Mercury News*. Thanks to the folks at Menasha Ridge Press, especially Bob Sehlinger and Molly Merkle; they are surely the kindest souls in publishing. And, most importantly, thanks to our traveling companions: Daniel, Patricia, and Irene Milder; Pat Taylor; Darryl, Erin, and Emily Bates; Ellie Dunn; and the camping families at Sequoyah School.

ABOUT *the* AUTHORS

LOS ANGELES NATIVE **Colleen Dunn Bates** is the author of many books, including *Hometown Pasadena: The Insider's Guide* and *Storybook Travels: From Eloise's New York to Harry Potter's London, Visits to 30 of the Best-Loved Landmarks in Children's Literature,* which she cowrote with Susan LaTempa. She lives in Pasadena with her husband, Darryl Bates, and their two daughters.

Culver City resident **Susan LaTempa** wrote *Storybook Travels* with Colleen, has written for many national magazines, and is now a staff writer for the *Los Angeles Times.* Susan and her husband, Dan Milder, have two daughters.

INTRODUCTION

OUR FAMILIES *and* TRAVELS

FROM COLLEEN

MY MOTHER IS NEVER HAPPIER than when she's planning a trip, and I inherited that longing and joy. God knows it wasn't easy to take our brood anywhere—my parents had six kids in seven years, and I'm not sure how they ever got us dressed, let alone out of the house. But they did. From our Los Angeles home, we crammed into the station wagon and went to Yosemite, Palm Springs, Big Bear, and Disneyland. We rented an RV and camped the entire length of the state. We skied Mammoth and Tahoe. We flew to San Francisco, two at a time. And we went to the beach, from Malibu to San Onofre, chasing the waves that my father, and later we kids, loved so much.

Now my husband, Darryl, and I are doing it with our own two kids: high schooler Erin and middle schooler Emily. We've rented a beach house, stayed in a fancy San Francisco hotel, taken Amtrak to San Diego, skied in Mammoth and Tahoe, snorkeled in Catalina, and camped in the Anza-Borrego Desert. We've gone beyond California's borders to Hawaiian beaches, a French country house, and Rocky Mountain ski towns. We've had mishaps, and stress, and a lifetime supply of whining, but we've never had a bad trip, and we've had lots of great ones. We've learned how to plan drives around Emily's essential rest times and set the stage to minimize Erin's fear of the unknown. And we've learned how to weave our grown-up desires and interests into those of our children, further fusing us as a family. (We've also learned how to take the occasional adult trip away from the kids . . . but that's another book.)

I will never tire of exploring California. My children are perpetually panting for a new outing in our home state. From the trail atop Half Dome to the splash at the end of Splash Mountain, California is a great gift to the traveling family.

FROM SUSAN

AS I WRITE THIS, I GET UP FROM THE DESK from time to time to check on the laundry—an extra load this week because my daughter Irene and I have just returned from a trip to San Francisco and need some of our things for school and work tomorrow. Irene, 14, hasn't learned the joys of packing light yet, so I shake my head over the size of the pile of laundry. But even at 14, Irene has learned that travel is a special joy, that it's a great good fortune to substitute pictures in your head for place-names in a book. This trip brought forth her memories of previous family travels, and Irene shared with me her perspective on such adventures as our family's two-week car trip through Mendocino and the redwoods, or a more recent biking weekend in the Santa Ynez Valley. Her reminiscences this week reminded me again how children hold dear the most unexpected moments (often forgotten by adults) of a vacation, and how, more than anything, travel is a kind of practice that allows a child to learn to face other new experiences and be free to explore in all parts of her or his life.

My own earliest memories of California are a child's images of giant pinecones and picnic tables at highway rest stops. But I have to admit that for the most part I ignored my first chances to appreciate the state's spectacular scenery as I sat next to my brother in the backseat of the station wagon, bologna sandwiches floating in the ice chest at my feet. Today my family travels frequently throughout the state—Irene and I joined by my husband, Dan, and older daughter, Patricia. We've summer-vacationed in Mammoth and Sequoia, in Oxnard and Mendocino. (Admittedly, we sometimes take two summer vacations!) We've had Christmas week or winter weekends away from home, and spring break has been a traditional time to travel with Grandma—once to La Jolla, once to Coronado. We've headed out to see natural wonders in Death Valley and to play on the waterslides at Hurricane Harbor. We've seen and done enough for me (with a little help from the kids' sharper memories) to contribute half the material in this book. But we haven't seen it all yet.

The **DYNAMICS** of **FAMILY TRAVEL**

DON'T EVEN THINK ABOUT PLANNING A FAMILY TRIP until you answer this question: What does each member of the family want to get out of the vacation?

It seems like a simple question, but it'll take more time and thought to answer than you might realize. It means assessing your current relationship with your kids and your spouse. It means taking stock of your children's passions and fears, as well as your own. It means attaching a budget to everyone's wishes. And it invariably means compromise.

Start by asking yourself some questions. Is this vacation a time for togetherness, for time alone for you while the children are entertained, or for a little of each? Are you a single dad who doesn't get to see the kids much? Are you an at-home mom who never gets a break? Are you looking for exhilarating adventures or a laid-back getaway? Do you want intellectual stimulation for you and the kids? How well do your kids handle spontaneity?

Because your family's dynamics change with every birthday, the answers may surprise you. One child may be more ready for adventure than you've realized; another might be more ready for peace and quiet than you think.

THE PLEASURES OF PLANNING

IT'S BEST TO DECIDE WHAT YOU WANT TO DO and come up with some options to start the ball rolling. Then call a family meeting and include your kids in the planning process. Let everyone ask questions. Show some brochures or books about the places you have in mind so they'll feel as though they have enough information to be taken seriously. Pull out maps and a globe. Jump on the Internet. Teenagers in particular are quite vocal about expressing their choices, and they appreciate it when they can influence the planning process. The getaway is much more enjoyable when everyone wants to be there.

This shared planning time can be a great routine to continue as the trip itself gets under way. Remember, your kids may not be able to easily visualize your destination or the plane ride or cab ride you'll take on the way. And if you're traveling from place to place during your vacation, each new day dawns on the unknown. So keep the brochures and guidebooks handy, and break the itinerary down into manageable chunks. Offer an advance agenda every now and then, referring again to your original planning sessions ("Remember how we thought that the Bubbling Brook Motel sounded like a good one?") and letting the kids develop anticipation rather than anxiety.

It's essential to be realistic when you plan a family vacation. Parents of young children may have to concede that the days of romantic sunsets are over for a while if there's a toddler tugging at their shorts. With infants and toddlers, the best vacations are the simple ones. They don't much need to see the sights; the idea is to be somewhere comfortable and intriguing for the adults, with a pleasant environment in which to relax and enjoy your children. In California, destinations like Mission Bay or Monterey are ideal for parents of the youngest group of kids. School-age kids revel in attractions created for their enjoyment—theme parks, amusement parks, arcades, rides. The metropolitan regions can also be a blast with elementary-age kids. Teens may seem reluctant, but if a pilgrimage to a special point of interest for them (a certain skateboard shop, a movie-star hangout) is included, the whole trip becomes "worthwhile." And they thrive in safe, explore-it-on-your-own situations like a tour of Alcatraz or a Gold Country town.

LESS IS MORE THAN ENOUGH

AS YOU PLAN, WE URGE YOU TO LEAVE PLENTY of downtime in the schedule. Some of our families' most memorable moments are simple breakfasts on the beach or early evening walks to nowhere, when the conversation naturally flows. Kids treasure moments, not places or days. Give your children plenty of room to run and play; a morning collecting seashells or an afternoon at the hotel pool can be more satisfying than standing in line at a crowded theme-park attraction.

If you spend the morning at a museum and plan to go to dinner at Universal CityWalk, go back to the hotel in the afternoon to rest and swim. If you're driving from San Francisco to Monterey, make your reservations for the aquarium the next day. Then you can stop on the way at the lighthouse and the artichoke fields and the funny little town that time forgot. Remember that travel itself is an activity.

unofficial **TIP**
A good rule of thumb may sound stringent: no more than two activities in a day.

Also, plan some activities that allow you to take a break from each other. Quarters get a little close after a week together in a hotel room, particularly if your children are of significantly different ages. Schedule an afternoon in which Mom and Dad split duties, giving each other a break; take advantage of child and teen programs offered in many resorts to allow an evening alone with your spouse. Everyone benefits from a little elbow room.

RECONNECTIONS

FAMILY VACATIONS ARE A NECESSARY INDULGENCE in today's hurried-up world, a time for togetherness without the day-to-day distractions. Whether it's a car trip on a budget or a transcontinental flight, it's a time to reconnect with your family, especially teenagers. And the best times are the serendipitous moments—a heart-to-heart conversation on an evening hike, or silly "knock-knock" jokes while standing in line for the roller coaster. Roles are relaxed when schedules are flexible, and kids can have the opportunity to see their parents as interesting companions, not just bossy grown-ups. We all can learn from one another when there's time to listen and when we take the time to see the world through a loved one's eyes.

A seasoned traveler friend once scoffed at the notion of traveling with young children, "since they don't remember anything." We couldn't disagree more.

Susan's children have often mentioned the hours spent sitting at the mouth of the Klamath River watching the incredible sight of sea lions, pelicans, Native American fishermen, and one ambitious wet dog, all competing for the salmon swimming into the river from the ocean.

When Colleen's daughter was 7, she struck up an intense friendship with a boy on a Hawaiian beach, and when they returned to their respective homes in Michigan and California, they kept in touch by e-mail.

Given the open hearts and all the innocence of childhood, new impressions may sink in even more deeply with kids than with adults.

Our children have a greater understanding of the rest of the world as a result of travel to new places and experiencing new ideas. And siblings have formed a special bond from traveling together, a bond less likely to be formed at home, where they have separate classrooms, separate friends, and separate bedrooms.

As parents, it's up to us to be sure there's some fun in a trip for each member of the family. And as a family, we all need to remember to indulge our traveling companions from time to time. Remember, your responses to challenges on the road—delayed flights, long lines, unsatisfactory accommodations—will influence the way your children will deal with frustrations. Be patient, be calm, and teach your children these important lifelong skills.

Vacations are times for adventure, relaxation, shared experiences, time alone—whatever your family decides. Our goal with this book is to evaluate each destination with that in mind—recognizing that your family has needs, based on ages, backgrounds, and interests, that are quite different from any other family's—and provide you with some structure to analyze your family's needs and create a vacation that works.

We have traveled the world with our children, from France and Holland to the Hawaiian Islands and the Rocky Mountains. Yet some of our most wondrous trips have been in our own backyard: hopping a San Francisco cable car, body boarding on a Santa Barbara beach, playing hide-and-seek in a redwood forest. We can't imagine ever tiring of exploring our home state, whether we're stalking the newest amped-up amusement park or finding the next best beach.

This book is not meant to be a compendium of every family-priced hotel or every advertised attraction, though we have strived to cover a variety of interests for a variety of ages. Instead of compiling a family-travel Yellow Pages, we've edited out the less worthy places to better draw attention to the destinations that will make your trip a hit.

Dozens of families have contributed their opinions to this book; it is evaluative and opinionated, and it offers advice for the best ways for families to have fun together and further relationships.

Survival Guide for Little Kids

THINK SMALL Little ones love little pleasures: splashing in the hotel pool, playing hide-and-seek in the lobby, stacking up rocks on the beach. Don't overload them.

SEEK CREATIVE TRANSPORTATION For young children, getting there is often more fun than being there. When Emily was 3 years old, her greatest joy and memory from our gala two-week Hawaiian vacation was the open-air wiki-wiki shuttle

unofficial **TIP**
It's stressful enough to get a kindergartner out the door to school each morning, so don't keep up the stress on vacation.

at Honolulu International Airport—she positively shook with excitement during the ride. Seek out the ferries, trolleys, shuttles, trains, surreys, and double-decker buses, and you'll be rewarded with a cheap thrill that's as fun for little ones as a Disneyland ride.

LIMIT THE SHOPPING Our rule at attractions is a firm one: no shopping, not even looking, until we are leaving the place. Young children can get consumed by and panicky about choosing a souvenir, and they'll enjoy the museum or theme park more if they can focus on the activities, not the trinkets.

GIVE THEM A VOICE Even a 4-year-old will benefit from feeling as if he has some control over his vacation. Let him make simple choices for the family—like "Should we walk to the beach or ride the trolley?"

ALLOW FOR LOTS OF DOWNTIME Bring books or quiet hobbies to amuse yourself during nap times or playtimes. Remember, a child's ability to tackle the big world is much more limited than yours.

ACCEPT SOME SLOWNESS As any parent who's gotten a child ready for school in the morning can attest, kids are used to being rushed. And kids, like adults, need a break from it. If they're happy playing in their pajamas for an extra half hour, the museum can wait. Conversely, accept that the times you like to be more leisurely—like dinnertime—lead to impatience in children.

Survival Guide for School-age Kids

GIVE THEM THEIR OWN SPACE Whether it's a backpack, a carry-on train case, or one of those shoebaglike hanging pockets that fits over the car seat in front of them, each kid needs a portable room of his or her own in which to stow gum, cards, books, disposable cameras, and souvenirs.

MAKE A NEW ROUTINE At least until middle-school years, most kids do best with a certain amount of predictability, so it's a kindness to create little travel routines and rituals within your changed life. Knowing that his parents will always stop sightseeing by 3 p.m. to swim (or will never check out without one last hour in the pool) is a comforting thought to many a fourth-grader. Knowing that you will have $5 spending money each day can do away with shopping anxiety. Having set turns as map reader can add some fun to a hundred-mile drive.

AVOID EATING BREAKFAST OUT Many savvy traveling parents never eat breakfast in a restaurant. School-age kids are at their brightest and best in the morning, and waiting for table service at a ho-hum restaurant can start the day on the wrong foot. We carry fruit, cereal, milk, and juices in coolers or to kitchenettes or pop for room service—it's the least expensive and most wonderfully indulgent time to do so.

BEWARE BEFUDDLED EXPECTATIONS School-age kids are old enough to have some reference points but young enough to have great gaping holes in their mental pictures of the world. Our kids have imagined that they'd find matzo ball soup instead of chocolate at Ghirardelli Square (thinking it was Jerry's Deli); they've worried that the car would tumble down the cliff on a winding mountain road; they've expected to see gold nuggets in the bottom of the creek in Gold Country. Ask what's going on in their minds. Listen. Don't overpromise.

WATCH THE DIET It's fun to let vacation be a time of special treats, but overindulgence in junk food, sweets, and caffeinated drinks may contribute to behavioral changes in kids who aren't sleeping in their own beds and are full of adrenaline as it is.

REMEMBER THAT KIDS HATE SCENERY Drive them through it if you must, but don't make them actually look at too much of it.

GIVE THEM A SHIP'S LOG A roll of tape and a blank book are all that's needed to turn ticket stubs, menus, brochures, and postcards from a clutter of trash into a wonderful scrapbook that's always ready to be shared and enjoyed.

HOTELS AND MOTELS ARE NOT JUST FOR SLEEPING Allow time for getting ice, playing in the pool, reviewing all items and prices in the minibar, packing and unpacking, using the hair dryer, putting laundry into the laundry bags, trying out the vending machines, etc.

HIT THE PLAYGROUNDS Check your maps and ask ahead about public playgrounds with climbing and sliding equipment, and on days when you'll be sightseeing, driving, or absorbing culture, allow for an hour's lunch or rest stop at the playground. Even on city vacations, try to set aside at least one day for pure physical fun at a beach or water park or ski slope.

JUST SAY YES TO RANGER TOURS These tours are often designed with schoolkids in mind. We'd never have tasted sand flies at Mono Lake or seen a tarantula up close at Anza-Borrego Desert State Park or understood about the Welsh miners' lunch pails if we hadn't checked the schedule at the state or national park information center and made a point to join the ranger walk.

Survival Guide for Teenagers

DON'T TRY TO FOOL THEM Don't try to tell them they'll have more fun with you than with their friends. They won't. But if you offer them the possibility of doing things they might want to tell their friends about later, they'll be interested.

RESPECT THEIR CULTURE Let your teenager play an active role in planning the vacation. Ask her opinion of your arrangements. Often our daughter will offer a great suggestion or an alternative that we may not have considered. And look for pop-culture landmarks—movie locations or palaces of fashion or music or sport. Add a ball game to the itinerary.

NIGHT MOVES A vacation is a great time to go with your teenager to a music club or a midnight movie, or on a moonlight hike. Go to the theater or the ballet; check out a jazz club. If you have other kids needing earlier bedtimes, let the parents switch-hit on going out at night with the older kids.

GIVE THEM OPTIONS You don't need to go everywhere with everyone. If your younger child wants to go see the dinosaurs at the museum, this is the time for a split plan: Dad and son see the dinosaurs; Mom and daughter shop or take in a movie or a play. If you have a teenager who appreciates her sleep time, let her snooze late at least one morning. Slip out with younger siblings and take a walk or read a book. Also, set wake-up time before everyone says good night so that there are no grouchy morning risers (at least not because they've been awakened too early).

GIVE THEM FREEDOM Before age 12, kids are bound to parents, preferring to stay in your orbit; when adolescence hits, they're programmed to push away from you. Choose a vacation spot that is safe and controlled enough to allow them to wander or spend time with other teenagers. If you can't do that, look for an afternoon or evening at a controlled hangout like Universal CityWalk or Pier 39. Give them the night to themselves at Disneyland or Knott's. Send them off to the ranger campfire by themselves at Yosemite; sign them up for an afternoon's photography workshop in Big Sur.

COMPROMISE ON THE HEADPHONE THING Headphones can allow teens to create their own space even when they're with others, and that can be a safety valve, but try to agree before the trip on some non-headphone parameters so you don't begin to feel as if they're being used to keep other family members and the trip itself at a distance. If you're traveling by car, take turns choosing the radio station or CD for part of the trip.

DON'T MAKE YOUR TEENAGER THE BUILT-IN BABYSITTER It should be a family vacation—a time for reconnecting, not for avoiding the kids. A special night out for parents also should be special for the children; let them order videos and room service, for example, or participate in a few age-appropriate hotel programs.

MAKE PEACE WITH SHOPPING Look for street markets and vintage stores; spend some time in surf shops and record stores. If you go with your teenager, you may find that the conversation in such an environment flows easily. Or hit the outlets—many a summer vacation has included a day of back-to-school shopping.

JUST SAY YES TO AT LEAST ONE BIG-TICKET EXCURSION Teenagers will get a lot out of a half-day adventure. What on the surface appeared to be expensive tours (often available through the hotel sports desk or concierge) turned into memorable and important experiences for our kids that we as parents were simply not able to offer by ourselves. A raft ride, a desert jeep tour, a kayak and snorkel trip, a horseback trail ride—each took us far into the country we were exploring, and each was worth every cent. Or let the teenager sign up for a lesson: surfing, sailing, rock climbing. One of our daughters took a remarkable rope-climbing course that had her swinging through the trees in Mammoth.

A Word on Homework

Both our elementary-school and high-school kids have faced a load of homework or a special project that had to be worked on during vacation time. If a surprise major assignment comes up and plans can't be changed, there will be an unavoidable strain on the trip. Parents should consider strategies such as bringing along a laptop computer, scheduling vacation fun in half-day chunks so that the homeworked kid gets some work and some play, and/or including a marathon session at a library at the vacation spot. You can also shamelessly beg the teacher for a reprieve, but make that a last resort.

The Secret to Visiting Art Museums

Wandering through room after room of paintings and sculptures is numbing to children. They need a focal point and a sense of adventure. Before your visit, find out what some of the major works on display are, and locate pictures of them (perhaps the museum will mail you a brochure with pictures, or you can look online or get an art book from the library). Let each child pick one or two works to sleuth out. They can learn a little about the artist and the work in question, and then when you visit the museum, they can go on a hunt for "their" artwork.

A Few Words for Single Parents

Because single parents generally are working parents, planning a special getaway with your children can be the best way to spend some quality time together. But remember, the vacation is not just for your child—it's for you, too. You might invite along a grandparent or a favorite aunt or uncle; the other adult provides nice company for you, and your child will benefit from the time with family members.

Don't try to spend every moment with your children on vacation. Instead, plan some activities for your children with other children. Look for hotels with supervised activities, or research the community you'll be visiting for school-vacation offerings at libraries, recreation centers, or temple or church day camps. Then take advantage of your free time to do what you want to do: read a book, have a massage, take a walk or a catnap.

Tips for Grandparents

A vacation that involves generations can be the most enriching experience for everyone,

unofficial **TIP**
If planning a child-friendly trip seems overwhelming, try **Grandtravel** (☎ 800-247-7651; **www.grandtrvl.com**), a tour operator–travel agent catering to kids and their grandparents.

but it is important to consider the needs of each family member, from the youngest to the oldest. Here are some things to consider.

- If you're planning to travel alone with your grandchildren, spend a little time getting to know them before the vacation. Be sure they're comfortable with the idea of traveling with you if their parents are not coming along.

- It's best to take one grandchild at a time, two at the most. Cousins can be better than siblings because they don't fight as much.

- Let your grandchildren help plan the vacation. Be flexible, and don't overplan.

- Discuss mealtimes and bedtime. Fortunately, many grandparents are on an early dinner schedule, which works nicely with younger children. Also, if you want to plan a special evening out, be sure to make the reservation ahead of time. Stash some crayons and paper in your bag to keep kids occupied.

- Gear plans to your grandchildren's age levels, because if they're not happy, you're not happy.

- Choose a vacation that offers some supervised activities for children in case you need a rest.

- If you're traveling by car, this is the one time we highly recommend headphones. Teenagers' musical tastes are vastly different from most grandparents', and it's simply more enjoyable when everyone can listen to their own style of music.

- Bring a night-light.

- Carry a notarized statement from parents for permission for medical care in case of an emergency. Also, be sure you have insurance information.

- Tell your grandchildren about any medical problems you may have so they can be prepared if there's an emergency.

- Many attractions and hotels offer discounts for seniors, so be sure to check ahead of time for bargains.

- A cruise may be the perfect compromise—plenty of daily activities for everyone but shared mealtimes.

For Travelers with Disabilities

Facilities for the physically challenged are plentiful in California. All public buildings have some form of access for people who use wheelchairs. In addition, many public buses are equipped with wheelchair lifts. Also, most of the state's attractions offer facilities and services for those with physical challenges, and many hotels have specially equipped rooms. The state's three most popular cities have guides for the physically challenged: in San Diego, call ☎ 858-279-0704; in Los Angeles, call ☎ 323-957-4280; and in San Francisco, call ☎ 415-391-2000.

california at a glance

HOW *the* UNOFFICIAL GUIDE WORKS

ORGANIZATION

OUR INFORMAL POLLS SHOW THAT MOST FAMILIES tend to choose a vacation spot based on geography—a place that's new and different, or familiar and comfortable. So we've divided California into eight regions, with family-friendly information for each region. The chapters are organized geographically, from south to north. For great places to stay within those regions—resorts, hotels, campgrounds—see the "Family Lodging" sections within each chapter; kid- and parent-pleasing dining is recommended in the "Family-friendly Restaurants" sections in each chapter.

The regions break down as follows:

- **San Diego County** From Tijuana to Carlsbad, and inland to Anza-Borrego, this region centers on the San Diego metropolitan area and beaches.
- **Orange County** From San Clemente in the south to Costa Mesa in the north, this region includes such beloved beach destinations as Newport, Laguna, and Dana Point, as well as Disneyland and Knott's Berry Farm.
- **Los Angeles and Vicinity** This huge urban area centers on the nation's second-largest city and includes such satellite towns as Palm Springs, Pasadena, Redondo Beach, Big Bear, and Santa Monica, as well as such suburban amusements as Magic Mountain.
- **Central Coast** North of L.A. lies this rich collection of beaches and small-town escapes, starting in Ventura, continuing through Santa Barbara and San Simeon (Hearst Castle), and going north through the wilds of Big Sur to the aquarium in Monterey.
- **Sierra Nevada** Mountain fun awaits in this large region, from Yosemite's Half Dome to Sequoia's trees to sparkling Lake Tahoe. This region also includes Death Valley on the Sierra's eastern boundary.
- **San Francisco Bay Area** Along with the great City by the Bay, this region includes adventures in the East Bay (Berkeley), San Jose, and Marin County as far north as Point Reyes.
- **Gold Country** Inland from San Francisco, this region encompasses the capital city, Sacramento, and wanders through the gold-rush towns flanking the western Sierra Nevada.
- **Northern California** A vast rural area rich in national and state parks, this region stretches from Bodega Bay up through the redwoods to the Oregon border and over to Mount Shasta.

WHAT'S THERE TO DO BESIDES DISNEYLAND?

EACH REGIONAL CHAPTER RECOMMENDS the best beaches, parks, family outdoor adventures, and attractions, ranging from theme parks to science museums. We've also included serendipitous sidebars on offbeat places that you'll want to know about, from children's theaters in L.A. to the old schoolhouses of the Gold Country.

If you're looking for some healthy family bonding, stretch beyond the man-made attractions. Have a sense of adventure and plan some activities that are new and exciting—not necessarily strenuous, but memorable. Each region has specific spots for the following activities.

CAMPING We've selected a few choice family-friendly campgrounds throughout the state. If it's your family's first experience, you might opt for a cabin; we list them in many state parks.

BIKING For beginners, we have recommended miles of paved bicycle trails; older kids will like the mountain biking spots we've found. You don't even have to bring your own bike; you can rent one at many resorts and bike shops, and many shops have trailers for rent for small children (age 5 and under) to travel safely behind you—these are much safer than bicycle seats. Know that helmets are the law for children, and it is strongly advised that all cyclists wear helmets.

unofficial **TIP**
Cycling is one of the best ways to experience an area firsthand and can be enjoyed year-round in much of California.

SURFING The wave is king (or queen) in many parts of California, so we've recommended the best surfing classes and camps for kids, as well as good beaches for wave riders of all kinds, including body boarders.

WHALE WATCHING Wintertime visitors won't want to miss a whale-watching trip, offered up and down the California coast. Even if you don't spot one of the great gray whales, you'll surely enjoy dolphins, seals, seabirds, and an exhilarating ride on the Pacific Ocean.

HIKING California is a hiker's paradise; we've concentrated on the easiest spots suitable for kids, from urban nature hikes to Sierra trails.

KAYAKING AND WHITE-WATER RAFTING From kayaking the coves of the north coast to rafting the wilds of the American River, these are wonderful bonding adventures for families with kids older than 5 or 6 years of age.

WHAT'S "UNOFFICIAL" ABOUT THIS BOOK?

THE MATERIAL IN THIS GUIDE ORIGINATED with the authors and researchers and has not been reviewed, edited, or in any way approved by attractions, restaurants, and hotels we describe. Our goal is to help families plan a vacation that's right for them by providing important details and honest opinions. If we found a family-oriented destination to be dreary or a rip-off, we simply didn't include it.

Readers care about the author's opinion. The author, after all, is supposed to know what he or she is talking about. This, coupled with the fact that the traveler wants quick answers (as opposed to endless alternatives), dictates that authors should be explicit, prescriptive, and above all, direct. The *Unofficial Guide* tries to be just that—it spells out alternatives and recommends specific courses of action. It simplifies complicated destinations and attractions and allows the traveler to feel in control in the most unfamiliar environments. The objective of the *Unofficial Guide* is not to have the most information or all the information, but to have the most accessible, useful information, unbiased by affiliation with any organization or industry.

This guide is directed at value-conscious, consumer-oriented families who seek a cost-effective, though not spartan, travel style.

The *Unofficial Guide* Rating System for Attractions

Our system includes an "appeal to different age groups" category, indicating a range of appeal from one star (★), "don't bother," up to five stars (★★★★★), "not to be missed."

Letters and Comments from Readers

We expect to learn from our mistakes, as well as from the input of our readers, and to improve with each book and edition. Many *Unofficial Guide* users write to us asking questions, making comments, or sharing their own discoveries and lessons learned. We appreciate all the input, both positive and critical, and encourage our readers to continue writing. Readers' comments and observations are frequently incorporated into revised editions of the *Unofficial Guide* and contribute immeasurably to its improvement.

How to Write the Authors

Colleen Dunn Bates and Susan LaTempa
The Unofficial Guide to California with Kids
P.O. Box 43673
Birmingham, AL 35243
unofficialguides@menasharidge.com

When you write, be sure to put your return address on your letter as well as on the envelope—sometimes envelopes and letters get separated. And remember that our work takes us out of the office for long periods of time, so forgive us if our response is delayed.

Reader Survey

At the back of this guide, you will find a short questionnaire that you can use to express opinions concerning your California visit. Clip the questionnaire out along the dotted line, and mail it to the above address.

The *Unofficial Guide* Web Site

The Web site of the *Unofficial Guide* Travel and Lifestyle Series, providing in-depth information on all *Unofficial Guides* in print, is at **www.theunofficialguides.com.**

GETTING READY *to* GO

WEATHER AND WHEN TO GO

CALIFORNIA'S CLIMATE VARIES TREMENDOUSLY from region to region, but in general it is a temperate state, suitable for year-round visiting. The deserts (Palm Springs, Anza-Borrego) are brutally hot in late summer, and the far north is rain soaked in winter, so avoid those areas then. Otherwise, travelers have a lot of flexibility. You can always count on warmth and sun in Southern California from mid-June through October, though the coastal areas can get fogged in during early summer (the "June gloom"); the San Francisco Bay Area is more unpredictable, with its chilly fog that's sent many a summer visitor scurrying to the Gap to buy a sweatshirt. (The average daily August temperature in L.A., for instance, is 82°F, while in San Francisco the average is just 69°F.)

We're most fond of visiting Los Angeles in May or October, when there's plenty of warm sun but not too much smog or blazing heat. If you're staying at the beach, know that May and June are often gray and overcast; the beach cities of San Diego, Newport, Laguna, Santa Barbara, and Santa Cruz shine in the peak of summer—July, August, and September are best—when days are long and the Pacific warms up. We like San Francisco best in winter, especially around the holidays when it is festive and mildly brisk, or in September, when the fog is minimal. The mountains, from the southern Sierra to the Cascades, are wonderful year-round, from the ski days of February to the hikes of August.

In general, popular tourist sights are busier on weekends than weekdays, and Saturdays are busier than Sundays. Locals say the least crowded time to visit theme parks is on a rainy weekday in the winter.

Of course, family travel schedules often revolve around school holidays, which tend to be the busiest times to travel. But consider taking your children out of school for special family trips—a well-planned week of family travel is just as enriching as five days in a classroom. Make it clear that traveling is a privilege, and agree that all missed work must be made up upon return. Talk with teachers ahead of time.

PACK LIGHT

WE LIMIT OURSELVES TO ONE CARRY-ON BAG EACH and a backpack, no matter what the duration of the trip or how we are traveling. (The exception is a ski or snow trip, which demands bulky clothes.) If you have small children, stashing an extra T-shirt and pair of shorts in your backpack comes in handy in emergencies. A California trip generally is casual, though you may want to pack one nice outfit for a special evening out.

Make a list of necessities and let the kids pack their own bags (subject to your inspection). T-shirts, shorts, and bathing suits are perfect in the warmer regions, but never travel without a jacket or

Web Sites for California-bound Kids

Kids from about age 8 and up will connect more with a trip if they're part of the planning. One of the ways for them to plan is to explore the Internet. Here are our favorite Web sites to prepare for a trip within California:

Alcatraz Island–Golden Gate NRA	**www.nps.gov/alcatraz**
Birch Aquarium at Scripps	**www.aquarium.ucsd.edu**
California Division of Tourism	**www.gocalif.ca.gov**
California Heritage Digital Image Access Project	**sunsite.berkeley.edu/calheritage**
California History	**www.californiahistory.net**
California State Parks	**www.parks.ca.gov**
Caltrans Driving Information	**www.dot.ca.gov**
Channel Islands National Park	**www.nps.gov/chis**
Donner Party	**www.donnerpartydiary.com**
Exploratorium	**www.exploratorium.edu**
Gold Country Guide	**www.malakoff.com/goldcountry**
Gold Rush	**www.isu.edu/~trinmich**
Golden Gate Bridge	**www.goldengate.org**
Hearst Castle	**www.hearstcastle.org**
International Surfing Museum	**www.surfingmuseum.org**
Marine Mammal Center	**www.tmmc.org**
Monterey Bay Aquarium	**www.mbayaq.org**
National Park Service	**www.nps.gov**
Northern California Information	**www.shastacascade.org**
Redwoods: California's Redwood Canyons	**www.savetheredwoods.org**
San Diego Zoo and Wild Animal Park	**www.sandiegozoo.org**
Santa Cruz Beach Boardwalk	**www.beachboardwalk.com**
Zeum	**www.zeum.org**

*un*official **TIP**
Bring a "surprise bag" for young travelers. Sticker books, a card game, or a new book is a perfect lightweight diversion to bring out when everyone's patience is wearing thin.

sturdy sweatshirt. California weather is fickle, and you may be surprised with cold. Bring a small bottle of detergent for hand washing. The vacation will be much more enjoyable if you don't have a bunch of bags to haul around busy airports or hotel lobbies.

Let your children pack their own backpacks, then ask them to wear them around the house to test how comfortable they will be on a long trip. Our children have become savvy packers, aware that each piece counts. Of course, you should check their bags before departing, just to be sure the essentials are all there.

REMEMBERING YOUR TRIP

WHEN YOU CHOOSE A DESTINATION, write or call for information (info sources are listed in each chapter). The travel brochures can later be used as part of a scrapbook commemorating your trip.

Purchase a notebook for each child and spend time each evening recording the events of the day. If your children have trouble getting motivated or don't know what to write about, start a discussion; otherwise, let them write or draw, whatever they want to do to remember the day's events.

Collect mementos along the way and create a treasure box in a small tin or cigar box. Months or years later, it's fun to look at postcards, seashells, or ticket stubs to jump-start a memory.

Add some inexpensive postcards to your photographs to create an album, and then write a few words on each page to accompany the images.

Give each child a disposable camera to record his or her version of the trip. Our 5-year-old snapped an entire series of photos that never showed anyone above the waist—his view of the world (the photos are priceless).

These days, many families travel with a camcorder, though we don't recommend using one—parents end up viewing the trip through the lens rather than enjoying the sights. Take it along if you must, but record only a few moments of major sights (too much is boring anyway). Let the kids tape and narrate.

Even better, because it's more compact, carry a palm-sized tape recorder and let everyone describe their experiences. Hearing a small child's voice years later is so endearing, and those recorded descriptions will trigger an album's worth of memories, far more focused than what most novices capture with a camcorder.

GETTING THERE

BY CAR

DRIVING IS CERTAINLY THE MOST ECONOMICAL way to travel, but if you're covering a lot of miles, it's time-consuming and can try the patience of every passenger. For starters, don't pull any punches with your kids about just how long you'll be in the car.

If it's a long trip, leave before daylight. Bring small pillows and blankets (we use our children's baby blankets), and let the kids snooze. When they're fully awake a few hours down the road, stop for breakfast and teeth brushing.

unofficial **TIP**
Be sure you have maps, and chart your trip before you leave home. Share the maps with the children so that they'll understand the distance to be covered.

Bring along books, crayons, paper, and a couple of laptop games (though not the electronic kind with annoying beeps). Parents can stash a few surprises to dole out along the way: sticker books, action figures, magazines. We take along a deflated beach ball to blow up, a Frisbee, or a Koosh ball for impromptu playtimes at rest stops.

The most significant California highway is **Interstate 5,** which runs from Mexico to Oregon, connecting San Diego, Los Angeles, Sacramento, and Shasta. It's fast and convenient, but frequently dreary; the stretch from L.A. to San Francisco is particularly numbing. **Highway 1** is the oceanfront road that starts and stops throughout the state; it's worth the detour and time to drive it through the Big Sur area. **Highway 101** heads in roughly the same direction as I-5, connecting L.A. to the Oregon border, but is far more charming (and slower), passing through farm and beach towns.

Traffic is a force to be reckoned with in California's urban areas, and you should plan around it. Don't even think about driving across L.A. or over San Francisco's Bay Bridge at 5:30 p.m.

Seat belts for drivers and front-seat passengers are required by law in California. Child car safety seats are mandatory for children under 4 years of age or weighing less than 40 pounds.

Snacks are great, but leave the drinks (preferably water, since it doesn't stain or get sticky when spilled) until the last moment, or else frequent restroom stops will prolong the journey. Rest areas can be found all along California's major highways, and most of them are open around the clock. Pack a picnic for mealtimes, and everyone can take a walk or stretch.

Small pillows and your own CDs or tapes make the journey peaceful. Take turns and let everyone choose a favorite. If kids fight over music, make them take turns choosing. To settle seat fights, we rotate turns, either weekly or daily, for who gets to choose a seat first.

Don't forget to always lock your car, and never leave wallets or luggage in sight. Keep valuables locked in the trunk.

BY TRAIN

AMTRAK BRINGS EASTERNERS TO CALIFORNIA via Chicago and Denver aboard the *Zephyr;* Northwesterners can train down on the *Coast Starlight,* which runs from Seattle to Los Angeles. Amtrak also runs popular commuter and vacationer trains from L.A. north to Santa Barbara and south to San Diego.

unofficial **TIP**
If you opt for a longer train trip, book first class and a sleeping car.

We have taken long train trips, and for youngsters, it's interesting for about the first hour of a many-hour trip. But with books, games, and activities to occupy the time, it's a leisurely and relatively inexpensive way to travel, with time to unwind and spend quality moments with your family. You can stand up and stretch, or go for a walk, and there's more legroom than in an airplane or car (and no traffic jams). Plus, many trains offer sleeping and dining cars, but remember—some trips can be mighty long, and the fare is not much less than cut-rate airfares.

Amtrak offers a children's discount—kids ages 2 to 15 ride for half price when accompanied by a full-fare-paying adult. Each adult can bring two children for the discount; one child under the age of 2 rides free with every adult ticket purchased.

If you're arriving in L.A. by train, you'll need a car to get around, so reserve one in advance. It's entirely possible, however, to arrive in San Francisco, Santa Barbara, and San Diego and enjoy your stay without a car.

For reservations and information, call ☎ 800-USA-RAIL or log on the Internet at **www.amtrak.com.**

BY PLANE

EVERY PART OF CALIFORNIA is served by major airlines, so choosing a flight is a matter of time and economics. Booking as far in advance as possible can save hundreds of dollars for a family of four. When you book your tickets, be sure to get your seat assignments. Request bulkhead seats for small kids who won't be entertained by a movie but might be able to move around a bit. Although far-front seats are preferred for the most part, be sure to ask how the movie is shown; if you're more than a few rows back from a small screen, it can be hard to enjoy the film.

Takeoff and landing bother some children's ears, particularly if they have a cold. Look for plastic earplugs designed to ease the pain of ear pressure. They come in children's sizes and are available at travel stores, drugstores, and airport sundry stores. We've found them to be highly effective. One pair lasts for at least two flights; they cost $2 or $3 per pair. You can also bring gum for older children or a bottle or sipper cup for babies and toddlers. A washcloth heated with hot water from a Thermos and held to ears will also help the younger ones who can't tolerate earplugs. Most of your fellow passengers would agree that the best babies on airplanes are sleeping babies, so, if possible, book your flights around nap times, which assures a peaceful flight for you and a happy child as you land.

Bring your own child-safety seat; though airlines allow children under 2 years of age to fly free on a parent's lap, it's much safer if they're strapped in a safety seat (and they're much more likely to nap, giving you a break). A car seat must have a visible label stating it is approved for air travel.

unofficial **TIP**
Pack a few nutritious snacks and a small bottle of water. If you or your child wants or needs a special meal, be sure to call the airline at least 48 hours in advance to request.

IF YOU RENT A CAR

THE CAR IS KING IN CALIFORNIA, so rental rates are competitive, and every major company is represented at the larger airports. Recreational vehicles, four-wheel-drives, and convertibles can also be rented, though they are considerably more expensive. To rent a car, you will need a valid driver's license, proof of insurance, and a major credit card. Some companies have minimum age requirements.

Ask about extras. Many companies offer cellular phones, ski racks, area maps, and child safety seats (California law says that any child who is less than 40 pounds or under 4 years old must sit in a safety seat).

If there are more than four in your family, you might want to consider renting a minivan. They cost a little more, but the comfort is worth it.

FAMILY LODGING

HOTELS, MOTELS, AND RESORTS

IN EACH REGIONAL CHAPTER, YOU'LL FIND OUR FAVORITE family hotels, motels, and resorts. Note that we said favorite *family* hotels, not favorite hotels, period—many wonderful retreats were excluded because they're aimed at romantics or businesspeople, and they would make any parent of an energetic 4-year-old feel like a leper. We've reviewed only places that particularly catch our fancy or seem suitable for families, and we've strived to find places with character. If you don't see an accommodation in the region you wish to visit, call the toll-free number of your favorite chain to find out what they offer.

Tips on Hotels, Motels, and Resorts with Kids

First, there has to be a pool. After that, you get some choices.

One room or two? Large or small? Upscale hotel or basic motel? Old or new? There are pros and cons with each of these overnight options, and we've found that on different days on the same vacation, we might make different choices.

Overall, one of the hardest things for some of us parents to adjust to is being awake when the kids are asleep but not wanting to leave them alone in the room. Although adjoining rooms are a good option in some hotels, they're not offered everywhere, and the choice between one or more rooms for a family always seems to come up.

So we try, on an extended family vacation during which we're moving from place to place, to book ourselves into several different kinds of facilities and have different solutions. In a hub city where we're not expecting to be in a picturesque setting, we look for a business-suite chain, especially on the weekends, when discounts are often offered (but check to see that all amenities, like breakfasts, continue). The price for a spacious suite may be the same as for a cramped room at

> ### CHILDPROOF YOUR ROOM
>
> When you arrive at the hotel, some childproofing may be in order. Be sure that both the front door and any patio or balcony doors and windows can be securely locked and bolted. Some hotels offer electrical outlet coverings if you have toddlers, and protective covers for sharp furniture corners. They also will remove glass objects or other knickknacks that might be easy for a toddler to break. And if the minibar is stocked with junk food and alcoholic beverages, it should be locked.

the motel down the street, and it's great to be able to watch the late show while the little ones snooze.

Big landmark hotels or luxury hotels with character are worth the splurge for us if the location is workable, and they might come at the end of a road trip, when the only choices in small-town stops on the way have been inexpensive roadside motels. Our kids tell us they like the excitement of big hotels (it's almost like a theme park, they say) and even enjoy "the neat old stuff" in some establishments. And room service is God's gift to traveling parents. But we also always ask about the executive, concierge, or butler floor of this kind of establishment, because the lounge areas often offer breakfast, coffee, snacks, and wine at various hours. For one thing, it's convenient for grabbing a muffin for a kid in the room; for another, it's a place for parents to escape to, like a living room, without being far away.

The all-American motel is, of course, a favorite with families. No need to find a bellman—you park in front of your room and unload only what you need. Kids love roaming the corridors for ice, getting soda from the machines, and spotting other children. Lack of towel service poolside may be compensated for by the existence of a coin laundry. At this kind of hostelry, we might opt for one room, but we'd request a room near the pool with a patio or veranda. Proximity to the pool allows kids of a certain age to come and go; the patio extends the living space nicely.

CHILDREN'S PROGRAMS

MANY LARGE HOTELS OFFER SUPERVISED PROGRAMS for children, some complimentary, some with fees. We've included several hotels throughout California that offer exemplary activities.

If you decide to take advantage of the kids' programs, call ahead for specific children's events that are scheduled during your vacation. Ask about cost and the ages that can participate; the best programs divide children into age groups. Make reservations for activities your child might enjoy (you can always cancel after arrival).

After check-in, stop by and visit with the kid's program staff. Ask about counselor-child ratio and whether the counselors are trained in

Chain-hotel Toll-free Numbers

This guidebook gives details on some of the hotels in California with outstanding children's programs. However, for your convenience we've listed toll-free numbers for the following hotel and motel chains' reservation lines:

Best Western	☎ 800-780-7234 United States and Canada
Comfort Inn	☎ 877-424-6423 United States and Canada
Courtyard by Marriott	☎ 888-236-2427, reservations United States ☎ 800-771-5665, customer service
Days Inn	☎ 800-329-7466 United States
DoubleTree and DoubleTree Guest Suites	☎ 800-222-TREE (8733) United States
Econo Lodge	☎ 800-424-4777 United States
Embassy Suites	☎ 800-362-2779 United States and Canada
Fairfield Inn by Marriott	☎ 800-228-2800 United States
Four Seasons	☎ 800-819-5053 United States and Canada
Hampton Inn	☎ 800-426-7866 United States and Canada
Hilton	☎ 800-445-8667 United States
Holiday Inn	☎ 800-465-4329 United States and Canada
Howard Johnson	☎ 800-446-4656, reservations United States ☎ 800-541-9881, customer service
Hyatt	☎ 800-233-1234 United States and Canada
Loew's	☎ 800-23-LOEWS United States and Canada
Marriott	☎ 888-236-2427, reservations ☎ 800-771-5665, customer service United States and Canada
Quality Inn	☎ 800-228-5151 United States and Canada
Radisson	☎ 800-333-3333 United States and Canada
Ramada Inn	☎ 800-272-6232 United States
Renaissance Hotels	☎ 888-236-2427, reservations ☎ 800-771-5665, customer service United States and Canada
Residence Inn by Marriott	☎ 888-236-2427, reservations United States ☎ 800-771-5661, customer service
Ritz-Carlton	☎ 800-241-3333 United States
Sheraton	☎ 800-325-3535 United States and Canada
Wyndham	☎ 877-999-3223, reservations United States ☎ 800-822-4200, information

first aid and CPR. Briefly introduce your children to the staff and setting, which typically will leave them wanting more, thereby easing the separation anxiety when they return to stay.

Some hotels offer in-room babysitting, but if your hotel does not, there is a national nonprofit referral program called **Child Care Aware** that will help you locate a good, high-quality sitter. To do so, call ☎ 800-424-2246, Monday through Thursday; 9 a.m. to 8 p.m EST and Friday 9 a.m. to 5 p.m. EST; **www.childcareaware.org.**

Be sure to ask if the sitter is licensed, bonded, and insured. To ease your children's anxiety, tell them how long you plan to be away, and be sure they feel good about the person who will be caring for them. Finally, trust your own instincts.

CAMPING

WE'VE INCLUDED A SMALL BUT CHOICE COLLECTION of California campgrounds—ones that are easily accessible, fun for children, and not too demanding of parents (we consider bathrooms and running water, for instance, to be essential). Camping can be a wonderful family experience, slowing down the pace so you can all take pleasure in the small things, from fishing in a stream to chasing butterflies. And, of course, camping takes you to California's most beautiful places for very little money.

Most of these campgrounds are state properties, and all are popular; for those that take reservations, make them early. Reservations are accepted seven months in advance, and the good campgrounds often book up fully seven months ahead. To make reservations, call **Reserve America** at ☎ 800-444-7275 or visit **www.reserveamerica.com.**

Tips on Camping with Children

We've had wonderful family camping trips—and horrible ones. Basically, if you are regular campers and your children are used to it from birth, you'll be happy at any of the campgrounds we suggest. If you're not regular campers, we'd recommend the motel option while your children are between infancy and the age of at least 3, maybe 4. As young as 6, Colleen's daughters rolled up their own sleeping bags, rinsed their own cups, and hiked a couple of miles, but at age 2 they mostly ate rocks, cried,

unofficial **TIP**
Camping is a superb opportunity to teach kids independence and self-reliance. If they're all expected to pitch in and the adventure aspect is played up, they'll help prepare food, pitch tents, and do camp chores.

and slept about four hours a night (tent living can greatly upset the routines of sensitive toddlers).

One of Colleen's daughters attends a school that organizes many camping trips, and we've adopted the school's camp rules in our families, because they maximize safety and comfort. They are as follows:

- No one is allowed to leave the campsite (even to go to the bathroom) without a whistle. Children wear the whistle around their necks; adults can carry it as they like. The whistle is blown only in an emergency, which can range from a twisted ankle to getting lost.

- Hats and sunscreen must be worn on all outings.
- Water must be carried on all outings.
- No playing, exploring, or hiking until the morning campsites are tidied and breakfast dishes are done.

Finally, recognize that camping is tiring, and after a few days of sleeping on the ground, tempers of both children and adults can get frayed. After two or three nights of roughing it, nothing cheers up a family like clean hotel sheets, a swimming pool, and a restaurant hamburger.

FAMILY-FRIENDLY RESTAURANTS

WE LOVE FOOD AND LOVE TO EAT OUT, and our kids love to eat out, too, but rarely do we agree on what constitutes a good restaurant. We like comfort, good service, creative cooking, and a nice glass of wine. They like noise, cups with lids, and as much fried food as possible. Hence the challenge: to put together a roster of restaurants throughout the state that make both parents and children happy. We had more success in some areas than others; some parts of the state don't have much more than coffee shops and chains, so you'll have to make do. Other areas, however (especially the San Francisco Bay area, the Central Coast, and the L.A. area), are rich in kid- and parent-friendly dining.

You'll note that most major chain restaurants and all the chain fast-food restaurants are not found in the listings that follow. We encourage you to skip McDonald's whenever possible and make the effort to patronize local places—not only is it better for your health, but you're more likely to get a feel for an area when you sit with the locals and eat a burrito or dim sum or pancakes. As for the big chain restaurants, we find most of them to be soulless and dull. There are exceptions, especially such smaller regional chains as California Pizza Kitchen, Crocodile Cafe, Islands, and Rubio's, all of which are good family restaurants with California flair.

The major tourist areas all seem to have Hard Rock Cafes and Planet Hollywoods, but we cover those rarely—after all, if you've been to one Hard Rock, you've been to them all. Your hotel in San Francisco, L.A., San Diego, or Orange County can steer you to one of them.

Tips on Dining Out with Children

BE REALISTIC ABOUT AGE LIMITS We ate at elegant restaurants when our children were sleeping infants in car seats. By the time toddlerhood hit, we restricted ourselves to quality fast food (like taquerias), child-friendly ethnic restaurants (Chinese, Cuban, Mexican, etc.), and take-out food enjoyed in park picnic areas. We began restaurant training in earnest at about age 4, the dawn of a years-long process of gentle reminding about napkins on laps, feet off chairs, and proper butter-knife etiquette. We expect to have achieved success around the junior year of college.

DON'T BATTLE A PICKY EATER You'll never win this one. If everything looks yucky, get them some plain rice and plain bread. Enjoy your food with gusto, and if the kids get hungry enough, they'll break down and ask to try some.

LOOK BEYOND THE KIDS' MENU The vast majority are monotonous and unhealthy, consisting mostly of burgers, deep-fried chicken, and french fries. Encourage experimentation in the grown-up menu, and ask if it's possible to order smaller portions of the "adult" food.

REMEMBER THE TAILGATE We had more fun eating on a tailgating vacation than perhaps any other. Grocery stores, delis, upscale gourmet shops, and mini-marts are all stocked with foods that seem almost too decadent to buy at home—but if you're tailgating, you have to go for the convenience foods. So we'd get take-out salads and chicken, made-to-order sandwiches, sushi, poached salmon, fresh baguettes, imported cheeses, and exotic fruits. The price was still less than a bad meal at a roadside coffee shop.

WATCH THE IN-BETWEENERS When they feel too old for (or don't like) the children's menu but can't really eat a big meal, some parental diplomacy is in order, or the in-betweener will be taking one bite from a huge order of whatever and then stopping, overwhelmed. Some kids will agree to splitting or sharing a meal, but let them choose most of it. Sometimes it's just a matter of ordering three meals for four people, so you avoid huge quantities of leftovers (which you can't take home when you're traveling) and yet allow for some tasting of different things.

SOUP, SOUP, SOUP Not only is it comforting and homey, but soup also is often a tasty, nutritious, affordable basis for a kid's meal that needs only an appetizer to complete it.

LET THEM BE WEIRD One man we know is still grateful to his parents for letting him order hamburgers at breakfast, and conversely, how many people are cheered up by a nice breakfast at 7 p.m.? As much as possible, let your kids enjoy the get-what-you-want pleasure of restaurant eating as part of their vacation. Remember, they're also missing home, routine, and the certainty of their daily meal rituals.

FREE CALIFORNIA PUBLICATIONS FOR VISITORS

FOR DESTINATION AND STATEWIDE VISITORS' INFORMATION, contact the **California Division of Tourism,** 1102 Q Street, Suite 6000,

Sacramento, CA 95814; ☎ 916-322-2881; fax 916-322-3402. For publications detailing the exceptional state-park system, contact the **California State Park System,** Department of Parks and Recreation, Box 942896, Sacramento, CA 94296; ☎ 916-653-6995. To reserve a state campground, call ☎ 800-444-7275; for a federal campground, call ☎ 877-444-6777.

PART ONE

SAN DIEGO COUNTY

WHAT AN INTERESTING TOEHOLD SAN DIEGO COUNTY has on the continent—right at the edge, where travelers must choose between the ocean and a foreign country if they keep going. The eastern part of the county is home to the enormous **Anza-Borrego Desert State Park.** The coastal area is the population center, with the city of **San Diego** (the second-largest municipality in the state) dominating. The northern part of the county (before the huge military base at **Camp Pendleton** takes over the map) is dotted with golf courses. To the south, of course, is Mexico.

> *unofficial* **TIP**
> Families will find San Diego County easy to like. It has everything California is supposed to have—palm trees, beaches, a multicultural population, unlimited outdoor recreation, sophisticated cultural offerings, and good Mexican food.

We've taken our kids to San Diego County in all seasons and for lots of different kinds of vacations. We've ridden the train from **L.A.** and stayed in downtown San Diego, riding the trolley to the **San Diego Zoo** and shopping in **Horton Plaza.** We based ourselves in **Carlsbad** to visit the **Wild Animal Park** and **Legoland** and enjoyed a bonus of gorgeous beach time. We've lolled in a fancy **Coronado Island** resort's outdoor spa after biking all over the island and taking the ferry back and forth just for fun. And we've sat in the gentle tidal waters of **Mission Bay** while a happy toddler splashed next to us. You see where this is headed, of course. It'll take more than a single vacation to even begin to sample San Diego's charms.

If it's your first visit to the San Diego area and you're arriving in summer, a four-day itinerary with a base at one of the Mission Bay resorts is ideal. **SeaWorld** is right in Mission Bay, so that's one day's outing. Pick among the zoo, Wild Animal Park, a Balboa Park museum or two, **Old Town,** and **Legoland California** for another two days of fun. Finish with a day dedicated to water sports and beach fun. If the attractions that most interest you are Legoland and the Wild Animal Park, and you like a small-town setting, consider staying up the coast

san diego county

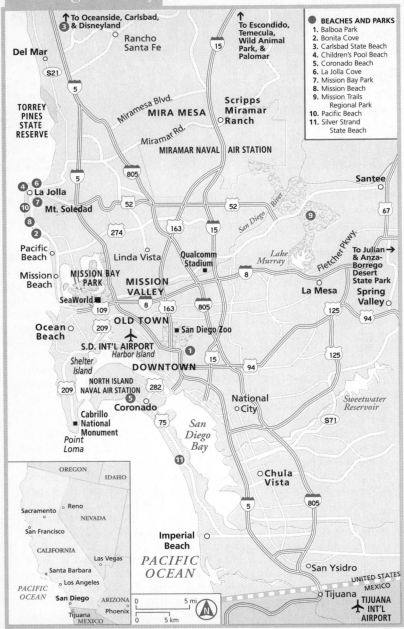

↑ To Oceanside, Carlsbad,
3 & Disneyland

Rancho
Santa Fe

Del Mar

S21

↑ To Escondido,
Temecula,
Wild Animal
Park, &
Palomar

15

● BEACHES AND PARKS
1. Balboa Park
2. Bonita Cove
3. Carlsbad State Beach
4. Children's Pool Beach
5. Coronado Beach
6. La Jolla Cove
7. Mission Bay Park
8. Mission Beach
9. Mission Trails
        Regional Park
10. Pacific Beach
11. Silver Strand
        State Beach

5

**TORREY
PINES
STATE
RESERVE**

Miramesa Blvd.

MIRA MESA

Miramar Rd.

**Scripps
Miramar
Ranch**

MIRAMAR NAVAL AIR STATION

5

Santee

67

52

52

San Diego River

9

4 **6**
La Jolla
10 **7**
8 **Mt. Soledad**
2

274

163

15

Fletcher Pkwy.

To Julian →
& Anza-
Borrego
Desert
State Park

**Pacific
Beach**

**Mission
Beach**

Linda Vista

**MISSION BAY
PARK**

SeaWorld ■

Qualcomm
Stadium ■

Lake
Murray

8

La Mesa

**Spring
Valley**

**MISSION
VALLEY**

109

8   163

805

125

94

**Ocean
Beach**

209

OLD TOWN

■ San Diego Zoo

S.D. INT'L AIRPORT
Harbor Island

1

15

94

125

**Shelter
Island**

DOWNTOWN

209   **NORTH ISLAND
NAVAL AIR STATION**

282

5

Coronado

75

**National
City**

*Sweetwater
Reservoir*

S71

**Cabrillo
■ National
Monument**

*Point
Loma*

*San
Diego
Bay*

11

○ **Chula
Vista**

5

805

*PACIFIC
OCEAN*

OREGON

IDAHO

○ Reno

Sacramento ○

NEVADA

○ San Francisco

CALIFORNIA

Las Vegas
○

○ Santa Barbara

○ Los Angeles

*PACIFIC
OCEAN*

San Diego

ARIZONA

Tijuana   Phoenix
MEXICO

**Imperial
Beach**

*PACIFIC
OCEAN*

○ **San Ysidro**

UNITED STATES
MEXICO

○ Tijuana   **TIJUANA
INT'L
AIRPORT**

0   5 mi

0   5 km

N

in **Carlsbad.** Families traveling with convention-goers won't be disappointed with the ever-improving downtown area and can try out the car-free itineraries described below. Visitors with another day should add a **Borrego Springs** visit, a **Tijuana** excursion (*note:* passports are required to enter Mexico starting January 1, 2008), or (in early spring) a whale-watching boat trip.

GETTING THERE

BY PLANE San Diego International Airport is served by most major airlines; **Lindbergh Field** (☎ 619-231-2100; **www.portofsandiego.org**) is just a few miles northeast of the city.

BY TRAIN Amtrak makes its final southbound stop in San Diego, delivering travelers from as far north as Seattle. From L.A., the trip is about two hours on the popular, well-patronized Surfliner commuter line (frequent departures morning and afternoon). Excellent public transportation from the train station makes a trip without a car possible. Call ☎ 800-USA-RAIL; **www.amtrak.com.**

BY CAR Interstate 5, which runs from Canada to Mexico, is the main freeway heading into San Diego. It's also reached from the north by **Highway 15,** which comes from the Riverside area and connects to **Interstate 10,** and by **Interstate 8,** which heads east to Arizona. A car is not necessary to enjoy central San Diego, but it's great to have if you want to explore the farther reaches.

Car-free Sightseeing

Although San Diego and its suburbs are spread generously over many acres, and motorists will find their way along good roads and modern freeways, the city has also created a network of public transportation that permits easy access to major attractions, many of which are in a comparatively concentrated geographic area. The weather's almost always sunny and mild, so the journey from place to place is a pleasant jaunt; and because the city does a brisk convention business, the various trams, trolleys, and ferries have enough patronage to justify frequent, convenient runs.

If you think you'd like to do San Diego without a car (arriving by train, for example), you'll need to stay downtown, in Coronado, or near Old Town, in order to easily combine the attractions mentioned here into a network. You can also simply take a taxi or municipal bus to the first boarding point of the day.

Here's a sample no-car itinerary: Board the **Old Town Trolley Tours** bus at your hotel in Coronado and ride it (enjoying the guide's descriptions of passing sights) to **Balboa Park.** Enjoy a morning at the zoo, then take the free Balboa shuttle to the **Space Museum,** then reboard the Old Town Trolley and continue to Old Town. Save the historic buildings for another day, but enjoy a Mexican meal and some shopping, then take the **San Diego Trolley** to downtown, changing to another trolley to

Seaport Village. At Seaport Village, let the kids play some games and get an ice-cream cone, then get on the ferry to cross the water to Coronado and your hotel.

You might think the Old Town Trolley Tours bus (with narration and music) is corny, but it sure is convenient. It goes to most of the major attractions, and you can get on and off at eight stops, including Old Town, the **Embarcadero, Seaport Village,** Horton Plaza, Coronado, and Balboa Park. Call ☎ 619-298-8687 or 800-868-7482, or on the Web, visit **www.historictours.com** for locations of stops and a timetable. $30 adults, $15 ages 4 to 12, age 3 and under free.

Metropolitan Transit Service's Transit Store (102 Broadway, downtown San Diego; ☎ 619-234-1060; **www.sdcommute.com**) is a center of information about buses, **Coaster** (Coastal Light Rail), and the San Diego Trolley. The Day Tripper Transit Pass, available as a one- ($5), two- ($9), three- ($12), or four-day ($15) pass, is sold here. There is no charge for children age 6 and under. One-day passes can also be purchased at trolley stations and the ferry landing.

The **San Diego Trolley** (☎ 619-233-3004; automated info line, ☎ 619-685-4900) operates daily from 5 a.m. to midnight, with service every 15 minutes most of the time. Tickets are dispensed from automated machines at each station. The **Blue Line** extends from Old Town through downtown to the Mexican border. The **Bayside Line** covers the Harbor Drive area and goes to Seaport Village, to the convention center, and through downtown and the **Gaslamp Quarter.** Another line heads for **Petco Park,** home of the San Diego Padres baseball team, via Mission Valley. Fares are $1.25 to $3.

There is free daily tram shuttle service around Balboa Park.

The **San Diego–Coronado Ferry,** ☎ 619-234-4111; runs between downtown San Diego's Broadway Pier (1050 North Harbor Drive, at Broadway) and the Ferry Landing Marketplace on Coronado at First Street and B Avenue. The crossing is 15 minutes, and it leaves San Diego every hour on the hour from 9 a.m. to 9 p.m., returning from Coronado every hour on the half hour. One-way fares are $3 per person and 50¢ per bike, and reservations are not needed.

The **San Diego Water Taxi** (Fish Harbor Pier, Seaport Village, 891 West Harbor Drive; ☎ 619-235-8294) offers on-call service from Monday through Friday, 2 p.m. to 10 p.m., and Saturday and Sunday, 11 a.m. to 11 p.m., and transports people to various spots around the bay, including Shelter Island, Harbor Island, Coronado, and Chula Vista; fares start at $6 but can vary by destination.

HOW TO GET INFORMATION BEFORE YOU GO

- **Anza-Borrego State Park Visitors Center** ☎ 760-767-4205; **www.anzaborrego.statepark.org.**
- **Balboa Park Visitors Center** ☎ 619-239-0512; **www.balboapark.org.**
- **Border Station Parking and Tourist Information** A commercial

park-and-shuttle service at the Mexican border; 4570 Camino De La Plaza, San Ysidro; ☎ 619-428-1422.

- **Carlsbad Convention and Visitors Bureau** ☎ 760-434-6093; **www.carlsbadca.org.**
- **Coronado Visitors Bureau** ☎ 619-437-8788; **www.coronado visitorcenter.com.**
- **San Diego Convention and Visitors Bureau** ☎ 619-236-1212; **www.sandiego.org.**
- **Tijuana Tourism and Convention Bureau** ☎ 888-775-2417; **www.seetijuana.com.**

CHILD CARE AND BABYSITTING

Kiddiecorp (10455 Sorrento Valley Road, Suite 103, San Diego; ☎ 858-455-1718; **www.kiddiecorp.com**) offers on-site group child care and special events for kids. **Marion's Childcare** (10491 Pine Grove Street, Spring Valley; ☎ 619-303-4379 or 888-891-5029; **www.hotelchildcare.com**) has in-room child care from a licensed, bonded, insured service of 18 years.

The BEST BEACHES and PARKS

ANZA-BORREGO DESERT STATE PARK This 600,000-acre park is home to bighorn sheep, roadrunners, and, in the spring, amazing wildflower displays; it's rich with riding and hiking trails for families with desert and wilderness experience. For a stop on a driving tour of San Diego County, the visitors center offers a fine slide presentation and lots of great children's books on desert flora and fauna. Open daily October through May, on weekends and holidays only June through September. Visitors center: 200 Palm Canyon Drive, Borrego Springs; ☎ 760-767-4205; **www.anzaborrego.statepark.org.**

BALBOA PARK SAN DIEGO has taken the urban park to new heights, going beyond outdoor recreation to create a compact cultural hub that no other American city can rival (except, of course, Washington, D.C.). In the heart of the city, not far from downtown, Balboa is home to 14 museums (many are reviewed later), the world-famous San Diego Zoo, and five theaters (including the Old Globe). You'll also find outdoor pleasures, including picnic areas, three playgrounds, and botanical gardens, along with amusements such as a miniature-train ride, a carousel, and butterfly rides for kids age 5 and under. Open daily 9:30 a.m. to 4:30 p.m., 5 p.m from June 26 to September 6; free parking. The Web site offers packages such as the Best of Balboa Park Combo for $55, which gets you into 13 attractions plus the zoo. Visitors center: House of Hospitality building, 1549 El Prado; ☎ 619-239-0512; **www.balboapark.org.**

*un*official **TIP**
Before you visit any of Balboa Park's destinations, hop on the free tram that cruises the park, both to get oriented and to give your kids a cheap thrill.

BONITA COVE Within Mission Bay Park, near Belmont Park and Mission Beach, you'll find this outdoor paradise for young children. The calm, shallow water is friendly even to toddlers, and there's a playground, a grassy picnic area, and sand to dig. For information, call ☎ 858-694-3049.

CARLSBAD STATE BEACH A broad sand beach with a wide concrete bike/skating path, this is a great summertime beach for families—there's typically enough surf to have fun in, but it's rarely rough. Just south of the beach is Agua Hedionda Lagoon, a calm, wave-free spot for swimming, fishing, and boating. Lifeguards, restrooms, showers. For information, call ☎ 760-438-3143; **www.carlsbad.ca.us/beaches.**

CHILDREN'S POOL BEACH Still known by the name given it by locals who brought kids to play in the quiet surf, this beach is now home to herds of sea lions. Families stop by to look down on the hundreds of huge, protected creatures from a high vantage point. End of Jenner Street, 850 Coast Boulevard, La Jolla.

CORONADO BEACH San Diego's widest beach, Coronado is so big that it absorbs even the largest crowds comfortably. Good for swimming, body boarding, people watching, and basic beach fun, it is guarded by the looming Hotel del Coronado. There are volleyball courts, fire pits on the north end, changing rooms, lifeguards in summer, showers, and pay parking at the hotel or free parking on the streets. For beach information, call ☎ 619-437-8788.

LA JOLLA COVE A drop-dead gorgeous jewel of a beach, in a cove protected by cliffs, La Jolla Cove seems smaller than ever in peak season, when crowds get intense. But don't let that keep you from enjoying the tide pools, the calm, clean water, the excellent snorkeling, and the grassy picnic areas. Next door is Boomer Beach, an expert bodysurfing spot that's dangerous for most but great for pros, or for watching the locals put on a show. Changing rooms, lifeguard. Coast Boulevard to Scripps Park, La Jolla. For information, call ☎ 619-221-8901.

☀ **MISSION BAY PARK** Although there are major resorts and hotels lining Mission Bay, a calm-water tidal area that curls and curves for many acres, the bay's park is a huge public playground, with grassy meadows and picnic areas sloping down to sandy beaches (many areas with no waves!), as well as several marinas servicing the 4,600-acre aquatic sports area. There are designated areas for each sport (swimming, sailing, windsurfing, kayaking, waterskiing, and fishing). And paved bike paths dot the grassy areas and run along the shore. Free parking lots adjacent, no overnight parking or camping. Fires allowed in designated fire containers on beaches. The playground at Tecolote Shores was especially designed for disabled children. For more information, call ☎ 619-221-8900 or 858-694-3049, or log on to **www .aboutmissionbay.com.**

MISSION BEACH If you have older kids who want to be where the action is, head to this two-mile-long shoreline on the ocean side of Mission Bay. Teenagers are plentiful here, playing volleyball, skating on the boardwalk, body-boarding in the sometimes-rough surf (riptides are common), and flaunting the latest surf wear. On the boardwalk right in the center of the beach is Belmont Park amusement park (see profile). Changing rooms, showers, lifeguards. Mission Boulevard, Mission Bay; For information, call ☎ 619-221-8900.

MISSION TRAILS REGIONAL PARK See "Hiking" under "Family Outdoor Adventures."

PACIFIC BEACH Locals call it the Strand, and locals are plentiful on hot summer days, of which San Diego has many. (Consequently, parking is a challenge.) It has everything a big public beach should have, from a fishing pier to a biking and skating path to body-board rentals to lifeguards; surfers are limited to one area, so swimmers don't have to battle them for wave space. The many restaurants and shops of the neighborhood of Pacific Beach are a short walk away. Changing rooms, showers, restrooms (but no public restrooms between Pacific Beach Drive and Mission Beach). Mission Boulevard, San Diego; for information, call ☎ 619-221-8900; **www.pacificbeach.org.**

SILVER STRAND STATE BEACH Three things make this state park a good beach for families: The surf and riptides are fairly calm; parking is plentiful here, unlike at the city beaches; and the shoreline sparkles with millions of tiny silver shells, which enchant many children. This two-mile-long beach connects the isthmus of Coronado (no, it's not really an island) to the mainland's Imperial Beach, and it's quieter than the beach in front of the Hotel Del Coronado. The broad, shallow shoreline allows for lots of safe scampering in gentle waves (or in no waves on the bay side), as well as good clamming and surf fishing. If you visit in winter, know that the location invites wind and chill, so dress warmly. Dogs are not allowed on the beach, in the tunnels, or on the bay side. Parking is free, and RV camping (reservations required) is available for $25 to $30; no tent camping. Restrooms, showers, lifeguards. Follow signs off Highway 75; for information, call ☎ 619-435-5184; **www.parks.ca.gov.**

FAMILY OUTDOOR ADVENTURES

BICYCLING AND SKATING On some bright summer days, it seems that every San Diegan is on skates, bikes, or skateboards, making good use of the endless paved paths that wend around Mission Bay and along the beaches. Mission and Pacific Beaches are particularly fun to cruise, but in season they can get intimidatingly crowded and speedy for the training-wheel set. For a quieter, beautiful, long ride, follow the path along the Coronado shoreline through Silver Strand State Park. The Mission Bay paths are also good for younger children. On Coronado Island, you can rent bikes and skates from **Bikes and Beyond,** Ferry Landing Marketplace; ☎ 619-435-7180. In the Mission Bay area, get gear from **Mission Bay Sportcenter,** 1010 Santa Clara Place; ☎ 858-488-1004; **www.missionbaysportcenter.com.**

BOATING Even novices can learn to sail in the calm waters of Mission Bay, and every weekend, they're out there doing it. Boats and lessons are offered at **Mission Bay Sportcenter,** 1010 Santa Clara Place; ☎ 858-488-1004; **www.missionbaysportcenter.com.** At the Dana Inn and Marina (1710 West Mission Bay Drive), there's **Adventure Watersports;** ☎ 619-226-8611; **www.adventurewatersports.com**), offering sailboats and lessons as well as kayaks, aqua cycles, and windsurfing gear.

FISHING Oceangoing fishing charters are plentiful in San Diego, but with kids we prefer a cheaper, lower-key outing—we head for one of the several fetching piers, where licenses are unnecessary and fish are often caught. The piers at Pacific Beach and the Coronado Ferry Landing are good ones, and both have bait-and-tackle shops.

HIKING Serious hiking opportunities abound in the region, but with kids in tow, our favorite destination is **Mission Trails Regional Park** (Father Junipero Serra Trail, San Diego; ☎ 619-668-3275; **www.mtrp .org**). This inland, 5,800-acre urban park has 35 miles of trails for hiking, mountain biking, and horseback riding, and some of the trails are paved to accommodate strollers and wheelchairs. Pick up a map at the visitors center. If your kids are sturdy, tackle the trail to San Diego's highest peak, a 1,600-foot climb that pays off with a 360-degree view of the city.

SNORKELING California's clearest waters are found in **La Jolla Cove,** a protected part of the San Diego–La Jolla Underwater Park. For swimming children old enough to manage a mask and snorkel (typically age 7 and up), a snorkeling adventure is mind-blowing, as interactive a nature experience as they'll ever have. See La Jolla Cove listing in "The Best Beaches and Parks" for location details; if you don't have snorkel gear, you can rent it from **Adventure Watersports** at the Dana Inn and Marina in Mission Bay (☎ 619-226-8611; **www.adventure watersports.com**).

SURFING Surfing's popularity has exploded in the last few years, and so the choices for surf lessons and camps are numerous. One of our favorites is the **San Diego Surfing Academy** (☎ 800-447-SURF or 760-230-1474; **www.surfsdsa.com**), which makes fine use of the gentle waves at South Carlsbad State Beach in its private lessons for kids (age 8 and up) and adults; also note that its summertime surf camps can be attended for just a day or two. On Mission Beach, Pacific Surf School (☎ 619-742-2267; **www.pacificsurf.org**) offers frequent group lessons for a reasonable $50 to $70. Also highly recommended is **La Jolla's Surf Diva** (☎ 858-454-8273; **www.surfdiva.com**), known for its classes for girls and their moms, but boys are welcome, too. If you want to try it on your own, rent a soft-foam longboard from the rental concessions at Pacific Beach and go for it.

WATERSKIING AND WINDSURFING On the ocean side of Mission Bay is some of the best windsurfing in California; on the bay side is superb waterskiing. For instruction and equipment for both sports, you can contact the **Mission Bay Sportcenter** (1010 Santa Clara Place; ☎ 858-488-1004; **www.missionbaysportcenter.com**); open daily, 10 a.m. to 7 p.m. They can also get you started on a surfboard, Jet Ski, or kayak. Another good spot for waterskiing lessons and rentals (as well as whale-watching excursions) is **Seaforth Mission Bay Boat Rentals** (1641 Quivira Road; ☎ 619-223-1681; **www.seaforthboatrental.com**). Yet another windsurfing outfitter and instructor is **Windsport Kayak and Windsurfing Center** (844 West Mission Bay Drive; ☎ 858-488-4642; **www.windsport.net**).

 WHALE WATCHING The Pacific gray whale swims past San Diego from December through mid-March, and blowhole and breech sightings are common. In fact, so confident is one outfitter, **H&M Landing** (2803 Emerson Street, San Diego; ☎ 619-222-1144; **www.hmlanding.com**), that it guarantees a whale sighting or you get a voucher for another outing. Family trips are typically three hours long. If you'd rather scout whales from dry land, head to the Cabrillo National Monument on Point Loma (see profile).

A **CALENDAR** of **FESTIVALS** and **EVENTS**

January

WHALEFEST Birch Aquarium at Scripps La Jolla. January and February. Special exhibits and hands-on activities teach kids about whales; ☎ 858-534-FISH; **www.aquarium.ucsd.edu.**

February

HERITAGE DAY PARADE San Diego. Late February. Celebrates the city's rich ethnic diversity; ☎ 619-286-9989.

WILDFLOWER BLOOMS Anza-Borrego. The blooms hit sometime between February and April, and they last only for a few weeks; ☎ 760-767-4205.

March

OCEAN BEACH KITE FESTIVAL Ocean Beach. Sponsored by the Kiwanis for more than 50 years. Kite decorating (9 a.m. to noon) and flying, as well as parade (plus free hot dogs). Bring your own kite; ☎ 619-531-1527.

April

GASLAMP QUARTER EASTER BONNET PARADE Fifth and L Streets, San Diego. A charity event held the weekend before Easter. Hat-making workshop, Easter egg hunt, parade, and treats; ☎ 619-233-5227; **www.gaslamp.org.**

OPENING DAY, SAN DIEGO PADRES Petco Park; ☎ 619-795-5000.

SAN DIEGO EARTHFAIR Balboa Park. Earth Day festival with lots of activities for children; ☎ 858-272-7370; **www.earthdayweb.org.**

May

FIESTA CINCO DE MAYO Old Town State Park, San Diego. A two-day party with music, entertainment, food, booths, and kids' activities; ☎ 619-296-3236.

CARLSBAD VILLAGE STREET FAIRE Carlsbad. Some 90,000 people fill this small town for its annual one-day blowout, which includes children's rides, a pancake breakfast, farmer's-market-style vendors, live music, and international foods; ☎ 760-931-8400; **www.carlsbad.org.**

June

AMERICAN INDIAN CULTURAL DAYS San Diego Museum of Man, Balboa Park. Native Americans from across the country gather to share tribal ceremonies, stories, music, foods, and crafts, with hands-on projects for children; ☎ 619-239-2001; **www.museumofman.org.**

SAN DIEGO COUNTY FAIR Del Mar. Carnival rides, flower shows, animals, arcades, and nationally known musical performers; ☎ 858-755-1161; **www.sdfair.com.**

July

ANNUAL FESTIVAL OF THE BELLS MISSION Basilica. Weekend-long festival celebrating the anniversary of the founding of Mission San Diego de Alcala. Includes food, music and dance performances, llama rides, and games; ☎ 619-283-7319.

FOURTH OF JULY EVENTS La Jolla: a free concert at Scripps Park followed by a fireworks show; ☎ 858-454-1600. Coronado: a parade, free concert in Spreckels Park, and fireworks; ☎ 619-437-8788.

U.S. OPEN SANDCASTLE COMPETITION Imperial Beach Pier. Sand castles like you've never seen 'em, along with a parade and evening fireworks. Children have their own competition; ☎ 619-424-6663.

MOVIES BEFORE THE MAST *Star of India.* Nautically themed, family-friendly movies are screened on board this historic sailing ship in July and August; ☎ 619-234-9153; **www.sdmaritime.org.**

August

CHULA VISTA ANNUAL DOWNTOWN LEMON FESTIVAL Food and crafts; ☎ 619-422-1982.

WORLD BODY SURFING CHAMPIONSHIPS Oceanside Pier and Beach. Body surfers from around the world put on a show; ☎ 760-722-1534.

October

FLEET WEEK A weeklong tribute to the military with many events, including ship and submarine tours, a ship parade, and an air show; ☎ 800-353-3893; **www.fleetweek.com.**

OKTOBERFEST Holiday Park, Carlsbad. Since Carlsbad was originally a German settlement named Karlsbad, this is the Oktoberfest event to attend; ☎ 760-434-6093.

November

DEL MAR FAIRGROUNDS Holiday of Lights. Drive your car around the racetrack and view 250 holiday displays; ☎ 858-793-5555.

MOTHER GOOSE PARADE Main Street, El Cajon. Hundreds of thousands of spectators jam into El Cajon for this decades-old parade honoring fairy tales, children, and Mother Goose rhymes; ☎ 619-444-8712.

December

LA JOLLA CHRISTMAS PARADE AND HOLIDAY FESTIVAL Downtown La Jolla. Floats, marching bands, and Santa, followed by a carnival and street fair; ☎ 858-454-5718; **www.lajollabythesea.com.**

SAN DIEGO

San Diego is the one destination in California that combines an ocean-resort feel with big-city culture and activities. You can lie on the beach at **Coronado** and 20 minutes later be downtown at a major rock concert. You can spend the morning in a museum as you might in other cities, but after lunch you'll be inline-skating along **Mission Bay.** While you watch your little one ride the carousel at **Shoreline Village,** you'll admire the bay on one side and the skyscrapers of the financial district on the other.

More cosmopolitan than Santa Barbara and easier to maneuver than L.A., San Diego is an ideal introduction to Southern California.

unofficial **TIP**
If you'll be in San Diego for at least a week, renting a beach house is the way to go.

The big-deal attractions (**San Diego Zoo, Wild Animal Park, SeaWorld**) are indeed world-class; the historic areas (**Old Town,** the **Maritime Museum** ships) are colorful and inviting; there are wonderfully located concentrations of hotels and motels (Mission Bay, Coronado); north of town are some beautiful, laid-back beach towns for day trips or overnight escapes (**La Jolla, Carlsbad**); and the residents are relaxed and casual.

FAMILY LODGING

Best Western Blue Sea Lodge
707 Pacific Beach Drive, San Diego; ☎ 858-488-4700 or 800-BLUE-SEA; www.bestwestern-bluesea.com; $139–$249 off season, $159–$279 in summer

The external architecture may be hideous, but the location can't be beat: The boardwalk and the soft sand of Pacific Beach are right in front, Mission Bay is just around the corner, and the neighborhood is full of cafes, restaurants, and beach shops. Furthermore, a recent remodeling spruced up the interior, adding a colorful surfer theme and 26 new rooms, bringing the room count up to 126. The ocean-view suites are big enough for families, and many rooms have kitchens. Extras include a small pool, a spa, a cheerful cafe, and rental bikes. Reserve at least two months in advance for summertime visits.

Catamaran Resort Hotel & Spa
3999 Mission Boulevard, Mission Bay; ☎ 858-488-1081 or 800-422-8386; www.catamaranresort.com; $165–$600; packages with SeaWorld or various sporting adventures offered

This large Mission Bay resort has live parrots in the tropical-décor lobby, spacious rooms (many with sliding glass doors to patios and bayside), outside pizza delivery service, and a location convenient to SeaWorld. It's not as glitzy as some other San Diego area resorts, but it is a beach and watersports paradise—wear your bathing suits and board shorts and head for the hotel pier for rentals and lessons in kayaking, windsurfing, diving, and more, or go to the bayfront beach for swimming and volleyball; wave lovers can just walk across Mission Boulevard to get to Mission Beach. Among the offerings for adventurous teens is sea-cave kayaking.

Embassy Suites San Diego Bay
601 Pacific Coast Highway, San Diego; ☎ 619-239-2400 or 800-EMBASSY; www.essandiegobay.com; $199–$319

If you want to be downtown (not a first choice for beach-loving families, but it has its appeal), this is a good place to stay. It has all the family comforts that the chain is known for (two-room suite, two TVs, sleeper sofa, refrigerator, microwave, free breakfast); it's close to the trolley line, the Embarcadero, and Seaport Village; and it's not far from Balboa Park. There is a pool, but, curiously, it is indoors.

Hotel del Coronado
1500 Orange Avenue, Coronado; ☎ 619-435-6611 or 800-HOTEL-DEL; www.hoteldel.com; $250–$600; suites $700 and up

Incredibly popular with many travelers, this huge (692 rooms, six restaurants) resort complex on Coronado Island offers lodgings from vintage-historic rooms to modern beachfront suites. Some kids find the main Victorian building kind of creepy, its dark hallways often crowded with busloads of daytrippers. But there's plenty of sunshine out by the (crowded) pool and on the beach, where supervised kids' programs and activities (some free, most costing $15 to $45, depending on activity) are held in spring and summer and during the Christmas holidays. Teens have a new lounge, with computers, video games, a pool table, and music, and they get such active options as surf lessons, kayaking, and biking. The full line of sports and water equipment is available to rent, and there are child-care services and children's menus. This is no place for the budget conscious—you'll pay dearly for everything from parking to food—but for some it's worth it to be in the middle of the history and the beach action.

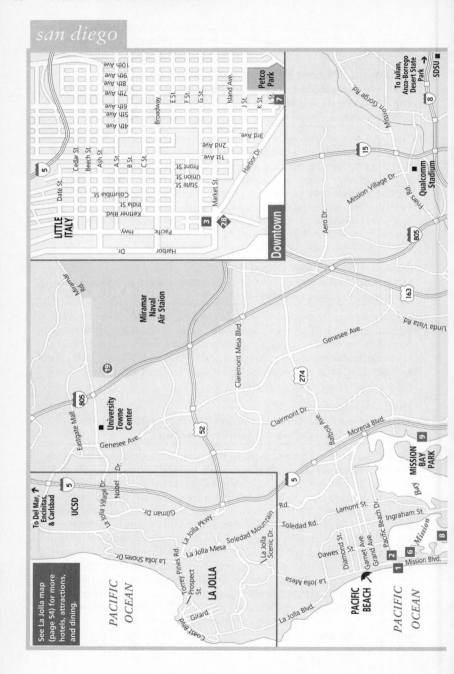

san diego

Downtown

LITTLE ITALY

10th Ave.
9th Ave.
8th Ave.
7th Ave.
6th Ave.
5th Ave.
4th Ave.

E St.
F St.
G St.
Island Ave.

J St.
K St.
L St.

Petco Park
7

Broadway
3rd Ave.
2nd Ave.
1st Ave.
Harbor Dr.

Cedar St.
Beech St.
Ash St.
A St.
B St.
C St.

Date St.
Columbia St.
India St.
State St.
Union St.
Front St.
Market St.

Kettner Blvd.

3
28

Pacific Hwy.

Harbor Dr.

5

To Julian, Anza-Borrego Desert State Park
SDSU

Mission Gorge Rd.

8

15

Friars Rd.

Qualcomm Stadium

Mission Village Dr.

805

Aero Dr.

163

Linda Vista Rd.

Genesee Ave.

Claremont Mesa Blvd.

Miramar Naval Air Station

Miramar Rd.

274

Clairemont Dr.

Balboa Ave.

Morena Blvd.

MISSION BAY PARK
9

805

University Towne Center

Eastgate Mall

Genesee Ave.

52

Nobel Dr.

Gilman Dr.

Clairemont Mesa Blvd.

5

Bay

Lamont St.

Ingraham St.

Mission

8

To Del Mar, Encinitas, & Carlsbad
5

UCSD

La Jolla Village Dr.

La Jolla Pkwy.

Soledad Mountain Rd.

Soledad Rd.

La Jolla Mesa

La Jolla Scenic Dr.

Pacific Beach Dr.

Lamont St.

Dawes St.

Diamond St.

Garnet Ave.

Grand Ave.

PACIFIC BEACH

1 2 6

Mission Blvd.

La Jolla Shores Dr.

Torrey Pines Rd.

Prospect St.

LA JOLLA

Girard

Coast Blvd

La Jolla Blvd.

La Jolla Mesa

PACIFIC OCEAN

PACIFIC OCEAN

See La Jolla map (page 54) for more hotels, attractions, and dining.

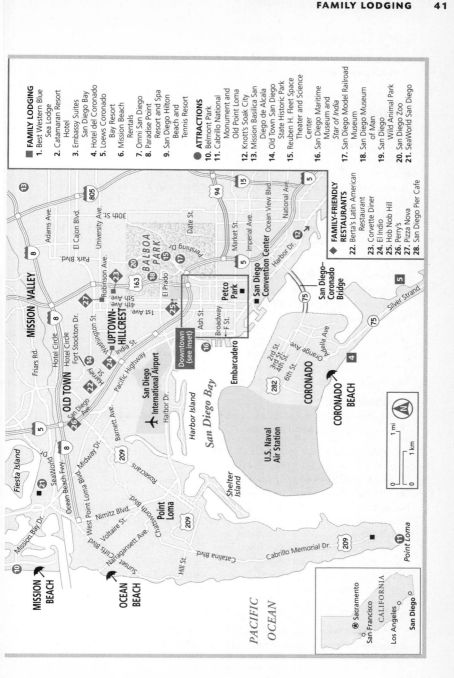

FAMILY LODGING

1. Best Western Blue Sea Lodge
2. Catamaran Resort Hotel
3. Embassy Suites San Diego Bay
4. Hotel del Coronado
5. Loews Coronado Bay Resort
6. Mission Beach Rentals
7. Omni San Diego
8. Paradise Point Resort and Spa
9. San Diego Hilton Beach and Tennis Resort

ATTRACTIONS

10. Belmont Park
11. Cabrillo National Monument and Old Point Loma
12. Knott's Soak City
13. Mission Basilica San Diego de Alcala
14. Old Town San Diego State Historic Park
15. Reuben H. Fleet Space Theater and Science Center
16. San Diego Maritime Museum and Star of India
17. San Diego Model Railroad Museum
18. San Diego Museum of Man
19. San Diego Wild Animal Park
20. San Diego Zoo
21. SeaWorld San Diego

FAMILY-FRIENDLY RESTAURANTS

22. Berta's Latin American Restaurant
23. Covette Diner
24. El Indio
25. Hob Nob Hill
26. Perry's
27. Pizza Nova
28. San Diego Pier Cafe

☀ Loews Coronado Bay Resort

4000 Coronado Bay Road, Coronado; ☎ 619-424-4000 or 800-23-LOEWS; www.loewscoronadobay.com; $265–$369; suites $525 and up

This upscale, modern, 440-room resort looks at first like a business hotel, but it is actually totally family friendly. Located on its own little peninsula on Coronado Island, it's far from the taco bars and shops of Coronado Village, but there's plenty to keep families happy right at the resort. There's a nice pool area (three pools, one of which is adults-only) with a great snack bar; on Friday nights, a 9- by 12-foot screen shows family movies while kids float on inner tubes. You'll also find a spa (for grown-ups), a playground, a game room, PBteen lounge/spa, and sailboat and bike rentals; beautiful Silver Strand State Beach is a short walk. The Loews Loves Kids activities program for ages 4 to 12 (summers and holidays) is $40 for a full day and $25 for a half day, with sibling discounts, and there is an in-room babysitting service as well as babyproofing kits. The casual restaurant and room service have kids' menus, but save the fine-dining room for adults.

Mission Beach Rentals

747 San Fernando Place, Mission Beach; ☎ 858-488-3100; www.missionbeachmanagement.com; weekly rentals in summer $550–$6,000 per week

A long-established rental agency with a good supply of beach houses, apartments, and condos. All but the smallest studios are ideal for families, with kitchens, living rooms, and homelike comfort; some condos have amenities like pools and spas. Locations include Mission Bay and Pacific Beach.

Omni San Diego

675 L Street; ☎ 619-231-6664 or 888-444-6664; www.omnihotels.com; $239–$329; suites $500 and up

Linked by a skybridge to Petco Park (home of Padres baseball), this gleaming new tower has a great location for those who need to be near the Convention Center and/or want to be in the Gaslamp Quarter or at a baseball game (some rooms even look right into the stadium!). Its 511 rooms include 27 family-fitting junior and one-bedroom suites, all decorated with a cool white-on-beige palette and all complete with such modern frills as video games, pay-per-view movies, and wireless Internet. The pool deck is decidedly urban, with modern buildings all around, but it's kid friendly and has a good cafe with a children's menu. The San Diego Trolley stops right in front, so you can easily get to Old Town, Seaport Village, and the Mexican-border transit center.

☀ Paradise Point Resort & Spa

1404 West Vacation Road, San Diego; ☎ 858-274-4630 or 800-344-2626; www.paradisepoint.com; $259–$895 summer, $229–$509 off season

This is no place for fans of intimate little hotels—462 low-slung, recently rehabbed 1970s-vintage rooms, five pools, tennis courts, a volleyball court, an 18-hole putting course, and much more are spread over a tropically land-scaped 44-acre island in Mission Bay. But it's a good place on a lovely bayside beach for an active family resort vacation. Summertime brings the daily Kids Camp, where kids ages 3 to 12 do everything from learn to Hula Hoop to make ice cream; the cost is $50 for a full day, including lunch (the littlest ones have a morning program only). Teens get nighttime activities and lots to do on their own, from sunbathing at the beach to cruising the video arcade. Many rooms have kitchens; all have patios or terraces. Bike and pedalboat rentals, children's menus, sauna, fitness center, packages with local attractions.

San Diego Hilton Beach and Tennis Resort
1775 East Mission Bay Drive, San Diego; ☎ 619-276-4010 or 800-221-2424; www.sandiegoresort.hilton.com; $249 (and up) off season, $279 (and up) in season; children stay free in parents' room

Part high-rise, part bungalow complex, this 357-room resort hotel on Mission Bay caters to families, with all sorts of kid-friendly amenities. Every day in summer, and on weekends during the rest of the year, the Kids Klub program is free by day and $30 for the nighttime dinner activities. (It's less like day care and more like organized fun, so many kids just join in for an hour or two to take part in the activities that most attract them.) The over-11 set gets its own Teen Time program, which includes mixers. Fun facilities include the huge swimming pool, the little-kid wading pool, biking and skating on the pathways (rentals available), the beach, the tennis, the water-sport rentals. Many of the large rooms have terraces or patios, as well as wet bars and refrigerators. Children's menus are available.

⏺ ATTRACTIONS

Belmont Park

APPEAL BY AGE	PRESCHOOL ★★	GRADE SCHOOL ★★★★	TEENS ★★
YOUNG ADULTS ★★★		OVER 30 ★★	SENIORS ★★

West Mission Bay Drive and West Mission Boulevard, Mission Bay; Belmont Park; ☎ 858-488-1549; www.giantdipper.com

Hours Summer: Sunday–Thursday, 11 a.m.–11 p.m.; Friday and Saturday, 11 a.m.–midnight. Off season: Sunday–Thursday, 11 a.m.–8 p.m., Friday and Saturday, 11 a.m.–9 p.m. **Admission** Free to park; ride prices vary. **Touring time** Average 3 hours with swimming; minimum 1 hour. **Rainy-day touring** Yes, for indoor facilities. **Restaurants** Concessions. **Alcoholic beverages** No. **Disabled access** Limited on rides. **Wheelchair rental** No. **Baby-stroller rental** No. **Lockers** No. **Pet kennels** No. **Rain check** No. **Private tours** No.

DESCRIPTION AND COMMENTS Part old-fashioned seaside amusement park, part modern playground, this fun zone is particularly appealing to school-age kids and teens; many of the games and rides are too difficult or scary for young children, though there is a small kiddie area. The showpieces are the 1925 wooden roller coaster and the wooden replica of a Looff carousel; our kids particularly liked steering the little remote-control boats around the miniature harbor. The Plunge, a gigantic indoor salt-water pool, is worth a dip, if only to experience Wyland's impressive underwater whale mural. Arcades, video games, a movie theater, and shops ring the rides.

Cabrillo National Monument and Old Point Loma

APPEAL BY AGE	PRESCHOOL ★★★	GRADE SCHOOL ★★★★	TEENS ★★★
YOUNG ADULTS ★★★★		OVER 30 ★★★★	SENIORS ★★★★

Point Loma, south on Catalina Boulevard, San Diego; ☎ 619-557-5450; www.nps.gov/cabr

Hours Daily, 9 a.m.–5:15 p.m.; open later in summer. **Admission** $5 per car or $3 per person walk-in, children under age 17 free when accompanied by adult. **Touring time** Average 2 hours; minimum 1 hour. **Rainy-day touring** Not good. **Restaurants** Vending machines. **Alcoholic beverages** No. **Disabled access** Yes. **Wheelchair rental** Yes, free. **Baby-stroller rental** No. **Lockers** No. **Pet kennels** No. **Rain check** No. **Private tours** No.

DESCRIPTION AND COMMENTS   This falls under the scenery category, which typically bores kids, but ours enjoyed this outing as much as we did. Reached after driving past the airport through Shelter Island, a huge Navy base (some of which is operational and some abandoned), and Point Loma, this point of land several hundred feet above the ocean seems like the end of the world. As you stand on the point's bluff, the Pacific stretches eternally to your right, while the whole of San Diego Bay spreads out straight ahead and to the left. The kids loved looking through the coin telescope for close-ups of the many incoming and outgoing military ships and planes, commercial planes, and pleasure boats (in winter and spring, this is also a great vantage to spot gray whales). Then we walked higher up the point to the tiny old 1856 light-house; what enthralled our 8-year-old was not the light itself, but the preserved (behind glass) living quarters of the lighthouse captain, his wife, and two sons. A steep trail down to tide pools is a worthy outing with older kids, and the visitors center has displays on the history of Juan Cabrillo's discovery of San Diego.

Knott's Soak City

APPEAL BY AGE	PRESCHOOL ★★	GRADE SCHOOL ★★★★	TEENS ★★★
YOUNG ADULTS ★★		OVER 30 ★★	SENIORS ★

20525 Entertainment Circle, Chula Vista; ☎ 619-661-7373; www.soakcityusa.com

Hours May, June, and September: daily, 10 a.m.–6 p.m.; July and August: daily, 10 a.m.–8 p.m. **Admission** $27 adults, $15 children ages 3–11; after 3 p.m., $15 for adults and kids; parking $7–$12. **Touring time** 4–6 hours; minimum 1 hour.

Rainy-day touring Yes. **Restaurants** Snack bar. **Alcoholic beverages** No. **Disabled access** Yes. **Wheelchair rental** No. **Baby-stroller rental** No. **Lockers** Yes. **Pet kennels** No. **Rain check** No. **Private tours** No.

DESCRIPTION AND COMMENTS This 1950s-themed water park celebrates the surf-loving California fantasy. A highlight is the Coronado Express, a family raft ride that rushes down almost 700 feet of twists and turns into a splashdown pool. Among the 22 other rides are tube slides, body slides, speed slides, a wave pool, and a lazy river for folks who just want to kick back and float.

Mission Basilica San Diego de Alcala

APPEAL BY AGE	PRESCHOOL ★	GRADE SCHOOL ★★	TEENS ★★
YOUNG ADULTS ★★		OVER 30 ★★★	SENIORS ★★★

10818 San Diego Mission Road, San Diego; ☎ 619-281-8449; www.missionsandiego.com

Hours Daily, 9 a.m.–4:45 p.m., except Thanksgiving and Christmas. Tours are Tuesday and Thursday, 10 a.m.–noon; call ☎ 858-565-9077 between noon and 2 p.m on Monday and Thursday only for reservations. **Admission** $3 adults, $2 seniors, $1 children ages 6–12. **Touring time** Average 1 hour; minimum 30 minutes. **Rainy-day touring** Yes. **Restaurants** No. **Alcoholic beverages** No. **Disabled access** Yes. **Wheelchair rental**. No **Baby-stroller rental** No. **Lockers** No. **Pet kennels** No. **Rain check** No. **Private tours** Self-guided audio tour.

DESCRIPTION AND COMMENTS This was the first of the California missions, and it still serves as an active parish church. It's a short stop for most families, because the museum area is small, but the grounds are lovely, and the church sanctuary is a fine example of the folkloric quality of mission architecture.

Old Town San Diego State Historic Park

APPEAL BY AGE	PRESCHOOL ★★★	GRADE SCHOOL ★★★★★	TEENS ★★★★
YOUNG ADULTS ★★★★★		OVER 30 ★★★★★	SENIORS ★★★★★

Bounded by Wallace, Congress, Twigs, and Juan streets; ☎ 619-220-5422; www.parks.ca.gov

Hours Daily, beginning at 10 a.m. for historic houses; most shops open until 9 p.m. **Admission** Free; donations appreciated. **Touring time** Average a half day; minimum 3 hours, with a meal and minimal shop browsing. **Rainy-day touring** Not great; outdoor paths, unpaved areas. **Restaurants** Surrounding. **Alcoholic beverages** In some restaurants. **Disabled access** Yes. **Wheelchair rental** No. **Baby-stroller rental** No. **Lockers** No. **Pet kennels** No; leashed pets allowed. **Rain check** No. **Private tours** Yes.

DESCRIPTION AND COMMENTS Shops and restaurants occupy many of the landmark buildings that surround the official state-historic-park section of Old Town, so the kids may never know they're being educated when you come here. The park showcases aspects of San Diego's past from 1821 to 1872, when the area was first under the Mexican and then later the American government. The original town plaza is the focal point of the pedestrian-only zone; it is surrounded by restored homes with furnishings of the period, a smithy and stable, a courthouse, a schoolhouse, a dental museum, a drugstore museum, and a newspaper museum. Free tours are conducted daily at 11 a.m. and 2 p.m. by costumed docents at the visitors center in the Robinson-Rose House (4002 Wallace Street). The Bazaar del Mundo, shops and cafes surrounding a courtyard, often has mariachis and costumed dancers performing.

 ## Reuben H. Fleet Space Theater and Science Center

APPEAL BY AGE	PRESCHOOL ★★★	GRADE SCHOOL ★★★★	TEENS ★★★★
YOUNG ADULTS ★★★★		OVER 30 ★★★★	SENIORS ★★★★

1875 El Prado, near San Diego Zoo; ☎ 619-238-1233; www.rhfleet.org

Hours Monday–Thursday, 9:30 a.m.–5 p.m.; Friday and Saturday, 9:30 a.m.–8 p.m.; Sunday, 9:30 a.m.–6 p.m. Summer hours vary. **Admission** Price varies depending on IMAX movies attended: $8–$15 adults, $6–$13 seniors 65 and over, $6–$12 children ages 3–12, free for children under age 3; first Monday of each month (holidays excluded) is Senior Day, with $5 admission to exhibits and 1 IMAX film. **Touring time** Average 2 hours; minimum 1 hour. **Rainy-day touring** Yes. **Restaurants** Yes. **Alcoholic beverages** No. **Disabled access** Yes. **Wheelchair rental** No. **Baby-stroller rental** No. **Lockers** No. **Pet kennels** No. **Rain check** No. **Private tours** No.

DESCRIPTION AND COMMENTS   Of the many, many fine museums in Balboa Park, this is the hardest to find—despite its tremendous appeal to families, it is not mentioned on any of the directional signs posted in the park. (*Hint:* It's across the fountain plaza from the Natural History Museum, en route to the zoo.) This is an excellent hands-on science museum, where kids can touch, feel, experiment, and explore. The special exhibits are always first rate, and they sometimes stay for a long time; recent examples included interactive exhibits on high-definition television, the science of seeing, and a "flight" through the human heart. Big-screen Omnimax (like IMAX) films, usually about nature and/or space, are shown daily in the adjacent theater, and they are invariably worth seeing—but note that the noise and special effects may scare small children. This place can get mobbed, so try to visit on a school day after lunch, when the field trips have all returned to school.

 ## San Diego Maritime Museum and *Star of India*

APPEAL BY AGE	PRESCHOOL ★★★	GRADE SCHOOL ★★★★★	TEENS ★★★★★
YOUNG ADULTS ★★★★		OVER 30 ★★★★★	SENIORS ★★★★★

1306 North Harbor Drive, San Diego; ☎ 619-234-9153; www.sdmaritime.com

Hours Daily, 9 a.m.–8 p.m.; Memorial Day through Labor Day, open until 9 p.m. **Admission** $12 adults, $9 seniors 62 and older, $9 active military with valid ID,

$8 ages 6–17, free for children age 5 and under. **Touring time** Average 3 hours; minimum 1 hour. **Rainy-day touring** Not good. **Restaurants** No. **Alcoholic beverages** No. **Disabled access** Limited. **Wheelchair rental** No. **Baby-stroller rental** No. **Lockers** No. **Pet kennels** No. **Rain check** No. **Private tours** No.

DESCRIPTION AND COMMENTS   The picture in our minds of the cozy passenger cabin of the square-rigged *Star of India,* an 1863 merchant sailing ship, is as fresh as the day we stepped into the officers' and passengers' area. As we talked to the children about what it might have been like to sail across an ocean on a ship like this, the wooden floor beneath us gently rose and fell with the waves. *Star of India* is one of three historic ships that together constitute the Maritime Museum; the others are an 1898 ferryboat and a 1904 steam-powered luxury yacht. Visitors walk or scramble up and down the ships, in and out of decks and holds, seeing ropes and engines and sailors' bunks. In summer, nautical film classics like *Captain Blood* are projected onto the ship's sail for an evening of unusual entertainment.

San Diego Model Railroad Museum

APPEAL BY AGE	PRESCHOOL ★★★★	GRADE SCHOOL ★★★★	TEENS ★★★
YOUNG ADULTS ★★★★		OVER 30 ★★★★	SENIORS ★★★★

1649 El Prado, San Diego; ☎ 619-696-0199; www.sdmodelrailroadm.com

Hours Tuesday–Friday, 11 a.m.–4 p.m.; Saturday and Sunday, 11 a.m.–5 p.m. **Admission** $6 adults, $5 seniors over 65, $3 students 15 and over, $2.50 military on active duty, free for children under age 15; free first Tuesday of the month. **Touring time** Average 2 hours; minimum 1 hour. **Rainy-day touring** Yes. **Restaurants** Sandwich shop. **Alcoholic beverages** No. **Disabled access** Yes. **Wheelchair rental** No. **Baby-stroller rental** No. **Lockers** No. **Pet kennels** No. **Rain check** No. **Private tours** No.

DESCRIPTION AND COMMENTS   We've seen many a grown man get far more excited about model trains than any kid does, and this museum caters to both groups. The country's largest collection of model trains winds through elaborate miniature countrysides and towns, some of which represent historical periods in Southern California. This fascinates some kids but makes others insane, because they're not allowed to touch—so take them to the Toy Train Gallery, where they can work the controls of Lionel O-Gauge toy trains and push Brio wooden trains on their tracks.

San Diego Museum of Man

APPEAL BY AGE	PRESCHOOL ★★	GRADE SCHOOL ★★★★	TEENS ★★★★
YOUNG ADULTS ★★★		OVER 30 ★★★	SENIORS ★★★

1350 El Prado, Balboa Park; ☎ 619-239-2001; www.museumofman.org

Hours Daily, 10 a.m.–4:30 p.m.; closed Christmas, Thanksgiving, and New Year's Days. **Admission** $6 adults, $3 children ages 6–17, $5 seniors 65 and over, free for children under age 6. **Touring time** Average 3 hours; minimum 1 hour. **Rainy-day touring** Yes. **Restaurants** No. **Alcoholic beverages** No. **Disabled access** Yes.

Wheelchair rental No. **Baby-stroller rental** No. **Lockers** No. **Pet kennels** No. **Rain check** No. **Private tours** No.

DESCRIPTION AND COMMENTS If your kids aren't fascinated with the history of man and woman, they will be after a visit to this cool museum, home to mummies, skeletons, and life-size, very realistic (often naked) re-creations of our predecessors going back to early Africa. Weekends bring live demonstrations of crafts and cooking from cultures around the world, and the Children's Discovery Center offers changing hands-on displays keyed to the museum's collection, allowing kids to, for instance, dress up like ancient Egyptians.

San Diego Wild Animal Park

APPEAL BY AGE	PRESCHOOL ★★★★	GRADE SCHOOL ★★★★★	TEENS ★★★★
YOUNG ADULTS ★★★★★		OVER 30 ★★★★★	SENIORS ★★★★★

15500 San Pasqual Valley Road, Escondido; ☎ 760-747-8702 or TDD 760-738-5067; www.sandiegozoo.org

Hours Summer: daily, 9 a.m.–8 p.m. (grounds open until 9 p.m.). Winter: daily, 9 a.m.–4 p.m. (grounds open until 5 p.m.). **Admission** $28.50 adults, $17.50 children ages 3–11, free for children ages 2 and under, $25.65 seniors age 60 and over; combination tickets for the Zoo and Wild Animal Park: $54.45 adults, $33.55 children ages 3–11; parking $8 and $10 for RVs. **Touring time** Average two-thirds of a day; minimum a half day. **Rainy-day touring** Some shows and exhibits close. **Restaurants** Yes. **Alcoholic beverages** Yes. **Disabled access** Yes. **Wheelchair rental** Yes. **Baby-stroller rental** Yes. **Lockers** Yes. **Pet kennels** Service animals only. **Rain check** No. **Private tours** Photo Caravan, ages 8 and over, $90–$130 plus admission.

DESCRIPTION AND COMMENTS Although it's actually in Escondido, about 45 minutes northeast of downtown, we're putting this in the San Diego section because San Diego heads up the name and it'd be confusing otherwise. This is a unique animal-viewing experience, designed to replicate what you'd see if you were visiting animal parks in Africa. The animals roam freely in herds over many acres of land similar to an African savannah, and the visitors observe from a monorail that travels through the park's 21,000 acres. The 55-minute ride (usually too long for toddlers) departs from a theme park–like Nairobi Village and Mombasa Lagoon area, where more traditional exhibits as well as animal shows are presented in an African-village setting, and visitors can relax at cafes—and, of course, shop. A walk-through exhibit, Condor Ridge, showcases endangered North American bird species; more heart-pounding is the new Cheetah Run Safari, where you get to watch cheetahs run at full speed up close (limited hours; call for reservations). There's also a pleasant play area for younger kids, with slides and climbing equipment, also themed. For a more in-depth adventure, consider the Beastly Bedtime Sleepovers (☎ 619-718-3000), an overnight family camping program for parents and children age 8 and over; the cost is $129–$199 adults and $109–$129 for children, depending on the package you choose.

We like to sit on the right side of the monorail car, and we always bring binoculars, so when someone shouts "Look over there!" we can actually see the animal they're pointing to. We also advise that you watch little children carefully on some of the viewing platforms; one is a three-story-high circular platform with wood railings that attracts climbing kids like magnets.

If you're planning to visit both the San Diego Zoo and the Wild Animal Park more than once a year, consider a membership for yourself and your children—it's probably cheaper, and you get other benefits as well. For details, call or go to the Web site.

San Diego Zoo

APPEAL BY AGE   PRESCHOOL ★★★★★   GRADE SCHOOL ★★★★★   TEENS ★★★★★
YOUNG ADULTS ★★★★★   OVER 30 ★★★★★   SENIORS ★★★★★

2920 Zoo Drive, Balboa Park, San Diego; ☎ 619-234-3153 or 619-231-1515; www.sandiegozoo.org

Hours Daily, 9 a.m.–4 p.m. (grounds open until 6 p.m.). Summer: open to 9 p.m., but animals generally go to sleep at dusk; call ☎ 888-MY-PANDA for current panda-viewing schedule. **Admission** Regular admission: $22 adults, $14.50 children ages 3–11, free for children age 2 and under. Deluxe admission (includes bus tour and sky tram) $32 adults, $29 seniors, $20 children ages 3–11, free for children age 2 and under. **Touring time** Average 6 hours; minimum 2 hours. **Rainy-day touring** Some shows and exhibits close. **Restaurants** Yes. **Alcoholic beverages** Yes. **Disabled access** Yes. **Wheelchair rental** Yes. **Baby-stroller rental** Yes. **Lockers** Yes. **Pet kennels** Service animals only. **Rain check** No. **Private tours** Kangaroo Bus: call ☎ 619-685-3264.

DESCRIPTION AND COMMENTS This legendary zoo has been exhibiting rare species since 1915 and now has more than 4,000 animals of 900 species. Unbarred enclosures and sensitive landscaping (Dr. Seuss used to sketch in the cactus gardens here) have been the norm at this 100-acre facility for many years, but trying to see everything means a lot of walking. The narrated bus tour gives a good overview in just 35 minutes; best viewing is from the left side. The giant pandas, Bai Yun and Shi Shi,

*un*official **TIP**
Trying to see everything at the San Diego Zoo means a lot of walking— we head right for the Children's Zoo, built to a 4-year-old's scale; here, kids can pet creatures and see the newborns.

became parents in 1999 to Hua Mei, the first panda cub born in captivity in the West since 1990, and their home is well worth a look. Also don't miss the new Monkey Trails and Forest Tales, a naturalistic home for more than 30 rare African and Asian monkeys, reptiles, pygmy hippos, and birds. Between June and September, the zoo opens at 9 a.m. (great if you have your own early birds) and stays open until 9 p.m. for nocturnal animal viewing and special entertainment programs.

☀ SeaWorld San Diego

APPEAL BY AGE	PRESCHOOL ★★★★	GRADE SCHOOL ★★★★★	TEENS ★★★★
YOUNG ADULTS ★★★★★		OVER 30 ★★★★★	SENIORS ★★★★

1720 South Shores Road, Mission Bay; ☎ 800-25-SHAMU or 619-226-3901; www.seaworld.com

Hours Fall–spring: daily, 10 a.m.–dusk. Summer: daily, 9 a.m.–10 p.m. **Admission** $54 adults, $44 children ages 3–9; parking $10. **Touring time** Average 6 hours; minimum 3 hours. **Rainy-day touring** So-so; most attractions are outdoors. **Restaurants** Yes. **Alcoholic beverages** Beer garden. **Disabled access** Yes. **Wheelchair rental** Yes. **Baby-stroller rental** Yes. **Lockers** Yes. **Pet kennels** Yes. **Rain check** No. **Private tours** Yes.

DESCRIPTION AND COMMENTS Part theme park, part zoo, part serious animal rescue and research program, SeaWorld has an appeal that cuts across age groups and interests—just try to find someone jaded and cynical enough to not be thoroughly wowed and charmed by the dolphin show, in which smiling dolphins perform amazing acrobatic feats and deliberately splash the audience. Over in Shamu's stadium, a huge crowd roars its approval when the killer whales leap far into the sky, ask for the extra-large bucket of fish, and serve as living surfboards for trainers. Popular attractions are "Fools with Tools," a sea lion, walrus, and otter show, and *R. L. Stine's Haunted Lighthouse 4-D*, a just-spooky-enough film-and-special-effects experience based on an old fishermen's tale.

Our 5-year-old loved adventuring through the aquarium tunnel under the shark tank, and the sight of our shivering but deliriously happy 8-year-old after a Shamu soaking will stay with us for years. (Her little sister, however, was shocked into shrieking tears by the coldness of the water, so don't forget a change of clothes for less-tough little ones.) Even the less popular exhibits are worthwhile—we stopped at the bird show because the stadium was empty and we needed a rest, and were then dazzled by hawks and falcons dive-bombing into the audience from a 300-foot-high balloon.

SeaWorld also gets points for going a little beyond the deep-fried, junk-food theme-park basics—over by the penguin house, you can get a tasty fresh-fruit smoothie for a cooling, healthy snack that kids love.

In summer, the park stays open later and jazzes things up with live music, a circus show, and special night performances. But we prefer getting dolphin-splashed under a hot San Diego sun.

▌▌ FAMILY-FRIENDLY RESTAURANTS

Berta's Latin American Restaurant
3928 Twiggs Street, Old Town; ☎ 619-295-2343;
www.bertasinoldtown.com

Meals served Lunch and dinner. **Cuisine** Mexican. **Entree range** $6–$16. **Kids' menu** No. **Reservations** Recommended for 6 or more. **Payment** All major credit cards.

Berta goes way behind the tourist-Mexican standards to offer the best from Chile (lamb stew), Guatemala (shrimp in spicy salsa), Spain (paella), and practically every Spanish-speaking country. Kids will like the cheese empanadas, quesadillas, and flan, and parents will like the Argentinean rib-eye steak and Brazilian seafood with tomatoes, peanuts, ginger, coconut, and chiles. Beer and wine only.

Corvette Diner
3946 Fifth Avenue, San Diego; ☎ 619-542-1001 or 619-542-1476

Meals served Breakfast, lunch, and dinner. **Cuisine** American. **Entree range** $7–$13 (lunch and dinner). **Kids' menu** Yes. **Reservations** Not accepted. **Payment** All major credit cards.

Hugely popular with local families, this 1950s diner camps it up with a live DJ, a magician, wisecracking waitresses, and blaring oldies rock. The décor is equally over the top: neon, chrome, a soda fountain, and an actual Corvette. The food is retro diner: meat loaf, chicken-fried steak, burgers, corn dogs, PB&Js, and root beer floats. Our kids beg to go back.

El Indio
3695 India Street, Old Town; ☎ 619-299-0333

Meals served Breakfast, lunch, and dinner. **Cuisine** Mexican. **Entree range** $6–$11. **Kids' menu** Yes. **Reservations** Not accepted. **Payment** MC, V.

Tortilla chips are the claim to fame of this beloved chain—they're so good that people buy them as souvenirs and ship them home. Originally a tortilla factory in 1940, the Old Town location is the parent restaurant, and it's notable for its bare-bones outdoor seating, as well as its claim to have invented the word *taquito*. Other than the fabulous chips, the food is workaday (but tasty) Cal-Mex; try the carne asada, the vegetarian tamale, the nachos deluxe, and, of course, the handmade tortillas. Beer and wine only.

Hob Nob Hill
2271 First Avenue, downtown; ☎ 619-239-8176

Meals served Breakfast, lunch, and dinner. **Cuisine** American. **Entree range** $10–$20. **Kids' menu** Yes. **Reservations** Recommended. **Payment** All major credit cards.

Since 1944, Hob Nob Hill has been dishing out home cooking, and it still looks as though it's 1944 inside: red Naugahyde booths, chintz curtains, glass pie cases, and waitresses who know their way around a coffeepot. The location is convenient to nowhere, but that doesn't stop this place from being San Diego's favorite breakfast restaurant, home to very good Western omelets, pancake sandwiches, roast-beef hash, and cinnamon rolls.

Dinner is of the turkey-croquette variety, and it's popular with the early-bird-special crowd.

Perry's
4610 Pacific Highway, Old Town; ☎ 619-291-7121

Meals served Breakfast and lunch. **Cuisine** American/Mexican. **Entree range** $5–$9. **Kids' menu** Yes. **Reservations** Not accepted. **Payment** MC, V.

The best place in Old Town for breakfast, Perry's serves an odd but appealing mix of Mexican (huevos rancheros), Italian (frittatas), and American (French toast) cooking; the children's menu is the usual pancake–hot dog roster. The food is cheap, tasty, and generously served, and there's a crowd on weekends.

Pizza Nova
3955 Fifth Avenue, downtown; ☎ 619-296-6682; 5050 North Harbor Drive, Mission Bay; ☎ 619-226-0268; 954 Lomas, Solana Beach; ☎ 858-259-0666

Meals served Lunch and dinner. **Cuisine** Italian/Californian. **Entree range** $7–$13. **Kids' menu** Yes. **Reservations** Recommended. **Payment** All major credit cards.

Winner of *San Diego* magazine's Best Pizza award, this small chain makes very good wood-fired pizzas, ranging from classic pepperoni to pizza pies with lox or Mexican lime chicken. Pastas, salads, and special-occasion desserts are also offered, along with kid-sized pizzas. The original branch in Mission Bay has water views and an appealing funkiness.

San Diego Pier Cafe
885 West Harbor Drive, downtown; ☎ 619-239-3968 or 619-232-7981

Meals served Breakfast, lunch, dinner, and Sunday brunch. **Cuisine** Seafood/American. **Entree range** Lunch, $8–$15; dinner, $13–$23. **Kids' menu** Yes. **Reservations** Only for 6 or more. **Payment** All major credit cards.

It may look like a tourist trap, given the Seaport Village location, but the food is better than it needs to be at this family favorite. Perched on the end of a small pier next to an old boathouse, it's a wonderful place for watching seagulls fly past, with the Coronado Bridge in the background; try to snag an outdoor table, especially if you have restless kids. The clam chowder, fresh fish, and fish tacos are all tasty, and the all-American breakfasts are particularly good; the children's menu includes fish 'n' chips.

LA JOLLA

A SOPHISTICATED VILLAGE PERCHED ABOVE A DRAMATIC PUBLIC BEACH, **La Jolla** isn't the kind of place you might think to take your kids—unless they are precocious, design-conscious shoppers. But look beyond the expensive shops and restaurants to discover La Jolla's spectacular cove (see "The Best Beaches and Parks") and the low-key, family-friendly resorts right on the gorgeous main beach. And the aquarium at **Scripps Institute** is worth a stop if you haven't seen one of the larger aquariums in Monterey or Long Beach. La Jolla is a few miles north of central San Diego, about a ten-minute drive.

FAMILY LODGING

La Jolla Beach and Tennis Club
2000 Spindrift Drive, La Jolla; ☎ 858-454-7126 or 800-640-7702; www.lbtc.com; $219–$809 off season, $299–$1,229 summer

This is the sort of old-money beach retreat that Pasadena families have been summering at for decades. It's decidedly unglamorous, even motel-frumpy, but once you get to know the place, its charms are seductive. The best draw is its own gorgeous beach, close to but just far enough away from the mob scene at La Jolla Shores public beach, and notable for one of the shallowest, family-friendly shorelines in California. There's also a large pool tucked into a wind-protected courtyard. Supervised activities in summer for kids age 3 and up include swim meets, treasure hunts, and craft making. The club can set you up so you can have your own beach barbecue. Other on-site fun includes a large collection of quality tennis courts (tennis is taken very seriously here) and a par-three golf course. Avoid the fancy restaurant; the more casual cafe is decent.

Sea Lodge on La Jolla Shores Beach
8110 Camino del Oro, La Jolla; ☎ 858-459-8271 or 800-640-7702; www.sealodge.com; $219–$399 off season, $239–$699 in season; children under 12 stay free

Sea Lodge doesn't have supervised children's activities, which is just fine with its many loyal patrons—with a beach this lovely and kid friendly, who

la jolla

■ **FAMILY LODGING**
1. La Jolla Beach and Tennis Club
2. Sea Lodge on La Jolla Shores

● **ATTRACTION**
3. Stephen Birch Aquarium and Museum at Scripps

◆ **FAMILY-FRIENDLY RESTAURANTS**
4. Brockton Villa
5. Hard Rock Cafe
6. Sammy's California Wood-Fired Pizza

needs a kids' program? The tile-roofed, Spanish-style hotel, a sibling of the La Jolla Beach and Tennis Club, is right on the same wonderful beach (with a boardwalk, good body boarding, and a gentle shoreline for little kids) and next door to a public park and playground; families also make good use of the pool, whirlpool, two tennis courts, Ping-Pong, and upscale restaurant, which has a children's menu. Wet, hungry kids can get a grilled-cheese sandwich delivered poolside. The 128 rooms have a no-frills, beachy-rattan décor, with refrigerators, coffeemakers, and wooden balconies; 19 of the larger rooms have kitchenettes. Be warned that rooms next to the public park can be noisy (scuba divers arrive at 5 a.m.).

ATTRACTION

Stephen Birch Aquarium and Museum at Scripps

APPEAL BY AGE	PRESCHOOL ★★★★	GRADE SCHOOL ★★★★	TEENS ★★★
YOUNG ADULTS ★★★		OVER 30 ★★★★	SENIORS ★★★★

2300 Expedition Way, La Jolla; ☎ 858-534-3474;
www.aquarium.ucsd.edu

Hours Daily, 9 a.m.–5 p.m.; closed Thanksgiving, Christmas, and New Year's Day. **Admission** $11 adults, $9 seniors, $7.50 college students, UCSD staff, and children ages 3–17, under age 3 free; 3-hour free parking. **Touring time** Average 1 hour; minimum 30 minutes. **Rainy-day touring** Yes. **Restaurants** Concessions. **Alcoholic beverages** No. **Disabled access** Yes. **Wheelchair rental** Yes. **Baby-stroller rental** No. **Lockers** No. **Pet kennels** No. **Rain check** No. **Private tours** Yes.

DESCRIPTION AND COMMENTS The museum is perched on a bluff high above the blue Pacific, and the outdoor touch tank is on a balcony boasting one of the most extraordinary views ever. Parents will find themselves admiring their offspring as the strong sunlight glints on their heads while they concentrate on sea stars and gulls circle overhead. Meanwhile, inside, dramatically dark hallways are lined with glowing aquariums, lit from behind to best showcase the jellyfish, lobsters, and other marine species. There's also a theme-park moment—a simulated submersible ride—but be warned that the ride might be too scary for kids under age 6. If your kids want to prepare for a visit, have them go to the Web site.

FAMILY-FRIENDLY RESTAURANTS

 Brockton Villa

1235 Coast Boulevard, La Jolla; ☎ 858-454-7393;
www.brocktonvilla.com

Meals served Breakfast, brunch, lunch, and dinner. **Cuisine** American. **Entree range** Lunch, $5–$12; dinner, $15–$30. **Kids' menu** Yes. **Reservations** Recommended; a day in advance. **Payment** All major credit cards.

The perfect funky beach restaurant, the Brockton Villa is pure San Diego. Breakfast or lunch at this 1894-vintage white clapboard beach house perched over La Jolla Cove will evoke beach summers of your childhood, or at least of your fantasy childhood. While you take in the ocean view, you can feast on the city's best French toast, scented with orange; warming oatmeal; a great turkey meat-loaf sandwich; or fresh grilled albacore with ginger-cilantro butter.

Hard Rock Cafe
909 Prospect Street, La Jolla; ☎ 858-454-5101

Meals served Lunch and dinner. **Cuisine** American. **Entree range** $9–$17. **Kids' menu** $6–$8. **Reservations** For groups of 8 or more only; expect to wait. **Payment** All major credit cards.

If you've been to one Hard Rock, you've been to them all. But for a 12-year-old, there's no such thing as too many trips to the Hard Rock. Like the others, it's a loud place, perhaps too loud for the very young; the small patio is a bit quieter. The ribs, burgers, and chicken are tasty, but it's the T-shirts that most kids remember.

Sammy's California Wood-Fired Pizza
702 Pearl Street, La Jolla; ☎ 858-456-5222

Meals served Lunch and dinner. **Cuisine** Californian. **Entree range** $10–$17. **Kids' menu** $5–$9. **Reservations** For 6 or more only. **Payment** All major credit cards.

This is the parent of a bright, yuppified San Diego chain dedicated to the California pizza: small pies flavored with things like goat cheese, grilled zucchini, and barbecued chicken. They are utterly delicious and can be paired with tasty Caesar salads. Kids have their own menu of mini-pizzas, and they can decorate a paper pizza with crayons. Come early to beat the considerable crowds.

DEL MAR
and
CARLSBAD

THE RACETRACK AT **Del Mar** is the famed adult draw here, but plenty of families frequent Del Mar and never place a bet. Instead, they head for the broad, white-sand beach between 15th and 29th streets, and the quaint little downtown area. We've used it as a base for visiting the **Wild Animal Park**—still a half-hour drive, but along scenic country roads from here. Downtown San Diego is a 15- to 20-minute drive south outside of rush hour, but be warned that increasing traffic on I-5 can greatly lengthen that trip.

A half hour north of San Diego, **Carlsbad** is a quiet community that has typically attracted the upscale-golfing set (think George Bush), but it became more family friendly when **Legoland** came to town. Between this major theme park, the clean and beautiful state beach, and two swell kid-friendly resorts (the upscale Four Seasons and the charming Carlsbad Inn), Carlsbad is turning into a lovely family destination away from the San Diego crowds. If you're in town in

unofficial **TIP**
Carlsbad is turning into a lovely family beach destination away from the San Diego crowds.

spring (March through May), don't pass up a quick trip to the 50 acres of colorful blooms at **The Flower Fields** (Carlsbad Ranch); ☎ 760-930-9123; **www.theflowerfields.com.**

FAMILY LODGING

Carlsbad Inn
3075 Carlsbad Boulevard, Carlsbad; ☎ 760-434-7020 or 800-235-3939; www.carlsbadinn.com; $159–$205 summer; $159–$179 off season

A charming if quirky (what's with the Tudor thing in sunny California?) beach resort, the Carlsbad Inn offers a lot of bang for the buck. Accommodations include family-size junior suites and spacious condos; the pool and spa area is fronted by a broad green lawn; and terrific Carlsbad Beach is just across the road. On site are a playground, frozen-yogurt shop, Mexican restaurant, Ping-Pong, fitness center, bikes, and beach toys, and Carlsbad's shops and restaurants are an easy walk. The hotel organizes activities for

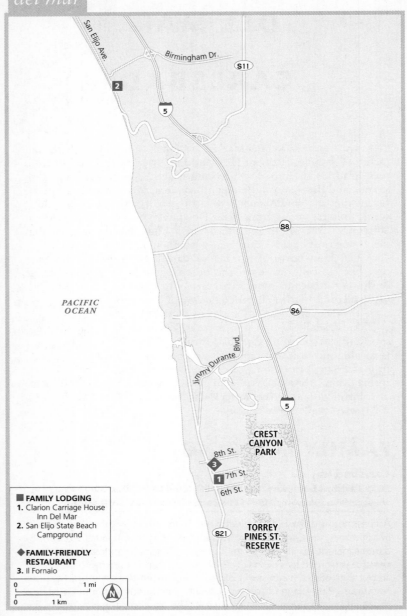

del mar

PACIFIC
OCEAN

San Elijo Ave.

Birmingham Dr.

S11

2

5

S8

S6

Jimmy Durante Blvd.

5

CREST
CANYON
PARK

8th St.

3

1 7th St.

6th St.

S21

TORREY
PINES ST.
RESERVE

■ FAMILY LODGING
1. Clarion Carriage House
Inn Del Mar
2. San Elijo State Beach
Campground

◆ FAMILY-FRIENDLY
RESTAURANT
3. Il Fornaio

0   1 mi

0   1 km

N

carlsbad

Marron Rd.

Buena
Vista
Lagoon

Carlsbad Village Dr.

San Diego Freeway

S11

Agua
Hedionda Lagoon

Cannon Rd.

Lego Dr.

PACIFIC OCEAN

Palomar Airport Rd.

Batiquitos Lagoon

0   2 mi
0   2 km

■ **FAMILY LODGING**
1. Four Seasons Resort
   at Aviara
2. Carlsbad Inn

● **ATTRACTIONS**
3. Legoland California

◆ **FAMILY-FRIENDLY
RESTAURANTS**
4. California Bistro
5. Rubio's

kids (sand-dollar painting, root-beer-float making) and seniors (financial planning, bus trips to Mexico).

Clarion Del Mar Inn
720 Camino del Mar, Del Mar; ☎ 858-755-9765 or 800-252-7466; www.delmarinn.com; $117–$180 summer; $89–$150 off season

There's a snapshot of our kids in the pool area of this motel, and the brightness of their smiles is matched by the bright flowers everywhere around them—real home gardens, not institutional landscaping. A landmark along the Pacific Coast Highway and popular lodging for the horse professionals frequenting the racetrack (just count the trailers in the parking lot), this 80-room faux-Tudor place has some unusual homey touches. Afternoon tea is served in real china cups by a woman with a genuine

t; the pool area is splendid with flowers; décor is heavy on
s and red plaid. The beach isn't too far of a walk.

Seasons Resort at Aviara

**Four Seasons Point, Carlsbad; ☎ 760-603-6800 or 800-819-
5055; www.fourseasons.com; $305–$585 low season, $405–$685
high season, special packages sometimes available; children stay free
in parents' room**

It may not have a beach—South Carlsbad beach is a couple of miles away—but
this expensive resort has just about everything else: a gorgeous golf course,
tennis, a swimming pool, a health club, a spa, high-end restaurants, ocean
views, walking/jogging trails around the neighboring Batiquitos lagoon and
bird sanctuary, and luxuriously outfitted rooms. Like almost all Four Seasons
resorts, this one is out to corner the upscale family market. Children are won
over from the moment of check-in: waiting for them in the room are cookies
and milk, and their names are spelled out with sponges in the bathroom. The
free Kids for All Seasons program goes far beyond the video-room basics—
warm, well-qualified counselors take kids on nature walks and swimming in
the pool; kids also enjoy storytelling in a teepee, make their own postcards,
and pet and feed the program's mascot, Avie the frog. Available for kids ages
4 to 12, the program is offered daily in summer, weekends and school vacations in spring, and weekends the rest of the year.

 ## San Elijo State Beach Campground

**On Highway 1, Cardiff-by-the-Sea; ☎ 760-753-5091 or 800-444-
7275; www.parks.ca.gov; campsites $25–$44**

Located in spiffy Cardiff-by-the-Sea, just south of Carlsbad and about 20
minutes north of San Diego's Mission Bay, this campground is beautifully
set on a small bluff above the beach, with most of the tent campsites overlooking the ocean. You won't get any privacy out here in the open (the
beachfront road runs right by), but you'll get a lot of beach beauty and fun
for very little money. Summertime always books up seven months in
advance, so reserve early. Hot showers, flush toilets, lifeguards, barbecues,
lots of nearby restaurants.

◻ ATTRACTIONS

Legoland California

APPEAL BY AGE	PRESCHOOL ★★★★★	GRADE SCHOOL ★★★★★	TEENS ★
YOUNG ADULTS ★★		OVER 30 ★★	SENIORS ★★

1 Legoland Drive, Carlsbad; ☎ 760-918-5346; www.legoland.com

Hours Vary daily; call ahead or check Web site for correct hours. **Admission** $53
adults, $43 children ages 3–12 and seniors; discounts for parents and/or Southern

California residents are sometimes offered. Parking is $8 cars, $10 campers/RVs, $5 motorcycles, preferred $15. **Touring time** Average 5 hours; minimum 3 hours. **Rainy-day touring** Limited. **Restaurants** Yes. **Alcoholic beverages** No. **Disabled access** Yes. **Wheelchair rental** Yes. **Baby-stroller rental** Yes. **Lockers** Yes. **Pet kennels** Yes. **Rain check** No. **Private tours** No.

DESCRIPTION AND COMMENTS When it first opened several years ago, this theme park held little appeal for older kids, especially older kids who aren't into Legos. There were no thrill rides, and to a 14-year-old, thrill rides are the only reason to go to a theme park. Over the last few years, however, the Legoland folks have added attractions to broaden the park's appeal, and it seems to be working. But for the most part, this friendly place remains best suited for kids under 12— and, of course, Legomaniacs of all ages.

unofficial TIP
Arrive right at opening time, do the Sky Cruiser, driving school, and rides first, indulge in some quiet-time building activities, have lunch, explore Mini-land, burn off lunch in the Hideaways and Pirate Shores, then leave at the hottest part of the day, in the early afternoon, to hit the beach in Carlsbad for a refreshing family swim.

The theme here, of course, is Legos, the little primary-colored plastic bricks out of which children (and adults) make everything from houses to *Star Wars* vehicles. The showpiece is Mini-land, which is perhaps the most appealing part of the park for adults and older Lego-loving kids, if a bit frustrating for little ones, who aren't allowed to touch. Many regions of the United States have been meticulously re-created with more than 20 million Lego bricks. Lego boats chug in the New England harbor, subway trains run under Rockefeller Center in Manhattan, rockets get ready to launch from Cape Canaveral, and cars drive down the streets of Beverly Hills. It's pretty astounding. In the new Florida Miniland, kids can race remote control minicars around a replica of the Daytona Speedway.

Our kids' hands-down favorite attraction is the driving school, which takes Disneyland's Autopia to the next level. Kids from 6 to 13 attend a brief class on driving safety and rules of the road and are then rewarded with a driver's license (these are treasured by 6-year-olds). In a Volvo-sponsored Lego car, they drive scaled-down city streets, stopping at signals and staying in their lanes like real drivers. Kids ages 3 to 6 get their own smaller-scale driving school as well.

Otherwise, your child's favorite area will depend on age and interests. The littlest ones like the Duplo building area, while the oldest ones like Mindstorms in the Imagination Zone, where they can build robotics vehicles. In this same area, kids are often allowed to help the master builders with whatever they're currently creating. After a session of quiet building, head over to the Hideaways in Castle Hill, a terrific climbing and play structure, or to the new Pirate Shores—and make sure to change into bathing suits! This new water-play area is a huge hit for 8-year-olds and up, offering waterslides, mock pirate battles, water jets, and a water-play place stocked with soaker devices galore. Younger kids might be happier at Explore Village, which includes the Dino Island, where they can dig for "remains" of prehistoric dinosaurs and ride the moderately thrilling Coastersaurus.

Other rides include the fairly tame Castle Hill roller coaster (an ideal thrill for 5- to 8-year-olds), the very tame Lake (great for preschoolers), and the fun Aquazone Wave Racer Jet Ski ride, a good one for older kids. The new Technic Coaster will amuse the big kids, though it's still no match for Magic Mountain's megacoasters. The Sky Cruiser, which putters around high over Fun Town, isn't worth it if the line is long, which it often is. If your kids really want to ride Sky Cruiser, head over there as soon as you arrive.

Legoland gets huge kudos for making the food far more palatable and healthful than at any other theme park. Pastas, sandwiches, and salads (including a great fruit salad for kids) are made fresh to order, and the various restaurant spaces are inviting, with plenty of shade from the often-hot Carlsbad sun.

FAMILY-FRIENDLY RESTAURANTS

California Bistro
Four Seasons Resort at Aviara, 7100 Four Seasons Point, Carlsbad;
☎ **760-603-6800**

Meals served Breakfast, lunch, and dinner. **Cuisine** Californian, American. **Entree range** Lunch, $10–$20; dinner, $15–$20. **Kids' menu** Yes. **Reservations** Recommended. **Payment** All major credit cards.

A rare "nice" restaurant that's as comfortable for children as adults, the Four Seasons' more casual eatery is a real find for families seeking a relaxed dinner out. In a beamed, high-ceilinged, California-chic dining room with an ocean-view terrace, the staff dotes on kids, bringing them little frog key chains and even escorting them to the bathroom when necessary; babies and toddlers get a high chair, snack box of Cheerios, and spill mat. Our kids flipped for the tortilla chip–crusted crab cakes from the grown-up menu, then returned to the safety of the children's menu for burgers and fries; we loved the herb-seared Atlantic salmon and the Aviara sandwich of juicy rosemary chicken and melted Brie on honey-sunflower bread.

Il Fornaio
Del Mar Plaza, 1555 Camino del Mar, Del Mar; ☎ **858-755-8876**

Meals served Lunch, dinner, and Sunday brunch. **Cuisine** Italian. **Entree range** Lunch and dinner, $10–$25. **Kids' menu** Yes. **Reservations** Advised. **Payment** All major credit cards.

For an upscale family meal out with a sunset ocean view you won't soon forget, head to this accomplished chain. A different region of Italy is featured monthly, and those specials are always the best, but the regular menu of risottos, pasta, bruschetta, grilled fish, and salads is delicious, too. Children are welcomed and given their own menu, with things like Italian-style macaroni and cheese.

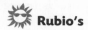 **Rubio's**

2604-A El Camino Real, Carlsbad; ☎ 760-434-6298

Meals served Lunch and dinner. **Cuisine** Mexican. **Entree range** $4–$12. **Kids' menu** Yes. **Reservations** Not accepted. **Payment** MC, V.

Born in San Diego, this order-at-the-counter chain is now found all over the West, and for good reason: the food is fresh, healthy, cheap, and tasty, appealing to kids and grown-ups alike. Known for its soft fish tacos, it also has a good grilled-chicken Caesar salad, peppery beans, and burritos and tacos filled with grilled mahimahi, savory carnitas, and hearty *machaca* (beef and eggs).

☼ SIDE TRIP:

Anza-Borrego Desert State Park

MANY SOUTHERN CALIFORNIANS MANAGE to achieve middle age without even realizing that this 600,000-acre desert park is hiding right in their midst. Inland about two hours from San Diego, Anza-Borrego is a wilderness preserve, desert playground, and wildflower paradise in spring; the only town, Borrego Springs, still doesn't have a traffic signal, though it has a few hotels and amenities. Our favorite excursions are the extremes: either sleeping in relative luxury at La Casa del Zorro or sleeping under the stars at the state campground. Either way, pack a picnic (including lots of drinking water), have the kids wear swimsuits under their clothes, and spend a day hiking up the Palm Canyon Trail. This child-friendly destination was overwhelmed by a flash flood in 2004 that took out many of the palms and swimming holes, but the intrepid scrambler will still find a few palm oases and water. Before your hike, stop by the visitors center in Borrego Springs so your kids will know which sorts of cacti, birds, and wildflowers to hunt for. Avoid the area from June through October, when the heat can be brutal. Visitors center is at 200 Palm Canyon Drive, Borrego Springs, ☎ 760-767-5311; **www.anzaborrego.statepark.org.** Open daily October through May; on weekends and holidays only June through September.

FAMILY LODGING

Borrego Palm Canyon State Campground

2 miles north of Borrego Springs (check Borrego Springs visitors center for directions); reservations: Reserve America, ☎ 800-444-7275, www.reserveamerica.com; campsites $15–$20 without hookups, $20–$29 with hookups. *Note:* This park is located inside Anza-Borrego Desert State Park.

Quiet campsites are scattered among the ocotillo, mesquite, and barrel cactus, close to the trailhead to Palm Canyon, an easy hike that kids love.

When not on the trail, they can scramble up the hillside, hunt for lizards, and, at night, count the shooting stars. Hot showers, flush toilets, barbecues, fire pits, and drinking water are available.

La Casa del Zorro Resort Hotel
3845 Yaqui Pass Road, Borrego Springs; ☎ 760-767-5323 or 800-824-1884; www.lacasadelzorro.com; $295–$1,220 off season; $360–$1,500 high season

More luxurious than the no-frills town and empty expanse of state park would suggest, this is a fine place to recover from a long, hot hike up Palm Canyon. Swim in the pool, play tennis, rent a bike, or stay cool in one of the large, handsome family-size villas or casitas, many of which have one or two bedrooms, refrigerators, and microwaves. Children's activities are sometimes scheduled on weekends. Rates plummet in the depths of summer. Good restaurant.

PART TWO

ORANGE COUNTY

NATIONALLY, ORANGE COUNTY IS BEST KNOWN as the home of **Disneyland Resort,** expanded with the addition of **Disney's California Adventure** and a dining and entertainment complex called **Downtown Disney.** But while the Magic Kingdom is certainly one of the county's great draws, it's located in singularly unattractive Anaheim, which hardly epitomizes the California dream. The dream is here, however—you just have to head south to the beach towns. Traditionally a side trip for California visitors, the county is now a destination in and of itself, or a generous series of stops on the north–south coastal route.

Home to more than 2.7 million people, Orange County is dense with suburban tract developments and strip malls. The lure is the county's 42 miles of coastline, peppered with lots of lively public beaches. On the north end of the county's coast is **Huntington Beach,** aka Surf City, a sun-bleached suburb known for its pier, its surf contests, and its relaxed friendliness. On the south end is **San Clemente,** located a bit too far from the business hubs of Irvine and San Diego to have become an affluent suburb—despite its prime oceanfront location, it remains a welcoming, regular-folks beach town. In between these are such visitor meccas as mission-centric **San Juan Capistrano,** artsy **Laguna Beach,** and posh **Newport Beach,** along with beautiful, lesser-known beaches, endless family sporting adventures, and some way-cool attractions.

If you've never visited Orange County, we advise spending a few days in the North County theme-park area, then driving 20 to 45 minutes southwest to stay in one of the coastal towns described in this chapter (Newport, Laguna, Huntington, or the South County towns) for a few days. From any of these locations, you'll be no more than a 45-minute drive to **Wild Rivers** or the big shopping malls . . . or, even better, you can simply enjoy beach life closer to your home base. From campgrounds to luxury resorts to house rentals, there are a lot of ways to hit the beach in the Big Orange.

orange county

CLEVELAND
NATIONAL
FOREST

San Juan Capistrano

San Clemente

Laguna
Niguel

Dana Point

Laguna
Hills

Laguna Beach

Irvine

Santa
Ana

Newport Beach

Anaheim

Fullerton

Buena Park

Huntington
Beach

PACIFIC OCEAN

BEACHES AND PARKS
1. Aliso Creek County Beach
2. Bolsa Chica State Beach
3. Corona del Mar Beach
4. Crystal Cove State Park
5. Doheny State Beach
6. Huntington State Beach–
   Huntington City Beach
7. Main Beach, Laguna
8. Newport Dunes Resort
9. San Clemente Pier–
   T Street
10. Upper Newport Bay
   Ecological Reserve
11. Wood's Cove

10 mi

10 km

GETTING THERE

BY PLANE Orange County is served by John Wayne–Orange County Airport, ☎ 949-252-5200, **www.ocair.com,** just off Interstate 405 in Irvine, inland from Newport Beach. Many major airlines fly into John Wayne; those that don't are served by Los Angeles International Airport, ☎ 310-646-5252; **www.lawa.org/lax,** located about 20 miles north on the 405 from Irvine.

BY TRAIN Amtrak delivers passengers throughout Orange County, with stops in Fullerton, Anaheim, Santa Ana, Irvine, San Juan Capistrano, and San Clemente, connecting between Union Station in Los Angeles and downtown San Diego. If you're not doing Disneyland, one of the best possible day trips from L.A. is to take the train to the San Juan Capistrano or San Clemente stations (there's also a stop at Anaheim stadium for an afternoon in the most family-friendly stadium in Southern California). The San Juan station is in the heart of the mission area of town, and between the station and the mission are shops and cafes. We had a mother-daughter day with friends this way and couldn't have had more fun. The San Clemente stop (only on selected trains) is at the beach and pier, so you really can wear your suits, bring a beach chair, enjoy a day at the beach and lunch at the pier, and then return to the big city. Call ☎ 800-USA-RAIL, or go to **www.amtrak.com** for details.

The same route is served during commuter hours by Metrolink (☎ 800-371-5465; **www.metrolinktrains.com**), which is considerably cheaper than Amtrak but lacks food service and weekend travel.

BY CAR Two major freeways cut through Orange County. **Interstate 5,** which heads north to Canada and south to Mexico, runs right past Disneyland, San Juan Capistrano, and Dana Point; the **405,** which splits off from the 5 and follows a coastal route north, will get you to Newport and Huntington Beach. The **San Joaquin Tollway** (Highway 73), Southern California's first toll road, gives riders a fast, traffic-free route from Irvine to San Juan Capistrano, via Laguna (for $4.25 peak, $3.75 off peak, $3.50 weekends).

unofficial **TIP**
While the Pacific Coast Highway can make for a pretty drive, it slows to a creep in some areas and is not a good long-distance artery.

HOW TO GET INFORMATION BEFORE YOU GO

- **Anaheim–Orange County Visitor and Convention Bureau**
  800 West Katella Avenue, Anaheim 92803; ☎ 714-765-8888; **www.anaheimoc.org.**
- **Huntington Beach Conference and Visitors Bureau**
  301 Main Street, Suite 208, Huntington Beach 92648; ☎ 714-969-3492; **www.hbvisit.com**.
- **Laguna Beach Visitors Bureau** 252 Broadway, Laguna Beach 92651; ☎ 800-877-1115 or 949-497-9229; **www.lagunabeachinfo.org.**

- **Newport Beach Conference and Visitors Bureau**
  3300 West Pacific Coast Highway, Newport Beach 92663;
  ☎ 800-94-COAST or 949-722-1611; **www.newportbeach-cvb.com.**
- **Orange County Tourism Council   www.visitorangecounty.net.**

SITTERS UNLIMITED

A HOME-BASED CHAIN BUSINESS, this organization will find you a licensed, bonded, experienced babysitter. For south Orange County area, call ☎ 949-635-0906; in the Newport–Costa Mesa area, call ☎ 949-650-1166; **www.sittersunlimited.com.**

A **CALENDAR** of **FESTIVALS** and **EVENTS**

March

FESTIVAL OF WHALES Dana Point. Held the last two weeks of February. First-rate (and free!) open-air rock, blues, and jazz concerts; a film festival; and a street fair on the weekends. Loads of great kid activities, from the one-mile Little Whales Run to the 2K Wag-a-Thon pet walk, which raises money for animal causes. A parade features lobster jugglers, and at the ranger-led campfire, kids learn about whales and marine life. Whale-watching trips leave from the Dana Point Harbor. Call for details; ☎ 949-472-7888 or 888-440-4309; **www.dpfestivalofwhales.com.**

GLORY OF EASTER Crystal Cathedral. Late March/early April. A gala show with live animals, special effects, and a cast of 200 in a spectacular church; ☎ 714-971-4000; **www.crystalcathedral.org.**

RETURN OF THE SWALLOWS Mission San Juan Capistrano. In midMarch. They ain't what they used to be, but that doesn't stop a good time from happening. Street fair, Mexican food, shows, live music; ☎ 949-234-1300, ext. 322; **www.missionsjc.com.**

April

KOREAN FESTIVAL Garden Grove. A three-day cultural fair with kiddie rides, a parade, and great food; ☎ 714-638-1440.

May

IMAGINATION CELEBRATION Countywide. An arts festival for children, teens, and their parents, with lots of hands-on workshops, performances, and exhibits; ☎ 714-556-5160; **www.icfestival.com.**

July

HUNTINGTON BEACH FOURTH OF JULY PARADE AND FIREWORKS Main Street, Huntington Beach. Several hundred thousand people attend this all-American parade in the morning; most stick around for the beachfront fireworks show after dark; **www.hb4thofjuly.org.**

OLD GLORY BOAT PARADE Newport Beach. July Fourth; ☎ 949-673-5070.

Orange County Fair 88 Fair Drive, Fairgrounds, Costa Mesa. A classic county fair; ☎ 714-708-3247; **www.ocfair.com**.

SAWDUST FESTIVAL Laguna Canyon. The funkier cousin to the upscale Festival of Arts, this craft-oriented art festival is particularly appealing to teenagers; ☎ 949-494-3030; **www.sawdustartfestival.org**.

U.S. OPEN SURFING AND BEACH GAMES Huntington Pier, Huntington Beach. In late July. If your kids are surfers (or wannabes), they'll want to check out this acclaimed surf contest; also features skateboarding and BMX competitions; ☎ 310-473-0411; **www.surfcityusa.com**.

September

TALLSHIPS FESTIVAL Orange County Marine Institute, Dana Point. Weekend after Labor Day. Grand old tall ships sail into the harbor; families can get aboard one of the ships and sail in the great parade (reservations are essential; call the number below). You can also tour old ships, learn how to sail a square-rigger, listen to live sea-chantey music, and see the work of nautical artisans; ☎ 949-496-2274; **www.tallshipfestival.com**.

October

ISA WORLD SURFING GAMES Huntington Beach Pier. Top surfers from around the world show their stuff; ☎ 858-551-5292; **www.isasurf.org**.

KIDS' DAY MISSION San Juan Capistrano. In late October, features free children's admission, daylong entertainment, food, and special activities, and kids are encouraged to wear costumes; ☎ 949-234-1300, ext. 323; **www.missionsjc.com**.

SAND CASTLE AND SAND SCULPTURE CONTEST Corona del Mar Beach. Kids and adults (including professionals) create amazing works in sand; ☎ 949-729-4400.

December

CHRISTMAS AT THE MISSION Mission San Juan Capistrano. Early December. The season kicks off with Christmas music, entertainment, and refreshments; ☎ 949-234-1300, ext. 322; **www.missionsjc.com**.

CHRISTMAS BOAT PARADE Newport Harbor. Seemingly all of Newport turns out to watch some 200 decorated, Christmas-lighted boats parade by; ☎ 949-729-4400; **www.christmasboatparade.com**.

The BEST BEACHES *and* PARKS

ALISO CREEK COUNTY BEACH Like its sister beach (Main Beach) to the north, Aliso Creek is so picturesque that it's beloved of film crews. The sand sweeps in a gentle golden arc, a tidy little pier adds charm, and kids frolic on the playground and in the waves. Barbecues, picnic tables, restrooms, easy metered parking, and lifeguards in summer. 31131 South Pacific Coast Highway, Laguna Beach; ☎ 949-923-2280; **www.ocparks.com/alisobeach.**

BOLSA CHICA STATE BEACH A long, substantial, sometimes-windy strip of sand between the ocean and Pacific Coast Highway, Bolsa Chica is between towns rather than in towns, and backing it on the other side of the highway is Bolsa Chica Nature Reserve, a bird sanctuary that's somewhat renowned. So families day-tripping or camping here can have some pretty pure all-nature days (bring binoculars). They are, however, within an easy bike ride of Huntington Beach's surf shops, movies, and taco joints, and both the overnight and day-use areas access a snack bar. The thrill of bonfires at night is available here, too. Barbecue pits, lifeguards in summer, camping, showers, concessions. Pacific Coast Highway between Warner and Golden West; ☎ 714-377-5691; **www.parks.ca.gov.**

CORONA DEL MAR BEACH Also known as Big Corona, this is one of Southern California's prettier beaches, with cliffs behind, the sparkling Pacific ahead, and a rock pier into the sea. Lifeguards, bathrooms, a snack bar, volleyball courts, barbecues. Ocean Boulevard and Iris, Corona del Mar. The neighboring beach is known as Little Corona, but its formal name is Corona del Mar Marine Life Refuge. When the tide is low, you can explore fascinating marine life pools; call for a schedule of kid-friendly ranger tours; ☎ 949-644-3038.

CRYSTAL COVE STATE PARK Developers have begun to build on the heretofore unspoiled land surrounding these 2,200 acres of bluffs, chaparral canyon, and open land—not to mention 3.5 miles of coast-line—between Laguna and Corona del Mar; a new luxury hotel and golf course are coming, and a housing development on the inland side is under construction. But this is still one of the most amazing open stretches south of Santa Barbara. Inland are miles of trails beloved by mountain bikers and hikers; on the beach is superb tide pooling in the rocky stretches. Docents hold nature walks on Saturday and Sunday mornings. 8471 Pacific Coast Highway, between Laguna and Corona del Mar; ☎ 949-494-3539; **www.parks.ca.gov.** Parking is $10. Primitive camping is available (bring your own water and take everything out), or you can rent one of the wonderful renovated cottages; **www.crystalcovebeachcottages.org.**

DOHENY STATE BEACH After San Onofre, this is the second-best Southern California beach for kids (or adults) to learn how to surf, thanks to the long, gentle waves that break just south of the Dana Point Harbor breakwater. This is also a great beach for a day trip, especially if you reserve one of the extremely popular barbecue-equipped picnic sites in advance, (call Reserve America, ☎ 800-444-PARK; **www.reserve america.com**). There's only one problem—the ocean has been off limits more and more days in the last couple of years for high bacteria counts, so there's a chance of disappointment, especially after a rainstorm. Rolling green lawns dotted with picnic areas are interwoven with pedestrian and bike paths; all this fronts a broad sand beach equipped with pro-quality volleyball courts, a snack bar, showers, and, in summer, both lifeguards and a concession that rents body boards, surrey bikes, inline skates, and other amusements. Near the entrance to the beach is a small but worthy interpretive center with an indoor tide pool and 3,000-gallon marine aquarium system. 25300 Dana Point Harbor Drive, Dana Point; ☎ 949-496-6171.

HUNTINGTON STATE BEACH–HUNTINGTON CITY BEACH When the surf is really booming, your kids will need to stay out of the water, but they'll have a blast watching the surfers put on a show, especially on the north side of the magnificent 1,800-foot-long pier. Typically, however, the waves aren't too forbidding. The city and state beaches adjoin each other, with the Bolsa Chica wetlands (see above) connecting via a fun bike path from the State Beach. This is a classic white-sand California beach, great for everything from castle making to body surfing to fishing on the pier. Summer lifeguards, a snack bar, bathrooms, a bike path, barbecue pits, concessions. State Beach is at Pacific Coast Highway at Magnolia; ☎ 714-536-1454; **www.parks.ca.gov**.

MAIN BEACH, LAGUNA This is the beach you've seen in a million commercials for everything from cars to sunscreen—it's the idealized California beach. A compact, gently sweeping arc in the heart of Laguna Beach, it's famed for its old-fashioned lifeguard tower (painted ad nauseam by local artists), its near–NBA-level pickup-basketball games, its volleyball courts, its swimming, and, most of all, its people watching. At the north end, you'll find the Glenn East Vedder Ecological Reserve, which continues north to Crescent Bay Drive. Pick up a tide chart at the visitors center, visit at low tide, and discover wonderful tide pooling; make sure children understand before you start that this is a marine preserve, so nothing may be removed, not even a shell. Older kids may want to join you in a snorkeling tour of the reserve at higher tide. Take younger ones to the south end of the beach, where there's a nifty playground. Summer lifeguard service, showers, and restrooms. Restaurants, ice-cream parlors, and shops are plentiful, but parking is not. Pacific Coast Highway at Broadway, Laguna Beach; ☎ 800-877-1115.

NEWPORT DUNES RESORT The Disneyland of beaches, this chic, RV-oriented, private campground is also a very fun day trip with young children. There's loads of clean, white sand, a wave-free lagoon in which sits a big fiberglass whale (the kids can swim to the whale), a good playground, and even decent shell hunting. A concession rents pedalboats, kayaks, and other watercraft, and you can even get a hot indoor shower. Snack bar, food shop, lifeguards, tent camping (but no stakes), RV camping. Admission is $10 per car. 1131 Back Bay Drive, Newport Beach; ☎ 949-729-3863; **www.newportdunes.com.**

SAN CLEMENTE PIER–T STREET A superb day-at-the-beach destination, T Street beach lies south of the San Clemente Pier; Amtrak trains stop right here a couple of times a day, making this a fun car-free trip from L.A. or Anaheim. It's a great beach for all ages—the shorebreak area is broad and shallow, with gentle waves that amuse toddlers to no end; farther out are some of the best bodysurfing–body-boarding waves for miles (surfboards are banned after 10 a.m., to protect the kids). Avenida Del Mar and Avenida Victoria, San Clemente; ☎ 949-361-8264. The Marine Safety Headquarters on the pier can be reached at ☎ 949-361-8261.

unofficial **TIP**
We like to stake out a spot south of the San Clemente Pier, closer to the restrooms, showers, and snack bar.

UPPER NEWPORT BAY ECOLOGICAL RESERVE Bring bikes or your sneakers to explore the 700 acres of pristine peace in the midst of developed Newport. The bird population is astounding; look for great blue herons and snowy egrets, and see how many different kinds of ducks you can spot. The Newport Bay Naturalists provide guided tours and interpretive programs for families. Back Bay Road off Jamboree, Newport Beach; ☎ 949-640-6746; **www.newportbay.org.**

WOOD'S COVE If Laguna's Main Beach is too crowded, head over to this lesser-known gem, hidden by dramatic bluffs. Kids love climbing the many rocks and hunting for crabs and other sea critters. Bathrooms, summer lifeguards. Pacific Coast Highway at Diamond Street, Laguna Beach; ☎ 949-494-1018.

FAMILY OUTDOOR ADVENTURES

BICYCLING AND INLINE SKATING Cycling, skating, and scootering are a passion with countless Orange County families, and for good reason—the county is zigzagged with miles of easy, dedicated paths, especially near the beaches. One of our favorite family rides is the path between **Huntington State Beach** north to **Bolsa Chica,** where you can watch birds in the wetlands. Or you can ride south from Huntington all the way to **Newport Beach,** a beautiful ride for 10-and-ups who can pedal a few miles. Another great one is the **Back Bay Drive** bike path, which wanders through the Upper Newport Bay Ecological Reserve (see "The Best Beaches and Parks," above). Finally, you can ride along the **Balboa Peninsula** in Newport, stopping to watch the gnarly bodysurfing waves at the Wedge on the south end of the peninsula. Then take your bikes over to **Balboa Island** on the ferry, explore the tiny island, have a snack, ferry back, and ride north along the peninsula to Newport Pier. You can get outfitted in rental skates, bikes, and protective gear at **Balboa Bikes & Beach Stuff** (601 East Balboa

Boulevard; ☎ 949-723-1516 on Balboa Peninsula); in Huntington Beach, check out **Team Bicycle Shop** (8462 Indianapolis Avenue; ☎ 714-969-5480).

Mountain bikers will want to check out the trails in Laguna's **Crystal Cove State Park** (see "The Best Beaches and Parks," page 70) and in **Laguna Canyon** (see "Hiking," below). If you need mountain bikes, you can rent them at **Laguna Beach Cyclery** (240 Thalia Street; ☎ 949-494-1522).

BOATING Puttering around **Newport Harbor** in a rented boat can be big fun for young sailors. Pick up a small sailboat ($40 per hour), electric boat, motorboat, or kayak at **Balboa Boat Rentals** in Newport Harbor (☎ 949-673-7200) and set out for a tour of the harbor's many nooks and crannies. Most of the smaller boats are not allowed out of the harbor.

FISHING Fun, affordable seagoing fishing trips are run out of Dana Point Harbor by **Dana Wharf Sportfishing** (34675 Golden Lantern; ☎ 949-496-5794; **www.danawharfsportfishing.com**). A half-day trip is $32 for adults and $24 for kids under age 12, with rods and reels renting for another $10; fishing licenses available for $11.50. The crew will help neophytes, and any fish you catch (there's calico bass, sand bass, rock cod, mackerel, even the occasional shark out there) will be filleted and packaged for you. Whale-watching trips are also offered in season. If you're based in Newport, try **Newport Landing Sport Fishing** (309 Palm, Suite A, Balboa; ☎ 949-675-0550; **www.newportlanding.com**).

HIKING There's more than beaches to Orange County's outdoors—there's also a surprising amount of high-quality hiking. The best trails for families are in the **Laguna** area; good ones are also found near **San Juan Capistrano,** but fear of mountain-lion attacks sometimes forces rangers to prohibit children from the trails. Our favorite family hike, other than the tide-pooling–rock-climbing adventures at **Dana Point** and **Crystal Cove** (see "The Best Beaches and Parks"), is in the **Laguna Hills,** led by Nature Conservancy docents by reservation on weekends (☎ 714-832-7478). This easy, two-mile trek to "Orange County's Grand Canyon" is recommended for kids age 5 and up. The Nature Conservancy also leads more difficult hikes for older families, as well as great mountain-biking rides in Laguna's backcountry. You'll find other trails to explore on your own at Crystal Cove State Park.

PARASAILING Adventurous teens (maybe you, too) will get a huge thrill out of a parasail trip—they'll be lofted up like a human kite, tethered to the deck of a boat, to soar over the ocean for a 12-minute ride that seems much longer. The best places to try it are **Dana Wharf Parasailing** (34675 Golden Lantern, Dana Point; ☎ 949-496-5794); and **Balboa Boat Rentals** (510 East Edgewater, Balboa; ☎ 949-673-7200).

SURFING AND OCEAN SPORTS The explosion of lessons, classes, and camps in recent years makes surfing easy to try. A good

unofficial **TIP**
No kid should visit
Orange County without
trying surfing.

program is sponsored by the city of San Clemente: half-day surf classes (and private lessons) for kids and adults in the easygoing waves of North Beach. **JP's Surf Camp** runs the program for the city; ☎ 949-361-8264; **www .jpsurfcamp.com.** For more options, see "Surf Camp" below.

TIDE POOLING An afternoon spent scrambling over rocks hunting for crabs, anemones, shells, sea stars, and maybe even an octopus is often a highlight of a trip. Orange County has several great locations, so look under a specific beach heading for recommendations. See our profiles of **Corona del Mar Beach, Crystal Cove State Park,** and **Main Beach** in "The Best Beaches and Parks," and also see the **Orange County Marine Institute** attraction profile in the South County section. You can pick up a tide chart at any of the dozens of surf, fishing, or boat stores in any of the beach towns. Make sure your kids understand that if the tide pools are part of a preserve, nothing may be removed, not even an empty shell—a hermit crab may need it for a home later.

WHALE WATCHING Much anticipated by local schoolchildren each year, and celebrated with a terrific festival in **Dana Point,** whale-watching season arrives each January and lasts through March. These boat trips are fun half-day outings for kids of all ages; even if you aren't lucky enough to spot a herd of migrating gray whales, you're sure to see dolphins and sea birds and get great views and a feel for the vast Pacific. Trips depart from the harbors in Dana Point (☎ 949-496-2274) and Newport (☎ 949-673-1434). The Dana Point trips are run by the **Orange County Marine Institute (www.ocean-institute.org)** and the Newport trips are run by **Davey's Locker–Sport Fishing and Whale Watching (www.daveys locker.com)** with curious kids in mind.

SURF CAMP

NOTHING SYMBOLIZES CALIFORNIA MORE than surfing, yet few sports are more challenging to master. Enter the surf camp, which offers several days or more of intense instruction, along with a lot of camaraderie and fun. After a week at any of these Orange County camps, your kid will be a real surfer. And don't be afraid to try it yourself—it's one of the simplest, purest thrills in the sporting world. Some camps offer one-day sessions.

SUMMER FUN SURF CAMP This popular, state-licensed program offers five-day summer sessions at San Clemente State Beach, an excellent campground and public beach. "Everybody loves surfing" is the motto, and that "everybody" often includes moms and dads, who get their own campsite adjacent to the kids. When they're not in the water, kids can ride bikes, skate, and play volleyball or Ping-Pong; evenings bring rousing campfires and, for those who can't live without it, TV watching. Prices range from $695 per person for the sleep-away programs, including all meals, boards, lots of one-on-one instructor time, and a videotape analysis of each student's surfing progress, to $495 for a day-camp version of the same program. San Clemente; ☎ 949-361-9526; **www.summerfunsurfcamp.com.**

SUPER SURF CAMP Part of the excellent California Junior Lifeguards Program, these one-week day camps (age 8 through adult) are offered during spring break and throughout summer. Based at such Orange County beaches as Sunset and Salt Creek (near Dana Point), this is a great way to get to know the ocean. Your kids (or your whole family) will learn not only how to surf or body-board, but also the essentials of first aid, CPR, lifeguarding, and ocean safety. The price is moderate, and it includes free loaner boards and wet suits for those who don't have their own. If you have a daughter, take note that even though surfing may seem boy dominated, 35 to 40 percent of the camp participants are girls. Huntington Beach; ☎ 714-901-9030; **www.jrlifeguards.com.**

SUMMER SOUL SURF CAMP This Billabong-sponsored camp isn't fancy—home base is the scruffy campgrounds of San Clemente State Park—but it's a lot of fun, very well run, and, best of all, the surfing is done at San Onofre, home of the most learner-friendly waves in the state. Former longboard champ Josh Baxter and Chris Bamum (and their staff) teach kids to surf and offer such extras as outrigger canoe surfing, skateboard outings, and art sessions. Little ones (ages 4 to 6) can attend a one-day camp that will get them up on a surfboard; older ones (up to age 17) enjoy five-day sessions that can either be done as day camps or sleepovers. Private lessons also offered. San Clemente; ☎ 800-522-1352; **www.summersoulsurfcamp.com.**

SURF ACADEMY Founded and run by 49-year-old former surfing champ Mary Setterholm, this L.A.-area operation has grown to include a rich roster of surfing-related events and activities. You can take private surf lessons or even lessons on how to swim in the ocean. Saturdays are devoted to surf classes for women and girls age 7 and older, Sundays to classes for families of all ages, and summer weekdays to terrific, reasonably priced surfing and body-boarding day camps for kids. Camps and lessons are held at Huntington Beach, Santa Monica, and El Segundo; ☎ 877-599-7873; **www.surfacademy.org.**

FINDING *a* HOME *in*
ORANGE COUNTY

RENTING A BEACH HOUSE

FROM ANY OF THE LOCATIONS BELOW, you can make easy day trips to Disneyland, Knott's, Wild Rivers, or the other Orange County amusements—but your kids will have just as much fun on the beach and in the ocean, and you may be happiest staying put. If you have younger children, try sleepy Capistrano; if you have teenagers, you're better off in Newport or Laguna, where they'll find more close-by shops, amusements, and other teens.

BURR WHITE REALTORS With 33 years of experience renting beach houses, this Newport firm is the best source for a beach house on the Balboa Peninsula; it has choices on the oceanfront, for wave fans; on the bay front, for gentler waters; and less expensive ones in between, for those on a budget who don't mind walking a block to the beach. August prices for a three-bedroom waterfront house range from $1,600 to $10,000 a week, depending on the property. The beach is less secluded and private than Capistrano, but there's more action for teens. 2901 Newport Boulevard, Newport Beach; ☎ 800-944-0952; **www.burrwhite.com.**

CAPISTRANO REALTY In between San Clemente and Dana Point lies one of Orange County's few private beachfront communities, perhaps the only one in which every house sits on the sand. This agency is the primary source for renting a house along guard-gated, 1.5-mile Beach Road, which parallels the Pacific Coast Highway just across the (frequently traveled) railroad tracks. Although hardly cheap, the houses rent for much less than in the Malibu colony or Del Mar: A high-quality three-bedroom, two-bath place might go for $2,500 a week in June and $4,200 in August. Cycling families note that you can ride from Beach Road all the way to Dana Point Harbor (about three miles) on a flat, protected, oceanfront route; a vendor at the public beach at the beginning of the road rents bikes, surreys, and skates. Houses on the north end of the road have the largest sand beach; those on the south end have the best swimming for children. 34700 Pacific Coast Highway, Capistrano Beach; ☎ 949-496-5353 or 800-397-6931; **www.socalvacation.com.**

LAGUNA PROPERTIES This Laguna Beach agency offers weekly and monthly vacation rentals in Laguna and surrounding towns, including Dana Point. 1096 South Coast Highway, Laguna Beach; ☎ 888-393-6533 or 949-494-8057; **www.lagunaproperties.biz.**

SOUTH COUNTY:

San Clemente, Dana Point, and San Juan Capistrano

LOW ON A-LIST AMUSEMENTS BUT HIGH ON BEACH FUN, the towns in southernmost Orange County aren't well known to the tourist trade. That's just fine by the locals, who get to enjoy clean, sunny beaches and small-town appeal. We have a number of friends who live within walking distance of L.A.'s beaches but who drive an hour or more south to **San Clemente's T Street** every Saturday in summer, because its water is cleaner, its beach more picturesque, and its surf better for both little kids and bodysurfers.

San Clemente is the southernmost town in this area, and it's a great place to spend a beach day. Amtrak trains stop right in front of the pier and beach, making it a fine car-free day trip from L.A. or Anaheim. Although it has begun to gentrify, it's still a real beach town, populated by retirees and middle-class families, so don't expect chain businesses and shops selling $100 aloha shirts—just a classic pier, a public beach with all the amenities, and a sunny downtown with great surf shops, a few interesting boutiques, and Mexican restaurants.

Dana Point, a few miles north, is centered around a large pleasure-craft harbor (see attraction profile). The heart of town itself is a rather dispiriting collection of late-model storefronts along Pacific Coast Highway (PCH), but if you look carefully you'll find a few shops that surf-fascinated kids will adore, including Hobie's, **Girl in the Curl** (for girl surfers), and **Killer Dana.** Along with the usual streets, a bike path follows **San Juan Creek** from its endpoint—the bird sanctuary–estuary in between **Doheny State Beach's** campground and public park—about three flat miles into **San Juan Capistrano,** the handsome mission town in which even the fast-food restaurants have red-tile roofs.

The mission is **San Juan's** main draw, and it's one of the state's loveliest and most interesting to children. From the mission, you can walk to the train depot and let kids run through the old train cars that make up the station and station restaurant; across the train tracks are a few of the town's oldest houses, including some adobes, as well as a sweet little petting farm and pony ride that local kids love.

FAMILY LODGING

Beachcomber Motel
533 Avenida Victoria, San Clemente; ☎ 949-492-5457 or 888-492-5457; www.beachcombermotel.com; $100–$350, weekly rates available

A vintage 1940s beach motel, the red-tile roof Beachcomber has just 12 rooms and a killer location on a grassy bluff overlooking San Clemente beach and the pier. The amenities are few: a vending machine instead of a coffee shop, and the blue Pacific instead of a pool. The prices are high for a basic motel (maid service, for example, is provided only "as needed"). But even the studios have kitchenettes and can house a family of four, and the one-bedrooms can handle as many as seven people. Each unit also has its own little front porch with a fabulous ocean view. The beach below is one of the best for family fun in Southern California. This motel books up months in advance for summer, so plan ahead.

Doheny State Beach Campground
25300 Dana Point Harbor Drive, Dana Point; ☎ 949-496-6171; www.dohenystatebeach.org; reservations: Reserve America, ☎ 800-444-7275; www.reserveamerica.com; campsites, $20–$35; parking rates are established by park

It's small, it has no RVs (no hookups), and it's right on one of the most family-friendly beaches in Southern California, so this tent campground is booked months in advance for weekends and summer. Because it's so compact, don't expect much peace and quiet, but do expect to find lots of other families skating and cycling the bike paths, playing volleyball, learning to surf the famed gentle waves, barbecuing, visiting the small indoor aquarium, and exploring the neighboring Dana Point Harbor. Be warned that the ocean has had a number of health closures in the last couple of years.

Marriott's Laguna Cliffs Resort & Spa
25135 Park Lantern, Dana Point; ☎ 949-661-5000 or 800-228-9290; www.marriott.com; $219–$750; suites, $500 and up

A Cape Cod–style hotel that sprawls over a bluff with views from Dana Point to San Clemente, this resort has had several changes in management, but it has remained a very good family resort no matter who's in charge. From the extensive lawns, paths lead down to a pine-dotted city park above the harbor, with a children's playground, excellent basketball court, and lawns popular with kite flyers. On site are two pools, lots of room to run around, a fitness center, and a spa. The children's menu is available in both the restaurant and room service; the all-day children's program in summer runs $45. Doheny State Beach is a third-of-a-mile walk, but the walk back is up a steep hill, so if you have little ones, you might want to consider driving (which means paying for parking).

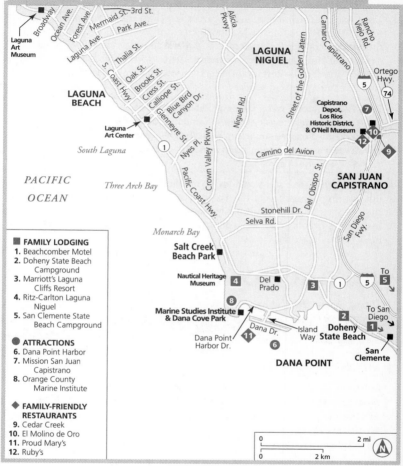

south county: san clemente, dana point, and san juan capistrano

FAMILY LODGING
1. Beachcomber Motel
2. Doheny State Beach Campground
3. Marriott's Laguna Cliffs Resort
4. Ritz-Carlton Laguna Niguel
5. San Clemente State Beach Campground

ATTRACTIONS
6. Dana Point Harbor
7. Mission San Juan Capistrano
8. Orange County Marine Institute

FAMILY-FRIENDLY RESTAURANTS
9. Cedar Creek
10. El Molino de Oro
11. Proud Mary's
12. Ruby's

Ritz-Carlton Laguna Niguel

1 Ritz-Carlton Drive, Dana Point; ☎ 949-240-2000 or 800-241-3333; www.ritzcarlton.com; $375–$495; 4 people allowed in a room ($50 per extra guest); children under 18 stay free

This is paradise for kids and their parents, as long as they've got plenty of money and don't mind a setting that's more formal than California beach. A few hundred guest rooms, elegant restaurants, lounges, lobbies, and meeting rooms are spread along a bluff overlooking a soft-sand beach; everywhere are lawns and flowers and walkways, along with the expected pools, spas, a fitness center, spa facilities, and tennis courts (golf is adjacent). Your 6- to 12-year-old children can join in the Ritz Kids program ($50 a day), which includes swimming, beach games, arts and crafts, tide pooling, and trips to the Orange County Marine Institute; if you crave a grown-up meal, the hotel offers Kids' Night Out on Friday and Saturday, when they're served dinner and entertained with movies or live performances (such as puppet shows). The Terrace Restaurant offers a good children's menu, which is also available through room service.

San Clemente State Beach Campground
3030 Avenida del Presidente, San Clemente; ☎ 949-492-3156; reservations: Reserve America; ☎ 800-444-7275; www.reserveamerica.com; campsites $20–$25 without hookups; $29–$34 with hookups

Popular with surfers and beach-loving families, this is a well-equipped (hook-ups, fire rings, hot showers, flush toilets) campground on a bluff overlooking the beach; the trail down is easily manageable for kids, though the littlest may whine heading back up (consider bringing a wagon). A fine beach for body boarding, surfing, splashing, and general beach fun.

ATTRACTIONS

Dana Point Harbor

APPEAL BY AGE	PRESCHOOL ★★★	GRADE SCHOOL ★★★	TEENS ★★★
YOUNG ADULTS ★★★		OVER 30 ★★★	SENIORS ★★★

Golden Lantern off Pacific Coast Highway, Dana Point; ☎ 949-923-2255; www.danapointharbor.com

Hours Shops and restaurants open daily; hours vary. **Admission** Free. **Touring time** Average 4 hours including lunch or dinner; minimum 1 hour. **Rainy-day Touring** Not great. **Restaurants** Many. **Alcoholic beverages** Yes. **Disabled access** Yes. **Wheelchair rental** No. **Baby-stroller rental** No. **Lockers** No. **Pet kennels** No. **Rain check** No. **Private tours** No.

DESCRIPTION AND COMMENTS More an afternoon's destination than an attraction, the harbor is home to a fine museum (the Orange County Marine Institute, see profile) and a kid-beloved outdoor cafe, Proud Mary's (see profile). The harbor is also the place to head out for a whale-watching, fishing, or Jet Skiing expedition (rentals available). You can also skate, cycle, or walk the pedestrian paths linking the shopping, eating, and boating areas, and explore the little caves, tide pools, and rocky shoreline on the far west end of the harbor. On a sunny day, the hippest place to be is the terrace front of the Scoop Deck, an ice-cream parlor next door to a coffeehouse. Locals and their many dogs join visitors to sit and watch the passing parade of inline skaters, sailors, and walkers.

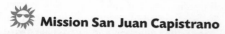

Mission San Juan Capistrano

APPEAL BY AGE	PRESCHOOL ★★	GRADE SCHOOL ★★★	TEENS ★★★
YOUNG ADULTS ★★★		OVER 30 ★★★	SENIORS ★★★★

Visitors Center, 31882 Camino Capistrano, San Juan Capistrano;
☎ **949-234-1300; www.missionsjc.com**

Hours Daily, 8:30 a.m.–5 p.m.; closed Thanksgiving, Christmas, and Good Friday afternoon. **Admission** Self-guided tours: $6 adults, $5 seniors, and $4 children ages 3–11; docent tours $7. **Touring time** Average 2 hours; minimum 1 hour. **Rainy-day Touring** Some; outdoors may be difficult. **Restaurants** Nearby. **Alcoholic beverages** No. **Disabled access** Yes. **Wheelchair rental** 2 chairs to borrow. **Baby-stroller rental** No. **Lockers** No. **Pet kennels** No. **Rain check** No. **Private tours** Guided tours $7 all ages; self-guided, $4–$6.

DESCRIPTION AND COMMENTS Perhaps the most fully restored of the mission chain, with the most to see in the way of demonstrations and living, working, sacred, and exhibition areas, San Juan Capistrano is also an enclosed parklike setting that makes it an easy place to keep track of kids while they scramble and skip around a bit. The mission buildings are laid out around two enclosed courtyards, and the rooms you see are on the ground level with a simple step in and out of the adobe doorways. Parents of very young children don't even have to bother with the lectures; instead they can wander past the tables full of ancient tools and bits of leather and such that are set out especially for little ones to touch and examine. On the last Saturday of each month, the mission holds Living History Day, which is worth a visit—docents dress and act in character as Native Americans and missionary priests. Check the Web site for hands-on activity days for kids.

Orange County Marine Institute

APPEAL BY AGE	PRESCHOOL ★★★	GRADE SCHOOL ★★★★	TEENS ★★★
YOUNG ADULTS ★★★		OVER 30 ★★★	SENIORS ★★★

24200 Dana Point Harbor Drive (far western end of harbor), Dana Point;
☎ **949-496-2274; www.ocean-institute.org**

Hours Store open daily, 10 a.m.–4:30 p.m.; facility open for field trips Monday–Friday, 8 a.m.–5 p.m. **Admission** $5.50 adults, $3.50 children ages 4–12, free for age 3 and under. **Touring time** Average 30 minutes; minimum 30 minutes. **Rainy-day Touring** No problem inside; difficult near tide pools. **Restaurants** Nearby. **Alcoholic beverages** No. **Disabled access** Yes. **Wheelchair rental** No. **Baby-stroller rental** No. **Lockers** No. **Pet kennels** No. **Rain check** Excursions only. **Private tours** Yes.

DESCRIPTION AND COMMENTS The name suggests an aquarium center, but while plans are afoot to add tank space, that's not what this place is about. It's a quirky, intriguing collection of marine-centered activities and sites, from the tide pools out on the shoreline to tours of a historic tall ship. Inside is a simple docent-manned touch tank, allowing kids to hold a sea star or tiny crab, along with a gift shop and such whale memorabilia as a fully reconstructed skeleton hanging overhead. Across the lawn outside is the home dock of *The Pilgrim,* site of overnight field trips for seemingly every fifth-grade class in Southern California; you can tour the ship on Sundays, which will bring your child's Captain Hook fantasies to life. Parent-child overnighters are offered sporadically in summer; call for information.

Even cooler, at least for the 8-to-teen set, is a trip aboard the *R/V Sea Explorer,* a state-of-the-art research ship complete with underwater remote cameras. Outings include the Marine Mammal trip (best during whale-watching season), and our favorite, the Bioluminescent Night Cruise, a two-hour trip in search of glowing fish, plankton, and glowworms.

Finally, the Institute supervises (and sometimes leads tours of) the wonderful tide-pooling preserve on its northern edge, at the base of the actual point. Our kids have spent many happy hours exploring the life here and hiking the rocky but easy trail that hugs the bluff, leading to several kid-sized caves and even more tide pooling.

FAMILY-FRIENDLY RESTAURANTS

Cedar Creek
26860 Ortega Highway, San Juan Capistrano; ☎ 949-240-2229; www.cedarcreekinn.com/sjc.htm

Meals served Lunch, dinner, and Sunday brunch. **Cuisine** American. **Entree range** Lunch, $9–$17; dinner, $17–$27. **Kids' menu** $6–$8. **Reservations** Not accepted on Friday and Saturday nights. **Payment** AE, MC, V.

Ideally located across the street from Mission San Juan Capistrano, this place has the prettiest patio in town, all brick and greenery and Mission influenced, with a fireplace for chilly evenings. Unlike the Cedar Creek in Laguna, this one welcomes children with things like special menus and booster seats. The well-prepared food is solid American with a bit of modernity (there's a rare-ahi sandwich as well as a terrific burger). Later evenings often bring live music and what passes for a singles scene in San Juan, so families are best coming for lunch and early dinner.

El Molino de Oro
31886 Plaza Drive, San Juan Capistrano; ☎ 949-489-9230

Meals served Breakfast, lunch, and dinner. **Cuisine** Mexican. **Entree range** $4–$12. **Kids' menu** Yes. **Reservations** Not accepted. **Payment** D, MC, V.

Almost hidden in a strip mall south of the mission (look for the Starbucks to find it), this *tortilleria* and cafe makes the best Mexican food in town. There's always a line at the counter, and the plastic tables on the sidewalk fill up fast, thanks to the fresh, homemade tortillas and hearty, cheap, delicious burritos, soft tacos, enchiladas, and more. My picky kids love the cheese quesadillas and fresh chips.

 Proud Mary's

34689 Golden Lantern, Dana Point Harbor; ☎ 949-493-5853

Meals served Breakfast and lunch. **Cuisine** American. **Entree range** Breakfast, $5–$8; lunch, $6–$12. **Kids' menu** Yes. **Reservations** Not accepted. **Payment** All major credit cards.

This is my 11-year-old's favorite restaurant, for a host of reasons. For one, all lunches come with a small bag of potato chips. For another, the children's menus are great to color, and they can hang them on the inside wall when finished. Best of all, the patio tables overlook the fishing boats, coastline, and harbor walkway, which is always packed with kids, dogs, and adults on weekends. While waiting for their chicken fingers, they can watch crabs scurry on the rocks below and wave to departing fishing boats. We love it, too, because of the sunny patio, the view, and the superb hamburger, Ortega chile–chicken sandwich, and breakfasts. If you still have room, there's an ice-cream shop farther along the harbor front.

Ruby's

31781 Camino Capistrano, San Juan Capistrano; ☎ 949-496-7829; www.rubys.com

Meals served Breakfast, lunch, and dinner. **Cuisine** American. **Entree range** Breakfast, $5–$8; lunch and dinner, $6–$12. **Kids' menu** Yes. **Reservations** Not accepted. **Payment** All major credit cards.

A local chain that grew out of the Newport Beach original, Ruby's is another rider on the 1940s-nostalgia bandwagon, and kids can't get enough of it. Booths are big, red, and shiny, children's cheeseburgers come in car-shaped cardboard boxes (complete with toy), and a model train chugs around the ceiling. The food is generic, inexpensive, and more fun for children than parents (though it makes kids happy).

LAGUNA BEACH *and* NEWPORT BEACH

THE ANTIDOTE TO THE TRACT-HOUSE STERILITY of Orange County is **Laguna Beach.** This hilly, meandering town is funky, artistic, and utterly charming. It's known more as a beach-town retreat for artists, art lovers (including devotees of the bizarre **Pageant of the Masters,** when people dress in costume and re-create famous paintings), and couples (straight and gay) seeking a romantic weekend. Don't look for amusements like theme parks or kid-oriented museums, but do spend time exploring some of its 30 jewellike beaches, many hidden at the base of steep bluffs. If you choose Laguna as a beachy base for exploring Orange County, know that **Newport** is only about a 15-minute drive north, **Dana Point** about a 15-minute drive south, and **Disneyland** and **Knott's Berry Farm** are some 30 minutes inland. Add more time to the drives in July and August, when central Laguna sees wicked traffic.

> *unofficial* **TIP**
> Laguna is an excellent base for beach vacations with teens and preteens, who will love the shopping (beads, tie-dyes, surfwear, locally made jewelry); the snack, coffee, and yogurt vendors; the hip cafes; and the fellow-teen watching.

Newport Beach is the nouveau-riche capital of California. It oozes prosperity, with seemingly more Mercedes-Benzes than in all of Germany. Although this can be irritating for less materialistic families, prosperity does have its advantages. Newport has miles of wide, clean, well-maintained beaches, a yacht harbor stocked with pretty boats, bike paths galore, some of the country's best shopping, good restaurants, and fetching little **Balboa Island,** almost a toy beach-village.

In some social circles, families have rented Newport beachside cottages for generations, which can be a fine idea (see "Renting a Beach House," page 75). **Balboa Peninsula** is a particularly nice place to be, with its bay and ocean beaches, bike path, pier, pedalboats on the bay, ferry, and **Fun Zone.** Teens especially love Balboa and Newport, because there's always life (and other teens) on the boardwalk and the beach. Don't miss a morning visit to the **Newport Pier** to watch the dory fishermen row in and unload their morning catch—kids find it enthralling. (They'll also like watching the fishing families on the pier, catching their dinners.) If you don't have a week or the inclination to

laguna beach

Hawthorne
Myrtle
Jasmine
Aster
Laguna Canyon Rd.

S. Coast Hwy.

Cliff

Broadway

1

Park

Legion

6

Cleo

3

Glenneyer

PACIFIC
OCEAN

7

Brooks

2

Cress

Mountain

Blue Bird Canyon Dr.

Agate

Pearl

S. Coast Hwy.

Nyes Place

■ **FAMILY LODGING**
1. Crystal Cove Beach Cottages
2. Surf and Sand Hotel
3. Vacation Village

◆ **FAMILY-FRIENDLY RESTAURANTS**
4. The Cottage
5. Ruby's
6. Taco Loco
7. Wahoo's Fish Tacos

Wesley

5

| 0 | 0.5 mi |
| 0 | 0.5 km |

N

newport beach

■ **FAMILY LODGING**
1. Bay Shores Peninsula Hotel
2. Hyatt Regency Newport Beach
3. Newport Dunes Resort

● **ATTRACTIONS**
4. Balboa Fun Zone
5. Wild Rivers Waterpark

◆ **FAMILY-FRIENDLY RESTAURANTS**
6. B. J.'s Balboa
7. Crab Cooker
8. Daily Grill
9. El Torito Grill
10. Ruby's

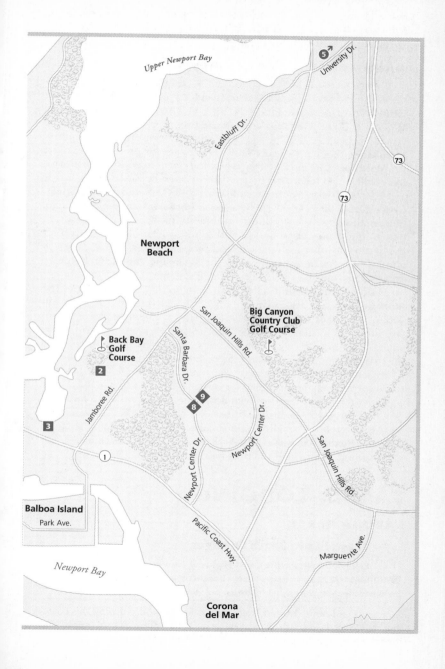

rent a house, one of the hotels or the campground at **Newport Dunes** will also make a fun family base. The theme parks of the North County are only about 20 minutes away.

MALL MANIA

A QUARTET OF DISTINCTIVE MALLS makes Orange County a shopper's destination. We prefer **Fashion Island** in Newport Beach (Newport Center Drive between Jamboree and MacArthur, Newport Beach; ☎ 949-721-2000; **www.shopfashionisland.com**), because it's open-air and visually appealing, with good restaurants; our favorite is the beautiful **Tutto Mare,** though it's really only appropriate for preteens and older (the **Hard Rock Cafe** is, of course, where kids want to go). See profiles for **Daily Grill** and **El Torito Grill** under "Family-friendly Restaurants."

In Costa Mesa, **South Coast Plaza** (☎ 3333 South Bristol Street, Costa Mesa; ☎ 714-435-2000; **www.southcoastplaza.com**) is a huge, glitz, mall that sells everything imaginable. Younger kids will want to play in the **Disney Store** and the other toy stores; older ones can hit the dozens of other fashion-oriented shops and department stores. A good on-site restaurant choice is the **Wolfgang Puck Cafe,** home to great salads, chic pizzas, and a children's menu.

Middle schoolers infatuated with skateboard culture will love **The Block at Orange** (City Drive off I-5 or the 22 freeway; ☎ 714-769-4000), home not only of all the best surf and swimwear shops in Southern California, but also of **Van's Skate Park,** an indoor facility where skateboarders and inline skaters can pay by the hour to skate the two "swimming pools" and the many ramps and other structures. There's also a movie megaplex, and adults can cool their heels at some surprisingly good cafes.

Older teens will want to head down the street to the **Lab Anti-mall** in Costa Mesa (2930 Bristol Street, Costa Mesa; ☎ 714-966-6660; **www.thelab.com**), a small, outdoor collection of teen/GenX shops—**Urban Outfitters, Crew** salon, **DWP** skate shop, **Trilogy Playhouse**—that sort of thing. Nose rings and pink hair are the norm here.

FAMILY LODGING

LAGUNA BEACH

 Crystal Cove Beach Cottages

Los Trancos at Pacific Coast Highway, Newport Coast;
☎ **800-444-7275; www.crystalcovebeachcottages.org; $115–$175 for 4 people; $30 for each additional person**

Modest board-and-batten cottage resorts like this once dotted this coastline, but they eventually gave way to condominiums, resort hotels, and mansions—all but Crystal Cove, that is. This new state park just north of

Laguna Beach recently refurbished 13 of its 46 1920s- and 1930s-era cottages and put them up for rental, and the demand has been over-whelming—you won't find a better oceanfront deal in California. The charming whitewashed cottages sleep four to nine, with rudimentary kitchens, generous porches, and access to a fabulous state beach and the funky Beachcomber Cafe. They are reserved just like state campgrounds, through ReserveAmerica, which means you need to start speed-dialing at 7:55 a.m. on the first of the month seven months before the month you hope to visit; even then, your chances aren't great, especially for summer. But it's worth the effort. Over time the state hopes to renovate the remaining cottages and add them to the rental pool.

☀ Surf and Sand Hotel

1555 South Coast Highway, Laguna Beach; ☎ 949-497-4477 or 888-869-7569; www.surfandsandresort.com; $400–$600; suites $700–$1,200; kids under 18 stay free

The best hotel in Laguna Beach, this is a small-scale resort most notable for its exceptional location perched on the rim of the Pacific; from some rooms, you might feel like you're shipboard. Although it is a quiet, subtly elegant place, it also manages to welcome families. Many rooms, from the least expensive ones with two queens to the oceanfront kings with pullout sofas, can handle a family of three or four; the large Catalina mini-suites can easily handle four. Along with 500 feet of beautiful beach, there's a fancy spa, a pool, summertime children's activities, and Splashes, a good Mediterranean restaurant (with children's menu) facing the beach. Main Beach is a mile north, but there are plenty of cafes and shops nearby.

Vacation Village

647 South Coast Highway, Laguna Beach; ☎ 949-494-8566 or 800-843-6895; www.vacationvillage.com; $130–$300; suites $300 and up

This older, family-run hotel is the beachfront location of choice for families who can't swing the steeper fares at the Surf and Sand or Ritz-Carlton—and many of these families have been returning for years. The 130-room, medium-rise hotel sits right on the sand, though that sand vanishes at high tide, when the waves lick the hotel's foundation and everyone moves camp to one of the two compact pools or walks a few blocks into downtown Laguna for a shopping expedition. Rooms come with coffeemakers, small re-frigerators, and movie channels; the family suites have complete kitchens. Since this is an aging, moderately priced place, guests accept that some rooms are small, that bathrooms are basic, and that corridors and rooms bear traces of that motel-disinfectant smell. But the place sold in July of 2006, so a thorough renovation (and probable upgrade in pricing) is expected.

NEWPORT BEACH

Bay Shores Peninsula Hotel

1800 West Balboa Boulevard, Newport Beach; ☎ 949-675-3463 or

800-222-6675; www.thebestinn.com; $219–$300 and up in summer, suites $420 and up; kids under 12 stay free in parents' room

Location is king, say real-estate agents, and this recently renovated motel has location in spades—it's one block to Newport Bay and, in the other direction, one block to the ocean-side beach. To make up for the lack of a pool, the motel supplies everything you need for the beach, including towels, body boards, chairs, toys, and umbrellas. Other extras include a good breakfast buffet and in-room VCRs and DVD players. The 25 surf-themed rooms are relatively small; four of you can fit in a room with two doubles, but just barely. But you don't come here to hang out in your room. Consider splurging on the newer two-bedroom suites.

Hyatt Regency Newport Beach
1107 Jamboree Road, Newport Beach; ☎ 949-729-1234 or 800-233-1234; newportbeach.hyatt.com; $219 and up; half-price adjoining rooms sometimes available

The nearby Four Seasons may be a bit more swank, but for families, this is the best resort hotel in Newport. It's attractive and upscale but not too fussy; the 403 rooms and suites are spread over 26 acres, surrounded by lawns, flowers, trees, and all sorts of amusements—like the three pools (one just for kids), or the tennis courts, Ping-Pong table, shuffleboard court, or nine-hole golf course. Or the bike-rental shop, which will steer you to the path connecting to the superb Upper Newport Bay Ecological Reserve (see "The Best Beaches and Parks").The amusements at Newport Dunes (also detailed in "The Best Beaches and Parks") are just across the street, and shuttles will deliver your family to Balboa's Fun Zone and Fashion Island.

Newport Dunes Resort
1131 Back Bay Drive, Newport Beach; ☎ 949-729-3863; www.newportdunes.com; reservations, ☎ 800-765-7661; tent sites $59–$110 in summer, RV sites $95–$225, higher on holidays

This private campground is so fun for families that it rates its own listing under "The Best Beaches and Parks." Along with all the amenities described there, it has RV and tent sites (freestanding tents only—no stakes allowed), windsurfing lessons, picnic facilities, barbecues, changing rooms, a restaurant, a market, and a boat launch. Reservations for the summer are taken from January 1 on, so call early for a prime time.

ATTRACTIONS

Balboa Fun Zone

APPEAL BY AGE	PRESCHOOL ★★★	GRADE SCHOOL ★★★★	TEENS ★★★
YOUNG ADULTS ★★		OVER 30 ★★	SENIORS ★★

**600 East Bay Avenue, Balboa; ☎ 949-673-0408;
www.thebalboafunzone.com**

Hours Sunday–Thursday, 11 a.m.–8 p.m.; Friday, 11 a.m.–10 p.m.; Saturday, 11 a.m.–
10 p.m. **Admission** Free; rides are $1–$3. **Touring time** Average 3 hours, with
ferry ride; minimum 1½ hours. **Rainy-day Touring** No. **Restaurants** Yes. **Alcoholic beverages** Yes. **Disabled access** Yes. **Wheelchair rental** No. **Baby-stroller
rental** No. **Lockers** In laser tag. **Pet kennels** No; leashed pets only. **Rain check**
Yes. **Private tours** On the boats.

DESCRIPTION AND COMMENTS On the waterfront near the Balboa Pier and Balboa Pavilion is a little amusement park full of small-town, old-fashioned
charm. There's a Ferris wheel, a merry-go-round, bumper cars, a moon
bounce, arcade games, laser tag, and such art projects as spin paintings.
One of the fondest memories of my childhood is getting a "Balboa bar," a
precursor to the Häagen-Dazs bar, that's as popular as ever.

Almost as fun as the Fun Zone is a ride over to Balboa Island on the
Balboa Island Ferry (☎ 949-673-1070), which leaves right near the Fun
Zone. It's a short, picturesque, little-kid–size ride to the island; kids ages
5 to 11 ride for just 30¢, and adults ride for 60¢; cars with driver are
$1.50, and passengers are extra. The island itself doesn't have much for
kids, but if you bring bikes over on the ferry, it's great fun to pedal
around the Lilliputian streets.

Wild Rivers Waterpark

APPEAL BY AGE	PRESCHOOL ★★★★★	GRADE SCHOOL ★★★★★	TEENS ★★★★★
YOUNG ADULTS ★★★★		OVER 30 ★★★★	SENIORS ★★★

8770 Irvine Center Drive, Irvine; ☎ 949-788-0808; www.wildrivers.com

Hours Mid-June to early September, open daily 10 a.m.–8 p.m.; limited hours available from mid-May to the prime season and in the post-season through September.
Admission $29, $18 for children 48" tall or shorter and $18 for adults, $15 for children after 4 p.m. in summer; parking, $8 **Touring time** Average 4 hours, 6 for school
age and up; minimum 2 hours, 4 for school age and up. **Rainy-day Touring** No.
Restaurants Yes. **Alcoholic beverages** No. **Disabled access** Limited. **Wheelchair
rental** No. **Baby-stroller rental** No. **Lockers** $5 plus $1 deposit small, $9 plus $1
deposit large. **Pet kennels** No. **Rain check** No. **Private tours** No.

DESCRIPTION AND COMMENTS When Anaheim starts to swelter, and the sand
burns your feet at Balboa, consider a trip to this first-rate water park,
which has something for every age group. At about a foot deep, Pygmy
Pond keeps the little ones happy, with its small, not-scary waterslides,
inner tube rides, gorilla swing, and climbing structure that shoots out
water. Older, braver kids will go for Surf Hills, which they can belly-slide
down; the swimming pool with a water-basketball hoop; and the wave
pools, which generate real waves. The bravest of all can tackle the vertical drops, rapids, and enclosed tunnel slides. All in all, there are more
than 40 rides, along with two swimming pools. If you don't want to eat
at the restaurants, there's a picnic area outside the entrance.

FAMILY-FRIENDLY RESTAURANTS

LAGUNA BEACH

The Cottage
308 North Coast Highway, Laguna Beach; ☎ 949-494-3023;
www.thecottagerestaurant.com

Meals served Breakfast, lunch, dinner, and Sunday brunch. **Cuisine** American.
Entree range Breakfast and lunch, $6–$14; dinner, $12–$24. **Kids' menu** Yes.
Reservations Accepted. **Payment** All major credit cards.

There's always a crowd at this handsome old Arts and Crafts bungalow in
north Laguna, thanks to the family-style conviviality and generous, simple
food. Breakfast is the real draw (and the most crowded), not because the
waffles and eggs are that memorable (they're fine), but because it's hard to
find a solid breakfast in this upscale town.

Ruby's
30622 South Pacific Coast Highway, Laguna Beach; ☎ 949-497-7829;
www.rubys.com

Meals served Breakfast, lunch, and dinner. **Cuisine** American. **Entree range**
Breakfast, $4–$10; lunch and dinner, $5–$15. **Kids' menu** Yes. **Reservations** Not
accepted. **Payment** All major credit cards.

South of the town center—which means parking is free and plentiful—this
is the hottest kid restaurant in Laguna. The gleaming 1940s and 1950s cars
in the parking lot set the stage for the neo–sock-hop theme: oldies music,
big vinyl booths, uniformed waitresses, old Coke ads, model trains, and
shameless catering to children, who find the food to be way more delicious
than their parents do.

Taco Loco
640 South Coast Highway, Laguna Beach; ☎ 949-497-1635

Meals served Lunch and dinner. **Cuisine** Mexican. **Entree range** $5–$13. **Kids'
menu** No. **Reservations** Not accepted. **Payment** All major credit cards.

If your teen wants to hang with the coolest surfers, come to this sidewalk
cafe, where you'll find the best Mexican street food in town, along with hip
Southwestern and Californian dishes; you can have a calamari quesadilla
while your kids try a carne asada burrito. The food is so good that regular
customer Jimmy Buffett hired the owner to cater his road tours.

Wahoo's Fish Tacos
1133 South Coast Highway, Laguna Beach; ☎ 949-497-0033;
www.wahoos.com

Meals served Lunch and dinner. **Cuisine** Mexican. **Entree range** $4–$10. **Kids'
menu** Yes. **Reservations** Not accepted. **Payment** MC, V.

Everybody loves Wahoo's: little kids, who get their own menu; big kids, who love both the food and the grunge surfer décor; parents, who can have fresh-fish (not fried) tacos or burritos and a cold Corona while the kids have quesadillas and fries; and Laguna's surfers, who would surely starve if not for Wahoo's tasty, cheap Mexican food with a Hawaiian accent (the "da plate" lunch specials are good). This is an order-at-the-counter, throw-a-T-shirt-over-your-bathing-suit kind of place, located in a prime spot between Main Beach and the Surf and Sand Hotel.

NEWPORT BEACH

B.J.'s Balboa
106 Main Street, Balboa Peninsula; ☎ 949-675-7560

Meals served Lunch and dinner. **Cuisine** Italian. **Entree range** Lunch and dinner, $7–$20. **Kids' menu** Yes. **Reservations** Not accepted. **Payment** All major credit cards.

Tasty thick-crust pizza is the draw here, as is the great location a half block from Balboa Pier. Other pluses are a pretty good salad bar, kid-sized pizzas and pastas, and boisterous camaraderie. Expect a wait, especially on summer weekends.

Crab Cooker
2200 Newport Boulevard, Newport Beach; ☎ 949-673-0100;
www.crabcooker.com

Meals served Lunch and dinner. **Cuisine** Seafood. **Entree range** $8–$30. **Kids' menu** No, but there is a "Light Eaters" plate. **Reservations** Not accepted. **Payment** AE, D, V.

A classic beach dive, the Crab Cooker is beloved of locals and tourists alike. The plates are paper, the prices are mostly rock bottom, and the food (mesquite-grilled fresh fish, clam chowder, crab legs, sourdough bread) is mighty fine. Expect to wait in line.

Daily Grill
Fashion Island, 957 Newport Center Drive, Newport Beach;
☎ 949-644-2223; www.dailygrill.com

Meals served Lunch, dinner, and Sunday brunch. **Cuisine** American. **Entree range** Lunch, $10–$20; dinner, $15–$27; Sunday brunch, $17 adults, $9 kids. **Kids' menu** Yes. **Reservations** Yes. **Payment** All major credit cards.

Success came quickly to this small California chain of updated bar and grill restaurants, thanks in part to its recognition that baby boomers like to take their kids out to eat. Little kids get their own menu, big kids can get a chicken potpie or turkey meat loaf, and parents can get an adult beverage and wonderful crab cakes. Avoid the pastas.

El Torito Grill
Fashion Island, 951 Newport Center Drive, Newport Beach;
☎ 949-640-2875; www.eltorito.com

Meals served Daily, lunch and dinner; Sunday, buffet brunch. **Cuisine** Southwestern. **Entree range** Lunch, $8–$14; dinner, $10–$17; Sunday brunch, $17 adults. **Kids' menu** Yes; Sunday brunch, $9 kids. **Reservations** Not necessary. **Payment** All major credit cards.

More Southwestern than Mexican, this offshoot of the El Torito chain of Mexican restaurants is a bit more upscale than its parent, but it's still family oriented. Colorful, noisy, and friendly, it's a good spot for nachos, fajitas, red-corn taquitos, great carnitas, and spicy chicken dishes. Parents get hand-shaken margaritas, and the kids get coloring supplies and their own burritos and tacos, as well as such standards as chicken fingers; children's meals even come with fresh fruit.

Ruby's
☎ 1 Balboa Pier, Newport Beach; ☎ 949-675-7829; www.rubys.com

Meals served Breakfast, lunch, and dinner. **Cuisine** American. **Entree range** $6–$12. **Kids' menu** Yes. **Reservations** Not accepted. **Payment** All major credit cards.

The original of the 1940s-diner chain (see profiles in Laguna and San Juan), this Ruby's is also the best located, smack on the end of the Balboa Pier. Get a table outside, soak in the view, drink a chocolate shake, and have a good time.

HUNTINGTON BEACH

MILES FROM THE FREEWAYS, **Huntington Beach,** the original Surf City and the archetypal beach town, is as lively as it gets because the pier and the commercial section of town are contiguous. This means beachgoers can roll up their towels and head across the street for a frozen yogurt or to shop for surfwear. It also means an ongoing sense of festivity, enhanced by the city's near-constant schedule of concerts and art fairs during the summer. Do you have kids who never want to come out of the water? You don't have to hassle them here. Huntington Beach is one of the few places where you can still build a fire on the beach (it's open until 10 p.m.), so grab a fire ring early in the day and bring hot dogs, marshmallows, guitars, and blankets for an unforgettable summer evening. To learn more about the beach, see **Bolsa Chica** and **Huntington State Beaches** under "The Best Beaches and Parks."

FAMILY LODGING

Hilton Waterfront Beach Resort
21100 Pacific Coast Highway, Huntington Beach; ☎ 714-960-7873 or 800-822-SURF; www.hilton.com; $214–$434 summer; kids under 18 stay free

Its high-rise design doesn't suit low-key Huntington Beach, but otherwise this 248-room hotel is a convenient resort, across the highway from the beach, with pedestrian and bike access to the bike trails and sand. The rooms are attractive and comfortable, the views can be great, and between the beach and the pool, kids have plenty to do. Family amenities include children's activities, babysitting services, bike rentals, a pool, and tennis courts.

ATTRACTION

 International Surfing Museum

APPEAL BY AGE	PRESCHOOL ★	GRADE SCHOOL ★★	TEENS ★★★
YOUNG ADULTS ★★★		OVER 30 ★★★	SENIORS ★★★

411 Olive Street, Huntington Beach; ☎ 714-960-3483; www.surfingmuseum.org

huntington beach

FAMILY LODGING
1. Hilton Waterfront Beach Resort

ATTRACTION
2. International Surfing Museum

FAMILY-FRIENDLY RESTAURANTS
3. Alice's Breakfast in the Park
4. Chimayo at the Beach

39

Main St.

HUNTINGTON CENTRAL PARK

Slater Ave.

Golden West

Central Park Dr.

Garfield Ave.

3

Huntington Lake

Sea Cliff Country Club

Edwards St.

Talbert Ave.

Springdale

BOLSA CHICA WETLANDS

1

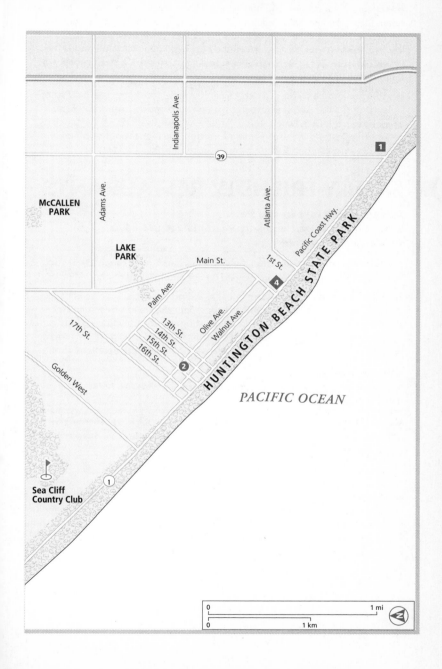

Indianapolis Ave.

39

Adams Ave.

Atlanta Ave.

McCALLEN PARK

Pacific Coast Hwy.

LAKE PARK

Main St.

1st St.

Palm Ave.

4

17th St.

13th St.
14th St.
Olive Ave.
Walnut Ave.
15th St.
16th St.

HUNTINGTON BEACH STATE PARK

2

Golden West

PACIFIC OCEAN

1

Sea Cliff Country Club

0   1 mi

0   1 km

Hours June–September: daily, noon–5 p.m.; October–May: Thursday–Monday, noon–5 p.m. Admission $2 adults, $1 students and seniors, children age 6 and under free. Touring time Average 1 hour; minimum 30 minutes. Rainy-day touring Yes. Restaurants Nearby. Alcoholic beverages No. Disabled access Yes. Wheelchair rental No. Baby-stroller rental No. Lockers No. Pet kennels No. Rain check No. Private tours No.

DESCRIPTION AND COMMENTS At this friendly little museum, the history of surfing is told via old photographs, text, surf music, trophies, old surfboards, even Dick Dale's guitar. After your visit, walk down the block to see the Surfer's Walk of Fame. Note that the star ratings apply only if you're interested in surfing; otherwise the museum's a snooze.

FAMILY-FRIENDLY RESTAURANTS

Alice's Breakfast in the Park
6622 Lakeview Drive, Huntington Beach; ☎ 714-848-0690; www.breakfastinthepark.com

Meals served Breakfast and lunch. Cuisine American. Entree range $5–$9. Kids' menu Yes. Reservations Recommended on weekends. Payment No credit cards.

Breakfast is often a kid's favorite meal to eat out, especially a breakfast like this: huge cinnamon rolls, scrambled eggs, pancakes, and other such treats, served on a patio next to the lake in Huntington Central Park, so kids can run around and feed the ducks between bites. After breakfast (or lunch), spend a couple of hours exploring the lovely park and the excellent library.

Chimayo at the Beach
315 Pacific Coast Highway, Huntington Beach; ☎ 714-374-7273; www.culinaryadventures.com

Meals served Lunch and dinner. Cuisine Cal-Mex Seafood. Entree range $12–$36. Kids' menu No. Reservations Good idea for brunch. Payment All major credit cards.

This handsome eatery is beautifully situated at the foot of the pier on the sand. Because it's often hard to enjoy a family meal at one of the more casual (and less expensive) restaurants across the street (which are typically crowded and difficult to manage with little kids), Chimayo can be a peaceful alternative. The casual tropical décor welcomes families in shorts and T-shirts; lunch is served until 4 p.m. Try a chicken taquito appetizer for a child; other options range from wild mushroom pizzas to fresh fish entrees.

NORTH COUNTY:
Anaheim, Buena Park, and Santa Ana

THE INLAND AREA OF NORTHERN ORANGE COUNTY would not be on any tourist's list if not for the ever-expanding **Disneyland Resort–Knott's Berry Farm** nexus. It's a sprawl of several former agricultural town centers, now linked by residential areas that are generally more working class than the expensive neighborhoods by the sea. It's an ethnically diverse region: **Santa Ana** is home to many Latino immigrants, and **Westminster** is known for its large Vietnamese community. But northern Orange County is not exactly known for its natural beauty—**Anaheim** is notable for its 150-plus hotels, most of which are cardboard-box motels (although some now qualify as vintage examples of 1950s and 1960s kitsch architecture), and **Buena Park** is flat and featureless, an easy place to get lost in under the glaringly reflective summer sun. But if you have kids, you'll be forced to visit the North County, because that's where you'll find Disneyland Resort and Knott's Berry Farm, along with such lesser amusements as **Adventure City** and the **Medieval Times** theme restaurant.

By all means, plan an overnight stay in Anaheim; Disneyland is best enjoyed over a two-day period, with a cool, quiet hotel room in which the family can retreat. Note that in season, Angels baseball games at **Anaheim Stadium** and Mighty Ducks hockey games at **Anaheim Pond** are nearby, and that the water park at Knott's, **Soak City,** offers the contrast of a day of water play.

If you have very young children, under age 5, they will enjoy the woodsy atmosphere and gentle rides of **Camp Snoopy** at Knott's or the birthday-party-park feel of **Adventure City** more than a bewildering day in the crowds swirling through the hugeness of Disneyland.

Just know that the beach is a half-hour drive or more, and the fun here is man-made. After a couple of days doing the theme-park thing in the North County, head to the beach communities to experience another side of the OC.

unofficial **TIP**
Don't try to fit Universal Studios, Disneyland, and Knott's into a sequential three-day period. Theme parks need the space of some nature days in between, or it will all be a blur to your kids.

north county: anaheim, buena park, and santa ana

0   5 mi
0   5 km

La Habra
9

710   5

91

Buena Park

57

16 6
12 15   91
7   13

Anaheim

22

405   **Westminster**   8   **Santa Ana**
10

Seal Beach

55

Irvine

405

Costa Mesa   55

FAMILY LODGING
1. Candy Cane Inn
2. Disneyland Hotel
3. Disney Paradise Pier Hotel
4. Disney's Grand Californian Hotel
5. DoubleTree
6. Embassy Suites Hotel Buena Park

ATTRACTIONS
7. Adventure City
8. Bowers Kidseum
9. Children's Museum at La Habra
10. Discovery Science Center
11. Disneyland Resort
12. Knott's Berry Farm and Knott's Soak City

FAMILY-FRIENDLY RESTAURANTS
13. El Pollo Inka
14. Goofy's Kitchen
15. Medieval Times
16. Mrs. Knott's Chicken Dinner Restaurant
17. Napa Rose

5   Ball Rd.

14 11   Cerritos Rd.
2
3   1
4   Katella Ave.
17

Orangewood Ave.

Chapman Ave.   57

Lewis St.   5   The City Dr.   **Orange**   55

5

22

8

0   1 mi
0   1 km

FAMILY LODGING

Candy Cane Inn

1747 South Harbor Boulevard, Anaheim; ☎ 714-774-5284 or 800-345-7057; www.candycaneinn.net; $119–$129 standard, $129–$139 deluxe

A good bargain well placed near Disneyland's parking lot, this motel is freshly spruced up and now has such luxurious touches as down comforters and plantation shutters. It's worth the modest splurge for a deluxe room, which comes with a fridge and coffeemaker. One of the deluxe rooms can sleep five if you pay an extra $20 for a rollaway. Rates include a continental breakfast and shuttles to Disneyland. Outside are a heated pool, spa, and a wading pool for little ones. Ask about packages including Disneyland tickets. Free parking.

Disneyland Hotel

1150 Magic Way, Anaheim; ☎ 714-778-6600 or 714-956-6425; disneyland.disney.go.com; $275–$320 (changes every season)

A gigantic annex to the park, connected by monorail (very nice for nappers), offering clean, comfortable, reasonably updated rooms in which to sleep off too many long lines. Younger children will enjoy a stay here as much as a trip across the street, thanks to the several pools, the little faux-sand beach complete with pedalboats, the fish ponds, the gift shops, and Goofy's Kitchen (see profile). Children under age 17 stay free in parents' rooms; ask about hotel-park packages. And remember that most days, guests here are allowed into Disneyland an hour before the ordinary folk, which alone is worth a stay in busy times.

Disney Paradise Pier Hotel

1717 South Disneyland Drive, Anaheim; ☎ 714-999-0990 or 714-956-6425; disneyland.disney.go.com; $245–$360 (changes every season)

Like the Disneyland Hotel, this is officially part of the Magic Kingdom. We prefer it to its sibling, because it's less than half the size and is therefore quieter and less overwhelming, with more attractive rooms. The food is better, too. There aren't as many amusements, but you can make do with the pool, workout room, video games, several restaurants and lounges, and shops, as well as direct access to Disneyland.

Disney's Grand Californian Hotel

1600 South Disneyland Drive, Anaheim; ☎ 714-635-2300 or 714-635-2300; disneyland.disney.go.com; $360–$685

This luxury resort has supplanted the Disneyland Hotel as Disneyland's prestigious lodging property. Even Disney haters have had to concede that it's a mighty handsome place. Designed in the Craftsman style of a rustic national park lodge (think of Yosemite's Ahwahnee), it has 750 spacious rooms—some with an extra day bed for kids—and offers three swimming pools (one with a tree slide and one shaped like Mickey Mouse), a high-end health club, and upscale (but family-friendly) restaurants. If you long for dinner without the kids, they'll be happy at Pinocchio's Workshop, an evening child-care center in the hotel. Hotel guests have their own entrance to California Adventure, and Disneyland is right across the way.

DoubleTree

100 The City Drive, Orange; ☎ 714-634-4500 or 800-222-8733; www.doubletreehotels.com; $129–$210 (breakfast extra); kids under 18 stay free in parents' room

This upper-midlevel hotel gives Disney-bound families a lot of bang for the buck. Aside from the nice but basic pool, there's a cool outdoor lagoon that's the size of several pools; other extras include two tennis courts, a fitness center, Nintendo in every room, free shuttles to Disneyland and local malls, in-room coffeemakers, and packages that include Disneyland tickets. The 454 rooms (and 11 suites) are well equipped and reasonably large. The Block mall is a short walk away.

Embassy Suites Hotel Buena Park

7762 Beach Boulevard, Buena Park; ☎ 714-739-5600 or 800-EMBASSY; www.embassysuites.com; $129 and up, check for specials

One of the best theme-park experiences we ever had was a day at Knott's with two nights here. This 202-suite facility is a four-story building surrounding a landscaped courtyard with pool and spa, and it's within walking distance of Knott's. We checked in the night before, enjoyed the cooked-to-order breakfast in the dining room (included in room rate), left the car in the (free) lot, and headed to Knott's. When we'd had our fill of the park, we got a take-out chicken dinner from Mrs. Knott's (far better than the restaurant, really), called the hotel shuttle, and returned to the hotel. We ate dinner in our dining area in the suite, then headed down (with bunches of other families) for a night swim and whirlpool soak.

ATTRACTIONS

Adventure City

APPEAL BY AGE	PRESCHOOL ★★★★	GRADE SCHOOL ★★★	TEENS ★
YOUNG ADULTS ★		OVER 30 ★	SENIORS ★

10120 South Beach Boulevard, Stanton; ☎ 714-236-9300; www.adventurecity.com

Hours Off season: Friday, 10 a.m.–5 p.m.; Saturday and Sunday, 11 a.m.–7 p.m.; summer: Monday–Thursday, 10 a.m.–5 p.m.; Friday, 11 a.m.–7 p.m.; Saturday, 11 a.m.–9 p.m.; Sunday, 11 a.m.–8 p.m. **Admission** $13, $10 for seniors, free for children age 1 and under; includes face painting, puppet shows, and theater. **Touring time** Average 3 hours; minimum 2 hours. **Rainy-day touring** Not great.

Restaurants Basic. **Alcoholic beverages** No. **Disabled access** Yes. **Wheelchair rental** No. **Baby-stroller rental** No. **Lockers** Yes. **Pet kennels** No. **Rain check** No. **Private tours** Yes.

DESCRIPTION AND COMMENTS All it takes is that first visit to Disneyland with a 3-year-old to understand that the Magic Kingdom is really for older kids—it can be an overwhelming and very scary place, overrun with huge, mute cartoon characters and dark, fast rides. Enter this compact kiddieland in Stanton (next door to Anaheim), adjacent to the parent Hobby City, a retail center for collectors and hobbyists. It's designed with the 3-year-old in mind, and while it's a dreadful bore for teens, it's heaven for little ones.

The roller coaster is small and not too intense, and the mini–Ferris wheel is so tame it's called the Giggle Wheel. In the 911 ride, they get to dress up in firefighter and police gear, climb in a kid-scale fire truck, and listen to dispatcher calls. Trains are a big deal here, from the 1938 open-air choo-choo ride that circles the park to the Thomas the Tank Engine play island. When it's time to sit down, head for a puppet show or one of the entertaining (to young ones) stage shows. Needless to say, this place is extremely popular for birthday parties. Be warned that there's an arcade, in the Chuck E. Cheese vein, so steer game-ticket–obsessed kids clear.

Bowers Kidseum

APPEAL BY AGE	PRESCHOOL ★★★	GRADE SCHOOL ★★★★	TEENS ★★
YOUNG ADULTS ★★		OVER 30 ★★	SENIORS ★★

1802 North Main Street, Santa Ana; ☎ 714-480-1520; www.bowers.org/kidseum/kidseum.asp

Hours Tuesday–Friday, noon–4 p.m.; Saturday and Sunday, 11 a.m.–4 p.m.; hours may be expanded in summer. **Admission** $5 for everyone age 3 and older, free for age 2 and under. **Touring time** Average 2½ hours; minimum 1 hour. **Rainy-day touring** Yes. **Restaurants** Yes. **Alcoholic beverages** No; only at Topaz cafe. **Disabled access** Yes. **Wheelchair rental** Yes, free. **Baby-stroller rental** No. **Lockers** Items can be checked. **Pet kennels** No. **Rain check** No. **Private tours** By appointment.

DESCRIPTION AND COMMENTS A companion to the Bowers Museum of Cultural Art next door, this interactive museum brings to life the culture and art of Asia, Africa, and the Native Americans for elementary-age kids. They can try on masks, go into the Time Vault (an old bank vault), put on puppet shows in the theater, play strange musical instruments, and pretend to grind corn with an old stone mortar and pestle. Some of its best offerings are special events—storytelling, art classes, craft workshops—so call for a schedule before you plan a visit. These classes are geared to kids over age 6, and they're especially good for ages 8 to 12; preschoolers will have fun in the interactive museum, but some of it will be above them. Before a visit, let your kids explore the fun Web site.

The admission fee also includes the neighboring museum, so if your older kids are ready for more, browse through and look at its beadwork, carvings, sculptures, and costumes from around the world.

Children's Museum at La Habra

APPEAL BY AGE	PRESCHOOL ★★★★	GRADE SCHOOL ★★★★	TEENS ★★
YOUNG ADULTS ★		OVER 30 ★	SENIORS ★

301 South Euclid Street, La Habra; ☎ 562-905-9793; www.lhcm.org

Hours Monday, 10 a.m.–1 p.m.; Tuesday–Saturday, 10 a.m.–5 p.m.; Sunday, 1–5 p.m.
Admission $5 for age 2 and older. **Touring time** Average 2½ hours; minimum
1 hour. **Rainy-day touring** Yes. **Restaurants** Picnic area and restaurants nearby.
Alcoholic beverages No. **Disabled access** Yes (but 1 room is not accessible).
Wheelchair rental No. **Baby-stroller rental** No. **Lockers** Cubbyholes. **Pet ken-
nels** No **Rain check** No. **Private tours** No.

DESCRIPTION AND COMMENTS   On more than one occasion, I've loaded the kids
in the car and headed to La Habra, bypassing the other children's museums closer to home. It occupies an old Union Pacific depot in a quiet
neighborhood, and it's full of wonderful hands-on activities. My kids'
favorite is the theater area, complete with costumes, a stage, and a lighting booth for impromptu performances. They also love the front half of
a city bus, to drive, ride, and scramble in; the full-size train caboose; the
kid-scale supermarket; and the science experiments. There's always a
new interactive temporary exhibit, and there's a separate play area for
those under age 5.

 ## Discovery Science Center

APPEAL BY AGE	PRESCHOOL ★★	GRADE SCHOOL ★★★★	TEENS ★★★★
YOUNG ADULTS ★★★		OVER 30 ★★★	SENIORS ★★★

**2500 North Main Street, Santa Ana; ☎ 714-542-2823;
www.discoverycube.org**

Hours Daily, 10 a.m.–5 p.m.; store, daily, 11 a.m.–5 p.m.; **Admission** $11 adults, $9
seniors age 55 and over and children ages 3–17; additional $1 for admission to 3-D
Laser Theater; parking $3; adult supervision required for children under age 13. **Tour-
ing time** Average 3 hours; minimum 1 hour. **Rainy-day touring** No. **Restaurants**
Yes. **Alcoholic beverages** No. **Disabled access** Yes. **Wheelchair rental** No. **Baby-
stroller rental** No. **Lockers** Yes. **Pet kennels** No. **Rain check** No. **Private tours** No.

DESCRIPTION AND COMMENTS   This new interactive science museum is packed
with 100 of the latest and greatest in cool, hands-on, science-based
exhibits and experiences. What better way than to lie on a bed of nails
to learn that the larger the area over which a force is distributed, the less
pressure is exerted on any one point? Kids can hoist themselves up with
pulleys, redirect an eight-foot-tall tornado by walking through it, experience an earthquake in the Shake Shack, learn about waves by touching
the spinning Lariat Chain, and make their hair stand on end by putting
one hand on the Van de Graaff generator. Special exhibits have included
such things as Par for the Planet, an 18-hole miniature golf game in
which kids learn about the natural world, from butterfly metamorphosis

to water pollution. And unlike at many science museums, the preschool set gets its own area, complete with age-appropriate science, art, and dress-up activities.

Food service is limited, alas, to a Pizza Hut Express and a Taco Bell Express, and there isn't an outdoor picnic area. But that's a small quibble, given that this place is such a wonderful addition to Orange County.

 Disneyland Resort

APPEAL BY AGE	PRESCHOOL ★★★	GRADE SCHOOL ★★★★★	TEENS ★★★★★
YOUNG ADULTS ★★★★★		OVER 30 ★★★★	SENIORS ★★★

Disneyland Park, Disney's California Adventure Theme Park, Downtown Disney, 1313 South Harbor Boulevard, Anaheim; ☎ 714-781-4565; www.disney.com

Hours Year-round: daily, 10 a.m.–6 p.m.; hours extended as early as 8 a.m. and as late as 1 a.m. during busy seasons; hours vary seasonally. **Admission** One-day pass: $59 age 10 and over, $57 seniors (age 60 and over), $49 children ages 3–9, free children age 3 and younger. **Touring time** Disneyland Park: average 16 hours–2 days; minimum 7 hours. Disney's California Adventure: average 8 hours–1 day; minimum 5 hours. **Rainy-day touring** Yes—a mildly rainy day can be great at the parks, because the crowds disappear and many rides are indoors. **Restaurants** Yes. **Alcoholic beverages** At Disney's California Adventure only. **Disabled access** Yes. **Wheelchair rental** $8; electric carts $35; $20 deposit (not offered at Downtown Disney). **Baby-stroller rental** $8 (not offered at Downtown Disney). **Lockers** $6–$12. **Pet kennels** $15; no overnight. **Rain check** No. **Private tours** Yes.

DESCRIPTION AND COMMENTS   In February of 2002, the Walt Disney Company unveiled its second theme park, Disney's California Adventure, on the Disneyland property. The opening caps an ambitious expansion of Disneyland that also includes new hotels and Downtown Disney, a dining, shopping, and entertainment complex. The entrances of Disneyland Park and Disney's California Adventure face each other across a palm-studded pedestrian plaza called the Esplanade. The Esplanade begins at Harbor Boulevard and runs west, passing into Downtown Disney, which you can visit without paying admission. From Downtown Disney the pedestrian thoroughfare continues to the new monorail station and to the Disneyland and Paradise Pier Hotels.

Disney's California Adventure, known as DCA among Disney-philes, is built on 55 acres (including a sizable carve-out for the Grand Californian Hotel), quite a small park by modern theme-park standards. The theme, celebrating all things (okay, okay, most things) Californian, is infinitely flexible, allowing Disney to offer diverse attractions that would not go well together under any other umbrella. Unfortunately, there's precious little new technology at work in Disney's newest theme park. Of the headliner attractions, only one, Soarin' Over California (a simulator ride), breaks new ground. All the rest are recycled, albeit

disneyland park

Main Street, U.S.A.

New Orleans Square

Adventureland

Alice in Wonderland **18**
Astro Orbiter **28**
Autopia **25**
Big Thunder Mountain Railroad **31**
Buzz Lightyear Astro Blasters **30**
Casey Jr. Circus Train **13**
Chip 'n' Dale's Treehouse **4**
Davy Crockett's Explorer
   Canoes **34**
Disney Gallery **40**
Disneyland Monorail **24**
Disneyland Railroad **8, 26, 39, 49**
Disneyland: The First 50 Years **48**
Dumbo, The Flying Elephant **12**
Enchanted Tiki Room **45**
Fantasyland Theatre **9**
Finding Nemo Submarine
   Voyage **23**
Gadget's Go Coaster **5**
Goofy's Playhouse **7**
Haunted Mansion **37**
Honey, I Shrunk the Audience **47**
Indiana Jones Adventure **43**
Innoventions **27**
It's a Small World **10**
Jungle Cruise **44**

King Arthur Carousel **15**
Mad Tea Party **17**
The Many Adventures of
   Winnie the Pooh **35**
Matterhorn Bobsleds **22**
Mickey's House **3**
Minnie's House **2**
Miss Daisy, Donald's Boat **6**
Mr. Toad's Wild Ride **16**
Peter Pan's Flight **19**
Pinocchio's Daring
   Journey **14**
Pirates of the
   Caribbean **41**

Rafts to Tom Sawyer Island **38**
Riverboat and Sailing Ship **32**
Roger Rabbit's Car Toon Spin **1**
Sleeping Beauty Castle **21**
Snow White's Scary Adventures **20**
Space Mountain **46**
Splash Mountain **36**
Star Tours **29**
Storybook Land Canal Boats **11**
Tarzan's Treehouse **42**
Tom Sawyer Island **33**

popular, attractions from the Animal Kingdom and Disney-MGM Studios. When you move to the smaller-statured second half of the attraction batting order, it gets worse. Most of these attractions are little more than off-the-shelf midway rides spruced up with a Disney story line and facade.

Seen from overhead, Disney's California Adventure is roughly arrayed in a fan shape around the park's visual icon, Grizzly Peak (yet another of Disney's "mountains"). At ground level, however, the park's layout is not so obvious. From the Esplanade you pass through huge block letters spelling "California" and under a whimsical representation of the Golden Gate Bridge, over which the monorail passes. To your left and right you'll find guest services as well as some shops and eateries.

Comparable to Main Street at Disneyland Park, but not as long, the entranceway leads to a central hub where pedestrian thoroughfares branch like spokes to the various theme areas. "Lands" at DCA are called "districts," and there are three of them. A left turn at the hub leads you to the Hollywood Pictures Backlot district of the park, celebrating California's history as the film capital of the world. All other paths lead to the Golden State district of the park. Golden State is a somewhat-amorphous combination of separate theme areas that showcase California's architecture, agriculture, industry, history, and natural resources. Within the Golden State district you'll find Condor Flats by taking the first right before the hub. Grizzly Peak will likewise be to your right, though you must walk two-thirds of the way around the mountain to reach its attractions. The entrances to A Bug's Land and Bountiful Valley Farm branch off the central hub at about two o'clock, as does Golden Vine Winery. The remaining two Golden State theme areas, The Bay Area and Pacific Wharf, are situated along a kidney-shaped lake and can be accessed by following the walkway emanating from the hub at seven o'clock and winding around Grizzly Peak. The third district, Paradise Pier, recalls seaside amusement parks of the first half of the 20th century. It is situated in the southwest corner of the park, across the lake from The Bay Area.

From a competitive perspective, Disney's California Adventure is an underwhelming shot at Disney's three Southern California competitors. The Hollywood section of DCA takes a hopeful poke at Universal Studios Hollywood, while Paradise Pier offers midway rides à la Six Flags Magic Mountain. Finally, the whole California theme has for years been the eminent domain of Knott's Berry Farm. In short, there's not much originality in DCA, only Disney's now-redundant mantra that "whatever they can do, we can do better."

We can't possibly do Disneyland and its two theme parks justice in this space; for the complete and inside scoop, pick up our sister book, *The Unofficial Guide to Disneyland.* If you have children and you're breathing, you know the basics of what Disneyland Park has to offer—from the atmospheric charms of Pirates of the Caribbean to the thrills of Splash Mountain, and the foregoing discussion of DCA should suffice as an overview of the new park. Therefore, instead of taking you through both parks in detail, we'll give you some tips and advice for how to best plan for the parks with each age group of kids.

1. Four-year-olds want to go to Disneyland Park only because their parents or their preschool friends tell them they want to go. In its research, *The Unofficial Guide to Disneyland* found that more than half of all kids that age are afraid of the characters (that is, Mickey, Goofy, Pooh) that roam the park, which often catches parents by surprise. (But wouldn't you be alarmed if a mute, stuffed [but clearly alive] creature four times your size loomed near?) If your dream dictates that you take your little one to Disneyland Park, that's fine, but realize that the park is really designed for kids age 7 and older.

Disney's California Adventure is aimed at an even more mature audience. Although it offers several children's play areas, it has comparatively little to offer 4-and-unders.

2. Consider a stay at a Disney hotel during busier seasons—or at a non-Disney hotel within walking distance. The monorail access back and forth (to Disneyland Park only) is also a fun and convenient way to break up the day. Kids object less strenuously to leaving for a few hours in the heat of the afternoon if it's to ride the monorail to take a swim (and of course a nap). The restaurants in the hotels and at Downtown Disney are less crowded than the food service areas in the parks during peak times, too.

3. Some 12 million people a year visit Disneyland, and on some days it seems like every one of them is waiting in your line. We locals know that the best time to visit is in the first three weeks of December. (Conversely, the parks' busiest season is the week between Christmas and New Year's.) The next-best times to visit are from September to mid-November, January 4 through early March, and the week after Easter to Memorial Day (although we remember a particularly nasty crowd one early May weekday). Thursdays are the quietest day, and days that start with a drizzle (not pouring rain) are ideal. Visiting the Disneyland parks on a July weekend is a nightmare. Trust us. Don't do it.

4. Not all lines are created equal. Disneyland Park's oldest rides were built in the 1950s, before it was known how huge the crowds of visitors would be, so they aren't set up to move large numbers of people quickly. Although these Fantasyland rides are no longer popular with the teen set, families (especially local parents who remember going on these rides as kids) often line up for Snow White or Peter Pan—and it can take forever to get in. Keep an eye out for when these lines are shortest. The rides built in the late 1960s—Small World, Pirates of the Caribbean, the Haunted Mansion—have outdoor plaza areas built to accommodate lines that move more quickly. The newest rides—Indiana Jones, Splash Mountain, Tomorrowland rides—were built knowing that much of the ride time is spent in line, so the waiting areas are part of the ride structure itself (you won't see them from the entrance area), decorated and sometimes offering a bit of entertainment.

At Disney's California Adventure, ride capacity and efficiency were sacrificed for eye appeal. Taking a step backward, Disney loaded the park with midway rides, infamous for slow loading and long waits. Of 11 rides, only 2 move crowds efficiently. Fortunately, most of the shows and theater attractions can accommodate large numbers.

5. Here are our recommended sample days, by age group:

UNDER 6 To do Disneyland right with young children, think small and plan carefully. To avoid meltdowns, visit the park of your choice for a half day and then return to your hotel for a swim and a nap, returning in the afternoon refreshed. Don't wander around the parks aimlessly, but head straight to the attractions best suited to young kids. At Disneyland Park with 6-and-unders, we go right to Fantasyland and do Dumbo, Peter Pan, Pinocchio, Alice in Wonderland (usually twice, because there's no line), and, depending on their scary-tolerance, Mr. Toad's Wild Ride. Then it's lunch and a peaceful trip on It's a Small World, which is so cool and calm it makes for a good rest stop. Refreshed, we head to Mickey's Toontown to see Minnie's House, ride the dinky roller coaster, jump in Goofy's Playhouse, ride the trolley, and, if they aren't especially timid, do Roger Rabbit. (But if the crowds are bad, we skip Toontown altogether, as it's impossible to understand its village setup when it's mobbed with people.) Then it's time for a cool drink and a souvenir stop near the exit gates, and the day is done. Any more with young kids is asking for trouble. Also with little ones, we establish a firm shopping policy. To prevent hours of panicked browsing through gift shops, we let our kids buy one toy or souvenir, but only at the very last stop before leaving. Before that, no shopping allowed.

At Disney's California Adventure, there is comparatively little of particular interest to the 6-and-under crowd, except for Flik's Fun Fair, a collection of diminutive rides for little ones.

EARLY ELEMENTARY For this age at Disneyland Park, we recommend a day alternating rides with shows and theme areas. Assuming that there's a too-scary limit for these kids but that they like a little thrill, we try to get them on Pirates of the Caribbean, Haunted Mansion, Indiana Jones, and Thunder Mountain as their "big" rides worth waiting in line for. In between the rides, we give them at least an hour for Tom Sawyer's Island (ride the raft over the water, run around the parklike trails, see the fort) and take them to Winnie the Pooh, the *Enchanted Tiki Room,* the Pocahontas show, Tarzan's Treehouse, and short-wait experiences like the excellent *Honey, I Shrunk the Audience.* We also schedule the nighttime parade and (if they're late stayer-uppers) the unbelievably wonderful *Fantasia* spectacle over the waters in Frontierland. Getting good parade-type seats on the curbs, refreshments, and a chance to browse a souvenir shop while waiting (and while another family member saves places) make for a pretty good interlude. The park's live entertainment is excellent, and it imparts more of the Disney spirit this age group looks for than long hours in line for high-speed thrills.

At Disney's California Adventure, head first for Soarin' Over California, then for the Paradise Pier district of the park and sample the rides that appeal to your kids, then backtrack and catch Grizzly River Run, using FASTPASS. Save shows and theater attractions for last.

OLDER ELEMENTARY–PRETEEN This age group, as is befitting, benefits from a half-and-half day. Kids age 10 and older with watches can be allowed to go off on their own in the parks for a few hours at a time, meeting parents (with younger kids to look after?) at designated times and places. When you first arrive at the park of your choice, discuss the park layout and the location of some key sites. Set early mealtime meeting places at a sit-down restaurant, and when you rendezvous, allow enough time for the kids to calm down and for you to assess their energy level. Let them have a half-hour leeway on the meeting time, so if they're in line for something, they don't have to get out to meet you; if you've picked a sit-down restaurant, you can relax comfortably while you wait for them. This age group can skip the parade and hustle off to the big-deal rides during that time, when the lines will be shorter. Another thing we've done with this group (because they like to go over and over again on a favorite ride) is bring a book and park ourselves on a bench while they do the rides and come check with us from time to time.

TEEN One of the few occasions when an ideal teen schedule fits into the world, a teen's trip to Disneyland should be almost the opposite of everyone else's. Don't make them get up early, but rather let them arrive at the park of their choice in late morning or early afternoon and stay until it closes (midnight and later in summer). Teens own the parks after dusk, and parents will love knowing that there's a safe place for kids this age to roam. (This is even more true of Knott's Berry Farm; see profile.) If you have preteens and teens and you're staying at a Disneyland hotel, you can even retire with the preteens and let the teens walk or ride the last monorail back to the hotel.

The Unofficial Guide to Disneyland, also published by John Wiley & Sons, offers in-depth information on both Disneyland Park and Disney's California Adventure and provides step-by-step touring plans that will eliminate an average of three hours of waiting in line on a busy day. If you plan to visit during periods of moderate to high attendance, you'll find the guide indispensable.

 Knott's Berry Farm

APPEAL BY AGE	PRESCHOOL ★★★★	GRADE SCHOOL ★★★★★	TEENS ★★★★★
YOUNG ADULTS ★★★★		OVER 30 ★★★	SENIORS ★★★

8039 Beach Boulevard, Buena Park; ☎ 714-220-5200; www.knotts.com

Hours October–May: Monday–Friday, 10 a.m.–6 p.m.; Saturday, 10 a.m.–10 p.m; Sunday, 10 a.m.–8 p.m.; summer: Monday–Thursday, 9 a.m.–8 p.m.; Friday and Sunday, 9 a.m.–10 p.m.; Saturday, 10 a.m.–11 p.m. **Admission** $40 adults, $15 children ages 3–11; parking $9, RVs $15, handicapped $6. **Touring time** Average 8 hours; minimum 4 hours. **Rainy-day touring** Limited. **Restaurants** Yes. **Alcoholic beverages** Yes. **Disabled access** Yes. **Wheelchair rental** Yes; call ahead for electric. **Baby-stroller rental** Yes. **Lockers** Yes. **Pet kennels** No. **Rain check** No. **Private tours** Yes.

DESCRIPTION AND COMMENTS This really was a berry farm once upon a time, and today it takes pride in its claim to be the country's first theme park. The theme gets a little confused from time to time, but in general the rides, shows, and amusements relate to early California and the Wild West.

Unlike Disneyland, Knott's can be great fun and not overwhelming for the 3- to 7-year-old-set, thanks to Camp Snoopy. Thoughtfully located close to the park's entrance, Camp Snoopy is a self-contained mini-park with rides scaled to little kids; when my youngest was 5, she was terrified of thrill rides, but she wanted to do this just-thrilling-enough little roller coaster over and over. She also loved the bumper cars, petting zoo, and Snoopy bounce. You can easily visit Camp Snoopy and then leave without dragging a cranky preschooler through other distractions.

unofficial **TIP**
One caveat: Though it's not as nationally famous as Disneyland, Knott's can also attract fearsome crowds.

If you have older kids, you'll want to explore the park's other areas, each of which has its own intense thrill rides. In Mexican-themed Fiesta Village, for instance, preteens and teens line up for Jaguar, a high-speed, 2,700-foot-long roller coaster; equally popular is Windjammer, a very intense dual-track roller coaster in the Boardwalk area. If you have timid kids, avoid Kingdom of the Dinosaurs; if you don't want to get wet, stay off the Roaring Rapids. If you have teens, they'll probably want to hang around the Boardwalk area, near some of the most intense thrill rides and full of midway games (which are too difficult, not to mention expensive, for younger kids).

What we most like about Knott's are the serendipitous items tucked around the park. Near Camp Snoopy, for instance, there's a trash can in the shape of a bear; when you walk by, it asks for trash, and when you put trash in its mouth, it thanks you. Our kids loved this bear so much that they went scavenging for trash. Elsewhere around the grounds you'll find a life-size great-white-shark replica; a ranger station (near Roaring Rapids) in which kids can hold insects and spiders; a one-room schoolhouse; informal bluegrass performances in the Old West Ghost Town; Native American artisans who will show kids how they make flutes, canoes, and jewelry; and a collection of Native American teepees and tents in which kids can play. And hokey though it is, they all love panning for gold, even jaded 15-year-olds. One daughter spent an hour watching in fascination as other visitors cracked open geodes with a hammer before she finally decided on which rock to select for herself to see what crystals lurked inside.

unofficial **TIP**
Camp Snoopy is labor intensive, requiring you to help toddlers up and down steps, and it loses much of its appeal to 4-year-olds who spend all their time waiting in line. You'll have a much better visit with young children if you visit on a weekday, first thing in the morning.

This is also a very good park for teens, with music, dancing, and special shows and holiday events (sometimes requiring separate nighttime admission). You really can drop 'em off and pick 'em up later.

Knott's Soak City

APPEAL BY AGE	PRESCHOOL ★★	GRADE SCHOOL ★★★★	TEENS ★★★★
YOUNG ADULTS ★★★★		OVER 30 ★★★★	SENIORS ★★

8039 Beach Boulevard, Buena Park; ☎ 714-220-5200; www.soakcityusa.com

Hours Open Memorial Day weekend through September; hours vary considerably, so check first. **Admission** $27 adults, $15 children ages 3–11 and seniors age 62+; after 3 p.m., $15 adults and children ages 3–11; $9 parking. **Touring time** Average 4–6 hours; minimum 1 hour. **Rainy-day touring** Limited. **Restaurants** Snack bars. **Alcoholic beverages** No. **Disabled access** Yes. **Wheelchair rental** Yes. **Baby-stroller rental** No. **Lockers** Yes. **Pet kennels** No. **Rain check** No. **Private tours** No.

DESCRIPTION AND COMMENTS   Built on the site of Knott's Berry Farm's former parking lot, this 13-acre water park is themed to the 1950s and 1960s—the golden days of California beach and surf culture. Sixteen rides include various slides (including Banzai Falls, six high-speed slides), a third-of-a-mile-long "lazy river" for folks who like to float, and a three-story fun house. There's a 750,000-gallon wave pool and a play area with nozzles, faucets, secret rooms, and surprise showers. Toddlers get a quiet lagoon with a submarine and an inactive octopus.

FAMILY-FRIENDLY RESTAURANTS

 El Pollo Inka

400 South Euclid Avenue, Anaheim; ☎ 714-772-2263

Meals served Lunch and dinner. **Cuisine** Peruvian. **Entree range** $6–$18. **Kids' menu** Yes. **Reservations** Accepted only Friday–Saturday. **Payment** All major credit cards.

If the blandness and sterility of the chain restaurants that clog Anaheim depress you, take the family on an adventure to this swell little joint, just a notch above a fast-food restaurant—it's home to superb roast chicken and interesting dishes involving french fries and other forms of potato (Peru is, after all, the birthplace of the potato). While a bit exotic, the food is simple enough for kids to enjoy, and the prices are hard to beat. Try to come on a weekend evening, when live Andean music is performed.

Goofy's Kitchen
Disneyland Hotel, 1150 Magic Way, Anaheim; ☎ 714-956-6755

Meals served Breakfast, lunch, and dinner. **Cuisine** American. **Entree range** Breakfast and lunch, $27.25 adults, $14.86 children; dinner, $35.92 adults, $14.86 children ages 3–12, free for children ages 2 and under; prices include tax and tip. **Reservations** Recommended. **Payment** All major credit cards.

If your 2- to 10-year-old isn't terrified of oversize, mute Mickeys and Goofys, bring them here for an all-you-can-eat meal, and it will be one of the highlights of your trip to Disneyland. Perfectly tolerable food is served buffet-style, which the kids adore, because they can have exactly what they want. Plan on a leisurely meal, so your kids will have time to hug, follow around, and get autographs from Goofy and other wandering characters.

Medieval Times
7662 Beach Boulevard, Buena Park; ☎ 714-521-4740

Meals served Daily, dinner. **Cuisine** American. **Entree range** Set price of $49. **Kids' menu** Set price of $35. **Reservations** Strongly advised the day before. **Payment** All major credit cards.

If you blow into town in the late afternoon or evening and are looking for something to do in the way of entertainment, you could do worse than joining the bus tour groups and birthday parties at Medieval Times. You'll eat ribs and chicken legs while watching knights joust and fair maidens faint; the crowd gets into the action with lots of whoops and hollers. The littlest ones might get scared by the jousting and shouting, but all in all, if your kids are ages 5 to 15, you'll have a fine time. You're near Hollywood, remember—the performers are Hollywood hopefuls and, as such, sometimes genuinely quite talented.

Mrs. Knott's Chicken Dinner Restaurant
803 Beach Boulevard, Buena Park; ☎ 714-220-5080

Meals served Breakfast, lunch, and dinner. **Cuisine** American. **Entree range** Breakfast, $4–$10; lunch, $5–$9; dinner, $13. **Kids' menu** $4–$7. **Reservations** Not necessary. **Payment** All major credit cards.

Every evening, the front door to this legendary place is blocked by a line that stretches around the building, and that line helps further the restaurant's reputation. In truth, however, the family-style fried-chicken dinner is not worth an hour's wait. If you time it right (early or late) and can get in quickly, your kids will enjoy the Jell-O, biscuits, chicken, corn, and ice cream, and you'll enjoy the low prices, but don't let the crowds get your hopes up for a memorable meal. However, the take-out window just down the way from the restaurant entrance is a great option for folks staying nearby. The food's hot, hearty, and ready to go immediately, and you don't have to drive around looking for another stop to make.

Napa Rose
Grand Californian Hotel, Disneyland Resort; 1600 West Disneyland Drive, Anaheim; ☎ 714-300-7170

Meals served Dinner and Sunday brunch. **Cuisine** Modern American, Californian. **Entree range** $27–$38. **Kids' menu** $9–$18. **Reservations** Strongly advised. **Payment** All major credit cards.

If your kids are the sort who can appreciate a special-occasion meal in an elegant restaurant—or if you're leaving them in the nearby Pinocchio's Workshop evening child-care center—live it up with dinner at this surprisingly good and amazingly handsome place. Disney lured Andrew Sutton, one of California's most talented chefs, to head Napa Rose, which celebrates the wine country and California cuisine. The warm, glowing Arts and Crafts–style dining room has soaring windows and beautiful vineyard murals. The wine list is rich in California notables, the cooking is excellent, and the kids' menu is the most appealing we've ever seen.

PART THREE

LOS ANGELES *and* VICINITY:

South Bay, Pasadena, Mountain Towns, Deserts, and Catalina Island

DESPITE ITS FABLED SUNSHINE AND ITS LAID-BACK ATTITUDE, **Los Angeles** has not traditionally been an easy city to visit. But continuing improvements and additions to the transit system make it easier to get around without a car, and an improving pool of hotels has made it possible to stay and play in some good, family-friendly "home base" areas like **Santa Monica, Universal City,** and **Long Beach.** Because there is no compact city center, distances between destinations are sometimes considerable, so parents should select their home base carefully.

L.A.'s attractions are many and diverse. You can sled in the local mountains and Boogie-board at the beach in the same weekend. You can go from a Mexican street fair to an African-American art show to a Korean barbecue restaurant in the same day. You can take in the illusions of **Hollywood** at **Universal Studios,** then decompress in a Japanese garden at Pasadena's **Huntington Gardens.** You can join the crowds exploring Santa Monica's **Third Street Promenade,** or ride a ferry to sleepy, sun-washed **Catalina Island.**

If you decide to stay in **Redondo Beach,** which is located south of LAX airport and a 30- to 60-minute drive from downtown L.A., accept that you may not be able to do **Universal Studios, Magic Mountain,** and Hollywood in the same weekend. Conversely, if Universal Studios and Hollywood are tops on your family's list, maybe you should save the beach for next time and stay in Universal City or Hollywood.

This chapter breaks the vast L.A. area into several geographical units, in the following order: the South Bay, composed of the beach towns of **Long Beach, Redondo,** and **Manhattan;** Catalina Island, a two-hour ferry ride from **San Pedro;** L.A.'s Westside, including **Santa Monica, Marina del Rey,** and **West L.A.;** Central L.A.,

unofficial **TIP**
The secret to a successful visit to L.A. is twofold: careful planning and judicious editing. Make a list of everything you want to do, find a place you'd like to stay, review your wish list with a map in hand, and start cutting your list down.

ranging from **Beverly Hills** to downtown and encompassing the majority of the attractions, from the **California Science Center** south of downtown to **Universal CityWalk** in the Hollywood hills; side trips to the suburbs of **San Dimas** (**Raging Waters**) and Valencia (**Six Flags Magic Mountain**); **Pasadena,** the city just northeast of downtown that is home to **Old Pasadena,** the **Huntington Gardens,** and **Kidspace;** the **Mountains,** including **Big Bear** and **Lake Arrowhead;** and the deserts, including **Palm Springs** and **Joshua Tree.**

GETTING THERE

BY PLANE Almost all major airlines serve the region's main airport, **Los Angeles International** (LAX; ☎ 310-646-5252; **www.lawa.org**), which is only about 15 minutes south of Santa Monica via the 405 freeway—if there's no traffic, which is rare. If you're staying somewhere on the Eastside—in downtown, Studio City, or Pasadena—you'll be better off flying via **Burbank-Glendale-Pasadena Airport** (2627 Hollywood Way, Burbank; ☎ 818-840-8840), a pleasantly small-scale operation used heavily by commuter flights. Also easy to manage is **Long Beach Airport,** home of the excellent JetBlue airline. Shuttle services, taxis, buses, and private car services link the airports to many locations across the region.

BY TRAIN Amtrak delivers visitors from Northern California, the Pacific Northwest, and the Midwest to Union Station, a gorgeous mission-style building in downtown that is every child's notion of what a train station should be. Call ☎ 800-USA-RAIL; **www.amtrak.com.**

After many years of construction, L.A.'s light-rail system is beginning to be a practical, affordable, and even enjoyable way to get around town. From downtown's gorgeous **Union Station** (a sight that's worth seeing on its own), you can take the **Red Line** to Hollywood (including Hollywood & Highland development) and Universal City. The Red Line also connects to the Blue Line, which heads south to Long Beach, where you'll find fun beaches, lively Belmont Shore, the Aquarium of the Pacific, and the *Queen Mary.* The **Gold Line** connects Union Station with Chinatown, Highland Park (the Southwest Museum), South Pasadena and Pasadena, including Old Pasadena. Getting information is a little confusing, because the light-rail system is under the purview of the bus-based MTA instead of the Metrolink system, which shares Amtrak's rails. For fare and route information, your best bet is to go to **www.mts.net,** and click "Riding Metro," or call ☎ 800-COMMUTE.

BY CAR The freeway rules in L.A., so there are major highways leading to the urban area from every which way. Visitors from the north and south arrive via **Interstate 5,** the artery connecting the Mexican and Canadian borders; the coastal route from the north into L.A. is the **101 Freeway,** which travels via Santa Barbara. Travelers entering from almost anywhere east, from Palm Springs to Chicago, will

los angeles and vicinity

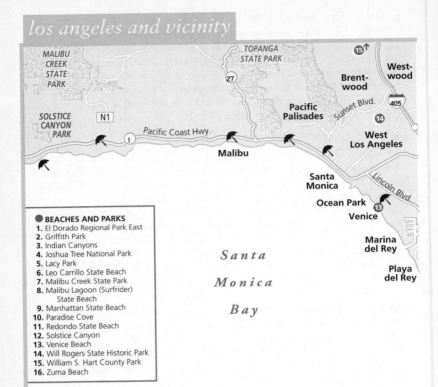

● BEACHES AND PARKS
1. El Dorado Regional Park East
2. Griffith Park
3. Indian Canyons
4. Joshua Tree National Park
5. Lacy Park
6. Leo Carrillo State Beach
7. Malibu Creek State Park
8. Malibu Lagoon (Surfrider) State Beach
9. Manhattan State Beach
10. Paradise Cove
11. Redondo State Beach
12. Solstice Canyon
13. Venice Beach
14. Will Rogers State Historic Park
15. William S. Hart County Park
16. Zuma Beach

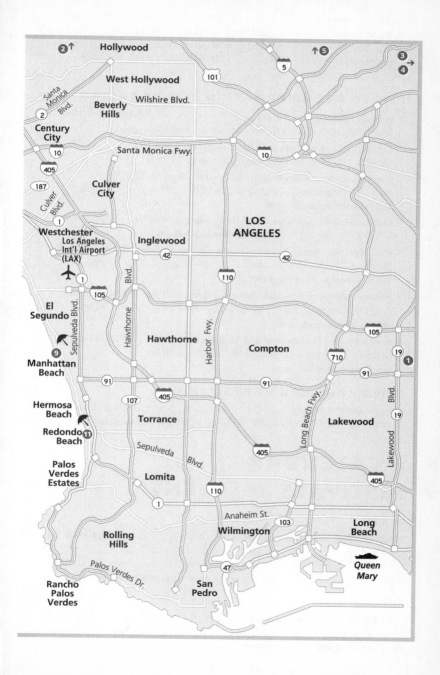

arrive via **Interstate 10.** Once in the city area, the freeway numbers explode: There's the 210, and the 91, and the 110, and the 22, and the 60, and the 134—so do not arrive without a good map. (The Thomas Bros. map book is the bible, but a basic folding map will suffice for freeway navigation.)

HOW TO GET INFORMATION BEFORE YOU GO

- **Beverly Hills Visitors Bureau** 239 South Beverly Drive, Beverly Hills 90212; ☎ 800-345-2210; **www.beverlyhillsbehere.com.**
- **Catalina Island Visitors Bureau** 1 Green Pier, Avalon; ☎ 310-510-1520; **www.visitcatalina.org.**
- **Long Beach Area Convention and Visitors Bureau** One World Trade Center, Suite 300, Long Beach 90831; ☎ 800-452-7829; **www.visitlongbeach.com.**
- **Los Angeles Convention and Visitors Bureau** 633 West Fifth Street, L.A. 90071; ☎ 213-624-7300; **www.lacvb.com.**
- **Palm Springs Desert Resorts Convention and Visitors Bureau** 71100 Highway 111, Rancho Mirage 92270; ☎ 800-967-3767 or 760-770-9000; **www.palmspringsusa.com.**
- **Pasadena Convention and Visitors Bureau** 171 South Los Robles Avenue, Pasadena 91101; ☎ 800-307-7977 or 800-544-5319; **www.pasedenacal.com.**
- **Santa Monica Convention and Visitors Bureau** 1920 Main Street, Suite B, Santa Monica 90401; ☎ 310-319-6263; **www.santamonica.com.**

CHILD CARE AND BABYSITTING

SITTERS UNLIMITED A licensed, bonded agency providing babysitters throughout L.A.'s Westside; ☎ 800-328-1191; **www.sittersunlimited.com.**

A **CALENDAR** of FESTIVALS *and* **EVENTS**

January

TOURNAMENT OF ROSES PARADE Colorado Boulevard in Pasadena. January 1. Every year untold millions watch this parade on TV, and lots of them decide right then to move to L.A. If you've never been, get tickets—kids adore it; ☎ 626-449-ROSE; **www.tournamentofroses.com.**

February

CHINESE NEW YEAR'S PARADE Chinatown. Huge dragons snake through Chinatown's streets, and the costumes are great; ☎ 415-391-9680; **www.chineseparade.com.**

March

LOS ANGELES MARATHON Throughout L.A. The city becomes gripped with marathon fever, and everyone tries to find a spot to watch the runners, walkers, skaters, wheelchair riders, and cyclists (including lots of middle- and high-school kids) go; ☎ 310-444-5544; **www.lamarathon.com.**

April

BLESSING OF THE ANIMAL Olvera Street, downtown. Saturday before Easter. Hundreds of people bring their pets—from dogs to hamsters— to be blessed in this festive procession; ☎ 213-680-2525; **www .olvera-street.com.**

FIESTA BROADWAY Downtown. The last weekend in April kicks off Cinco de Mayo season when 36 downtown blocks are shut to traffic and thousands of revelers enjoy performances on several stages, with Latino pop stars headlining; ☎ 310-914-0015; **www.fiestabroadway.la.**

LOS ANGELES TIMES FESTIVAL OF BOOKS Dickson Plaza, UCLA. Includes a large children's area and lots of good storytelling events; ☎ 800-LA-TIMES, ext. 7BOOK; **www.latimes.com.**

OPENING DAY Dodger Stadium. A festive, fun family outing; ☎ 323-224-1500; **www.dodgers.com.**

May

CHILDREN'S DAY Little Tokyo (downtown L.A.). A traditional Japanese celebration of the child, featuring footraces, games, arts and crafts; ☎ 213-628-2725.

Valley Greek Festival Northridge. Memorial Day party with music, food, and more; ☎ 818-886-4040; **www.valleygreekfestival.com.**

June

LONG BEACH BAYOU FESTIVAL Rainbow Lagoon, Long Beach. Rollicking music, dance lessons, Cajun food, and children's amusements; ☎ 562-427-3713; **www.longbeachfestival.com.**

NOHO INTERNATIONAL THEATER AND ARTS FESTIVAL A street fair in the burgeoning arts district; ☎ 818-508-5155; **www.nohoartsdistrict.com.**

July

FOURTH OF JULY CELEBRATION *Queen Mary,* Long Beach. One of the best fireworks shows in L.A. County; ☎ 562-435-3511.

AMERICAFEST Rose Bowl, Pasadena. A rousing event with live music and a boffo fireworks show; ☎ 626-577-3101; **www.rosebowlstadium.com.**

LOTUS FESTIVAL Echo Park. In the park surrounding pretty little Echo Park Lake, home to a large lotus bed, is a terrific celebration of Asian food and arts, with dragon-boat races, kiddie rides, and pedalboat rides on the lake; ☎ 213-485-8743; **www.laparks.org/grifmet/lotis.**

August

AFRICAN MARKETPLACE AND CULTURAL FAIRE Location varies, L.A. Hundreds of booths, a Children's Village, and live entertainment celebrating African cultures; ☎ 323-293-1612; **www.africanmarketplace.org**.

September

L.A. COUNTY FAIR County Fairplex Fairgrounds, Pomona. An 18-day extravaganza of carnival rides, pie-eating contests, livestock shows, and live entertainment; ☎ 909-623-3111; **www.fairplex.com**.

October

CALABASAS PUMPKIN FESTIVAL Paramount Ranch, Agoura. This Old West ranch, location for many a cowboy movie, hosts pumpkin sales, haunted houses, country music, and pumpkin seed spit-offs; ☎ 818-222-5680.

November

DIA DE LOS MUERTOS Olvera Street, downtown. November 1 or 2. A lively, colorful celebration of the Day of the Dead, including a candlelit procession; ☎ 213-485-9769.

DOO DAH PARADE Old Pasadena. Sunday after Thanksgiving. A goofy, eccentric spoof of the Rose Parade; ☎ 626-440-7379; **www.pasadenadoodahparade.com**.

ROSEBUD PARADE Lake Avenue, Pasadena. Sponsored by Kidspace Museum, this miniature version of the Rose Parade is a wonderful family event. Children parade in or on self-decorated wagons, bikes, trikes, and skateboards, and those who sign up in advance can take a float-making class at Kidspace; ☎ 626-449-9144; **www.kidspacemuseum.org/rosebud**.

December

CHRISTMAS BOAT PARADE Burton Chase Park, Marina del Rey. Come after dark to watch the decorated, colorfully lit boats parade by; ☎ 310-821-0555.

HOLIDAY CONCERT SEASON Walt Disney Concert Hall, downtown L.A. Several of these holiday-themed concerts held in spectacular Disney Hall are great for families; ☎ 323-850-2000; **wdch.laphil.com**.

The BEST BEACHES *and* PARKS

EL DORADO REGIONAL PARK EAST Your kids will have to try hard to be bored in this huge inland park in Long Beach. The 450 acres include four fishing lakes (stocked with trout, catfish, and bass), pedalboats, playgrounds, miles of level biking trails, an archery range used in the 1984 Olympics, and a fun, one-mile steam train ride (closed Monday in summer and Monday and Tuesday off season). The biggest attraction here is the **El Dorado Nature Center,** which takes up 100 acres of the park. Its museum has cool stuff kids can touch and explore, like skulls and antlers, as well as insect and reptile houses, animal displays, and summer-camp programs. Outside are stroller-accommodating trails and a pond that's home to turtles and ducks. Call the Nature Center to reserve a spot in one of the guided family night walks or campfires. 7550 East Spring Street, Long Beach; ☎ 562-570-1745 (Nature Center) or 562-570-1771 (park); **.ci.long-beach .ca.us/park.** Open daily, 7 a.m. to dusk; closed Christmas. Parking $4 weekdays, $6 weekends and holidays.

GRIFFITH PARK One of the country's great urban parks (it is, in fact, the nation's largest city park), Griffith Park is a world unto itself, home to many excellent amusements for children and worth a full day trip, if not two. On the park's eastern edge are the **Los Angeles Zoo** and the **Autry Museum of the American West** (see attraction profiles). A little west of there you'll find the pony rides and kiddie train ride (☎ 323-664-6788) loved by generations of L.A. children. On the north-Burbank side is **Travel Town** (☎ 323-662-5874), a marvelous collection of old trains that kids can climb into and explore; a small-scale train ride circles the area. Children also love the old carousel (although the deafening music terrified our 3-year-old), which is surrounded by playground areas and rolling lawns that are perfect for picnics. Extras include two golf courses, tennis courts, equestrian trails, a fern preserve, soccer fields, and woodlands. There are many entrances: Zoo and Autry Museum from Zoo Drive off I-5; pony and train rides and carousel from Griffith Park Boulevard north of Los Feliz Boulevard; Travel Town from Victory Boulevard on Burbank side; observatory, golf course, Greek Theatre, picnic areas, and trailheads from Vermont Avenue north of Los Feliz Boulevard; ☎ 323-664-1191; **ci.la.ca.us/rap/grifmet/ griffith.** Open daily, 6 a.m. to 10 p.m.

INDIAN CANYONS Some come for the tchotchke-filled gift shop, but we come for the hiking and the almost miraculously lush beauty of this desert oasis, a stream-fed, palm-rich hideaway in the mountain rocks. There's easy hiking near the base of the trails. If your kids are old enough to ride horses, a great way to see the canyons is on horseback; contact **Smoke Tree Stables** (☎ 760-327-1372). The Canyons are the property of the local Cahuilla Tribe, which maintains the land and charges admission for entrance. 38500 South Palm Canyon Drive, Palm Springs; ☎ 760-325-3400 or 800-790-3398; **www.indian-canyons.com.** Open daily, 8 a.m. to 5 p.m.; admission $8 adults, $6.50 for seniors, students, and military, $2 ages 6 to 12; equestrians $10, free for children under age 6; guided hikes, $2 to $3.

 JOSHUA TREE NATIONAL PARK A desert unlike any other, Joshua Tree borders on the mystical. Gigantic boulders are

joshua tree national park

strewn everywhere, like God's rough-hewn marbles; they're so awesome they almost seem alive. Add mysteriously soft and white sand and the armies of prickly Joshua trees reaching their arms heavenward, and you have a place of great beauty, beloved by rock climbers, naturalists, hikers, and stargazers. Allow time to stop at the **Oasis Visitor Center** to get oriented and take the short nature walk to an oasis; ask for a map so you can find the fun one-mile trail in Hidden Valley and the cool Jumbo Rocks area. For kids, the best bet is a private family lesson from **Joshua Tree Rock Climbing School** (☎ 800-890-4745; **www.joshuatreerockclimbing.com**) or **Vertical Adventures** (☎ 800-514-8785; **www.vertical-adventures.com**). There are several campgrounds; one of the best is White Tank, where the boulders are grand and the sand is soft. Visit in spring and fall only, and bring lots and lots of water—the entire park has none. If that makes camping sound too intense, the **Twentynine Palms Motel** will make a fine base. 74485 National Park Drive (off I-10), Twentynine Palms; ☎ 760-367-5525; **www.nps.gov/jotr**. Free admission but $15 per vehicle for parking.

unofficial **TIP**
Consider taking a family rock-climbing lesson in Joshua Tree, and prepare to be amazed at how quickly your children might take to such a challenging and intense sport.

LACY PARK One of the prettiest urban parks anywhere, Lacy is carefully hidden in the wealthy enclave of San Marino, near Pasadena. So skillful is its design that it seems to go on for miles, with the trees blocking any hint of residential development. It has an excellent, large playground, vast lawns, softball fields, a bike and skate path ringing the park, and complete picnic and restroom facilities. A popular day camp is held here in summer, and the Fourth of July festivities are legendary. This is a good play stop if you're staying either downtown or in the Pasadena area. 1485 Virginia Road (north of Monterey), San Marino; ☎ 626-300-0790. There is a $3 fee for nonresidents on weekends.

LEO CARRILLO STATE BEACH Many a Southern California school goes field tripping to this Malibu beach, and for very good reason. Kids (and parents) adore it here, especially in the quieter fringe seasons, such as May and October. The tide pooling is the best in the L.A. area; everything is protected, so kids can't take even a shell from the tide pool preserve. There are sea caves to explore, rocks to climb, a sandy beach, good ocean swimming, a playground, nature trails, and a good campground with 300 sites for tents (no hookups for RVs). Lifeguards are on duty in summer. It can get pretty chilly, so bring jackets for your whole crew. 35000 Pacific Coast Highway, between Point

Mugu and Point Dume, Malibu; ☎ 818-880-0350; **www.parks.ca.gov.**
Parking $6; campsites $20–$25; for campsite reservations, call Reserve
America, ☎ 800-444-7275; **www.reserveamerica.com.**

MALIBU CREEK STATE PARK One of the many wonders of the Santa
Monica Mountains, this park has lots to offer. You can ride mountain bikes, hike the **Malibu Creek Trail** (a beautiful hike, and not too
challenging for school-age kids), fish for bass and bluegill in **Century
Lake,** picnic, and swim in the rock pool near the visitors center. Parents take note that three miles in on the Malibu Creek Trail is the
former set of the TV show *M*A*S*H*. Don't miss the visitors center,
which has maps, children's information, and a little museum. There's
also a nice campground. 125 Las Virgenes Road, Calabasas; ☎ 805-
488-1827; **www.parks.ca.gov.** Parking $5 per vehicle per day.

MALIBU LAGOON (SURFRIDER) STATE BEACH If you have a surfer in the
family, or someone who thinks surfers are cool, head for these adjacent beaches on the north side of the Malibu Pier. The longboarding
capital of L.A., Surfrider was one of the birthplaces of the California surfing scene in the 1940s and 1950s, thanks to its consistent (but
rarely huge) cruiser waves. The **International Surfing Contest** is held
here each September. The pier is a good fishing spot, and the state
beach just north of Surfrider is home to a natural lagoon with great
bird-watching, tide pools, a nature center, and easy little trails. Guided
tours are offered; call ☎ 310-456-8432 for details. 23000 block of
Pacific Coast Highway (0.5 miles south of Cross Creek Road), Malibu;
☎ 310-880-0350; **www.parks.ca.gov.** Parking $3 to $8, depending on
season; limited parking available along PCH.

MANHATTAN STATE BEACH Broad and long, this is a classic
Southern California beach, with a pier, bike path, volleyball
courts, snack bars, summertime lifeguards, great people watching,
and lots of sunshine. The generally good waves for bodysurfing,
body boarding, and surfing make this a better beach for solid swimmers, usually kids over age 8; our favorite spot is on the north side of
the pier. If you have time to hit only one good all-around beach on an
L.A. trip, this is the one to hit. The downside is the lack of parking—
come early to find a metered spot. 1200 The Strand, Manhattan Beach;
☎ 310-545-5621; **www.parks.ca.gov.**

PARADISE COVE If you loathe giant, crowded beaches and want a nice
family place—and if outrageous parking fees don't bother you—
head north from Santa Monica via PCH to this lovely private beach
fronting what must surely be the most attractive, upscale trailer-park
community in the country. The sand is soft, the cove and small pier
are picturesque, and the shallow shoreline lets kids have lots of wave
fun without getting pounded. Extras include showers, restrooms, a
basketball court, and a summer lifeguard, but no snack bar; you can

avoid the parking charge if you eat in the beachfront restaurant, a decent seafood cafe owned by Bob Morris of Gladstone's fame. 28128 Pacific Coast Highway, Malibu; ☎ 310-457-2511. Parking $25 if you aren't eating at the restaurant.

REDONDO STATE BEACH A large, sweeping sand beach complete with a pier, Redondo is popular with groups of teens and young families alike. The fishing from the pier is surprisingly good; down on the sand, there are waves, volleyball courts, a bike path, concession stands, lifeguards, and good restroom and shower facilities. On the King Harbor end of the beach, you can sign up for a whale-watching trip in winter–spring or a sportfishing trip in summer. In July and August, the pier is often home to free concerts and festivals. Consider bringing your bikes and riding to neighboring Manhattan Beach. 1101 Esplanade, Redondo Beach; ☎ 310-372-2166; **www.parks.ca.gov.** Parking ranges from free to $8.

SOLSTICE CANYON A hike that's so easy you can do a major part of it with a stroller is the big draw here. A shaded, paved former ranch road leads through the canyon, often next to the babbling, rock-strewn creek, to an 18th-century adobe and several fine picnic areas and on to the ruins of a house that was built almost into a rock grotto and falls. This is a perfect turnaround point, about an hour each way, although real hikers can continue. Make sure to allow time for playing in the grotto and in the creek along the way. We like to pick up gourmet picnic supplies in Malibu, take a hike here, then spend some time on the beach. Water, restrooms, dogs allowed on leash. Off Corral Canyon Road, Malibu; ☎ 805-370-2301; **www.nps.gov/samo.** Admission free.

VENICE BEACH When Angelenos host out-of-town visitors, they almost always bring them to Venice, but not to swim or sunbathe. The scene is the draw here, and what a scene it is: the boardwalk teems with merchants (T-shirts, jewelry, tie-dyes, junk of every description), tattooed acrobatic skaters, snake handlers, cycling musicians, chain-saw jugglers, street rappers, bodybuilders, and all manner of folk your Aunt Martha will never see in Topeka. Of the various food vendors, **Jody Maroni**'s sausage stand is the hands-down winner. You might see some awesome basketball action (along with intense, often-foul street language) at the public courts, and the famed **Muscle Beach** is still going strong. 2300 Ocean Front Walk, between Marina del Rey Channel and the Santa Monica city line, Venice; ☎ 310-577-5700. Parking in the county lot is $3 on weekdays and $8 on weekends.

unofficial **TIP**
Teenagers adore Venice Beach, and they'll want some spending money. It may be too freakish and crowded for very young children, however.

WILLIAM S. HART COUNTY PARK Buffalo graze behind fences, you can often spot deer, and kids can feed the barnyard animals—sheep, horses, burros, ducks, chickens. When you're ready to move, you can hike any of the 265 acres. The tour of the former home of cowboy–movie star William Hart can be frustrating for some kids, because they can't touch, but others like seeing some of the Western gear, especially the bearskin rug and old guns. Also on site is a sweet little train-station museum (open weekend afternoons only) with a steam locomotive out front and a nifty model train inside. 24151 North San Fernando Road, Newhall, Santa Clarita Valley; ☎ 661-259-0855; **www.hartmuseum.org.** Admission and parking are free.

WILL ROGERS STATE HISTORIC PARK The great storyteller's former house, still furnished as if he lived there, won't interest your kids in the slightest (Will who?), but they'll probably get a kick out of the visitors center video showing Will doing his rope tricks. After the video, head out for the one-mile (each way) hike to **Inspiration Point,** where the Pacific view is glorious, then return to the polo fields for a picnic or barbecue. Other trails link to **Topanga State Park.** 1501 Will Rogers State Park Road (off Sunset Boulevard), Pacific Palisades; ☎ 310-454-8212; **www.parks.ca.gov.** Parking is $7.

ZUMA BEACH L.A.'s coolest teens hang out at this northern Malibu beach, near the Ventura County line. Keep young children and inexperienced swimmers out of the water—strong riptides prevail—but enjoy the playgrounds, sandy beach, volleyball, and people watching, especially if you have teens. Lifeguards, concession stands, restrooms. 30050 Pacific Coast Highway, between Trancas Canyon Boulevard and Westward Beach Road; ☎ 310-457-2525; **beaches.co.la.ca.us.** Parking $8; limited free parking along PCH.

FAMILY OUTDOOR ADVENTURES

BICYCLING–INLINE SKATING Cycling in this car-obsessed city isn't for the timid, but at the beach, the cyclist (and skater) is king. A smooth, paved bike path wends along the sand from the north end of **Santa Monica Beach** (in the Pacific Palisades neighborhood) for more than 20 level miles, all the way south to **Redondo Beach.** The path gets pretty congested on warm-weather weekends, so consider a weekday outing. Bike- and skate-rental shops are plentiful near the path in Santa Monica, in Venice, and down in the South Bay. Mountain-bike trails also abound in the Santa Monica and San Gabriel Mountains; for more information on how to find them, pick up *Mountain Bike! Los Angeles County* (Menasha Ridge Press), or call the Santa Monica Mountains National Recreation Area; ☎ 818-597-9192; **www.nps.gov/samo.**

unofficial **TIP**
Our kids' favorite is to ride bikes from Manhattan Beach south to Redondo Pier for lunch and/or ice cream, then ride back and swim at Manhattan Beach Pier.

BOATING See the "Catalina Island" section later in this chapter.

FISHING Surprisingly good fishing is found off the **Redondo Beach** and **Malibu piers;** both have tackle shops. If you're ready for a sea-fishing trip, try **Redondo Sport Fishing Company** (233 North Harbor Drive, Redondo Beach; ☎ 310-372-2111; **www.redondosportfishing .com**) or go with **L.A. Harbor Sportfishing** (Berth 79, San Pedro Harbor; ☎ 310-547-9916; **www.laharborsportfishing.com**). Both offer half-day charters that are good for school-age children.

HIKING Entire books have been published on the hiking opportunities in the L.A. area, so rich are the choices. With young children, we particularly like **Solstice Canyon** (see "The Best Beaches and Parks") and the easy trails at **Eaton Canyon** (1750 North Altadena Drive, Pasadena; ☎ 626-398-5420; **www.ecnca.org**), which offers wonderful family nature walks every Saturday morning. **Big Bear** and **Lake Arrowhead** also offer lots of great family hiking; see the "Mountain Towns" section later in this chapter. You'll also find good trails in some of the other parks in "The Best Beaches and Parks," especially **Will Rogers, Leo Carrillo,** and **Griffith parks.**

HORSEBACK RIDING One of our favorite outings in Los Angeles is the Friday-night sunset horseback ride through Griffith Park offered by **Sunset Ranch** (3400 Beachwood Drive, Hollywood; ☎ 323-469-5450; **www.sunsetranchhollywood.com**)—it's a wonderful evening to spend with teenagers. A guide takes you over the mountain and down into Burbank at sunset, with dusk settling on the wild scrub and scurrying jackrabbits; you tie up at a (pretty bad) Mexican restaurant in Burbank and ride back over after dinner, hopefully guided by a bright moon. Children as young as 5 are welcome on daytime rides; the stable is home to some very gentle horses. Another place to find high-quality horses and access to many park trails is the **Los Angeles Equestrian Center** (480 West Riverside Drive, Burbank; ☎ 818-840-8401; **www .la-equestriancenter.com;** horse rentals $20 to $40, cash only). See also Indian Canyons in "The Best Beaches and Parks."

SURFING–OCEAN SPORTS You're in the land of the Beach Boys, and you (or your kids) won't have experienced it fully if you don't get some wave action. Our favorite place to learn is the **Surf Academy** in Manhattan Beach (☎ 310-372-2790; **www.surfacademy .com**), created by a former surf champ who's also a mother of five. It offers both private lessons and terrific weeklong summer surfing day camps, along with great classes for moms and families, too. Another good choice is **Malibu Ocean Sports** (south side of Malibu Pier; ☎ 310-456-6302; **www.malibuoceansports.com**). A two-hour private lesson, including board and wet suit, is $90 to $120, depending on the instructor; lessons are usually held at famed Surfrider beach. The same company also has windsurfing lessons for the same fee. To try your hand at the

unofficial **TIP**
Know your swimming strength and ability—if lifeguards have posted riptide or high-surf warnings, respect the power of the ocean and stay out.

easier sport of kayaking, head to **Action Water Sports** in Marina del Rey (4144 Lincoln Boulevard; ☎ 310-827-2233).

If you just want to get into the surf without the cost and trouble of surfing lessons, rent a body board at any of dozens of concessions in Malibu, Santa Monica, Redondo, or any beach town, and ride the waves on your own.

TIDE POOLING The best tide pooling in town is found at **Leo Carrillo State Beach** (see "The Best Beaches and Parks"). The snorkeling there is superb as well, but you'll need to bring your own gear, as there's no equipment rental on site.

WHALE WATCHING We've enjoyed the morning whale-watching expeditions by **Redondo Sport Fishing Company** (233 North Harbor Drive, in Redondo Beach; ☎ 310-372-2111; **www.redondo sportfishing.com**), some of which have a docent from the Cabrillo Marine Aquarium on board to answer questions. On our last trip, we saw at least a half-dozen gray whales, along with dolphins and sea lions. On your way in or out of the Redondo harbor area, make sure to stop for a look at the gigantic Wyland whale- and sea-life mural on the side of the PG&E building. Another good whale-watching outfit is **L.A. Harbor Sportfishing** (Berth 79, San Pedro Harbor; ☎ 310-547-9916; **www.laharborsportfishing.com**).

KID CULTURE:
Theater, Literature, and the Arts

FORGET THE TALK-SHOW JOKES about bubble-headed L.A.—contrary to popular opinion, Angelenos and their children are voracious readers and patrons of the arts. Here are our favorite pint-size cultural centers, for a civilized break from the theme-park sights.

BOB BAKER MARIONETTE THEATER Skillful puppeteers ply their craft, making their creations sing, dance, and interact with each other and the audience. An L.A. kid favorite since 1963. 1345 West First Street, downtown L.A.; ☎ 213-250-9995; **www.bobbakermarionettes.com**; tickets $10.

CHILDREN'S BOOK WORLD If you're staying on the Westside, head over here on Saturday morning for a generally captivating (and free) story time. Author signings are also sometimes offered. Call for schedules. 10580 West Pico Boulevard, West L.A.; ☎ 310-559-2665; **www.childrensbookworld.com**; admission free.

FAMILY THEATER Musicals, Santa Monica Playhouse Every Saturday and Sunday at 12:30 and 3 p.m., professional actors stage high-quality children's musical theater—typically variations on popular fairy tales—in a 92-seat playhouse. Day-camp theater programs for kids are offered in summer. 1211 Fourth Street, Santa Monica; ☎ 310-394-9779; **www.santamonicaplayhouse.com;** admission $10 to $15 per person.

GETTY CENTER Events and activities that engage kids are plentiful at the Getty, from folk-music concerts and storytelling to the half-hour Family Art Stop, which helps kids get up close and personal with a single work of art. 1200 Getty Center Drive, West Los Angeles; ☎ 310-440-7300; **www.getty.edu;** admission free, parking $7.

IMAGINATION STATION Children's Theater, Morgan-Wixon Theater Accomplished performances of children's theater are held on Saturdays and Sundays. 2627 Pico Boulevard, Santa Monica; ☎ 310-828-7519; admission $7 adults, $5 children and seniors.

LOS ANGELES PHILHARMONIC SYMPHONIES FOR YOUTH To introduce 6- to 12-year-olds to symphonic music, reserve early for one of the Philharmonic's Symphonies for Youth, typically held seven times a year. The daytime weekend concerts start with hands-on, preconcert activities, like art projects and instrument demonstrations; the concert features music that appeals to children. Preschool children get their own performances at the Open House Series. Walt Disney Concert Hall, Music Center, 111 South Grand Avenue, downtown L.A., ☎ 323-850-2000; **www.laphil.org;** admission $7 to $10.

STORYBOOK THEATRE Theatre West Every Saturday at 1 p.m., this theater near Universal Studios puts on a lively, interactive musical play aimed at children ages 3 to 8. 3333 Cahuenga Boulevard West, Universal City; ☎ 818-761-2203; **www.theatrewest.org;** admission varies.

STORYOPOLIS We know childless adults who hang out at this children's art gallery and bookstore—that's how wonderful it is. You'll find original works and limited-edition prints from the finest artists in children's literature, as well as high-quality books; on Saturdays, children gather for craft workshops, story hours, and author signings. 12348 Ventura Boulevard, Studio City; ☎ 818-509-5600; **www.storyopolis.com;** admission $6 for Saturday events, otherwise free.

SUMMERSOUNDS AT THE HOLLYWOOD BOWL A superb summer program that combines hands-on activities (puppet making, folk-dancing lessons) with performances, aimed at children ages 3 to 11. After a jazz concert, for instance, children will make their own instruments. Performances are Monday through Friday, 10 a.m. and 11:15 a.m., early July to mid-August; prices by event. Top of Highland Avenue, Hollywood; ☎ 323-850-2000; **www.hollywoodbowl.org.**

WILL GEER THEATRICUM BOTANICUM Theater settings don't get much better than this—a natural amphitheater space set in the oaks and eucalyptus of Topanga Canyon. This is a serious theater company with first-rate actors, but many of its productions are family friendly, particularly the Shakespeare comedies, which have captivated our kids; look for the special productions that include a preshow discussion, which really helps everyone understand what's going on. The classes and summer camps for young people are renowned. 1419 North Topanga Canyon Boulevard, Topanga; ☎ 310-455-2322; **www .theatricum.com.**

THE SOUTH BAY:

Manhattan Beach to Long Beach

SOUTH OF LAX IS A STRING OF BEACH COMMUNITIES linked by the 405 Freeway: **Manhattan, Hermosa,** and **Redondo** beaches, **Torrance, San Pedro,** and **Long Beach.** They're better known for their suburbia than their tourist appeal, but if you're seeking a fun beach day, some of these towns make for fine day trips (see "The Best Beaches and Parks"). We especially like Redondo, which has a lively pier popular with fishermen, a broad beach, and a harbor out of which run whale-watching trips; Manhattan is ideal for sun, surf, sand play, and cycling. Although San Pedro is a fairly gritty port town, full of smokestacks and cargo

unofficial TIP
On the bay shore in Belmont Shore is a protected sand beach that's well used by young families, thanks to its shallow, warm, wave-free water.

containers, it has real visitor value, as the departing point for the Catalina ferries (see Catalina Island section) and home of the hokey but amusing **Ports o' Call Village** (a shopping and seafood area on the waterfront) and the **Cabrillo Marine Aquarium.**

The largest city in this region, Long Beach is aiming to be a world-class family destination with the **Long Beach Aquarium of the Pacific.** (The *Queen Mary* has been here for years, but our kids find it a snooze.) Long Beach is also home to a miles-long beach popular with kite fliers, and the charming villages of **Belmont Shore** and **Naples**—good walking neighborhoods with canals, boutiques, restaurants, and lots of summer street life. Second Street is lots of fun for teens to stroll, shop, and people-watch.

FAMILY LODGING

Crowne Plaza Redondo Beach Marina and Hotel
300 North Harbor Drive, Redondo Beach; ☎ 310-318-8888 or 800-368-9760; www.redondobeach.crowneplaza.com; $216 and up; children under age 18 stay free; parking, $12 daily

The massive saltwater aquarium in the lobby is a kid magnet, as is Redondo's saltwater lagoon just across the street. (There's also a huge pool, but it's kind of barren and not nearly as fun as the lagoon.) Overlooking Kings Harbor, this *the south bay: manhattan beach to long beach*

■ FAMILY LODGING
1. Crowne Plaza
   Redondo
   Beach Marina
   and Hotel

● ATTRACTIONS
2. Bob Baker Marionette
   Theater
3. The Cabrillo Marine
   Aquarium
4. The Long Beach
   Aquarium
   of the Pacific

**◆ FAMILY-FRIENDLY
RESTAURANTS**
5. King's Fish House
6. Riviera Mexican Grill
7. Uncle Bill's Pancake
   House

upscale (if generic) hotel is well located for families interested in whale watching, sportfishing, biking the beach path, or enjoying summer days on Redondo Beach. Children under age 12 eat free in the restaurant when accompanied by a paying parent, and room service offers a kids' menu. The 339 well-maintained rooms, done in a subtle tropical style, are comfortable. Extras include a tennis court, bike rentals, and SeaLab, a touch-tank program for families run by the L.A. Conservation Corps. Ruby's, a retro family restaurant, is across the street, next to the lagoon.

ATTRACTIONS

The Cabrillo Marine Aquarium

APPEAL BY AGE	PRESCHOOL ★★★	GRADE SCHOOL ★★★★	TEENS ★★★
YOUNG ADULTS ★★★		OVER 30 ★★★	SENIORS ★★★

**3720 Stephen White Drive (off Pacific Avenue and 36th Street),
San Pedro; ☎ 310-548-7562; www.cabrilloaq.org**

Hours Tuesday–Friday, noon–5 p.m.; Saturday and Sunday, 10 a.m.–5 p.m. **Admission** Free; suggested donation, $5 adults, $1 children and seniors; parking, $7 per car. **Touring time** Average 1½ hours; minimum 45 minutes. **Rainy-day touring** Yes. **Restaurants** No. **Alcoholic beverages** No. **Disabled access** Yes. **Wheelchair rental** Yes; call ahead for beach wheelchairs. **Baby-stroller rental** No. **Lockers** No. **Pet kennels** No. **Rain check** No. **Private tours** No.

DESCRIPTION AND COMMENTS   More modest than the grandiose Aquarium of the Pacific in nearby Long Beach, this collection of sea life is also much less crowded, which counts for a lot. To do this place right, bring a picnic lunch and plan on spending much of the day here. First, spend a couple of hours playing, exploring, and swimming at adjacent Cabrillo Beach. Then, after lunch, when the kids are ready for some inside time, head into the aquarium to delve deeper into local sea life. They'll see all the critters that share the Pacific with us, from corbina fish to moray eels to leopard sharks; they'll touch sea stars and anemones at the touch tank; they'll feel whale bones and shark skin; and they can marvel up close at the life-size models of a killer whale and dolphin. Ask about the seasonal grunion runs and the guided tours of the nearby marine refuge during very low tides.

 ## The Long Beach Aquarium of the Pacific

APPEAL BY AGE	PRESCHOOL ★★★	GRADE SCHOOL ★★★★	TEENS ★★★★
YOUNG ADULTS ★★★	OVER 30 ★★★★		SENIORS ★★★★

100 Aquarium Way (off Shoreline Drive), Long Beach; ☎ 562-590-3100; www.aquariumofpacific.org

Hours Daily, 9 a.m.–6 p.m.; closed Christmas Day. **Admission** $19 adults, $11 children ages 3–11, children under age 3 free, $16 seniors age 60 and over; parking $8. **Touring time** Average 3–4 hours; minimum 1½ hours. **Rainy-day touring** Yes. **Restaurants** Yes. **Alcoholic beverages** No. **Disabled access** Yes. **Wheelchair rental** Yes. **Baby-stroller rental** Yes. **Lockers** No. **Pet kennels** No. **Rain check** No. **Private tours** Yes.

DESCRIPTION AND COMMENTS   This huge, impressive aquarium, part of the Rainbow Harbor area of Long Beach, lies across the channel from the *Queen Mary* (the two are linked by a water taxi) and down the waterfront promenade from Shoreline Village, a charming collection of shops and restaurants. For visitors staying at any of the major Long Beach hotels, it's all part of a convenient waterfront entertainment area.

Inside the dramatic aquarium building (its roof is designed to look like waves), more than 12,500 ocean animals are on display. In the huge entry hall is a 142,000-gallon predator tank filled with leopard sharks and giant sea bass. Passageways lead to three major underwater worlds, each focusing on a different Pacific Rim marine habitat. The Southern California and Baja world is where you'll find Kid's Cove, with a touch tank and an outdoor area devoted to up-close viewing of seals and sea lions. The Northern Pacific section features exhibits of animals native to cold-water areas of Canada, Alaska, Russia, and Japan, including puffins, sea otters, and a giant octopus. The Tropical Pacific gallery has above- and below-water viewing, a tube walkway that takes visitors right through the middle of an enormous aquarium, and spectacular, colorful fish and coral. Ours kids' favorites are the new Shark Lagoon and the environment called Dazzling and Dangerous, filled with lots of creepy, venomous critters, including sea jellies.

Family-friendly extras include a kids-only register in the educational-goodies-packed store; such special events as Grandparents' Morning and kayak expeditions; 3-D films about marine life; and a changing roster of interactive, staff-supervised activities throughout the facility.

FAMILY-FRIENDLY RESTAURANTS

King's Fish House
100 West Broadway, Long Beach; ☎ 562-432-7463;
www.kingsfishhouse.com

Meals served Lunch and dinner. **Cuisine** American/seafood. **Entree range** Lunch, $9–$17; dinner, $14–$37. **Kids' menu** $5.50–$7.50. **Reservations** Recommended. **Payment** All major credit cards.

In the heart of "old" downtown Long Beach, close to the Aquarium of the Pacific, King's is the best seafood restaurant in these parts, offering everything from clam chowder and tuna sandwiches to Ecuadorean mahimahi and live Maine lobster—or, for the less adventurous, burgers and chicken parmigiana. Good kids' menu, handsome setting, professional service, and some tables out on the sidewalk.

Riviera Mexican Grill
1615 South Pacific Coast Highway, Redondo Beach; ☎ 310-540-2501

Meals served Lunch and dinner. **Cuisine** Mexican. **Entree range** Lunch, $5–$9; dinner, $7–$13. **Kids' menu** $4. **Reservations** Recommended on weekends. **Payment** All major credit cards.

Fresh, tasty, modern surfer-style Mexican food—shrimp tacos, creative quesadillas—is the order of the day in this lively grill a block from Redondo Beach. It's filled with surf photos and memorabilia, which charms kids, and the patio is perfect for summer evenings.

Uncle Bill's Pancake House
1305 Highland Avenue, Manhattan Beach; ☎ 310-545-5177

Meals served Breakfast and lunch. **Cuisine** American. **Entree range** $4–$7. **Kids' menu** Yes. **Reservations** Not accepted. **Payment** All major credit cards.

Ocean views, low prices, great waffles and pancakes—it's no wonder there's always a wait at Uncle Bill's, a funky old coffee shop that's legendary in these parts. Try to visit during the week when the wait isn't as bad.

CATALINA ISLAND

BOTH A ROMANTIC'S RETREAT AND A HUGELY POPULAR summertime family destination, this island is a great escape for two or three days. Centered on the dinky town of **Avalon,** life here is outdoors and active: swimming at the small beaches, snorkeling and diving in the crystal-clear waters, boating, fishing, cycling, and hiking or horseback riding into the rugged backcountry. You can wear shorts just about anywhere, and the kids never seem to get all the sand out of their hair. Beyond the one square mile of Avalon, there's nothing but wilderness, except for the tiny village of **Two Harbors,** a popular campsite and boat harbor.

The fastest seagoing way to reach Catalina is on the high-speed ferries (75 to 90 minutes) run by **Catalina Express** (☎ 310-519-1212 or 800-481-3470), out of San Pedro or Long Beach, or the **Catalina Flyer** (☎ 949-673-5245; **www.catalinainfo.com**) out of Newport Beach. For general Catalina information, links to **Discovery Tours,** and other Catalina Island Company offerings, go to **www.scico.com.**

OUTDOOR ACTION

BOATING/WATERCRAFT You can rent every watercraft imaginable: kayak, Jet Ski, pedalboat, rafts, even paddleboards; our kids have had lots of fun kayaking around the harbor. **Joe's Rent-a-Boat** on the pier (☎ 310-510-0455) is a good vendor.

CRUISES Several one-hour cruises are good for families, including a cruise to **Seal Rock** ($5 to $9), and a night cruise to see flying fish ($10 to $16). Tickets available at mainland boat terminals and at the pier, boat landing, and **Discovery Tours Center** on the island (☎ 310-510-TOUR).

CYCLING Bikes are rented at concessions for riding around town. There's great mountain biking inland, but you have to spend $75 for an annual family permit from the **Catalina Island Conservancy** (125 Claressa Avenue; ☎ 310-510-2595, ext. 101; **www.catalinaconservancy.org**).

FISHING Kids ages 10 and up won't soon forget the thrill of reeling in a 25-pound white sea bass or bluefin tuna. Of the many fishing charters in Avalon, we like **Afishinados** (☎ 323-447-4669; **www.afishinados.com**).

catalina island

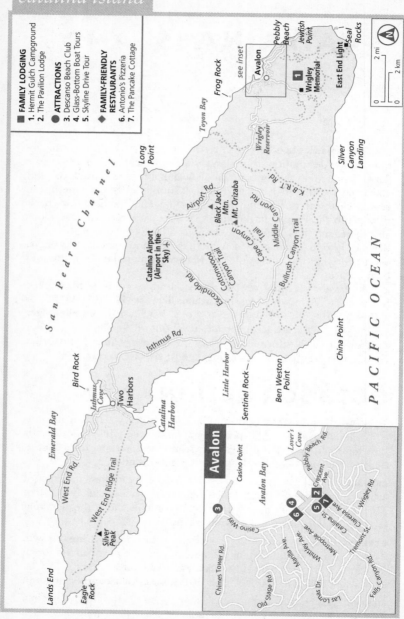

FAMILY LODGING
1. Hermit Gulch Campground
2. The Pavilion Lodge

ATTRACTIONS
3. Descanso Beach Club
4. Glass-Bottom Boat Tours
5. Skyline Drive Tour

FAMILY-FRIENDLY RESTAURANTS
6. Antonio's Pizzeria
7. The Pancake Cottage

Pebbly Beach
Jewfish Point
East End Light
Seal Rocks

Avalon
see inset
Wrigley Memorial
1

2 mi
2 km

Frog Rock

Toyon Bay

Wrigley Reservoir

Silver Canyon Landing

Long Point

K.B.R.T. Rd.

Airport Rd.
Black Jack Mtn.
Mt. Orizaba

Catalina Airport (Airport in the Sky)

Cape Canyon Trail
Middle Canyon Rd.
Bullrush Canyon Trail

Cottonwood Canyon Trail

Escondido Rd.

S a n   P e d r o   C h a n n e l

Isthmus Rd.

Bird Rock

Isthmus Cove
Two Harbors

Catalina Harbor

Little Harbor
Sentinel Rock
Ben Weston Point

China Point

P A C I F I C   O C E A N

Emerald Bay

West End Rd.
West End Ridge Trail

Silver Peak

Lands End

Eagle Rock

Avalon

Casino Point
Avalon Bay

Lover's Cove
Pebbly Beach Rd.
Crescent Ave.
2
1
5
7
Wrigley Rd.

4
6

Clarissa Ave

Catalina St.

Tremont St.

Casino Way

Chimes Tower Rd.

Old Stage Rd.

Marilla Ave.

Whitley Ave.

Metropole Ave.

Las Lomas Dr.

Falls Canyon Rd.

GOLF CARTING Families with toddlers might enjoy a one-hour golf-cart ride around Avalon, although there isn't a lot of territory to cover. You must be 25 or older to rent. Go to **Cartopia Golf Cart Rental** (☎ 310-510-2493).

HIKING The trails can be pretty intense here, so keep walks to the Avalon area with young children. But if you have sturdy walkers over age 8 or so, pick up a map and free permit from the **Catalina Island Conservancy** (125 Claressa Avenue; ☎ 310-510-2595, ext. 101; **www .catalinaconservancy.org**). When you get into the interior, you may see lots of wildlife, including bald eagles and wild boar.

HORSEBACK RIDING Families with horse-knowledgeable children over age 8 can join guided rides into the mountains above Avalon. Call **Catalina Stables** (☎ 310-510-0478).

 SNORKELING/DIVING Catalina Divers Supply on the pier (☎ 310-510-0330) can outfit you with gear to snorkel at Lover's Cove, found on the other side of the boat landing area. The snorkeling here is superb, and the gentle water is accommodating to very young children. Teens and parents can consider a scuba-diving lesson.

FAMILY LODGING

 ## Hermit Gulch Campground

A half mile from Avalon, at the top of Avalon Canyon (transportation by shuttle bus, by taxi, or on foot); ☎ 310-510-TENT; $6 per night for children, $12 for adults; reservations required

This privately owned campground is one of many fine family camping sites on Catalina; its selling point is its proximity to the town of Avalon, a half mile away. (So what it loses in isolation, it makes up for in convenience.) It's a pleasant, surprisingly quiet location in the hills overlooking the ocean; if you don't have your own tent, you can stay in a cabin or tepee. Town is a pretty easy walk, but there's a shuttle bus, too. Barbecue pits, fire rings, picnic tables, hot showers, flush toilets, hiking trails.

The Pavilion Lodge

513 Crescent Avenue, Avalon; ☎ 310-510-1788 or 800-851-0217; www.pavilionlodge.com; $224–$299; children age 11 and under stay free in parents' room

When the weather's fine, families pack into this newly renovated 73-room motel a few feet from the beach. There are no suites, but rooms are large enough for a small family, and some rooms connect. Room rates include beach towels, continental breakfast, HBO and Disney Channel on the TV, Internet access, and mini-refrigerators. Restaurants, shops, and the beach are a stone's throw away.

ATTRACTIONS

Descanso Beach Club

APPEAL BY AGE	PRESCHOOL ★★★★	GRADE SCHOOL ★★★★	TEENS ★★★★
YOUNG ADULTS ★★★		OVER 30 ★★★	SENIORS ★★★

1 Descanso Way (just past casino building), Avalon; ☎ 310-510-7410

Hours Daily, 11 a.m.–6 p.m.; Memorial Day–October: Friday and Saturday BYOB barbecue, 6–9 p.m.; closed October–April. **Admission** $2 for beach; everything else free. **Touring time** Average 3–4 hours; minimum 1 hour. **Rainy-day touring** No, closed for rain. **Restaurants** Yes. **Alcoholic beverages** Yes. **Disabled access** Yes. **Wheelchair rental** Patio and grass area only. **Baby-stroller rental** No, chairs only. **Lockers** Yes. **Pet kennels** No. **Rain check** No. **Private tours** No.

DESCRIPTION AND COMMENTS If main Crescent Beach gets too crowded, consider a beach day at this private club on the other side of the casino; you can become a "member" for just $2 a day. You can rent everything from beach chairs to rafts to kayaks to snorkeling gear, and kids will like the playground. The beach is large and pretty, with tiny waves, lawns and rough sand, and clear, clear water. Showers, changing rooms, lifeguards, and full food and bar service (you can't bring in your own food).

 ## Glass-Bottom Boat Tours

APPEAL BY AGE	PRESCHOOL ★★★	GRADE SCHOOL ★★★★	TEENS ★★★
YOUNG ADULTS ★★★		OVER 30 ★★★	SENIORS ★★★

Green Pleasure Pier, Avalon; ☎ 800-851-0217

Hours Daily, 10 a.m.–5 p.m.; conditional upon weather and visibility. **Admission** $8 adults, $5 age 11 and under. **Touring time** Average 40–45 minutes. **Rainy-day touring** Yes. **Restaurants** No. **Alcoholic beverages** No. **Disabled access** Yes. **Wheelchair rental** No. **Baby-stroller rental** No. **Lockers** No. **Pet kennels** No. **Rain check** No. **Private tours** No.

DESCRIPTION AND COMMENTS To get a glimpse of why Catalina is a diver's paradise, take this 45-minute boat tour to meet the local sea life. The water is amazingly clear, and when you get over to the kelp beds, you'll see vivid orange garibaldi, yellow giant kelpfish, bat rays, bass, maybe even a sea lion or some dolphins. The night cruise is cool, offering a look at nocturnal fish. The same company runs semisubmersible boat tours, but they aren't worth the substantial extra bucks.

Skyline Drive Tour

APPEAL BY AGE	PRESCHOOL ★★★	GRADE SCHOOL ★★★★	TEENS ★★★
YOUNG ADULTS ★★★		OVER 30 ★★★	SENIORS ★★★

Leaves from Island Plaza, Avalon; ☎ 800-851-0217

Hours Summer: tours 11 a.m., 1 p.m., and 3 p.m.; fewer off season. **Admission** $22 adults, $19 seniors age 55 and over, $11 children ages 2–11; tickets available from kiosks around the island and at the mainland terminal. **Touring time** Average 3 hours; minimum 1 hour. **Rainy-day touring** Yes. **Restaurants** No. **Alcoholic beverages** No. **Disabled access** No. **Wheelchair rental** Yes. **Baby-stroller rental** No. **Lockers** No. **Pet kennels** No. **Rain check** No. **Private tours** No.

DESCRIPTION AND COMMENTS First-timers to Catalina should take the two-hour narrated tour. It introduces you to the natural environment, animal life, and geography of the island. Kids love the ride and looking for wild boar and buffalo, and you'll love the views. Midway, everyone gets out for a leg stretch, so kids can blow off steam and see the nature center at the Island Conservancy. Reservations are essential in the busy season.

FAMILY-FRIENDLY RESTAURANTS

Antonio's Pizzeria
230 Crescent Avenue, Avalon; ☎ 310-510-0008

Meals served Breakfast, lunch, and dinner; call ahead because hours vary. **Cuisine** Italian. **Entree range** Lunch and dinner, $8–$18. **Kids' menu** No. **Reservations** Accepted for large parties. **Payment** AE, MC, V.

The food's a bit on the heavy side—pizzas, spaghetti with meat sauce, meatball sandwiches—but the setting is kid friendly, with peanut shells on the floor and country music on the stereo.

The Pancake Cottage
118 Catalina Street, Avalon; ☎ 310-510-0726

Meals served Breakfast and lunch; closed December–January. **Cuisine** American. **Entree range** Breakfast, $6–$8; lunch, $5–$12. **Kids' menu** Yes. **Reservations** Not accepted. **Payment** Personal checks and cash only.

You name it, they'll make it: omelets and pancakes of any description, waffles, Mexican dishes, sandwiches—the menu is vast, and most of the food is just fine. The fresh-fruit pancakes are particularly good. Breakfast is served all day.

LOS ANGELES:
Westside

IT HAS CONSIDERABLY FEWER ATTRACTIONS and museums than central L.A. does, but the Westside is nonetheless our favorite family-vacation base. Development in recent years has favored the pedestrian, so you can now stroll from your Ocean Avenue hotel to the **Santa Monica Pier** and its amusement park, to the beach, to the walking path along **Palisades Park,** the bluff overlooking the beach, and to a wealth of restaurants, shops, movie theaters, and small amusements, many of which are found on the car-free **Third Street Promenade** and the indoor mall across the street. The **Tide Shuttle** minibus (25¢) operates every 15 minutes between downtown Santa Monica, the beach, and the promenade. Active families can hop on bikes and ride the bike path down to **Venice Beach** and even on to the **South Bay.**

unofficial **TIP**
In the car-crazed L.A. area, we recommend choosing a hotel in **Santa Monica,** where you can actually stay quite happily without a car.

From the Santa Monica area, downtown L.A. is 30 minutes by freeway, **Disneyland** is about an hour, and **Hollywood** and **Universal Studios** are 30 to 40 minutes away. That's assuming that the freeways aren't congested, which seems increasingly rare, so factor in more time if you're traveling even remotely near rush hours. For a prettier drive, head north on the Pacific Coast Highway toward **Malibu** to explore some of the beaches and parks (see "The Best Beaches and Parks").

FAMILY LODGING

Best Western Jamaica Bay Inn
4175 Admiralty Way, Marina del Rey; ☎ 310-823-5333 or 888-823-5333; www.bestwestern-jamaicabay.com; $149–$189

Young families get an excellent location-to-price ratio here: This recently renovated motel is located right on Marina del Rey's Mother's Beach. Many of the 42 rooms in the low-slung, two-story motel have patios or balconies overlooking the marina, and the rooms with two queen beds are large enough to handle a family (some have microwaves and refrigerators). Outside are a

los angeles: westside

SOLSTICE CANYON PARK

TOPANGA STATE PARK

PACIFIC PALISADES

West-Brentwood wood

West Los Angeles

Santa Monica

Ocean Park

Venice

MALIBU

Santa Monica Bay

Pacific Coast Hwy.

see inset at left

■ **FAMILY LODGING**
1. Best Western Jamaica Bay Inn
2. Circle X Ranch Campground
3. Georgian Hotel
4. Loews Santa Monica Beach Hotel
5. Shutters on the Beach
6. Sycamore Canyon Campground

● **ATTRACTIONS**
7. Bright Child Indoor Playground
8. The Getty Center
9. Imagination Station Children's Theater
10. Magicopolis
11. Museum of Tolerance
12. Pacific Park
13. Santa Monica Playhouse
14. Will Geer Theatricum Botanicum

◆ **FAMILY-FRIENDLY RESTAURANTS**
15. Aunt Kizzy's Back Porch
16. Back on the Beach
17. Broadway Deli
18. California Pizza Kitchen (2 locations)
19. Duke's Malibu
20. El Cholo
21. Johnnie's New York Pizza
22. The Reel Inn
23. Typhoon

Santa Monica

Venice

Marina del Rey

Venice Pier

Santa Monica Pier

playground, pool, spa, lawn, coffee shop, bike rental, and an excellent beach for young children.

Circle X Ranch Campground

12898 Yerba Buena Road, Malibu; reservations ☎ 805-370-2300, ext. 1702; www.nps.gov/samo/maps/cx.htm; $2 per person per night

A hideaway in the Santa Monica Mountains, this national park group campground is more ranchlike than beachy, but it's popular with surfers, because the beach is a short drive away. Amenities include a swimming pool, basketball courts, drinking water, toilets, barbecues (charcoal only; no wood), and miles of hiking trails to wonderful locations, including grottoes, subterranean caverns, and a waterfall; there's plenty of easy hiking for little ones.

Georgian Hotel

1415 Ocean Avenue, Santa Monica; ☎ 310-395-9945 or 800-538-8147; www.georgianhotel.com; $205–$450

The pleasant, midsize (84 rooms) Georgian Hotel is much less formal than the newer Santa Monica hotels. It's a family-friendly, moderately priced (given the neighborhood) place ideally located for walks to the Santa Monica pier, the beach, and the Third Street Promenade. Many rooms on the upper floors have ocean views. The restaurant serves only breakfast (a continental breakfast is free), but there are plenty of great places within walking distance. The TVs are stocked with Nintendo, and the 28 suites are big enough for groups.

Loews Santa Monica Beach Hotel

1700 Ocean Avenue, Santa Monica; ☎ 310-458-6700 or 800-23-LOEWS; www.loewshotels.com; $230–$480, suites $625

Families are actively courted at this 342-room atrium-style beachfront resort. The pool is huge and kid friendly, the concierge will provide babysitters, kids can borrow games and DVDs from the lending library, the Santa Monica Pier is a short walk down the beach, and a concession rents kid-sized bikes (the great Santa Monica bike path is right out front). You'll also find a beach playground and children's menus in both the restaurant and room service. Rooms are modern, comfortable, and well equipped.

Shutters on the Beach

One Pico Boulevard, Santa Monica; ☎ 310-458-0030 or 800-334-9000; www.shuttersonthebeach.com; $355–$610

The only L.A.–area hotel that sits right on the sand, Shutters is a luxury hotel, its gray shingles and white trim and shutters evoking a grand Cape Cod beach house. It has ceded the kid's-club market to neighboring competitor Loew's, but many families still choose this place, willing to give up family amenities for Shutters' architecture, service, art collection, and location. There's a lovely ocean-view pool with poolside service, and a concession that rents adult- and kid-size bikes. The concierge can supply sand toys and babysitters, and the restaurant's children's menu is available for room service as well. Rooms are beautiful, done in pale ocean colors, with sliding shutters opening to small balconies.

 ### Sycamore Canyon Campground

Point Mugu State Park (off Pacific Coast Highway north of Deer Creek Road), Malibu; office is at 2860-A Camino Dos Rios, Newbury Park; ☎ 818-880-0350; reservations: Reserve America, ☎ 800-444-7275; www.reserveamerica.com; campsites $20–$25

A clean, safe, beautiful family beach retreat in the L.A. area, near multimillion-dollar movie-star houses—for $20 a night? Yes, that's the happy truth about this campground in north Malibu. The former Chumash Indian settlement sits at the mouth of a canyon, a site that keeps visitors warmer in winter and cooler in summer. It's a short walk to a gorgeous white-sand beach, known for frequent visits from dolphins; in the canyon itself, you'll find sycamores, wild rose, monarch butterflies, a stream, and poison oak, so watch out on hikes. If you don't feel like cooking, drive a couple of miles south to Neptune's Net, a good ocean-side seafood shanty. Because of all this, the campground is extremely popular, so reserve very early. Best times are in spring wildflower season and in late summer after the June gloom burns off.

 # ATTRACTIONS

Bright Child Indoor Playground

APPEAL BY AGE	PRESCHOOL ★★★★★	GRADE SCHOOL ★★★★	TEENS –
YOUNG ADULTS –	OVER 30 –		SENIORS –

1415 Fourth Street, Santa Monica; ☎ 310-393-4844; www.brightchild.com

Hours Daily, 10 a.m.–6 p.m. **Admission** $9.75 per child for two hours, $5 per child for each additional hour; one free adult with each paid child; sibling discounts offered. Adults must be accompanied by a child, and all children must be supervised by an adult. Socks must be worn by everyone (including adults). **Touring time** Average 2 hours; minimum 1 hour. **Rainy-day touring** Yes. **Restaurants** Snack bar. **Alcoholic beverages** No. **Disabled access** Yes. **Wheelchair rental** No. **Baby-stroller rental** No. **Lockers** No. **Pet kennels** No. **Rain check** No. **Private tours** Birthday parties.

DESCRIPTION AND COMMENTS An unusual facility, this popular storefront playground combines elements previously available in preschools, kids' gyms, children's museums, and outdoor playgrounds. Basically it's a safe, challenging indoor environment for kids to explore while supervised by a parent. There's a huge play structure with slides and tunnels, a ball room, a basketball court with adjustable-height hoops, a putting green, an arts and crafts room, a keyboard area with musical keyboards set at many different heights, and a protected toddler area for climbing and exploring without getting run over by older kids. It's very popular for birthday parties and a great place for families staying in hotels to bring younger kids while older ones shop at the Promenade nearby.

 ## The Getty Center

| APPEAL BY AGE | PRESCHOOL ★★★ | GRADE SCHOOL ★★★★★ | TEENS ★★★★ |
| YOUNG ADULTS ★★★★★ | | OVER 30 ★★★★★ | SENIORS ★★★★★ |

1200 Getty Center Drive, off 405 Freeway; ☎ 310-440-7300; www.getty.edu

Hours Sunday, Tuesday–Thursday, 10 a.m.–6 p.m.; Friday and Saturday, 10 a.m.–9 p.m. **Admission** Free, but parking is $7 (cash only). **Touring time** Average 3–4 hours; minimum 1 hour. **Rainy-day touring** Yes. **Restaurants** Yes. **Alcoholic beverages** Yes. **Disabled access** Yes. **Wheelchair rental** Yes, free. **Baby-stroller rental** Yes, free. **Lockers** No. **Pet kennels** No. **Rain check** No. **Private tours** No; museum tours daily.

DESCRIPTION AND COMMENTS Perched like a Pacific Rim Parthenon on a ridge above the San Diego Freeway, the Getty Center commands a view of the ocean on one side and miles of metropolitan Los Angeles on the other. Its Richard Meier–designed buildings, too, signal that this is a Grand and Important Place. Because the plazas and balconies are filled with visitors from all over the world, speaking different languages, it really does feel like the center of something.

If the Getty Center offered just grandeur, we wouldn't recommend it for children (what's impressive to an adult can be merely big to a 5-year-old), but the Getty is a kid-friendly place from the start. Upon arrival, patrons are whisked up the hill on a monorail, which, of course, delights children. As they disembark and enter the main plaza, kids are drawn to the outsides of buildings, which are sheathed in sand-colored Italian travertine and embedded with fossil prints (we've spotted shells, leaves, and fish). Sometimes we rent an audioguide, which we tune to the special family track that offers stories, fun facts, and sound effects related to the artworks (as opposed to the scholarly discourse on the main track). Sometimes, we head straight for the Family Room to check out "Perplexing Paintings" or the "Getty Art Detective" game box, so that moving through the museum becomes a treasure hunt. Before or after our tour, we snap photos of the kids posed in costumes and backdrops that re-create famous paintings.

With older kids, we stop in the Art Information rooms of galleries that intrigue them and spend time doing projects or playing with interactive exhibits. Weekend workshops that combine gallery visits with art projects are offered for children ages 5 to 13 accompanied by a parent (sign up at the information desk in the entrance hall).

Magicopolis

| APPEAL BY AGE | PRESCHOOL ★ | GRADE SCHOOL ★★★★ | TEENS ★★★★ |
| YOUNG ADULTS ★★★★ | | OVER 30 ★★★★ | SENIORS ★★★★ |

**1418 Fourth Street, Santa Monica; ☎ 310-451-2241;
www.magicopolis.com**

Hours Showtimes vary but are generally Tuesday–Sunday evenings with matinees on weekends. **Admission** Ticket prices range from $15–$25 depending on the show. **Touring time** Average 2 hours; minimum 1 hour. **Rainy-day touring** Yes. **Restaurants** Snack bar. **Alcoholic beverages** No. **Disabled access** Yes. **Wheelchair rental** No. **Baby-stroller rental** No. **Lockers** No. **Pet kennels** No. **Rain check** No. **Private tours** Birthday parties.

DESCRIPTION AND COMMENTS   This theater has been welcomed heartily by young magic lovers in L.A., because the two other showcases for the region's great pool of magic talent are nightclubs. And because a little magic appeals to everyone, Magicopolis is a good idea for any family looking for special-occasion live entertainment in a family atmosphere. Choose a show in either the 150-seat theater (with raked seating so that even the shortest audience member can see everything) or the 50-seat close-up theater. Some famous and soon-to-be-famous performers can be seen here, and performances range from the traditional to the more modern and innovative.

Museum of Tolerance

| APPEAL BY AGE | PRESCHOOL ★ | GRADE SCHOOL ★★★ | TEENS ★★★★★ |
| YOUNG ADULTS ★★★★★ | | OVER 30 ★★★★★ | SENIORS ★★★★★ |

**9786 West Pico Boulevard, Century City; ☎ 310-553-8403;
www.museumoftolerance.com**

Hours Monday–Thursday, 10 a.m.–6:30 p.m.; Friday, 10 a.m.–5 p.m.; Sunday, 10 a.m.–7:30 p.m.; closed Saturday. **Admission** $10 adults, $8 seniors, $7 students and children. **Touring time** Average 2 hours; minimum 1 hour. **Rainy-day touring** Yes. **Restaurants** Cafeteria. **Alcoholic beverages** No. **Disabled access.** Yes **Wheelchair rental** Yes, free. **Baby-stroller rental** No. **Lockers** No. **Pet kennels** No. **Rain check** No. **Private tours** Yes.

DESCRIPTION AND COMMENTS   Far too intense for young children, the Museum of Tolerance can be life changing for middle and high schoolers. It's the only museum of its kind in the world, with a devotion to increasing humankind's tolerance of differences by both exploring intolerance and celebrating diversity. This is achieved through several state-of-the-art exhibits, most famously the one on the Holocaust, which left our 13-year-old both stunned and motivated to make a difference. (This is the exhibit that is not recommended for children younger than 12.) Other worthwhile displays include the Point of View Diner, a 1950s diner counter that "serves" high-tech, interactive displays related to personal responsibility, from drunk driving to hate speech; a video wall that explores America's struggle for civil rights; and the Millennium Machine, which both illustrates the human-rights abuses going on around the world and helps visitors look for solutions. Your teens would rather be at Universal Studios, but they'll never forget a visit here.

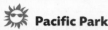 **Pacific Park**

| APPEAL BY AGE | PRESCHOOL ★★★★ | GRADE SCHOOL ★★★★ | TEENS ★★★ |
| YOUNG   ADULTS ★★ | | OVER   30   ★★ | SENIORS   ★★ |

380 Santa Monica Pier, Santa Monica; ☎ 310-260-8744; www.pacpark.com

Hours Summer: Sunday–Thursday, 11 a.m.–11 p.m.; Friday and Saturday, 11 a.m.–12:30 a.m.; times vary after Labor Day; call for more information. **Admission** Rides $1–$3; parking $7 on weekends, less on weekdays; unlimited ride wristbands, under 42" tall, $10–$11; over 42" tall, $20–$22; discount for online ticket purchases. **Touring time** Average 2 hours; minimum 1 hour. **Rainy-day touring** No. **Restaurants** Snack bar. **Alcoholic beverages** No. **Disabled access** Yes. **Wheelchair rental** No. **Baby-stroller rental** No. **Lockers** No. **Pet kennels** No. **Rain check** No. **Private tours** No.

DESCRIPTION AND COMMENTS   A new but old-fashioned amusement park on the planks of the Santa Monica Pier, Pacific Park is a fun beach excursion, if only for the coastline view from the Ferris wheel. If your children are under age 10, come as close as possible to opening time, when the crowds are minimal and the clientele is other young families; late afternoon and evening draws swarms of teens and young adults on dates. Its small size makes it not too overwhelming for little ones, who get their own area on the shore side of the pier: bumper cars, mini–Ferris wheel, imitation Dumbo ride, and such. Older kids get a short but fast roller coaster, a couple of other modest thrills, and video-arcade games; steer them away from the outrageously expensive "skill" games. Don't miss the wonderful old indoor carousel on the other end of the parking lot, and allow extra time for running around the vast sandy expanse of Santa Monica Beach.

 # FAMILY-FRIENDLY RESTAURANTS

Aunt Kizzy's Back Porch
Villa Marina, 4325 Glencoe Avenue, Marina del Rey; ☎ 310-578-1005; www.auntkizzys.com

Meals served Lunch, dinner, and Sunday brunch. **Cuisine** Southern American. **Entree range** Lunch, $8; dinner, $12–$15; all-you-can-eat brunch, $14. **Kids' menu** $8 and up. **Reservations** Not accepted. **Payment** All major credit cards.

Bursting with liveliness and conviviality, Aunt Kizzy's is a great place for a casual, hearty family meal: meat loaf, fried chicken, peach cobbler, and lemonade. The children's menu lets kids have the same good food the adults are having, only in smaller portions. Expect a wait on weekends.

Back on the Beach
445 Pacific Coast Highway, Santa Monica; ☎ 310-393-8282

Meals served Breakfast, lunch, and dinner. **Cuisine** American. **Entree range** $5–$9. **Kids' menu** Lunch and dinner menu only. **Reservations** For 6 or more, inside only. **Payment** All major credit cards.

The food is basic, but stick to eggs-and-pancakes fare, which is what most kids want anyway, and you'll get a decent, inexpensive breakfast right on the sand, with a swing set structure nearby to boot. We know families who start their weekends with breakfast here, then take advantage of the parking and restroom and spend the whole day on the beach.

Broadway Deli
1457 Third Street Promenade, Santa Monica; ☎ 310-451-0616

Meals served Breakfast, lunch, and dinner. **Cuisine** American/Californian. **Entree range** Breakfast, $6–$10; lunch and dinner, $13–$22. **Kids' menu** $4–$5. **Reservations** Not accepted. **Payment** All major credit cards.

More a yuppie diner than a deli, this teeming place on the edge of the Promenade packs 'em in for everything from omelets and coffee to froufrou California pizzas and Bordeaux wines. The huge booths can handle a big family, the noise level is forgiving, and the children's menu offers all the standards and then some.

California Pizza Kitchen
11677 San Vicente Boulevard, Brentwood; ☎ 310-826-3573;
210 Wilshire Boulevard, Santa Monica; ☎ 310-393-9335; www.cpk.com

Meals served Lunch and dinner. **Cuisine** Californian. **Entree range** $10–$20. **Kids' menu** $5–$6. **Reservations** Accepted for large parties. **Payment** All major credit cards.

There's something for everyone at this slick chain. We like the shrimp-pesto pizza, the field-green salads, the wine by the glass, and the modest prices. Our kids like the mini-pizzas, the coloring menus, the booths, and the kid's drinks in take-home cups, complete with lids and bendy straws.

Duke's Malibu
21150 Pacific Coast Highway, Malibu; ☎ 310-317-0777;
www.hulapie.com

Meals served Lunch, dinner, and Sunday brunch. **Cuisine** American, seafood. **Entree range** Lunch, $8–$13; dinner, $14–$35; Sunday buffet brunch, $17. **Kids' menu** $5 and up; Sunday buffet, $13. **Reservations** Recommended. **Payment** All major credit cards.

unofficial **TIP**
If your kids are enamored of surf culture, bring them to Duke's, a swell Malibu branch of the popular Waikiki original.

Duke's Malibu is devoted to the father of surfing, Duke Kahanamoku. Beautifully located right on top of the Malibu ocean, Duke's is a casual, lively place decorated with old surfboards and surf photos, offering modern surf 'n' turf fare: a mighty fine Caesar salad and straightforward grilled Hawaiian fish, with burgers and the like for kids. If you're headed south, check out the Duke's in Huntington Beach, also right on the beach.

El Cholo
1025 Wilshire Boulevard, Santa Monica; ☎ 310-899-1106;
www.elcholo.com

Meals served Lunch and dinner. **Cuisine** Mexican. **Entree range** $8–$20. **Kids' menu** Yes. **Reservations** Necessary. **Payment** All major credit cards.

The original El Cholo, in the heart of central L.A., is loved by several generations of Angelenos for its tasty Cal-Mex food and margaritas; this sprawling branch in Santa Monica continues the tradition honorably. Tile-work, fountains, plants, and painted walls are the set, costumed waitresses are the performers, and families crowd in for the chips 'n' guac, saucy cheese enchiladas, fajitas, soft tacos, and other nonauthentic but nonetheless delicious classics.

Johnnie's New York Pizza
1444 Third Street Promenade, Santa Monica; ☎ 310-395-9062
22333 Pacific Coast Highway, Malibu; ☎ 310-456-1717

Meals served Lunch and dinner. **Cuisine** Italian/pizza. **Entree range** $7–$19. **Kids' menu** No. **Reservations** Not accepted. **Payment** AE, MC, V.

Johnnie's make one of the best pizzas in L.A. It's a traditional New York pizza—thin-crusted, herby, and cheesy—and it's really terrific. Both branches are noisy, casual, and New Yorkish, even if they are packed with tanned Angelenos.

The Reel Inn
18661 Pacific Coast Highway, Malibu; ☎ 310-456-8221

Meals served Lunch and dinner. **Cuisine** Seafood. **Entree range** Lunch, $6–$15; dinner, $8–$25. **Kids' menu** $5. **Reservations**. Accepted for large groups. **Payment** AE, MC, V.

Funky, affordable, and beach adjacent, this is the sort of no-frills seafood shack found in every respectable beach town—an order-at-the-counter, share-big-tables sort of place. You can splurge on fresh lobster, but most people are perfectly happy with simple grilled ahi, wahoo, and snapper, with maybe a cup of chowder. The kids' menu is fine.

Typhoon
Santa Monica Airport, 3221 Donald Douglas Loop South, Santa Monica;
☎ **310-390-6565; www.thehump-sushi.com**

Meals served Lunch and dinner; closed Saturday lunch; Sunday brunch. **Cuisine** Pacific Rim. **Entree range** Lunch, $12–$19; dinner, $14–$20. **Kids' menu** No. **Reservations** Recommended. **Payment** All major credit cards.

At first glimpse, this might not seem like a great family restaurant, what with the serious bar (featuring the sort of Technicolor drinks that have the word "killer" in their names) and preponderance of beautiful people. But take a second look, and you and your kids will love it. Request a table by the windows or on the balcony overlooking the runway of Santa Monica Airport, which still looks as if it could be the set for the airport in *Casablanca;* the kids will love watching the small planes take off, and if you time it right, you might get a great sunset to boot. The menu wanders the Asian continent, offering everything from Thai *mee krob* to Japanese sushi to Korean barbecue, and it's all terrific; for kids who find such exotica yucky, there are simple noodles and delicious egg rolls. Yuckiest of all are the insect dishes—really!—which will surely fascinate your kids. Just knowing this place serves Manchurian ants and Thai-style crispy sea worms is cool, even if you don't try them.

CENTRAL
LOS ANGELES

"CENTRAL" LOS ANGELES AS WE'RE DESCRIBING IT HERE is not a neighborhood in any way—in fact, we'll be touching on sights and attractions in **Hollywood, West Hollywood, Wilshire Center,** downtown, **Exposition Park, Griffith Park,** and **Universal City.** But all of these communities are geographically contiguous in a mostly flatland area best defined by freeway boundaries: the Santa Monica Freeway is to the south, the Ventura Freeway to the north, the Hollywood Freeway to the east, and the San Diego Freeway to the west. It's home to many of L.A.'s major museums and cultural centers as well as a multicultural triangle of eating/shopping districts: **Chinatown, Little Tokyo,** and **Olvera Street.** Finally, it contains one of California's premier theme parks, the movie lovers' **Universal Studios,** which is a better Hollywood destination than the actual Hollywood itself.

unofficial **TIP**
Now that the Hollywood Roosevelt Hotel has gone hipster, we don't even recommend staying in Hollywood—Universal City, Studio City, downtown, or the area just east of Beverly Hills make better home bases for families.

FAMILY LODGING

Four Seasons Hotel Los Angeles at Beverly Hills
300 South Doheny Drive, L.A.; ☎ 310-273-2222 or 800-332-3442; www.fourseasons.com; $345–$555; suites $625–$5,500

The Four Seasons people know how to cater to kids, and this elegant hotel succeeds in making both children and movie stars happy. The location, on the eastern border of Beverly Hills, is terrific, and the 284 rooms and 42 suites are appointed with every convenience and luxury. The pool area is one of the most glamorous in L.A., with a view over palm-tree tops across the prettier parts of the city. In spite of being a major power hangout, it's a great place for families ready to do the upscale thing. Gift bags are given to children upon check-in, and milk and cookies are served to them that night. A babysitter service is available, and tasty kids' menus are offered through room service, at the elegant restaurant, and at the acclaimed Sunday brunch.

The Millennium Biltmore Hotel

506 South Grand Avenue, downtown; ☎ 213-624-1011 or 800-245-8673; www1.millenniumhotels.com; $139–$269; higher for suites

This stately, well-maintained dowager is a good choice if you're bringing kids on a downtown business/pleasure trip or if you want to focus on such cultural activities as theater at the Music Center and storytime at the Central Library. It sits in the heart of downtown, about 30 minutes east of Santa Monica beach and 20 minutes southeast of Universal Studios. We've found that kids actually enjoy the grand landmark hotels—the many differently decorated areas, the ornateness, and the various nooks and crannies seem to appeal to them. It's fun to dress up and take tea in the historic lobby-lounge, with its hand-painted beams overhead; this has been a location in countless movies and TV shows. Less formal settings are also around, including a cafe and an indoor pool. You can catch a DASH bus to all sorts of downtown destinations, from Chinatown to Staples Center sports arena; the wonderful Los Angeles Central Library is an easy walk.

The Orlando

8384 West Third Street, L.A.; ☎ 800-62-HOTEL (4-6835) or 323-658-6600; www.theorlando.com; $209–$349

Formerly the Beverly Plaza, this smallish (98 rooms) hotel was recently totally overhauled and is now a pretty swank spot, but the price is reasonable given the location (a block and a half east of the Beverly Center shopping mall) and amenities. It's not quite in Beverly Hills, but it's close enough for your luxury-loving shoppers, and yet near enough to the major streets that will carry you to other parts of town. The nearest attractions are the Petersen Automotive Museum, La Brea Tar Pits, Farmer's Market and its adjacent shopping center–cineplex, the Grove, and Hollywood, and there's plenty of walking and dining nearby. There's a wonderful saltwater swimming pool, a fitness center, wireless Internet, and a good Italian restaurant; the front desk rents iPods and DVD players.

Sheraton Universal

333 Universal Hollywood Drive, Universal City; ☎ 818-980-1212 or 888-625-5144; www.sheraton.com; $199 and up

A well-run link in the Sheraton chain, this 442-room, 23-suite modern high-rise hotel is a good bet for families planning a Universal City visit, because its packages with the park offer savings and convenience. One recent package, for instance, combined a room and two adult tickets to Universal Studios for $245, and discounted children's tickets can be bought in the hotel gift shop. Universal City and CityWalk are a free tram ride or a five-minute walk away. Game room, large heated pool, children's menus, and good-sized, comfortable, generic rooms, some with killer views of the Valley.

downtown los angeles

■ **FAMILY LODGING**
1. Millennium Biltmore
   Hotel Los Angeles

● **ATTRACTIONS**
2. California Science Center
3. Dodger Stadium
4. Los Angeles Central Library
5. Olvera Street
6. Walt Disney Concert Hall
7. The Watts Tower of Simon
   Rodia State Historic Park

◆ **FAMILY-FRIENDLY RESTAURANT**
8. Empress Pavilion

Information ⓘ
Parking 🅿

hollywood

RUNYAN CANYON PARK

HOLLYWOOD

Franklin Ave.

Franklin Ave.
Hollywood Blvd.

Sunset Blvd.

DeLongpre Ave.

Fountain Ave.

Santa Monica Blvd.

Romaine St.

Willoughby Ave.

Melrose Ave.

Rosewood Ave.

Oakwood Ave.

Beverly Blvd.

CBS Television City

PAN PACIFIC PARK

PARK LA BREA

HANCOCK PARK

Mid-Wilshire

Wilshire Blvd.

Olympic Blvd.

Fairfax Ave.

Crescent Heights Blvd.

Gardner St.

Martell Ave.

Alta Vista Blvd.

Sycamore Ave.

La Brea Ave.

Highland Ave.

Cochran Ave.

Hauser Blvd.

San Vicente Blvd.

Cahuenga Blvd.

Vine St.

Wilcox Ave.

Vine St.

Gower St.

HOLLYWOOD CEMETERY (HOLLYWOOD FOREVER)

Rosewood Ave.

Gower St.

Larchmont Blvd.

Rossmore Ave.

The Wilshire Country Club

1st St.

2nd St.

3rd St.

6th St.

Van Ness Ave.

Western Ave.

Western Ave.

To Griffith Park

HOLLYWOOD

101

Downtown Los Angeles

Map area

PACIFIC OCEAN

LAX

0   1/2 mi
0   0.5 km

0   15mi
0   15 km

Information ⓘ

N

■ **FAMILY LODGING**
1. Four Seasons at Beverly Hills
2. The Orlando

● **ATTRACTIONS**
3. ArcLight Cinemas
4. Autry Museum
5. Children's Book World
6. Farmers Market
7. Hollywood & Highland
8. Hollywood Walk of Fame

9. La Brea Tar Pits and Museum
10. Los Angeles County Museum of Art
11. Los Angeles Zoo
12. Museum of Radio and Television
13. Petersen Automotive Museum
14. Silent Movie Theater
15. Sony Pictures Entertainment Studio Tour

16. Summer Sounds
17. Travel Town

◆ **FAMILY-FRIENDLY RESTAURANTS**
18. Daily Grill
19. El Cholo
20. Fabiolus Cafe
21. House of Blues
22. Johnny Rockets
23. La Fonda de Los Comperos
24. Pink's

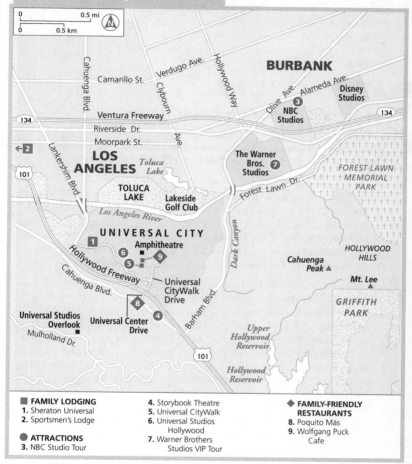

universal city–burbank

FAMILY LODGING
1. Sheraton Universal
2. Sportsmen's Lodge

ATTRACTIONS
3. NBC Studio Tour

4. Storybook Theatre
5. Universal CityWalk
6. Universal Studios
   Hollywood
7. Warner Brothers
   Studios VIP Tour

**FAMILY-FRIENDLY
RESTAURANTS**
8. Poquito Más
9. Wolfgang Puck
   Cafe

Sportsmen's Lodge

**12825 Ventura Boulevard, Studio City; ☎ 818-769-4700 or
800-821-8511; www.slhotel.com; $142 and up; kids under age 18
stay free in parents' room**

We're not sure what's so sportsmanlike about this comfortable, low-slung,
garden-style hotel—the only thing people hunt for in this Studio City
neighborhood is a good restaurant. Still, we love its subtly hokey charms,
not to mention its large pool set in a protected courtyard, its little lagoon

bedecked with swans, and its tiny tinkling waterfalls. The executive suites with patios are perfect for families. There's a children's menu in room service and the casual cafe, and there's also a lot of good eating along Ventura Boulevard. Universal City is only about five minutes away (the hotel offers a free shuttle and discounted tickets), Hollywood is just over the hill, and Pasadena's Old Town is about 15 minutes via freeway.

ATTRACTIONS

The Autry Museum of the American West

APPEAL BY AGE	PRESCHOOL ★★	GRADE SCHOOL ★★★★	TEENS ★★★
YOUNG ADULTS ★★★	OVER 30 ★★★		SENIORS ★★★★★

4700 Western Heritage Way, Griffith Park; ☎ 323-667-2000; www.autry-museum.org

Hours Tuesday–Sunday, 10 a.m.–5 p.m.; Thursday, 10 a.m.–8 p.m. **Admission** $7.50 adults, $5 seniors age 60 and over, $5 students ages 13–18, $3 children ages 2–12, free for children under age 2. **Touring time** Average 2½ hours; minimum 1 hour. **Rainy-day touring** Yes. **Restaurants** Cafeteria-style cafe. **Alcoholic beverages** No. **Disabled access** Yes. **Wheelchair rental** Yes, free. **Baby-stroller rental** Yes, free. **Lockers** No. **Pet kennels** No. **Rain check** No. **Private tours** Yes.

DESCRIPTION AND COMMENTS This is a perfect outing for grandparents and their grandchildren, or older parents and their kids. If you're over 50, chances are good that you idolized stars like Gene Autry and Tom Mix—and along with often-worthy exhibitions of paintings, sculpture, and other works from Western and Native American artists, you'll find great collections of Hollywood cowboy memorabilia, from costumes to posters. Our kids love the full-size jail cell, the dioramas reenacting the shootout at the OK Corral, the collections of sheriff's badges and pistols, and especially the hands-on Children's Discovery Gallery, where kids get to experience the life of Chinese immigrants to America in the 1800s—there's even a Chinese restaurant in which they can pretend to cook, serve, and eat. Elsewhere in the museum is a "movie studio" in which kids are inserted via videotape into an old Western chase scene. The gift shop is a major kid pleaser, with lots of fun Native American and cowboy stuff. Weekends often bring free performances of cowboy music and/or children's art classes.

California Science Center

APPEAL BY AGE	PRESCHOOL ★★	GRADE SCHOOL ★★★★★	TEENS ★★★★
YOUNG ADULTS ★★★★	OVER 30 ★★★★		SENIORS ★★★

700 State Drive, Exposition Park; ☎ 323-724-3623; www.casciencectr.org

Hours Daily, 10 a.m.–5 p.m.; closed Thanksgiving, Christmas, and New Year's Day. **Admission** Free with $6 parking; IMAX admission $8 adults, $6 seniors age 60 and older, and students ages 13–17, $5 children ages 4–12. **Touring time** Average 3 hours; minimum 1½ hours. **Rainy-day touring** No. **Restaurants** Yes. **Alcoholic beverages** No. **Disabled access** Yes. **Wheelchair rental** Yes, free. **Baby-stroller rental** No. **Lockers** Yes. **Pet kennels** No. **Rain check** No. **Private tours** No.

DESCRIPTION AND COMMENTS Los Angeles parents, teachers, and kids love this ambitious museum, which has revitalized the Exposition Park complex south of downtown. When my daughter first visited on a school field trip, crowds prevented her and her classmates from even getting near Tess, the 50-foot model woman with the see-through body that lets you see how the body's systems work. (What they missed was a 15-minute animatronic demonstration of a virtual soccer game that Tess plays; lights, sounds, and visual tricks help explain what's happening in her body while she runs and kicks.) But on a later visit, when the crowds had abated, our group did get a chance to operate the high-wire bicycle and experience a simulated earthquake. The kids also enjoyed pulling, maneuvering, and playing with lots of hands-on science experiments and displays. And, of course, they love the IMAX movies. The secret to visiting this place in relative peace is to come on a school day between 1 and 3 p.m. The field-trip kids will have left, and the after-school crowd hasn't hit yet. The exhibits are so dynamic, fun, and educational that they're worth missing a day of school.

Dodger Stadium Tour

APPEAL BY AGE	PRESCHOOL ★	GRADE SCHOOL ★★★		TEENS ★★★
YOUNG ADULTS ★★		OVER 30 ★★★		SENIORS ★★★

Stadium, 1000 Elysian Park Avenue; ☎ 866-DODGERS; www.dodgers.com

Hours Tours April–September, Tuesday–Friday at 2 p.m. on nongame days; reservations required, call ☎ 323-224-1-HIT (448). **Admission** $8 adults, $4 children ages 4–14. **Touring time** Average 1–1½ hours; minimum 1 hour. **Rainy-day touring** No. **Restaurants** No, snack bars closed on nongame days. **Alcoholic beverages** No. **Disabled access** Yes. **Wheelchair rental** No. **Baby-stroller rental** No. **Lockers** No. **Pet kennels** No. **Rain check** No. **Private tours** Yes.

DESCRIPTION AND COMMENTS If you have a baseball nut in your family, this behind-the-scenes tour offers the kind of up-close experience so hard to come by in our electronic age. A guide takes you into the press box, clubhouse area, bullpen, and dugout, onto the field, and through the new Dodger Museum. Reservations required.

Hollywood & Highland

APPEAL BY AGE	PRESCHOOL ★	GRADE SCHOOL ★★★		TEENS ★★★★★
YOUNG ADULTS ★★★★		OVER 30 ★★		SENIORS ★★

Hollywood Boulevard at Highland, L.A.; ☎ 323-817-0220; www.hollywoodandhighland.com

Hours Monday–Saturday, 10 a.m.–10 p.m.; Sunday, 10 a.m.–7 p.m.; theaters, clubs, and some restaurants have extended hours. **Admission** Free to shopping center; various admissions for theaters. **Touring time** 2 hours. **Rainy-day touring**

Yes. for theaters; mall is outdoors. **Restaurants** Yes. **Alcoholic beverages** Yes. **Disabled access** Yes. **Wheelchair rental** No. **Baby-stroller rental** No. **Lockers** No. **Pet kennels** No. **Rain check** No. **Private tours** No.

DESCRIPTION AND COMMENTS Hollywood has tried to gussy itself up for many years to little avail, but the tide has finally turned with this ambitious development built around the famed Mann's Chinese Theatre. At its core, it's really just another glorified mall, home to—you'll be amazed to discover!—a **Gap, Victoria's Secret,** and **M.A.C.** Scattered around the shopping venues are the Kodak Theatre, new home of the Academy Awards and the site of some worthwhile concerts; a cineplex; the famed **Chinese Theatre;** a bunch of hip restaurants; the chic **Lucky Strike Lanes** bowling alley, which is kid friendly most of the time but gets nightclubby later at night; **The Road to Hollywood,** an intriguing on-the-ground art piece that serves as a tribute to the Hollywood of fantasy and reality; a couple of courtyards and outdoor performing spaces; and an adjacent upscale hotel. Preteens and teens will like it, as long as they have money to spend.

La Brea Tar Pits and George C. Page Museum of La Brea Discoveries

APPEAL BY AGE	PRESCHOOL ★★★★	GRADE SCHOOL ★★★★★	TEENS ★★★★
YOUNG ADULTS ★★★★	OVER 30 ★★★★★		SENIORS ★★★★★

5801 Wilshire Boulevard, Hancock Park; ☎ 323-934-PAGE (7243); www.tarpits.org

Hours Monday–Friday, 9:30 a.m.–5 p.m.; Saturday, Sunday, and holidays, 10 a.m.–5 p.m. **Admission** $7 adults, $5 seniors/students, $2 children ages 5–12, free for age 4 and under; free first Tuesday of every month. Parking $6–$8. **Touring time** Average 1½ hours; minimum 30 minutes. **Rainy-day touring** Yes. **Restaurants** No. **Alcoholic beverages** No. **Disabled access** Yes. **Wheelchair rental** Yes, free. **Baby-stroller rental** No. **Lockers** No. **Pet kennels** No. **Rain check** No. **Private tours** Yes.

DESCRIPTION AND COMMENTS Every young Angeleno comes here at one time or another and pulls up on the poles suspended in tar-pit goo to get a feel for what it must have been like to be a prehistoric animal stuck in the bubbling ooze. This museum is architecturally interesting and pleasantly compact, with an inventive range of varied exhibits, from a film and holograms to models and a window through which visitors can watch paleontologists cleaning and studying bones. The exhibits are tightly focused—all pertain to fossils found on this very site. The Page is a standout, and it has a great museum shop for kids.

Los Angeles Central Library

APPEAL BY AGE	PRESCHOOL ★★★	GRADE SCHOOL ★★★	TEENS ★★★
YOUNG ADULTS ★★★	OVER 30 ★★★★		SENIORS ★★★★

630 West Fifth Street, Downtown; ☎ **213-228-7000; www.lapl.org**

Hours Monday–Thursday, 10 a.m.–8 p.m.; Friday and Saturday, 10 a.m.–6 p.m.; Sunday, 1–5 p.m.; closed major holidays. **Admission** Free; parking in selected lots $2 with library card. **Touring time** Average 2 hours; minimum 1 hour. **Rainy-day touring** Excellent. **Restaurants** Yes. **Alcoholic beverages** No. **Disabled access** Yes. **Baby-stroller rental** No. **Lockers** Yes. **Pet kennels** No. **Rain check** No. **Private tours** Docent tours.

DESCRIPTION AND COMMENTS   The hordes of office workers leave downtown L.A. on weekends, so parking is easier and cheaper than during the week, and that's when the historic and gorgeous Central Library is a real treat. Children's programs (theater, puppets, or video) on Saturday and Sunday give a shape and purpose to the outing, but it's great fun to simply browse the beautiful 1930s-era restored children's room, play on the computers in the room adjacent, ride the escalators through the glass-walled, four-story atrium with its cartoonlike giant chandeliers, and get lunch at the Chinese buffet restaurant with terrace seating.

Los Angeles County Museum of Art

APPEAL BY AGE	PRESCHOOL ★★	GRADE SCHOOL ★★★	TEENS ★★★★
YOUNG ADULTS ★★★★★	OVER 30 ★★★★★		SENIORS ★★★★★

5905 Wilshire Boulevard, Miracle Mile; ☎ **323-857-6000 or 323-857-6010 (tickets); www.lacma.org**

Hours Monday, Tuesday, Thursday, noon–8 p.m.; Friday, noon–9 p.m.; Saturday and Sunday, 11 a.m.–8 p.m.; closed Wednesdays, Thanksgiving, and Christmas Day. **Admission** $9 adults, $5 seniors and students age 18 and over with valid ID, free for children age 17 and under; some special-fee shows; free second Tuesday of every month after 5 p.m.; parking $5. **Touring time** Average a half day; minimum 2 hours. **Rainy-day touring** Good. **Restaurants** Yes. **Alcoholic beverages** Yes. **Disabled access** Yes. **Wheelchair rental** Yes, free. **Baby-stroller rental** No. **Lockers** No. **Pet kennels** No. **Rain check** No. **Private tours** No.

DESCRIPTION AND COMMENTS   This big-city art museum is a complex of buildings on the same parklike block as the La Brea Tar Pits and Page Museum. Don't try to see everything in a single visit—just pick a single period, floor, or section, enjoy it, and be done. Some strong holdings that might appeal to certain kids are the costume and fashion collection (try it on middle schoolers), the photo collection (good for teens, too disturbing for little ones), the modern-art wing (whose huge paintings and bright colors appeal to elementary-age kids), and the sacred art of India—stone sculptures are impressive at any age. A separate but related facility is the Japanese Pavilion, with a specialized collection not likely to be appreciated by many children. The best bet for families is the special events, especially the occasional family music concerts and the Family Sundays (every Sunday at 12:30 p.m.), which typically offer hands-on artmaking projects and storytelling. Note that kids age 17 and under get in free.

Los Angeles Zoo

APPEAL BY AGE	PRESCHOOL ★★★★	GRADE SCHOOL ★★★★	TEENS ★★★
YOUNG ADULTS ★★★		OVER 30 ★★★	SENIORS ★★★

5333 Zoo Drive, off I-5 Freeway, Griffith Park; ☎ 323-644-4200; www.lazoo.org

Hours Daily 10 a.m.–5 p.m.; closed Christmas. **Admission** $9 adults (age 13 and older), $6 seniors age 62 and older, $4 children ages 2–12, free for children under age 2; free parking. **Touring time** Average 3 hours; minimum 1 hour. **Rainy-day touring** Limited. **Restaurants** Yes. **Alcoholic beverages** Yes. **Disabled access** Yes. **Wheelchair rental** Yes. **Baby-stroller rental** Yes. **Lockers** No. **Pet kennels** Yes. **Rain check** No. **Private tours** Yes.

DESCRIPTION AND COMMENTS A zoo membership is a must for many L.A. families—special events abound at this large, inviting attraction, and many are for kids. For visitors, this means you'll find plenty of entertainment in addition to looking at animals. There are excellent demonstrations and shows (schedules available at gate), as well as fun educational installations at various points (What Does a Bear Smell?). There's a children's zoo and baby-animal nursery. Overnight camps and family camping nights are occasionally offered in the summer.

Olvera Street

APPEAL BY AGE	PRESCHOOL ★★	GRADE SCHOOL ★★★★	TEENS ★★★★
YOUNG ADULTS ★★★★		OVER 30 ★★★★	SENIORS ★★★★

845 North Alameda Street, downtown; ☎ 213-628-1274; www.olvera-street.com

Hours Daily, 10 a.m.–7 p.m.; summer: daily, 10 a.m.–10 p.m. **Admission** Free. **Touring time** Average 2½ hours, with meal; minimum 1 hour. **Rainy-day touring** Limited. **Restaurants** Yes. **Alcoholic beverages** Yes. **Disabled access** Limited. **Baby-stroller rental** No. **Lockers** No. **Pet kennels** No. **Rain check** No. **Private tours** No.

DESCRIPTION AND COMMENTS When we first came to L.A., we thought Olvera Street was corny, but when we worked downtown, we started to hang out here, and we came to appreciate its sidewalk cafes and strolling mariachis; its varied shops with colorful, often-seasonal goods; and its lively street scene. Our daughter was enthusiastic after a school field trip that included a tour of the historic adobe and the vintage fire station. And everybody loves the shopping, which is every bit as good as on the main tourist strip in Ensenada. We've been happy with purchases of blankets, purses, silver jewelry, piñatas, paper flowers, and jumping beans. As for food, eat at the tiny hole-in-the-wall called Juanita's, and save the fancier joints for margaritas (virgin or regular) and mariachis. This historic little street is part of the larger El Pueblo de Los Angeles, the birthplace of the city, which includes a lovely restored plaza and several historic buildings. Union Station is across the street, so Olvera Street is easily reached from the Gold Line or Red Line subways.

Petersen Automotive Museum

APPEAL BY AGE	PRESCHOOL ★★★	GRADE SCHOOL ★★★★	TEENS ★★★★★
YOUNG ADULTS ★★★★		OVER 30 ★★★★	SENIORS ★★★

6060 Wilshire Boulevard, Miracle Mile; ☎ 323-930-2277;
www.petersen.org

Hours Tuesday–Sunday, 10 a.m.–6 p.m.; Discovery Center: Tuesday–Friday, 10 a.m.–
4 p.m.; Saturday and Sunday, 10 a.m.–5 p.m. **Admission** $10 adults, $5 seniors age
62 and older and students with valid ID, $3 children ages 5–12, free for children
age 4 and under; parking, $6. **Touring time** Average 2½ hours; minimum 1 hour.
Rainy-day touring Limited. **Restaurants** Mini-mart. **Alcoholic beverages** No.
Disabled access. Yes **Baby-stroller rental** No. **Lockers** No. **Pet kennels** No. **Rain
check** No. **Private tours** No.

DESCRIPTION AND COMMENTS California's car culture is honored and explored
in this unusual museum. More than 150 classic cars, hot rods, Indy cars,
trucks, motorcycles, and custom vehicles are displayed in settings that
bring the period or use of the car to life. It won't feel like a museum as you
and the kids walk through settings from the horse-and-buggy era to the
space-age future, each with motor vehicles of the period. Some visitors
will like the vintage signage and other historically accurate parts of the environments (complete in some cases with sounds) as much as the gleaming motor vehicles. The second-floor exhibits are more traditional but
include some favorites like hot rods and celebrity cars. The Children's Discovery Center brings welcome interactivity to the museum.

Travel Town

APPEAL BY AGE	PRESCHOOL ★★★	GRADE SCHOOL ★★★	TEENS ★★
YOUNG ADULTS ★★		OVER 30 ★★	SENIORS ★★

5200 West Zoo Drive, Griffith Park; ☎ 323-662-5874; www.laparks.org

Hours Monday–Friday, 10 a.m.–4 p.m.; Saturday and Sunday, holidays, 10 a.m.–
5 p.m.; closed Christmas. **Admission** Free. **Touring time** Average 1 hour; minimum
8 minutes for the ride only. **Rainy-day touring** No. **Restaurants** No. **Alcoholic
beverages** No. **Disabled access** Yes. **Wheelchair rental** No. **Baby-stroller rental**
No. **Lockers** No. **Pet kennels** No. **Rain check** No. **Private tours** Yes.

DESCRIPTION AND COMMENTS A fond memory from our own childhoods,
Travel Town is now enchanting a new generation of young train lovers,
who can climb into old engines, scramble through cabooses, and ride a
miniature train around the park. Our Thomas-obsessed nephew wants
to come here every weekend. It's basically just a bunch of old train cars
and engines, but that's enough for fun.

Universal CityWalk

APPEAL BY AGE	PRESCHOOL ★★	GRADE SCHOOL ★★★★	TEENS ★★★★★
YOUNG ADULTS ★★★★		OVER 30 ★★★	SENIORS ★★★

100 Universal City Plaza, Universal City; ☎ 818-622-4455;
www.citywalkhollywood.com

Hours Sunday–Thursday, 11 a.m.–9 p.m.; Friday and Saturday, 11 a.m.–11 p.m. **Admission** Free; self-parking, $7; valet parking with validated ticket from any CityWalk vendor, $4–$12. **Touring time** Average 2 hours; minimum 1 hour. **Rainy-day touring** So-so; mall area is outdoors. **Restaurants** Yes. **Alcoholic beverages** Yes. **Disabled access** Yes. **Wheelchair rental** Yes. **Baby-stroller rental** No. **Lockers** No. **Pet kennels** No. **Rain check** No. **Private tours** No.

DESCRIPTION AND COMMENTS   Universal CityWalk aggressively courts the family (and date-night) market, and judging by the size of the crowds, it is succeeding beautifully. In addition to the movie theaters, magic club, B. B. King's Blues Club, restaurants, and shops, there's an IMAX theater, a NASCAR virtual-racing experience, a rock 'n' roll bowling alley, a bunch more restaurants, and even more of the CityWalk shops that sell such quintessential inessentials as windup toys, nostalgic clothing, science fiction memorabilia, magic tricks, and hair-braiding accessories. The entire place is as phony as a three-dollar bill (there's no actual city here), and it's shamelessly shallow, materialistic, and deafeningly loud, but there's no denying that it's fun. You'll have to pry teenagers out of here with a crowbar.

 Universal Studios Hollywood

APPEAL BY AGE	PRESCHOOL ★	GRADE SCHOOL ★★★★	TEENS ★★★★★
YOUNG ADULTS ★★★★		OVER 30 ★★★★	SENIORS ★★★★

(See map on pages 166–167)

100 Universal City Plaza, Universal City; ☎ 800-UNIVERSAL**; www.universalstudios.com/unicity2**

Hours Mid-April–September, 9 a.m.–8 p.m. (box office: 8:30 a.m.–4 p.m.); October–March, 10 a.m.–6 p.m. **Admission** $49 adults, $40 seniors age 60 and older, $39 children under 48" tall; parking $8 general, $15 preferred. **Touring time** Average 8 hours; minimum 4 hours. **Rainy-day touring** Not great, but the rain thins crowds. **Restaurants** Yes. **Alcoholic beverages** Yes. **Disabled access** Yes. **Wheelchair rental** Yes. **Baby-stroller rental** Yes. **Lockers** Yes. **Pet kennels** Yes. **Rain check** Yes. **Private tours** Yes.

DESCRIPTION AND COMMENTS   If your children are younger than age 8, you might want to postpone a trip here—it costs a fortune to get in, and the money is mostly wasted on the very young, for whom most of the special-effects rides are too scary. Although attractions for younger kids have been added, little kids are too young to be impressed by the behind-the-scenes moviemaking aspect of the park, the main point of the place.

That said, a trip to Universal Studios can be a tremendously enjoyable day for the right group, especially older elementary-school kids, teenagers, and adults who haven't experienced it before. Although sometimes hokey, the one-hour, often-updated tram ride is essential for first-timers, both for its backlot peek at sets from many popular movies and TV shows and for its thrills—the parting of the Red Sea isn't as cool as it used to be, but the simulated earthquake is impressively realistic (and scary for Angelenos!), and the *War of the Worlds* set is astonishing. As for the rides, most of their thrills come from special effects, not roller-coaster speed—although the Revenge of the Mummy indoor roller coaster is both fast and scary—and those thrills are remarkable. Back to the Future and Jurassic Park are amazing feats of movie-ride technology, not to mention big fun. Backdraft—not a ride, really, but a close-up view of special effects used in that firefighting movie—is also breathtaking, but if you take a fearful kid on this one, you'll be sorry. Instead, head for *Hollywood Animal Actors* or the Nickelodeon interactive playground.

We recently brought a pack of elementary-school boys here, and what they really remembered wasn't the rides but the spectacular *Waterworld* show. What flopped on the screen is great fun on an outdoor stage—stuntmen and stuntwomen in fabulous rags fighting on Jet Skis and diving from towers. In fact, any show is worth a look, because the studio connection attracts talented producers and performers. Also, the *Shrek 4–D* film is a gas.

The Watts Towers of Simon Rodia State Historic Park

APPEAL BY AGE	PRESCHOOL ★	GRADE SCHOOL ★★★★	TEENS ★★★★
YOUNG ADULTS ★★★★		OVER 30 ★★★★	SENIORS ★★★★

1727 East 107th Street, L.A.; ☎ 213-847-4646, (Arts Center); www.trywatts.com

Hours Guided tours every half hour: Tuesday–Friday, 11 a.m.–2:30 p.m.; Saturday, 10:30 a.m.–2:30 p.m.; Sunday, 12:30–3 p.m. **Admission** $2 adults, free for children with paying adult. **Touring time** Average 1 hour. **Rainy-day touring** None. **Restaurants** No. **Alcoholic beverages** No. **Disabled access** Yes. **Wheelchair rental** No. **Baby-stroller rental** No. **Lockers** No. **Pet kennels** No. **Rain check** No. **Private tours** No.

DESCRIPTION AND COMMENTS After years of being closed for repairing and reinforcing after the 1994 Northridge earthquake, the Watts Towers are reopened, and we have been reminded of what a treasure they are. In the early 1920s, an illiterate Italian tile-factory worker named Simon Rodia bought an odd-shaped lot in Watts, south of downtown Los Angeles, and spent every free moment of the next 33 years creating his own fantasyland of folk art. This is art that speaks to children—so much so that we'd advise not bringing toddlers and preschoolers, because they'll want to touch it all, and in the interest of preservation, touching is not allowed. Embedded in the concrete towers, walls, benches, fountains, and floor is a colorful, fanciful panoply of objects Rodia found at the factory and the nearby train tracks: broken tile, glass, bottles, teapots, ceramic animals, and such. The towers can be seen up close only with a guided tour, but be glad for that, because the guide's stories

universal studios hollywood

Lower Lot

Stairway/Escalator

Entrance

Ticket Booths

0   .03 mi
0   .03 km

1. Back to the Future
2. *Backdraft*
3. *Fear Factor Live*
4. *Hollywood Animal Actors*

5. Jurassic Park: The Ride
6. Lucy: A Tribute
7. Nickelodeon Blast Zone
8. Revenge of the Mummy

9. *Shrek 4-D*
10. Special Effects Stages
11. Studio Tour

12. *Terminator 2: 3-D*
13. Van Helsing Fortress Dracula
14. *Waterworld*

add much to the experience, especially for kids. After your visit, your kids will be sure to want to create some towers or folk art of their own.

FAMILY-FRIENDLY RESTAURANTS

Daily Grill
Beverly Connection, 100 North La Cienega Boulevard, L.A.;
☎ **310-659-3100; www.dailygrill.com**

Meals served Lunch, dinner, and Sunday brunch. **Cuisine** American. **Entree range** Lunch, $9–$13; dinner, $10–$21. **Kids' menu** Yes. **Reservations** Not necessary. **Payment** All major credit cards.

This spin-off of Beverly Hills's swank The Grill is popular with families catching a movie or shopping at the Beverly Connection or the looming Beverly Center across the street. It's a yuppie copy of an old New York or San Francisco bar and grill, with tile floors, wooden booths, chicken potpie, and turkey meat loaf. Our kids adore the food, and they can color on the paper tablecloths. More branches at Universal CityWalk and on Ventura and Laurel Canyon in Studio City.

 El Cholo

1121 South Western Avenue, Mid-Wilshire; ☎ **323-734-2773; www.elcholo.com**

Meals served Lunch and dinner. **Cuisine** Mexican. **Entree range** $8–$20. **Kids' menu** Yes. **Reservations** Recommended. **Payment** All major credit cards.

Since 1921, El Cholo has been home to the city's best margaritas and green-corn tamales—and the enchiladas, chiles rellenos, taco tray, carnitas, and guacamole are pretty swell, too. A multiethnic cross-section of L.A. folk fills the maze of painted, tiled adobe-style dining rooms, served by waitresses in flouncy costumes. The children's menu has a burger, but they're better off with the junior quesadilla or enchilada. The location is midway between downtown and the La Brea Tar Pits.

Empress Pavilion
988 North Hill Street, Chinatown; ☎ **213-617-9898**

Meals served Breakfast (dim sum), lunch, and dinner. **Cuisine** Chinese. **Entree range** Dim sum plates, $2–$6; dinner, $7–$15. **Kids' menu** No. **Reservations** Accepted for dinner only. **Payment** DC, MC, V.

The problem with visiting the best dim sum restaurant in Chinatown is that everyone in L.A. knows it's the best dim sum restaurant, so the wait is an hour long by noon on weekends, and the good stuff is gone by 12:30 p.m. So arrive at this Chinatown mini-mall by 10:30 a.m. on weekends to share with your kids the spectacle of a vast, teeming dining room being serviced by surly women pushing metal steam carts of superb dumplings and buns of every possible description (ask for *bao* buns, pot stickers, and *sui mai*, which are the most agreeable to children). Come nighttime, the dim sum vanishes and some very good Cantonese cooking takes over, from excellent seafood to Peking duck.

Fabiolus Cafe
6270 Sunset Boulevard, Hollywood; ☎ 323-467-2882; 5255 Melrose Avenue; ☎ 323-464-5857

Meals served Daily, lunch and dinner. **Cuisine** Italian. **Entree range** $10–$21. **Kids' menu** No. **Reservations** Not necessary. **Payment** All major credit cards.

If you're doing the Tinseltown tourist thing and don't want to eat at the Hollywood & Highland mall, head over to these friendly, inexpensive trattorias, one a few doors east of the ArcLight and Cinerama Dome, the other next to Paramount Pictures. The pastas and salads are delicious, the setting is casual, and though there's no children's menu, the kitchen is happy to make a plain pasta or pizza.

Farmer's Market

6333 West Third Street, L.A.; ☎ 323-933-9211;
www.farmersmarketla.com

Meals served Breakfast, lunch, and early dinner. **Cuisine** Variety. **Entree range** $8–$14. **Kids' menu** Yes, at some stands. **Reservations** Not accepted. **Payment** Varies by stand.

One of the city's great meeting spots and melting pots, Farmer's Market is beloved of senior citizens and children alike. Area retirees meet to chat, nosh, play cards, and shop for high-quality produce, meat, seafood, and specialty foods; children love to cruise the open-air merchants, looking for candy vendors and seeking kid paradise: Bob's, home of the best doughnuts in town. Come early to snag a good table strategically located between the most interesting food vendors, so everyone can get what they want—a slice of pizza for one, a corned-beef sandwich for another, a bowl of gumbo for another. Next door to Farmer's Market is the Grove, a luxe shopping center with serene restaurants and a trolley that kids adore.

House of Blues
8430 Sunset Boulevard, West Hollywood; ☎ 323-848-5136;
www.hob.com

Meals served Dinner, Sunday brunch. **Cuisine** American/Southern. **Entree range** Brunch $40 for adults (senior discount), $18.50 for children ages 5–12, free for children age 4 and under. **Reservations** Essential. **Payment** All major credit cards.

Not too many families come to this music club for dinner, though if you're bringing teens to a concert, it can be fun. But the whole family will love the Sunday Gospel Brunch—and, in fact, you'll see tables filled with families, from great-grandmas down to preschoolers. The Southern cooking—fruit salads, homemade waffles, biscuits and gravy, Cheddar cheese grits, fried chicken, peach cobbler—is served as an all-you-can-eat buffet, and the gospel acts are foot-stompin,' spirit-liftin,' world-class performers. Dress nicely—it's Sunday, after all—and be prepared for a Sunday brunch you'll never forget.

Johnny Rockets
7507 Melrose Avenue, L.A.; ☎ 323-651-3361; www.johnnyrockets.com

Meals served Lunch and dinner (open late). **Cuisine** American. **Entree range** $6–$9. **Kids' menu** $4–$7. **Reservations** Not accepted. **Payment** All major credit cards.

Melrose isn't quite as hip as it once was, but teens will still find it worth a gander, and this slick, rather overpriced chain is well located in the heart of the action. Basic burgers, fries, and shakes are served in a blindingly lit red-and-white diner to a sound track of rock oldies. There are several branches, including on the Third Street Promenade and in Old Pasadena.

La Fonda de los Camperos
2501 Wilshire Boulevard, Mid-Wilshire; ☎ 213-380-5055

Meals served Dinner. **Cuisine** Mexican. **Entree range** $12–$17. **Kids' menu** No. **Reservations** Strongly recommended. **Payment** All major credit cards.

One of the city's greatest cultural treasures is Los Camperos, the mariachi group that is resident at this long-established supper club. The music is authentic, moving, memorable, and loud enough (seven or eight musicians include several brass players) to get the attention of even jaded teens. (One 16-year-old boy removed his headset, and the next day mentioned, without prompting, that the music was "good, huh?") Every table holds an office party group, a birthday celebration, or a group of tourists, and the mariachis oblige with "Happy Birthday" in French and Japanese. But remember, you're seeing the real thing. And the food ain't bad, either. Remarkably priced for the experience, too.

Pink's
709 North La Brea Avenue, L.A.; ☎ 323-931-4223; www.pinkshollywood.com

Meals served Lunch and dinner. **Cuisine** Hot dogs, turkey dogs, turkey burgers. **Entree range** $2–$6. **Kids' menu** No. **Reservations** Not accepted. **Payment** No credit cards.

A Hollywood landmark, this roadside stand is considered by many to serve the best chili dog in town. Kids can get plain dogs, of course, and sloppy burgers as well. Be warned that the chili is likely to wreak havoc on your stomach, though you'll be loving it while it's going down. The clientele can get bizarre in the wee hours. Long lines at prime times.

Poquito Más

3701 Cahuenga Boulevard West, Studio City; ☎ **818-760-8226;**
www.poquitomas.com

Meals served Lunch and dinner. **Cuisine** Mexican. **Entree range** $3–$9. **Kids'**
menu $4. **Reservations** Not accepted. **Payment** AE, D, V.

For a taste of what Angelenos really eat, skip the tourist traps in Universal
City and travel a mile or so to this strip-mall joint. You order at the counter
and sit on plastic tables in the parking lot, and you're as likely to see a star
here as in the studio. The *carnitas* (juicy pork) are among the best in town,
the fish tacos are delicious, and the burritos are generous. You can also get
takeout to eat in your hotel up the hill.

Wolfgang Puck Cafe
Universal CityWalk, 1000 Universal Center Drive, Universal City;
☎ **818-985-9653; www.wolfgangpuck.com**

Meals served Lunch and dinner. **Cuisine** Californian. **Entree range** $10–$21.
Kids' menu Yes. **Reservations** Not accepted. **Payment** All major credit cards.

You have to reserve three months ahead and spend a car payment to have
dinner at Wolfgang Puck's flagship Spago in Beverly Hills, but at this colorful,
loud cafe, you can put your name in, browse CityWalk for awhile, then enjoy
affordable modern American boomer food: duck sausage pizzas, baby-green
salads, homey desserts. Kids get a fine coloring menu of their own.

WHERE *to* FIND *the*
REAL HOLLYWOOD

THE GLAMOUR IS COMING BACK to landmarks of the movie business, as studios and vintage movie theaters in Los Angeles are restored
and renovated and proud owners show them off to the public. Just
remember that visiting Hollywood doesn't mean simply exploring the
not-very-interesting neighborhood of that name, but rather
wandering through working studios (there are now four different tours), TV-
show tapings, museums, and restored movie palaces throughout the
city. Most tours and tapings have age restrictions, but the younger kids
won't appreciate those experiences anyway. Even if they're not movie-
mad, however, most junior-high kids and older kids have seen and
heard enough about show business to enjoy a look behind the scenes.
And don't forget, Universal Studios is a real studio as well as a theme
park, and its backlot tram tour often features a glimpse of moviemaking in progress.
    Please note that security measures have tightened at the studios.
Video cameras, large bags, and weapons of any type (such as pocket

knives) are not allowed. Be prepared to be checked by a metal detector and have your belongings inspected.

ARCLIGHT CINEMAS 6360 West Sunset Boulevard, Hollywood; ☎ 323-464-1478; **www.arclightcinemas.com.** Including and encompassing the historic Cinerama Dome theater, the ArcLight is L.A.'s premier movie-watching venue and is a great place to take older kids. You pay more for the tickets, but you get reserved seats, real ushers, no commercials, an audience that doesn't talk, a chic cafe and bar, and state-of-the-art theaters. The gift shop will enthrall hip teens. Note that this is also a great spot for spotting stars—but do what the locals do and let them watch their movie in peace. The massive used-and-new-record store across the street, **Amoeba,** is teen heaven.

AUDIENCES UNLIMITED For free tickets to tapings, call ☎ 818-753-3470, ext. 321, or go to **www.tvtickets.com** for show schedules, maps and directions, minimum age requirements, and other information. Peak taping season is August through March. Tickets are available for shows taped in Hollywood, Burbank, Culver City, and Universal City–North Hollywood.

HOLLYWOOD BOULEVARD MOVIE PALACES: EGYPTIAN THEATRE, MANN'S CHINESE THEATER, EL CAPITAN THEATRE Three restored movie-palace jewels adorn the crown of Hollywood Boulevard (a fourth is the legit house, the **Pantages Theater**) and allow visitors to really understand what the hoopla was all about in the 1930s and 1940s, when these theaters were the scene of grand premieres. Begin at the **Egyptian Theatre** (6712 Hollywood Boulevard, Hollywood; ☎ 323-466-FILM; **www.egyptiantheatre.com**), which offers several daily screenings of a one-hour film ($5 to $7). A compilation of golden-age documentaries, classic movie clips, and interviews with current Hollywood celebrities, this movie is the perfect way to give your kids some background before they look at the footprints in the court of **Mann's Chinese Theater** (6925 Hollywood Boulevard, Hollywood; ☎ 323-464-8111). Most of the stars who've left their marks here will otherwise be unfamiliar to your kids. Surrounding the Chinese is the new Hollywood & Highland center, which includes the **Kodak Theatre,** home of the Academy Awards. If you have younger kids, their Hollywood highlight will be the **El Capitan Theatre** (6838 Hollywood Boulevard, Hollywood; ☎ 323-467-7674; **www.elcapitantickets.com**), gloriously renovated in a joint venture with Disney, and the location of premiere showings of the latest Disney releases, complete with glittering curtains and spotlights, special stage shows, and sometimes souvenirs, interactive exhibits, and other extras.

unofficial **TIP**
Studio representatives often pass out free tickets to TV-show tapings at Mann's Chinese Theatre, so you might keep your itinerary flexible in case something appeals to your group.

HOLLYWOOD WALK OF FAME On Hollywood Boulevard between Gower and La Brea and on Vine from Yucca to Sunset Boulevard;

☎ 323-469-8311 (Hollywood Chamber of Commerce). Just ignore the **Movieland Wax Museum** (unless you're way into kitsch), **Ripley's Believe It or Not!,** and the **Hollywood Entertainment Museum** (a so-far-unsuccessful attempt at a showbiz museum) as you walk along, reading the names on the stars embedded in the sidewalk.

MUSEUM OF RADIO AND TELEVISION 465 North Beverly Drive, Beverly Hills; ☎ 310-786-1025; **www.mtr.org;** Wednesday through Sunday, noon to 5 p.m.; free admission with suggested donation; $10 adults, $8 students, $5 children age 13 and under. Another good pre–Chinese Theater stop is this museum, where you can view a tape of the classic *I Love Lucy* in which Lucille Ball visits the Chinese Theater and gets her foot stuck in a bucket of wet (quick-drying) cement. This small, ultramodern facility is heavily supported by the industry, because it's really an archive that collects and preserves tapes of radio and TV shows, many of which had been previously preserved only by individuals. Your visit can include an hour in the screening room to see a scheduled show of select TV clips, 20 minutes in the living room–like "radio listening room" with headsets and access to a vintage radio show, and a visit to the TV library. In the library, visitors select footage choices from the museum's computer database, then move to private consoles to view their choice of vintage or historic TV clips (ranging from episodes of *Welcome Back, Kotter* to moonwalk footage).

NBC STUDIO TOUR 3000 West Alameda Avenue, Burbank; ☎ 818-840-3537; tours leave weekdays 9 a.m. to 3 p.m.; $7 adults, $6 seniors age 60 and older, $4 children ages 6 to 12, free for children age 5 and younger. This isn't a big movie studio with entire streets built as sets, but rather an indoor TV taping facility with several separate stages, including the one where *The Tonight Show* has been filmed for decades. It isn't glitzy, but the tour is geared for kids, and the studio's real—we walked past "hot" prop tables, coiled cables, and "live" sets. The 70-minute walking tour includes a video, an NBC sports presentation, and a look at wardrobe, makeup, and set construction.

SILENT MOVIE THEATER 611 North Fairfax Avenue; ☎ 323-655-2520; **www.silentmovietheater.com;** prices vary according to shows. This unique theater is adored by locals for its lovely presentation of pristine prints of the classics. It's a tiny theater, showing movies primarily on weekends (evenings and matinees), with personal touches that make attending a movie here as old-fashioned an experience as the Charlie Chaplin, Mary Pickford, and Laurel and Hardy movies (among many others) it screens.

SONY PICTURES ENTERTAINMENT STUDIO TOUR 10202 West Washington Boulevard, Culver City; ☎ 323-520-TOUR; **sonypicturesstudios.com;** $25 per person; several departures a day, weekdays only; no children under age 12 permitted. The former MGM Studios was once the most glamorous of all the movie lots, and Sony has worked hard to restore the Art Deco and age-old buildings (there are some 1920s-era window-walled buildings that are among the earliest movie industry buildings anywhere). The two-hour walking tour weaves in and out of sound-stages and onto some working sets as the workers go about their jobs. Highlights include a stroll through wardrobe and a peek at artists at work in a backdrop studio with a seven-story-high canvas in front of them. The tour begins with a video and ends on a street of picturesque facades, where participants can get an ice-cream cone and shop in the studio store. Call **Audiences Unlimited** (☎ 818-753-3470; **www .audiencesunlimited.com**) to attend a taping at Sony or nearby Culver Studios to coincide with your tour day.

 WARNER BROS. STUDIOS VIP TOUR 3400 Riverside Drive (park at Gate 6), Burbank; ☎ 818-846-1403; **wbsf.warnerbros.com;** $42 per person, children under age 8 not permitted). Group tours of this famous lot are held Monday through Friday, 8:30 a.m. to 4 p.m., with extended hours in the summer and fall; reservations are required. It's not cheap, but you will get an insider's look at a working studio—and unlike at Sony, kids between ages 8 and 12 are welcome. No more than 12 people spend two and a half hours wandering through sound-stages, past historic dressing rooms and offices, onto the set of a current TV show, and through working studio areas. Part of the trip will be via golf cart, and part on foot. Time your visit so you can have lunch before or after at the Studio Plaza cafe, where many Warner employees eat.

SIDE TRIPS

Raging Waters

APPEAL BY AGE	PRESCHOOL ★★	GRADE SCHOOL ★★★★	TEENS ★★★★★
YOUNG ADULTS ★★★		OVER 30 ★★	SENIORS ★

111 Raging Waters Drive (off 210 Freeway), San Dimas; ☎ 909-802-2200; www.ragingwaters.com

Hours Late April–May: Saturday and Sunday, 10 a.m.–6 p.m.; June and September: Monday–Friday, 10 a.m.–6 p.m.; Saturday and Sunday, 10 a.m.–7 p.m.; July: Monday–Friday, 10 a.m.–8 p.m.; Saturday and Sunday, 9:30 a.m.–9 p.m.; August: Monday–Friday, 10 a.m.–9 p.m.; Saturday and Sunday, 9:30 a.m.–9 p.m.; hours vary daily, so call first; park closes at end of September. **Admission** By height: over 48" tall $32; under 48" tall $17; under age 2, free. **Touring time** Average 6 hours; minimum 2 hours. **Rainy-day touring** No. **Restaurants** Yes. **Alcoholic beverages** No. **Disabled access** Yes. **Wheelchair rental** No. **Baby-stroller rental** No. **Lockers** Yes. **Pet kennels** No. **Rain check** Half-price coupon for another visit. **Private tours** No.

DESCRIPTION AND COMMENTS Raging Waters is worth a side trip to hot-and-smoggy San Dimas if you have preteens and teens and the weather's hot. (It's a solid 45-minute drive from the Westside and 20 minutes from Pasadena.) Plan on an all-day excursion, and be prepared for crowds. If your kids are younger, there's plenty for them to enjoy, but the real target audience is anyone crazy enough to slide down steep, slick waterslides. Tickets are sold in advance, so call ahead to make sure the park hasn't been bought out before you arrive.

Six Flags Hurricane Harbor Water Park

APPEAL BY AGE	PRESCHOOL ★★★★★	GRADE SCHOOL ★★★★★	TEENS ★★★★
YOUNG ADULTS ★★★★		OVER 30 ★★	SENIORS ★★

Magic Mountain Parkway (off I-5), Valencia; ☎ 661-255-4100; www.sixflags.com

Hours Weekdays, 10 a.m.–6 p.m.; weekends, 10 a.m.–8 p.m.; hours vary tremendously by season, so call or visit Web site first. **Admission** Adults $30; children under 48" tall $21; children age 2 and under free; online discount offered; combo tickets, $70 for both Hurricane Harbor and Magic Mountain; parking $15. **Touring time** Average 4–6 hours; minimum 2 hours. **Rainy-day touring** Not good. **Restaurants** Yes. **Alcoholic beverages** No. **Disabled access** Yes, but no assisted slides. **Wheelchair rental** Yes. **Baby-stroller rental** Yes. **Lockers** Yes. **Pet kennels** Yes. **Rain check** No. **Private tours** No.

DESCRIPTION AND COMMENTS This water park is so much fun in the summer that we recommend it over Magic Mountain (next door and more expensive), unless you have roller-coaster–loving teens. And even then, why not let the older kids do Magic Mountain by themselves, while you relax on a chaise lounge and the younger kids either play at Castaway Cove, a toddler wading area; ride tubes around an island; roll with the waves in a giant cement sea; or hit the waterslides. Older kids and teens love Lizard Lagoon, where they can play water basketball and volleyball, and the thrill slides, like the 75-foot-high Tornado. It's not as crowded as Magic Mountain, either, and the tropical jungle theme is played out in nice landscaping. Note that swimwear with metal ornamentation or rivets is not allowed on some rides. Valencia is located north of L.A., about a half-hour drive from downtown or 45 minutes from Santa Monica (much longer at rush hour).

Six Flags Magic Mountain

APPEAL BY AGE	PRESCHOOL ★★	GRADE SCHOOL ★★★★	TEENS ★★★★★
YOUNG ADULTS ★★★★		OVER 30 ★★★	SENIORS ★

26101 Magic Mountain Parkway (off I-5), Valencia; ☎ 661-255-4100; www.sixflags.com

Hours Mid-spring–late fall: daily, open 10 a.m.; closing times vary with season and weather; rest of year, open 11 a.m. **Admission** Adults $60; children under 48" tall $30; children age 2 and under free; significant online discount; combo tickets, $57 for both Hurricane Harbor and Magic Mountain; parking $15. **Touring time** Average 5 hours; minimum 3 hours. **Rainy-day touring** No. **Restaurants** Yes.

Alcoholic beverages No. **Disabled access** Yes. **Wheelchair rental** Yes. **Baby-stroller rental** Yes. **Lockers** Yes. **Pet kennels** Yes. **Rain check** In some instances. **Private tours** No.

DESCRIPTION AND COMMENTS This cornucopia of hyper-intense roller coasters (it seems as if a new one opens every year) is heaven for teens and thrill-mad preteens, but it could be hell for younger ones. They do, however, get their own smaller-thrill area, with such Looney Tunes–inspired kiddie rides as Elmer's Weather Balloons and Foghorn Leghorn's Railway. But the real reason to come here is for the white-knuckle, stomach-flipping thrill rides, our 14-year-old's reason for living. From Superman The Escape (which accelerates to 100 mph in seven seconds) to the wonderful Colossus (the tallest, fastest wooden roller coaster in the West), these rides are designed to make you scream. Valencia is located north of L.A., about a half-hour drive from downtown, or 45 minutes from Santa Monica (much longer at evening rush hour).

PASADENA

THE LITTLE OLD LADY FROM PASADENA ISN'T MUCH in evidence anymore—these days, **Pasadena** is packed with families, both ones who live on its stately old tree-lined streets and ones who are visiting this L.A. satellite city, just ten minutes north of downtown. Over the last 15 years, formerly seedy **Old Pasadena** has become one of the hottest outdoor mall-restaurant-nightlife areas in Southern California, beloved by SUV-driving moms and tattooed teens alike—and now you can take the MTA's Gold Line from downtown L.A. to Old Pasadena.

unofficial **TIP**
With its family-friendly destinations and proximity to downtown L.A. and Universal City, Pasadena is a fine vacation base, particularly in the winter, when being by the beach isn't so appealing.

On weekends, street musicians, balloon-animal makers, and magicians amuse passersby; in summer don't miss the nightly free concerts at **Levitt Pavilion** in Memorial Park on the edge of Old Town (☎ 626-683-3230); Wednesday nights are aimed at children, but all concerts are family friendly. Also in summer are Friday- and Saturday-night free outdoor movie screenings or concerts in **One Colorado**'s courtyard; all are fun for families. Elsewhere in Old Town are a movie-theater complex, teen-haven stores, candy and frozen-yogurt shops, a **Barnes & Noble** with a children's area, excellent restaurants, and a plaza with climb-on-me sculptures. About a mile east on Colorado is a stylish outdoor mall, **Paseo Colorado,** with the requisite multiplex and hip chain restaurants; it's where Pasadena's middle-school set hangs out. If we have a spare weekend hour, we take our kids to **Vroman's Bookstore** (695 East Colorado Boulevard; ☎ 626-449-5320), one of the great independent booksellers, with a wonderful children's section and first-rate storytelling programs.

Elsewhere in town are a bounty of museums and parks, the most family friendly of which are listed below; see also **Lacy Park** under "The Best Beaches and Parks" and **Eaton Canyon** under "Hiking" in "Outdoor Family Adventures." And see the Calendar of Events to learn about the town's famous parades: the **Rose Parade,** the **Rosebud Parade,** and the **Doo Dah Parade.**

pasadena

FAMILY LODGING
1. Ritz-Carlton, Huntington Hotel and Spa
2. Westin Pasadena

ATTRACTIONS
3. The Huntington Library, Art Collections, and Botanical Gardens
4. Kidspace

FAMILY-FRIENDLY RESTAURANTS
5. Fair Oaks Pharmacy and Soda Fountain
6. Il Fornaio

FAMILY LODGING

☀ Ritz-Carlton, Huntington Hotel & Spa

1401 South Oak Knoll Avenue, Pasadena; ☎ 626-568-3900 or 800-241-3333; www.ritzcarlton.com/hotels/huntington; $229–$579 and up

A grand, gorgeous, and historic hotel from Pasadena's early days as a posh winter resort, the Huntington is a pretty formal place, but it's still welcoming to children. The pool is beautiful, the poolside restaurant has a children's menu, and the pastry chef offers baking classes for kids. As with all Pasadena hotels, it books up months before the Rose Parade.

Westin Pasadena

191 North Los Robles Avenue, Pasadena; ☎ 626-792-2727 or 888-625-5144; www.starwoodhotels.com; $199–$275

This pleasant, modern hotel is well located for visitors, near Paseo Colorado (shops, theaters, restaurants), the Pasadena Playhouse, and Vroman's Bookstore; Old Town and its Gold Line subway station are just a few blocks away. There's no kids' program, but there's a rooftop pool, a children's menu in the restaurant, a California Pizza Kitchen next door, ticket packages for Universal Studios, and a wonderful plaza outside, full of waterways and little fountains that kids love to explore.

ATTRACTIONS

☀ The Huntington Library, Art Collections, and Botanical Gardens

| APPEAL BY AGE | PRESCHOOL ★★★ | | GRADE SCHOOL ★★★ | TEENS ★★★ |
| YOUNG ADULTS ★★★★ | | OVER 30 ★★★★★ | | SENIORS ★★★★★ |

1151 Oxford Road, San Marino; ☎ 626-405-2100; www.huntington.org

Hours September–May: Tuesday–Friday, noon–4:30 p.m.; Saturday and Sunday, 10:30 a.m.–4:30 p.m.; June–August: Tuesday–Sunday, 10:30 a.m.–4:30 p.m.; closed major holidays. **Admission** $15 adults, $12 seniors, $10 students ages 12–18 (with full-time student ID), $6 children ages 5–11, free for children age 5 and under; groups of 15 or more $11 each; free first Thursday of month; no picnics allowed. **Touring time** Average 2 hours; minimum 1 hour. **Rainy-day touring** Yes, but you'll get wet. **Restaurants** Cafe, tearoom. **Alcoholic beverages** No. **Disabled access** Yes. **Wheelchair rental** Free, reserve. **Baby-stroller rental** No. **Lockers** Yes. **Pet kennels** No. **Rain check** No. **Private tours** Arranged for mornings.

DESCRIPTION AND COMMENTS An internationally famed treasure found in sleepy San Marino, a wealthy suburb just south of Pasadena, this cultural center has appeal to both preschoolers and teenagers. The little ones love to run through the extraordinary gardens: world-class roses, a desert garden, a Zen garden, a jungle garden, and, most of all, the extraordinary Children's Garden, an interactive experience designed for children ages 2 to 7. They can walk under a rainbow, disappear into a sea of fog, make music with pebbles, and more. The new Conservatory for Botanical Science has hands-on exhibits that appeal to all ages, including the Carnivorous Plant Bog (cool!) and the Field Lab. Older children, especially bookworms, will be wowed by some of the venerable books in the library, including a Gutenberg Bible and first editions of Shakespeare. In-between kids will have fun searching for Gainsborough's *Blue Boy* in the art gallery. The beautiful Rose Garden Tea Room is a wonderful place to celebrate a birthday or occasion; the Café is more informal and inexpensive.

 Kidspace

APPEAL BY AGE	PRESCHOOL ★★★★★		GRADE SCHOOL ★★★★★	TEENS ★★
YOUNG ADULTS ★★		OVER 30 ★★★		SENIORS ★★★

480 North Arroyo Boulevard; ☎ 626-449-9144;
www.kidspacemuseum.org

Hours Daily 9:30 a.m.–5 p.m.; closed major holidays. **Admission** $8; free for age 1 and under. **Touring time** Average 3 hours; minimum 1 hour. **Rainy-day touring** Yes, for the indoor activities. **Restaurants** Yes. **Alcoholic beverages** Yes. **Disabled access** Yes. **Wheelchair rental** No. **Baby-stroller rental** No, strollers not allowed. **Lockers** No. **Pet kennels** No. **Rain check** No. **Private tours** No.

DESCRIPTION AND COMMENTS Once a modest play place in a borrowed space, Kidspace is now one of the finest interactive children's museums in the West, and it's worth a detour. In Brookside Park near the Rose Bowl, it pays tribute to the site's original tenant, the Fannie Morrison Horticultural Center, by making the outdoors as much a part of the experience as the indoors. Shows and story times take place in the outdoor amphitheater, and gardens include the Bumpy Fuzzy Garden, Interpretive Arroyo (a scaled-down version of the Arroyo Seco, in which Kidspace sits), the Spider Web Climber, tricycle tracks, and much more. Indoors are a wonderful digging exhibit for budding paleontologists, an earthquake zone, the Bug Inn, climbing towers, and more. Coming in 2007 is a large new building that will house everything from a robotics lab to a music-making space.

▌ FAMILY-FRIENDLY RESTAURANTS

Fair Oaks Pharmacy and Soda Fountain
1526 Mission Street, South Pasadena; ☎ 626-799-1414

Meals served Breakfast Saturday and Sunday, lunch daily. **Cuisine** American. **Entree range** $4–$8. **Kids' menu** No. **Reservations** Not accepted. **Payment** AE, MC, V.

A proper small-town pharmacy in the historic small town of South Pasadena, this place has a vintage 19th-century soda fountain complete with marble counter. You can get breakfast on the weekends; a simple, kid-pleasing lunch (hot dogs, grilled cheese) any day; and ice-cream concoctions in the afternoon. Fun gifts, too.

Il Fornaio
One Colorado Boulevard, Pasadena; ☎ 626-683-9797

Meals served Lunch, dinner and Sunday brunch. **Cuisine** Italian. **Entree range** $11–$24 **Kids' menu** Yes. **Reservations** Recommended. **Payment** All major credit cards.

Ideally located in the heart of Old Pasadena, Il Fornaio is on the upscale side, but it's welcoming to families, with an excellent children's menu, high chairs, and an outdoor terrace overlooking the One Colorado courtyard, home to summertime movie screenings and concerts. While the kids have Italian-style mac and cheese, you can enjoy a delicious seafood tagliolini or grilled salmon. If they get bored waiting for you to finish your Barbera, they can go outside to play on the *Working Man* sculpture.

THE MOUNTAINS:
Big Bear, Lake Arrowhead, and Idyllwild

LOCAL SKIING IS ONE OF THE GREAT LUXURIES of Southern California life. It means that residents can be enjoying a sunny day in their hometown, drive two hours "up the hill," and get in an afternoon of skiing. And the nearby ski resorts are especially nice for introducing kids to the sport. But these charming mountain retreats are equally appealing in the summer.

A popular weekend getaway for L.A. residents, **Big Bear** is less pretentious and easier for the casual visitor to negotiate, because the entire north shore of the lake is public land (so there's boat launching, bike trails, and picnic areas), and a combination of private and city concessions offers lake access on the southern side of the lake through a public swim beach, boat docks, and fishing sites. There are many modest vintage motels and cottages in Big Bear, as well as two conference resort hotels and some bed-and-breakfasts. It's also a ski center, five minutes from Southern California's largest ski mountain, **Snow Summit.**

Lakefront property in nearby **Lake Arrowhead,** on the other hand, is almost entirely in private hands, and unless you rent a house on the shoreline (not a bad option for a family), your only access to the lake is by boat, by staying at the **Lake Arrowhead Resort,** or in the shopping area known as the **Village.**

Meanwhile, **Idyllwild** is in another mountain range, about two hours from L.A. near **Palm Springs,** and it offers a much-less-trafficked locale for mountain hiking in the summer or snow play in the winter, weather permitting.

FAMILY LODGING

Grey Squirrel Resort
39372 Big Bear Boulevard, Big Bear; ☎ 909-866-4335; www.greysquirrel.com; $85 and up

Beloved of many L.A. families for weekend retreats, this cabin compound in the woods along Big Bear's main drag is an excellent value. Our favorite is the Raccoon Cabin, a 75-year-old, two-bedroom house with a stone fireplace.

the mountains: big bear, lake arrowhead, and idyllwild

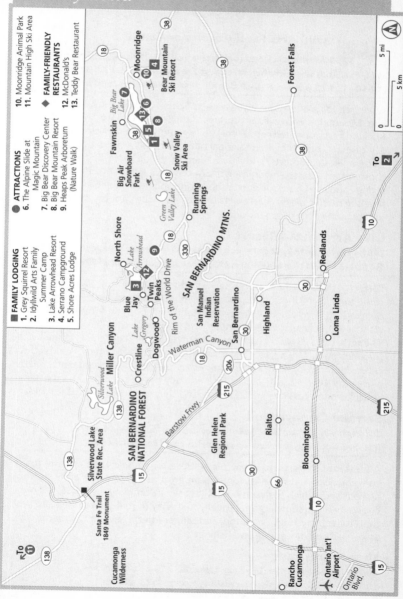

■ FAMILY LODGING
1. Grey Squirrel Resort
2. Idyllwild Arts Family Summer Camp
3. Lake Arrowhead Resort
4. Serrano Campground
5. Shore Acres Lodge

● ATTRACTIONS
6. The Alpine Slide at Magic Mountain
7. Big Bear Discovery Center
8. Big Bear Mountain Resort
9. Heaps Peak Arboretum (Nature Walk)
10. Moonridge Animal Park
11. Mountain High Ski Area

◆ FAMILY-FRIENDLY RESTAURANTS
12. McDonald's
13. Teddy Bear Restaurant

The ten cottages and two small motel units share outdoor barbecue facilities, a laundry area, and a heated pool. Even the family dog is welcome. This friendly, well-maintained place is a great base for hiking, sledding, and fishing down at the lake, a short walk away.

☀ Idyllwild Arts Family Summer Camp

52500 Temecula Road (off Highway 243), Idyllwild; ☎ 951-659-2171, ext. 365; www.idyllwildarts.org; 1-bedroom unit with 3 people: $1,650–$2,775 per week (includes all classes, activities, and meals)

When school is out at the Idyllwild Arts School in the cool, sleepy San Jacinto Mountains above Palm Springs, families move into the dorms for weeklong arts-oriented camp fun. While young children enjoy playtime and day care and older children take part in supervised swimming, crafts, theater games, art projects, and sports, parents divide their time among their choice of arts classes—everything from ceramics and dance to writing and acting—and such outdoor pursuits as hiking and mountain biking. Everyone sleeps in modern, new Pearson Hall, with private bathrooms and daily maid service, and all meals are included.

Lake Arrowhead Resort

27984 Highway 189, at entrance to Lake Arrowhead Village; ☎ 909-336-1511 or 800-800-6792; www.laresort.com; $109–$475

Perfectly sited if you're not a very outdoorsy family but want to spend some time in the mountains, the 177-room Lake Arrowhead Resort is part of lakefront Arrowhead Village, a collection of shops and restaurants. The views are spectacular in the summer and Christmas card–like in the winter. The resort has its own beach for swimming in the (cold) lake, as well as a (heated) pool. The adjacent marina offers watercraft rentals. A kids' club called Junior Mountaineers (campfire stories, fishing, arts and crafts, pizza party) for 4- to 12-year-olds is offered daily in the summer. The morning and afternoon sessions are $25 each, and they can be combined for $40.

Serrano Campground

Off Highway 38, Big Bear Lake; reservations ☎ 877-444-6777; Reserve America, www.reserveamerica.com; campsites $24

A pleasant campground in the pines, close to Big Bear Lake and the town conveniences, this national forest campground allows some of its sites to be reserved, which is always a good bet when camping with kids. It's only open when the snow is gone, usually mid-May to mid-September. Shower, flush toilets, fire rings, firewood, and ranger interpretive programs, as well as lake access for boating and fishing.

Shore Acres Lodge

40090 Lakeview Drive, Big Bear Lake; ☎ 909-866-8200 or 800-524-6600; www.shoreacreslodge.com; $135 and up (based on triple occupancy)

Not quite a motel, more a collection of housekeeping cabins, this lodge is well located on a quiet stretch of Big Bear Lake, and it offers good value without the hassle of working through a private-home rental agency. The choices include 11 cabins with kitchens, ranging from studio-size to a cabin that sleeps 12. All are near the shore, and some are directly on the lake. In the summer, the office also offers additional rental units in private homes. The lodge area has a playground, pool, Jacuzzi, and boat dock.

ATTRACTIONS

The Alpine Slide at Magic Mountain

APPEAL BY AGE	PRESCHOOL ★★	GRADE SCHOOL ★★★	TEENS ★★★
YOUNG ADULTS ★★		OVER 30 ★★	SENIORS ★

800 Wildrose Lane, Big Bear Lake; ☎ 909-866-4626; www.bigbear.com/activities/recreation/winter/slide

Hours *Alpine Slide:* summer, Sunday–Thursday, 10 a.m.–6 p.m.; Friday and Saturday, 10 a.m.–9 p.m.; fall: Saturday and Sunday, 10 a.m.–6 p.m.; Monday, 11 a.m.–4 p.m.; winter: Saturday and Sunday, 10 a.m.–dusk; Monday–Friday, 11 a.m.–4 p.m.; spring: Saturday and Sunday, 10 a.m.–5 p.m. *Waterslide:* mid-June–mid-September, daily, 10 a.m.–5 p.m. *Snow Play:* November–Easter: daily, 10 a.m.–4 p.m. **Admission** Single ride on Alpine Slide, $4; $18 Waterslide or Snow Play unlimited day pass; children age 6 and under ride free with adult; various ride packages available. **Touring time** Average 1 hour; minimum 20 minutes. **Rainy-day touring** No. **Restaurants** Snack bar. **Alcoholic beverages** No. **Disabled access** Yes. **Wheelchair rental** No. **Baby-stroller rental** No. **Lockers** No. **Pet kennels** No. **Rain check** No. **Private tours** No.

DESCRIPTION AND COMMENTS This modest family attraction has been the highlight of a couple of winter-spring weekends in Big Bear. There was enough snow left to slide ourselves into exhaustion on the inner tube slide, climbing up the small hill with giant inner tubes and flying right back down again (big kids can grab hold of a rope tow, but not the under-age-8 set, so we hoofed it). Then, since there wasn't too much snow, we had a ride on the curving, lugelike concrete slide, a little kid on our lap and the bigger kids steering their own, which was quite a thrill. Also open at various times are a go-cart track and waterslide. Go-cart rentals are $4 single, $5 double. Not for the very young.

Big Bear Discovery Center

APPEAL BY AGE	PRESCHOOL ★★	GRADE SCHOOL ★★★	TEENS ★★★
YOUNG ADULTS ★★★		OVER 30 ★★★	SENIORS ★★★

North Shore of Big Bear Lake on Highway 38 between Fawnskin and Stanfield Cutoff; ☎ 909-866-3437; www.bigbeardiscoverycenter.com

Hours Daily, 8 a.m.–6 p.m. (summer); closed Christmas and New Year's Day. **Admission** Free; some activities have fees or require a Park Service Adventure

Pass. **Touring time** Average 1–4 hours; minimum 15 minutes. **Rainy-day touring** Yes. **Restaurants** No. **Alcoholic beverages** No. **Disabled access** Yes, into center; varies with different programs. **Wheelchair rental** No. **Baby-stroller rental** No. **Lockers** No. **Pet kennels** No. **Rain check** No. **Private tours** Yes.

DESCRIPTION AND COMMENTS Big Bear Discovery Center is a wonderful environmental-education facility resulting from a partnership between the federal San Bernardino Forest and the San Bernardino National Forest Association, a private nonprofit organization. Because budget cuts decreased the number of forest rangers available to educate, guide, or entertain the public, the Discovery Center was created to take up the slack. More than 100 volunteers (among whom are two former Big Bear mayors and two former college presidents) staff the center's exhibits and displays seven days a week, and also develop and participate in programs such as campfire talks, interpretive hikes, and history tours. The Adventure Outpost store offers educational and nature-related merchandise.

After looking over the center's exhibits about local flora and fauna, families can sign up for activities like guided hikes, campfire programs with music and storytelling (fees vary, reservations required), or in the winter months, the center's Eagle Tours, which take participants by vans into bald eagle habitat areas closed to the general public.

 ## Big Bear Mountain Resorts

APPEAL BY AGE	PRESCHOOL ★★★	GRADE SCHOOL ★★★★	TEENS ★★★★
YOUNG ADULTS ★★★		OVER 30 ★★★	SENIORS ★★

880 Summit Boulevard (just south of Big Bear Village); ☎ 909-866-5766; www.snowsummit.com

Hours Weekdays, 8 a.m.–4:30 p.m.; weekends, 8 a.m.–6 p.m.; ski season is mid-November–mid-April; mountain biking and hiking available in off season. **Admission** Lift tickets: adults, $48–$55; kids ages 7–12, $15–$22; ages 13–21, $36–$55; free for age 6 and under. **Touring time** Average 1 day; minimum a half day. **Rainy-day touring** Depending on conditions; resort may close. **Restaurants** Yes. **Alcoholic beverages** Yes. **Disabled access** Yes. **Wheelchair rental** No. **Baby-stroller rental** No. **Lockers** Yes. **Pet kennels** No. **Rain check** Vouchers under certain conditions. **Private tours** Private lessons.

DESCRIPTION AND COMMENTS Two mountains, Snow Summit and Bear Mountain, are now under the same ownership, so one lift ticket will work at either mountain. If you have skilled snowboarding teenagers, they'll want to go to Bear Mountain, which is full of rails, jumps, pipes, and other extreme action. Families with younger kids or beginning skiers or snowboarders will be more comfortable at Snow Summit, which has a fun, professionally staffed children's center and a good ski and snowboard school. If your 5-year-old gets wet and miserable and doesn't want to ski anymore, he can come inside, have some juice, and play with the toys. Both mountains have only a fraction of the runs that the major Sierra resorts have, and the snow is often man-made, but there's plenty to keep a skiing family happy for a two- to three-day trip. In summer, some of Snow Summit's runs become the turf of mountain bikers, often the same teens who were snowboarding here just a few months earlier.

Heaps Peak Arboretum (Nature Walk)

APPEAL BY AGE	PRESCHOOL ★★	GRADE SCHOOL ★★★	TEENS ★★
YOUNG ADULTS ★★		OVER 30 ★★★	SENIORS ★★★

Highway 18 (2 miles from Lake Arrowhead turnoff);
Ranger Station, ☎ 909-337-2444

Hours Daily, dawn–dusk. **Admission** Free, but Adventure Pass is necessary to park ($5 for day or $30 for year); purchase from Arrowhead Ranger Station off Highway 18 or vendors around Lake Arrowhead. **Touring time** Average 1½ hours; minimum 20 minutes to stretch. **Rainy-day touring** No. **Restaurants** No. **Alcoholic beverages** No. **Disabled access** Some trails limited. **Wheelchair rental** No. **Baby-stroller rental** No. **Lockers** No. **Pet kennels** No; pets not allowed on trail. **Rain check** No. **Private tours** Yes; call Ranger Station.

DESCRIPTION AND COMMENTS Located in an Arrowhead-adjacent site that makes a good first stop upon reaching the top of the mountain, this nature trail is a great place to walk after being in the car for a little too long. Your kids can stretch their legs and get acquainted with the forest on an easy one-mile loop that meanders through dogwood groves (blooming in May) and wildflower meadows, across a stream or two, and through pines and chaparral. The brochure that identifies various points to stop and learn a thing or two is geared beautifully to kids.

Moonridge Animal Park

APPEAL BY AGE	PRESCHOOL ★★★	GRADE SCHOOL ★★★	TEENS ★★
YOUNG ADULTS ★★★		OVER 30 ★★★	SENIORS ★★★

Near Bear Mountain Ski Resort, Moonridge Road to Clubview to
Goldmine Drive; ☎ 909-584-1171; www.moonridgezoo.org

Hours May–August: daily, 10 a.m.–5 p.m.; September–April: Monday–Friday, 10 a.m.–4 p.m.; Saturday and Sunday, 10 a.m.–5 p.m. (weather permitting). **Admission** $5 adults, $4 seniors and children ages 3–10, age 3 and under free. **Touring time** Average 1–2 hours; minimum 1 hour. **Rainy-day touring** Open during light rain, but closes during snowstorms. **Restaurants** No. **Alcoholic beverages** No. **Disabled access** Yes. **Wheelchair rental** No. **Baby-stroller rental** No. **Lockers** Yes. **Pet kennels** No. **Rain check** No. **Private tours** No.

DESCRIPTION AND COMMENTS As we gazed at the fierce, dignified bald eagle here, our daughter spotted a fallen feather. The docent gently took it from her, explaining to the kids that any feathers shed by the eagles are given to Native American groups for sacred use. Founded in 1959, the animal park shelters orphaned and injured animals native to the San Bernardino mountains, releasing the recovered ones into the wild. It's also open to visitors, who can see coyotes, bears, wolves, cougars, raccoons, foxes, and birds of prey. There's a gift shop and a few educational exhibits. But check the Web site or call before visiting—Moonridge is in the middle of a capital campaign and plans to become the Living Forest Wildlife Center, with better exhibits and enclosures and a more peaceful setting.

Mountain High Ski Area

APPEAL BY AGE	PRESCHOOL ★★	GRADE SCHOOL ★★★	TEENS ★★★
YOUNG ADULTS ★★★		OVER 30 ★★	SENIORS ★

24510 Highway 2, Wrightwood; ☎ 760-249-5808 or 888-754-7878; www.mthigh.com

Hours Mid-November–mid-April: Monday–Friday, 8:30 a.m.–10 p.m.; Saturday and Sunday, 8 a.m.–10 p.m. **Admission** *Lift tickets:* $43, 4 hours; $48, 8 hours; free for children under age 6 with paying adult, children ages 7–12, and seniors age 70 and older; *night skiing:* $26 adults, $17 children ages 7–12; 5–10 p.m. **Touring time** Average 8 hours; minimum 6 hours. **Rainy-day touring** No. **Restaurants** Yes. **Alcoholic beverages** Yes. **Disabled access** Yes. **Wheelchair rental** No. **Baby-stroller rental** No. **Lockers** Yes. **Pet kennels** No. **Rain check** Vouchers under certain conditions. **Private tours** Yes, classes.

DESCRIPTION AND COMMENTS Tucked into a sparsely populated community in the mountains north of L.A., an easy 90-minute drive from downtown, this working-class ski mountain is typically filled with local teens snowboarding, skiing, and hanging out on the big wooden deck of the lodge, checking each other out. Reasonably priced lessons are available for younger children, but the facilities are minimal, with a little too much uphill walking for the littlest ones. The snow can get pretty wet at the bottom, not to mention thick with out-of-control beginning snowboarders, but if you stay on the lifts to the top of the mountain, you might be surprised at the quality of the snow, much of which is man-made. Not for anyone who get easily spooked by raging teen snowboarders—but if you have teen snowboarders in the family, they'll want to come here.

FAMILY-FRIENDLY RESTAURANTS

McDonald's
28200 Highway 189, Building G, Lake Arrowhead (Lake Arrowhead Village, lower level); ☎ 909-337-0558

Meals served Breakfast, lunch, and dinner. **Cuisine** American fast food. **Entree range** $2–$6. **Kids' menu** Yes. **Reservations** Not accepted. **Payment** No credit cards.

This may be the McDonald's with the best view in all of California. It is indeed lakefront dining, and you won't see a bluer sky or more-sparkling

You don't have to own or even rent a ski or fishing boat to spend some time on the water. For one thing, if you take an afternoon tour of Big Bear Lake, your fretful preschooler may nap the time away (as ours did) in the fresh mountain air, with the hum of the boat's engine to lull him or her. For another, the view from the lake is unique, and whether you're interested in gazing at celebrity vacation homes, geological formations, or the spectacular granite slopes of San Gorgonio Mountain against a bright blue sky, you'll see it from the boat. Big Bear's scenic boat tour leaves from Pine Knot Landing at the foot of Pine Knot Avenue for an 80-minute narrated excursion, April through November, departing every two hours 10 a.m. to 6 p.m.; fare is $13.50 adults, $11 ages 52 and older, $7 children ages 2 to 10; call ☎ 909-866-2628; **www.pineknotlanding.com.** The *Arrowhead Queen* can be boarded at Arrowhead Village for a 45-minute tour, year-round; boats leave at regular intervals daily, 11 a.m. to 5 p.m.; fare is $11, $10 over age 59, $7.50 children ages 3 to 12; they're sold at LeRoy's Sports; ☎ 909-336-6992.

water from any of the terraces at the pricier restaurants down the way. So go ahead, let the kids get their favorites; just insist on getting a terrace table and put on plenty of sunscreen.

Teddy Bear Restaurant
583 Pineknot Avenue, Big Bear Lake; ☎ 909-866-5415

Meals served Breakfast, lunch, and dinner. **Cuisine** American **Entree range** Breakfast and lunch, $4–$7; dinner, $8–$12. **Kids' menu** Yes. **Reservations** Not accepted. **Payment** AE, MC, V.

One of our favorites in a town with pretty undistinguished dining, this coffee shop does a fine BLT, some great pancakes, and such local mountain specialties as warm hot chocolate on a chilly fall morning.

PALM SPRINGS

THE DESERT COMMUNITIES ARE LOVED BY RETIREES, of course, and driving through superquiet **Palm Springs** and its neighboring towns, **Palm Desert** and **Rancho Mirage,** on a hot day, with its empty streets (everyone's indoors) punctuated by golf courses, can make parents panic—what will we do with the kids? But real kids live here, and there are a growing number of activities for young people. Resorts include kids in the mix, especially as parents are tending to bring kids along for a weekend added to a meeting or conference. Palm Springs is beloved as a weekend getaway in winter for sun lovers (it's a two-hour drive east of downtown L.A). If you're going midweek or weekends, plan to include a Thursday night in your stay. The lively street fair and market (6 to 10 p.m. in the winter, 7 to 10 p.m. in the summer) offers fun food, booths (selling everything from vintage celebrity photos to a one-minute massage), and entertainment.

unofficial **TIP**
Palm Springs can turn hellish in July and August, when temperatures sometimes hit 115°F—but those months bring incredible deals at the resorts.

FAMILY LODGING

Marriott's Desert Springs Resort and Spa
74855 Country Club Drive, Palm Desert; ☎ 760-341-2211 or 800-228-9290; www.desertspringsresort.com; $219–$510; substantial discounts in summer

This gigantic (more than 900 rooms and suites) resort hotel is loads of fun, because it offers entertainment and luxury without formality. There are, for example, little motorboats to take you to the restaurants. The hundreds of people lounging poolside are serenaded by a reggae surf band playing Jimmy Buffett tunes, and the isolation of the place is not an issue, because it's got everything from a cappuccino bar to a hot dog stand. We took our kids to the golf course coffee shop for breakfast, sat in the Jacuzzi and watched colorful hot air balloons glide overhead, then spent some time playing badminton near the tennis courts. The year-round Kid's Club

palm springs

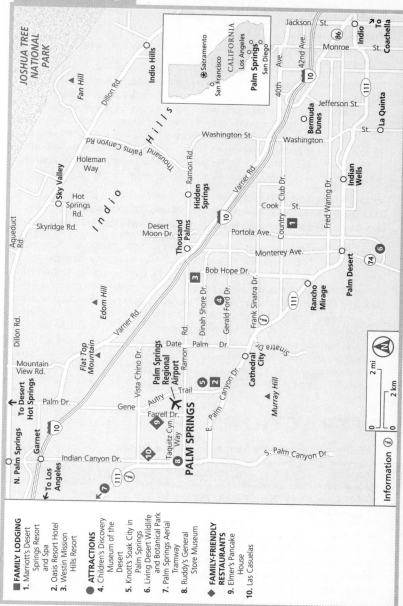

■ FAMILY LODGING
1. Marriott's Desert Springs Resort and Spa
2. Oasis Resort Hotel
3. Westin Mission Hills Resort

● ATTRACTIONS
4. Children's Discovery Museum of the Desert
5. Knott's Soak City in Palm Springs
6. Living Desert Wildlife and Botanical Park
7. Palm Springs Aerial Tramway
8. Ruddy's General Store Museum

◆ FAMILY-FRIENDLY RESTAURANTS
9. Elmer's Pancake House
10. Las Casuelas

($60 per day, $40 for night program), features organized lawn games, rock-wall climbing, arts and crafts, pizza parties, swimming parties, cartoons, and movies.

Oasis Resort Hotel
4190 East Palm Canyon Drive, Palm Springs; ☎ 760-328-1499;
$245–$365 for 2-bedroom condo (sleeps 6)

This is a good choice for families from March through October, when the nearby Soak City water park is open. Your water-park admission is included in your room cost, and a tram will whisk you to the park entrance. But this isn't a hotel, really, it's the overnight rental arm of a time-share condo complex. Two- and three-bedroom condos are available, and the eight pools of the complex are open to overnight guests. The air-conditioned, fully furnished units are luxurious for the price, and although there is neither restaurant nor room service, we were happy to order pizza and relax.

Westin Mission Hills Resort
7133 Dinah Shore Drive, Rancho Mirage; ☎ 760-328-5955 or
800-WESTIN-1; $189 and up in summer, $350 and up in late fall and winter

It was hard to be comfortable with a family of four in one of the small rooms at this 552-room resort, but the kids were happy in the daytime with the pool area, which includes misters at the bar and a wonderful 60-foot waterslide into the pool. Because of the many conference attendees, the Cactus Kids program is pretty active for kids ages 4 to 12 (though kids over age 8 might find it a little silly), offering a year-round program with daily morning and/or afternoon sessions ($40 each) featuring nature walks, swimming, arts and crafts, and movies. Family movies and a Sony PlayStation are available in the rooms. In the summer, two kids dine for free when accompanied by a parent. Tennis-playing families should take part in the excellent Reed Anderson Tennis Camp, held in the cooler months.

ATTRACTIONS

Children's Discovery Museum of the Desert

APPEAL BY AGE	PRESCHOOL ★★★★		GRADE SCHOOL ★★★★		TEENS –
YOUNG ADULTS	–	OVER 30	★–	SENIORS	★

71–701 Gerald Ford Drive, Rancho Mirage; ☎ 760-321-0602;
www.cdmod.org

Hours Tuesday–Sunday, 10 a.m.–5 p.m.; closed Monday. **Admission** $6 per person age 2 and up; all children must be accompanied by an adult. **Touring time** Average 2 hours; minimum 1 hour. **Rainy-day touring** Yes. **Restaurants** No. **Alcoholic beverages** No. **Disabled access** Yes. **Wheelchair rental** No. **Baby-stroller rental** No. **Lockers** No. **Pet kennels** No. **Rain check** No. **Private tours** For groups, special events.

DESCRIPTION AND COMMENTS A hands-on activity center where kids can paint a car, play in a grocery store, and rummage in an "attic." Special Handworks programs are available and include arts and crafts from clay to Native American gourd art. A highlight is an archaeological dig, which simulates a dig for Cahuilla Indian artifacts. Picnic area and museum store.

Knott's Soak City in Palm Springs

APPEAL BY AGE	PRESCHOOL ★★★	GRADE SCHOOL ★★★★	TEENS ★★★★
YOUNG ADULTS ★★★		OVER 30 ★★	SENIORS ★★

1500 Gene Autry Trail, Palm Springs; ☎ 760-327-0499; www.soakcityusa.com

Hours Mid-March–Labor Day: daily, 11 a.m.–5 p.m.; Labor Day–October: Saturday and Sunday, 11 a.m.–6 p.m. (on average—hours vary daily, so check Web site); closed November–mid-March. Admission $26.95 adults, $14.95 children ages 3–11, free for children under age 3. After 3 p.m., $15 adults, $14.95 children ages 3–11; parking $7. Touring time Average 3–4 hours; there may be lines for some of the 13 slides. Rainy-day touring No. Restaurants Snack bars. Alcoholic beverages No. Disabled access Yes. Wheelchair rental Yes. Baby-stroller rental No. Lockers Yes. Pet kennels No. Rain check No. Private tours No.

DESCRIPTION AND COMMENTS This is one of the smaller of the water parks we mention in this book, but you can believe that in the over-100°F temperatures of the desert, it's among the most loved. It has most of what a water park needs: a wave pool, slides, a tube river; the new six-story Pacific Spin is a big hit with older kids. Take note that this place is short on shade—please take our advice and pay for a "cabana," which is actually a tent with chairs, tables, and indoor–outdoor carpeting. Otherwise, you'll fry every time you leave the water, and your kids'll get sun-addled brains.

Living Desert Wildlife and Botanical Park

APPEAL BY AGE	PRESCHOOL ★★★	GRADE SCHOOL ★★★★	TEENS ★★★★
YOUNG ADULTS ★★★★		OVER 30 ★★★★	SENIORS ★★★★

47900 Portola Avenue, Palm Desert; ☎ 760-346-5694; www.livingdesert.org

Hours September 1–June 15: daily, 9 a.m.–5 p.m.; last admission at 4 p.m. June 16–August 31: 8 a.m.–1:30 p.m., last admission at 1 p.m. Closed Christmas. Admission September 1–June 15: $11.95, age 13 and up, $10.50, seniors and military, $7.50, children ages 3–12, free for children age 2 and under; June 16–August 31: $8.75 age 13 and up, $4.75 children ages 3–12, free for children age 2 and under. Touring time Average 3 hours; minimum 50 minutes, for tram ride only. Rainy-day touring No. Restaurants Yes. Alcoholic beverages No. Disabled access Yes. Wheelchair rental Yes, free. Baby-stroller rental Yes, free. Lockers No. Pet kennels No. Rain check No. Private tours Yes.

DESCRIPTION AND COMMENTS To dispel any myths about deserts being barren wastelands, bring the family to this wonderful 1,200-acre preserve. The elusive bighorn sheep clamber on hillsides as you wander through the pathways, along with the even rarer oryx, which the park is helping to save from extinction. The kids will meet coyotes, great horned owls, tortoises, mountain lions, and golden eagles of incredible grandeur. Inside is the Discovery Room, where kids can touch and feel. The desert botanical gardens will bore the kids, but sneak a peek if you can. If the day's too hot for walking, consider taking the 50-minute guided tram tour; in general, arrive right at opening time to beat the heat, unless you're visiting in winter.

 ## Palm Springs Aerial Tramway

APPEAL BY AGE	PRESCHOOL ★	GRADE SCHOOL ★★★★	TEENS ★★★
YOUNG ADULTS ★★★	OVER 30 ★★★		SENIORS ★★★

1 Tramway Road at Highway 111, Palm Springs; ☎ 888-515-TRAM or 760-325-1391; www.pstramway.com

Hours Weekdays, 10 a.m.–9 p.m.; weekends, 8 a.m.–9 p.m. **Admission** $21.50 adults, $19.50 for seniors age 60 and older, $14.50 children ages 3–12; children under age 3 ride free. **Touring time** Average 4 hours; minimum 2 hours. **Rainy-day touring** No. **Restaurants** Yes. **Alcoholic beverages** Yes. **Disabled access** Yes. **Wheelchair rental** No. **Baby-stroller rental** No. **Lockers** Yes. **Pet kennels** No. **Rain check** No. **Private tours** Yes.

DESCRIPTION AND COMMENTS New gondola cars that rotate 360 degrees give you dizzying views as they whisk you off the desert floor and swoop you up the side of Mount San Jacinto, delivering you to a cool (sometimes even snow-filled) mountain park at 8,500 feet, with pines, trails, and picnic areas. The ride is a very big thrill for kids age 10 and under (maybe a little too much for squeamish ones), and when the heat is wilting, it's a lovely escape. Just remember to bring a sweatshirt, because temperatures often drop 40°F or more. There's a restaurant up top, but we much prefer to bring a picnic.

Ruddy's General Store Museum

APPEAL BY AGE	PRESCHOOL ★	GRADE SCHOOL ★★	TEENS ★★★
YOUNG ADULTS ★★★	OVER 30 ★★★		SENIORS ★★★★

Village Green, 221 South Palm Canyon Drive, Palm Springs; ☎ 760-327-2156

Hours October–June: Thursday–Sunday, 10 a.m.–4 p.m.; July–September: weekends, 10 a.m.–4 p.m. **Admission** 95¢ per person, children age 12 and under free. **Touring time** Average a half hour; minimum 15 minutes. **Rainy-day touring** Yes. **Restaurants** No. **Alcoholic beverages** No. **Disabled access** Yes. **Wheelchair rental** No. **Baby-stroller rental** No. **Lockers** Yes. **Pet kennels** No. **Rain check** No. **Private tours** No.

DESCRIPTION AND COMMENTS Of the three small museums that make up Village Green in downtown Palm Springs, this one-room general store is the only one that will appeal to kids—and it's a fun and unique way to introduce them to everyday life of yesteryear. It's a facsimile of a general store circa 1930, and it's crammed with vintage packages of every imaginable product, all part of an extensive private collection. More than 6,000 unused items—from shirt collars to cigars, from soda pop bottles to straw boater hats, from kites to toy trains—line the shelves and display cases.

FAMILY-FRIENDLY RESTAURANTS

Elmer's Pancake House

1030 East Palm Canyon Drive, Palm Springs; ☎ 760-327-8419; www.elmers-restaurant.com

Meals served Breakfast, lunch, and dinner. **Cuisine** American. **Entree range** $6–$12. **Kids' menu** $5. **Reservations** Not accepted. **Payment** All major credit cards.

Popular with seniors and young families alike, this long-standing coffee shop does a booming breakfast business. Booths are roomy, service is friendly, and the pancakes are really good.

 Las Casuelas

368 North Palm Canyon, Palm Springs; ☎ 760-325-3213

Meals served Breakfast, lunch, and dinner. **Cuisine** Mexican. **Entree range** Breakfast, $5–$6; lunch and dinner, $6–$12. **Kids' menu** $5, limited choice of hamburger, taco, or eggs. **Reservations** Recommended. **Payment** All major credit cards.

"Las Cas" (as the locals call it) has been serving nachos, enchiladas, and tostadas in the desert for a couple of generations. This is the slightly more downscale original, which we like for its coziness and feel of local authenticity. A block away is the larger, fancier Las Casuelas Terraza, with a pretty sidewalk terrace and good margaritas (beer and wine only at the original location). The food at both is solid, tasty, and comforting; try the *mojo de ajos* (garlic shrimp).

PART FOUR

THE CENTRAL COAST

BEST KNOWN AS THE HOME OF THE MOST CELEBRATED STRETCH of California Highway 1, the Central Coast region of California has come into its own in recent years. The southern part of the Central Coast, from **Ventura** to **San Simeon,** is within easy reach of the Los Angeles metropolitan area, and the northern part, from **Big Sur** through the **Monterey Peninsula,** is weekend-getaway distance from San Francisco. Both sections of the Central Coast share a characteristic lack of urban sprawl: These are distinct and very different communities, with boundaries defined by agricultural or forest landscapes. And the pace of life is calmer here than in the urban areas.

A visit to the **Santa Barbara Zoo** or an afternoon on the **Santa Cruz Boardwalk** is no small-town experience, but each has an intimacy and ease that would be unthinkable in California's more heavily populated areas. (An exception to this rule is the internationally popular and crowded **Monterey Bay Aquarium.**) And the national restaurant or fast-food chain is not king here—many cafes are locally owned, use local produce, and create regional specialties for their menus.

We have explored this region with our children in a number of ways: by renting a beach house, by staying for the weekend during a soccer tournament, by adding time to an overnight business trip, by visiting friends and relatives. Highlights for our kids have included the unique and impressive Monterey Aquarium; Santa Barbara's charming little zoo; camping at **El Capitan State Beach,** playing in the clear, cold creek at Big Sur; apple-touring in the **Santa Ynez Valley;** getting a wax impression of one's hand on Santa Cruz Boardwalk; and, amazingly, enjoying classical music at the **Ojai Music Festival.**

To give this region its due, a week's visit is only fair. If you have only two or three days, focus on one end or the other. On the Southern California end, you can spend a few days based in Santa Barbara, exploring the beaches, the zoo, **Lake Cachuma, Solvang,** the playgrounds, and parks. Or set up camp in **San Luis Obispo,** from where you can venture

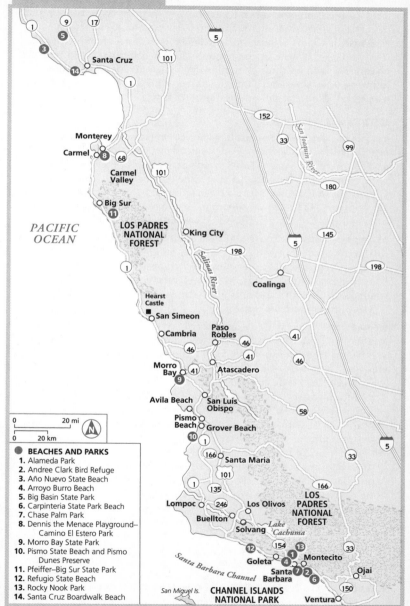

the central coast

PACIFIC
OCEAN

Santa Cruz

Monterey
Carmel

Carmel
Valley

Big Sur

LOS PADRES
NATIONAL
FOREST

King City

Hearst
Castle
San Simeon

Cambria

Paso
Robles

Morro
Bay

Atascadero

Avila Beach

San Luis
Obispo

Pismo
Beach

Grover Beach

Santa Maria

Lompoc

Los Olivos

LOS
PADRES
NATIONAL
FOREST

Buellton

Solvang

Lake Cachuma

Santa Barbara Channel

San Miguel Is.

CHANNEL ISLANDS
NATIONAL PARK

Goleta

Santa
Barbara

Montecito

Ojai

Ventura

Coalinga

San Joaquin River

Salinas River

0 ——— 20 mi
0 ——— 20 km

● **BEACHES AND PARKS**
1. Alameda Park
2. Andree Clark Bird Refuge
3. Año Nuevo State Beach
4. Arroyo Burro Beach
5. Big Basin State Park
6. Carpinteria State Park Beach
7. Chase Palm Park
8. Dennis the Menace Playground–
   Camino El Estero Park
9. Morro Bay State Park
10. Pismo State Beach and Pismo
    Dunes Preserve
11. Pfeiffer–Big Sur State Park
12. Refugio State Beach
13. Rocky Nook Park
14. Santa Cruz Boardwalk Beach

to **Morro Bay, Pismo Beach,** and even **Hearst Castle.** If you're coming from the northern end, you can easily devote three days to **Monterey,** with its aquarium and other attractions, or spend a day in Big Sur and a couple of days in Monterey. In summertime, Santa Cruz also makes a fine base, with lots of beach-oriented activities and a great boardwalk. You won't get a whit of the region's cherished intimacy and relaxed charm if you zoom through it all, so pick a couple of spots and focus, allowing time to wander through a farmers market or have a picnic by a waterfall. The rest will wait for another trip.

GETTING THERE

BY PLANE **Monterey Peninsula Airport** (**www.montereyairport.com**) is serviced by four airlines: American Eagle, Skywest/Delta, United, and US Airways. Arrivals are to and from San Francisco and L.A., with connections beyond. To reach the Airport Department for the City of Santa Barbara (Monday through Friday, 8 a.m. to 5 p.m.), call ☎ 805-967-7111; **www.flysba.com.** For San Luis Obispo Airport information, call ☎ 805-781-5205; **www.sloairport.com.**

BY TRAIN **Amtrak**'s Coast Starlight from L.A. to Seattle permits up to three stopovers, and it does stop in Santa Barbara and San Luis Obispo. Otherwise, there are commuter trains several times daily from L.A. to Santa Barbara. Trains to the Santa Cruz or Monterey areas originate in Oakland and only get as far as Salinas. Telephone ☎ 800-USA-RAIL; **www.amtrak.com.**

BY CAR The Central Coast area as we're defining it stretches from Ventura to Santa Cruz; it is best accessed from the north by CA Highway 1 and from the south by US Highway 101. Tour this region by enjoying some part of its famous coast drive.

We recommend driving US 101 from L.A. to Santa Barbara (about a two-hour drive) and from Santa Barbara to San Luis Obispo (another two hours). From SLO to San Simeon, take CA 1, allowing about an hour with no stops. You'll continue on the same road for about the same amount of time to drive from San Simeon to Big Sur. Allow at least 3½ hours total from San Luis Obispo to Monterey.

Heading south, from San Francisco, take Highway 1 through Half Moon Bay to Santa Cruz (about an hour and a half). Monterey is an hour's drive from Santa Cruz in light traffic on CA 1.

Between Monterey and San Luis Obispo, US 101 runs roughly parallel to CA 1, but inland through the Salinas Valley. Between San Luis Obispo and Santa Barbara, CA 1 is not exactly on the coast (Vandenberg Air Force Base controls that land) but is west of US 101 and goes through the little towns of Lompoc and Guadeloupe.

HOW TO GET INFORMATION BEFORE YOU GO

• **California State Parks** P.O. Box 942896, Sacramento 94296; ☎ 916-653-6995 or 800-777-0369; **www.parks.ca.gov.**

- **Monterey Convention Bureau and Visitor** 150 Olivier Street, Monterey 93942; ☎ 831-649-1770 or 888-221-1010; **www.montereyinfo.org.**
- **Morro Bay Chamber of Commerce** 845 Embarcadero Road, Suite D, Morro Bay 93442; ☎ 805-772-4467 or 800-231-0592; **www.morro bay.org.**
- **Ojai Valley Chamber of Commerce and Visitors Bureau** 201 South Signal Street, Ojai; mailing address P.O. Box 1134, Ojai 93024; ☎ 805-646-8126; **www.ojaichamber.org.**
- **Pismo Beach Visitor Information Center** 581 Dolliver Street, Pismo Beach 93449; ☎ 800-443-7778 or 805-773-4382; **www.classic california.com.**
- **San Luis Obispo County Visitors and Conference Bureau** ☎ 805-541-8000 or 800-634-1414; **www.sanluisobispocounty.com.**
- **San Simeon Chamber of Commerce** 250 San Simeon Drive, Suite 3A, San Simeon 93452; ☎ 805-927-3500; **www.sansimeonchamber.org.**
- **Santa Barbara Conference and Visitors Bureau** 1601 Anacapa Street, Santa Barbara 93101; ☎ 805-966-9222 or 800-549-5133; **www.santabarbaraca.com.**
- **Santa Cruz County Conference and Visitors Council** 1211 Ocean Street, Santa Cruz 95060; ☎ 831-425-1234; **www.santacruzca.org.**
- **Santa Cruz Visitor Information** Santa Cruz Boardwalk, 809 Center Street, Santa Cruz 95060; ☎ 831-426-7433 or 800-833-3494; **www.ci.santa-cruz.ca.us.**
- **Solvang Conference and Visitors Bureau** P.O. Box 70, Solvang 93464; ☎ 805-688-6144 or 800-468-6765; **www.solvangusa.com.**
- **Ventura Visitors Bureau** 89 South California Street, Suite C, Ventura 93001; ☎ 805-648-2075 or 800-333-2989; **www.ventura-usa.com.**

The BEST BEACHES *and* PARKS

ALAMEDA PARK Santa Barbara's kids designed the Kid's World playground in this lovely midcity park. The result is a playground worth a detour, with such creations as an eel-shaped slide, a giant shark, and a really cool tree house–style climbing structure. 1400 Santa Barbara Street, Santa Barbara; ☎ 805-564-5418; **www.sbparksand recreation.com.**

ANDREE CLARK BIRD REFUGE An easy bike or surrey ride along Santa Barbara's oceanfront path from Stearns Wharf, this lagoon is just past the zoo. Bring some bread crumbs for the kids to toss to the birds. 1400 East Cabrillo Boulevard, Santa Barbara.

AÑO NUEVO STATE BEACH This one-of-a-kind animal refuge is found on the coast north of Santa Cruz. In the winter, by reservation, rangers bring visitors along a roped path right into the breeding rookery of the remarkable elephant seals. These enormous sea mammals (bulls can get up to 20 feet long and some weigh in at four tons) can be seen up close, lying in the sand with their pups or bellowing at each other. (A summer highlight is the molting of the seals, when they "haul out" to shore and shed their skin.) In some frightening cases, visitors witness the bulls attacking each other in the waves. Sea otters are also within camera range. Visitors must be able to walk for two and a half hours on a three-mile round-trip trail that is sandy and uneven (or call for access information). Highway 1–New Year's Creek Road, Pescadero. Reservations: ☎ 800-444-4445; equal access program: ☎ 650-879-2033; general information: ☎ 650-879-0227; **www.anonuevo.org.** Wildlife viewing offered December 15 through March 31. Advance reservations highly recommended. Individual exploration allowed during other parts of the year, but sensitive areas are controlled by rangers or well-trained volunteer "Roving Naturalists," who are happy to answer any questions. Open 8 a.m. to sunset.

ARROYO BURRO BEACH Santa Barbara locals with kids skip city-center Cabrillo Beach and head to this fine beach park, where whales and sea lions are sometimes spotted. The surf is usually calm enough for younger kids, and creature comforts—restrooms, showers, snack bar, lifeguard—are good, too. 2981 Cliff Drive, Santa Barbara; ☎ 805-687-3714. Open 8 a.m. to sunset.

BIG BASIN STATE PARK More than 100 miles of trails lead visitors on explorations of the cool groves of towering 2,000-year-old redwoods in this acclaimed coastal park north of Santa Cruz. The short Redwood Nature Trail takes you into a grove of ancient trees, including the Mother of the Forest, a 330-foot monster. If your kids are over 8 years old, you should hike the Sequoia Trail, which leads past lush ferns and azaleas to Sempervirens Falls. There are several wonderful campgrounds, including a cluster of tent cabins for those who want to rough it only to a point. 21600 Big Basin Way, Boulder Creek (Highway 1 north of Santa Cruz to Highway 9 to 236); ☎ 831-335-3174; **www.mountainparks.org.** Open sunrise to sunset; $6 day-use fee.

CARPINTERIA STATE PARK BEACH This beach was named by the Spanish for the Chumash canoe-building carpentry shop once located here. There's lots of calm, shallow water plus a lagoon and tide pools. An area of the beach not protected by the offshore shelf offers surfing. There are 261 developed campsites, 120 with RV hookups; camping fees are $12 to $18 per night; day-use fee is $6. Ranger walks include topics from tide pool life to maritime history, and campfire programs include Chumash Indian lore. Restaurant, groceries, restrooms, showers. At the bottom of Linden Avenue, Carpinteria (via Highway 224 off US 101), 12 miles south of Santa Barbara;

unofficial **TIP**
Carpinteria has been called the world's safest beach. Its natural breakwater makes the surf peaceful and allows for a mile of great swimming with lots of shallow water and no riptides.

big sur

To Bixby Bridge,
Garrapata State Park,
& Point Lobos

Point Sur
Lighthouse

POINT SUR
STATE HISTORIC
PARK

Point Sur

False
Sur

California
Sea Otter
Game Refuge

Molera
Point

PACIFIC
OCEAN

Cooper
Point

Pfeiffer Beach

Pfeiffer Point

VENTANA
WILDERNESS

South Fork

Santa

Little Sur River

Lucia

ANDREW
MOLERA
STATE PARK

Adams Hill

LOS PADRES

Range

Gate

Gate
Camp
Parking
Gate

Gate

Gate
Gate

Big Sur

Big Sur River

NATIONAL FOREST

Pfeiffer
Falls

Park
Headquarters

PFEIFFER BIG SUR
STATE PARK

Sawmill
Flat
Weyland

South Park
Entrance

Wreck Beach

To
Julia Pfeiffer Burns
State Park

California Sea Otter
Game Refuge

San
Francisco

Sacramento

CALIFORNIA

Map
Area

Los Angeles

PACIFIC
OCEAN

0   1 mi
0   1 km

N

☎ 805-684-2811. To make reservations, call ☎ 800-444-7275 or visit
www.reserveamerica.com.

CHASE PALM PARK Santa Barbara's newest city park is a Pacific
Coast jewel. Across the street from the ocean, this meticulously
crafted and landscaped public space is composed of grassy knolls,
ponds, a new skate park, a lavish fountain, perfectly situated benches,
a vintage carousel, murals painted by local artists, an unobtrusive
snack bar, clean restrooms, picnic tables, and a superb playground
that reflects the style and history of the region. Climb-on-me whales,
half submerged in the sand, spout mist throughout the day. A mock
mission is great for pretend play, as are ship-themed climbing structures. We took a gang of 10-year-olds who couldn't get enough of the
stand-up slide. Bring a picnic lunch and hang out for awhile. East
Cabrillo Boulevard at Santa Barbara Street, Santa Barbara; ☎ 805-
564-5418; **www.sbparksandrecreation.com.**

DENNIS THE MENACE PLAYGROUND–CAMINO EL ESTERO PARK We have vivid childhood memories of playing on the locomotive here, so on a recent visit to Monterey, we took the kids on a pilgrimage. Time hadn't faded the park's charm for toddlers and preschoolers in particular, although it seemed modest to the over-four-footers. Designed by cartoonist Hank Ketcham, it does indeed still have the train engine, as well as slides, a bridge, and a maze. In the park at Camino El Estero, Monterey; ☎ 831-646-3866. Open 10 a.m. to dusk, Tuesday through Saturday; admission free. A little lake in the same park offers pedalboats for $10 a half hour, $15 an hour; call ☎ 831-375-1484 for hours.

MORRO BAY STATE PARK This is one of the most varied-use state parks around, with a golf course (featuring a tree planted in the 1930s by the Civilian Conservation Corps), museum (see the Natural History Museum attraction profile in the Morro Bay section), a boat harbor with launch and rental facilities, a bayside restaurant, a bird sanctuary that protects peregrine falcon nesting sites, and campgrounds. You can rent a boat or kayak, fish in the surf or from a boat, go clamming, picnic, and hike. State Park Road, 1 mile south of Morro Bay, ☎ 805-772-7434; reservations: Reserve America, ☎ 800-444-7275; **www.reserveamerica.com.** Open daily; free day use. Campsites with electricity and water are $29 to $34, and sites for a tent or self-contained vehicle are $12 to $18.

PFEIFFER–BIG SUR STATE PARK Every campsite in this park is taken during the summer and over holiday weekends, when Californians bring their kids here to relive their own childhood memories of making dams in the cool, clear creeks under the canopy of redwoods, sycamores, and willows. Adults will remember the spectacular drive to and from the park on the often-photographed stretch of Highway 1 that winds on cliffs above the rugged shoreline. But kids will remember the canyon, whether you stop for a picnic (at least), an overnight in the park's motellike lodge, or several quiet days of riverside camping. Junior Ranger programs, guided walks, and ranger programs. Off Highway 1, Big Sur; ☎ 831-667-2315; reservations: Reserve America, ☎ 800-444-7275; **www .reserveamerica.com.** Day-use fee $7; campsites $25 to $35.

PISMO STATE BEACH AND PISMO DUNES PRESERVE This huge (eight-mile) beach runs through the towns of Oceano, Grover City, and Pismo Beach. At the turn of the century, Pismo Beach was a tourist mecca, with visitors coming to dig clams and play in the sand. Today the monarch butterflies are the greater wildlife attraction—the largest colony to winter in the United States is found in and around a grove of pine and eucalyptus south of North Beach campground between November and March. Ironically, the sand dunes of this beach are known on the one hand for dune buggies and other off-road riding (see "Family Outdoor Adventures," right), and on the other hand for the Pismo Dunes Preserve, a protected area with unique and rare vegetation as well as archaeological sites. You'll find the Dunes Preserve via Oso Flaco Lake Road, at the end of which is a parking lot that is open from 8 a.m. to 6 p.m.; the dunes may be reached after a ten-minute walk. Passenger vehicles may drive along the beach from Grand Avenue in Grover City and Pier Avenue in Oceano. The state park has two campgrounds, food service, a visitors center, exhibits, and programs. Pismo State Beach information is ☎ 805-489-2684. Campground reservations through Reserve America, ☎ 800-444-7275; **www.reserveamerica.com.** Campsites $10 per day.

REFUGIO STATE BEACH About 20 minutes north of Santa Barbara lies this lovely, palm-rimmed cove nestled below Highway 101 and the train tracks. Campsites are tough to come by; if you can't score one, visit for the afternoon. The sand is soft, the swimming and body-boarding great, and the tide pools on the north end are stunning. Bring bikes to ride the 2.5-mile path to neighboring El Capitan State Beach; our kids also loved riding bikes in Refugio's paved areas. Lawns, barbe-cue facilities, showers, restrooms, summer lifeguard. Highway 101 at Refugio Road, Goleta, ☎ 805-968-1033. Campground reservations via Reserve America, ☎ 800-444-7275; **www.reserveamerica.com.** Camp-sites $25 per day.

ROCKY NOOK PARK With 19 acres in the heart of Santa Barbara near the mission and the Museum of Natural History, this park is great for a picnic with need-to-run kids after too much touring. No grassy lawns, but big boulders for climbing along Mission Creek, as well as picnic and barbecue areas and playground equipment. 610 Mission Canyon Road, Santa Barbara; ☎ 805-568-2460; **www.sbparksandrecreation.com.**

SANTA CRUZ BOARDWALK BEACH Why not spread your towel on the sand, with the sparkling Pacific before you and the col-orful roller coasters and sky buckets of the boardwalk as a backdrop? There's a lot of sense in breaking up the hours spent on rides with a dip in the sea and a nap in the sun. ☎ 831-426-7433.

FAMILY OUTDOOR ADVENTURES

ATV DRIVING ON THE SAND DUNES All-terrain vehicles are welcome at **Oceano Dunes State Vehicular Recreation Area.** All off-road vehicles must be transported by street-legal vehicles to the off-road area, from which they may explore almost 2,000 acres of sand. Drivers under 18 years of age may operate ATVs on public land only if they have an ATV Safety Certificate of Completion. All riders are advised to wear helmets and protective clothing; vehicles must have an adequate roll bar and other safety features. For information call Oceano Dunes at ☎ 805-788-4926, **www.oceanodunes.org** or State Parks Information Line at ☎ 800-777-0369; **www.parks.ca.gov.** There are ATV-rental companies in Grover City and Oceano, including **BJ's ATV Rentals,** 197 Grand Avenue, Grover Beach; ☎ 805-481-5411.

EAGLE CRUISE AT LAKE CACHUMA The personable and regionally famous ranger Neal Taylor was our guide when we took the 75-minute boat tour of **Lake Cachuma,** a man-made reservoir with camping areas about 18 miles northeast of Santa Barbara. He enthralled grandmother and 5-year-old alike as he pointed out and identified birds for us, then pulled up to the shoreline and clipped a piece of "miner's lettuce" for us to see, and held open the palm of his hand to show us how a particular seed "walked." In winter months, visitors cruise to see eagle-nesting areas as well as migratory birds like Canada geese. Summer cruisers see other birds (over 275 species, both year-round and migratory), including great blue herons, osprey, hawks, and woodpeckers. There's a small natural history museum on shore that complements the experience.

Amenities for campers at Cachuma include yurts (tentlike cabins sleeping six) to rent, 500 campsites, a general store, laundry facilities, showers, a snack bar, a marina, bait and tackle shop, picnic tables, barbecues, corrals for campers on horseback, fireside theater programs, summer movies, and weekend nature walks. Access available for travelers with disabilities. Cachuma Lake Recreation Area, Santa Barbara County Park Department, Star Route, Highway 154. Boat tour reservations: ☎ 805-686-5050 weekdays, 805-686-5055 weekends; $15 adults, $7 children under age 12. Camping and yurt reservations: ☎ 805-686-5050, 805-686-5055 weekends.

HIKING If you never do any other outdoor activities in California, we urge you to get out of your car and take a few hikes or nature walks while in Central California. There are several good trails for children in this area.

To reach **Cold Springs Canyon** in Santa Barbara (for older kids), off US 101 south of the San Ysidro Road exit, take San Ysidro east to Mountain Drive, turn left and continue 1.25 miles to the trailhead, where a creek crosses the road. Walk on the trail for a quarter-mile, then head right at the main (east) fork, which leads to lovely pools in the creek.

To reach **Rattlesnake Canyon Trail** in Santa Barbara, take the Mission Street exit north from US 101 and continue past Mission to Foothill Road. Turn right on Foothill, left on Mission Canyon, and right on Las Canoas Road; the trailhead is about a mile from the turn at a stone bridge in Skofield Park–Rattlesnake Canyon Wilderness Area. The trail leads to pools and a small waterfall.

Aliso Canyon Nature Trail is three miles from the Santa Barbara District Rangers Office at Sage Hill Campground. Call ☎ 805-967-3481 for directions.

Nojoquoi Falls County Park Trail is seven miles southwest of Solvang on Alisal Road. This easy trail travels alongside a creek under the California coastal oaks and comes to the 164-foot falls. The park is open 8 a.m. to dusk; admission is free.

Big Basin State Park in Santa Cruz offers the four-mile Sequoia Trail through the big trees, which culminates at a waterfall; see more details in "The Best Beaches and Parks." Call ☎ 831-338-8860.

Even the little ones can handle **Pfeiffer Falls Trail**—a less-than-half-mile loop up to see the waterfall. In Pfeiffer–Big Sur State Park; ☎ 831-667-2315.

KAYAKING OR CRUISING Before or after learning about the special marine ecology of the huge and magnificent Monterey Bay (with Santa Cruz on the north end and Monterey on the south), school-age and older kids can sign up for an outing in the **Monterey Bay National Marine Sanctuary** (☎ 831-647-4201; **montereybay .noaa.gov;** interpretive center at Santa Cruz Harbor), a stellar ocean-kayaking site thanks to its sheltered waters and remarkable wildlife (otters, sea lions, gray whales). **Adventure Sports Unlimited** (303 Potrero, Suite 15, The Old Sash Mill, Santa Cruz; ☎ 831-458-3648; **www.asudoit.com**) offers an intensive but not-too-long combination that includes training in sit-on-top kayaks and an excursion to the sanctuary. You begin in the evening with classroom and heated-pool instruction, then, the next day, enjoy an outing to the sanctuary, complete with a "cooperative" brunch and an end-of-the-day Jacuzzi soak. **Kayak Connections** sets off from two locations in the Monterey Bay Sanctuary, at Santa Cruz Harbor (413 Lake Avenue, Santa Cruz; ☎ 831-479-1121; **www.kayakconnection.com**) and in Moss Landing, 20 miles south of Santa Cruz, at Elkhorn Yacht Club (2370 Highway 1, Moss Landing; ☎ 831-724-5692). Rentals, guided tours, and instruction. The Monterey Bay Sanctuary tour is Sundays at 8:30 a.m., and private tours are held by request.

Nonpaddlers can take a two-hour guided natural history tour on an easy-riding 27-foot pontoon boat. The **Elkhorn Slough Safari** takes you ten miles into the coastal wetlands of the Monterey Bay National Marine Sanctuary. Fares, which include guide, refreshments, and use of binoculars, are $28 adults, $26 seniors, and $20 children ages 3 to 14 (no one under age 3 permitted); tours depart from Moss Landing. Guided nature walks. Day-use fee $5. Call ☎ 831-633-5555, or go to **www.elkhornslough.com.**

SURF SPORTS Certain beaches of the Central Coast are prime areas to try or enjoy surf sports, from Boogie boarding to bodysurfing to surfing.

In Santa Barbara, **Greg Lewis's Santa Barbara Surf School** offers day camps, private lessons, and even surf/yoga classes; ☎ 805-745-8877; **www.santabarbarasurfschool.com.** If you want to try it yourself, you can rent a soft longboard at **Rincon Designs Surfboards** ☎ 805-684-2413; at the East Beach Cabrillo Pavilion, on Cabrillo Boulevard in Santa Barbara. The **Cabrillo Bathhouse** also rents and sells equipment and sundries; call ☎ 805-897-2680.

In Santa Cruz, the place to learn to surf is at **Club Ed Surf Schools and Camps,** established by "the Professor of Surfing" at UC Santa Cruz, Ed Guzman, a third-generation Santa Cruz surfer (his grandmother learned to surf in 1915!). The school offers lessons, rentals, excursions, and camps; it's located on Cowell's Beach in front of the West Coast Santa Cruz Hotel in Santa Cruz, ☎ 800-287-SURF or 831-464-0177; **www.club-ed.com.** Private lessons are $95 an hour; two-hour group lessons are $85 for the first lesson, with two-hour group follow-ups at $60, including equipment. A solid alternative surf academy is **Richard Schmidt Surf School,** 849 Almar Avenue, Santa Cruz; ☎ 831-423-0928; **www.richardschmidt.com.**

NOSHING *through the* CENTRAL COAST

AGRICULTURE IS AS IMPORTANT AS SURFING (maybe even more so!) in the Central Coast, so the food is often wonderful. Here are the edible souvenirs to look for:

TUB OF BUTTER COOKIES from Solvang (year-round). Available from several bakeries, but we like the quality of the cookies and other goods at **Solvang Bakery** (☎ 805-688-4939; **www.solvangbakery.com**), near the big visitors' parking lot on the mission side of town. Layers of different kinds of butter cookies (marble, cherry-in-center, chocolate crescents) are packed between sheets of baker's paper in a plastic tub with a handle. We always think it'll take a week to empty, but it's never made it past two days.

BAG OF APPLES bought from streetside apple stand in Santa Ynez Valley (September and October). Farmers in the area grow several varieties, and fresh-picked ones are available from card tables in driveways and other roadside stands. We usually stop by Mr. Dittmar's stand at **Greenhaven Orchard** (2275 Alamo Pintado Road) near the little town of Ballard, just down the way from the miniature horse farm. The startling superiority of fresh Fujis and Granny Smiths makes it easy for kids to enjoy a healthy snack from a bag carried along on your travels.

 STRAWBERRIES AND CORN from roadside stands in Oxnard/Ventura (May and June). The corn is possible only if you have a kitchen, but a basket of strawberries is a wonderful addition to a picnic or tailgate lunch. Stand locations vary but can often be found alongside the 101 after descending the big grade heading north. Check by the Las Posas exit or in Ventura at the end of Telephone Road at Olivos Park.

CENTRAL COAST TRI-TIP SANDWICH from an outdoor barbecue stand at the Thursday night farmers market in San Luis Obispo (year-round). The essence of Central Coast cowboy culture (formerly 19th-century rancho culture) is carried in the aroma of grilling beef that emanates from competing barbecues set up during this weekly farmers market and street fair. Tri-tip is the locally favored cut of beef (the top portion of choice sirloin), and it makes for a tasty sandwich. For the ultimate picnic, stop by **El Rancho Market** near Solvang (2886 East Highway 246; ☎ 805-688-4300), where, on the weekends, a barbecue wagon is set up outside the market and whole tri-tips, chicken, sausage, ribs, and turkey breast are grilled over oak and sold by the pound.

PISMO BEACH CLAM CHOWDER In the late 19th century, Pismo Beach visitors would come for the sweet, succulent shellfish, so numerous then that it's said they could be dug with the toes (the earliest limits were for 200 a day per person). Today, visitors with a fishing license and a clamming fork can try to bag the current limit of ten clams per person a day, but they're not as easily found. If you're not the hunter-gatherer type, order some chowder at one of the beach-shanty cafes in town.

PICK YOUR OWN OLALLABERRIES at Avila Valley Barn (late May or early June); call ☎ 805-595-2810. Located at 560 Avila Beach Drive, a half mile west of US 101 near San Luis Obispo. If you're too late for berry season, you can pick peaches, apples, or pumpkins. There's also a bakery and gift shop here, and a place to picnic. The overall season is approximately Memorial Day through Thanksgiving.

FRESH STEAMED ARTICHOKES The eastern Monterey Peninsula borders on the rich agricultural lands of the Salinas Valley. Wineries abound, as do a variety of farms, but the area is most famous for its artichokes. Locals will be bagging produce here, but you can stop and eat fresh steamed artichokes at the **Pezzini Farms** stand off Highway 1 three miles from Castroville, north of Monterey. Open year-round at the corner of Nashua and Molera; ☎ 831-757-7434.

APPLE JUICE Young apple-juice guzzlers will delight not only in drinking the fresh-pressed apple juice from Gizdich Ranch in Watsonville near Santa Cruz (see attraction profile in the Santa Cruz section), but also in watching it made.

A CALENDAR of FESTIVALS and EVENTS

January

WHALEFEST Monterey. Special exhibits, art shows, children's activities; ☎ 831-649-6544.

February

JOHN STEINBECK BIRTHDAY FESTIVAL Monterey. At Cannery Row, with tours, entertainment, refreshments; ☎ 831-775-4721.

MIGRATION FESTIVAL Natural Bridges State Beach, Santa Cruz. Exhibits, slide programs, music, and crafts in celebration of "the fantastic journeys of migrating animals"; ☎ 831-423-4609.

March

SOLVANG CENTURY BIKE RIDE A huge event open to participants age 10 and up, who take part in a 100-mile ride; ☎ 562-690-9693; **www .bikescor.com/solvang/welcome.**

WHALE FESTIVAL Santa Barbara. The annual migration of the gray whale is honored in this fine festival, which includes live music, whale memorabilia, and a duck race; ☎ 805-969-5244; **www.sbwhale festival.com.**

April

SANTA MARIA STRAWBERRY FESTIVAL County Fairgrounds, Santa Maria. Locals celebrate the kickoff of the typically bounteous strawberry season with a lively carnival and festival that's great for kids; ☎ 805-925-8824; **www.santamariafairpark.com.**

May

CALIFORNIA STRAWBERRY FESTIVAL Oxnard. This multievent celebration includes soccer tournaments, arts and crafts, entertainment, and special events; ☎ 805-385-4739 or 888-288-9242; **www.strawberry-fest.org.**

CHILDREN'S FESTIVAL Alameda Park Santa Barbara. ☎ 805-965-1001; **www.sbparks.org.**

GREAT MONTEREY SQUID FESTIVAL Monterey Fairgrounds. There are cooking demonstrations, exhibits on the commercial fishing industry, touch tanks, entertainment, arts, and crafts; ☎ 831-649-6544.

SANTA CRUZ LONGBOARD CLUB INVITATIONAL Western surf clubs compete in this amateur competition; **www.santacruz.org.**

June

JOSÉ CUERVO VOLLEYBALL TOURNAMENT West Beach, Santa Barbara. Most school-age kids and their parents will love watching these beach gods and goddesses do their thing; ☎ 805-564-5422.

LIVE OAK MUSIC FESTIVAL San Luis Obispo. A three-day family-style festival of music including traditional, blues, Cajun, and classical. Concerts, barn dance, food, crafts, camping; ☎ 805-781-3020; **www.liveoakfest.org.**

LOMPOC VALLEY FLOWER SHOW Lompoc. Kids will go for the floral floats, marching bands, and carnival; gardening parents will love the tours of the region's great flower fields; ☎ 805-735-8511; **www.flower festival.org.**

SUMMER SOLSTICE CELEBRATION Central Santa Barbara, with music festival in Alameda Park. The antidote to overblown theme parks. No motorized floats, no amplified music, just one of the most joyous, freewheeling parades you'll ever see; ☎ 805-965-3396; **www.solstice parade.com.**

July

FOURTH OF JULY CELEBRATION Monterey. Music, parade, and fireworks; ☎ 831-646-5648.

PACIFIC GROVE FEAST OF LANTERNS For more than 90 years, this small community next to Monterey has celebrated with a week of activities; concludes with a pageant, barbecue, boat parade, and fireworks on the city beach; ☎ 831-649-8737; **www.feast-of-lanterns.org.**

SANTA BARBARA COUNTY FAIR County Fairgrounds, Santa Maria. An A-list county fair with everything from pie-eating contests to concerts by some of the country's best musicians; ☎ 805-925-8824.

Late July–early August

MID-STATE FAIR Paso Robles. ☎ 805-239-0665 or 800-909-FAIR; **www.midstatefair.com.**

August

OLD SPANISH DAYS FIESTA Held at sites throughout Santa Barbara. Many activities include Children's Parade and Tardes de Ronda, a children's variety show; ☎ 805-962-8101; **www.oldspanish days-fiesta.org.**

RUSSIAN-AMERICAN FESTIVAL Santa Cruz. Booths, food, crafts, music of Russia and the Ukraine; ☎ 831-420-5270.

SHAKESPEARE SANTA CRUZ Outdoor theater festival at UC Santa Cruz; ☎ 831-459-2151; **www.shakespearesantacruz.org.**

September

CAPITOLA BEGONIA FESTIVAL An unusual flower-boat parade—floats are constructed of flowers wired onto pontoons and sailed down Soquel Creek and under Stockton Bridge while onlookers gaze from banks. Also a sand-castle contest; ☎ 831-476-3566 or 800-919-8155; **www.begoniafestival.com.**

CARMEL MISSION FIESTA At the lovely site of the mission, a farmers market, art fair, children's games, and entertainment; ☎ 831-621-8322.

DANISH DAYS Solvang. Parade, special events to celebrate the town's Danish heritage. Always held the third weekend in September; ☎ 800-468-6765.

SANTA ROSALIA FESTIVAL Monterey. Outdoor mass, parade, blessing of the fleet, entertainment, arts and crafts, food; ☎ 831-238-6740; **www.festaitaliamonterey.com.**

SHARK FESTIVAL AND SANCTUARY CELEBRATION Santa Cruz Municipal Wharf. Shark exhibits, live shark tanks; ☎ 831-420-5273.

October

HARVEST FESTIVAL AND DRAFT HORSE DAYS Wilder Ranch State Park, Santa Cruz. Showcases antique tractors, historic farming techniques; celebrates local produce harvest. Food, games, children's activities; ☎ 831-426-0505.

MORRO BAY HARBOR FESTIVAL Morro Bay. Various events and locations, including entertainment, boat rides, and seafood fair; ☎ 800-366-6043; **www.mbhf.com.**

OLD MONTEREY SEAFOOD AND MUSIC FESTIVAL Music on two stages, arts and crafts fair; ☎ 831-655-8070; **www.oldmonterey.org.**

PISMO BEACH CLAM FESTIVAL Held in the downtown pier parking lot and other locations, Pismo Beach. Always the third weekend in October. Clam digging for prizes, clam chowder cook-off, fishing derby. Parade featuring Pam and Sam Clam walking along and greeting kids. Admission, $3; ☎ 805-773-4382.

WELCOME BACK MONARCHS Natural Bridges State Beach, Santa Cruz. The butterflies return to Santa Cruz. Music, food, games; ☎ 831-423-4609.

December

CAROLING UNDER THE STARS Santa Cruz. Rain or shine, families gather on successive weekends to carol at Lighthouse Point and Municipal Wharf; ☎ 831-420-5273.

VENTURA

IF YOU'RE TAKING A COAST VACATION in short stages, **Ventura** offers a nice enough balance of beach, marina areas, agricultural landscapes, and suburban shopping to keep a family busy for a day or two, and it's a dandy half-day stop as well. As you approach the area from the south, the first thing you may notice is an expansive farming setting: On roads just off the freeways, you'll see orange groves as full of fruit and blossoms as on any picture postcard. The old downtown area east of the freeway has a fun midcentury main street with vintage storefronts in various stages of renovation and reuse.

unofficial **TIP**
California's famous "June gloom" means Ventura is often overcast in May and June; if you want a sunny beach vacation, August and September are your best bets.

On the other side of the freeway (but accessible by foot) is a wide, sandy beach, with a pedestrian and bike path on a rise above the beach. It's great for walking, people watching, and admiring vendors' wares when mini–arts fairs are set up. A few miles away, the **Ventura Harbor** area has shops, restaurants, boat slips, a merry-go-round, and the **Channel Islands** visitors center (see profile).

▌ FAMILY LODGING

Embassy Suites Resort Mandalay Beach
2101 Mandalay Beach Road, Oxnard; ☎ 805-984-2500 or 800-EMBASSY; www.embassysuites.com; weekends $225–$300; weekdays $179 and up

A resort that's been run by one chain after another, this little-known all-suite (two-bedroom, two-bath) hotel has a choice on-the-beach location—but beware, it often doesn't get sunny in this region until July. The 249 suites are roomy and comfortable, and the oceanfront ones could make a family happy for several days. Other rooms overlook a landscaped courtyard. Extras include a pool, tennis court, fitness room, paddle tennis, pool table, children's activities, and children's menus; a full breakfast is included in the rates.

ventura

FAMILY LODGING
1. Embassy Suites Resort Mandalay Beach
2. Holiday Inn Ventura Beach Resort

ATTRACTIONS
3. Alpine Skate Park
4. Channel Islands National Park Visitors Center
5. Ventura County Gull Wings Children's Museum

FAMILY-FRIENDLY RESTAURANTS
6. Topper's Pizza Palace
7. Yolanda's Mexican Cafe

Holiday Inn Ventura Beach Resort

450 East Harbor Boulevard (off California and Harbor Boulevard), Ventura;
☎ **805-648-7731 or 800-HOLIDAY; www.venturaca.holiday-inn.com;**
$115 and up, winter; $159 and up, summer

The people's beach resort, this high-rise hotel has a terrific location and affordable rooms. That means it is very popular, and although there are 260 rooms and 16 suites, it's often sold out in summer. There's a pedestrian walkway to a plaza with shops and cafes adjacent; the pool overlooks the public beach promenade and sands. You just walk across the sidewalk to reach the beach. There are no kids' programs or children's menus, but there is a game room.

ATTRACTIONS

Alpine Skate Park

APPEAL BY AGE	PRESCHOOL –	GRADE SCHOOL ★★★	TEENS ★★★
YOUNG ADULTS ★★		OVER 30 –	SENIORS –

**1954 Goodyear Avenue, Ventura; ☎ 805-650-1213;
www.alpineventura.com**

Hours Skate sessions in 2-hour increments at various times, depending on camps and lessons. **Admission** $5; parents must sign a liability waver; helmets and pads required and can be rented on site for $5. **Touring time** Average 2 hours; minimum 1 hour. **Rainy-day touring** Yes. **Restaurants** Snacks. **Alcoholic beverages** No. **Disabled access** No. **Wheelchair rental** No. **Baby-stroller rental** No. **Lockers** Yes. **Pet kennels** No. **Rain check** No. **Private tours** Birthday parties.

DESCRIPTION AND COMMENTS   This is not your grandfather's roller rink, but rather a cavernous setting with an array of bowls, ramps, and specialty areas (like a water wall) for young shredders. Less intimidating is the beginners' area, and Alpine even sponsors contests and events for children under age 6. Open sessions of two hours are scheduled around lessons and camp time, and in the evenings beginning at 7 p.m., skating gives way to all-ages concerts. A video arcade keeps nonskaters busy.

 ## Channel Islands National Park

APPEAL BY AGE	PRESCHOOL ★★	GRADE SCHOOL ★★★★★	TEENS ★★★★★
YOUNG ADULTS ★★★★★		OVER 30 ★★★★★	SENIORS ★★★

**1901 Spinnaker Drive, Ventura Harbor; ☎ 805-658-5730;
www.nps.gov/chis**

Hours (Visitors center) Memorial Day–Labor Day: Monday–Friday, 8:30 a.m.–5 p.m.; Saturday and Sunday, 8:30 a.m.–5 p.m. Rest of year: Monday–Friday, 8:30 a.m.–5 p.m.; Saturday and Sunday, 8:30 a.m.–5 p.m.; closed Thanksgiving, Christmas. **Admission** $7.35 per day; all-day boat excursion and guided hike to Anacapa Island: $42 adults, $38 seniors, $25 children; contact Island Packers, ☎ 805-642-7688; **www.islandpackers.com.** **Touring time** All-day trip to Anacapa is 7–8 hours; half-day trip to Anacapa is 3–4 hours; minimum touring time 30 minutes to walk through visitors center only and see nature exhibits. **Rainy-day touring** Yes, to visitors center; boat excursions are weather permitting. **Restaurants** No. **Alcoholic beverages** No. **Disabled access** Yes, to visitors center. **Wheelchair rental** No. **Baby-stroller rental** No. **Lockers** No. **Pet kennels** No. **Rain check** No. **Private tours** No.

DESCRIPTION AND COMMENTS   Ever wanted to visit the Galápagos Islands? A visit to Channel Islands National Park is easier and way cheaper, and it offers similarly amazing wildlife experiences. The park includes five islands and their surrounding one nautical mile of ocean with kelp forests. The ocean for six miles around each island is designated as a

National Marine Sanctuary, and the isolation of the islands has preserved many unique plant and animal species. The park is home to more species of seals and sea lions (pinnipeds) than anywhere else in the world; between 180,000 and 200,000 individuals live on and around the islands. Pelicans, seagulls, and other sea birds nest here, and the ocean around the islands often teems with dolphins. For families, the day trips to Anacapa Island are wondrous. Sometimes, seagulls are nesting along the one-mile path the ranger leads you on; or schools of dolphins surround your boat; or whales are spotted along the way. You have to be able to climb a ladder (or be carried in a backpack) and a few flights of stairs; otherwise, the 1.5-mile island is easily accessible. Landlubbers can stop by the visitors center, located in a waterfront complex of shops and cafes, and combine a look at the island exhibits and indoor tide pool with a ride on the carousel and stop for lunch. In the center store, you can pick up a copy of *The Island of the Blue Dolphins,* required reading in many fifth-grade classrooms, and based on a true story of the Channel Islands.

Ventura County Gull Wings Children's Museum

APPEAL BY AGE	PRESCHOOL ★★★★★	GRADE SCHOOL ★★★	TEENS ★
YOUNG ADULTS ★	OVER 30 ★		SENIORS ★

418 West Fourth Street, Oxnard; ☎ 805-483-3005; www.gullwings.org

Hours Tuesday–Saturday, 10 a.m.–5 p.m.; closed Sundays and Mondays. **Admission** $4 adults, free for children under age 2. **Touring time** Average 3 hours; minimum 2 hours (no point in rushing the little ones). **Rainy-day touring** Yes, excellent. **Restaurants** No. **Alcoholic beverages** No. **Disabled access** Yes. **Wheelchair rental** No. **Baby-stroller rental** No. **Lockers** No. **Pet kennels** No. **Rain check** No. **Private tours** No.

DESCRIPTION AND COMMENTS An excellent, homegrown, low-tech children's museum, best for kids under age 9. Our little ones spent happy hours with the bubble exhibit, puppet theater, pretend campground with tent, pretend farmers market, and fossils to touch. Not glitzy like the big-city children's museums, but not overwhelming for the little ones in any way, so for some families it will be actually more fun and hands-on.

FAMILY-FRIENDLY RESTAURANTS

Topper's Pizza Place
3940 East Main Street, Ventura; ☎ 805-385-4444

Meals served Lunch and dinner. **Cuisine** American. **Entree range** Lunch, $4–$6; dinner, $6–$20. **Kids' menu** No. **Reservations** Not necessary. **Payment** MC, V.

This small local chain (five restaurants in Ventura County) is a good, reliable eat-in, take-out, or deliver-to-your-hotel-room restaurant. The pizzas are fine, and the six-inch sandwiches are fresh and tasty. If you eat in, there's a salad bar, games, and a big-screen TV.

Yolanda's Mexican Cafe

2753 East Main Street, Ventura; ☎ 805-643-2700

Meals served Lunch, dinner, and Sunday brunch. **Cuisine** Mexican. **Entree range** Lunch, $7–$11; dinner, $8–$15. **Kids' menu** $5. **Reservations** Recommended. **Payment** All major credit cards.

One of the best Mexican restaurants in Southern California, this large, cheerful place is nevertheless completely kid friendly. You'll find terrific homemade food here, made from the freshest ingredients, some obtained from local farms. Try the veggie combo plate, the enchiladas rancheros, and the flautas.

SANTA BARBARA

Santa Barbara IS CONSIDERED BY ITS RESIDENTS to be an unparalleled paradise of perfect weather, fine restaurants, and beautifully maintained residential neighborhoods. Strict zoning laws have kept the city's famous red-tile-roof building style so predominant that even major shopping malls are discreetly tucked into the traditional Mediterranean silhouette (and in some cases into the historic buildings themselves).

unofficial **TIP**
The trick is to focus on the area's unbeatable outdoor attractions: glorious beaches, lovely hiking trails to rock-strewn waterfalls, pastoral agricultural areas of horse ranches, and apple orchards.

For some families, the lack of theme parks and glitzy attractions will make Santa Barbara look like a sleepy, ho-hum sort of place, but we think that whether you're making a day trip up from L.A., stopping for a couple of nights en route north or south, or making a weeklong vacation of it, Santa Barbara is a great place for a family trip making the most of the area's terrific outdoor resources. Making these outdoor pleasures family friendly is easy to do—rent a bike, sign up for Boogie-board lessons, hang out at the kiddie wading pool on a sunny afternoon, or pack a picnic and look for the trailhead. Overnight options range from retro-appealing postwar motels with kitchenettes near the main city beaches to full-service, five-star resorts to a vintage ranch resort.

FAMILY LODGING

Casa del Mar
18 Bath Street, Santa Barbara; ☎ 805-963-4418 or 800-433-3097; www.casadelmar.com; $114–$289

Built as a courtyard apartment building, this 1930s Spanish charmer offers a lot of comfort and location for the price (which includes breakfast). The downside for kids is the lack of a pool, but the large spa is lovely. Cabrillo Beach is just around the corner, and the 20 apartment-style accommodations are ideal for a family, offering kitchens, fireplaces, and plenty of room for everyone.

santa barbara

N

Golf ⛳
Information ⓘ

1 mi
1 km
0
0

Hot Springs Rd.
Olive Hill Rd.
To LA
To Montecito & Summerland
Channel Dr.
East Beach
225
101
Blvd.
Stearns Wharf
Santa Barbara Harbor
Hot Springs Rd.
Alston Rd.
Eucalyptus Hill Rd.
Salinas St. Village Rd.
Coast
Mason St.
144
Milpas St.
Garcia Rd.
Sycamore Canyon Rd.
Stanwood Dr.
Sheffield Reservoir
192
Alameda Padre Serra
Mountain Dr.
Mission Canyon Rd.
Lauro Reservoir
192
Alamar Ave.
Las Positas Rd.
State St.
Santa Barbara Golf Club
Foothill Rd.
La Cumbre Rd.
101
154
El Sueno Rd.
Laguna Blanca
Arroyo Burro
Cantina Way
225
Las Positas Rd.
De La Vina St.
Constance Ave.
Los Olivos St.
Mission St.
Anacapa St.
Laguna St.
Santa Barbara St.
Garden St.
State St.
Valerio St.
Micheltorena St.
Arrellaga St.
San Andres St.
Carrillo St.
Meigs Rd.
Cliff Dr.
Cliff Dr.
Shoreline Dr.
Loma Alta Dr.
Cabrillo Blvd.
Haley St.
Gutierrez St.
Santa Barbara Channel
Arroyo Burro Beach County Park
Las Palmas Dr.

9
4
12
225
11 ⓘ 5
1
13
15
18
10
8 7 11
14
17

Sandpiper Golf Course ⛳

2 3
6 16

■ **FAMILY LODGING**
1. Casa del Mar
2. El Capitan and Refugio State Beach Campgrounds
3. El Capitan Canyon
4. Four Seasons Santa Barbara
5. Harbor View Inn
6. Rancho Oso

● **ATTRACTIONS**
7. Mission Santa Barbara
8. Santa Barbara Museum of Natural History
9. Santa Barbara Zoological Gardens
10. Skater's Point
11. Ty Warner Sea Center

◆ **FAMILY-FRIENDLY RESTAURANTS**
12. Beach Grill at Padaro
13. Brophy Bros. Clam Bar & Restaurant
14. The Brown Pelican
15. California Pizza Kitchen
16. Cold Spring Tavern
17. Endless Summer Bar-Café
18. La Super-Rica

El Capitan and Refugio State Beach Campgrounds

Highway 101 between Santa Barbara and Gaviota;
☎ 805-968-1033; reservations: Reserve America, ☎ 800-444-7275;
www.reserveamerica.com; campsites $13–$16

Very popular with locals seeking a simple beach vacation, El Capitan and Refugio are located about 20 minutes north of Santa Barbara. At El Capitan, you camp in a grassy, oak-shaded area on a bluff overlooking the sea, with a good beach below; request a campsite as far away from Highway 101 and the train tracks as possible, or you'll be up all night. Refugio's campsites are closer together and therefore less private than El Capitan's, but there's a beautiful beach right in front, and the train noise isn't a problem. There are fire rings, showers, flush toilets, picnic tables, and a lifeguard on beach in summer.

El Capitan Canyon

11560 Calle Real, Santa Barbara; ☎ 805-685-3887 or 866-352-2729;
www.elcapitancanyon.com; $115–$245 (November–April), $135–$305
(May–October)

If you'd like to experience some of the rustic outdoorsiness of camping but can't travel with all the camping gear—or don't actually want to sleep on the ground—bring the kids to El Capitan Canyon. Tucked in a sycamore-and-oak–shaded canyon just inland from El Capitan State Beach, it's a rustic-chic resort with "safari tents" (think *Out of Africa* goes to the beach) and cedar cabins furnished with willow pieces, comfy beds, front porches, fire pits, and barbecues. The tin-roofed market has a good deli counter that offers kits with everything you need to make dinner on your barbecue. It's a kid paradise here, with room to run, a creek to play in, a solar-heated swimming pool, guided naturalist hikes, El Capitan beach a short walk away, and Saturday-night campfire concerts in summer. The safari tents are too small for a family, but many of the cabins sleep four to six comfortably.

☼ Four Seasons Resort Santa Barbara

1260 Channel Drive, Montecito; ☎ 805-969-2261 or 800-332-3442;
www.fourseasons.com; $475 and up

To find the California dream, look no further than this famed luxury hotel facing the Pacific. From the spectacular flowerbeds to the enveloping king-size beds, every detail is perfect. The arches, tiles, and thick stucco walls evoke the romance of old California, but the amenities are thoroughly modern—like the free children's program, which keeps kids happily swimming, exploring, and making crafts while parents play tennis, get massages, or nap on the beach. Only the beach is a bit lacking—on the small side—but that's a minor quibble in paradise.

Harbor View Inn
28 West Cabrillo Boulevard; ☎ 805-963-0780 or 800-755-0222; www .harborviewinnsb.com; $275 and up; no charge for children under age 16

This handsome red-tile-roofed Spanish motel has a large pool, a wading pool, and a whirlpool, as well as the breadth of Cabrillo Beach right across the street, with Stearns Wharf a three-minute walk. The newest of the cool, well-appointed rooms (coffeemakers, fridges, movies) are relatively large, so even though there aren't any suites, you may fit comfortably in one room. The rates include a tasty continental breakfast and afternoon refreshments.

Rancho Oso
3750 Paradise Road (off Highway 154); ☎ 805-683-5686; www.rancho-oso.com; wagons $59, cabins $84

Just up the San Marcos Pass from downtown Santa Barbara lies a rustic family retreat that offers a lot of fun for not much money. Originally a riding stable, Rancho Oso has evolved into a small guest ranch, with five simple cabins (each sleeps four) and the kids' favorite, ten covered wagons, which are fitted with army cots to sleep four. Luxuries are few—restrooms are outside—but the fun quotient is high. Kids age 8 and up (and their parents) can head out on the several daily horseback rides; littler ones enjoy escorted pony rides. When you're not riding, you can swim in the two pools, soak in the spa, play in the playground, fish in the creek, or head out for nature hikes. A chuck wagon feeds guests hearty cowboy fare.

SANTA BARBARA FINDS

One Thousand Steps Beach An unbelievably long staircase to the beach from Mesa on Santa Cruz Boulevard below Shoreline Drive. There's a landing midway, so you can stop to enjoy the view and catch your breath.

Santa Barbara Arts and Crafts Show Held Sundays and holidays year-round at Chase Palm Park between Cabrillo Boulevard and the ocean, this permanent arts show attracts vendors of all kinds and is patronized by locals for gift shopping. The sales are direct and the prices often very reasonable.

Santa Barbara Trolley Tour Nine times a day, every hour from 10 a.m. to 4 p.m., the Santa Barbara Trolley leaves from Stearns Wharf and the Old Mission. The 90-minute tour ($18 adults, $9 children, $43 family pass for two adults and up to five children; online discounts available) gives a pleasant overview of the town, pointing out landmarks such as the bird refuge, zoo, Moreton Bay Fig Tree, mission, and so forth. Your ticket is good for boarding all day as you make one loop around. Call ☎ 805-965-0353; **www.sbtrolley.com.**

ATTRACTIONS

Mission Santa Barbara

APPEAL BY AGE	PRESCHOOL ★	GRADE SCHOOL ★★	TEENS ★★
YOUNG ADULTS ★★★	OVER 30 ★★★★		SENIORS ★★★★

East Los Olivos and Laguna Street, Santa Barbara; ☎ 805-682-4149; www.sbmission.org

Hours Daily, 9 a.m.–5 p.m.; closed Easter, Thanksgiving, and Christmas Days. **Admission** $4 adults, free for children age 12 and under. **Touring time** Average 2 hours; minimum 1 hour. **Rainy-day touring** Not recommended. **Restaurants** No. **Alcoholic beverages** No. **Disabled access** Limited; some steps. **Wheelchair rental** No. **Baby-stroller rental** No. **Lockers** No. **Pet kennels** No. **Rain check** No. **Private tours** No.

DESCRIPTION AND COMMENTS We don't list all the California missions in this book because we think they're pretty confusing for the youngest kids and more interesting to adults than to even many school-age kids. But Santa Barbara's mission is well preserved, well restored, and quite kid friendly in the exhibits. Completed in 1820, this mission now features a self-guided tour with stops including a padre's bedroom, a Chumash Indian room, and the chapel and cemetery.

Santa Barbara Museum of Natural History

APPEAL BY AGE	PRESCHOOL ★★★	GRADE SCHOOL ★★★	TEENS ★★
YOUNG ADULTS ★★	OVER 30 ★★★		SENIORS ★★★

2559 Puesta del Sol Road (behind the Mission), Santa Barbara; ☎ 805-682-4711; www.sbnature.org

Hours Daily, 10 a.m.–5 p.m.; Closed Thanksgiving, Christmas Eve, Christmas, and New Year's Day, first Friday in August, and at noon for Fiesta. **Admission** $8 adults, $7 seniors age 65 and over and teens ages 13–17, $5 children ages 2–12; children under age 2 free. The third Sunday of every month except September is free admission. **Touring time** Average 1½ hours; minimum 45 minutes. **Rainy-day touring** Yes. **Restaurants** June–September. **Alcoholic beverages** No. **Disabled access** Yes. **Wheelchair rental** Yes, free. **Baby-stroller rental** No. **Lockers** No. **Pet kennels** No. **Rain check** No. **Private tours** No.

DESCRIPTION AND COMMENTS A graceful, elegant complex of red-tile-roofed buildings, this museum prides itself on programming that focuses on the local environment, so it makes for an enlightening stop for visitors unfamiliar with California's ecology. Native animal and bird species are shown (stuffed) in dioramas and with models, like the full-size (33-foot) giant squid. Other highlights are the Chumash Indian Hall, a planetarium, and an observatory. The museum also runs the Ty Warner Sea Center on Stearns Wharf; see profile below.

Santa Barbara Zoological Gardens

APPEAL BY AGE	PRESCHOOL ★★★★★	GRADE SCHOOL ★★★★	TEENS ★★
YOUNG ADULTS ★★		OVER 30 ★★★	SENIORS ★★★

500 Niños Drive (off Cabrillo Drive), Santa Barbara; ☎ 805-962-6310 or 805-962-5339, ext. 54; www.santabarbarazoo.org

Hours Daily, 10 a.m.–5 p.m.; closed Thanksgiving and Christmas days. **Admission** $10 adults ages 13–59, $8 seniors age 60 and older, $8 children ages 2–12, children under age 2 free; parking $3. **Touring time** Average 3–4 hours; minimum 2 hours. **Rainy-day touring** Yes, but you'll get wet. **Restaurants** Yes. **Alcoholic beverages** No. **Disabled access** Yes. **Wheelchair rental** Yes, $5. **Baby-stroller rental** Yes, $5 single, $7 double. **Lockers** No. **Pet kennels** No. **Rain check** No. **Private tours** No.

DESCRIPTION AND COMMENTS Neatly hidden on the west end of town, between Cabrillo Beach and the bird refuge, this gem of a zoo fits a lot into a compact space. The skillful wending of paths and exhibits through the former private estate makes this a wonderful place for even the littlest kids, who might get overwhelmed at huge, crowded animal parks and theme parks. The elephants, giraffes, and lions are a big hit, as is the reptile house. My preschool nephew insisted on three rides on the miniature train; other extras include a playground, an excellent gift shop, and a lovely picnic area. A unique gorilla-viewing area is a replica of Dian Fossey's African field station and allows kids to walk into a room with desk, hammock, and everyday objects left as if the famous scientist were just outside.

Skater's Point

APPEAL BY AGE	PRESCHOOL ★★	GRADE SCHOOL ★★★★	TEENS ★★★★
YOUNG ADULTS ★★		OVER 30 ★★	SENIORS ★

Chase Palm Park, East Cabrillo Boulevard at Garden Street, Santa Barbara; ☎ 805-564-5418

Hours Daily, 8 a.m. to half hour after sunset. **Admission** Free. **Touring time** Average 1 hour; minimum 30 minutes. **Rainy-day touring** Yes, but it'll be slippery. **Restaurants** Nearby. **Alcoholic beverages** No. **Disabled access** No. **Wheelchair rental** No. **Baby-stroller rental** No. **Lockers** No. **Pet kennels** No. **Rain check** No. **Private tours** No.

DESCRIPTION AND COMMENTS The latest addition to the beachfront, Chase Palm Park has been a huge hit with Santa Barbara's kids. This 14,600-square-foot oceanview skate park is chock-full of rails, ramps, hips, ledges, a half pipe, and a six-foot-deep bowl. Some skate parks can be intimidating for all but the best skaters, but this one is as likely to have a 5-year-old girl in a pink helmet going down a ramp as it is a shaggy-haired 16-year-old skate dude. (A rule of thumb is to bring younger kids before noon—the older ones run the show in the afternoons.) Helmets and pads required.

Ty Warner Sea Center

APPEAL BY AGE	PRESCHOOL ★★★★	GRADE SCHOOL ★★★★	TEENS ★★★
YOUNG ADULTS ★★★		OVER 30 ★★★	SENIORS ★★★

Stearns Wharf, State Street at Cabrillo Boulevard, Santa Barbara;
☎ **805-962-2526; www.sbnature.org/seacenter**

Hours Daily, 10 a.m.–5 p.m. **Admission** $7 adults, $4 children ages 2–12, $6 students and seniors; children under 2, free. **Touring time** Average 1 hour; minimum 30 minutes. **Rainy-day touring** Yes. **Restaurants** Nearby. **Alcoholic beverages** No. **Disabled access** Yes. **Wheelchair rental** No. **Baby-stroller rental** No. **Lockers** No. **Pet kennels** No. **Rain check** No. **Private tours** No.

DESCRIPTION AND COMMENTS Run by the Museum of Natural History, this small, easy-to-digest marine education center is right on picturesque Stearns Wharf. After a morning of beach fun, bring the kids here to learn about the critters they were just swimming with. Kids get to help with the scientific research that goes on here by testing water samples, examining miniature sea life under microscopes, and observing tide pool life. They can also crawl through a tunnel inside a 1,500-gallon surge tank and then wonder at the new exhibit of tiny local sharks (sharks aren't all great whites!). Check the Web site for the fun events, like the Sunday Sea Stories.

 # FAMILY-FRIENDLY RESTAURANTS

 ## Beach Grill at Padaro

3765 Santa Claus Lane, Carpinteria; ☎ **805-566-0566**

Meals served Breakfast, lunch, and dinner. **Cuisine** American. **Entree range** Lunch and dinner, $5–$11. **Kids' menu** Yes. **Reservations** Not accepted. **Payment** All major credit cards.

When the weather is fine, there is no better family restaurant in the Santa Barbara area. Order at the counter inside the restaurant, then take your food (soups, good salads, fresh fish sandwiches, burgers) to one of the picnic tables on the huge grassy lawn overlooking the ocean. After the kids wolf down their food, they can run and play (there's even a playground) while parents have a few moments of ocean-view peace, perhaps accompanied by a glass of wine. Even the family dog is welcome. Padaro Street Grill is located in the little beach town of Carpinteria, a few miles south of Santa Barbara.

Brophy Bros. Clam Bar & Restaurant
119 Harbor Way, Santa Barbara; ☎ **805-966-4418**

Meals served Lunch and dinner. **Cuisine** American/seafood. **Entree range** Lunch, $4–$15; dinner, $13–$17. **Kids' menu** Yes. **Reservations** No. **Payment** AE, MC, V.

For the best waterfront seafood in town, head to this informal, family-friendly harbor-front restaurant, where the locals flock to get the tastiest clam chowder, calamari, cioppino, and oyster shooters this side of Monterey. Kids love the views of the seagulls and boats as much as parents. There are plenty of kid-pleasing choices. Come early to avoid a long wait.

The Brown Pelican
Hendry's Beach, 2981H Cliff Drive at Arroyo Burro County Park, Santa Barbara; ☎ 805-687-4550

Meals served Breakfast, lunch, and dinner. **Cuisine** American. **Entree range** Lunch and dinner, $10–$20. **Kids' menu** Yes. **Reservations** Accepted. **Payment** AE, MC, V.

A television fantasy of California beach life come true, this restaurant is on the sand in an isolated cove beach. Park the car, spend time on the beach, and come up to the restaurant for a meal, or just stop for lunch and revel in the sun and surf and families playing in the waves. You'll eat basic seaside burger-and-bistro fare: huevos rancheros, omelets, seafood, sandwiches, crab cakes, lots of appetizers for the wine-and-tidbit crowd, espresso drinks, and rich desserts.

California Pizza Kitchen
719 Paseo Nuevo, State Street, Santa Barbara; ☎ 805-962-4648; www.cpk.com

Meals served Lunch and dinner. **Cuisine** Californian. **Entree range** $4–$14. **Kids' menu** Yes. **Reservations** Not accepted. **Payment** All major credit cards.

A chain, yes, but a great one for families, well located in downtown's Paseo Nuevo shopping center. The vegetarian soups, field-green and Caesar salads, designer pizzas, and California wines keep parents happy, and the simpler pizzas and pastas are perfect for younger kids.

Cold Spring Tavern
5995 Stagecoach Road, Santa Barbara; ☎ 805-967-0066; www.coldspringtavern.com

Meals served Lunch and dinner; breakfast Saturday and Sunday only. **Cuisine** American. **Entree range** Lunch, $7–$12; dinner, $16–$24. **Kids' menu** Yes. **Reservations** Yes. **Payment** AE, MC, V.

Well worth the 20-minute drive up Highway 154 to the San Marcos Pass in the hills above Santa Barbara, this place has so much atmosphere, you can practically cut it with a knife. A century-old stagecoach stop set in an oak grove, it looks like a restaurant Tom Sawyer would love, with stone fireplaces, hidden nooks and crannies, and battered wooden walls hung with things like barbed-wire displays and hunting trophies. Outside, a cook mans a huge oak-burning barbecue, grilling marinated tri-tips, while over in front of the separate bar (a Harley riders' hangout), musicians play Grateful Dead and Crosby, Stills & Nash songs for tips. Add a creek with a small waterfall and a kids' menu offering ribs, pasta, and giant hot dogs, and you've got a very fun family outing, especially at lunchtime, when the kids can scamper around outside and the (harmless) bikers aren't yet drinking seriously. The service can drag on busy days.

Endless Summer Bar-Cafe
113 Harbor Way, Santa Barbara; ☎ 805-564-4666;
www.endlesssummerbarcafe.net

Meals served Lunch and dinner. **Cuisine** American/seafood. **Entree range** $8–$20. **Kids' menu** Yes. **Reservations** Accepted. **Payment** All major credit cards.

Upstairs from the fancier Waterfront Grill, on the north end of the harbor with a fabulous view of the boats, the coastline, and the city, this place is a find for families who want a good meal in a great setting—a great setting, that is, with a tolerance for 4-year-olds who jump on the banquettes. Kids are welcomed with a smile, crayons, and a kids' menu, and parents are rewarded with delicious clam chowder, seafood salads, simple grilled fish, and other chic, beachy fare. Before and after your meal, the kids can run around the harbor paths, looking at the boats and chasing seagulls.

La Super-Rica
622 North Milpas Street, Santa Barbara; ☎ 805-963-4940

Meals served Lunch and dinner. **Cuisine** Mexican. **Entree range** $2–$6. **Kids' menu** No. **Reservations** Not accepted. **Payment** No credit cards.

This order-at-the-counter roadside joint draws people from 100 miles away. This is great Mexican soul food: beans, *queso fundido,* posole, homemade tortillas, tamales, and cold sodas and Coronas. You eat in a tarp-covered patio on rickety plastic furniture, and you'll probably have to wait in a long line, but it's still an absolute must-visit. Plenty of plain options (cheese quesadillas, steak tacos) for picky eaters.

SIDE TRIP: *Ojai*

A HAVEN FOR PAINTERS, WRITERS, AND THE SORTS OF CRAFTY FOLKS who make jewelry, **Ojai** is also a fine family getaway for a day or two. We passed a near-perfect weekend here, staying at the serene **Ojai Valley Inn** and riding the inn's bikes into the dinky town for ice cream, a browse at open-air **Bart's Books,** a romp at **Libbey Park,** and a fun shopping trip at the Sunday farmers market. The town trolley is also a hoot for kids. Try to get in a short hike in the local hills to get a view over this gorgeous valley, once a Chumash paradise and later the set for the movie *Lost Horizon.* A trail map is available at the Ojai Chamber; ☎ 805-646-8126.

FAMILY LODGING

Ojai Valley Inn and Spa

905 Country Club Road, Ojai; ☎ 805-646-5511 or 888-697-8780; www.ojairesort.com; $279–$450, more for suites

This resort sits in the middle of a lovely golf course at the base of the Topa Topa Mountains, with an adjacent 800-acre ranch that you can explore via hiking and equestrian trails; tennis courts, a full-service spa, a beautiful swimming pool, and a lap pool are also on site. For kids ages 3 to 12, Camp Ojai is one of the best hotel children's programs we've ever experienced (though it's pricey—$55 half day, $70 full day, though some holidays, the evening program is offered for $50 per child). Our kids rode ponies, played Ping-Pong, had their faces painted, decorated hats, played in the Chumash hut, and spent a long time petting and visiting with the collection of miniature animals over in the barn area. We love the beamed, tiled rooms in the old adobe wing, but the modern, upscale-motel rooms are a good value.

ATTRACTION

Fillmore & Western Railway Company

APPEAL BY AGE	PRESCHOOL ★	GRADE SCHOOL ★★★	TEENS ★★
YOUNG ADULTS ★★★★		OVER 30 ★★★	SENIORS ★★★★

Boarding at railway depot, 250 Central Avenue, Fillmore; ☎ 805-524-2546; reservations: ☎ 800-773-8724; www.fwry.com

Hours Trains depart at various times; call or check Web site for more information. There are seasonal special trains, such as the Spaghetti Western all year, Pumpkin-liners in October, and Christmas Tree trains (cut your own tree and bring it back on the train) in December. There are also special dinner trains, including Murder Mystery with special whodunit-type fun. **Admission** Tickets $20 adults, $18 seniors age 60 and over, $10 children ages 4–12, $6 kids age 3 and younger; for special trains, prices are subject to change; 48-hour cancellation notice for refunds. **Touring time** Excursions average 2½ hours round trip; dinner trains 3½–4 hours. **Rainy-day touring** Yes. **Restaurants** Dinner trains. **Alcoholic beverages** Yes. **Disabled access** Some. **Wheelchair rental** No. **Baby-stroller rental** No. **Lockers** No. **Pet kennels** No. **Rain check** No. **Private tours** No.

DESCRIPTION AND COMMENTS   Southeast of Ojai is this little vintage train line that travels through a beautiful stretch of California nostalgia. Fillmore, where the rides begin and end, is one of the last pretty little rural towns in California; the various excursions take you through orange groves and agricultural lands. You ride in restored vintage cars, and, depending on the time, you might enjoy a murder mystery, musical entertainment, or such activities as pumpkin picking and Christmas-tree cutting. Meals range from celebrity-chef demonstrations and wine-tasting rides to family-friendly "spaghetti Westerns." Weekend day excursions have lunch service (extra charge).

FAMILY-FRIENDLY RESTAURANT

Oak Cafe and Terrace at the Ojai Valley Inn
905 Country Club Road, Ojai; ☎ 805-646-5511

Meals served Breakfast, lunch, dinner. **Cuisine** Californian. **Entree range** Breakfast, $10–$15; lunch, $12–$16; dinner, $13–$30. **Kids' menu** Yes. **Reservations** Accepted. **Payment** All major credit cards.

Parents craving a civilized grown-up meal will love this idyllic terrace restaurant overlooking the golf course. Not only is there a swell kids' menu (it even offers fruit!) and a fun little goody bag for each child, but the outdoor setting means that kids who've devoured their chicken fingers can safely explore the grounds while you finish your salmon in peace. The upscale, hip American cooking is expertly prepared.

SOLVANG

SOLVANG IS THE TOWN THAT TOURISM MADE. Its perfect placement as a stopping point on the long trip between L.A. and San Francisco—combined with the bright idea some decades ago for local businesses to emphasize the region's Danish heritage—turned it into a popular disembarking point for massive tour buses, but it's also a stop for Southern California families looking for a Sunday-drive destination.

Although Solvang is kitschy, it is visitor friendly, and we recommend it as an overnight base if you plan on exploring the area's authentic attractions such as the **Lake Cachuma** nature cruise (see "Family Outdoor Adventures").

It's especially nice for those families with several age groups. One parent can stay with little kids at the pool and not really miss anything (it's hot, hot, hot here from late spring through fall), while older kids are let out on their own to wander the village and another parent goes to the art-gallery town of **Los Olivos** or, with grandmother, heads for the flower fields of **Lompoc.**

BALLARD SCHOOL

It's fun to drive or bike past this little red 1883 schoolhouse and tell your kids that it's still in use. It's found at Cottonwood and School streets in the village of Ballard, a few miles north of Solvang.

FAMILY LODGING

Alisal Guest Ranch
1054 Alisal Road, Solvang; ☎ 805-688-6411 or 800-4-ALISAL; www.alisal.com; $450–$485 double occupancy, including breakfast and dinner; extra charge of $85 per child ages 6–12 and $55 per child ages 3–6; children age 2 and under free

Alisal, an old-money, intentionally low-key family resort, is the kind of place where even though the setting is outdoorsy, active, and rustic (with horseback riding, fishing, and canoeing), people are expected to dress for dinner and children to be on their best behavior. Golf is the central focus

solvang

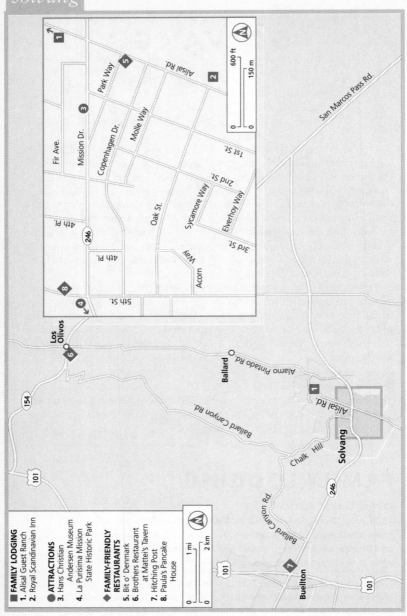

FAMILY LODGING
1. Alisal Guest Ranch
2. Royal Scandinavian Inn

ATTRACTIONS
3. Hans Christian
   Andersen Museum
4. La Purísima Mission
   State Historic Park

FAMILY-FRIENDLY
RESTAURANTS
5. Bit o' Denmark
6. Brothers Restaurant
   at Mattei's Tavern
7. Hitching Post
8. Paula's Pancake
   House

of the place, but there are tennis courts, a swimming pool, and a private lake. There are neither phones nor TVs in the 73 rooms and cottages. Kids ages 6 to 12 are invited to join free activities, such as a pool bash, nature hikes, reptile nights, and a mini-rodeo; occasional teen nights are also offered. The whole family joins together for barbecues and bingo night. Although it is located just outside Solvang, about a half hour from Santa Barbara, guests rarely leave the property.

Royal Scandinavian Inn

Solvang Royal Scandinavian Inn, 400 Alisal Road, Solvang;
☎ **805-688-8000 or 800-624-5572; www.royalscandinavianinn.com;**
$159–$249 summer, $139–$200 winter

We have vivid memories of sitting in the pool area here, looking out at the brown hills of the Santa Ynez Valley while the heat folded down on us like a sky full of blankets. In the cooler morning and evening, we were just steps away from some great bakeries and fun shops. Rooms (there are 133 rooms and 7 suites) have country décor, VCRs, Disney Channel. Kids' menus in restaurant and room service; Ping-Pong table.

ATTRACTIONS

Hans Christian Andersen Museum

APPEAL BY AGE	PRESCHOOL ★★	GRADE SCHOOL ★★	TEENS ★★
YOUNG ADULTS ★★		OVER 30 ★★	SENIORS ★★

1680 Mission Drive, Solvang; ☎ 805-688-2052;
www.solvangca.com/museum/h1.htm

Hours Daily, 10 a.m.–5 p.m. **Admission** Free. **Touring time** Average 30 minutes; minimum 15 minutes. **Rainy-day touring** Yes. **Restaurants** No. **Alcoholic beverages** No. **Disabled access** No. **Wheelchair rental** No. **Baby-stroller rental** No. **Lockers** No. **Pet kennels** No. **Rain check** No. **Private tours** No.

DESCRIPTION AND COMMENTS   A small gallery, this is actually the upstairs part of a building shared with a bookstore and feels like an exhibition space at a library. For fans of "The Princess and the Pea," "The Little Mermaid," and "The Ugly Duckling," there are little models of scenes from Andersen's life and stories, original letters by and photographs of the writer, whimsical artwork he created, and hundreds of first and early editions, as well as specially illustrated volumes of his works.

La Purisima Mission State Historic Park

APPEAL BY AGE	PRESCHOOL ★★★	GRADE SCHOOL ★★★★	TEENS ★★★
YOUNG ADULTS ★★★		OVER 30 ★★★★	SENIORS ★★★★

2295 Purisima Road (off Highway 246), Lompoc; ☎ 805-733-3713;
www.lapurisimamission.org

Hours Daily, 9 a.m.–5 p.m.; closed Thanksgiving, Christmas, and New Year's Days. **Admission** $4 per vehicle; $10 for large passenger commercial vans; call for rates for buses. **Touring time** Average 2 hours; minimum 1 hour, 3 hours with living-history program. **Rainy-day touring** Okay. **Restaurants** No. **Alcoholic beverages** No. **Disabled access** Yes. **Wheelchair rental** No. **Baby-stroller rental** No. **Lockers** No. **Pet kennels** No; pets allowed on leash, even in buildings. **Rain check** No. **Private tours** Yes.

DESCRIPTION AND COMMENTS   This tiny mission is marvelous to visit when the monthly living-history program is going on, so check ahead and see if your trip will coincide. Always held on either a Saturday or a Sunday from 11 a.m. to 2 p.m., it features costumed docents going about their mission-era business, with visitors eavesdropping on them and observing as they do their tasks with period tools and techniques.

FAMILY-FRIENDLY RESTAURANTS

Bit o' Denmark
473 Alisal Road, Solvang; ☎ 805-688-5426

Meals served Breakfast, lunch, and dinner. **Cuisine** American/Danish. **Entree range** Breakfast, $6–$7; lunch, $6–$9; dinner, $10–$22. **Kids' menu** $7–$8. **Reservations** Accepted. **Payment** All major credit cards.

Many visitors feel obliged to try smorgasbord while in Solvang, and this pleasant restaurant offers a nice sampling of salads, smoked fish, and other Danish dishes, as well as American entrees. In spring and fall, the patio is a nice place to be, and there's a full bar.

Brothers Restaurant at Mattei's Tavern
Railway Avenue at State Road 154, Los Olivos; ☎ 805-688-4820

Meals served Dinner, nightly. **Cuisine** American. **Entree range** Dinner, $16–$42. **Kids' menu** Yes. **Reservations** Recommended. **Payment** MC, V.

Run by brothers and chefs Matt and Jeff Nichols, this 1886-built stagecoach stop–turned restaurant is a beloved Santa Barbara wine country way station. With its massive stone fireplace, garden grounds, and upscale menu (tempura shrimp, prime rib, rack of lamb), this is a special-occasion restaurant, but one that welcomes families and offers a children's menu.

Hitching Post
Highway 246 (1 mile from 101 Freeway), Buellton; ☎ 805-688-0676

Meals served Dinner **Cuisine** American/steak house. **Entree range** $13–$35. **Kids' menu** $8. **Reservations** Recommended. **Payment** AE, MC, V.

A well-known steak and barbecue restaurant in a meat-eating part of the world, the Hitching Post is particularly nice in the early part of the evening while seniors are enjoying the early-bird specials and the kids are ravenous. The approach is straight out of the 1950s: Appetizers are a relish tray or shrimp cocktail, steak is cooked over an open oak fire, and the French fries are highly recommended.

Paula's Pancake House
1531 Mission Drive, Solvang; ☎ 805-688-2867

Meals served Breakfast and lunch. **Cuisine** American/Danish. **Entree range** $7–$9. **Kids' menu** No, but small/split portions available. **Reservations** Not accepted. **Payment** All major credit cards.

If the local pastry shops aren't enough fortification, head for this cheerful breakfast haven for buttermilk or thin Danish pancakes, sausages, omelets, and waffles.

SAN LUIS OBISPO

THIS SMALL CITY IS A MODEL OF WORKABILITY. Its renovated downtown is lively with students from the nearby university as well as families and businesspeople. The mission plaza, also restored, features a running creek that's the centerpiece of the park. Although the suburbs hint at the growth that's come to the area, the city center itself is as tree-lined and friendly as ever.

There's a visitors center at 1039 Chorro Street and a trolley that runs for free along a downtown corridor of several blocks, but this is not a tourist-attraction town. It's a good base for visits to **Hearst Castle** to the north and nearby beach towns: **Pismo, Morro Bay,** and the closest, **Avila,** just four miles from town. Take a stroll on Avila's pier, below which sea lions await scraps thrown over by fishermen, and allow time to pick seasonal fruit at the **Avila Valley Barn** (560 Avila Beach Drive; ☎ 805-595-2810). In the fall, the Barn is duded up with pumpkins, and a tractor-pulled hayride and a hay maze are provided.

MISSION PLAZA

Found at Monterey and Chorro streets in downtown San Luis Obispo, this former eyesore was redesigned and transformed in the 1960s into a city-center gathering place where workers eat their brown-bag lunches, children wade in the creek, and tourists head for the mission or the historic adobe.

FAMILY LODGING

Embassy Suites Hotel
333 Madonna Road, San Luis Obispo; ☎ 805-549-0800 or 800-EMBASSY; www.embassysuites.com; $169 and up in winter; $200 and up in summer

This branch of the national chain has 196 suites and is connected to the Central Coast Mall, so teens can roam and younger kids can enjoy the swimming pools, but downtown is too far away to walk. Breakfast included, kids' menu in restaurant and room service, Nintendo in rooms.

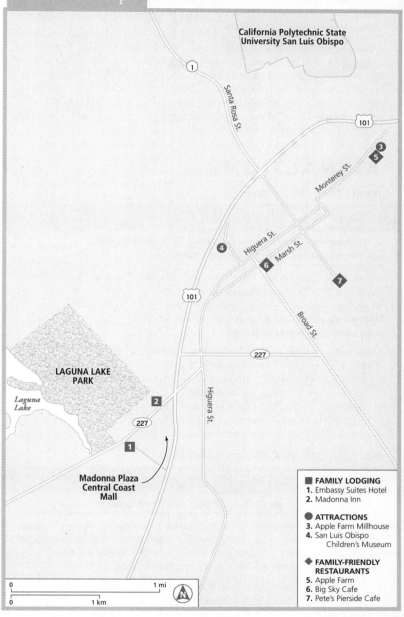

san luis obispo

California Polytechnic State
University San Luis Obispo

LAGUNA LAKE
PARK

Laguna
Lake

Madonna Plaza
Central Coast
Mall

0   1 mi
0   1 km

■ **FAMILY LODGING**
1. Embassy Suites Hotel
2. Madonna Inn

● **ATTRACTIONS**
3. Apple Farm Millhouse
4. San Luis Obispo
    Children's Museum

◆ **FAMILY-FRIENDLY
RESTAURANTS**
5. Apple Farm
6. Big Sky Cafe
7. Pete's Pierside Cafe

Madonna Inn

100 Madonna Road, San Luis Obispo; ☎ 805-543-3000 or 800-543-9666; www.madonnainn.com; $168–$445; children under age 12 stay free

Most people just stop here to have a bite in the restaurant and peek at the elaborately overdecorated restrooms, and to visit the office and look at the pictures of the 109 rooms and 36 suites (no two alike), outrageously themed along the lines of Cave-Man Room (with a rock shower) and other fantasies. Ostriches, emus, and ranch animals roam the grounds. If you're willing to pay for an elaborate joke, you might like a stay here. There are kids' menus in the two restaurants.

ATTRACTIONS

Apple Farm Millhouse

APPEAL BY AGE	PRESCHOOL ★★★	GRADE SCHOOL ★★★	TEENS ★★
YOUNG ADULTS ★★		OVER 30 ★★★	SENIORS ★★★

2015 Monterey Street, San Luis Obispo; ☎ 800-255-2040, ask for restaurant or inn; www.applefarm.com

Hours Daily, 9 a.m.–6 p.m. **Admission** Free. **Touring time** Average 30 minutes; minimum 30 minutes. **Rainy-day touring** Better on a nice day; interior quite small. **Restaurants** Next door. **Alcoholic beverages** Yes. **Disabled access** Yes. **Wheelchair rental** No. **Baby-stroller rental** No. **Lockers** No. **Pet kennels** No. **Rain check** No. **Private tours** No.

DESCRIPTION AND COMMENTS Within the buildings of the Apple Farm Inn, behind the Apple Farm restaurant, is a replica of a 19th-century mill. It's a working mill, constructed with such attention to period detail (using salvaged parts from other mills) that local schoolchildren come here for field trips to see the 14-foot-high waterwheel move the gears that turn the stones to grind the wheat or press the apples. Products made here are sold in the gift shop and restaurant.

San Luis Obispo Children's Museum

APPEAL BY AGE	PRESCHOOL ★★★★	GRADE SCHOOL ★★★	TEENS ★ YOUNG
ADULTS ★		OVER 30 ★	SENIORS ★

1010 Nipomo, San Luis Obispo; ☎ 805-544-5437; www.slokids.org

Hours Call first. **Admission** To be determined. **Touring time** Average 2 hours; minimum 1 hour. **Rainy-day touring** Yes. **Restaurants** No. **Alcoholic beverages** No. **Disabled access** Yes. **Wheelchair rental** No. **Baby-stroller rental** No. **Lockers** No. **Pet kennels** No. **Rain check** No. **Private tours** No.

DESCRIPTION AND COMMENTS At press time, this fine children's museum was under construction, with the snazzy new three-story building slated to open in December 2006. Some of the forthcoming exhibits are a closely held secret, but we know the second floor will be devoted to a kid-sized "town" of San Luis Obispo, with a fire station, diner, 16-foot-tall climbable clock tower, and more, and the top floor will pay homage to SLO's railroad heritage with a train-themed play area for preschoolers. Call before visiting to check on hours and admission. This promises to be a wonderful destination for children.

SAN LUIS OBISPO FARMERS' MARKET

Held on Higuera Street on Thursdays (year-round, 6:30 to 9 p.m.), this is a lively and fun street fair and market that our kids loved. In addition to the usual farmers market offerings of produce, flowers, and herbs, this festive gathering includes food booths of many kinds (don't miss the famous SLO tri-tip) and such street entertainment as puppet shows, musicians, and jugglers.

FAMILY-FRIENDLY RESTAURANTS

Apple Farm
2015 Monterey Street, San Luis Obispo; ☎ 805-544-6100; www.applefarm.com

Meals served Daily; breakfast, lunch, and dinner. **Cuisine** American. **Entree range** Breakfast, $7–$15; lunch, $10–$15; dinner, $10–$24. **Kids' menu** $6–$8. **Reservations** Recommended. **Payment** All major credit cards.

What was once a cute grandma-ish roadside cafe has become a phony theme restaurant, but the pancakes and cinnamon French toast are still terrific, and kids are well catered to.

Big Sky Cafe
1121 Broad Street, downtown San Luis Obispo; ☎ 805-545-5401

Meals served Breakfast, lunch, and dinner. **Cuisine** Californian. **Entree range** Breakfast, $4–$10; lunch, $8–$20; dinner, $12–$25. **Kids' menu** Yes. **Reservations** Not accepted. **Payment** AE, MC, V.

A funky-chic cafe that's noisy, lively, colorful, and earnestly Californian, featuring local organic products and local wines. The kitchen turns out great sandwiches, pastas, salads, Latin dishes, and homey desserts.

Pete's Pierside Cafe
Harford Pier, Avila Beach Drive, Avila Beach; ☎ 805-595-7627

Meals served Lunch and dinner. **Cuisine** Californian. **Entree range** $4–$12. **Kids' menu** No. **Reservations** Not accepted. **Payment** MC, V.

Delicious, cheap waterfront chow—shrimp tacos, clam chowder, sandwiches, calamari—is served out on a real working fishermen's pier without the usual tourist shops but with frequent visits from sea lions and seabirds. Some of the fresh-fish dishes will have been just caught the night before.

SIDE TRIP: *Morro Bay*

unofficial **TIP**
One of the best family adventures we've ever had was renting kayaks and paddling past otters to Montana de Oro State Park, where we ran down soft sand dunes.

NO ONE WHO DRIVES THIS STRETCH OF COAST will forget the sight of **Morro Rock** looming 578 feet tall in this city's harbor, even if the sight lines are obstructed at some vantage points by the equally looming power plant next to the rock. The pleasures here include a bustling harbor, a tranquil bird sanctuary, and hotels and cafes that bring you close to the shore and its wildlife. You could also stay here and combine a visit to **Hearst Castle** with nature-loving time.

FAMILY LODGING

Gray's Inn
561 Embarcadero, Morro Bay; ☎ 805-772-3911; webpages.charter.net/graysinn; $100–$145, winter; $140–$165, spring and fall; $160–$170, summer

This tiny inn is located right on the waterfront in a building that also houses an art gallery. It has only three rooms, but they each have living rooms and kitchens, so this is a good value for small families who like a lively setting. No restaurant.

☀ The Inn at Morro Bay
60 State Park Road, Morro Bay State Park; ☎ 805-772-5651 or 800-321-9566; www.innatmorrobay.com; $119–$229

Situated in Morro Bay State Park in a spot that's notable for birds, the inn has rooms furnished with brass beds and fireplaces; two-thirds of them have ocean views and most have mini–hot tubs on their balconies. Sea otters live in the waters in front. It's a peaceful, quiet spot away from town center, with very good views. There are five family-size rooms, children's menus, a heated pool, and free mountain bikes, and kayak rentals are available.

THE EMBARCADERO

This waterfront area has restaurants, fish markets, art galleries, and such, and its small-craft harbor is the embarkation point for boat cruises and fishing charters. A giant chessboard in a park along the way has hand-carved two- and three-foot-tall game pieces. The aquarium and commercial fishing docks are located here, too.

ATTRACTIONS

Morro Bay Aquarium

APPEAL BY AGE	PRESCHOOL ★★★	GRADE SCHOOL ★★	TEENS ★★
YOUNG ADULTS ★★		OVER 30 ★★	SENIORS ★★

595 Embarcadero Street (on the waterfront), Morro Bay;
☎ **805-772-7647; www.morrobay.com/morrobayaquarium**

Hours Daily, 9:30 a.m.–5:30 p.m. (may be open as late as 6 p.m.). **Admission** $2, $1 children ages 5–11, free for children age 4 and under. **Touring time** Average 30 minutes; minimum 10 minutes to see the seals. **Rainy-day touring** Bring umbrellas for outside sites. **Restaurants** No. **Alcoholic beverages** No. **Disabled access** Yes. **Wheelchair rental** No. **Baby-stroller rental** No. **Lockers** No. **Pet kennels** No. **Rain check** No. **Private tours** No.

DESCRIPTION AND COMMENTS Although this small facility doesn't hold a candle to the high-tech, superdesigned glamour of the big-time aquariums, it's not crowded, either, and small children won't be overwhelmed by mobs and noise. Kids can feed seals and sea lions and check on marine mammals being cared for in a rescue center, as well as look at eels, small sharks, and the like in 14 small tanks.

Morro Bay State Park Museum of Natural History

APPEAL BY AGE	PRESCHOOL ★★	GRADE SCHOOL ★★★	TEENS ★★★
YOUNG ADULTS ★★★		OVER 30 ★★★	SENIORS ★★★

Morro Bay State Park Road, Morro Bay State Park; ☎ **805-772-2694; www.mbspmuseum.org**

Hours Daily, 10 a.m.–5 p.m.; closed Thanksgiving, Christmas, and New Year's Days. **Admission** $2 adult, free for children age 16 and under. **Touring time** Average 1 hour; minimum 30 minutes. **Rainy-day touring** No problem. **Restaurants** No. **Alcoholic beverages** No. **Disabled access** Yes. **Wheelchair rental** No. **Baby-stroller rental** No. **Lockers** No. **Pet kennels** No. **Rain check** No. **Private tours** No.

DESCRIPTION AND COMMENTS Overlooking the bay from a high, rocky bluff, the museum also overlooks a large heron rookery and has several trailheads to viewing areas. Exhibits and dioramas focus on the flora and fauna (including marine life) of the area, as well as on geology and Native American history. Check times of nature walks and presentations.

FAMILY-FRIENDLY RESTAURANTS

 Bayside Cafe

10 State Park Road, Morro Bay State Park; ☎ **805-772-1465**

Meals served Lunch daily, and dinner Thursday–Sunday. **Cuisine** Cal-Mexican and seafood. **Entree range** Lunch, $5–$12; dinner, $7–$20. **Kids' menu** Yes. **Reservations** Not accepted. **Payment** No credit cards.

Located in the state park's marina area, this terrific find looks out over the waters of the back bay. It's less expensive than the waterfront restaurants, but the clam chowder and other seafood dishes are just as fresh, and the generous lunches—dishes like a black-bean-and-fish burrito or seafood taco salad—satisfy hearty appetites.

Dorn's Original Breakers Cafe
801 Market Street, Morro Bay; ☎ 805-772-4415

Meals served Breakfast, lunch, and dinner. **Cuisine** American. **Entree range** $10–$30. **Kids' menu** Yes. **Reservations** Recommended. **Payment** MC, V.

This is a great place for breakfast, with a view of the Rock and specialties like seafood omelets and blueberry pancakes. Lunch and dinner dishes include seafood and meats. Located in the same white-clapboard, Cape Cod–style building since 1942, Dorn's is in great shape, with a new deck and a well-maintained décor of ship models, pictures of fishermen, and such. Parents of hungry kids, take note: they begin serving dinner at 4 p.m.

Margie's Diner
1698 North Main, Morro Bay; ☎ 805-772-2510; www.margiesdiner.com

Meals served Breakfast, lunch, and dinner. **Cuisine** American. **Entree range** Breakfast and lunch, $5–$11; dinner, $8–$15. **Kids' menu** No. **Reservations** Not accepted. **Payment** No credit cards, but personal checks okay.

A proper diner, not a trendy imitation, serving chicken-fried steak, big omelets, hamburgers, shakes, and homemade pie. There's no kids' menu, but the portions are large, and they'll split plates at no extra charge.

SIDE TRIP: *Pismo Beach*

THIS BEACH TOWN PRIDES ITSELF on being in a bit of a time warp, with shell shops like Grandma used to shop in, and lots of chowder shacks and postwar beach-town motels.

FAMILY LODGING

The Sandcastle Inn
100 Stimson Avenue, Pismo Beach; ☎ 805-773-2422 or 800-822-6606; www.sandcastleinn.com; $109–$249

Boasting an enviable beachfront location, this recently renovated place offers fine ocean views and a beachfront spa (but no pool). Among the 60 rooms in three stories are several family-size junior suites, one with a kitchenette.

FAMILY-FRIENDLY RESTAURANT

Giuseppe's
891 Price Street, Pismo Beach; ☎ 805-773-2870; www.giuseppesrestaurant.com

Meals served Lunch and dinner. **Cuisine** Italian. **Entree range** Lunch, $9–$16; dinner, $9–$22. **Kids' menu** No. **Reservations** Not accepted. **Payment** All major credit cards.

Surely the best place in town, with or without kids, this homey, noisy, informal Italian eatery is a terrific family restaurant. Try the spaghetti and meatballs.

SIDE TRIP:
San Simeon and Cambria

THE FIRST FEW TIMES WE CAME TO **San Simeon,** we didn't even know the place had a name. It seemed to be simply an area of motels and coffee shops near **Hearst Castle.** And that's what it is. But it is a convenient place to stay, and our kids had a great time splashing with other traveling families in a sheltered pool after a long drive.

Meanwhile, **Cambria** is just too cute for most active families, unless you have some country-cozy–loving shop browsers. A veritable capital of bed-and-breakfasts, Cambria is located on the curve as the highway heads to the sea, between San Luis Obispo and San Simeon.

unofficial **TIP**
Your best bet is to arrive in the late afternoon the day before your early morning Hearst Castle tour. Swim, eat, sleep, and hit the castle the next day.

FAMILY LODGING

Best Western Cavalier
9415 Hearst Drive, San Simeon; ☎ 805-927-4688 or 800-826-8168; www.cavalierresort.com; $139–$279

A utilitarian motel with 90 large rooms, many of which have stunning views of the ocean from the bluff above. Some rooms have terraces, some have fireplaces, and all have VCRs. Extras include two pools, spa, gym, kids' menus in restaurant and room service, and binoculars for whale watching.

Best Western Courtesy Inn
9450 Castillo Drive, San Simeon; ☎ 805-927-4691 or 800-555-5773; $99–$200

On our visit to this hotel, every parking space was filled with a car that was loaded with luggage and ice chests. Kids ran up and down the outside corridors, heading for the ice machines or the indoor pool, which was appreciated as the afternoon quickly cooled. Of the 115 motel-standard units, 25 are efficiencies. Laundry facilities are on site, and there's a restaurant adjacent.

San Simeon Pines
7200 Moonstone Beach Drive, Cambria; ☎ 866-927-4648; www.sspines.com; $120–$150

This is a hint of Big Sur before you get to Big Sur. Perhaps it's the dark-shingled buildings, or the twisted cypresses and pines, or the rocky beach below the motel where we spotted seals. But you know you're not in Southern California anymore, Toto. Put on a sweater, play a little shuffle-board or croquet, and enjoy the eight-acre grounds of this 125-room, 60-suite motel. There's a pool, and continental breakfast is included in your stay.

ATTRACTION

☀ Hearst Castle–San Simeon State Historical Monument

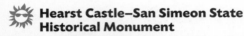

APPEAL BY AGE	PRESCHOOL ★	GRADE SCHOOL ★	TEENS ★★
YOUNG ADULTS ★★	OVER 30 ★★★★		SENIORS ★★★★

Off Highway 1, San Simeon; ☎ 805-927-2020 or reservations ☎ 800-444-4445; www.hearst-castle.org

Hours March–September: daily, 8 a.m.–6 p.m.; October–February: Monday–Friday, 9 a.m.–5 p.m.; Saturday and Sunday, 9 a.m.–3 p.m. Closed Thanksgiving, Christmas, and New Year's Days. **Admission** $20 adults, $10 children ages 6–17, free for children age 5 and under. **Touring time** Average 1 hour 45 minutes. **Rainy-day touring** Yes. **Restaurants** Concession stand. **Alcoholic beverages** No. **Disabled access** Yes. **Wheelchair rental** Free; call for special tours. **Lockers** Yes. **Pet kennels** No. **Baby-stroller rental** No; not allowed on tour. **Rain check** No. **Private tours** Call ☎ 805-927-2070.

DESCRIPTION AND COMMENTS Face it, this isn't a great stop for young children. They just don't get it. And why should they? It's hard enough for adults to grasp the beautiful weirdness of a place that is largely made up of pieces and parts of European churches and palaces that are older than the state they are visiting (having been disassembled, shipped across the seas, and reassembled here as dining room walls and corridor embellishments). Even official brochures warn that "young children may find the stairs, museum restrictions, and group format challenging." But school-age kids and teens will make it through one of the shorter tours, all of which include the cool swimming pools. The latest add-on is a 40-minute *National Geographic* movie, which is shown as part of the shortest tours. Make sure to book your tour in advance—this place draws the crowds!

SIDE TRIP: *Big Sur*

GETTING THERE, ESPECIALLY FROM THE SOUTH, can be hell with a car sickness–prone kid, but if you have to keep pulling over, at least you'll have the awesome view as a reward. Once you get to **Big Sur,** you'll find a town in which the clocks seemed to have stopped back in 1971—the hippie lives here, and lives well. Oh, sure, things have gotten fancy with the big-bucks **Post Ranch Inn,** but you'll still see rusted-out VW vans and tie-dyes. The only thing for families to do in Big Sur is soak in the natural beauty, preferably among the redwoods in **Pfeiffer–Big Sur State Park,** where you can pass happy days camping or staying in the lodge. A horseback ride on the beach is lots of fun; we also love hiking the gorgeous trails and playing on the beaches.

FAMILY LODGING

Deetjen's Big Sur Inn

Highway 1 at south end of town, Big Sur; ☎ 831-667-2377; www.deetjens.com; $75–$200

Rich with funky, ex-hippie, Big Sur charm, Deetjen's is a ragtag collection of cottages tucked among the redwoods in a setting of great beauty. Walls may be thin, beds a little creaky, and housekeeping on the simple side, but you won't find a motel more atmospheric than this one. The restaurant serves a killer breakfast (get the pancakes), but you'll need reservations.

Pfeiffer–Big Sur State Park Campground and Big Sur Lodge

Off Highway 1, Big Sur; ☎ 831-667-2315; reservations: Reserve America, ☎ 800-444-7275; www.reserveamerica.com; campsites $16–$20

A beloved family campground, this park has 218 campsites nestled among the redwoods just inland from the breathtaking Big Sur coast. Each site has tables, stoves, and food lockers; some are next to Big Sur River and some are in the redwoods, while others rest in oak groves or meadows. There are no hookups, but there are showers, laundry facilities, a store, and a cafe. A more luxurious choice (in relative terms) is the park's Big Sur Lodge, where you can rent a simple motel-style cottage in the redwoods, perhaps even with a fireplace, for $99 to $149 (call ☎ 831-667-3100 or 800-424-4787; **www.bigsurlodge.com** for reservations—well in advance). See also the park description in "The Best Beaches and Parks."

FAMILY-FRIENDLY RESTAURANTS

Big Sur Bakery and Restaurant

Highway 1 (middle of town), Big Sur; ☎ 831-667-0520; www.bigsurbakery.com

Meals served Breakfast, lunch, and dinner. **Cuisine** American and Mediterranean. **Entree range** Breakfast and lunch, $12–$18; dinner, $27–$36. **Kids' menu** No. **Reservations** Recommended. **Payment** MC, V.

A serious restaurant disguised as a casual-funky, indoor-outdoor bakery, this place has fantastic food. The couple who do the cooking—she is the baker and he is the chef—produce a hearty cuisine that's appealing to everyone. Carnivores adore the grilled prime rib and roasted Niman Ranch pork loin, and vegetarians have tons to choose from, too. The wood-fired pizzas are outstanding; our kids pronounce the cheeses-and-tomato-sauce pizza to be the best one they've ever had. Save room for one of the amazing desserts, and consider picking up some cookies from the bakery counter to sustain you on the Highway 1 drive. The counter can also make a good latte or cocoa to go.

Nepenthe and Cafe Kevah
Highway 1 (south end of town), Big Sur; ☎ 831-667-2345

Meals served Breakfast, lunch, and dinner. **Cuisine** American. **Entree range** Lunch, $13–$16; dinner, $13–$37. **Kids' menu** No. **Reservations** Not necessary. **Payment** AE, MC, V.

Surely the best-view restaurant on the California coast, Nepenthe and its outdoor-cafe sibling, Cafe Kevah, can be forgiven if the food isn't memorable. We've had a decent burger and some mighty good fries, however, which tasted even better on the terrace, with the famed Big Sur coastline tumbling down below. Teenagers will like the downstairs gift shop, featuring local crafts. A fine refueling stop after the long drive from the south.

MONTEREY

MONTEREY IS A BEAUTIFUL CITY, AND SINCE ITS REMARKABLE AQUARIUM has become a top tourist attraction, it's on most must-see lists for travelers to California. And how wonderful that is, because Monterey is as much a part of how Californians feel about themselves, thanks to the novels of John Steinbeck and the recordings of the **Monterey Jazz Festival,** as the waterfalls of Yosemite or the star-studded sidewalks of Hollywood.

California's regions can each be symbolized by a tree that dominates the landscape. In the south, it's the palm tree; in the north, the redwood; and in the north-central coast, here on the Monterey Peninsula, it's the cypress tree. The Monterey Cypress survives only on **Point Lobos,** where the dramatic trees, twisted into starkly artistic shapes by the wind, are preserved in a state reserve. But there are other varieties of cypresses planted throughout the city, giving it a special dark-green canopy. Another striking characteristic of Monterey is its preserved 19th-century historic district, a rarity in California, but not an attraction we recommend spending a lot of time in with young children. Instead, look to the gem in the crown of the revitalized waterfront: the **Monterey Bay Aquarium,** one of the largest in the country.

EASY MONTEREY OUTINGS

CANNERY ROW Several self-contained mini-malls now reside in the former sardine canneries made famous by novelist John Steinbeck; most are just tourist shops, which will interest a 13-year-old but not a 6-year-old. But kids of all ages like the **Oceans 18** indoor miniature golf course in the American Tin Cannery (125 Ocean Boulevard; ☎ 831-643-9215). And for a souvenir with soul, go to **Friends of the Sea Otter,** also inside the American Tin Cannery (☎ 831-642-9037), which sells books, gifts, and educational materials; all proceeds benefit the otters. For a Cannery Row Resource Guide, call ☎ 831-649-6690 or go to **www.canneryrow.com.**

FISHERMAN'S WHARF Even kids who think seafood is yucky (seafood restaurants being the main attraction at Fisherman's Wharf) will get a kick out of the sea lions who frequent the pier area. Charter fishing boats and sightseeing boats tie up here.

monterey

■ **FAMILY LODGING**
1. Casa Munras Garden Hotel
2. Hyatt Regency
3. Lighthouse Lodge
4. Manresa Uplands State
   Beach Campground
5. Monterey Marriott

● **ATTRACTIONS**
6. Monterey Bay Aquarium
7. M.Y. Museum
8. Peter Hay Par Three
9. Point Pinos Lighthouse

◆ **FAMILY-FRIENDLY
RESTAURANTS**
10. Abalonetti Seafood
    Trattoria
11. Jose's
12. Old Monterey Cafe
13. Whaling Station Prime
    Steaks and Seafood

MONTEREY PENINSULA RECREATION TRAIL This 18-mile trail connects parks and paths between Asilomar State Beach in Pacific Grove and the city of Castroville. It is a multiuse trail for walkers, bikers, and surrey pedalers and goes along the shore past Point Pinos Lighthouse, the Monterey Bay Aquarium, Cannery Row, the Custom House Plaza, and De Monte Beach. The trail is equipped with drinking fountains, bike racks, and benches at various points.

OLD MONTEREY MARKETPLACE Tuesday afternoons year-round, this farmers market is a great way for families to enjoy Old Monterey (as opposed to, say, a docent walking tour of the historic buildings). There are produce stalls, flowers, and arts and crafts, as well as food and entertainment.

FAMILY LODGING

Casa Munras Garden Hotel
700 Munras Avenue, Monterey; ☎ 831-375-2411, 800-222-2558, or 800-222-2446 in CA; www.casamunras-hotel.com; $179–$209 summer, $149–$169 winter

A nice change from cookie-cutter motels, this hotel near Fisherman's Wharf fills an 1824 building on acres of landscaped grounds. The 166 rooms have some special touches, like brass beds, and there are a few family-size junior suites. Outside is a heated pool with a large shallow end for kids. A shuttle bus runs to local attractions, and you can buy aquarium tickets here.

Hyatt Regency
1 Old Golf Course Road, Monterey; ☎ 831-372-1234 or 800-633-7313; www.hyatt.com; $165–$385

If you're looking for a Monterey hotel with a children's program, the free Camp Hyatt program attracts 3- to 15-year-olds with garden-variety activities. Around the 575-room property, you'll find two pools, spas, a game room, a volleyball court, tennis, a golf course, a sports bar, and a bike-rental concession. Children's menus offered.

Lighthouse Lodge
1150 and 1249 Lighthouse Avenue, Pacific Grove; ☎ 831-655-2111 or 800-858-1249; www.lhls.com/lodge; $120–$240

Clever new owners took two motel properties and jazzed them up with families in mind. On one side of the street is a former Best Western, comfortably furnished with a few upscale touches, including 32-inch TVs and robes; the rooms (including double-doubles that are popular with families) surround a pool, at which a free barbecue (hamburgers and hot dogs) is held every evening. On the other side of the street is a smaller building with 31 suites, some of which are ideal for families. Room rates include a full breakfast and the aforementioned barbecue; typically on offer are good package deals that include admission to the aquarium and/or whale-watching trips. The tide pools of Pacific Grove are just a block away.

Manresa Uplands State Beach Campground

205 Manresa Beach Road (off San Andreas Road), La Selva Beach;
☎ **831-761-1795; reservations: Reserve America, ☎ 800-444-7275;**
www.reserveamerica.com; campsites $13–$20

Beach campgrounds don't get any more peaceful and lovely than this small tent-camping retreat, which forbids RVs. The location is gorgeous, on a bluff overlooking Monterey Bay, shaded by Monterey pines and eucalyptus; a trail leads down to the long sand beach. Fire rings, picnic tables, showers, flush toilets.

Monterey Marriott
350 Calle Principal, Monterey; ☎ 831-649-4234 or 800-228-9290;
www.marriotthotels.com; $189 and up

This ten-story modern hotel doesn't have much in the way of charm, but it does have views to spare, along with a relaxed, family-friendly atmosphere and good family amenities. Rooms are large, with refrigerators, tables and chairs, and sometimes couches; kids get Nintendo and the Disney Channel. A children's menu is available in both the restaurant and room service, and the concierge can get you a qualified babysitter.

ATTRACTIONS

Monterey Bay Aquarium

APPEAL BY AGE	PRESCHOOL ★★★★	GRADE SCHOOL ★★★★★	TEENS ★★★★★
YOUNG ADULTS ★★★★★		OVER 30 ★★★★★	SENIORS ★★★★

886 Cannery Row, Monterey; ☎ 831-648-4800; advance tickets:
☎ **800-756-3737; www.mbayaq.org**

Hours June–August: daily, 9:30 a.m.–6 p.m.; rest of year: 10 a.m.–6 p.m.; closed Christmas Day. **Admission** $22 adults; $20 seniors, students ages 13–17, and college students with ID; $12.95 for guests with disabilities and children ages 3–12. **Touring time** Average 4 hours; minimum 2 hours. **Rainy-day touring** Yes. **Restaurants** Yes. **Alcoholic beverages** Yes. **Disabled access** Yes. **Wheelchair rental** Yes, free. **Baby-stroller rental** No. **Lockers** Yes. **Pet kennels** No. **Rain check** No. **Private tours** Yes, $75 and up.

DESCRIPTION AND COMMENTS Don't despair. If you forget to call way, way ahead for advance tickets to the aquarium for the day of your visit, you can avoid waiting in line for too long. Ask at your hotel—many sell tickets good for the next day or two.

Is it really that crowded? Yes. Is it really worth it? Yes. You haven't seen an aquarium until you've seen the Outer Bay exhibit, a million-gallon tank filled with sharks, sea turtles, barracuda, and tuna, and the spectacular three-story "kelp forest" tank, which holds hundreds of species. Because the tanks tower from floor to ceiling, you have the sensation of actually being on the ocean floor looking up.

But to really enjoy the aquarium, a few things should be considered. The youngest children won't find cartoon-cute animals that jump and play with balls like at SeaWorld, and you may discover that the beautiful, impressive tanks of jellyfish and other animals don't hold preschoolers' attention for long (although some will put nose to the glass and not move for hours). Let the little ones hang out and watch the antics of the sea otters, those charismatic mammals that swim on their backs and seem to grin at spectators. Then take them to the Splash Zone, an experiential, interactive museum-within-a-museum designed for children from toddlers to about age 9. Young ones can climb and crawl through shore habitats, sit in a giant clam chair, feel sea critters in a touch pool, and go "inside" a penguin community. While 3- to 9-year-olds stage underwater plays in the costume and puppet area, babies and toddlers can play in Coral Cove, a place just for tiny ones.

School-age kids will want to spend a lot of time at the bat-ray pool, another pet-the-fish area. The 100 or so exhibits include an aviary and a video feed from a submarine down in Monterey Bay. And don't forget to check for the feeding times, which are posted—they make for a good show. There's a restaurant and a gift shop–bookstore.

M. Y. Museum

APPEAL BY AGE	PRESCHOOL ★★★★		GRADE SCHOOL ★★★★
TEENS ★	YOUNG ADULTS ★	OVER 30 ★	SENIORS ★

601 Wave Street, Monterey; ☎ 831-649-6444; www.mymuseum.org

Hours Monday–Saturday, 10 a.m.–5 p.m.; Sunday, noon–5 p.m.; closed Wednesday, Easter, Thanksgiving, Christmas, and New Year's Days. **Admission** $5.50, free for children under age 2. **Touring time** Average 2 hours; minimum 1 hour. **Rainy-day touring** Yes. **Restaurants** Yes. **Alcoholic beverages** Yes. **Disabled access** Yes. **Wheelchair rental** Yes. **Baby-stroller rental** Yes. **Lockers** Yes. **Pet kennels** No. **Rain check** No. **Private tours** Photo Caravan, age 8 and over, $65–$89.

DESCRIPTION AND COMMENTS M. Y. stands for "Monterey Youth" at this interactive children's museum. A good spot for hands-on, action-oriented entertainment, including life-size environments that let very young kids fish from a boat, "buy" food and supplies, be a cook or a customer in a restaurant, and make a puppet show. Our kids' favorite exhibits are the Magnetic Center, where they make structures out of magnetic pieces, and Build-a-House, where they don hard hats and build brick walls, fix plumbing, and hang wallpaper.

Peter Hay Par Three

APPEAL BY AGE	PRESCHOOL ★	GRADE SCHOOL ★★★	TEENS ★★★
YOUNG ADULTS ★★★		OVER 30 ★★	SENIORS ★★★

17 Mile Drive, Pebble Beach; ☎ 831-622-8723

Hours Daily, 6:30 a.m.–dark; call to make sure there are no golf clinics. **Admission** $20 for as many rounds as you like. **Touring time** Average 1 hour; minimum 45 minutes. **Rainy-day touring** No. **Restaurants** Yes. **Alcoholic beverages** Yes. **Disabled access** Yes. **Wheelchair rental** No. **Baby-stroller rental** No. **Lockers** No, storage available. **Pet kennels** No. **Rain check** No. **Private tours** Lessons.

DESCRIPTION AND COMMENTS For the budding Tiger Woodses in your family, make a stop at the Peter Hay Par Three public golf course in Pebble Beach. It's a pitch-and-putt that's part of the complex of famous courses that include the Pebble Beach Golf Links and the Links at Spanish Bay. No reservations needed for tee times, but call ahead in case a golf clinic is scheduled. Nine holes; the longest is 18 yards.

Point Pinos Lighthouse

APPEAL BY AGE	PRESCHOOL ★	GRADE SCHOOL ★★★	TEENS ★★★
YOUNG ADULTS ★★★	OVER 30 ★★★	SENIORS ★★★	

Lighthouse Avenue at Asilomar Boulevard; ☎ 831-648-5716

Hours Thursday–Monday, 1–4 p.m.; 11:30 a.m.–5 p.m. in summer. **Admission** Free; requested donation $2 for adults, $1 for kids. **Touring time** Average 45 minutes; minimum 20 minutes. **Rainy-day touring** Not pleasant. **Restaurants** No. **Alcoholic beverages** No. **Disabled access** No. **Wheelchair rental** No. **Baby-stroller rental** No. **Lockers** No. **Pet kennels** No. **Rain check** No. **Private tours** No.

DESCRIPTION AND COMMENTS The oldest lighthouse still in operation on the West Coast, Point Pinos dates from 1855. This is a quick stop—the kids can run up the stairs to the top of the lighthouse, and there's a little museum room downstairs.

▌ FAMILY-FRIENDLY RESTAURANTS

Abalonetti Seafood Trattoria
57 Fisherman's Wharf, Monterey; ☎ 831-373-1851;
www.abalonettimonterey.com

Meals served Lunch and dinner. **Cuisine** American/seafood. **Entree range** Lunch, $9–$14; dinner, $15–$25. **Kids' menu** Yes. **Reservations** Recommended. **Payment** All major credit cards.

It may look like a tourist trap, but this wharf restaurant turned out to be one trap we were glad to get caught in. Famed for its calamari (squid), prepared every way imaginable, it's also a good, straightforward Italian trattoria with wood-fired pizzas and decent pastas. Kids get a menu to color and choices that include pizza, pasta, or fish and chips, or they can get half portions off the regular menu. We passed a happy early evening here, eating irresistible fried calamari and sipping Chianti (or sodas) while we watched the sea lions put on a show right outside the window.

Jose's
638 Wave Street, Monterey; ☎ 831-655-4419

Meals served Lunch and dinner. **Cuisine** Mexican. **Entree range** $6–$10. **Kids' menu** Yes. **Reservations** Not accepted. **Payment** Cash only.

This good taqueria is ideally located across the street from the M. Y. Children's Museum and two blocks from the aquarium. Order your quesadillas, soft tacos, burritos, and chips at the counter, then snag a table outside when the weather's good.

Old Monterey Cafe
489 Alvarado Street, Monterey; ☎ 831-646-1021;
www.cafemonterey.com

Meals served Breakfast and lunch. **Cuisine** American. **Entree range** $5–$12. **Kids' menu** Yes, and will serve a half portion. **Reservations** Not accepted. **Payment** MC, V, D.

A good downtown choice, near Dennis the Menace Park, this popular cafe is known for its cappuccino, hefty four-egg omelets, homemade muffins, and from-scratch hash browns; breakfast is served through the lunch hour as well, but not to the exclusion of traditional lunch dishes, which include homemade soups and half-pound burgers. Children are welcomed and much in evidence.

Whaling Station Prime Steaks and Seafood
763 Wave Street, Monterey; ☎ 831-373-3778

Meals served Dinner. **Cuisine** American/seafood. **Entree range** $18–$75. **Kids' menu** Yes. **Reservations** Recommended. **Payment** All major credit cards.

Located just above Cannery Row, this is a famed and elegant place to be sure, yet the Whaling Station is exceptionally welcoming to children. When you see the rough wood beams, crisp white linens, and flickering candlelight, you'll be tempted to flee and take your 5-year-old to McDonald's—but before you know it, your child will be warmly greeted and presented with a children's menu; very little ones are given Goldfish crackers to keep hunger at bay. The mesquite-grilled steaks, chops, and fresh fish are excellent, and they come with a justly acclaimed artichoke appetizer.

SANTA CRUZ

THIS BEAUTIFULLY SITUATED TOWN IS KNOWN for the university on a hill in the redwoods, as well as (nowadays) for its many recently arrived, well-heeled residents who supported the downtown businesses that were rebuilt after earthquake damage—so now the little town center is more picturesque (and pricey) than ever before.

Vacationing families will gravitate toward neither of these town centers, however, but instead will make for the waterfront, where the pier, boardwalk, beach, and train station come together to form a bright, cheerful summertime-amusement area. Lots of motels and cafes compete for the visitor's attention, but the area is still low-key. It's a beach town, true, but not everyone who's strolling in the sun looks rich or beautiful, and fancy cars don't block the narrow streets. Rather, working-class families from inland (Salinas and east) come to the shore for much-deserved recreation to join traveling families of all income levels.

unofficial **TIP**
In winter, when the seaside attractions are shuttered or open only on weekends, the area assumes an off-season charm. Bargains abound in lodgings, and the beaches are good for soulful walks, if not sun-bathing. And the redwoods know no seasons.

▮ FAMILY LODGING

 Big Basin Redwoods State Campgrounds

21600 Big Basin Highway (off Highway 1 north of Santa Cruz);
☎ 831-338-8860; reservations: Reserve America, ☎ 800-444-7275;
www.reserveamerica.com; campsites $25, tent cabins $40–$44

One of the most beautiful state parks in California, Big Basin is home to some seriously big redwoods and some seriously fine campgrounds. If sleeping on the ground makes you grumpy, reserve one of the 35 sweet little cabins in Huckleberry Camp, each equipped with two double beds and a woodstove (bring your own sleeping bags, pillows, and wood). Huckleberry also has tent sites a short walk from the parking area, and the

santa cruz

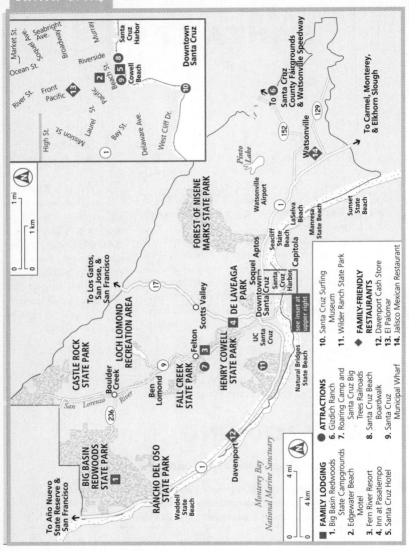

FAMILY LODGING
1. Big Basin Redwoods State Campgrounds
2. Edgewater Beach Motel
3. Fern River Resort
4. Inn at Pasatiempo
5. Santa Cruz Hotel

ATTRACTIONS
6. Gizdich Ranch
7. Roaring Camp and Santa Cruz Big Trees Railroads
8. Santa Cruz Beach Boardwalk
9. Santa Cruz Municipal Wharf
10. Santa Cruz Surfing Museum
11. Wilder Ranch State Park

FAMILY-FRIENDLY RESTAURANTS
12. Davenport Cash Store
13. El Palomar
14. Jalisco Mexican Restaurant

RV campsites at Blooms and Sempervirens are among the loveliest we've seen. Lots of good hiking. Picnic tables, fireplaces, showers, flush toilets.

Coast Santa Cruz Hotel

175 West Cliff Drive, Santa Cruz; ☎ 831-426-4330 or 800-662-3838; www.coasthotels.com; $259–$369 summer; $159–$249 winter

This 1970s-modern hotel next to the boardwalk represents the high end in these parts. It's right on the sand and all 163 rooms and 16 suites face the ocean. In addition to direct beach access, guests enjoy an outdoor pool with kids' and adult spas, two restaurants (with kids' menus), room service (also with kids' menu), and touches like in-room DVDs and video games.

Edgewater Beach Motel

525 Second Street, Santa Cruz; ☎ 831-423-0440 or 888-809-6767; www.edgewaterbeachmotel.com; $189–$259 summer; $129–$189 winter

This pleasant motel is near the beach and boardwalk, and it has a garden setting to enjoy in the summer as well as fireplaces to warm that year-round chill. There are 17 family suites, including 11 with kitchenettes. We liked the barbecue and picnic area and the heated pool.

Fern River Resort

5250 Highway 9, Felton; ☎ 831-335-4412; www.fernriver.com; $87–$129 low season; $131–$165 high season

This vintage resort brings you into the mountains near the redwood parks and Roaring Camp, where the popular train ride originates. The inexpensive accommodations include 13 cabins, most with fireplaces and kitchenettes; two of them sleep up to six people. Youngsters enjoy exploring the private beach on the San Lorenzo River (the river is just wading depth); playing volleyball, tetherball, horseshoes, and indoor games; and feeding the ducks. The basic rooms are equipped with Sony PlayStations and Nickelodeon.

Inn at Pasatiempo

555 Highway 17, Santa Cruz; ☎ 831-423-5000 or 800-834-2546; www.innatpasatiempo.com; $110–$450 summer; $100–$350 winter

This nicely appointed inn near the beach has gardens, a heated outdoor pool, and an adjacent golf course. The on-site restaurant has both indoor and outdoor seating. The 52 rooms are on the large side; some have fireplaces, and all have coffeemakers and refrigerators. Kids' menus available.

■ ATTRACTIONS

Gizdich Ranch

**55 Peckham Road, Watsonville; ☎ 831-722-1056;
www.gizdich-ranch.com**

Hours January–March: weekends, 9 a.m.–5 p.m.; April (apple-blossom time): daily, 9 a.m.–5 p.m.; May 1–July 31 (berry season): daily, 8 a.m.–5 p.m.; August–December 31 (apple season): daily, 9 a.m.–5 p.m. **Admission** Free. **Touring time** Average 2 hours with picking; minimum 1 hour. **Rainy-day touring** Not recommended. **Restaurants** Yes. **Alcoholic beverages** No. **Disabled access** Shops. **Wheelchair rental** No. **Baby-stroller rental** No. **Lockers** No. **Pet kennels** No. **Rain check** No. **Private tours** For groups.

DESCRIPTION AND COMMENTS If your visit to the Santa Cruz area coincides with berry season, your kids will enjoy picking their own strawberries, boysenberries, and raspberries—and apples are on the trees for pickin' in the fall. There's a bake shop where you can watch bakers prepare pies (available for sale). You can also see apple juice pressed. Boxes of apples can be shipped.

Roaring Camp and Santa Cruz Big Trees Railroads

**Graham Hill Road, Felton (6 miles north of Santa Cruz);
☎ 831-335-4484; www.roaringcamp.com**

Hours Vary per trip and season. **Admission** Redwood forest trip: $18 adults, $12 children ages 3–12, free for children under age 3, if with an adult; beach trip: $20 adults, $15 children ages 3–12, free for children under age 3, if with an adult. **Touring time** Average 2½ hours to beach; 75 minutes to redwoods; minimum 2 hours. **Rainy-day touring** Not recommended. **Restaurants** Picnicking. **Alcoholic beverages** No. **Disabled access** Yes; no motorized wheelchairs. **Wheelchair rental** No. **Baby-stroller rental** No. **Lockers** No. **Pet kennels** No, but pets allowed. **Rain check** Yes. **Private tours** No.

DESCRIPTION AND COMMENTS America's last steam-powered passenger railroad with year-round passenger service, Roaring Camp and Big Trees operate two trains in hour-long excursions from a colorful "camp" that has a general store and outdoor barbecue. The attraction re-creates a logging camp of 100 years ago, when trains hauled timber out of the mountain areas. This is one of those great tourist activities that is extremely well run. The train rides take you through beautiful forest land southbound to the beach and northbound to the redwoods. On each ride, passengers may disembark at midpoint to hike or picnic (in the redwoods) or stroll along the beach and boardwalk in downtown Santa Cruz and take a later train back (space permitting, so be careful during crowded months).

Santa Cruz Beach Boardwalk

APPEAL BY AGE	PRESCHOOL ★★★★	GRADE SCHOOL ★★★★★	TEENS ★★★★
YOUNG ADULTS ★★★	⁰ OVER 30 ★★★		SENIORS ★★

400 Beach Street, Santa Cruz; ☎ 831-423-5590; www.beachboardwalk.com

Hours Memorial Day–Labor Day: daily, 11 a.m.–8 p.m.; spring and fall: Saturdays and Sundays, 11 a.m.–7 p.m. **Admission** Free to boardwalk, but rides cost $2–$4; full-day passes for unlimited rides $27; 60 tickets for $33 (good if you have more than 1 child); parking, $10. **Touring time** Average 3–4 hours; minimum 2 hours. **Rainy-day touring** Not good. **Restaurants** Yes. **Alcoholic beverages** Yes. **Disabled access** Yes. **Wheelchair rental** Free. **Baby-stroller rental** Yes. **Lockers** Yes. **Pet kennels** No. **Rain check** No. **Private tours** No.

DESCRIPTION AND COMMENTS There's nothing quite like the screams of roller coaster riders mingling with the smell of hot dogs and salt air. Adults will be content just to stroll along the sunny beachfront boardwalk and, on one hand, admire the ocean view and, on the other, enjoy the colorful amusement-park atmosphere. The famous Big Dipper Roller Coaster dates from 1924, and the carousel from 1911, but there are also up-to-date amusements like laser tag and virtual reality. Rides tend to be traditional favorites, and there's a special little-kid area with gentle rides as well as fun booths of games, wax hand-dipping, and ice-cream vendors.

Santa Cruz Municipal Wharf

APPEAL BY AGE	PRESCHOOL ★★★★	GRADE SCHOOL ★★★★	TEENS ★★★★
YOUNG ADULTS ★★★★	OVER 30 ★★★★		SENIORS ★★★★

Beach Street, Santa Cruz; ☎ 831-420-6025; www.ci.santa-cruz.ca.us/pr/wharf

Hours Daily, 5 a.m.–2 a.m. **Admission** Parking $2 per hour. **Touring time** Average 1 hour; minimum half-hour stroll. **Rainy-day touring** Not recommended. **Restaurants** Yes, many. **Alcoholic beverages** In some restaurants. **Disabled access** Yes. **Wheelchair rental** No. **Baby-stroller rental** No. **Lockers** No. **Pet kennels** No. **Rain check** No. **Private tours** No.

DESCRIPTION AND COMMENTS This is among the best spots in the Monterey Bay Sanctuary to give the kids a glimpse of the appealing sea lions native to these waters. Just walk out on the wharf and look over the railings. There, beneath the surface, you'll see the lithe, balletic bodies of the sea lions as they swim. The bait shops on the wharf sell bags of fish to toss down to the mammals. Eight gift shops, restaurants, charter boats.

Santa Cruz Surfing Museum

APPEAL BY AGE	PRESCHOOL ★★	GRADE SCHOOL ★★★	TEENS ★★★
YOUNG ADULTS ★★★		OVER 30 ★★★	SENIORS ★★★

Mark Abbott Lighthouse, West Cliff Drive, Santa Cruz;
☎ **831-420-6289; www.cruzio.com/~scva/surf**

Hours Summer: Wednesday–Monday, noon–4 p.m.; winter: Thursday–Monday, noon–4 p.m. **Admission** Free; donation requested. **Touring time** Average 1 hour; minimum 30 minutes. **Rainy-day touring** Yes. **Restaurants** No. **Alcoholic beverages** No. **Disabled access** Yes. **Wheelchair rental** No. **Baby-stroller rental** No. **Lockers** No. **Pet kennels** No, but pets allowed. **Rain check** No. **Private tours** No.

DESCRIPTION AND COMMENTS This museum actually holds some interest for nonsurfers, thanks to its atmospheric location in the Mark Abbott Memorial Lighthouse on a pretty coastal stretch. Surf-history fans can check out the small but appealing collection of old photos, vintage boards, and local surf history, while others watch the sea-lion colony and the surfers outside.

Wilder Ranch State Park

APPEAL BY AGE	PRESCHOOL ★★★	GRADE SCHOOL ★★★★	TEENS ★★★
YOUNG ADULTS ★★★		OVER 30 ★★★	SENIORS ★★★

1401 Coast Road, Santa Cruz; ☎ **831-426-0505**

Hours Historic complex: Thursday–Sunday, 10 a.m.–4 p.m.; ranch activities on weekends; park open daily, sunrise–sunset. **Admission** Free, but $6 for a day pass to park. **Touring time** Average 3 hours with hike; minimum 1 hour. **Rainy-day touring** Yes, but wet. **Restaurants** No. **Alcoholic beverages** No. **Disabled access** Yes. **Wheelchair rental** No. **Baby-stroller rental** No. **Lockers** No. **Pet kennels** No. **Rain check** No. **Private tours** No.

DESCRIPTION AND COMMENTS At this park just north of Santa Cruz, you can see what ranch life was like 100 years ago. There's a great old farmhouse, chicken coops, a working blacksmith, and a storybook barn, as well as trails and natural wonders like a beachside fern grotto. Call to ask about the schedule of living-history weekends, when docents dress in costume and go about daily ranch life circa 1890. The horse-drawn wagon tour of the ranch is a big hit with younger kids.

FAMILY-FRIENDLY RESTAURANTS

Davenport Cash Store

31 Davenport Avenue (9 miles north of Santa Cruz on Highway 1);
☎ **831-425-1818 or 800-870-1817; www.davenportinn.com**

Meals served Breakfast, lunch, and dinner. **Cuisine** Californian. **Entree range** Breakfast, $5–$11; lunch, $7–$12; dinner, $9–$25. **Kids' menu** No. **Reservations** Not accepted. **Payment** All major credit cards.

Perfectly sited for travelers who decide to head north to San Francisco without having a big lunch in Santa Cruz, this is a very popular stop. Sometimes there's a long wait, but the cinnamon buns are worth it. We enjoyed the woodsy, airy room and the beautifully prepared pastas, salads, and homemade breads. Vegetarian dishes are a specialty.

El Palomar
1336 Pacific Avenue, Santa Cruz; ☎ 831-425-7575

Meals served Lunch, dinner, and Sunday brunch. **Cuisine** Mexican. **Entree range** Lunch and dinner, $10–$25. **Kids' menu** Yes. **Reservations** Yes. **Payment** All major credit cards.

This noisy, lively restaurant and bar has several high-ceilinged, beamed dining rooms and some striking murals, thanks to its location in a historic landmark hotel. It's everybody's favorite restaurant, busy even on weeknights, so it's overwhelming for the youngest ones but fun for older kids. You'll enjoy excellent Mexican regional dishes like mole, fabulous fish tacos, and specialties like funnel-shaped tacos—a cut above your average Cal-Mex establishment, but still casual and reasonably priced.

Jalisco Mexican Restaurant
610 Main Street, Watsonville; ☎ 831-728-9080

Meals served Lunch and dinner. **Cuisine** Mexican. **Entree range** $10–$15; combination dinners $10–$13. **Kids' menu** No. **Reservations** Necessary on Friday night. **Payment** All major credit cards.

Locals come here on Friday nights to hear the real mariachis perform, and their music typically captivates kids. The food is straightforward, authentic Mexican, everything from the kid-quesadilla basics to saucy entrees.

PART FIVE

THE SIERRA NEVADA

LITERARY GIANTS AND LEGENDARY EXPLORERS have put their pens to use in describing the sights found in the regions in and around the **Sierra Nevada** mountain range of eastern California. From **Lake Tahoe**'s blue, blue water to **Half Dome**'s moonlit granite curve to the awe-inspiring sequoias, the wonders contained in these landscapes are so extraordinary that Americans have enshrined all or parts of them as national parks, forests, and preserves. From south to north, we will consider the following destinations in this Sierra Nevada chapter: **Death Valley, Sequoia–Kings Canyon, Mammoth Lakes** (with side trips to **Bodie** and **Mono Lake**), **Yosemite,** and Lake Tahoe (the California section of **South Lake Tahoe** as well as **North Lake Tahoe**). The regions we are discussing are for the most part mountainous, except for Death Valley, which is, of course, the lowest point on the continent, and they stretch in length along more than half the state.

Though our enthusiasm for California's national parks is unbounded, our children have had occasion to groan about driving another four hours "to see some more big rocks." Unless you are literally going to be traveling for several weeks, don't try to see all the parks or destinations mentioned in this chapter. Make plans to stay in the park you select or its vicinity and consider a few activities or excursions to bring variety to your days: a guided tour, a horseback ride, a rope-climbing session, a river swim, or even an outlet-shopping day.

unofficial **TIP**
We caution families about being too ambitious in planning visits to the Sierra's remarkable landscapes. Do as Californians do, and concentrate on one or two at a time.

Let the season be your first guide in planning your visit to this region. Again, from south to north: Death Valley is most pleasant and popular between October and April, with high season being in March (although European visitors often prefer the extreme heat of summer, we don't advise it with kids—they'll be fabulously uncomfortable). **Mammoth Mountain** and the town of Mammoth Lakes

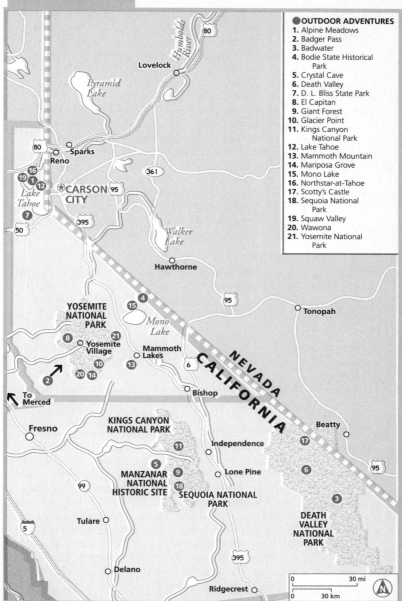

sierra nevada

OUTDOOR ADVENTURES
1. Alpine Meadows
2. Badger Pass
3. Badwater
4. Bodie State Historical Park
5. Crystal Cave
6. Death Valley
7. D. L. Bliss State Park
8. El Capitan
9. Giant Forest
10. Glacier Point
11. Kings Canyon National Park
12. Lake Tahoe
13. Mammoth Mountain
14. Mariposa Grove
15. Mono Lake
16. Northstar-at-Tahoe
17. Scotty's Castle
18. Sequoia National Park
19. Squaw Valley
20. Wawona
21. Yosemite National Park

have two peak seasons—winter for skiing and other snow sports, summer for hiking, fishing, and mountain biking. Sequoia–Kings Canyon has traditionally been a spring-summer-fall destination, but family snow play is burgeoning there, and rangers now lead snowshoe walks and other activities in the winter months. Yosemite is popular year-round, its beauty chronicled by photographers and writers in every season, although summer is its busiest. And Tahoe has distinctly different pleasures in summer (boating, swimming, waterskiing, hiking) and winter (skiing, snowboarding, snow play).

You don't have to be a camper to enjoy these national parks and Big Wonders, but camping is a wonderful option at all of these sites. It is necessary to plan ahead and make reservations whenever possible. There are also lodges and motels in every area, but a limited number of rooms, so advance planning (several months before summer) is necessary to secure the most desirable accommodations. Camping reservations may (and should) typically be made three months in advance. Mammoth and Lake Tahoe have full-fledged towns, with shopping and movie theaters (and, in the case of the Nevada side of South Lake Tahoe, casinos) in addition to lodging and restaurants.

FOR SKIERS ONLY

WE COULDN'T POSSIBLY DO JUSTICE to the many, many ski mountains in the Sierra. Instead, we'll give you the short list of our five favorite Sierra family ski resorts. For more comprehensive information on skiing, see *The Unofficial Guide to Snowboarding and Skiing in the West.*

ALPINE MEADOWS This large North Tahoe mountain has excellent snow, less of a scene than glitzier Squaw, and what may be the best children's ski school in the state, staffed by first-rate instructors. There are more snowboarders than there used to be, which may please your 12-year-old (if not you), but skiers have hardly been forced out. 2600 Alpine Meadows Road, Tahoe City; ☎ 530-587-4266 or 800-949-3296; **www.alpinemeadows.com.**

BADGER PASS The conditions aren't always ideal, and the quality of skiing is on the lower end, but that didn't stop us from falling in love with this place. It's the ski mountain that time forgot, with a small beamed lodge, the cheapest ski-mountain cafeteria in the West, friendly people, good Nordic trails, and a very good learn-to-ski program for children and adults. The beginner-to-intermediate runs are great for learning and cruising, and the lift tickets and packages are the least expensive we've seen. Good skiers and cool teens, however, might get bored. The mountain is easily reached from accommodations on the valley floor. Yosemite National Park; ☎ 209-372-0200.

MAMMOTH MOUNTAIN We learned to ski at Mammoth as teenagers, and it remains a teen haven to this day—in fact, it's a haven for every sort of skier, because its vastness can accommodate everyone, and the quality and diversity of its runs are among North America's best. It'd take you a week to ski every run. Very good children's programs and lessons are run out of both the main lodge and Canyon Lodge, and nearby condos are plentiful. The downside is the crowding during holidays, when Southern California locals pour in, but the addition of more high-speed lifts has dramatically improved the situation. For details, see the Mammoth Mountain attraction profile in the Mammoth Lakes section.

NORTHSTAR-AT-TAHOE This is a large, upscale snow resort with well-designed and well-maintained areas for downhill skiers, snowboarders, and Nordic skiers. The children's programs and ski schools are impressive. For details, see the Northstar attraction profile in the Lake Tahoe section.

SQUAW VALLEY Like Mammoth, this mountain (actually mountains) is so huge that it takes days to ski it all. Unlike at Mammoth, lift lines are short, if encountered at all. Lots of beginner runs, lots of expert runs, even more groomed intermediate runs, and a separate children's ski area. For details, see the Squaw Valley attraction profile in the Lake Tahoe section.

A **CALENDAR** of **FESTIVALS** and **EVENTS**

January

SOUTH LAKE TAHOE ANNUAL WINTER CELEBRATION Includes Celebrity Ski Classic at Heavenly as well as other ski and snowboard races, concerts, and ice-sculpting contest; ☎ 530-544-5050.

February

NATIONAL WOMEN'S SNOWBOARD AND SKI FESTIVAL Mammoth; ☎ 760-934-0745.

March

SNOWFEST Lake Tahoe. Tahoe's ten-day Snowfest celebration includes more than 100 events, ranging from a penny carnival, parades, and snow-sculpture contests to a polar swim and a "wild thing" costume party; ☎ 530-583-3494; **www.snowfest.org.**

April

EASTER EGG HUNT AND PLAYDAY Mammoth Lakes; ☎ 760-934-8989.

May

MULE DAYS Bishop. A rootin'-tootin' rodeo and fair, with coon jumping, mule dressage, barrel racing, a parade, country-western concerts, and big barbecue dinners; ☎ 760-872-4263; **www.muledays.org.**

June

AMERICA'S MOST BEAUTIFUL BIKE RIDE Hundreds of cyclists ride the 72-mile shoreline road around Lake Tahoe; **www.bikethewest.com;** ☎ 800-565-2704.

LAKE TAHOE SUMMER MUSIC FESTIVAL Extends throughout June and July at various locations around the lake; ☎ 530-583-3101, **www.tahoemusic.org.**

CONVICT LAKE SPRING TROUT DERBY Lots of kids join their parents in trying to catch the biggest fish at this Eastern Sierra lake; ☎ 760-934-3800.

July

CHILDREN'S FISHING FESTIVAL Mammoth, Snowcreek Ponds. For ages 1 to 15; kids learn to fish, free tackle provided; ☎ 760-934-2712.

FOURTH OF JULY CELEBRATION Lake Tahoe. Includes fireworks at the beach in Tahoe City, craft fair and music festival at Truckee High School, and parade and party in Truckee; ☎ 530-587-2757.

FOURTH OF JULY CELEBRATION Mammoth Lakes. Includes Lions Club pancake breakfast, horseshoe tournament, a very popular parade, Fire Department open house, U.S. Forest Service Fire Department open house, and fireworks at Crowley Lake; ☎ 760-934-6717.

MAMMOTH LAKES JAZZ JUBILEE Mammoth Lakes. Lots of mostly traditional (Dixieland, swing, big-band) jazz, dancing, food, and more; ☎ 760-934-2478; **www.mammothjazz.org.**

August

MAMMOTH CONCERTS IN THE PINES Free music presentations and a variety of music festivals throughout the month, including folk, chamber, and country-western; ☎ 760-924-5500.

TAHOE WOODEN BOAT WEEK Show of antique and vintage wooden boats and other maritime events; ☎ 530-581-4700.

September

LABOR DAY ARTS AND CRAFTS FESTIVAL Mammoth. A village arts celebration of the end of summer; ☎ 760-873-7242.

MILLPOND MUSIC FESTIVAL Bishop. A sweet, family-friendly outdoor music festival, emphasizing folk and world music; bring a picnic and a guitar; ☎ 760-873-8014.

October

KOKANEE SALMON FESTIVAL Lake Tahoe Visitors Center. Two-day festival celebrating the spawning of local salmon. With family activities such as art displays, nature walks, a children's fishing booth, and interpretive talks at the fish windows of the Lake Tahoe Visitors Center; ☎ 530-543-2674.

December

MAMMOTH LAKES TOWN CHRISTMAS TREE LIGHTING CEREMONY
☎ 760-934-8989.

SLEIGH RIDE AND BREAKFAST WITH SANTA Mammoth; ☎ 760-924-5500.

GETTING THERE

BECAUSE THE TERRITORY COVERED IS SO HUGE, we will devote a section of each destination's coverage to getting there.

HOW TO GET INFORMATION BEFORE YOU GO

- **Caltrans Highway Conditions** (For winter driving in mountains); ☎ 800-427-7623; **www.dot.ca.gov.**
- **Death Valley National Park** Death Valley 92328; ☎ 760-786-2331; **www.nps.gov/deva.**
- **Lake Tahoe Visitor Information** ☎ 800-GO-TAHOE; **www.gotahoe.com.**
- **Mammoth Lakes Visitors Bureau** P.O. Box 48, Mammoth Lakes 93546; ☎ 888-466-2666; **www.visitmammoth.com.**
- **Mammoth Visitor Center and Ranger Station** ☎ 760-924-5500. Has up-to-date information on opening dates of campgrounds (700 sites at elevations above 7,500 feet) in Inyo National Forest.
- **National Parks Camping Reservations** Sequoia–Kings Canyon and Death Valley, ☎ 800-365-2267; Yosemite, ☎ 800-436-7275; **reservations.nps.gov** for all national park camping reservations.
- **North Lake Tahoe Central Reservations Service** ☎ 530-583-3494 or 888-434-1262; **www.mytahoevacation.com.**
- **Sequoia and Kings Canyon National Parks** ☎ 559-565-3134; **www.nps.gov/seki.** Guest Services (authorized concessionaire handling lodging except for camping and other services in the two parks), P.O. Box 789, Three Rivers 93271; ☎ 559-565-3341.

The BEST PARKS

THIS ENTIRE CHAPTER IS NOTHING BUT THE BEST PARKS, so they're not listed under this heading—they're described in detail throughout the chapter, as "town" descriptions and sometimes under "Attractions." Look for specifics under the particular area that interests you.

FAMILY OUTDOOR ADVENTURES

AGAIN, THIS CHAPTER IS NOTHING BUT. They're not listed separately here, because they're plentiful at every spot in these wilderness areas. Check for details in individual geographic areas.

LITTLE MOMENTS IN BIG PLACES

SOMETIMES THE VASTNESS OF THESE REMARKABLE WESTERN landscapes—big skies, big mountains, big lakes—is just too much for kids to absorb, and they respond with indifference or ennui. We always look for ways to bring the wonders of the region down to their scale; here are some activities and strategies that have worked for us.

1. While a sports-loving middle schooler and Mom went for a challenging hike in Yosemite (up many, many steps to Vernal Falls), Dad and a younger sister rented bikes and took a leisurely ride along the flat, paved bike path of Yosemite Valley that winds through meadows and campgrounds. Deer, squirrels, and other kids were out in view, and those easy two hours live on in her memory.

2. After panning for gold in Gold Country, we began our time in Yosemite by stopping for a picnic at a spot where the Yosemite River makes a sweeping curve and Half Dome can be seen rising majestically above the treetops. The kids didn't even look up at the mighty landmark, though, because while wading in the icy stream, they realized that the water was flecked with gold. So they began to gather and scrutinize every pebble just in case one was a real nugget.

3. At Family Camp Montecito Sequoia, the youngest children are taken on a "fishing trip," in which they lie on their stomachs on a dock over the little lake and reach down with nets to try to scoop up the tadpoles and guppies they can see below. My daughter now indignantly says the nets had holes big enough to allow every fish to swim through, but at the time she was, at age 4, an enthralled sportswoman.

4. Because of the uniquely sudden coolness of the desert night, the Furnace Creek Inn in Death Valley has a huge fireplace in the pool area. My daughter floated in the 85°F pool water (heated by natural hot springs), gazing at the early-rising "children's moon" as the sky started to glow pink with a dramatic desert sunset. After getting out, she wrapped herself in a big towel and warmed herself happily by the fireplace. The juxtaposition charmed her.

5. In an inspired moment while enjoying a condo vacation in Mammoth, we agreed to stop (after hiking and before hitting the pool) at a bead shop and let the kids each browse among the bins with a muffin tin. They picked out a variety of beads and something to string them on, and left with little bags and triumphant airs. That night, the usual plea for a movie on video was replaced by the quiet sound of kids creating.

6. At Mono Lake, the adults read interpretive plaques and shook their heads over water-use controversies, but the kids didn't come alive until we joined a ranger walk at lake's edge and the story of those teeny-tiny brine shrimp (specimens scrutinized) and the funny little fly larvae was revealed.

DEATH VALLEY

OFTEN, CITY OR SUBURB DWELLERS find that gazing on open vistas refreshes the mind and broadens mental horizons. In contrast to the close-up visual density of our daily lives (from nearby computer screen to a horizon cluttered with buildings), there are places where emptiness is neither a sign of failure nor simply an affront to commercial enterprise. This vast area is one such.

In **Death Valley,** we found the spaces to be affirmingly vast and the views cleansing—barren mountains, untrafficked roads stretching empty for miles in both directions, sky as a presence. The children felt it, too, though they didn't articulate the sensation, but fell silent and gazed about them when we stopped for cold drinks and directions.

As we explored, the vastness was broken up into little sections, each with a history, a personality, and a name. Such places as **Scotty's Castle** and **Badwater** became real to us. Where there had seemed to be a great nothingness, we found a little bit of everything.

GETTING THERE

BY CAR Death Valley is about 300 miles northeast of L.A. and 525 miles southeast of San Francisco. It's a long drive no matter which way you come, and you can't cross those mountains just anywhere. From L.A., take **CA 14** north to US 395 north to a fork in the road called Olancha, where you pick up **Highway 190** (scenic route) east to Death Valley. From San Francisco, your best bet is to pick one or two other parks to include in your trip and to access Death Valley after visiting Yosemite or Sequoia, both directly between San Francisco and your goal.

▌ FAMILY LODGING

Furnace Creek Campground
Highway 190, Death Valley; ☎ 800-365-CAMP; www.nps.gov/deva; $18

Part of Death Valley National Park, this campground is a good bet for families. There are 20 tent spaces and 180 tent or RV spaces with fireplaces, tables, water, and flush toilets. Not all campsites have shade.

death valley

Key

✈	Airport	☎	Phone
△	Campground	═ ═	Primitive road (4-wheel drive only)
¶¶	Dining	⚒	Radiator water
🛏	Lodging	⚑	Ranger Station
🏕	Picnic area	- -	Unpaved road
ⓘ	Information		

■ **FAMILY LODGING**
1. Furnace Creek Campground
2. Furnace Creek Inn
3. Furnace Creek Ranch

● **ATTRACTIONS**
4. Borax Museum
5. Furnace Creek Visitor Center and Museum
6. Scotty's Castle

Furnace Creek Inn
Highway 190, Death Valley; ☎ 760-786-2345 or 888-29-PARKS;
www.furnacecreekresort.com; $275–$400

Designed by the noted early-20th-century architect Albert C. Martin, this 66-room luxury hotel is truly something special, offering real comfort in an incredibly isolated location. You might be hot and dusty from a hike, but after a shower and a swim in the warm spring-fed pool and a cool drink on your room's balcony, you'll feel lucky indeed. The rooms, remodeled in the late 1990s, are true to their 1920s roots in a décor that fits nicely with the desert setting. The dining room was too formal for us to enjoy with the kids except at breakfast (although there is a kids' menu). We went down the hill to the Ranch part of the resort (see separate listing below). The hotel is on a hill above the valley, so views are spectacular, especially at sunrise.

Furnace Creek Ranch
Highway 190, Death Valley; ☎ 760-786-2345 or 888-29-PARKS;
www.furnacecreekresort.com; $108–$192; kids under age 18 stay free

At the bottom of the hill is the other part of the Furnace Creek Resort, the more boisterous motel- and camping-focused area, where restaurants, laundry services, tennis courts, and spring-fed swimming pools serve visitors in a grassy, shady oasis. The 255 units range in quality from okay to very good, depending on whether they've been upgraded. There are three restaurants on the grounds, and plenty of kids running around playing basketball, tennis, Nintendo, and (desert) sand volleyball.

▌ ATTRACTIONS

Borax Museum

APPEAL BY AGE	PRESCHOOL ★★	GRADE SCHOOL ★★	TEENS ★★
YOUNG ADULTS ★★★	OVER 30 ★★★		SENIORS ★★★

Furnace Creek Ranch, Death Valley; ☎ 760-786-2345

Hours Daily, 8:30 a.m.–4 p.m.; closed noon–1 p.m. for lunch. **Admission** Free. **Touring time** Average 40 minutes; minimum 20 minutes. **Rainy-day touring** Yes (it doesn't rain anyway). **Restaurants** At resort. **Alcoholic beverages** At restaurants. **Disabled access** Yes. **Wheelchair rental** At registration. **Baby-stroller rental** No. **Lockers** No. **Pet kennels** No. **Rain check** No. **Private tours** No.

DESCRIPTION AND COMMENTS Whether or not you stay at Furnace Creek Inn or Furnace Creek Ranch, you'll end up spending some time at the ranch because of the amenities, including horseback riding. You can while away some time by strolling through the old mining-equipment graveyard behind this museum or, if the hour is right, through the museum itself. The brand name "20 Mule Team Borax" doesn't mean much to those too young to have seen the Ronald Reagan

*un*official **TIP**
Don't bother with the Borax horseback trail ride—it's a dull walk.

commercials in the early 1960s, but if you think about it and talk about it a bit, the idea of actually handling a team of 20 mules will begin to sink in.

Furnace Creek Visitor Center and Museum

APPEAL BY AGE	PRESCHOOL ★★	GRADE SCHOOL ★★	TEENS ★★
YOUNG ADULTS ★★		OVER 30 ★★★	SENIORS ★★

Death Valley National Park, Death Valley; ☎ 760-786-2331

Hours Daily, 8 a.m.–6 p.m. **Admission** $10. **Touring time** Average 1 hour for exhibits, slide show, and questions; minimum 30 minutes. **Rainy-day touring** Yes. **Restaurants** At ranch. **Alcoholic beverages** At restaurants. **Disabled access** Yes. **Wheelchair rental** No. **Baby-stroller rental** No. **Lockers** No. **Pet kennels** No. **Rain check** No. **Private tours** No.

DESCRIPTION AND COMMENTS The central source for visitor information while in Death Valley, the center has an hourly slide show orientation, a small museum, and schedules of programs offered at campsites around the valley. The bookstore operated by Death Valley History Association has a number of children's publications.

 ## Scotty's Castle

APPEAL BY AGE	PRESCHOOL ★★	GRADE SCHOOL ★★★★	TEENS ★★★★★
YOUNG ADULTS ★★★★★		OVER 30 ★★★★★	SENIORS ★★★★★

Death Valley Ranch, Death Valley National Park, Death Valley;
☎ 760-786-2392 or 760-786-2331; www.nps.gov/deva/scottys

Hours Tours daily, winter 9 a.m.–5 p.m., summer 9:30 a.m.–4:30 p.m. **Admission** $11 adults, $6 disabled adults, $9 seniors, $6 children ages 6–15, free for children age 5 and under; admission includes both tours. **Touring time** Average 50 minutes; minimum 50 minutes. **Rainy-day touring** Yes, for inside. **Restaurants** Snack bar. **Alcoholic beverages** No. **Disabled access** Good. **Wheelchair rental** Yes, free. **Baby-stroller rental** No. **Lockers** No. **Pet kennels** No. **Rain check** No. **Private tours** No.

DESCRIPTION AND COMMENTS Together with Hearst Castle and the Will Rogers House, Scotty's Castle forms a picture of a grand period in California in the late 1920s and early 1930s, when personalities and the houses they occupied were larger than life. This remarkable mansion museum is shown today by docents who offer living-history tours, pretending as if you are arriving guests of the owner, Chicago millionaire Albert Johnson, and they're showing you around. In its way, it rivals the stately homes and castles of Europe, with its carpets from Majorca, ceramics from Italy, custom wrought-iron fixtures in fantasy shapes, and huge redwood beams. The kids listened intently to the story of the trickster Scotty the caretaker, who persuaded many that this was his house. At the end, it was extraordinary in a goofy way to stand in the resonating vibration of the player organ as it played "Pomp and Circumstance" and we wended our way down the circular steps of a turret.

SEQUOIA *and* KINGS CANYON

THESE TWIN PARKS ARE ADMINISTERED jointly but were established separately, **Sequoia** in 1890 and **Kings Canyon** in 1940. Today's visitors might not know, as they drive from place to place in the pine forests, whether they are entering Kings Canyon or leaving Sequoia. Overall, most of the park acreage is given over to wilderness areas, but 90 miles of paved roads allow for access to the groves of sequoias and some other natural wonders. A special experience is a stay at **Montecito-Sequoia Family Vacation Camp,** a family camp open year-round (see listing under "Family Lodging"). Sequoia is home to the world's largest tree, the **General Sherman,** found in the **Giant Forest.**

GETTING THERE

BY CAR Highway 198 leads into Sequoia National Park from the southwest; **Route 180,** the General's Highway, connects the parks. The **Foothill Visitors Center** (☎ 559-565-3134) is at the entrance to the park. It's the park headquarters, and rangers here will collect an entrance fee.

FAMILY LODGING

Buckeye Tree Lodge
46000 Sierra Drive, Three Rivers; ☎ 559-561-5900; www.buckeyetree.com; $55–$205

There are several motels in Three Rivers, which is a short distance from the entrance to Kings Canyon National Park, and this is one of the more comfortable. It has 12 rooms, and it's in a woodsy setting next to a river; some rooms have balconies overlooking the river. One room has a kitchenette; our favorite is the two-bedroom cottage with a fireplace and a kitchen. Pool and a playground, refrigerators in the rooms, and a restaurant nearby.

Dorst Creek Campground
Off General's Highway, a few miles north of the Lodgepole Visitors Center; ☎ 559-565-3341; reservations, ☎ 800-365-2267; reservations www.nps.gov; campsites $18

sequoia and kings canyon

FAMILY LODGING
1. Buckeye Tree Lodge
2. Dorst Creek Campground
3. Grant Grove Lodge
4. John Muir Lodge
5. Lazy J Ranch Motel
6. Montecito-Sequoia Family Vacation Camp

ATTRACTIONS
7. Big Stump Trail
8. Crystal Cave
9. Giant Forest
10. Grant Grove

The best family campground in Sequoia–Kings Canyon is Dorst, which also happens to be one of the many national-park campgrounds that accepts reservations—so make them very, very early. Kids run wild here, making friends at other tent sites, jumping in gentle Dorst Creek, and running in the meadowy areas. This is a great base for exploring the redwood forests and hiking to little peaks and creeks. Hume Lake, a great swimming and fishing destination, is close by, and you can pick up supplies easily at Lodgepole. Flush toilets, fireplaces, picnic tables, food lockers.

Grant Grove Lodge

Grant Grove, Three Rivers; ☎ **559-335-5500; www.rescentre.com/grant.htm; $59.50–$121**

The 52 small cabins look far more picturesque on the outside than they feel on the inside—we'd advise taking a picture here rather than staying, but if you must, you'll find that only nine have electricity and indoor plumbing. The others have kerosene lanterns, outdoor woodstoves, and shared bathhouses.

John Muir Lodge

Grant Grove, Three Rivers; ☎ **559-335-5500; www.rescentre.com/johnmuir.htm; $69–$167**

This newish motel in Grant Grove is a good bet for families who want to be in the park. The lodge is woodsy on the outside and basic-motel on the inside, but the beds are comfortable, the bathrooms are new, and the location is great. No kitchens, so you'll have to eat in the cafe or pack picnics, and no TV, which is a very good thing in such a beautiful place.

Lazy J Ranch Motel

39625 Sierra Drive, Three Rivers; ☎ **559-561-4449 or 800-341-8000; www.rescentre.com/lazyj.htm; $100–$210**

An 18-room motel with a real ranch feel—cottages are scattered around meadows, and there's a path down to the river. Several units have one or two bedrooms, and five cottages have kitchens. There's a pool, a playground, and laundry facilities.

Montecito-Sequoia Family Vacation Camp

8000 General's Highway, Grant Grove, Kings Canyon National Park; ☎ **559-565-3388 or 800-227-9900; www.montecitosequoia.com; weekly 7-day, 6-night stay in cabin, $925 adults, $835 children ages 2–12 per person; mini-week of 3–4 days, $545 adults, $475 children ages 2–12 per person; all meals and activities included**

When we stayed here it was like a California version of Lake Wobegon: all the men were good-looking, and all the women were above average. Something about the mountain-air atmosphere and the choice to be with your kids at summer camp made for a lot of conviviality among the adults.

Parents never had to cook a meal, but plenty gathered at the camp "bar" for a glass of wine in the early evening hours. And plenty gathered early in the morning at the daily songfest before activities.

Kids are divided into age groups with counselors, and they can spend specified hours in the counselors' care while you pursue your own camp activities (archery, anyone?) or leave the premises to hike or sightsee. Meals are taken together, and evening activities like games and costume parties are designed for the whole family. This is truly the best of both worlds for those who'd rather join their kids at camp than send them (especially the too-young ones). This former girls' camp is within the national park itself, within easy distance of Crystal Cave and some of the most famous big trees. Open all year, it offers cross-country skiing and ice skating on the lake in the winter, and waterskiing, horseback riding, pool swimming, and many other activities in the summer. There are 29 rustic motel-type rooms with private baths, and 13 family camping cabins (beds, but bring your own linens; they have electricity and wood-burning stoves, but no running water—bathhouses are nearby). You can sign up for the whole camp, or stay for a day or two between camp sessions in the summer.

ATTRACTIONS

Big Stump Trail

APPEAL BY AGE	PRESCHOOL ★★	GRADE SCHOOL ★★	TEENS ★★
YOUNG ADULTS ★★★		OVER 30 ★★★	SENIORS ★★★

Near the entrance to Kings Canyon National Park; ☎ 559-335-2856

Hours Daily, 24 hours, weather permitting. **Admission** Free. **Touring time** Average 3 hours; minimum 30 minutes. **Rainy-day touring** No, and hard to tour in snow. **Restaurants** In Grant Grove. **Alcoholic beverages** Yes. **Disabled access** No. **Wheelchair rental** No. **Baby-stroller rental** No. **Lockers** No. **Pet kennels** No. **Rain check** No. **Private tours** No.

DESCRIPTION AND COMMENTS This one-and-a-half-mile nature loop has a wonderful disaster theme that appeals to school-age kids. It shows, in its short distance, all sorts of natural and human-caused damage that the sequoias have endured. There's one tree that was hit by lightning, another that was shattered by loggers, and a huge stump that was created when one of the largest sequoias was felled for display in New York.

Crystal Cave

APPEAL BY AGE	PRESCHOOL ★★★	GRADE SCHOOL ★★★★	TEENS ★★★
YOUNG ADULTS ★★★		OVER 30 ★★★	SENIORS ★★

9 miles from Lodgepole Visitor Center; ☎ 559-565-3341; www.sequoiahistory.org

Hours Mid-May–October: daily 1-hour tours, 10 a.m.–4:30 p.m.; early spring and fall: tours Friday–Sunday, 11 a.m.–4 p.m. on the hour. **Admission** $11 adults,

$9 seniors, $6 children ages 6–12, free for children age 5 and under (tickets at Lodgepole or Foothill Visitors Centers only). **Touring time** Average 2 hours; minimum 1-hour tour plus time to hike steep half-mile trail from parking area to cave entrance. **Rainy-day touring** Okay. **Restaurants** No. **Alcoholic beverages** No. **Disabled access** No. **Wheelchair rental** No. **Baby-stroller rental** No. **Lockers** No. **Pet kennels** No. **Rain check** No. **Private tours** Group tours only.

DESCRIPTION AND COMMENTS Not far from the Giant Forest (see profile below) is the Crystal Cave. We like cave tours when there are plenty of people and the caves aren't too dark and spooky but, rather, full of stalactites and stalagmites. So we like the one-hour tour of Crystal Cave with the Organ Room and the Marble Room. And it's nice in the summer to spend some time in the cool underground. Note that this tour is neither stroller nor wheelchair accessible, and backpacks are not allowed.

 ## Giant Forest

APPEAL BY AGE	PRESCHOOL ★★★★	GRADE SCHOOL ★★★★	TEENS ★★★★
YOUNG ADULTS ★★★★	OVER 30 ★★★★	SENIORS ★★★★	

Highway 198, Sequoia National Forest; ☎ 559-565-3782; www.nps.gov/seki/lpvc.htm

Hours Vary by season and conditions; call. **Admission** Free (park has $12 vehicle-entrance fee). **Touring time** Average 2–3 hours; minimum 30 minutes without the walk. **Rainy-day touring** Come prepared and you won't be miserable. **Restaurants** Yes. **Alcoholic beverages** No. **Disabled access** Limited. **Wheelchair rental** No. **Baby-stroller rental** No. **Lockers** No. **Pet kennels** No. **Rain check** No. **Private tours** No.

DESCRIPTION AND COMMENTS In the Giant Forest, you'll find the General Sherman Tree and the Congress Trail. The 2,500-year-old tree is one of those superlatives every visitor to the region must pay homage to. It's the biggest measured tree in the world, as tall as a 27-story building. Near this giant specimen in Sequoia National Park is the Congress Trail, a two-mile self-guided loop that makes a nice outing for walking families, because it winds through several magnificent groves of sequoias. Stop at Lodgepole Visitor Center for trail and other information.

Grant Grove

APPEAL BY AGE	PRESCHOOL ★★★★	GRADE SCHOOL ★★★★	TEENS ★★★★
YOUNG ADULTS ★★★★	OVER 30 ★★★★	SENIORS ★★★★	

Kings Canyon; ☎ 559-335-2856; www.nps.gov/seki/ggvc.htm

Hours Daily, 8 a.m.–5 p.m. **Admission** Free (park has $12 vehicle-entrance fee). **Touring time** Average 2 hours with visitors center, refreshments, and self-guided nature walk; minimum 1 hour. **Rainy-day touring** No; plus, it's hard to tour in the snows. **Restaurants** Yes. **Alcoholic beverages** Yes. **Disabled access** Yes. **Wheelchair rental** No. **Baby-stroller rental** No. **Lockers** No. **Pet kennels** No. **Rain check** No. **Private tours** No; interpretive hikes available.

DESCRIPTION AND COMMENTS This mountain village is a kind of headquarters for Kings Canyon. It's a few miles from the park entrance and adjacent to the General Grant Grove stand of giant sequoias. In the village are a couple of lodges, a little market, and a visitors center. The grove itself is an impressive stand of sequoias that was not too much for us to enjoy in an hour's part-drive, part-stroll from tree to tree. There's a twin-sisters tree, with two trees growing from a single trunk; a fallen 120-foot-diameter tree that forms a tunnel; and the General Grant, the third-largest known tree in the world, at 267 feet high, with a circumference of almost 108 feet.

MAMMOTH LAKES

THIS IS THE EASIEST MOUNTAIN RESORT in California to recommend to visitors, because you don't have to be a certain kind of traveler to enjoy it. It has such a wide range of options that two very different families could spend time here and never cross paths. Some visit only during ski season, but we had one of the most fun summer family vacations ever by staying a week in a condo, which is the housing of choice for most visitors. Family friendly and plentiful, **Mammoth**'s condos range from the swank and expensive to the dated and cheap; now that developer Starwood is pumping zillions into this once-funky resort town, prices are climbing. Summer or winter, **Mammoth Mountain** is the scene of many sports competitions, from mountain biking to snowboarding (a number of Olympic snowboarders hail from Mammoth), and there are marathons weekly throughout the nonsnow season. If you happen upon one of these events, let the kids hang out for a while and watch—they may see a young sports hero followed around by a TV crew.

GETTING THERE

BY PLANE At this writing, there is no air service to little **Mammoth Airport.** An airport expansion is planned, but it is currently tied up in environmental battles.

BY CAR This is one of the easiest mountain communities to take kids to in the world—the approaches via **US 395** from Bishop in the south and Yosemite out of Lee Vining in the northeast are on a mostly multi-lane, modern highway, whose broad pavement curves slowly and gradually up into the higher elevations. There's none of the hours of switchbacks that so often unnerve (and make ill) the little ones. From L.A., plan on a five-hour drive; it's about 100 miles from Yosemite Valley, but you can't take the direct route in winter, when snow closes the roads.

mammoth lakes

To Bodie
via 270

Conway
Summit

167

Mono
Lake

395

Lundy
Lake

0 ___ 5 mi
0 ___ 5 km

N

Mono Basin
Visitor Center

Lee Vining
Museum

120

Ellery
Lake

Tioga
Lake

Tioga Pass

Tufa State
Reserve

Mono
Craters

MONO BASIN NATIONAL
FOREST
SCENIC AREA

120

YOSEMITE
NATIONAL
PARK

Walker
Lake

June Lake Loop

Grant
Lake

Devil's
Punchbowl

⊕ Hospital
⊠ Post Office
⚡ Ski Area
♦ Visitor Center

158

Silver
Lake

June
Lake

Gull
Lake

June
Lake

Big
Springs

Owens River

June Mountain

Minarets

Roadside
Rest

Lookout
Mountain

LITTLE ANTELOPE
VALLEY

Benton
Crossing

Inyo
Craters

Scenic Loop

395

Hot Creek
Geological Site

ANSEL ADAMS
WILDERNESS AREA

Minaret
Vista

5

7

Museum

Fish
Hatchery

Fish Hatchery Rd.

Benton Crossing Rd.

Crowley
Lake

203

6

Twin
Lakes

Historic
Mine
Sites

Owens River

Rainbow
Falls

Horseshoe

Mamie

George

Mary

MAMMOTH
LAKES

1 Convict
Lake

Tom's
Place

Mammoth Lakes
Basin

JOHN MUIR
WILDERNESS AREA

McGee Creek

Rock Creek

San Joaquin River

INYO NATIONAL FOREST

Sacramento

San
Francisco

*Mammoth
Lakes Region*

CALIFORNIA

Los Angeles

3 **8**

To Main Lodge **203**

Chair
7

Chair
17

Chair
16

Chair
8

Chair
22

SKI AREA

Chair
15

Chair
24

2

Chair
25

Lake Mary Rd.

Valentine Reserve
(private)

Canyon Blvd
Lakeview Blvd

203

10

Main St.

⊕

4

11

Minaret Rd.

9

Visitors
Bureau

⊠

12

203

U.S. Forest
Service
Visitor Center

Meridian Blvd.

Old Mammoth Rd.

Mammoth Lakes

Mammoth Creek

Winter
Road
Closure

Mammoth
Museum

Mammoth Creek

Old Mammoth Rd.

FAMILY LODGING

CONDO RENTALS

MOST MAMMOTH VISITORS RENT A CONDOMINIUM for a few nights or a week, and there are hundreds of choices. Unfortunately, there's no one central reservations service, so you'll have to surf some Web sites or call around to find a place right for you. The ones close to Canyon or Little Eagle (aka Juniper Springs) Lodges are best suited to skiers and those who want mountain/lift access. Main Lodge is the hub of summer activity, from the climbing wall to the mountain-bike lift rides. Snow Creek is great for golfers, tennis players, and hikers. The developments near town are best for those who want to eat, shop, and be central to everything. Three of our favorite developments and/or rental agencies include: Mammoth **Mountain Reservations,** representing two developments near Canyon Lodge (☎ 800-468-6225; **www.mammothres.com**); **Mammoth Properties,** which represents many different developments all over the area (☎ 888-MAMMOTH; **www.mammoth-lodging.com**); and **Mammoth Estates,** a good value near the new Village development and not far from Canyon Lodge (☎ 800-228-2884; **www.mammothestates.com**).

 ## Convict Lake Resort

2000 Convict Lake Road (off Highway 395), just south of Mammoth Lakes; ☎ 760-934-3800 or 800-992-2260; www.convictlake.com; $119–$999

Families return to this friendly community of cabins summer after summer, often for generations. About ten minutes south of the town of Mammoth and two miles off the highway, it's as peaceful and quiet as you can get. A five-minute walk takes you to Convict Lake, bordered on three sides by majestic Sierras peaks. The fishing, swimming, and boating is lots of fun here, and you can also ride horseback, bike, or hike around the lake. Kids also love fooling around Convict Creek. The kitchen-equipped cabins range from the tiny and quite rustic to the large and homelike; you can also camp at the Forest Service campground (no reservations accepted) alongside the creek. The general store is stocked with everything you might need, and the surprisingly upscale restaurant is famous for what might be the best cooking in the Eastern Sierra.

Juniper Springs Lodge

4000 Meridian Way, Mammoth Lakes; ☎ 760-924-1102 or 888-311-1102; www.mammothmountain.com; $149–$349 in summer, $249–$549 winter, $335–$795 holidays for studio to 3-bedroom condos

This woodsy lodge/condo was built as phase one of the ambitious plan to turn Mammoth into a ski resort with the swank of, say, Whistler. Located at the base of the new Eagle Express six-person chairlift, Juniper Springs combines the services of a hotel—daily maid service, bellmen, coffee shop, concierge, ski check—with the convenience of condo living: each of the 174 units, even the studios, has a full kitchen. It's more expensive than renting a condo in one of the many nearby complexes, but because of the ski-in–ski-out location (on an easy run that beginners can handle) and the full-service aspect, many families consider it money well spent. Extras include a pool, spa, and laundry room. Be forewarned that in spring, the snow melts first on this side of the mountain, so you may have to take a shuttle or drive over to Canyon Lodge or Main Lodge.

Mammoth Mountain Inn
Highway 203 next to ski area, Mammoth; ☎ 760-934-2581; www.mammothmountain.com; $115–$825

This partially upgraded lodge is terribly convenient, located right in front of the Main Lodge, gondola, summer activities, and Woolywood children's ski school (though it's several miles from town). Many families are pleasantly surprised to find that they can afford one of the 213 rooms, 43 two-bedroom units, or 14 three-bedroom units, and since skiing families tend to arrive with an SUV stuffed with gear and tired children, they practically weep with joy to discover that there's bell service and a free ski check right by the door. There's also a child-care center (sometimes with storytellers and magicians), a game room, and kids' menus. In summer, the mountain-bike park, climbing wall, and Devil's Postpile shuttle are just outside the door. The rooms vary from the small and dated to the refurbished and comfortable; request a remodeled room when you book.

Quality Inn
3537 Main Street, Mammoth Lakes; ☎ 760-934-5114 or 877-424-6423; $90–$220; kids under age 12 stay free

The second-floor lounge of this well-run motel makes for a less claustrophobic feel for guests in the winter. There are 61 rooms (with coffeemakers, microwaves, refrigerators, and free movies), an indoor Jacuzzi, and the best free continental breakfast in town.

■ ATTRACTIONS

Adventure Center

APPEAL BY AGE	PRESCHOOL ★	GRADE SCHOOL ★★★★	TEENS ★★★★
YOUNG ADULTS ★★★★★		OVER 30 ★★★★	SENIORS ★★

1 Minaret Road, Mammoth Mountain Ski Area; ☎ 760-934-2571; www.mammothmountain.com

Hours Late June–late August: daily, 10 a.m.–6 p.m. **Admission** Single-zip, $10; 2 zips, $15; climbing wall: $10 single climb, $20 1 hour. **Touring time** Average 1 hour; minimum 30 minutes. **Rainy-day touring** No. **Restaurants** Cafe. **Alcoholic**

beverages Yes. **Disabled access**. Limited, but programs available. **Wheelchair rental** No. **Baby-stroller rental** No. **Lockers** No. **Pet kennels** No; pets may be tied up. **Rain check** Yes. **Private tours** Yes, and classes.

DESCRIPTION AND COMMENTS Unfortunately the wonderful ropes course is no longer offered, but the multisided climbing towers outside Main Lodge are a big hit, offering everyone from beginners (4-year-olds to grandmas) to experienced climbers a challenge and a chance to succeed. Don't waste your money on a $10 single climb, which could be completed in minutes—instead, spend the $20 for an hour of climbing, and try various routes. A friendly staff helps kids and parents into harnesses and provides tips and support. There's nothing like watching a scared 8-year-old make it to the top of a climbing wall and beam with joy and the sense of achievement. Next to the climbing towers is a 100-foot zip line that's a blast for kids ages 13 and under.

 Devil's Postpile National Monument

APPEAL BY AGE	PRESCHOOL ★★★★	GRADE SCHOOL ★★★★★	TEENS ★★★★★
YOUNG ADULTS ★★★★★		OVER 30 ★★★★★	SENIORS ★★★★★

Mammoth Visitor Center and Ranger Station; board shuttle in front of Mammoth Mountain Inn at the ski area; ☎ 760-934-2289; www.nps.gov/depo

Hours Last bus leaves Mammoth Mountain at 5:25 p.m. and Red's Meadow at 6:15 p.m. **Admission** Shuttle $7 adults, $4 children. **Touring time** Average half to full day; minimum 2 hours. **Rainy-day touring** Not recommended. **Restaurants** Cafe at Red's Meadow. **Alcoholic beverages** At cafe and resort store. **Disabled access** No; private cars admitted. **Wheelchair rental** No. **Baby-stroller rental** No. **Lockers** No. **Pet kennels** No. **Rain check** No. **Private tours** No.

DESCRIPTION AND COMMENTS Don't miss the Devil's Postpile National Monument. We set aside about two-thirds of a day and boarded the shuttle (the only way to enter the park), getting off at the Devil's Postpile trailhead. Before we'd walked five minutes we found a lovely picnic spot next to a roaring river. We continued to the Postpile (an easy half-mile walk from the bus stop) and then on to Rainbow Falls, where scores of people, including families with grandmothers whose shoes were not made for walking, either looked at the 100-foot falls from a viewpoint or continued down stairs and a steep path to the bottom of the falls to fully enjoy the thundering waters of the San Joaquin River. Rainbow Falls is a one-and-a-half-mile walk from the bus stop through mostly dusty flatland. Other shuttle bus stops include lakes, falls, and Red's Meadow Resort, a pack station for trail rides with a cafe and store for campers.

unofficial **TIP**
We prefer the beautiful, easy hike from Devil's Postpile to Minaret Falls, a wonderful place for children to play in splashing, cascading water.

☀ Mammoth Mountain

APPEAL BY AGE	PRESCHOOL ★★	GRADE SCHOOL ★★★★★	TEENS ★★★★★
YOUNG ADULTS ★★★★★		OVER 30 ★★★★★	SENIORS ★★★★★

Mammoth Lakes: ☎ 800-MAMMOTH; **bike park:** ☎ 760-934-2571, **ext. 3671; gondola:** ☎ 800-MAMMOTH; www.mammothmountain.com

Hours Vary by activity. **Admission** Varies by activity. **Touring time** Average depends on your sign-up choices; minimum at least 1 hour to get the lay of the land. **Rainy-day touring** Yes, depends. **Restaurants** Yes, several. **Alcoholic beverages** Yes. **Disabled access** Limited. **Wheelchair rental** No. **Baby-stroller rental** No. **Lockers** Yes. **Pet kennels** No. **Rain check** No. **Private tours** Ski, snowboard, and mountain bike.

DESCRIPTION AND COMMENTS The official ski area and the condos and restaurants adjacent to it are known as Mammoth Mountain. To visitors, it simply feels like a few little complexes at several bases around the mountain above the town of Mammoth Lakes.

In winter, this is one of the best ski mountains in the West, serviced by seemingly endless high-speed lifts; in the summer, the gondola continues to run as a scenic ride and mountain-bike hauler to the top of the mountain. Winter skiing and snowboarding options for families include group and individual lessons as well as a good children's half-day and all-day ski and snowboard school (all-day includes lunch and supervision), as well as a three-day snowboard camp for groups of five or more compatible kids.

In the summer, a mountain-bike trail area, the Mammoth Mountain Bike Park, is created in the trails accessed via the Main Lodge, and it includes a "little riders fun zone" for 4-and-up riders just learning. Some lifts carry bikes and riders up the mountain, but you should start on the most modest hills—it can be scarier than you might think to point a bike down these steep trails; try the Little Eagle chair over by Juniper Springs for easier runs (mountain bikes are rented here). Main Lodge is also home to a zip line for kids age 12 and under and a big climbing wall for all ages, so everyone can try rock climbing, complete with ropes and harnesses. Main Lodge is also the place to catch the shuttle to Devil's Postpile (see previous profile) and many great backcountry lakes and hikes. In the summer, an outdoor barbecue cafe is set up in the middle of the whole scene.

Sledz

APPEAL BY AGE	PRESCHOOL ★★★★	GRADE SCHOOL ★★★★	TEENS ★★★★
YOUNG ADULTS ★★★★		OVER 30 ★★★★	SENIORS ★★★

Highway 203, between town and Main Lodge; ☎ 760-934-7533

Hours Winter: daily, 10 a.m.–4 p.m.; spring: daily, 4:30–7:30 p.m.; weather and snow permitting. **Admission** $10 per person (any age) for an hour of sledding.

Touring time 1 hour. **Rainy-day touring** Closes in rain; good if it's snowing. **Restaurants** No. **Alcoholic beverages** No. **Disabled access** No. **Wheelchair rental** No. **Baby-stroller rental** No. **Lockers** No. **Pet kennels** No. **Rain check** No. **Private tours** No.

DESCRIPTION AND COMMENTS If you haven't had a good, whooping laugh with your kids in a while, come here and take a ride (or ten) on an inner tube down a wide, luge-style snow chute. Ten bucks gets you an hour of sledding, which is plenty. An iron rope tow takes you up to the top of the 500-foot run, and then you come bouncing and barreling down, which generally involves a lot of screaming and hooting. It's safe enough for preschoolers, and many inner tubes are big enough for a parent and child to ride in together.

FAMILY-FRIENDLY RESTAURANTS

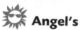 **Angel's**

3516 Main Street, Mammoth Lakes; ☎ 760-934-7427

Meals served Lunch and dinner. **Cuisine** American/Mediterranean. **Entree range** Lunch, $7–$9; dinner, $10–$25. **Kids' menu** Yes. **Reservations** Not accepted. **Payment** All major credit cards.

This Mammoth institution is often jam-packed at peak times, and it doesn't take reservations, so try to come on the early or late side. We love the hearty lunch-or-dinner sandwiches (triple-stacked grilled club, Ortega-chile melt, tuna-avocado melt, chicken Caesar wrap), the acclaimed ribs, the homemade soups, and the hickory-roasted barbecued chicken. Note that the modestly priced house wines are actually pretty good.

Base Camp Cafe

3325 Main Street, Mammoth Lakes; ☎ 760-934-3900

Meals served Breakfast, lunch, and dinner. **Cuisine** American. **Entree range** $5–$13. **Kids' menu** Yes. **Reservations** Not accepted. **Payment** All major credit cards.

This locals' hangout is the best place in town for a bargain meal, whether it's a hearty breakfast, take-out sandwiches for a hikers' picnic, or a dinner of soup, chili, pasta, or steak. Good kids' menu, nice people.

Nevados

Main Street and Minaret Road, Mammoth Lakes; ☎ 760-934-4466

Meals served Dinner. **Cuisine** American/Californian. **Entree range** $16–$30. **Kids' menu** Yes. **Reservations** Recommended. **Payment** All major credit cards.

The food at this stylish, upscale restaurant could pretty much hold its own in L.A., which is not true of most Mammoth restaurants. And despite the niceness of the place, children are welcome, with a fixed-price $10 menu (steak, pasta, or shrimp, including salad and dessert). We particularly liked the creative pasta dishes, and there's a pretty good wine list.

Perry's Italian Cafe
3399 Main Street, Mammoth Lakes; ☎ 760-934-6521

Meals served Breakfast, lunch, and dinner. **Cuisine** Italian **Entree range** Lunch, $7–$9; dinner, $8–$25. **Kids' Menu** Yes. **Reservations** Not accepted. **Payment** All major credit cards.

A friendly, family-oriented place, Perry's is popular, bright, and lively—perhaps a little too lively during peak seasons, when the wait can top an hour. The food is simple and satisfying fare: a good salad bar, pizzas, burgers, pastas. Our kids love the "old-fashioned" video games (Pac-Man!), and the TV in the bar is always tuned to a game.

SIDE TRIPS

Bodie State Historic Park

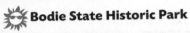

APPEAL BY AGE	PRESCHOOL ★	GRADE SCHOOL ★★★★	TEENS ★★★★
YOUNG ADULTS ★★★★		OVER 30 ★★★★	SENIORS ★★★★

20 miles from Bridgeport; ☎ 760-647-6445; www.parks.ca.gov

Hours Often closed because of inaccessible roads in winter, so call ahead; otherwise, open Memorial Day–Labor Day: daily, 8 a.m.–7 p.m.; rest of year: daily, 8 a.m.–4 p.m. **Admission** $1 per person. **Touring time** Average 2–3 hours; minimum 1 hour (not counting drive time). **Rainy-day touring** Not recommended. **Restaurants** No. **Alcoholic beverages** No. **Disabled access** No. **Wheelchair rental** No. **Baby-stroller rental** No. **Lockers** No. **Pet kennels** No; pets must be leashed, $1 fee. **Rain check** No. **Private tours** No.

DESCRIPTION AND COMMENTS This remarkable ghost town is all alone in its remote valley, so it's the fullest experience of the real Old West available today. It's located north of the turnout to Yosemite from US 395; from the highway, you take another road 13 miles east—the last three miles of which are hard-packed unpaved dirt, which is unplowed in winter and accessible only by cross-country skis or snowmobile. (The park is actually open and manned by rangers then, but no one visits.) The only services in Bodie are restrooms near the parking lot and a small museum and bookstore that is sometimes manned by volunteers. There's no snack bar, so bring water and a picnic lunch.

The ghost town is preserved by the park service in a state of "arrested decay," which means the rangers and volunteers keep the buildings from falling down (by strengthening foundations, replacing broken glass, and such) while allowing them to look as if they might actually fall down at any moment. In its golden years, Bodie had 10,000 residents in its lawless 19th-century heyday (it was a gold-mining town with dozens of saloons, no churches, and lots of gunfights); a much smaller number

For a memorable way to take your children into the Sierras, head out on horse-back. Several outfitters offer everything from half-hour hand-led rides for 6-year-olds and younger to weeklong pack trips into the John Muir Wilder-ness. Here are three favorite outfitters:

Convict Lake Resort ☎ 760-934-3800; **www.convictlake.com.** The 75-minute horseback ride around this beautiful lake is easy and ideal for kids (ages 7 and up), who do not need to be accompanied by parents. Littler ones can be guided by their parents on a 30-minute walk.

McGee Creek Pack Station ☎ 800-854-740; **www.mcgeecreekpack station.com.** The possibilities are vast here, from a one-hour ride along McGee Creek, to a day trip into historic McGee Canyon, to weeklong riding or pack-mule trips into the John Muir Wilderness. A popular family option is a ride-in camping trip to McGee's wilderness base camp; the horses return home, leaving you to hike, fish, and sing around the campfire until they return to collect you a few days later.

Red's Meadow Pack Station ☎ 760-934-2345. Near Devil's Postpile and Rainbow Falls, this is a tidy mountain resort complete with cabins, a gen-eral store, and a cafe. The Tanner family leads all sorts of outings, from two-hour rides to a five-day parent-child summertime pack trip up into either the Ansel Adams or John Muir Wilderness areas, in which families with chil-dren as young as 5 years old sleep at two well-equipped base camps.

of people lived here until 1932, when a fire devastated the town. Artifacts inside and outside the buildings—furniture, wagons, trucks, mining equipment, beauty-shop fixtures, curtains—are left from all periods of the town's occupation. Visitors walk around the dirt streets on a self-guided tour, peeking into the windows of houses and churches, the schoolhouse (with a map show-ing the world as it was just before World War I), the big old mine, and the mortuary. A detailed brochure tells about the inhabitants of each address and what is known of their fates, and a very good film about life in Bodie's very wild Wild West days shows in an old barn.

unofficial **TIP**
School-age kids love the ghostly exploration of Bodie's Wild West past, but little ones don't really get it.

We took a group of young teens who were enthralled by the voyeuristic thrill of looking into the windows and doors. Even though this is the coldest spot in the lower 48, the summer sun can be strong, so wear hats and stay hydrated.

Mono Lake

APPEAL BY AGE	PRESCHOOL ★	GRADE SCHOOL ★★	TEENS ★★
YOUNG ADULTS ★★		OVER 30 ★★★	SENIORS ★★★

(Add ★★ to each rating if ranger walk included.)

Highway 395 near Lee Vining; ☎ 760-647-6595; www.monolake.org

Hours Summer: daily, 9 a.m.–4:30 p.m.; limited hours in winter. **Admission** $3 in visitors center. **Touring time** Average 1 hour for visitors center and nature walk, ranger walk 1 hour; minimum 30 minutes. **Rainy-day touring** Not recommended. **Restaurants** In Lee Vining. **Alcoholic beverages** In Lee Vining. **Disabled access** Visitors center, viewing veranda. **Wheelchair rental** No. **Baby-stroller rental** No. **Lockers** No. **Pet kennels** No. **Rain check** No. **Private tours** No.

DESCRIPTION AND COMMENTS Families spending time in the Mammoth area should consider an excursion to Mono Lake to experience a strange and beautiful landscape: a large, flat lake in a desertlike setting with shore-line formations of tufa-rock columns rising like stalagmites above the surface of the water. We had stopped at the Mono Basin Scenic Area Visitors Center to enjoy the view and walk the nature trail when we learned that a ranger walk was scheduled soon, so we joined it and had a wonderful experience. The walk included touching, tasting, smelling, and looking through binoculars and magnifying glasses and was con-ducted right along the lake's shore. The center also offers a stargazing and storytelling program, a "sounds of the creek" walk, and additional hikes and talks at campgrounds and other sites around the Inyo National Forest. The early-morning guided canoe and kayak tours can be extra-ordinarily beautiful.

FAMILY-FRIENDLY RESTAURANT

 Whoa Nellie Deli

Tioga Gas Mart, Highway 120 at Highway 395, Lee Vining;
☎ 760-647-1088; www.thesierraweb.com/tiogagasmart

Meals served Breakfast, lunch, and dinner, April–October only. **Cuisine** American. **Entree range** $7–$19. **Kids' menu** Yes. **Reservations** Not accepted. **Payment** All major credit cards.

This ain't your typical Mobil mart—the setting overlooks Mono Lake, the shop stocks REI-quality gear, and the deli counter goes way beyond the gas-station orange-cheese–nachos standards. Chef Matt Toomey runs an amazing kitchen here, serving everything from grilled-salmon salads to lobster taquitos—but your kids can get chicken fingers, too. The pizzas are superb, as is the barbecue potato salad. Call ahead, and they'll pack picnic boxes for a Mono Lake outing or Sierra hike. An absolute must-stop between Mam-moth and Yosemite in summertime.

YOSEMITE

SO MANY GIFTED WRITERS AND PHOTOGRAPHERS have turned their talents to portraying **Yosemite** that we can't possibly do it justice. Suffice it to say that this national park is one of the world's natural treasures, a place of great beauty, grandeur, and even mysticism. And while the awesomeness of **Yosemite Valley** may not leave your children as speechless as you, it will provide plenty of opportunities to imprint itself on their memories. Whether they're climbing up **Vernal Falls,** riding a bike under **Half Dome,** or searching the **Merced River** for frogs, your kids will find their own reasons to love Yosemite.

Yosemite is also, of course, a place with man-made roads, visitors centers, and campgrounds, being that this is a national park. This infrastructure was greatly damaged in a 1997 flood; restoration work has been going on for years and is almost complete. After the flood, the park service put into immediate effect a long-term plan designed to update, upgrade, and improve Yosemite's infrastructure and make visitor facilities more environmentally friendly. So not all structures were rebuilt; there are fewer campsites in the Valley itself and more in the surrounding areas (which are well worth exploring); public transportation has improved and cars are greatly discouraged; and overall, the summer crowds aren't as overwhelming as they once were.

Campsite reservations may be made beginning at the 15th of each month up to three months in advance by calling ☎ 800-436-7275 or going to **reservations.nps.gov**. Reservations for hotels, motels, and tent cabins within Yosemite may be made up to a year in advance; call ☎ 559-252-4848 or go to **www .yosemitepark.com.**

> *un*official **TIP**
> Yosemite's popularity demands that visitors make reservations as early as possible.

The camp entrance fee is $20 per car (an annual Yosemite pass is $40, and an annual National Park Service pass is $50). Once you've arrived and settled into your camp or cabin, please try to use your car as little as possible and use the park's convenient free shuttle service to get to trailheads and other areas.

There are several Yosemite Web pages to explore. The National Park Service site is at **www.nps.gov/yose** and has park information and "Yosemite Notebooks" with visuals. The Yosemite Association's site,

yosemite

FAMILY LODGING
1. Ahwahnee Hotel
2. Curry Village
3. Marriott's Tenaya Lodge
4. Wawona Hotel
5. Yosemite Lodge

ATTRACTIONS
6. Wawona
7. Yosemite Valley

www.yosemite.org, has visitor information, a bookstore, class listings, and a live camera view of **Glacier Point.** The Yosemite Concessions Services page at **www.yosemitepark.com** has lodging and park activity information, links to other Yosemite sites, and an online gift shop.

GETTING THERE

BY CAR The most common approach to the park is from the west, via the town of **Merced,** which is reached by taking **Interstate 5** south from San Francisco or north from L.A. and then transitioning to **CA Highway 140** east. Visitors who are also seeing Mammoth, Death Valley, or Lake Tahoe might approach from the east, via the town of Lee Vining, by taking **US Highway 395** north or south, then **State Highway 120** west into the park.

BY BUS Be respectful and leave your smelly car behind, traveling via the **Yosemite Connection–Grayline,** ☎ 209-384-1315 or, in California, ☎ 800-369-PARK. There's service from the Merced Amtrak Station and Transportation Center to Yosemite Valley Visitors Center several times a day.

FAMILY LODGING

 Ahwahnee Hotel

Yosemite National Park; ☎ 559-253-5635;
www.webportal.com/ahwahnee; $394 and up

This National Historic Landmark hotel is a favorite for outdoors people and city-slicker visitors alike, and it's often sold out. Its soaring Arts and Crafts–era stone-and-wood architecture fits the majestic setting, and its Native American artifacts and décor are authentic and museum quality. In addition to 97 lodge rooms, there are 26 cottages, a good choice for families. It's not the most kid-friendly lodging in the park—lots of wealthy retirees visit here, and they like to sit quietly in the awesome public areas, reading or doing elaborate jigsaw puzzles; when we visited, we felt like we had to constantly hush our children and keep them away from those jigsaw puzzles. On the other hand, it does have a pool and a children's play area, and the restaurant is polite to children and has a children's menu. And, of course, you can always take them out into the vastness of the valley, just outside the door.

Curry Village
Yosemite National Park; ☎ 559-252-4848;
www.yosemitepark.com; $74–$123

Composed of some 300 packed-together rustic wooden cabins (with or without private baths) and tiny tent cabins (the least expensive lodging in the park), Curry Village is crowded and low on comfort. But the location is fun for kids, because of the bustling village atmosphere with pool, cafeteria, snack bar, mini-market, and lots of other kids to make friends with. It's also a center of activities and services, including tour departures, raft rentals, cross-country ski rentals, and bike rentals. From mid-November to March there's an outdoor ice rink (rare in California!). Overall, Curry Village is lively and active; don't expect any quiet, secluded moments.

Marriott's Tenaya Lodge
1122 Highway 41, Fish Camp; ☎ 559-253-2005 or 888-514-2167; www.tenayalodge.com; $185 and up; children free in parents' room

Two miles from Yosemite's south entrance in the town of Fish Camp, this newer full-service resort makes a fine vacation base, even if it does imprint a sense of chain-corporate America on a previously funky little mountain village. Spread among the trees are 244 rooms, two restaurants, a playground, and two pools, one indoor and one out. The best room for families is the double deluxe, a larger room with a sitting area, a sofa bed, and a balcony with a forest view. At the activities desk, you can sign up for a flashlight hike for the kids, a narrated bus tour of the valley, and a guided ten-mile hike to a 30-foot waterfall; other fun stuff to do includes mountain-bike rentals, volleyball, and fishing at nearby Bass Lake. Camp Tenaya, the program for children ages 5 to 12, operates all summer with day and evening activities and includes meals; cost ranges from $30 to $35, depending on time.

Wawona Hotel
Highway 41, Wawona, 27 miles south of Yosemite Valley, Yosemite National Park; ☎ 559-253-5635; www.yosemitepark.com; $119–$183

Located in the Mariposa Grove area, nearly 30 miles from the Valley, the Wawona (like the Ahwahnee) is a National Historic Landmark. There's an almost secluded feeling to the hotel, a favorite with Yosemite lovers who want to avoid the hustle and bustle of the valley. Come here in the off season and you're likely to see deer, coyotes, and foxes right in front of the hotel. The homey, rustic rooms are spread among whitewashed turn-of-the-19th-century buildings with great front porches; ask for spacious or connecting rooms as there are a variety of options among the 105 rooms (50 with private baths). There's a big lawn with a pool, tennis courts, and a nine-hole golf course. Restaurant on site, store nearby.

Yosemite Lodge
Yosemite National Park; ☎ 559-253-5635; www.yosemitepark.com; $98–$170

Conveniently located and neither as grand as the Ahwahnee nor as funky as Curry Village, Yosemite Lodge provides the middle-ground noncamping accommodations in the park. Activities right around the lodge are plentiful. The short walk to Yosemite Falls begins just across the street; the lodge has a bike-rental shop, many paved trails adjacent, and a terrific pool. There are three restaurants, one with a children's menu. Learn-to-ski packages for Badger Pass are offered midweek in the winter.

❚ ATTRACTIONS

Wawona

APPEAL BY AGE	PRESCHOOL ★★★	GRADE SCHOOL ★★★★	TEENS ★★★★★
YOUNG ADULTS ★★★★★		OVER 30 ★★★★★	SENIORS ★★★★★

**Highway 41 south of Yosemite Valley; ☎ 209-375-9501;
off season: ☎ 209-372-0200; www.yosemite.org**

Hours Spring and summer: Wawona Information Station open daily, 9 a.m.–
5 p.m.; off-season hours limited. **Admission** $20 per vehicle at park entrance.
Touring time Average several days; minimum 1 day, 1 night. **Rainy-day touring**
Possible. **Restaurants** Yes. **Alcoholic beverages** Yes. **Disabled access** Some.
Wheelchair rental No. **Baby-stroller rental** No. **Lockers** No. **Pet kennels** No.
Rain check No. **Private tours** No.

DESCRIPTION AND COMMENTS   This south-entrance area of Yosemite is loved
by some visitors as a base because of its relative peace and quiet. There's
no lack of things to do, however; here's where the Mariposa Grove
and the Pioneer Yosemite History Center are found. You can stay in the
charming, rustic (and inexpensive) old white-sided Wawona Hotel (see
listing in "Family Lodging").

The Wawona Information Station, at the park's south entrance, has
maps, wilderness permits, trail guides, and books. A free shuttle bus from
the information station takes visitors to the Mariposa Grove of giant
sequoias; it operates daily in the summer from mid-May, 9 a.m. to 6 p.m.

Yosemite Valley

APPEAL BY AGE	PRESCHOOL ★★★	GRADE SCHOOL ★★★★★	TEENS ★★★★★
YOUNG ADULTS ★★★★★		OVER 30 ★★★★★	SENIORS ★★★★★

**Yosemite Village west of the main post office; ☎ 209-372-0200;
www.yosemite.org**

Hours Visitors center open daily, 8 a.m.–5 p.m. **Admission** $20 per vehicle at park
entrance. **Touring time** Average several days; minimum a half day. **Rainy-day
touring** Possible; can be pretty and quiet. **Restaurants** Yes. **Alcoholic beverages**
Yes. **Disabled access** Yes, ask at visitors center. **Wheelchair rental** No. **Baby-
stroller rental** No. **Lockers** Food lockers vs. bears. **Pet
kennels** No. **Rain check** No. **Private tours** No.

DESCRIPTION AND COMMENTS   Much is written in travel
literature about Yosemite being more than the
Yosemite Valley itself, and it's true—the famous
park has miles of wilderness for hiking and camping, and plenty of room in which to spread out if
you get off the beaten path. We know many Californians who return (often with kids in tow) year
after year to the valley to settle in for a week of

unofficial **TIP**
Visitors don't need to
apologize for actually
liking the valley, with its
ranger talks, its world-
famous waterfalls and
much-photographed
views, and its abundant
wildlife and scenic
bike rides.

hiking, biking, and campfire-going. These repeaters tell us that Yosemite is a large park with a varied topography and that they do go on excursions, such as the easy walk to Mirror Lake or on one of a zillion incredible hiking trails. But they still love the valley.

Along with the Yosemite Valley Visitors Center, in Yosemite Village west of the main post office, you'll find a museum, gallery, wilderness supply shop, and trailheads to two nature trails.

YOSEMITE'S LITTLE JOYS

BIKE RIDING Bikes can be rented at Yosemite Lodge or Curry Village, and there are level trails crisscrossing the entire valley floor. This is lots of fun for school-age kids.

EARLY-MORNING PHOTOGRAPHY WALKS These leave around 8:30 a.m. and last for one hour from either the Ahwahnee or Yosemite Lodge.

EL CAPITAN Take some moments while you're in Yosemite to look at this granite wall at different times of the day. There are often climbers working their way up the face, and if you go to the meadow across from it with binoculars, you can watch their progress. At night, you can see the climbers' lights, or on a full-moon night, simply admire the dazzling rock itself. See "Rock-climbing Classes" (right) for your own adventurous climbing kids.

FAMILY WALKS These begin at the Valley Visitors Center, and they're led by a ranger-naturalist.

GLACIER POINT Most families stop here for just a half hour on their way into or out of the valley, but don't neglect to make the stop. It's the picture-postcard view of your dreams, and even the kids will be awestruck. The scenic overlook is 30 miles (1 hour) from the valley, and the road is open from late spring through early fall. There's a snack stand open 9 a.m. to sundown.

HORSEBACK RIDING Weather permitting, two-hour and half-day rides depart spring through fall from stables in the valley and at Wawona. Call ☎ 209-372-8348 for more information.

LE CONTE MEMORIAL LODGE CHILDREN'S CENTER In the summer months, there are programs for kids ages 5 to 10. ☎ 209-372-4542.

MARIPOSA GROVE The largest of three sequoia groves in Yosemite has been a magnet for visitors since the mid-19th century. The grove's Grizzly Giant tree, 2,700 years old, is believed to be the oldest living sequoia. There's a small log cabin museum at the grove (May 22 through fall, open 10 a.m. to 5 p.m.). To reach the grove, take the free shuttle bus from Wawona, then follow the interpretive trail signs for a self-guided walking tour. Weather permitting in the summer, a guided tram tour ($16 adults, $10 for kids ages 4 to 12, children under age 4 free) leaves every 20 minutes for a one-hour tour through the upper and lower groves. For reservations, call ☎ 209-375-1621.

PIONEER YOSEMITE HISTORY CENTER This cluster of historic buildings at Wawona is the center of living-history programs and other activities for children. A jailhouse, miner's cabin, and covered bridge can be explored in a 30-minute self-guided tour; there's a stagecoach ride, and there are sometimes demonstrations and crafts depending on the season, such as soap making, yarn spinning, and Christmas crafts. The bookstore is open 9 a.m. to 5 p.m. in the summer.

ROCK-CLIMBING CLASSES Yosemite Mountaineering School and Guide Service (☎ 209-372-8344). Rock climbing is hugely popular here, and it can be a wonderful adventure for older kids. Beginning rock-climbing classes are offered from Easter through mid-October; kids must be at least 10 years old. Mike Corbett's one-hour talk and walk about the history of climbing in Yosemite leaves from either the Ahwahnee or the Yosemite Lodge twice a week at 8:30 a.m.

TOURS OF THE VALLEY Two-hour, half-day, and all-day summer tours of the major landmarks of Yosemite Valley are given daily, in part to reduce the flow of auto traffic on the few roads on the valley floor. The summer tour vehicle is completely open-air and allows riders to see in all directions; winter tours are in heated buses. There's also a two-hour moonlight tour in the summer. We thought the tour was an easy, helpful way to get the lay of the land, and we found the guide's comments on wildlife particularly interesting. Call the Yosemite Lodge at ☎ 209-372-1240 for fees and times.

WATERFALLS Waterfalls from below and waterfalls from above are one of the main attractions at Yosemite, but depending on the time of year and the amount of snowmelt the area is receiving, some of the falls may or may not be filled with water. One of the most popular hikes in Yosemite is up to the top of Vernal Falls, and for purists it's probably a discouraging experience—literally hundreds of people at a time are working their way up and down the waterside trail that goes from the base of the falls to a pool (where people swim) at the top (from which some hikers continue on up to other pools). But families with active preteens and teens may find this a great way to participate in the democratic appreciation of a great national park. The other hikers are from all over the country and the world, and it makes for a fine outdoor social occasion, if not a wilderness experience. Lower Yosemite Falls and Bridalveil Falls can be enjoyed with just short, easy walks from shuttle stops. Yosemite Falls, with its 2,425-foot drop, can be seen from Glacier Point.

WILDLIFE Please, please review safety information about sharing the park with bears and mountain lions, and watch your children closely at all times. You will also see deer, coyotes, squirrels, and other smaller animals. Do not feed or disturb wildlife—doing so is a violation subject to fine.

LAKE TAHOE

THIS IS A BIG LAKE, TO BE SURE—it's 22 miles long and 12 miles wide, with 72 miles of shoreline—but the special characteristic remembered by most visitors here is not the size but the beautiful deep, dark blue of the water. Surrounded by pine forests and visible from above on some scenic roads and hikes, **Lake Tahoe** makes an indelible impression. That inky blue water will turn swimmers blue, too—it seldom gets warmer than 60°F, even in the middle of summer. We love it for instantly soothing aching muscles or swelling feet after a hike in the hot sun, but parents of little ones will want to pull them out of the water for a towel rubdown every now and then.

Two-thirds of the lake is in California, and one-third in Nevada. The several communities on the lake's shore are quite different and are concentrated either north or south. The North Shore California towns of **Tahoe City** and **Tahoe Vista** are summer sports centers, where the best Jet Ski rentals are located and where water-skiers rule. The South Shore includes some Nevada territory, so there are casinos, but the town of South **Lake Tahoe** also offers family-friendly swim beaches, hikes, and sightseeing excursions. There is skiing on both sides of the lake. The west side of the lake offers access to the hiking trails of the **Desolation Wilderness** and **El Dorado Village;** the east side offers highway junctions to Nevada's gambling centers and historic silver-mining towns.

GETTING THERE

BY CAR Lake Tahoe is most easily reached by car from San Francisco; it's 200 miles northeast of the Bay Area. Your route will depend on whether you're headed for the North or South Shore. For North Shore, take **Interstate 80** east to Truckee; for South Lake Tahoe, take **US Highway 50** east.

BY AIR Among the airlines serving **Reno/Tahoe International Airport** (60 miles east of the lake area; ☎ 775-328-6400; **www.renoairport.com**) are Alaska Air, Aloha, American, Continental, Delta, Frontier, US Airways, Skywest, Southwest, and United.

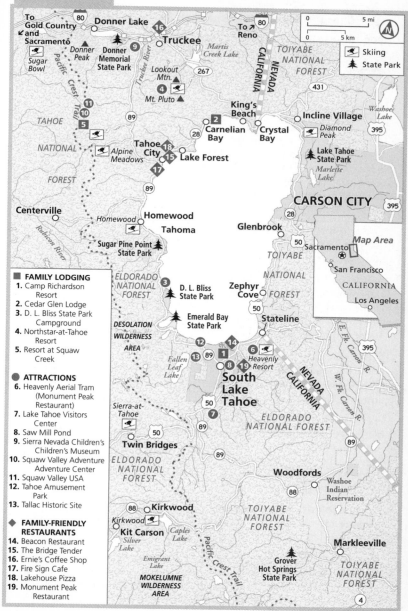

lake tahoe

0 — 5 mi
0 — 5 km

🎿 Skiing
🌲 State Park

FAMILY LODGING
1. Camp Richardson Resort
2. Cedar Glen Lodge
3. D. L. Bliss State Park Campground
4. Northstar-at-Tahoe Resort
5. Resort at Squaw Creek

ATTRACTIONS
6. Heavenly Aerial Tram (Monument Peak Restaurant)
7. Lake Tahoe Visitors Center
8. Saw Mill Pond
9. Sierra Nevada Children's Children's Museum
10. Squaw Valley Adventure Adventure Center
11. Squaw Valley USA
12. Tahoe Amusement Park
13. Tallac Historic Site

FAMILY-FRIENDLY RESTAURANTS
14. Beacon Restaurant
15. The Bridge Tender
16. Ernie's Coffee Shop
17. Fire Sign Cafe
18. Lakehouse Pizza
19. Monument Peak Restaurant

FAMILY LODGING

 Camp Richardson Resort

1900 Jameson Beach Road, South Lake Tahoe; ☎ 530-541-1801 or 800-544-1801; www.camprich.com; $140–$270 summer, $105–$210 winter

This unique, rustic resort has been home to vacationing families for more than 70 years—it's no grand ski complex, but rather a jumble of lodges, cabins, and campsites (for both tents and RVs) in a pine woods at the shore of the lake. The lodge has a pleasant public space with a big stone fireplace and the wonderful Beacon restaurant. The beach is the big draw for many; it's one of the best for swimming, and the full-service marina is a bustling center of water sports, kayak rentals, windsurfing gear, and more. The 36 lodge rooms and 39 cottages vary in décor and layout; some have terraces, fireplaces, and/or kitchens, but the cabins don't have TVs or phones. Also on premises are an ice-cream shop and cafe-bakery, children's playground, bike-rental shop, and stable.

Cedar Glen Lodge
6589 North Lake Boulevard, Tahoe Vista; ☎ 530-546-4281 or 800-500-TAHOE; www.cedarglenlodge.com; $115–$250

A very good value for families, this small motel is located across the highway from a nice beach in Tahoe Vista on the North Shore. It's tucked in the pine woods, with a playground, pool, hot tub, and barbecues. Two two-bedroom units with kitchens are found among the rooms and cabins. There's no restaurant, but a basic continental breakfast is free.

D. L. Bliss State Park Campground
Route 89, Tahoma; ☎ 530-525-7277; reservations: Reserve America, ☎ 800-444-7275; www.reserveamerica.com; campsites $20 plus $5 entrance fee

It's blissful here all right, especially for children, who never tire of scrambling over the boulders, playing hide-and-seek behind the pines, and exploring the gorgeous white-sand Lester Beach or close-by Emerald Bay. Bliss has three clumps of campsites; if you want to be closest to Lester Beach, reserve a site between 141 and 168. Hot showers, flush toilets, picnic tables, fire pits, wood for sale.

Northstar-at-Tahoe Resort
Highway 267 north of Lake Tahoe, 6 miles south of Truckee; ☎ 530-562-1010 or 800-466-6784; www.skinorthstar.com; $159–$935

This Squaw Valley rival resort has everything an active family could dream of spread over its 600 acres. You and/or your kids can mountain bike, ride a pony, join guided hikes, ski, tackle a climbing wall, learn orienteering, take a ropes course, swim in heated pools, play tennis—it's exhausting just to consider the options. The Minor's Camp program handles kids ages 3 to 12, with skiing lessons and snow play in winter and all sorts of amusements year-round. The accommodations range from upscale motel rooms to suites to fully equipped condos, found one mile from the main complex. There are five restaurants, most of which have kids' menus.

unofficial **TIP**
Northstar is one of the most popular learn-to-ski family resorts in North America, known for its ego-enhancing runs and friendly ski school.

Resort at Squaw Creek

400 Squaw Creek Road, Squaw Valley;
☎ **530-583-6300 or 800-327-3353; www.squawcreek.com;**
$149–$589

Modern mountain architecture makes this a distinctly Tahoe resort, with contemporary buildings at the center of 632 acres designed so every room has a view of the Sierra. The resort is a little town, actually, and in the winter especially, families can find all they need for a vacation right within the complex: shopping, skiing (direct access to Squaw Creek mountain lifts), world-class golf, junior tennis programs, even lawn games. In the summer, the Activity Center has a ropes course, climbing walls, and bungee jump, and the wonderful, landscaped pool complex boasts a waterslide; in the winter there's an ice rink. Of the 403 rooms and suites, the best bet for families is a suite, some of which have fireplaces. The Mountain Buddies Club offers half- and full-day programs (swimming, hiking, crafts, and games) for kids ages 4 to 13, as well as separate teen programs. One drawback: the lodging is not connected to the lobby area except by outdoor walkways, so in the winter, guests must go outside to get to restaurants.

TAHOE TREASURES

D. L. BLISS STATE PARK This park contains some great camping (168 sites; see "Family Lodging"); terrific beach and boating areas; and several wonderful trails for day hikers, including the dreamy 4.5-mile Rubicon Trail, which snakes along the shore through the woods to the beach, where you can swim and picnic. Another hike, less than a mile long, takes you to an old lighthouse, and another, just one mile round trip, takes you to the remarkable Balancing Rock. Nine miles north of South Lake Tahoe on Highway 89; ☎ 530-525-7277 or 530-525-7982; **www.parks.ca.gov.**

TRUCKEE HISTORIC TOWN CENTER Almost 100 19th-century buildings remain in this town, and visitors can get an Old West feel on Commercial Row, where wooden sidewalks remain. The historic area is largely cafes and shops, as well as the Southern Pacific Railroad Depot Gallery; the Bar of America, with its photos of famous outlaws; and the old **Truckee Jailhouse Museum** (10142 Jibboom Street, behind Commercial Row; ☎ 530-582-0893; free admission, open weekends), which features real cells, historic photos, and Chinese American historical items. Truckee is located on Interstate 80, 20 minutes north of Lake Tahoe.

ATTRACTIONS

Heavenly Aerial Tram (Monument Peak Restaurant)

APPEAL BY AGE	PRESCHOOL ★	GRADE SCHOOL ★★★★	TEENS ★★★★★
YOUNG ADULTS ★★★★★		OVER 30 ★★★★★	SENIORS ★★★★

Heavenly Ski Resort, Ski Run Boulevard, South Lake Tahoe;
☎ **775-586-7000; www.skiheavenly.com**

Hours Summer: daily, 10 a.m.–5 p.m.; winter: Monday–Friday, 9 a.m.–4 p.m.; Saturday, Sunday, holidays, 8:30 a.m.–4 p.m. **Admission** Tram: adults $24, children ages 5–12 $15, children under age 5, free; winter ski-lift ticket: $20–$57. **Touring time** Average 2 hours; minimum 15 minutes. **Rainy-day touring** Not good for hiking. **Restaurants** Yes. **Alcoholic beverages** Yes. **Disabled access** Tram only. **Wheelchair rental** No. **Baby-stroller rental** No. **Lockers** In winter. **Pet kennels** No. **Rain check** No. **Private tours** No.

DESCRIPTION AND COMMENTS Theme parks sometimes try to duplicate the thrill of a ski gondola or tram ride, but there's nothing like the real thing. The ride itself is a spectacular mile-long ascent to a point 2,000 feet above Lake Tahoe. At the top is a cafe with a large deck and a self-guided nature trail. For a memorable supper, come just before sunset and eat enjoying the view—the lake reflects the gorgeous light.

Lake Tahoe Visitor Center

APPEAL BY AGE	PRESCHOOL ★★★	GRADE SCHOOL ★★★	TEENS ★★★
YOUNG ADULTS ★★★		OVER 30 ★★★	SENIORS ★★★

Highway 89, 4 miles south of US 50 and Highway 90, South Lake Tahoe;
☎ **530-543-2674; www.fs.fed.us/r5/ltbmu/recreation/visitor-center**

Hours Summer: daily, 8 a.m.–5:30 p.m.; open weekends only in early June and October; closed in winter. **Admission** Free. **Touring time** Average, depends on trail chosen; minimum 30 minutes. **Rainy-day touring** Okay on paved path. **Restaurants** Nearby. **Alcoholic beverages** Yes. **Disabled access** Yes. **Wheelchair rental** Yes, free. **Baby-stroller rental** No. **Lockers** No. **Pet kennels** No; leashed pets allowed. **Rain check** No. **Private tours** No.

DESCRIPTION AND COMMENTS While one parent peruses the maps and brochures, another can take the kids along one of the six self-guided nature trails at this center run by the U.S. Forest Service. Among the trail attractions is an underground fish-viewing chamber that provides a window on the lake's aquatic life. Interpretive programs (night walks, astronomy adventures, living-history performances) are offered on site from June through Labor Day.

Saw Mill Pond

APPEAL BY AGE	PRESCHOOL ★★★★	GRADE SCHOOL ★★★★	TEENS ★★★
YOUNG ADULTS ★		OVER 30 ★	SENIORS ★

Past the Y at Lake Tahoe Boulevard and Saw Mill Road, Lake Tahoe Basin Management, 870 Emerald Bay Road, South Lake Tahoe; ☎ 530-543-2600

Hours Daily, 24 hours, year-round. **Admission** Free. **Touring time** Average 2 hours; minimum 1 hour. **Rainy-day touring** Yes, but you'll get wet. **Restaurants** 2 miles from civilization. **Alcoholic beverages** Yes. **Disabled access** Not yet; in the works. **Wheelchair rental** No. **Baby-stroller rental** No. **Lockers** No. **Pet kennels** No; leashed pets allowed. **Rain check** No. **Private tours** No.

DESCRIPTION AND COMMENTS Serious fishing families will scoff, but for non-fishing adults, this is a fine fishing hole for introducing your kids to the activity. Kids under age 13 fish free in this pretty little pond stocked with trout by the California Department of Fish and Game, but you must supply your own bait and equipment. It's not open to anyone over age 14, so parents can teach but not fish. The pond is popular for ice-skating and hockey in winter.

Sierra Nevada Children's Museum

APPEAL BY AGE	PRESCHOOL ★★★★	GRADE SCHOOL ★★★★	TEENS ★★
YOUNG ADULTS ★		OVER 30 ★	SENIORS ★

1140 Donner Pass Road, Truckee; ☎ 530-587-5437

Hours April–November: Tuesday–Saturday, 9 a.m.–1 p.m. **Admission** $4, free for children under age 2. **Touring time** Average 2 hours; minimum 1 hour. **Rainy-day touring** Yes. **Restaurants** Next door. **Alcoholic beverages** Next door. **Disabled access** Yes. **Wheelchair rental** No. **Baby-stroller rental** No. **Lockers** Cubby-holes. **Pet kennels** No. **Rain check** No. **Private tours** No.

DESCRIPTION AND COMMENTS A modest example of its kind, but for very little ones it's a welcome respite from the macho world of skiing or waterskiing. A variety of educational hands-on exhibits are here, as well as some imaginative temporary special exhibits and arts and crafts projects.

Squaw Valley Adventure Center

APPEAL BY AGE	PRESCHOOL ★	GRADE SCHOOL ★★★★	TEENS ★★★★★
YOUNG ADULTS ★★★★★		OVER 30 ★★★★	SENIORS ★★

1960 Squaw Valley Road, Squaw Valley; ☎ 530-583-7673 or 800-403-0206; www.squawadventure.com

Hours Open summers; hours vary by activity. **Admission** Varies by activity. **Touring time** Average 1 day; minimum 1 hour. **Rainy-day touring** Indoor climbing wall only. **Restaurants** Nearby. **Alcoholic beverages** In some restaurants. **Disabled access** Yes. **Wheelchair rental** No. **Baby-stroller rental** No. **Lockers** No. **Pet kennels** No; leashed pets allowed in summer. **Rain check** No. **Private tours** Yes.

DESCRIPTION AND COMMENTS This "center" is actually spread over three activities in three areas, all within the Squaw Valley resort. Near the Olympic Village Inn is the excellent ropes course, open for individual and family use in July and August (other months are available for groups only). It's an intense and amazing experience to walk across a swaying rope bridge 25 feet above ground while your family cheers you on. We highly recommend this adventure for teenagers, brave preteens, and parents, but it's too scary for younger ones. Even toddlers, however, will have a blast on the Skyjump, a combination trampoline and bungee jump that's safe and thrilling ($10 for a five-minute jump session). Finally, there's the Headwall Climbing Wall, which is actually two walls: a 30-foot indoor climbing structure and a summertime 40-foot outdoor wall. A day pass is a reasonable $14, plus $4 to rent climbing shoes.

Squaw Valley USA

APPEAL BY AGE	PRESCHOOL ★★★	GRADE SCHOOL ★★★★	TEENS ★★★★★
YOUNG ADULTS ★★★★★		OVER 30 ★★★★	SENIORS ★★★

1960 Squaw Valley Road, Squaw Valley; ☎ 530-583-6985 or 800-403-0206; www.squaw.com

Hours Open year-round; hours vary by activity. **Admission** Varies by activity. **Touring time** Average 1 day; minimum 2 hours. **Rainy-day touring** Not great. **Restaurants** Yes. **Alcoholic beverages** In some restaurants. **Disabled access** Yes. **Wheelchair rental** Yes. **Baby-stroller rental** No. **Lockers** Yes. **Pet kennels** No; leashed pets allowed in summer. **Rain check** No. **Private tours** No.

DESCRIPTION AND COMMENTS There's little to remind visitors of the 1960 Winter Olympics that were held here, but there's plenty to do year-round. Summer activities include an aerial tram ride to the High Camp Bath and Tennis Club, where you can swim, mountain-bike, play tennis, and bungee-jump—all at an altitude of 8,200 feet. In winter, don't miss the chance to ice-skate in the beautiful outdoor Olympic Ice Pavilion (it's even open in summer); in the summer, head for the Adventure Center (see previous profile). And, of course, there's the skiing, some of the best in the West, with spectacular views of the lake. Kids get their own ski area, Children's World, with a playground, ski school, day-care center, and complete facilities.

Tahoe Amusement Park

APPEAL BY AGE	PRESCHOOL ★★★★	GRADE SCHOOL ★★★★	TEENS ★★★
YOUNG ADULTS ★		OVER 30 ★	SENIORS ★

2401 Lake Tahoe Boulevard, South Lake Tahoe; ☎ 530-541-1300

Hours Off season: daily, 11 a.m.–6 p.m.; summer: daily, 10 a.m.–9 p.m. **Admission** Varies by ride. **Touring time** Average 2 hours; minimum 1 hour. **Rainy-day touring** Very poor. **Restaurants** Snack bar and picnic area. **Alcoholic beverages** No. **Disabled access** Yes. **Wheelchair rental** No. **Baby-stroller rental** No. **Lockers** No. **Pet kennels** No. **Rain check** Yes. **Private tours** No.

DESCRIPTION AND COMMENTS It's just a small facility (11 rides), but the mini–Ferris wheel, slide, merry-go-round, electric golf, and mini-golf make for a nice afternoon. It's a reminder of how far a few small rides can carry vacationing kids.

Tallac Historic Site

APPEAL BY AGE	PRESCHOOL ★★	GRADE SCHOOL ★★★	TEENS ★★★
YOUNG ADULTS ★★★		OVER 30 ★★★	SENIORS ★★★

Highway 89, 3.5 miles north of South Lake Tahoe, next to Camp Richardson; ☎ 530-541-5227

Hours Late May–early September: daily, 10 a.m.–4 p.m.; closed Tuesdays. **Admission** Free. **Touring time** Average 2 hours; minimum 45 minutes. **Rainy-day touring** Yes, places to escape from rain. **Restaurants** Adjacent. **Alcoholic beverages** At restaurant. **Disabled access** About half of buildings. **Wheelchair rental** No. **Baby-stroller rental** No. **Lockers** No. **Pet kennels** No; leashed pets allowed. **Rain check** No. **Private tours** Yes.

DESCRIPTION AND COMMENTS There are several mansion museums in the Tahoe area, but the most interesting with children is a three-building complex in South Lake Tahoe called Tallac Historic Site. It's accessible by paved bike paths from the town and is adjacent to white-sand beaches and a couple of easy hiking trails, so it makes for a nice destination for a bike ride or combination sightseeing-swimming-hiking afternoon. The buildings are composed of a 1921 "log cabin" estate that is now a museum, with exhibits on Washoe Indians and the history of the estate owners; an 1894 mansion retreat that's home to an interpretive center and summertime living-history programs; and a 1923 estate used for music and arts events, where you'll find several cabins turned over to crafts and arts exhibits and workshops for children.

■ FAMILY-FRIENDLY RESTAURANTS

Beacon Restaurant
Richardson's Resort, 1900 Jameson Beach Road, South Lake Tahoe; ☎ 530-541-0630

Meals served Lunch, dinner, and weekend brunch. **Cuisine** American. **Entree range** Lunch and dinner, $8–$34. **Kids' menu** Yes. **Reservations** Recommended. **Payment** D, MC, V.

Sitting on the deck here, eye level with that blue, blue lake, watching kids in their bathing suits pad barefoot and dripping up to the take-out window for a snow cone—it all made us want to be kids again. Then again, seeing the gang of 20-somethings laughing over margaritas made us want to be footloose and single again. But then, looking around our own table at the contented smiles as we scarfed down our just-fine summer-vacation food in a carefree boat-and-beachy setting made us, of course, feel happy to be who we are and where we were.

☀ The Bridge Tender
65 West Lake Boulevard, Tahoe City; ☎ 530-583-3342

Meals served Lunch and dinner. **Cuisine** American. **Entree range** $5–$10. **Kids' menu** No. **Reservations** Not accepted. **Payment** D, MC, V.

A noisy, casual locals' hangout in the heart of Tahoe City, the Bridge Tender is known for its delicious, messy burgers, its ribs, its onion rings, its mountain-folk bar scene, and its location right next to Fanny Bridge—so named for the dozens of fannies sticking up in the air on summer days as people lean over the bridge to see (and feed) the huge spawning trout. Older kids will like the food and scene at this place, and little ones will love tossing bread crumbs down to the fish.

Ernie's Coffee Shop
1146 Emerald Bay Road, South Lake Tahoe; ☎ 530-541-2161

Meals served Breakfast and lunch. **Cuisine** American/coffee shop. **Entree range** $5–$10. **Kids' menu** Yes. **Reservations** Not necessary. **Payment** No credit cards.

Just a place where neighbors gather to drink coffee and chew the fat before the day gets too far along. You and the kids will be comfortable here.

Fire Sign Cafe
1785 West Lake Boulevard, Tahoe City; ☎ 530-583-0871

Meals served Breakfast and lunch. **Cuisine** American. **Entree range** $5–$9. **Kids' menu** Yes. **Reservations** Not accepted. **Payment** MC, V.

A good stop between hikes, this modern coffee shop has a nice woodsy atmosphere and an outside deck for summertime. Choices include teriyaki steak, a turkey club sandwich, veggie baked potatoes, and awesome breakfasts, especially the buckwheat pancakes and lattes. The staff brings out a basket of toys and crayons for kids. Expect a wait on Sunday morning.

Lakehouse Pizza
120 Grove Street, Tahoe City; ☎ 530-583-2222

Meals served Breakfast, lunch, and dinner. **Cuisine** American. **Entree range** Lunch and dinner, $6–$9; pizzas, $8–$22. **Kids' menu** No. **Reservations** Not accepted. **Payment** AE, MC, V.

Only in Lake Tahoe can you find a modest pizza parlor with terrific outdoor deck dining right at the water's edge. Straightforward pizza, pastas, and Chinese chicken salads. Sometimes they'll give the kids some pizza dough to play with, which was a huge hit with the 4-year-old at the next table the last time we were there.

Monument Peak Restaurant
Heavenly Ski Resort, Ski Run Boulevard, South Lake Tahoe;
☎ **530-544-6263**

Meals served Lunch and dinner. **Cuisine** Californian/American. **Entree range** Lunch, $8–$10; dinner, $20–$35. **Kids' menu** Yes. **Reservations** Required for dinner. **Payment** All major credit cards.

Although the fun is in the getting here on the aerial tram, it's not a bad restaurant considering how far the staff has to come to cook. And you can't beat the view. It's a special-event–feeling place at dinner, when the steak and seafood dishes get pricey; for families with younger kids, it's best at lunch.

PART SIX

SAN FRANCISCO BAY AREA

SIMPLY PUT, WE CAN'T GET ENOUGH OF THE BAY AREA. We've both visited with our kids many times and still feel there's more to explore, as well as many favorites to revisit. The city of **San Francisco** appeals to every age group, though it's easiest with the 5-and-up set, who are old enough to walk the steep streets and jump on cable cars. Compact and easily navigable, it has something for every kid: great parks, museums (of science, art, even blue jeans), fun ferries, buses, subways, and cable cars, cool shops, street music, and so much more. Theme-park junkies can venture out to **Vallejo** to **Marine World Africa USA,** or south to **Paramount's Great America** in Santa Clara. **East in Berkeley** are the **University of California** and the wonderful **Charles Lee Tilden Regional Park;** north in **Marin** are redwoods, beaches, and charming small towns. Everywhere there is great food—many of the country's best restaurants live in the Bay Area, and some are even welcoming to children.

If you have only two or three days and your kids haven't experienced San Francisco, stick to the city and you won't be sorry. The city center is compact and easy to negotiate, so in just a few days you can easily hit the hot spots, from cable car and ferry rides to the **Exploratorium, Zeum,** and **Golden Gate Park.** If you have more time, you'll be able to add some wonderful adventures to the itinerary: kayaking **Tomales Bay** in Marin, for instance, or BARTing over to Berkeley, or even tackling one of the suburban theme parks.

If you're combining a Monterey–Santa Cruz visit (see Part Four, The Central Coast) with some time in San Francisco, you may want to make **San Jose,** capital of the Silicon Valley, your gateway city, as it's midway between the two points. And San Jose's extraordinary **Tech Museum** is well worth a visit all by itself.

GETTING THERE

BY PLANE Most major airlines serve one or all three of the region's airports: **San Francisco International Airport** (☎ 650-821-8211;

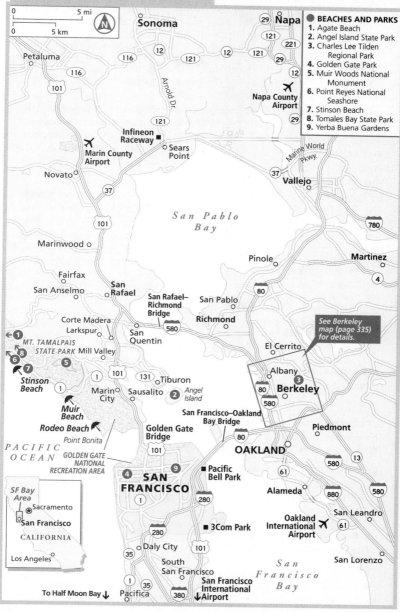

san francisco bay area

0 — 5 mi
0 — 5 km

Sonoma

Petaluma

Napa

BEACHES AND PARKS
1. Agate Beach
2. Angel Island State Park
3. Charles Lee Tilden Regional Park
4. Golden Gate Park
5. Muir Woods National Monument
6. Point Reyes National Seashore
7. Stinson Beach
8. Tomales Bay State Park
9. Yerba Buena Gardens

116
116
101

12
121
12
121
29
221
121
29
12
29

Napa County Airport

Arnold Dr.

Infineon Raceway
Sears Point

Marin County Airport
Novato
37

Marine World Pkwy.
37
Vallejo

San Pablo Bay

101

780

Marinwood

Pinole
Martinez
4

Fairfax
San Anselmo
San Rafael
San Rafael–Richmond Bridge
San Pablo
Richmond
80

Corte Madera
Larkspur
San Quentin
580

El Cerrito

See Berkeley map (page 335) for details.

MT. TAMALPAIS STATE PARK Mill Valley
Albany
3

1
101
131
Tiburon
2 *Angel Island*
80
Berkeley
580

Stinson Beach
1
Marin City
Sausalito

Muir Beach
Rodeo Beach
Point Bonita

San Francisco–Oakland Bay Bridge
80

Piedmont

PACIFIC OCEAN
GOLDEN GATE NATIONAL RECREATION AREA
Golden Gate Bridge
101

OAKLAND
580
13

4 9
SAN FRANCISCO
1
■ Pacific Bell Park
280
61

Alameda
880
580

SF Bay Area
Sacramento
San Francisco
CALIFORNIA
Los Angeles

280
35
■ 3Com Park
Daly City
101
South San Francisco
35
San Francisco International Airport
380

Oakland International Airport
61
San Leandro

San Lorenzo

San Francisco Bay

To Half Moon Bay
Pacifica

www.flysfo.com) is a 30-minute drive south of downtown; **Oakland International Airport** (☎ 510-563-3300; **www.oaklandairport.com**) is more convenient for the East Bay. **BART,** or Bay Area Rapid Transit, connects Oakland Airport to downtown San Francisco. **San Jose International Airport** (☎ 408-501-7600; **www.sjc.org**) is just three miles from downtown San Jose; this airport connects with downtown San Jose via free "airport flyer" shuttle and light rail, and with San Francisco via free shuttle to Santa Clara's Caltrain station and then by train.

BY TRAIN Amtrak delivers visitors from Southern California, the Pacific Northwest, and Midwest (☎ 800-USA-RAIL; **www.amtrak.com**). There is also train service via **BART** (☎ 415-498-2278; **www.bart.org**) and **Caltrain** (☎ 800-660-4287; **www.caltrain.com**) among various Bay Area and Peninsula cities, including San Francisco, the East Bay communities, and San Jose.

BY CAR The major highways heading into San Francisco are **Highway 101,** which heads south to L.A. and north to the Oregon border, and **Highway 80,** which leads to Oakland, Sacramento, Lake Tahoe, and Nevada. Parking is a challenge—expect to pay dearly for hotel parking.

San Jose is reached by any of the Bay Area's main freeways: **Interstates 280, 680,** and **880,** and **CA 101.**

A **CALENDAR** of **FESTIVALS** and **EVENTS**

January
SEA-LION ARRIVAL Pier 39, San Francisco. A celebration of the annual return of the sea lions to the bay for breeding; ☎ 415-705-5436.

February
CALIFORNIA INTERNATIONAL ANTIQUARIAN BOOK FAIR Concourse Exhibition Center, San Francisco. World's largest rare-book fair; ☎ 415-551-5190; **www.labookfair.com.**

CHINESE NEW YEAR CELEBRATION San Francisco. A lavish parade from Market and Second streets to Columbus Avenue, plus a festival and street fair in Chinatown; ☎ 415-391-9680; **www.chineseparade.com.**

March
ST. PATRICK'S DAY PARADE San Francisco. ☎ 415-675-9885; **www .sfstpatricksdayparade.com.**

April
CHERRY BLOSSOM FESTIVAL Japantown and Japan Center, San Francisco. Japanese food, music, taiko drumming, martial arts, and more; ☎ 415-563-2313; **www.nccbf.org.**

SAN FRANCISCO INTERNATIONAL FILM FESTIVAL Worthwhile for teens; more than 100 films and videos from around the world; ☎ 415-561-5000; **www.sffs.org.**

May

BAY TO BREAKERS FOOTRACE San Francisco. The world's largest footrace is also the most colorful—most of the 70,000-plus participants dress in costume; ☎ 415-359-2800; **www.baytobreakers.com.**

CINCO DE MAYO CELEBRATION Mission District, San Francisco. Arts, crafts, food, music, and parade in the city's vibrant Latino community; ☎ 415-206-0577.

June

NORTH BEACH FESTIVAL Grant and Green streets, San Francisco. The city's oldest street fair is refreshingly low-key and funky, with great food, live music, and good crafts; ☎ 415-989-2220.

SAN FRANCISCO YOUTH ARTS FESTIVAL Golden Gate Park. ☎ 415-750-8630; **www.sfyouthartsfestival.org.**

ZOOFEST FOR KIDS San Francisco Zoo. Festival, live entertainment, up-close encounters with animals; ☎ 415-753-7080; **www.sfzoo.org.**

July

SAN FRANCISCO CABLE CAR BELL-RINGING COMPETITION Union Square. The much-esteemed cable car conductors put on a show; ☎ 415-474-1887; **www.cablecarmuseum.org.**

SAN FRANCISCO FOURTH OF JULY WATERFRONT FESTIVAL Fisherman's Wharf. Food, amusements, arts, and a fabulous fireworks show; ☎ 415-392-4520.

September

FARMERS' MARKET HARVEST FAIR San Rafael. ☎ 415-456-FARM.

RENAISSANCE PLEASURE FAIRE Blackpoint Forest, San Francisco. An in-costume celebration of 16th-century England, with performers, theater, food, dance, music, and more; ☎ 800-523-2473.

SAN FRANCISCO SHAKESPEARE FESTIVAL Golden Gate Park. Free plays in the park; ☎ 415-558-0888; **www.sfshakes.org.**

October

THE CANNERY'S HALLOWEEN FESTIVAL San Francisco. For more than 20 years, kids have come to the Cannery for a costume contest, games, cookie decorating, and trick-or-treating in the shops; ☎ 415-771-3112; **www.delmontesquare.com.**

HARDLY STRICTLY BLUEGRASS Golden Gate Park, San Francisco. A remarkable and free weekend music festival that includes some of the finest folk, bluegrass, and alternative-country musicians in the United States; **www.hardlystrictlybluegrass.com.**

INDIGENOUS PEOPLE'S DAY Berkeley. Held the Saturday closest to October 12. Berkeley's answer to the traditional Columbus Day parade, featuring a Powwow and Indian Market; ☎ 510-642-0119.

ITALIAN HERITAGE DAY CELEBRATION North Beach and Fisherman's Wharf, San Francisco. Parade, Queen Isabella coronation, and celebration of Italian culture and Columbus's discovery; ☎ 415-703-9888.

November

GREAT SAN FRANCISCO SNOW PARTY Pier 39. Learn-to-ski park and snow play for kids; ☎ 415-705-5500.

December

CHRISTMAS AT SEA Hyde Street Pier, Fisherman's Wharf. Santa, caroling, stories, cookies, and more on the historic *Balclutha;* ☎ 415-929-0202.

TELEGRAPH AVENUE HOLIDAY STREET FAIR Berkeley. A vibrant street market and festival held the two weekends before Christmas; ☎ 510-234-1013.

HOW TO GET INFORMATION BEFORE YOU GO

- **Berkeley Convention and Visitors Bureau** 2015 Center Street, Berkeley 94704; ☎ 510-549-7040 or 800-847-4823; **www.visitberkeley.com.**
- **Marin County Convention and Visitors Bureau** 1013 Larkspur Landing, Larkspur 94939; ☎ 415-925-2060 or 866-925-2060; **www.visitmarin.org.**
- **San Francisco Convention and Visitors Bureau** P.O. Box 429097, San Francisco 94142-9097. Visitor Information Center, Lower Level, Hallidie Plaza, 900 Market Street; ☎ 415-391-2000; **www.sfvisitor.org.**
- **San Jose Convention and Visitors Bureau** 408 Almaden Boulevard, San Jose 95110; ☎ 408-295-9600 or 800-SAN-JOSE; **www.sanjose.org.**
- **Sausalito Visitors Center** 780 Bay Street, Sausalito 94965; ☎ 415-331-7262; **www.sausalito.org.**

CHILD CARE AND BABYSITTING

AMERICAN CHILDCARE SERVICES 580 California Street, Suite 1600, San Francisco; ☎ 415-285-2300; **www.americanchildcare.com.** Activity programs and in-room care; credit cards accepted.

The BEST BEACHES *and* PARKS

AGATE BEACH It's a bit of a challenge to reach this 6.6-acre beach park, found at the end of a 300-yard, sometimes-steep gravel path that is neither stroller nor wheelchair friendly. The reward, however, is considerable: an excellent tide-pooling beach teeming with sea life. (Remember, no collecting allowed.) Ranger tours are limited but possible; call the County of Marin Parks Service to arrange one; ☎ 415-499-6405. Highway 1 to Elm Road, Bolinas; ☎ 415-499-6387; **co.marin.ca.us.**

ANGEL ISLAND STATE PARK Between the congested urbanity of San Francisco and the pampered suburbanity of Tiburon lies this wonderfully unspoiled island, a terrific day or half-day trip for families. Once a Civil War garrison, then an immigration center ("Ellis Island of the West"), Angel Island is now devoted to hiking, mountain biking, kayaking, and beach fun. Ferries from San Francisco and Tiburon pull into **Ayala Cove,** where you can rent bikes or kayaks, take a tram tour, or pick up a hiking map. The paved five-mile **Perimeter Road** is the favorite hiking and biking destination, thanks to its incredible bay and city views; some of the unpaved hiking trails may be too challenging for little kids. See also "Kayaking" under "Family Outdoor Adventures"; ☎ 415-435-1915; **www.angelisland.org.**

CHARLES LEE TILDEN REGIONAL PARK If you visit the Berkeley area by car (BART won't get you this far), set aside a few hours to explore this storybook-perfect park in the hills. Within more than 2,000 acres are amusements for all ages, from the pony rides (☎ 510-527-0421) and petting farm to the beach at **Lake Anza** and the many hiking trails. You'll also find an old hand-carved merry-go-round (open weekends; ☎ 510-524-6773), a miniature steam train (open weekends; ☎ 510-548-6100), playgrounds, and naturalist programs. Off Grizzly Peak Boulevard, Berkeley; ☎ 510-525-2233; **www.ebparks.org/parks/tilden.**

GOLDEN GATE PARK One of the country's great urban parks, Golden Gate is 1,000 acres of family fun, worthy of a full day or more. Its various activities are sometimes driving-distance apart, separated by rolling acres of parkland. In "Attractions," you'll find descriptions of its museums (the **California Academy of Sciences** and the **de Young**); in "Family Outdoor Adventures," you'll find advice on biking and skating the park. But that's just the beginning. Very young children will spend several happy hours at **Stow Lake** (☎ 415-752-0347), for example. There's also a children's playground with great slides and equipment accessible to those with disabilities; a 1912 carousel ($2) with a veritable Noah's ark of animals to ride (including frogs, cats, and zebras!); and fields and facilities for playing soccer, tennis, baseball, golf, or croquet. The **Japanese Tea Garden** is a lovely interlude for grandparents and grandchildren. It's open daily 9 a.m. to 6:30 p.m.; tea and cookies are served in the teahouse ($2 adults, $1 seniors and children). Of course, families picnic in the many meadows. There's a buffalo paddock, an arboretum, a Victorian-glass conservatory, a windmill, and access to the beach. Pick up a map to

golden gate park

Arguello Blvd.
4th Ave.
6th Ave.
8th Ave.
10th Ave.
12th Ave.
Park Presidio Blvd.
15th Ave.

25th St.

39th Ave.
43rd Ave.
47th Ave.
Esplanade

9th Ave.
Funston Ave.
Lincoln Way
19th Ave.
26th Ave.
Irving St.
Judah St.
33rd Ave.
Sunset Blvd.
41st Ave.
45th Ave.
La Playa Ave.

J.F. Kennedy Dr.
Conservatory Dr.
McLaren Lodge (Park HQ)
Tennis Courts
Children's Playground
Bowling Green Dr.
Lawn Bowling
Kezar Stadium and Pavilion
AIDS Memorial Grove
Lily Pond
Middle Dr. E.
M.L. King Dr.
Stow Lake Dr.
Strawberry Hill
Cross-Over Dr.
Transverse Dr.
Park Presidio By-Pass Dr.
Fulton St.
Marx Meadow
Lloyd Lake
Lindley Meadow
Speedway Meadow
Overlook Dr.
Middle Dr.
Elk Glen Lake
Metson Lake
Mallard Lake
Medson Rd.
M.L. King Dr.
Spreckels Lake Dr.
Spreckels Lake
Golden Gate Park Stadium
Polo Field
Fly Casting Pool
Buffalo Paddock
J.F. Kennedy Dr.
Middle Lake
South Lake
North Lake
Chain of Lakes Dr.
Fulton St.
Balboa
Cabrillo
Great Highway
Ocean Beach

PACIFIC OCEAN

1. Beach Chalet
2. Boat House
3. Buffalo Paddock
4. Conservatory of Flowers
5. Dutch Windmill
6. Golden Gate Golf Course
7. Japanese Tea Garden
8. McLaren Memorial Rhododendron Dell
9. Music Concourse
10. Riding Stables
11. Stow Lake
12. Strybing Arboretum & Botanical Gardens

¼ mi
0   0.25 km

Golden Gate Park
Union Square
SAN FRANCISCO
Candlestick Park

the park at McLaren Lodge (Stanyan and Fell streets) and consider taking the free guided walking tour conducted by park docents. Bordered by Fulton, Stanyan, Lincoln, and Great Highway; ☎ 415-263-0991; **parks.sfgov.org.**

MUIR WOODS NATIONAL MONUMENT One of the Bay Area's last uncut stands of old-growth redwoods lives in this small national forest. The largest trees—250 tall, 14 feet across, and 1,000 years old—are found in **Bohemian Grove** and **Cathedral Grove,** both of which are accessed via stroller-friendly, less-than-a-mile trails that head out from the main parking lot. In the spring, kids can try to spot baby salmon in **Redwood Creek.** Come early to avoid the afternoon crowds, and stop at the visitors center to pick up the free, very cool Junior Ranger pack, complete with bug box and activity guide. This is a forest of awe, mystery, and beauty, appreciated by everyone from toddlers to teens. Open daily; admission $3 for adults, free for children. Located on Highway 1 near Mill Valley, 12 miles north of the Golden Gate Bridge; ☎ 415-388-2595; **www.nps.gov/muwo.**

unofficial **TIP**
We've circumnavigated the island of Golden Gate Park's tiny lake with a succession of 3-year-olds in pedalboats who, at rental time's end, hop onto the shore, beg us to buy popcorn, and feed the ducks for another hour.

POINT REYES NATIONAL SEASHORE Remote and gloriously wild, this national park preserves 65,000 acres of coastal property on the north end of Marin County. It is a paradise for bird-watchers—more than 45 percent of the bird species in North America have been sighted here—for hikers, and for lovers of romantically windswept, rocky, foggy beaches. The beach hikes are fairly challenging, but for families with younger kids, there are several easy walks that begin at the **Bear Valley Visitors Center** (Bear Valley Road off Highway 1 near Olema; ☎ 415-464-5100). Walk the quarter-mile trail to **Kule Loklo,** a replica of a Coast Miwok Indian village. Another short walk takes you across fern-filled gullies and scrambling over fallen logs to **Morgan Horse Ranch,** where you can watch cowboys train horses for the park rangers to use, and walk through historic stables. School-age kids like the half-mile **Earthquake Trail,** which follows a fracture zone of the famed San Andreas Fault; an exhibit displays a seismograph and photos of the 1906 quake in San Francisco. For a longer but still easy hike, take the three-mile **Bear Valley Trail.** Point Reyes Station; ☎ 415-464-5100; **www.nps.gov/pore.**

Farther afield are more treasures, most notably **Point Reyes Lighthouse,** built in 1870 and found at the bottom of a 300-step walkway (warning for parents of whiny preschoolers) on Point Reyes Headlands (Sir Francis Drake Boulevard; ☎ 415-669-1534). The visitors center has exhibits on whales and lighthouses, and from January to April the lighthouse is a superb place to look for the migrating gray whales. Elsewhere you'll find great beaches to comb (**Drakes** is a good one), but the water's too cold and rough for swimming.

unofficial **TIP**
Stinson changes from a cold, rough, riptide-laden place in the winter and spring to a peaceful, delightful, small-surf beach in the summer.

STINSON BEACH A grand, sweeping beach some three and a half miles long, Stinson is ideal for a family beach day in July and August, though the water is frosty by Southern California standards. The little town of Stinson Beach, which has a couple of restaurants and shops, is just a half block away. Picnic area, restrooms, snack bar, outdoor (cold) showers, lifeguards (in summer). Highway 1 at Panoramic Highway, north of San Francisco; ☎ 415-868-1922; **www.nps.gov/muwo/stbe.**

TOMALES BAY STATE PARK A former home of the Miwok Indians, this is a beautiful retreat with lots for families. Its several beaches include **Heart's Desire,** a sheltered cove with wading lagoon, picnicking, and easy hiking trails through groves of pines. Kayaking is also popular here; see "Kayaking" in "Family Outdoor Adventures." Pierce Point Road, near Inverness; ☎ 415-669-1140; **www.parks.ca.gov.**

YERBA BUENA GARDENS Atop the roof of Moscone Center South, near the Museum of Modern Art, public Yerba Buena Gardens has something for every kid. There's a state-of-the-art ice-skating rink, a cheerful bowling alley, a hand-carved 1906 carousel, a fabulous hands-on, high-tech arts museum (**Zeum**), a hip urban playground bordered by a child-sized botanical maze . . . and a Starbucks for Frappuccino-swilling 12-year-olds. For free fun, bring a picnic lunch to the open, grassy knolls in the center of the gardens, where kids can run behind the huge waterfall-fountain, then head over to the pit-style playground. Kids slide down giant tubes, bounce giant balls on the springy recycled-sneaker playground surface, and lose themselves in sand-and-water play. To learn more about Zeum, see its attraction profile; for details on the other admission-charging venues, see the Yerba Buena Gardens attraction profile; **www.yerbabuenagardens.com.**

FAMILY OUTDOOR ADVENTURES

BICYCLING At the north end of Golden Gate Park, you can rent bikes at **Golden Gate Skate and Bike** (3038 Fulton street at Sixth Avenue; ☎ 415-668-1117), then set off and explore the park's 1,017 acres, which are crisscrossed with paths; if you follow Kennedy Drive west, you'll hit the oceanfront bike path at Ocean Beach, which goes for three level miles. Stash a picnic in a backpack, and you've got a great family day. (Note that Kennedy is a functioning street, but it's closed to cars on Sundays.)

Also within the city limits is a wonderful adventure: riding across the **Golden Gate Bridge.** Pick up rental bikes and a route map at **Blazing**

yerba buena gardens and environs

map not to scale

Stevenson St.

Argent Hotel

City College Downtown Center

Marriott Hotel

St. Patrick's Church

Jessie Square (Future)

Parking

Mexican Museum

Mission St.

California → Historical Society

Fifth & Mission Garage

Metreon (Sony Entertainment Center)

Butterfly Garden

Yerba Buena Center for the Arts Galleries & Forum

Parking

■ Reflection

E S P L A N A D E

Stage ◯

East Garden

Ship Sculpture ▪

4th St.

Moscone West

■ MLK Jr. Memorial

San Francisco Museum of Modern Art

Theater

■ Shaking Man

Sister Cities Garden

3rd St.

California ← Academy of Sciences

Howard St.

W Hotel

Carousel

Moscone Convention Center

Zeum

Children's Center

Moscone Garage ↘

Saddles Bike Rentals (1095 Columbus Avenue, Fisherman's Wharf, or at Pier 41; ☎ 415-202-8888; **www.blazingsaddles.com**), ride across the bridge, refuel with lunch in Sausalito, then catch the ferry back—there's a bike-return spot at the ferry terminal. Your kids need to be confident riders, because you share the road with cars.

If you have older children who are avid mountain bikers, you'll want to go to **Mount Tamalpais State Park** (Panoramic Highway off Highway 1, Marin County; ☎ 415-388-2070), where the mountain bike was invented in 1974 by a few broke gearheads. The trails, views, and thrills are first rate. You can rent gear on the way there at **Mike's Bikes** (1 Gate 6 Road, Sausalito; ☎ 415-332-3200; **www.mikesbikes.com**).

FISHING Fishing can be a great family bonding activity, and the deep-sea fishing is good in the bay—even better when the boats venture under the Golden Gate into the Pacific, in search of striped bass, salmon, and giant sturgeon. It's not cheap, though—a full day costs about $65, with kids charged roughly half price. A number of companies run boats out of the Fisherman's Wharf area. For salmon fishing, reserve a trip with **Wacky Jacky** (473 Bella Vista Way, San Francisco; ☎ 415-586-9800), whose boats are modern, fast, and cool.

*un**official* TIP**
Try climbing San Francisco's urban mountains—in other words, stair climbing. What can be so tedious in a gym is a joy in this city, and kids feel a tremendous sense of accomplishment at cresting one of the famed peaks.

HILL WALKING Looking for an outdoor family challenge that offers exercise, adventure, and great views? Try stair-climbing. Our favorite places to do so are the stairs up to **Coit Tower** on the edge of North Beach, off Greenwich Street, which pays off in an extraordinary view and a look at the evocative WPA murals inside the tower; the stairs up Vallejo Street in Russian Hill to **Ina Coolbrith Park,** a terraced city park with killer views and great hide-and-seek possibilities; and, of course, a climb up **Lombard Street,** the famous winding road.

HORSEBACK RIDING To ride in the redwoods, head up to **Willow Tree Stables** in the Marin County town of Novato (3777 Vineyard Road; ☎ 415-897-8212; **www.willowtreestables.com**). This high-quality stable leads hourly, brunch, and sunset rides up into the oak- and redwood-covered Novato hills, following the ancient trails of the Miwok Indians. Children over age 6 are welcome on rides.

KAYAKING The hot outdoor activity of the moment is kayaking in Marin County's **Tomales Bay,** a spectacular coastal wilderness refuge. A full-service kayak company, **Blue Waters Kayaking** in Inverness (☎ 415-669-2600; **www.bwkayak.com**), can teach your family how to kayak, rent you the boats, or take you on a naturalist-led tour of the coves and sea life in the bay. The best bet for families (with kids age 8 and up) is the guided three-hour morning paddle on weekends (starting at $68 per person), which pairs one adult with one child in each kayak; you'll paddle to hidden beaches and look for seals, bat rays, and birds. Over in Sausalito is **Sea Trek** (Schoonmaker Point Arena; ☎ 415-488-1000; **www.seatrekkayak.com**), which will take you paddling to see a bird refuge, sea lions, and Angel Island; it also has a three-hour guided, kid-oriented paddling adventure ($65 adults, $30 children).

SKATING Two spots are perfect for family skating: **Marina Green,** the easy 1.5-mile waterfront park with great bay views, and **Golden Gate Park,** especially on Sundays, when the main street is closed (rent skates at **Golden Gate Skate and Bike,** 3038 Fulton Street at Sixth Avenue; ☎ 415-668-1117).

WHALE WATCHING Oceanic Society Expeditions heads out in search of the gray and humpback whales from Fort Mason Center in the Marina District, (Quarters 35 N; ☎ 415-441-1106; **www.oceanic-society.org;**

reservations required weeks in advance). The all-day outings are held Saturday and Sunday; the cost is $38 to $78 for adults, $35 to $75 for children ages 7 to 15 and seniors. After the gray-whale season, the tours become nature cruises to the Farallon Islands in pursuit of humpback and blue whales and other marine life. These are rustic, nature-focused trips, and you'll need to bring your own food and drink. No disabled access.

SAN FRANCISCO

EVEN THOUGH THIS POLISHED, CHIC WATERFRONT CITY was home of the original yuppie, it's still a wonderful place to visit with children, especially school-age kids, who can appreciate the big-city energy, not to mention hop on cable cars and safely hold on all by themselves. **San Francisco** doesn't have theme parks, but who needs 'em when the city itself is one big theme park? Rounding a corner on a cable car, driving down Lombard Street, cutting through the fog on a ferry boat, paddling a kayak around **Angel Island,** cycling over the **Golden Gate Bridge**—these are thrills that a kid remembers.

Colleen took each of her daughters on a special one-on-one trip to San Francisco when they turned 7. On both trips they did the hokey tourist stuff that she'd usually avoid, and they had a ball. Here are the highlights, and any child under the age of 10 would adore the same things:

- An afternoon at the **Exploratorium,** the hands-down highlight of the trip, and a winner for any child, teenager, or adult.
- Riding up and down **Nob Hill** on a cable car, hanging off the side.
- Strolling past the sidewalk vendors at **Fisherman's Wharf,** and splurging on her most cherished memento, a $1.50 caricature of herself.
- Picking out a chocolate bar at **Ghirardelli Square.**
- Riding the ferry to **Tiburon,** then spending an hour climbing the shore rocks.
- Studying with amazement the 1906 post-fire photos of the city at the **Cable Car Museum.**

Older kids and teens might find Fisherman's Wharf and Ghirardelli a bit predictable, but they'll love the video arcade at **Pier 39,** the spiffy shops of **Union Street,** the Claymation studio at **Zeum,** the now-upscale tie-dyed wares of **Haight-Ashbury,** and an inline-skating session along **Marina Green.** And since San Francisco has become a sort of sophisticated Disneyland for grown-ups, parents enjoy a family trip there as much as the kids. For starters, they're going to eat way, way better than in Anaheim.

WORDS OF WISDOM

MARK TWAIN QUIPPED, "The coldest winter I ever spent was a summer in San Francisco." This may be the most overquoted line in guidebook history, but it's for a very good reason: When a fog bank moves in, you'll be chilled to the bone, even if it's July. Be prepared with warm clothing.

unofficial **TIP**
San Franciscans are a dressy lot by laid-back California standards, so bring something nice to wear.

If you're bringing a car into the city, be aware that parking is costly and that street spots are as rare as sunny days in June. If you do find a spot, and it's on a hill, make sure to curb the wheels, or you'll face a nasty ticket (and risk a smashed car).

GETTING THERE IS ALL THE FUN

NOT ONLY IS SAN FRANCISCO HAPPILY navigable without a car, but its various forms of public transportation—cable car, subway, ferries, taxis—are as fun for kids as the city's best amusements. Here are the basics on each:

CABLE CARS Part of the city's vast **Muni** (San Francisco Municipal Railway) service, the cable cars are the city's pied pipers, an irresistible lure to children. They run on three routes in the heart of the city, connecting **Market Street–Union Square** to **Fisherman's Wharf** and **Union Square** to **Ghirardelli Square,** and running from the **downtown financial district** near the Ferry Building over **Nob Hill** to **Van Ness.** In peak tourist times (which, thanks to conventions, is almost always), expect long lines at the end stations near Union Square and the wharf; we've had better luck catching a ride several blocks up the hill from either of these stops (the cars are sometimes not fully loaded to allow for passengers to get on at later stops). If the city's really crowded, avoid the Powell Line completely and climb up Nob Hill to catch the California Line, which is typically half empty.

The best way to enjoy cable cars the old-fashioned way (as actual transportation) is to designate one day as cable-car day. Leave your hotel very early in the morning before breakfast the way my daughter Irene and I did (Susan speaking). The cars start running at 6:30 a.m., so there we were, virtually alone, stepping onto the Powell Line car, buying an all-day pass from the conductor, transferring at the top of the hill, then riding along with the office workers down the steep and dramatic California line to the end. We hopped off, enjoyed breakfast, and then hopped on again and headed for Chinatown. We reboarded later in Chinatown and continued on to our next stop. That evening after dinner we used our passes to board a once-again nearly vacant cable car back to our hotel. At the end of the day we'd had a half-dozen cable-car rides, hadn't waited in line for any of them, and had gotten where we were going, too. The fare is $3 (kids

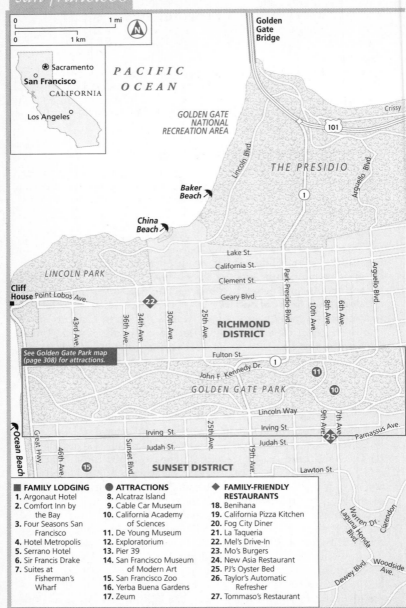

san francisco

0 ___ 1 mi
0 ___ 1 km

Golden Gate Bridge

⊛ Sacramento
San Francisco
CALIFORNIA
Los Angeles

PACIFIC OCEAN

GOLDEN GATE NATIONAL RECREATION AREA

Crissy

THE PRESIDIO

Lincoln Blvd.

Arguello Blvd.

Baker Beach ↗

China Beach ↗

Lake St.
California St.
Clement St.
Geary Blvd.

Park Presidio Blvd.

LINCOLN PARK

Cliff House Point Lobos Ave.

43rd Ave.
36th Ave.
34th Ave.
30th Ave.
25th Ave.
10th Ave.
8th Ave.
6th Ave.
Arguello Blvd.

㉒

RICHMOND DISTRICT

See Golden Gate Park map (page 308) for attractions.

Fulton St.

John F. Kennedy Dr.

⑪

GOLDEN GATE PARK

⑩

Lincoln Way

9th Ave.
7th Ave.

Parnassus Ave.

Ocean Beach

Great Hwy.
46th Ave.
Sunset Blvd.
25th Ave.
19th Ave.

Irving St.
Judah St.

Irving St.
Judah St.

㉕

⑮

SUNSET DISTRICT

Lawton St.

Warren Dr.
Laguna Honda Blvd.
Clarendon
Woodside Ave.
Dewey Blvd.

■ **FAMILY LODGING**
1. Argonaut Hotel
2. Comfort Inn by the Bay
3. Four Seasons San Francisco
4. Hotel Metropolis
5. Serrano Hotel
6. Sir Francis Drake
7. Suites at Fisherman's Wharf

● **ATTRACTIONS**
8. Alcatraz Island
9. Cable Car Museum
10. California Academy of Sciences
11. De Young Museum
12. Exploratorium
13. Pier 39
14. San Francisco Museum of Modern Art
15. San Francisco Zoo
16. Yerba Buena Gardens
17. Zeum

◆ **FAMILY-FRIENDLY RESTAURANTS**
18. Benihana
19. California Pizza Kitchen
20. Fog City Diner
21. La Taqueria
22. Mel's Drive-In
23. Mo's Burgers
24. New Asia Restaurant
25. PJ's Oyster Bed
26. Taylor's Automatic Refresher
27. Tommaso's Restaurant

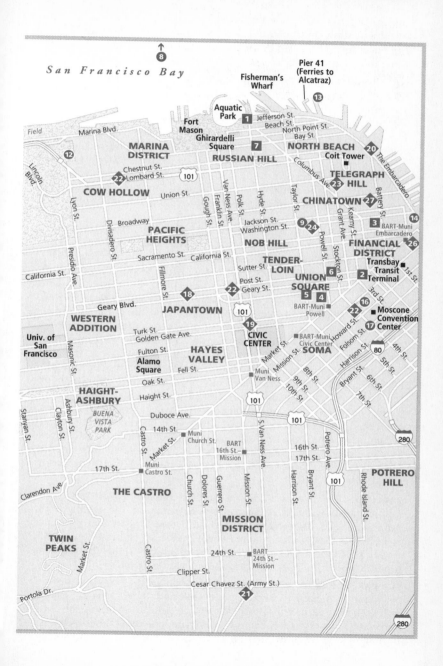

San Francisco Bay

Fisherman's Wharf

Pier 41 (Ferries to Alcatraz) ⑬

↑ ⑧

Aquatic Park ①

Jefferson St.
Beach St.
North Point St.
Bay St.

Field

Marina Blvd.

Fort Mason

Ghirardelli Square ⑦

NORTH BEACH ⑳

The Embarcadero

⑫

MARINA DISTRICT

RUSSIAN HILL

Coit Tower ■

Chestnut St.
Lombard St. ㉒

101

TELEGRAPH HILL

㉓

Lincoln Blvd.

COW HOLLOW

Union St.

Van Ness Ave.

Franklin St.

Polk St.

Hyde St.

Taylor St.

Columbus Ave.

CHINATOWN ㉗

Lyon St.

Broadway

Gough St.

Jackson St.
Washington St.

⑨㉔

Kearny St.

Grant Ave.

③ BART-Muni Embarcadero ⑭

Divisadero St.

PACIFIC HEIGHTS

NOB HILL

Powell St.

Stockton St.

Battery St.

FINANCIAL DISTRICT ㉖

Presidio Ave.

California St.

Sacramento St.

California St.

TENDER-LOIN

UNION SQUARE

⑥

Transbay Transit Terminal

② Terminal

1st St.

California St.

Fillmore St.

Sutter St.

Post St.
Geary St. ㉒

⑤ ④

BART-Muni Powell ■

㉒

3rd St.

16 ■ Moscone Convention Center ⑰

WESTERN ADDITION

⑱

Geary Blvd.

JAPANTOWN

101

Howard St.

Folsom St.

80

Univ. of San Francisco

Masonic Ave.

Turk St.
Golden Gate Ave.

⑲

CIVIC CENTER

BART-Muni Civic Center ■

Harrison St.

4th St.

5th St.

Fulton St.

HAYES VALLEY

Market St.

Mission St.

SOMA

6th St.

7th St.

Alamo Square

Fell St.

8th St.

9th St.

Bryant St.

HAIGHT-ASHBURY

Oak St.

Haight St.

Muni Van Ness ■

10th St.

280

Stanyan St.

Ashbury St.

Clayton St.

BUENA VISTA PARK

Duboce Ave.

101

S. Van Ness Ave.

Potrero Ave.

Rhode Island St.

POTRERO HILL

14th St.
Market St.

Muni Church St. ■

BART 16th St.-Mission

16th St.

17th St.

Castro St.

17th St.

Muni Castro St. ■

Church St.

Dolores St.

Guerrero St.

Mission St.

Harrison St.

Bryant St.

Clarendon Ave.

THE CASTRO

101

TWIN PEAKS

Market St.

Castro St.

MISSION DISTRICT

24th St. ■ BART 24th St.-Mission

Clipper St.

Cesar Chavez St. (Army St.)

㉑

Portola Dr.

280

under age 5 free) for a one-way ride; Muni Passes (available throughout town) allow unlimited rides on the cable cars, trolleys, and light-rail buses for $11 a day, $18 for three days, or $24 for seven days. For more information, call ☎ 415-673-MUNI; **www.sfmuni.com.**

FERRIES The view of San Francisco from the water surrounding it is one of the most memorable sights in the world, and you can thrill to it (without having your kids even realize you're wasting time looking at scenery) by hopping onto one of the commuter ferries used to bring office workers from the suburbs into downtown's financial district. The fun for the kids, of course (and for adults, too), is in the boat ride, and nobody in your family will argue against a ferry to wherever and back—an hour on the bay, standing at the rail with the gulls sporting behind you and the wind in your face, will knock the airplane and hotel-room blahs right out of everyone's system.

From Pier 41, within easy distance of a number of tourist attractions, is the disembarkation point for the **Blue and Gold Fleet** (☎ 415-705-5555; **www.blueandgoldfleet.com**), which will take you (famously) not only to Sausalito but also to Tiburon, Muir Woods, Angel Island, and Oakland's Jack London Square waterfront. But we've also had a great trip on a high-speed commuter ferry (**Golden Gate Ferries;** ☎ 415-455-2000; **www.goldengate.org**), buying sodas at the snack bar and then heading out to the benches on deck to shiver while passing under the majestic Bay Bridge on the way to Alameda, where the ferry docks at a decidedly less picturesque point (an abandoned military base) than in Sausalito. We had found ourselves near the end of Market Street when we spied the Ferry Building, so we simply asked about the next ferry and got on for a round trip. We might just as easily have gone to Sausalito, where you can while away a few hours in shops and cafes, or to Larkspur. Be sure to ask your hotel concierge to call for updated departure times to give yourselves an idea of the schedule (in general, the commuter ferries run for a few hours in the morning and afternoon-evening, but not at midday), then be ready to take a ride.

TROLLEYS The newest additions to San Francisco's already-great public-transportation system combine retro charm for parents with novelty for kids. Running along the refurbished Embarcadero, ending at Fisherman's Wharf, the new **F Line** is made up of brightly colored trolley buses salvaged from several American cities, including L.A.'s long-lamented Red Cars. Regular Muni rates apply.

SUBWAY The **BART** system whisks riders under the bay from downtown San Francisco to Berkeley and Oakland. The trains are clean, quiet, and modern, and kids love the ride—not to mention the cool automated ticket dispensers and sucker-uppers at the high-tech stations. Fares are modest; children under age 4 ride free, and those ages

5 to 12 can get a huge discount from outside vendors, which are listed in brochures at every BART station. You can even board at one of the Market Street stops and go just one or two stops in either direction— it's more fun to ride an escalator underground and board a train than it is to drag a dead-tired toddler along the sidewalks of those long city blocks. For information on stations and maps, call ☎ 510-464-6000; **www.bart.gov.**

TAXIS To children who live in the suburbs, nothing is more cosmopolitan than hopping in a cab and being whisked off someplace. My 7-year-old's first ride in a taxi was as thrilling as her first ride on Dumbo at age 4. Stay away from the unlicensed gypsy cabs (generally black sedans), but otherwise feel safe in any of the city's licensed cabs. And the short distances within San Francisco mean that taxi rides are a real bargain, especially with three or four people; fares are typically in the $5 to $8 range. Cabs are easy to find at hotels and in downtown; otherwise, call or ask your restaurant host to order one. Our favorite companies are **Luxor** (☎ 415-282-4141) and **Veteran's** (☎ 415-552-1300).

SPENDING IT

COMPACT, STYLISH, AND RELENTLESSLY PROSPEROUS, San Francisco draws shoppers from all over the West, including children. Here are our kids' favorite San Francisco shops.

BORDERS BOOKS AND MUSIC 400 Post Street, Union Square; ☎ 415-399-1633; **www.borders.com.** A swell kids' area, along with magazines, an espresso bar, CDs, and more. Watch for story times.

GHIRARDELLI CHOCOLATE MANUFACTORY Ghirardelli Square, Northpoint and Larkin streets; ☎ 415-775-5500; **www.ghirardelli.com.** Chocolate bars, chocolate cable cars, chocolate coins—you get the picture. In the rear is a Willy Wonka fantasy: a picture window overlooking a giant vat of chocolate being stirred by mechanical paddles. Next door is an ice-cream parlor that serves great hot-fudge sundaes. Irresistible.

PUPPETS ON THE PIER Pier 39, Fisherman's Wharf; ☎ 415-781-4435. From finger puppets to marionettes, they're all here, often in performance in front of the shop; **www.pier39.com.**

SANRIO 865 Market Street, Union Square; ☎ 415-495-3056. Hello Kitty heaven or hell, depending on where you stand on the issue.

TOWER RECORDS 2525 Jones Street, Fisherman's Wharf; ☎ 415-885-0500; **www.towerrecords.com.** The very first Tower, and a good one, with everything an iPod-eared kid could want.

HAIGHT STREET VINTAGE-CLOTHING SHOPS There's no one shop to look for in this still-hip neighborhood made famous in the 1960s. If you have teens, you must let them wander the Haight and explore the shops selling vintage and funky-new clothes, jewelry, and accessories. Telegraph Avenue in Berkeley is also great for the same thing, including good street vendors on the weekends.

TWO SPECIAL FOUNTAINS

TWO FOUNTAINS IN TWO WELL-TRAVELED PARTS of San Francisco—Ghirardelli Square and Union Square—were gifts to children from Ruth Asawa, a San Francisco–based sculptor. One, at the **Grand Hyatt at Union Square** (345 Stockton Street), is a drum-shaped fountain that straddles some steps and can be viewed from below (as you climb the steps), from the sides, and from above. You can touch it and get as close as you want, because the drum is covered with bronze relief panels cast from sculpted figures, as well as landscape features that were fashioned by Asawa and scores of kid and adult helpers out of a dough mixture called "baker's clay." (Asawa, mother of six children, first used the medium to keep small hands busy, then came to use it in her work.) The panoramic scenes are of San Francisco itself, with some fantasy folks (Raggedy Ann, Superman) thrown in. One could easily pass it by, but if you take a moment with kids after a day or two in the city, they'll see all the places they've visited, represented in whimsical, whirling relief: Golden Gate Bridge, Lombard Street, the Ferry Building, the parks, some schools and neighborhoods. Chinatown has a dragon; there are kite fliers and clowns, City Hall, trains, and taxis.

Over at Ghirardelli Square, toddlers and their parents spend happy times dipping fingers and toes into the **Mermaid Fountain,** a more traditional shape with a pool and some central figures—but especially fun for kids because some of the sculpted features, like frogs, extend out to the sides, where visitors sit and splash.

FAMILY LODGING

 ### The Argonaut Hotel

495 Jefferson Street; ☎ 415-563-0800 or 800-790-1415; www.argonauthotel.com; $220 and up

Part of the spiffy Kimpton Hotel group, this boutique hotel is part of the Maritime National Historic Park at Fisherman's Wharf. The location is terrific—the Cannery is on one side of the hotel, the cable-car turnaround is on the other side, and the park and bay are right out front. Many rooms have views of Alcatraz and/or the Golden Gate Bridge, and all are done in a cheerful navy-and-yellow nautical style, with white-washed furniture and captain's chairs (as well as such high-tech goodies as flat-screen TVs and Super Nintendo). Check out the Neptune's Adventure package, which includes a two-queen-bedded room for a family of four, a full breakfast, cable-car passes, Hyde Street Pier passes, and a gift for the kids. This is also one of the rare upscale city hotels that welcomes pets.

Comfort Inn by the Bay

2775 Van Ness Avenue, near Fisherman's Wharf; ☎ 415-673-0411 or 877-424-6423; www.comfortinn.com; $129 and up; children under age 12 free in parents' room; special discounts sometimes offered

The value is good at this 11-story, 135-room motel, located six blocks from Ghirardelli Square on busy Van Ness Avenue. Some rooms have bay views, a generous continental breakfast is free, and seasonal specials can bring the room rates below $100. Expect a clean, no-frills motel, and you won't be disappointed.

Four Seasons San Francisco

757 Market Street, Union Square; ☎ 415-633-3000 or 800-819-5053; www.fourseasons.com; $389–$800; children under age 18 stay free in parents' room

This slick Four Seasons provides the pampering and child friendliness that are trademarks of the chain. It's located next to the new Yerba Buena Gardens, just south of Market, making it ideal for families heading to Zeum and the Museum of Modern Art. The gleaming 40-story tower also houses luxury condos and the 100,000-square-foot Sports Club/LA, which is free to guests 16 and older. Kids get welcome gifts, child-size robes, kids' menus, and video games; parents get dazzling city views, a warmly modern décor featuring the work of local artists, and every creature comfort.

Hotel Metropolis

25 Mason Street; ☎ 415-775-4600 or 800-553-1900; www.hotelmetropolis.com; $99–$199; family suite $269

The nicest of several San Francisco hotels in the Personality Hotels group, the ten-story, 105-room Metropolis has a three-room family suite that includes a parents' room, a bunk room complete with toys and an eMac computer, and a living room (for the nanny?) with a wet bar, fridge, and pullout sofa. It's located on the edge of the Tenderloin at Mason and Third streets, a block from the Powell cable-car station and an easy walk to Yerba Buena Gardens, and it has a colorful, kid-appealing décor, as well as a terrific Southern restaurant, Farmer Brown (great mac and cheese). All rooms have refrigerators, free Internet access, and Nintendo; on site are a fitness center and library. Ask about family packages, as well as the family packages offered at the group's several other small hotels in the neighborhood.

Serrano Hotel

405 Taylor Street, Union Square; ☎ 415-885-2500 or 866-289-6561; www.serranohotel.com; $220–$399, suites $299 and up

A member of the stylish Kimpton Hotel family, this carefully renovated Spanish Revival charmer boasts games as its theme, so our kids love it. The lobby has several seating areas built around chess, checkers, backgammon, and tic-tac-toe tables; rooms are equipped with playing cards, puzzles, and Nintendo; and a call to the front desk will have your room supplied with any of dozens of board games, from Twister to Trivial Pursuit. The rooms are lovely but small, so families might need a suite or adjoining rooms. The Serrano is located in the theater district, three blocks west of Union Square, and has all the upscale modern essentials: fitness room, in-room high-speed Internet access, free newspapers, morning Starbucks, evening wine tastings, and good soundproofing.

Sir Francis Drake
450 Powell Street, Union Square; ☎ 415-392-7755 or 800-795-7129; www.sirfrancisdrake.com; $219 and up; packages and free upgrades often available

Colleen has a sentimental attachment to this Union Square hotel—her family stayed here on her first trip to San Francisco when she was 10 years old, and she and her sister were enthralled with the doormen in Beefeater costumes, not to mention the cable cars right out front. The Beefeaters and cable cars are still captivating children, only now the rooms have been tastefully modernized, with rustic furniture and floral fabrics; the studio-style executive rooms have sleeper sofas and are a good family choice. Some rooms have refrigerators, there's free Nintendo on the TV, and the touristy but perfectly fine Cal-Italian restaurant has a kids' menu. Let the concierge book a babysitter for you, and head upstairs for a memorable grown-up night at Harry Denton's Starlight Room on the roof, a Sinatraesque 1950s throwback that's one of the city's most happening nightclubs.

Suites at Fisherman's Wharf
2655 Hyde, Fisherman's Wharf; ☎ 415-771-0200 or 800-227-3608; www.thesuitesatfishermanswharf.com; $179–$289; children under age 12 stay free

A good base for families who want to be near the wharf, this 24-unit all-suite hotel is also a time-share property. Each unit is about 550 square feet, containing a bedroom with queen bed, a living room with queen sleeper sofa, and a full compact kitchen complete with dishwasher and cookware. It's located two blocks up from the wharf, right on the cable car line, which means the front-facing view rooms can get noisy; if you want quiet, pick a viewless room in back. Rates include an adequate continental breakfast and wine, tea, and cookies in the afternoon.

 # ATTRACTIONS

 ## Alcatraz Island (via Blue and Gold Fleet)

APPEAL BY AGE	PRESCHOOL ★	GRADE SCHOOL ★★★	TEENS ★★★★★
YOUNG ADULTS ★★★★★		OVER 30 ★★★★	SENIORS ★★★★

Pier 41, Fisherman's Wharf; ☎ 415-705-5555; www.blueandgoldfleet.com

Hours Tours leave daily at 30-minute intervals, 9:30 a.m.–4:15 p.m.; the Evenings on Alcatraz tours leave Thursday–Sunday, 4:15 p.m. and 5:10 p.m.; later departure times in summer. **Admission** $16.50 adults with recorded tour, $11.50 without; $14.75 seniors age 62 and older with recording, $9.75 without; $10.75 children ages 5–11 with recording, $8.25 without; evenings on Alcatraz are $23.50 adults, $20.75 seniors age 62 and over and teens ages 12–17, $14.25 children ages 5–11, free for children age 4 and under. **Touring time** Average 2 hours; minimum 2 hours. **Rainy-day touring** Tours run unless captain feels it's dangerous. **Restaurants** Snack bars on boats. **Alcoholic beverages** No. **Disabled access** Yes. **Wheelchair rental** No, but ask about SEAT. **Baby-stroller rental** No. **Lockers** No. **Pet kennels** No. **Rain check** Yes. **Private tours** No.

DESCRIPTION AND COMMENTS This fabled maximum-security prison, isolated as it is on an island with the city so tantalizingly visible, is both a powerful reality and a striking metaphor. Its thoughtful adaptation as an "attraction" has made it an important historic site. The bleak corridors, now thronged with tourists, are nevertheless strangely quiet as visitors, each with his or her audio tour set, listen to the tales of individual prisoners trying to escape, hear the sounds of the occupied prison re-created, and stand before the unimaginably small and dark isolation cells. Don't go without the audio tour— the dimension of sound is what brings the ghosts back to these sad halls.

unofficial **TIP**
Definitely too eerie for preschoolers, Alcatraz is significant and memorable for older kids and teenagers.

Cable Car Museum

APPEAL BY AGE	PRESCHOOL ★★★	GRADE SCHOOL ★★★★	TEENS ★★★
YOUNG ADULTS ★★	OVER 30 ★★★		SENIORS ★★★

1201 Mason Street, Nob Hill; ☎ 415-474-1887;
www.cablecarmuseum.com

Hours October–March: daily, 10 a.m.–5 p.m.; April–September: daily, 10 a.m.–6 p.m. **Admission** Free; donations welcome. **Touring time** Average 1 hour; minimum 30 minutes. **Rainy-day touring** Yes. **Restaurants** No. **Alcoholic beverages** No. **Disabled access** Limited. **Wheelchair rental** No. **Baby-stroller rental** No. **Lockers** No. **Pet kennels** No. **Rain check** No. **Private tours** No.

DESCRIPTION AND COMMENTS School-age kids are fascinated by the cable car, not just because it is open-air but because it is propelled by some mysterious force that requires a strong man to yank on big metal handles. A fairly brief visit to this extremely noisy museum will dispel the mystery in a most enjoyable way. The functioning hub of the cable-car system, this 1907 redbrick building sits atop the vast pulley-and-cable network that hauls the cars up Nob Hill, and enough of that network is visible to make it understandable to kids. What my daughter found even more fascinating than the cables and the prototype cars, however, were the ancient 25-cent photo viewfinders that show before-and-after pictures from the great 1906 quake and fire—she was astounded by the devastation and amazed at how the city rebuilt itself.

California Academy of Sciences

APPEAL BY AGE	PRESCHOOL ★★★	GRADE SCHOOL ★★★★	TEENS ★★★★
YOUNG ADULTS ★★★★		OVER 30 ★★★★	SENIORS ★★★★

875 Howard Street, San Francisco; ☎ 415-321-8000;
www.calacademy.org

Hours Daily, 10 a.m.–5 p.m. **Admission** $7 adults; $4.50 seniors, students, and youths ages 12–17; $2 children ages 4–11; free for children age 3 and under. **Touring time** Average 2–3 hours. **Rainy-day touring** Yes. **Restaurants** Yes. **Alcoholic beverages** No. **Disabled access** Yes. **Wheelchair rental** Yes. **Baby-stroller rental** No. **Lockers** No. **Pet kennels** No. **Rain check** No. **Private tours** Yes.

DESCRIPTION AND COMMENTS The Academy's permanent home in Golden Gate Park is closed for a major renovation, and it won't reopen until late 2008. But not to worry: two of the three components of the Academy— the Steinhart Aquarium and the Natural History Museum—are spending the next few years happily ensconced in the South of Market neighborhood, near Yerba Buena Gardens, Zeum, and other family favorites. Although it is smaller than its permanent home, this temporary center is well worth a few hours.

There was no way, of course, to transfer the entire Natural History Museum, which is one of the world's largest, so instead the curators are presenting focused shows. A recent one, Xtreme Life, looks at how life survives in hostile environments, which helps scientists search for life on other planets. Permanent exhibits include; Nature's Nest, a hands-on area for little ones (don't miss the story times on Saturdays at 10:30 a.m.); and the Naturalist Center, where school-age kids can do things like dissect owl pellets and dig for fossils.

Many of the aquarium exhibits were successfully moved to the temporary facility, including the collection of coral and tropical reef fish, which have a 20,000-gallon home. The African penguins got a cool new home, too, and round tanks showcase lots of other ocean dwellers. Besides ocean critters, there's a creepy-but-cool exhibit called Sssssnake Alley, home to such swamp-loving reptiles as ground boas, anacondas, pythons, vine snakes, and emerald tree boas.

The third component to the Academy, the Morrison Planetarium, will remain closed until 2008, when it is slated to reopen with a bang.

De Young Museum

APPEAL BY AGE	PRESCHOOL ★★	GRADE SCHOOL ★★★	TEENS ★★★
YOUNG ADULTS ★★★★		OVER 30 ★★★★	SENIORS ★★★★

50 Hagiwara Tea Garden Drive, Golden Gate Park; ☎ 415-863-3330;
www.thinker.org/deyoung

Hours Tuesday–Sunday, 9 a.m.–5 p.m.; open Friday to 8:45 p.m.; closed January 1, Thanksgiving Day, and Christmas. **Admission** $10 adults, $6 youths 13–17 and college students, $7 seniors, free for children age 12 and under. **Touring time**

Average 3 hours; minimum 1 hour. **Rainy-day touring** Yes. **Restaurants** Yes. **Alcoholic beverages** Yes. **Disabled access** Yes. **Wheelchair rental** Yes, free loaners. **Baby-stroller rental** No. **Lockers** Bag check. **Pet kennels** No. **Rain check** No. **Private tours** Yes.

DESCRIPTION AND COMMENTS After five years of renovation, the beloved de Young Museum is now a sleek, modern facility that offers twice the museum space of the 1895 original on a much smaller footprint. And the same beautiful Golden Gate Park surrounds it. This is a very fine fine-art museum with one of the best collections of American paintings in the nation, along with American sculpture; decorative art; and exciting collections from sub-Saharan Africa, New Guinea, the Americas, and Oceania. These latter collections are typically the most engaging for kids: the masks, totem poles, figures, charms, and weapons holders are totally cool. Try to visit on Saturday mornings, when the museum offers free drop-in art classes for kids ages 3½ to 12; Friday nights are also devoted to family activities. If you have a budding artist, stop by the Kimball Education Gallery Wednesday through Sunday afternoons, when you can see the visiting artist of the month at work; he or she will be happy to chat with youngsters. The changing exhibitions typically feature modern American art and are often appealing to teenagers.

 Exploratorium

APPEAL BY AGE	PRESCHOOL ★★★★	GRADE SCHOOL ★★★★★	TEENS ★★★★★
YOUNG ADULTS ★★★★★		OVER 30 ★★★★★	SENIORS ★★★★★

Palace of Fine Arts, 3601 Lyon Street; ☎ 415-563-7337; www.exploratorium.com

Hours Tuesday–Sunday, 10 a.m.–5 p.m.; closed Mondays, Thanksgiving, Christmas Eve, and Christmas Days. **Admission** $13 adults ages 18–64, $10 seniors age 65 and older and students over age 18 with ID, $10 people with disabilities and children ages 13–17, $8 children ages 4–12, free for children age 3 and under. Free admission on the first Wednesday of each month, but groups of 10 or more must make reservations. **Touring time** Average 4 hours; minimum 2 hours. **Rainy-day touring** Yes. **Restaurants** Yes. **Alcoholic beverages** No. **Disabled access** Yes. **Wheelchair rental** Yes, free. **Baby-stroller rental** No. **Lockers** Yes. **Pet kennels** No. **Rain check** No. **Private tours** No.

DESCRIPTION AND COMMENTS Even childless adults find themselves drawn back to the Exploratorium, so seductive are its science-geek charms. More than 650 hands-on exhibits fill a sprawling warehouse-style space within the grand Palace of Fine Arts on the west end of the Marina District; there's so much to experience that you may want to visit twice to do the place justice. Kids and grown-ups get to feel, touch, see, and wonder, in the Distortion Room, the Shadow Box, the two-way mirrors, the interactive video discs, the computer finger painting, the optical illusions—it goes on and on. Kids over age 7 (and their parents) who aren't claustrophobic or skittish can brave the Tactile Dome, where you

unofficial **TIP**
The grounds alone—rolling lawns, meandering pond, ducks, gorgeous trees—are worth a visit, so pack a picnic lunch to enjoy before or after your Exploratorium exploration.

squeeze through in total darkness, experiencing only touch sensations. Each "exhibit" is really an activity: a machine, a device, or a Rube Goldberg concoction designed to illustrate a scientific principle. These principles range from the swimming habits of fish to optical illusions to the physics of tornadoes.

On our first visit, the first floor alone (which begins with biology-related exhibits) exhausted us, so we had to return to discover the ultracool area upstairs, with its sight- and sound-perception exhibits. From this mezzanine area, we looked down on the work area where the exhibits are created and were amused and entertained to watch graduate-student types hard at work on these most appreciated of science projects.

Scattered throughout the vast space are guides (mostly college students) who love to explain the gizmos to the kids, so don't be shy about flagging them down.

Pier 39

APPEAL BY AGE	PRESCHOOL ★★	GRADE SCHOOL ★★★	TEENS ★★★★
YOUNG ADULTS ★★		OVER 30 ★★	SENIORS ★★

Beach Street and the Embarcadero; ☎ 415-981-PIER; www.pier39.com

Hours Daily; hours vary by activity, shop, or restaurant. **Admission** Free overall, but rides charge fees. **Touring time** Average 3 hours; minimum 1 hour. **Rainy-day touring** Yes, for inside activities. **Restaurants** Yes. **Alcoholic beverages** In restaurants. **Disabled access** Yes. **Wheelchair rental** No. **Baby-stroller rental** No. **Lockers** No. **Pet kennels** No; leashed pets allowed on pier. **Rain check** No. **Private tours** No.

DESCRIPTION AND COMMENTS This is really a kitschy, crowded mall, not an attraction, but it's a mighty seductive place for kids, and it borders on being a theme park. It can be an expensive place if you fall prey to the rides and shops, but one of its greatest charms is free: the thriving sea-lion community at the end of the 1,000-foot-long K pier, which fascinates toddlers and teens alike. On weekends, docents offer free programs about the sea lion; call ☎ 415-705-5500 for details. The view is also free, and it's a doozy, taking in everything from Coit Tower to the Golden Gate Bridge.

After you've enjoyed the simple pleasures, the kids will be on you to start shopping. We'll leave that up to you.

Next, head for **Aquarium of the Bay** (☎ 415-623-5300; admission $13.95 adults, $7 children ages 3 to 11, $7 seniors, family rate $33.95 for two adults and two children), where you walk through 300 feet of acrylic tunnels through a huge aquarium, surrounded by thousands of Bay Area fish. The Blue and Gold Fleet also runs its bay tours from Pier 39 (see "Ferries" under "Getting There Is All the Fun").

Older kids will want a turn on **TurboRide** (☎ 415-392-8872; admission $12 adults, $8 seniors and children), a simulated high-tech, special-effects roller coaster that gives a pretty impressive thrill but is too scary for many young children. While the big kids are on TurboRide, you can take littler ones to the low-key double-decker carousel.

Other kid fun includes the 10,000-square-foot video arcade called Riptide, cookie vendors, and lots of shops (the **Marine Mammal Store, National Park Store, Houdini's Magic Shop,** and **Fairyland** are big hits). If you have teens who need time away from parents, Pier 39 is a good self-contained place to drop them off for a few hours.

San Francisco Museum of Modern Art

APPEAL BY AGE	PRESCHOOL ★★	GRADE SCHOOL ★★★	TEENS ★★★
YOUNG ADULTS ★★★		OVER 30 ★★★	SENIORS ★★★

151 Third Street at Mission; ☎ 415-357-4000; www.sfmoma.com

Hours Friday–Tuesday, 10 a.m.–5:45 p.m.; Thursday, 10 a.m.–8:45 p.m.; closed major holidays and Wednesdays. **Admission** $12.50 adults, $8 seniors age 62 and older, $7 students with current ID, free for children age 12 and under; first Tuesday of each month free; Thursday 6–8:45 p.m. is half price. **Touring time** Average 3 hours; minimum 1 hour. **Rainy-day touring** Yes. **Restaurants** Yes. **Alcoholic beverages** Yes. **Disabled access** Yes. **Wheelchair rental** Yes, free. **Baby-stroller rental** No. **Lockers** No. **Pet kennels** No. **Rain check** No. **Private tours** Yes.

DESCRIPTION AND COMMENTS This heavily patronized museum is nice and compact, so museum fatigue never gets a chance to set in. My 11-year-old daughter had learned about Frida Kahlo and Jackson Pollock in school and was pleased to find their works represented here. The small permanent collection of 20th-century masters is a mini-tour of modern art, and the changing exhibits often include photography, which can be highly accessible to kids in a museum setting. A very low-key interactive area of four computers with headsets attached allowed us to click on a painting we'd seen to learn more—and the five-minute "Making Sense of Modern Art" presentation explained what parents couldn't in an hour.

San Francisco Zoo

APPEAL BY AGE	PRESCHOOL ★★★★★	GRADE SCHOOL ★★★★	TEENS ★★★
YOUNG ADULTS ★★★		OVER 30 ★★★	SENIORS ★★★

1 Zoo Road, 45th Avenue at Sloat Boulevard, Golden Gate Park; ☎ 415-753-7080; www.sfzoo.org

Hours Daily, 10 a.m.–5 p.m. **Admission** Non–San Francisco residents: $11 adults, $8 seniors age 65 and older and kids ages 12–17, $5 children ages 3–11, free for children age 2 and under; discount for San Francisco residents; first Wednesday of each month free. **Touring time** Average 3 hours; minimum 1 hour. **Rainy-day touring** Limited. **Restaurants** Yes. **Alcoholic beverages** Yes. **Disabled access** Limited. **Wheelchair rental** Yes, $6. **Baby-stroller rental** Yes, single $6 and double $9. **Lockers** No. **Pet kennels** Yes. **Rain check** No. **Private tours** No.

DESCRIPTION AND COMMENTS After years of gradual improvements, this old zoo has become a pretty wonderful place to spend an afternoon, and it's a must-visit for families with children under age 7 or so, thanks to the exceptional Children's Zoo. Located right near the entrance and charging an extra buck, it goes far beyond the typical mangy petting area. There's the Barnyard, with plenty of animals to pet, but also a chick hatchery, a nature trail, a deer park, families of mice, and an enthralling indoor Insect Zoo. Just outside its entrance is a good playground and carousel ($2 a ride). Young kids could spend an hour or two here and happily skip the larger zoo. But that's not to say it deserves skipping—there's plenty to see, in improved, more naturalistic settings. Our two favorites are the huge Gorilla World and the Primate Discovery Center, home to many species of rare and endangered monkeys. Our kids also loved seeing the penguins get their dinner, usually about 3 p.m. every day.

 Yerba Buena Gardens

APPEAL BY AGE	PRESCHOOL ★★★★	GRADE SCHOOL ★★★★	TEENS ★★★★
YOUNG ADULTS ★★★		OVER 30 ★★★	SENIORS ★★★

(See map on page 311)

Rooftop of Moscone Center South, bordered by Mission, Third, Folsom, and Fourth streets; ☎ 415-978-2787; www.yerbabuenaarts.org; skating or bowling: ☎ 415-820-3532; www.skatebowl.com

Hours Gardens open 6 a.m.–10 p.m daily; hours vary for attractions. **Admission** Free to gardens and playground; carousel ride $2; skating center $7 adults, $5.50 seniors age 55 and older and children; bowling fees vary; $3 skate rental. **Touring time** Average 1 hour; minimum 30 minutes. **Rainy-day touring** Yes for indoor attractions, no for park. **Restaurants** Yes. **Alcoholic beverages** No. **Disabled access** Yes. **Wheelchair rental** No. **Baby-stroller rental** No. **Lockers** No. **Pet kennels** No. **Rain check** No. **Private tours** No.

DESCRIPTION AND COMMENTS Spread over the vast squatness of the Moscone Center, this new rooftop children's center has something for every kid, from sand play for toddlers to the ultracool Zeum for tech-crazy teens. For a description of the park, see "The Best Beaches and Parks" at the beginning of this chapter; for details on Zeum, see its attraction profile at right.

Aside from the park space and Zeum, Yerba Buena Gardens has several kid-pleasing opportunities. First is the ornate, hand-carved 1906 carousel, which is unfortunately housed in a glass structure, which was deemed necessary to protect it from the elements and give it more operating days. Inside or out, it's a fine carousel that's well worth a ride; next to it is a food cart serving hot dogs and snacks.

Past Zeum, over near the playground, are the two other indoor amusements: the Ice Skating Center and the Bowling Center. Both are state of the art; the huge window in the skating rink offers a great view of downtown San Francisco, so you almost feel like you're skating outside, and the bowling alley is spotless and cheerful, unlike most urban bowling alleys, which tend toward the grim.

An entire day could easily be passed here. Gather for a picnic in the park, then send older kids into Zeum to make a video or work on an art project while you sip a latte (yes, there's a Starbucks) and watch the little ones ride the carousel and play in the playground, then treat the whole gang to a session of skating or bowling. You could end the day by walking to the mall next door to catch a movie.

 ## Zeum

| APPEAL BY AGE | PRESCHOOL ★ | GRADE SCHOOL ★★★★★ | TEENS ★★★★★ |
| YOUNG ADULTS ★★★★ | | OVER 30 ★★★ | SENIORS ★★★ |

**Yerba Buena Gardens, 221 Fourth Street, South of Market;
☎ 415-820-3320; www.zeum.org**

Hours During school year, Wednesday–Sunday, 11 a.m.–5 p.m., and specified weekday afternoons for special workshops; summer: Tuesday–Sunday, 11 a.m.– 5 p.m. Admission $8 adults, $7 students and seniors, $6 kids ages 3–18; free for members. Touring time Average 3 hours; minimum 2 hours. Rainy-day touring Yes. Restaurants No. Alcoholic beverages No. Disabled access No. Wheelchair rental No. Baby-stroller rental No. Lockers No. Pet kennels No. Rain check No. Private tours No.

DESCRIPTION AND COMMENTS If there was ever a place that will make you wish to be 12 years old again, Zeum is it. A nonprofit, wildly creative, hands-on art and technology center, this is more a big-kid arts play place than a museum. In the Animators Studio, kids sketch characters of their own making, storyboard a story, then bring it to life in a Claymation film. They get to do every step of the process (with help from plenty of staff members if needed). It was a dream come true for our 10-year-old, who could have spent days here. In the Learning Lab, kids try digital photography and digital animation, and if that's not fun enough, they can design their own Web pages. In the Production Lab, kids work together (bring friends!) to make a multimedia video—they're the actors, directors, special-effects technicians, sound-effects technicians, and camera operators. In the Main Gallery, the artists-in-residence help kids do everything from build architectural models to publish their own books.

Zeum is heaven for kids from about the second or third grade through high school, but it's boring for younger ones, who won't have the patience or the physical skills necessary to tackle these projects. And be forewarned that this is not a quick-drop-in place—come prepared to spend the afternoon so that your children have time to become fully absorbed. The last time we were here, the city was mobbed, but Zeum was half empty, with plenty of staff members and easy access to the labs and studios.

FAMILY-FRIENDLY RESTAURANTS

Benihana
1737 Post Street, Union Square; ☎ **415-563-4844; www.benihana.com**

Meals served Lunch and dinner. **Cuisine** Japanese. **Entree range** $15–$45. **Kids' menu** $8–$10. **Reservations** Recommended. **Payment** All major credit cards.

Sure, it's touristy and gimmicky, but it's great fun for kids, and the mainstream Japanese food is fine and not threatening to picky eaters. You sit around a grill while a showman chef cooks your meal, tossing knives, cutting food in midair, flipping shrimp, and making jokes. It's so entertaining that they're more likely to try some new, scary food.

California Pizza Kitchen
524 Van Ness Avenue; ☎ **415-436-9380; www.cpk.com**

Meals served Lunch and dinner. **Cuisine** Californian. **Entree range** Lunch and dinner, $7–$15. **Kids' menu** $5. **Reservations** Not accepted. **Payment** All major credit cards.

Despite San Francisco's popularity as a family vacation spot, it's not always easy to find a good parent-child restaurant, especially in the Civic Center area. This import from L.A. is your best bet, and it's sure to make you all happy. Kids get a coloring menu, crayons, cups with lids, and tasty little pizzas and pastas; parents get chic designer pizzas and pastas, fresh salads, and wine by the glass.

Fog City Diner
1300 Battery Street, Financial District; ☎ **415-982-2000;**
www.fogcitydiner.com

Meals served Lunch and dinner. **Cuisine** Modern American. **Entree range** Lunch, $10–$15; dinner, $15–$25. **Kids' menu** No. **Reservations** Recommended. **Payment** All major credit cards.

A great place for parents to get a taste of modern American cooking, San Francisco–style, in a lively setting that's kid friendly. Located on the North Beach–Battery waterfront (but lacking a view), Fog City is a cross between a train-car diner and old San Francisco bar and grill, with roomy booths, an open kitchen, and lots of hustle and bustle. Prices are fair, given the hipness of the place, and food is delicious: crab cakes, skinny fries, chicken on a biscuit with Virginia ham and morels, Cobb salad sandwich, outstanding meat loaf, grilled-cheese sandwiches, homey desserts. We go in the 3-to-5-p.m. range to avoid the constant crowds.

La Taqueria
2889 Mission Street, Mission District; ☎ **415-285-7117**

Meals served Lunch and dinner. **Cuisine** Mexican. **Entree range** $4–$8. **Kids' menu** No. **Reservations** Not accepted. **Payment** No credit cards.

The largely Latino Mission District, south of downtown's Market Street, is blessed with many fine taco joints, and this is one of the finest. Timid eaters will be pleased with a cheese quesadilla and a fresh strawberry *liquado* (shake); braver kids will adore the huge burritos and savory soft tacos filled with *pollo* (chicken), *carnitas* (pork), or *carne asada* (grilled beef).

Mel's Drive-In

3355 Geary Boulevard, near Golden Gate Park; ☎ 415-387-2244
2165 Lombard Street, Marina; ☎ 415-921-3039
801 Mission; ☎ 415-227-4477
1050 Van Ness Avenue; ☎ 415-292-6357; www.melsdrive-in.com

Meals served Breakfast, lunch, and dinner. **Cuisine** American. **Entree range** Breakfast, $2–$10; lunch, $6–$7; dinner, $7–$14. **Kids' menu** Yes. **Reservations** Not accepted. **Payment** No credit cards.

The Geary location is the original Mel's, lionized in *American Graffiti* and beloved by many a San Francisco kid. Oldies blare, waitresses talk smart, and milk shakes are thick and good. Our kids adore the kids' menu, the crayons, the music, the floats, and the grilled-cheese sandwiches served in a toy Corvette. The Lombard Street Mel's is well located for a lively diner meal after a visit to the Exploratorium or a skate along the Marina Green.

Mo's Burgers
1322 Grant Street, North Beach; ☎ 415-788-3779

Meals served Breakfast, lunch, and dinner; no dinner Saturday or Sunday. **Cuisine** American. **Entree range** Breakfast, $4–$7; lunch and dinner, $6–$8. **Kids' menu** Yes. **Reservations** Not accepted. **Payment** MC, V.

This is likely the best burger in San Francisco, a town that takes the burger pretty seriously. A simple, friendly spot not far from the Wharf, serving fresh, perfectly cooked burgers.

New Asia Restaurant
772 Pacific Avenue, Chinatown; ☎ 415-391-6666

Meals served Breakfast, lunch, and dinner. **Cuisine** Chinese. **Entree range** $3–$6 (per dim sum order). **Kids' menu** No. **Reservations** Not accepted. **Payment** AE, MC, V.

The best family-oriented restaurant in Chinatown, New Asia makes a mean dumpling for breakfast or lunch and fine Chinese seafood dishes for dinner. If your kids have never experienced dim sum, with waitresses wheeling around carts laden with dumplings, noodles, meats, and strange sweets, bring them here. They'll recoil in horror at the chicken feet, but they'll love the fluffy white *bao* buns stuffed with pork and the savory little *sui mai*. At dinnertime, kids are always happy with a big plate of Chinese noodles or fried rice. Come early to beat the lunchtime line.

PJ's Oyster Bed
737 Irving Street, Richmond District; ☎ 415-566-7775;
www.pjsoysterbed.com

Meals served Lunch and dinner. **Cuisine** Seafood. **Entree range** Lunch and
dinner $12 to $26. **Kids' menu** Yes. **Reservations** Accepted. **Payment** All major
credit cards.

For great San Francisco–style seafood and a casual, noisy, child-friendly
setting, skip the Fisherman's Wharf tourist traps and stop here instead. It's
ideally located for a lunch or dinner before or after a day in nearby Golden
Gate Park. The clam chowder will ward off the worst fog attack, and the
gumbo, oysters, and all-you-can-eat crawfish will make parents happy. The
kids' menu includes fried shrimp, a change from the usual chicken fingers.

Taylor's Automatic Refresher
1 Ferry Building, the Embarcadero at Market Street; ☎ 415-328-3663;
www.taylorsrefresher.com

Meals served Lunch and dinner. **Cuisine** American. **Entree range** $6–$12. **Kids'
menu** No. **Reservations** Not accepted. **Payment** All major credit cards.

This sleek, modern diner is part of the newly restored Ferry Building, a sort
of food lover's mall and the site of a terrific farmers market on Tuesdays,
Thursdays, Saturdays, and Sundays. The diner aesthetic is honored with
great burgers, fries, and hand-scooped shakes. But there's more than just
diner fare: The ahi burger (cooked rare) is fabulous, the fish tacos are as
good as any in Mexico, and the gazpacho is sharp and soothing at the same
time. Be prepared for a long line at rush hours. Try to snag a table outside,
where the people watching is great and the kids can run.

Tommaso's Restaurant
1042 Kearny, North Beach; ☎ 415-398-9696;
www.tommasosnorthbeach.com

Meals served Dinner. **Cuisine** Italian. **Entree range** $11–$18. **Kids' menu** No.
Reservations Not accepted. **Payment** All major credit cards.

Almost a cliché of what an old North Beach pizza joint should look like,
Tommaso's is the real thing, from its rickety white wooden table nooks to
its old brick pizza oven to its chipped walls hung with photos of the restaurant's patron saint, Francis Ford Coppola. On the way here, you may have
to distract the kids' attention from the nearby triple-X theater, but once
inside you'll be rewarded with superb, inexpensive food that's a far cry
from Domino's. Calzones are hearty and cheesy, thin-crust pizzas are saucy
and delicious, and vegetables hail from local organic farms (if you see the
fresh tomato–mozzarella salad on special, get it). An essential North Beach
experience.

SIDE TRIP

Six Flags Marine World

APPEAL BY AGE	PRESCHOOL ★★★★	GRADE SCHOOL ★★★★	TEENS ★★★★
YOUNG ADULTS ★★★★	OVER 30 ★★★★		SENIORS ★★★★

2001 Marine World Parkway (off I-80), Vallejo; ☎ 707-643-6722; www.sixflags.com

Hours Spring and fall: daily, 10 a.m.–8 p.m.; summer: daily, 10 a.m.–10 p.m.; closed November–late March. **Admission** $52 adults ($40 if you buy online), $30 children less than 48" tall, free for children age 2 and under. **Touring time** Average 6 hours; minimum 3–4 hours. **Rainy-day touring** Yes, but you'll get wet. **Restaurants** Yes. **Alcoholic beverages** Yes. **Disabled access** Yes. **Wheelchair rental** Yes. **Baby-stroller rental** Yes. **Lockers** Yes. **Pet kennels** No. **Rain check** No. **Private tours** No.

DESCRIPTION AND COMMENTS Formerly known as Marine World Africa USA, this animal-oriented theme park is now more thrill oriented (since Six Flags is the operator), but it also emphasizes the marine-life side of the park. Animal shows are the park's strong suit, each running 20 minutes or so, and many get quite crowded. As at SeaWorld, the killer-whale and dolphin shows are lots of fun (and wet—if you sit in front, you'll get splashed). Traveling on the moving ramp through the Shark Experience, where sharks swim around you on three sides, is a very cool experience; the sea-lion show is charming; the waterskiing show is full of great stunts; and the new Dolphin Encounter, where you can touch, train, and feed bottlenose dolphins, has proved a hit with kids.

Out of water, you'll find lots of animals from around the world in different park zones, from kangaroos to camels, and the experiences are interactive whenever possible, whether it's riding an elephant or feeding a giraffe. (Butterfly World is particularly enchanting for young ones.) In the process, kids learn quite a bit about animals, their habitats, their diets, and their fragility in a people-dominated world.

When your 6-year-old has had enough of sitting through shows and needs to blow off steam, he'll have fun in the Gentle Jungle play area, or in the Whale of a Time World, where a life-size blue-whale replica makes for a great play structure.

Its mix of animal life, play areas, and some intense thrills—including Medusa, a "flying" roller coaster, and Boomerang, a corkscrew coaster—makes this a very appealing theme park for families with different ages to please—a 4-year-old and a 14-year-old will both be happy.

Note that for families staying in San Francisco, you can reach Marine World via the Blue and Gold Fleet, with a combination ticket that includes both the scenic one-hour ferry ride and park admission.

BERKELEY

NATIONALLY KNOWN AS THE HOME of the **University of California at Berkeley** and one of the seminal birthplaces of the hippie movement, **Berkeley** is a dynamic little city that is particularly wonderful for teenagers. The campus is inspirational to wander, and the still-funky downtown is colorful and great fun to shop, thick with coffeehouses, bookstores, theaters, handmade jewelry, and street musicians. Kids of all ages will like the cool, hands-on **Lawrence Hall of Science** on campus, as well as the sprawling **Charles Lee Tilden Park** on the outskirts of town (see "The Best Beaches and Parks," page 306). East of San Francisco across the bay, this college town can be easily reached on a BART subway or by car across the Bay Bridge; taxi rides are costly.

> *unofficial* **TIP**
> Most 16-year-olds could spend a week in Berkeley and not be bored.

FAMILY LODGING

Claremont Resort and Spa
41 Tunnel Road, Oakland; ☎ 510-843-3000 or 877-206-1781; www.claremontresort.com; $329 and up

This grand white Victorian rambler in the Berkeley hills (on the Oakland border) is the place for society locals to have weddings and parties, and now that the former stuffiness has relaxed enough to inspire the creation of a kids' program, it's a terrific family retreat as well. Hotel guests can take advantage of The Club at the Claremont, a sort of country club within a resort; it includes two beautiful pools, ten tennis courts, a fitness center, a spa, and a comprehensive children's program, including kids' tennis and yoga and a Friday-night movie.

Gramma's Rose Garden Inn
2740 Telegraph Avenue, Berkeley; ☎ 510-549-2145 or 800-992-9005; www.rosegardeninn.com; $99–$245

As sweet a place as its name suggests, this longtime favorite of visiting professors occupies two old mansions in the middle of the good shopping and walking area near the UC campus. It has all the charm of a bed-and-breakfast

berkeley

FAMILY LODGING
1. Claremont Resort and Spa
2. Gramma's Rose Garden Inn

ATTRACTIONS
3. Berkeley Convention and Visitor's Bureau
4. Lawrence Hall of Science
5. Tilden Park
6. Visitor Information Center

FAMILY-FRIENDLY RESTAURANTS
7. Chez Panisse Café
8. Fat Apple's
9. Homemade Cafe

(fireplaces, quirky rooms, evening wine and cheese), but unlike at most, families are welcome—some rooms are big enough for several, and they'll bring in a futon for $10 more. There's a lawn to play on outside, and kids can opt for cookies and milk instead of wine and cheese.

ATTRACTION

Lawrence Hall of Science

APPEAL BY AGE	PRESCHOOL ★★★	GRADE SCHOOL ★★★★	TEENS ★★★★
YOUNG ADULTS ★★★		OVER 30 ★★★	SENIORS ★★★

Centennial Drive below Grizzly Peak Boulevard, UC Berkeley;
☎ **510-642-5132; www.lawrencehallofscience.org**

Hours Daily, 10 a.m.–5 p.m. **Admission** $9.50 adults ages 19–61; $7.50 students ages 5–18, disabled guests, and seniors age 62 and older; $5.50 children ages 3–4; free for children age 2 and under. **Touring time** Average 3 hours; minimum 2 hours. **Rainy-day touring** Yes. **Restaurants** Yes. **Alcoholic beverages** No. **Disabled access** Yes. **Wheelchair rental** No. **Baby-stroller rental** No. **Lockers** No. **Pet kennels** No. **Rain check** No. **Private tours** No.

DESCRIPTION AND COMMENTS   A smaller version of San Francisco's Exploratorium, this university science museum encourages kids to touch and experience, starting with the 60-foot-long DNA model outside, which doubles as a climbing structure. A particular favorite of our kids is the Biology Discovery Lab, which on weekends and summer days allows them to examine frogs, pet snakes, and hold a tarantula. Elsewhere they can play math puzzle games, try to get magnets through a maze, look through telescopes, create their own laser-light show, and get inside the human brain. Prepare for some serious begging for a souvenir from the exceptional gift shop, stocked with gee-whiz toys, science experiments, puzzles, books, and all sorts of fun and educational kid stuff.

 # FAMILY-FRIENDLY RESTAURANTS

 ## Chez Panisse Café

1517 Shattuck Avenue, Berkeley; ☎ 510-548-5049; www.chezpanisse.com

Meals served Lunch and dinner. **Cuisine** Modern American. **Entree range** Lunch, $12–$18; dinner, $12–$26. **Kids' menu** Weekdays only. **Reservations** Not accepted. **Payment** All major credit cards.

If your kids are the least bit interested in food—or if you are—bring them to the casual cafe above chef Alice Waters's more serious restaurant, the birthplace of California cuisine. It's lively, friendly to kids (they even get crayons), and moderately priced, considering the restaurant's international fame and the exceptional quality of the food. Thanks to Waters's slavish devotion to farm-fresh produce (most grown just for this restaurant), even the simplest cheese pizza sings with flavor. Great salads, sophisticated pizzas, grilled fish, and homey desserts. To beat the crowds, we like to come for a very early lunch.

Fat Apple's
1346 Martin Luther King Boulevard, Berkeley; ☎ 510-526-2260

Meals served Breakfast, lunch, and dinner. **Cuisine** American. **Entree range** Lunch, $6–$9; dinner, $10–$15. **Kids' menu** No. **Reservations** Not accepted. **Payment** MC, V.

Fans drive across the Bay Bridge to sit in this plain coffee shop and eat some terrific diner cooking: oatmeal-apple pancakes, homemade soups, dreamy cheese puffs, perfect burgers, fresh-berry pies. There's no need to have a kids' menu when you have a grown-up menu that speaks so profoundly to kids.

Homemade Cafe
2454 Sacramento Street, Berkeley; ☎ 510-845-1940

Meals served Breakfast (available all day) and lunch. **Cuisine** American. **Entree range** $7–$11. **Kids' menu** No. **Reservations** Not accepted. **Payment** No credit cards.

Breakfast nirvana, known for its pancakes, French toast, and egg scrambles. As is usually the case at great breakfast cafes, however, there's always a crowd, so be prepared to wait. Lunch runs to clever, tasty sandwiches.

MARIN COUNTY

WITH ITS REDWOOD FORESTS, CREEKS, ROLLING HILLS, and proximity to San Francisco just across the Golden Gate Bridge, it's no surprise that **Marin County** is home to some of the priciest real estate in the nation. Fortunately, you don't have to take on a million-dollar mortgage to enjoy its spectacular parks, beaches, and atmospheric small towns. Under "The Best Beaches and Parks" and "Family Outdoor Adventures," you'll find details on Marin's great outdoors, from **Muir Woods** walks to **Tomales Bay** kayaking to **Mount Tamalpais** mountain biking. En route to these adventures, you'll find spiffy towns worth a stop, stroll, and nosh, especially **Mill Valley, Larkspur, Olema,** and **San Rafael.** From San Francisco, you can reach two of the county's most popular and charming towns, **Sausalito** and **Tiburon,** by ferry; both are fun to explore.

FAMILY LODGING

Point Reyes Seashore Lodge
10021 Coastal Highway 1, Olema; ☎ 415-663-9000 or 800-404-5634; www.pointreyesseashore.com; $135–$295

Ideally located alongside Olema Creek at the edge of Point Reyes National Seashore, this country inn is more family friendly than many places in these parts. Done in a modern Victorian style, it has 23 rooms and 2 cottages, and several of the accommodations can handle a family (the private Creekside Cottage, with kitchen and spa, is our favorite). The grounds encompass lawns, woods, walkways, Adirondack chairs for quiet reading, and a trail to the National Park headquarters; inside is a game room and library. The neighboring restaurant, the Farm House (see profile on page 341), is a welcoming, casual place with a take-out deli attached.

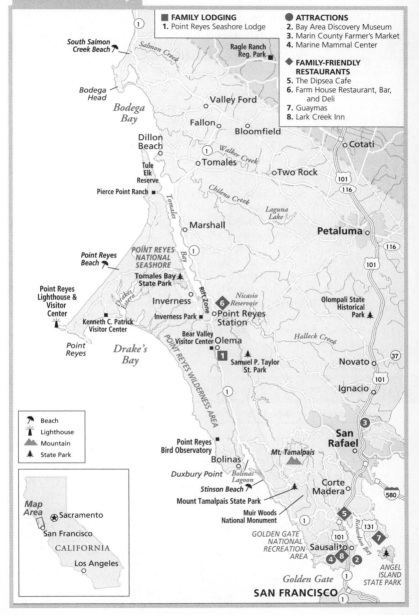

marin county

■ FAMILY LODGING
1. Point Reyes Seashore Lodge

● ATTRACTIONS
2. Bay Area Discovery Museum
3. Marin County Farmer's Market
4. Marine Mammal Center

◆ FAMILY-FRIENDLY RESTAURANTS
5. The Dipsea Cafe
6. Farm House Restaurant, Bar, and Deli
7. Guaymas
8. Lark Creek Inn

South Salmon Creek Beach

Salmon Creek

Ragle Ranch Reg. Park

Bodega Head

Bodega Bay

Valley Ford

Fallon

Bloomfield

Cotati

Dillon Beach

Walker Creek

Tomales

Two Rock

101
116

Tule Elk Reserve

Pierce Point Ranch

Chileno Creek

Tomales Bay

Marshall

Laguna Lake

Petaluma

116

Point Reyes Beach

POINT REYES NATIONAL SEASHORE

101

Tomales Bay State Park

Nicasio Reservoir

Point Reyes Lighthouse & Visitor Center

Drake's Estero

Inverness

Inverness Park

6 Point Reyes Station

Olompali State Historical Park

Kenneth C. Patrick Visitor Center

Point Reyes

Drake's Bay

POINT REYES WILDERNESS AREA

Bear Valley Visitor Center

Olema

Halleck Creek

Novato

37

1 Samuel P. Taylor St. Park

Ignacio

101

Beach
Lighthouse
Mountain
State Park

Point Reyes Bird Observatory

Mt. Tamalpais

3

San Rafael

Bolinas

Duxbury Point

Bolinas Lagoon

Stinson Beach

Mount Tamalpais State Park

Corte Madera

580

Muir Woods National Monument

1

5

131

7

Map Area

Sacramento

San Francisco

CALIFORNIA

Los Angeles

GOLDEN GATE NATIONAL RECREATION AREA

101

Sausalito

4 8 2

Richardson Bay

ANGEL ISLAND STATE PARK

Golden Gate

SAN FRANCISCO

1

ATTRACTIONS

 Bay Area Discovery Museum

APPEAL BY AGE	PRESCHOOL ★★★★		GRADE SCHOOL ★★★★	TEENS ★★★
YOUNG ADULTS	★★	OVER 30	★★	SENIORS ★★

Fort Baker, 557 McReynolds Road, Sausalito; ☎ 415-339-3900; www.badm.org

Hours Tuesday–Friday, 9 a.m.–4 p.m.; Saturday and Sunday, 10 a.m.–5 p.m. **Admission** $8.50 for adults, $7.50 for children. **Touring time** Average 2 hours; minimum 1 hour. **Rainy-day touring** Yes. **Restaurants** Lunch cafe. **Alcoholic beverages** No. **Disabled access** Yes. **Wheelchair rental** No. **Baby-stroller rental** No. **Lockers** No. **Pet kennels** No. **Rain check** No. **Private tours** No.

DESCRIPTION AND COMMENTS Tucked under the Marin side of the Golden Gate Bridge, this is one of the better children's museums in California, especially for kids under age 11. It's hands-on, interactive, and fun, emphasizing the bay-side location instead of generic kid stuff. Kids love the Underwater Sea Tunnel, which lets them crawl "under" the bay, and the full-size Discovery Boat, where they can be fishermen. Other cool exhibits include the Maze of Illusions and computer lab. There's a separate, equally fun play area for toddlers, a decent cafe, and a cool gift shop. There's even a carousel for kids who insist on a theme-park ride.

If you don't have a car, you can reach the museum from the Sausalito ferry terminal via a shuttle, which runs daily from 11 a.m. to 5:30 p.m. and costs $6.45 for adults and $3.20 for kids, seniors, and disabled persons round trip.

Marin County Farmer's Market

APPEAL BY AGE	PRESCHOOL ★★★★	GRADE SCHOOL ★★★★	TEENS ★★★★
YOUNG ADULTS ★★★★	OVER 30 ★★★★		SENIORS ★★★★

Fourth Street, San Rafael; ☎ 415-492-8007; www.sanrafaelmarket.org

Hours April–September: Thursday, 6–9 p.m. **Admission** Free. **Touring time** Average 1 hour; minimum 30 minutes. **Rainy-day touring** Yes, but you'll get wet. **Restaurants** In town. **Alcoholic beverages** In town. **Disabled access** Yes. **Wheelchair rental** No. **Baby-stroller rental** No. **Lockers** No. **Pet kennels** No. **Rain check** No. **Private tours** No.

DESCRIPTION AND COMMENTS One of the nation's best farmers markets is held every Thursday evening from April through September at the Marin County Civic Center, and it's worth a detour. The center alone is worth a look, as one of the last and most significant of Frank Lloyd Wright's buildings. And the market is as much fun for kids as for food-loving baby boomers. There's usually a balloon artist and storyteller, a man on roller skates selling eggs, street musicians, and a small-town party atmosphere. Along with superb organic produce, you can buy boutique cheeses, condiments, oils, and fresh breads and graze on tamales, pancakes, and sausage sandwiches.

Marine Mammal Center

APPEAL BY AGE	PRESCHOOL ★★	GRADE SCHOOL ★★★	TEENS ★★★
YOUNG ADULTS ★★★		OVER 30 ★★★	SENIORS ★★★

Marin Headlands, near Sausalito; ☎ 415-289-7325; www.tmmc.org

Hours Daily, 10 a.m.–4 p.m.; closed Thanksgiving, Christmas, and New Year's Day. **Admission** Free. **Touring time** Average 1½ hours; minimum 45 minutes. **Rainy-day touring** Yes. **Restaurants** No. **Alcoholic beverages** No. **Disabled access** Yes. **Wheelchair rental** No. **Baby-stroller rental** No. **Lockers** No. **Pet kennels** No. **Rain check** No. **Private tours** No; docents available on weekends.

DESCRIPTION AND COMMENTS Part of the Golden Gate National Recreation Area, this nonprofit organization rescues, rehabilitates, and releases ocean mammals that have been injured or orphaned or that become ill. It's one of the largest wild-animal hospitals in the world, and it welcomes animal-loving children, who can observe the volunteers and vets tending to the sea lions, dolphins, seals, and otters. Exhibits teach kids about the mammals and about marine ecology and conservation.

FAMILY-FRIENDLY RESTAURANTS

The Dipsea Cafe
200 Shoreline Highway, Mill Valley; ☎ 415-381-0298

Meals served Breakfast and lunch. **Cuisine** American. **Entree range** $8–$12. **Kids' menu** $4–$5. **Reservations** Not accepted. **Payment** All major credit cards.

A fantasy family restaurant done up like a 19th-century farmhouse, Dipsea is idyllically located creek-side, and picture windows bring in views of the footbridge and ducks outside. This is a fine spot to fuel up for a hike along one of the terrific, not-too-challenging local trails. Although the cooking can suffer from a slapdash approach, it's generally quite satisfying: pancakes, eggs, biscuits, and smoothies for breakfast, and burgers, Caesar salad, and grilled-ahi salads for lunch.

Farm House Restaurant, Bar & Deli
10005 Highway 1, Olema; ☎ 415-663-1264; www.olemafarmhouse.com

Meals served Lunch and dinner; breakfast on weekends only. **Cuisine** American. **Entree range** Lunch, $8–$20; dinner, $10–$25; breakfast, $5–$10. **Kids' menu** No. **Reservations** Recommended. **Payment** All major credit cards.

Both convenient and charming, this is a good place to eat before or after a day at Point Reyes, thanks to its location near the lighthouse, beaches, and visitors center. On your way into the 1856 farmhouse building, take a peek at the cowhide-upholstered saloon—it will wow any cowboy-loving kid. In the boarding house–style dining room, people put away large portions of clam chowder, oyster stew, barbecued oysters, ribs, burgers, and cioppino, as well as hearty, good-quality breakfasts. There's no children's menu, but kids will have no trouble finding something good (without slimy oysters) to eat. The adjacent deli can supply you for a Point Reyes picnic.

Guaymas
5 Main Street, Tiburon; ☎ 415-435-6300; www.guaymas.com

Meals served Lunch and dinner. **Cuisine** Mexican. **Entree range** $11–$19. **Kids' menu** No. **Reservations** Accepted. **Payment** All major credit cards.

If the sun is shining, take advantage of it and treat the kids to a 30-minute ferry ride to the impossibly bucolic town of Tiburon (the ferry passes right by Alcatraz, which is a thrill). This slick waterfront restaurant, just a few steps from the ferry landing, is most notable for its huge patio with a fabulous view of the bay and San Francisco. The yuppified Mexican food is perfectly fine, especially when accompanied by a margarita and the dreamy view. There's no kids' menu, but the kitchen is happy to make plain quesadillas. If you score the right patio table, you can let the kids scramble over adjacent waterfront rocks while you linger awhile and watch them from your seat.

Lark Creek Inn
234 Magnolia Avenue, Larkspur; ☎ 415-924-7766; www.larkcreek.com

Meals served Lunch, dinner, Sunday brunch. **Cuisine** Modern American. **Entree range** Lunch, $11–$20; dinner, $20–$36; brunch, $11–$18. **Kids' menu** Yes. **Reservations** Essential. **Payment** All major credit cards.

A very special special-occasion restaurant, Lark Creek is a wonderful place to experience California cuisine. Located in a turn-of-the-19th-century mansion at the edge of a redwood canyon a short drive north of the Golden Gate Bridge, this is one of the best restaurants in the Bay Area, with or without kids. Unlike at the region's other top restaurants, however, children are warmly welcomed and catered to with their own menu (field-green salads, great chicken fingers, pasta). The kitchen takes American classics—crab Cobb salad, grilled quail salad, oak-roasted chicken—to lofty levels, and the desserts alone (butterscotch pudding, devil's food cake with espresso ice cream) are worth the trip. In summer, request a garden table outside.

SAN JOSE

WITH A POPULATION OF MORE THAN 900,000, **San Jose** may be bigger than San Francisco, but it's nowhere near the tourist destination that the City by the Bay is—although its fame as the hub of high-tech industry has made it a major business-travel destination and the home of the wonderful **Tech Museum**, which is well worth a trip in itself. It's located at the southern tip of San Francisco Bay, about an hour's drive south from downtown San Francisco and a 90-minute drive from Monterey. That can make it a good stop on a road trip, especially on weekends, when hotel rates plummet to half the cost of weeknights.

San Jose's an important city historically—it was founded in 1777 and was the state's first capital—but families with computer-savvy kids will be more interested in the city's role in the future, as symbolized by the the **Tech Museum of Innovation** (see profile).

Close by San Jose are a number of attractive little towns—**Los Gatos, Saratoga, Campbell,** and **Gilroy**—that we won't discuss here, but you should know that not only are they centers of adult tourist pleasures, with wineries, historic districts, hiking, and fine restaurants, but they can also be pleasant for a lunch stop or afternoon hike or park visit with kids.

FAMILY LODGING

Hotel De Anza
233 West Santa Clara Street, San Jose; ☎ 408-286-1000 or 800-843-3700; www.hoteldeanza.com; $99–$299

There's no denying that this is primarily a business hotel, but with its discounted weekend rates, central location, and smaller size than the big convention hotels, the historic De Anza can be a good choice for families. Our kids learned to love breakfast buffets in Europe and can indulge in them here, but even more fun for night owls is the "Raid Our Pantry" program. Your room key opens the door to a lounge where a full deli buffet is set out—sandwich fixings, cookies, fruit, and surprises—seven nights a week from 10 p.m. until 5 a.m. This is a great TV-dinner choice for teens and older kids who've stayed up late at one of the big amusement parks. The hotel is

san jose

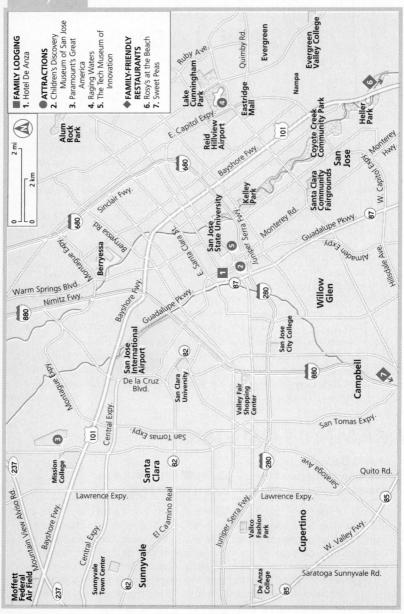

FAMILY LODGING
1. Hotel De Anza

ATTRACTIONS
2. Children's Discovery Museum of San Jose
3. Paramount's Great America
4. Raging Waters
5. The Tech Museum of Innovation

FAMILY-FRIENDLY RESTAURANTS
6. Rosy's at the Beach
7. Sweet Peas

2 mi

2 km

just a few easily walked blocks from each of the museums listed below and is also near Guadalupe River Park, a nice city park with playground and lawns. Make sure to check out the diving lady mural at the pool.

■ ATTRACTIONS

Children's Discovery Museum of San Jose

APPEAL BY AGE	PRESCHOOL ★★★★	GRADE SCHOOL ★★★	TEENS ★
YOUNG ADULTS ★		OVER 30 ★	SENIORS ★

180 Woz Way, San Jose; ☎ 408-298-5437; www.cdm.org

Hours Monday–Saturday, 10 a.m.–5 p.m.; Sunday, noon–5 p.m. **Admission** $7 kids and adults, $6 seniors, under age 1, free. **Touring time** 2–4 hours; minimum 1 hour. **Rainy-day touring** Yes. **Restaurants** Yes. **Alcoholic beverages** No. **Disabled access** No. **Wheelchair rental** No. **Baby-stroller rental** No. **Lockers** No. **Pet kennels** No. **Rain check** No. **Private tours** No.

DESCRIPTION AND COMMENTS This highly regarded children's museum is adjacent to Guadalupe River Park and has a nice cafe, too, so plan at least a half-day outing and a meal indoors or out. Great for kids who are too young for the Tech Museum, it is home to a variety of semipermanent and temporary interactive, hands-on exhibitions, climbing and play areas, and such imagination-stimulating environments as a play post office and Alice's Wonderland.

 ## Paramount's Great America

APPEAL BY AGE	PRESCHOOL ★★★★	GRADE SCHOOL ★★★★★	TEENS ★★★★★
YOUNG ADULTS ★★★★		OVER 30 ★★★★	SENIORS ★★

2401 Agnew Road (Great America Parkway exit off 101), Santa Clara; ☎ 408-988-1776; www.pgathrills.com

Hours May–end of August: daily, 10 a.m.–various closing times depending on month; closed November–February; open Saturday and Sunday only March–May, September, and October. **Admission** $52 ages 7–59; $35 seniors age 60 and older, disabled guests, and children ages 3–6; free for children age 2 and under. **Touring time** Average 6–8 hours; minimum 4 hours. **Rainy-day touring** Yes; rides still function, and the lines are shorter. **Restaurants** Yes. **Alcoholic beverages** Yes. **Disabled access** Yes. **Wheelchair rental** Yes. **Baby-stroller rental** Yes. **Lockers** Yes. **Pet kennels** No. **Rain check** Yes. **Private tours** No.

DESCRIPTION AND COMMENTS An amusement park taken to the highest level, Great America has an American-heritage theme, with six zones devoted to different epochs in our history. But the themes are merely window dressing: this place is really about thrills. Some of its rides are so intense they leave parents a quivering mess, but 12- to 19-year-olds can't get enough—like the Drop Zone, the world's tallest free-fall ride, and Top Gun, where you'll experience a zero-gravity barrel roll and 360-degree vertical loop,

unofficial **TIP**
Don't expect cool San Francisco weather at Great America—it's an entirely different climate, demanding plenty of sunscreen, drinking water, and hats in summertime.

among other psychological and physiological challenges. Those seeking slightly less terrifying thrills have lots more to choose from, including the IMAX films (which can be too intense for little ones), a few fun water-rapids rides (expect to get wet), and the famed Grizzly, Northern California's largest wooden roller coaster. The newest adventure, Survivor, is billed as "the world's first reality coaster" and is an intense, interactive, spinning-top ride that made us woozy just looking at it from a distance.

Although ultimately this place is really best for kids age 10 and up, young ones are hardly neglected. They get their own area, KidZville, with small-scale rides, a cartoon carousel, a play area, and wandering Hanna-Barbera characters like Scooby-Doo; the live music and ice shows are good for all ages as well. And our second-grader went wild for Nickelodeon's Central, where she got slimed. In the summertime, Boomerang Bay adds a water-park element, and it has play areas for young kids, too.

If you don't want to succumb to the pricey, junky food in the park, make use of the pleasant picnic area outside the front gates.

Raging Waters

APPEAL BY AGE	PRESCHOOL ★★★★	GRADE SCHOOL ★★★★★	TEENS ★★★★★
YOUNG ADULTS ★★★★		OVER 30 ★★★★	SENIORS ★★★

2333 South White Road, San Jose; ☎ 408-238-9900; www.rwsplash.com

Hours Mid-June–Labor Day: weekdays, 10:30 a.m.–6 p.m.; weekends, 10:30 a.m.–7 p.m.; May, early June, and September: weekends only, 10 a.m.–6 p.m. **Admission** $26 over 48" tall, $16 seniors age 55 and older, $20 under 48" tall, free for children age 2 and under; after 3 p.m. $19 over 48" tall, $14 under 48" tall; parking $6; double tube rental $6, single tube rental $4, all-day locker rental $5. **Touring time** Average 6–8 hours; minimum 4 hours. **Rainy-day touring** Okay. **Restaurants** Food service. **Alcoholic beverages** No. **Disabled access** No. **Wheelchair rental** No. **Baby-stroller rental** No. **Lockers** Yes. **Pet kennels** No. **Rain check** No. **Private tours** No.

DESCRIPTION AND COMMENTS Like its sister Raging Waters in San Dimas (see Part Three, Los Angeles and Vicinity), this huge water park with its many twisting, intense slides appeals to teens and preteens, but you'll also find some moderate slides, a few little-kids-only areas, some not-for-thrill-seekers quiet pools, and a "lazy river" for tube floating. Every vacationing kid deserves a day in a water park, and if you find yourself in the San Jose area in the peak of summer, you'll be desperate for a dunk in the wave pool, too.

 ## The Tech Museum of Innovation

APPEAL BY AGE	PRESCHOOL ★	GRADE SCHOOL ★★★★	TEENS ★★★★★
YOUNG ADULTS ★★★★★		OVER 30 ★★★★	SENIORS ★★★★

201 South Market Street, San Jose; ☎ 408-294-8324; www.thetech.org

Hours Daily, 10 a.m.–5 p.m.; closed several days in September for annual mainte-nance (check ahead for dates); closed Thanksgiving and Christmas Days. **Admission** $16 ages 13–64, $15 seniors age 65 and older, $13 for children ages 3–12; admission includes IMAX movie. **Touring time** Average 4 hours; minimum 2 hours. **Rainy-day touring** Yes. **Restaurants** No. **Alcoholic beverages** No. **Disabled access** Yes. **Wheelchair rental** Yes. **Baby-stroller rental** No. **Lockers** No. **Pet kennels** No. **Rain check** No. **Private tours** No.

DESCRIPTION AND COMMENTS   Here in the birthplace of high-tech, this won-drous warehouse of gadgets and tools encompasses more than 132,000 square feet, throughout which kids and adults can try out or step into or peer through all sorts of really cool scientific devices. More than 240 interactive displays are found in dozens of themed exhibits, many of which have changed recently as part of a large-scale updating. Our kids loved Superhero Science, a lively show and exhibit that demystifies the science behind superpowers. Another new exhibit, NetPl@net, pushes the boundaries of how people use the Internet—a kid, for instance, can arm wrestle a kid at another science museum in New York or Alaska. And still another, the Silicon Workshop, allows kids to learn about microchip programming by programming their own Mr. Potato Head. In the ocean section, you can sit in a mini-submarine, put your arm into a full-size model of a deep-sea diving suit, and manipulate its claw. In the Life Tech section, you learn about DNA and genetics and get to take a virtual trip through the Visible Man. Elsewhere you can do everything from make a movie in a digital studio to go crazy in the high-tech Imag-ination Playground.

unofficial **TIP**
The Tech Museum is a most worthy day-trip destination from San Francisco.

   Curious adults will be as enthralled with this place as their kids, so allow plenty of time to explore and experience. The entry fee includes admission to the special IMAX Dome Theater, the first of its kind in Northern California, with an eight-story-tall domed screen and wrap-around sound.

▌ FAMILY-FRIENDLY RESTAURANTS

Rosy's at the Beach
17320 Monterey Road, Morgan Hill; ☎ 408-778-0551

Meals served Breakfast, lunch, and dinner. **Cuisine** American. **Entree range** $8–$25. **Kids' menu** Yes. **Reservations** Recommended. **Payment** All major credit cards.

Rosy and Rich Bergin's restaurant isn't actually on the beach, but it is con-veniently located right off the 101 Freeway in Morgan Hill, south of San Jose. It also has a swell beachy vibe, with surfboards, beach umbrellas, tropical cocktails, and the seductive aromas of cioppino and fish and chips. The Bergins spent years as fish-market proprietors before becoming restaurateurs, so the quality of their grilled fresh fish, seafood chowders, and famous salmon tacos is first rate. There's a good kids' menu, and the prices are moderate.

Sweet Peas
453 North Santa Cruz Avenue, Los Gatos; ☎ 408-354-3144

Meals served Breakfast, lunch, and dinner. **Cuisine** American. **Entree range** $5–$10. **Kids' menu** No. **Reservations** Not accepted. **Payment** All major credit cards.

This friendly, order-at-the-counter place in the fetching little town of Los Gatos is one of the best cafes in the San Jose area, featuring local products and family-friendly fare: smoothies, Belgian waffles, all kinds of crepes, all sorts of sandwiches (try the chicken pesto), omelets, homemade soups, and fabulous cookies and cakes, some from old German family recipes. The only catch is the limited seating—just a couple of tables on a patio—so be prepared to wait.

PART SEVEN

GOLD COUNTRY

CALIFORNIA'S GOLD COUNTRY MIGHT SOUND to the uninitiated like a vaguely educational collection of musty historic sites. And indeed, parents intent on reading every paragraph of every historic marker will certainly bore their kids in this region. But the rest of us can have a grand, old-fashioned time in the villages and towns along Highway 49, panning for gold, riding horses, exploring caves, scrambling around ruins, walking Native American trails, and even white-water rafting.

The Gold Country consists of a string of picturesque small towns and cities strung along the grassy foothills of the **Sierra Nevada** east of **Sacramento.** It's the area called the Mother Lode by the '49ers, the thousands of gold seekers who rushed here from all over the world after John Marshall's 1848 discovery of gold at John Sutter's mill.

The area is particularly rich in Chinese American history, because the Sacramento Delta was originally reclaimed by Chinese laborers, and many of these Chinese railroad workers went on to become miners. The Delta town of **Locke** was founded by Chinese immigrants, and Gold Country landmarks include 100-year-old buildings that housed stores owned by Chinese pioneers.

We'll concentrate here on the former mining boomtowns along Highway 49 between **Nevada City** and **Columbia.** Sacramento is our gateway city and could be used as an airport–rental car starting point, but families might also consider touring the southern part of Gold Country before or after some time in Yosemite. (Yosemite is covered in Part Five, The Sierra Nevada.) Kids of at least elementary-school age will enjoy Gold Country the most. They should be old enough to want to pan for gold or ride a mule.

The region is anchored by six fascinating state parks, each worthy of a half-day stop. In **Grass Valley,** in the northern part of Gold Country, you'll find **Empire Mine State Historic Park,** the site of one of the oldest and richest gold mines in California. In Sacramento, the riverfront *gold country*

0   10 mi

0   10 km

TAHOE NATIONAL FOREST

● **PARKS**

1. American River Parkway
2. Calaveras Big Trees State Park
3. Chaw'Se Indian Grinding Rock State Historic Park
4. Columbia State Historic Park
5. Discovery Park
6. Empire Mine State Historic Park
7. Malakoff Diggins State Historic Park
8. Old Sacramento Historic Park
9. Sutter's Fort State Historic Park
10. William Land Park

99

5

Rio Linda

193

6 7

80

Applegate

Newcastle

To Nevada City & Grass Valley

Foresthill

Loomis

Rocklin

Auburn

FOLSOM

Rubicon River

80

Roseville

Granite Bay

STATE REC. AREA

49

193

Georgetown

Carmichael

Folsom Reservoir

193

8 9

Coloma

E9 1

Sacramento

American River

Marshall Gold Discovery State Hist. Park

5

Placerville

10

Rancho Cordova

Folsom

Florin

El Dorado Hills

Cameron Park

50

Diamond Springs

99

Elk Grove

16

El Dorado

5

Cosumnes River

49

E16

E13

Plymouth

E16

Galt

104

49

88

Lodi

99

124

Amador City

South Fork American River

Ione

Sutter Creek

Indian Grinding Rocks State Hist. Park

88

Mokelumne River

Comanche Res.

3

Volcano

88

Lockeford

Jackson

West Point

TOIYABE NATIONAL FOREST

88

12

Pardee Res.

26

Mokelumne River

Salt Springs Res.

26

Valley Springs

Mokelumne Hill

Linden

26

New Hogan Res.

San Andreas

4

Woodward Res.

J6

J14

Mercer Caverns

49

Arnold

Calaveras Big Trees State Park

STANISLAUS NATIONAL FOREST

4

J7

Murphys

4

2

J6

New Melones Lake U.S. Bureau of Reclamation

Angels Camp

Stanislaus River

Beardsleys Res.

108

Escalon

4

49

Columbia State Historic Park

J14

New Melones Lake

Tullock Res.

Tuttletown

4

Columbia

Sugar Pine

Mi-Wuk Village

Pinecrest

Oakdale

Jamestown

Sonora

108

Twain Harte

TOIYABE NATIONAL FOREST

Riverbank

108

132

Waterford

Modesto Lake

49

Tuolumne

Tuolumne River

Cherry Lake

YOSEMITE NATIONAL PARK

132

Turlock Lake St. Rec. Area

Lake Don Pedro

120

Lake Eleanor

Hetch Hetchy Res.

J17

Turlock Lake

132

Grand Canyon of the Tuolumne

McConnell St. Rec. Area

J16

Lake McLure

Couterville

Sacramento

The Gold Country

Livingston

49

SIERRA NATIONAL FOREST

99

Winton

59

Merced River

San Francisco

CALIFORNIA

140

Atwater

J7

J16

Bagby Rec. Area

140

El Portal

Los Angeles

Merced

140

✈ Airport

🌲 State Park

Old Sacramento State Historic Park has 110 restored or reconstructed buildings, and **Sutter Fort State Historic Park** has a blacksmith shop, jail, and other gold rush–era environments. In the middle part of the region is **Indian Grinding Rock State Historic Park,** once the seasonal meeting place of the Miwok tribe and the only California state park that focuses primarily on Native American culture. A short easterly side trip from Highway 49 brings you to **Calaveras Big Trees State Park,** where you will see majestic giant sequoias. In the southern section of the Mother Lode is **Columbia State Historic Park,** the most fully preserved of the gold rush towns, whose old brick buildings now house museums, shops, cafes, hotels, and a theater.

unofficial **TIP**
Families should consider touring the southern part of Gold Country before or after some time in Yosemite.

Between these main attractions, various tiny gold rush towns each offer one or two interesting sites to explore, as well as enjoyable activities like cave tours, hiking, and berry picking. The 19th-century historic districts of the towns are usually surrounded by 21st-century American small towns, commercial districts, and residential areas, so travelers won't lack access to motels, mini-marts, fast food, and, in some cases, fine dining.

Allow three days and two overnights in either case. For the northern part, begin with a day and a night in Sacramento, then drive on to Grass Valley and Nevada City for another day and a night. Add a day for such activities as river rafting, if you can. In the south, choose any of the gold-rush towns as a base depending on your desired activities (historic sights, cave exploration, river rafting) for a one-day add-on (Columbia State Park only) to a Yosemite trip or a two- or three-day exploration of several different towns.

GETTING THERE

BY PLANE Sacramento International Airport (☎ 916-874-0700; **www.sacairports.org**) is 15 minutes from downtown Sacramento.

BY TRAIN Amtrak offers direct service on the *California Zephyr* east from the Bay Area and west from Chicago, and on the *Coast Starlight* south from Vancouver and Seattle and north from San Diego and Los Angeles (☎ 800-872-7245; **www.amtrak.com**). Commuter trains also run several times daily from the Bay Area and San Jose.

BY CAR From the San Francisco Bay Area, take **Interstate 80** west to **Interstate 5** north. From the L.A. area, take I-5 north. From Reno–North Lake Tahoe, take I-80 west; from Reno via South Lake Tahoe, take **Interstate 50** west. From Yosemite, take **Highway 99** north.

HOW TO GET INFORMATION BEFORE YOU GO

• **Amador County Chamber of Commerce** 125 Peek Street, P.O. Box 596, Jackson 94562; ☎ 209-223-0350; **www.amadorcountychamber.com**.

- **Calaveras Visitors Bureau** P.O. Box 637, Angels Camp 95222; ☎ 209-736-0049 or 800-225-3764; **www.gocalaveras.com.**
- **Grass Valley and Nevada County Chamber of Commerce** 248 Mill Street, Grass Valley 95945; ☎ 530-273-4667; **www.grassvalley chamber.com.**
- **Nevada City Chamber of Commerce** 153 Main Street, Nevada City 95959; ☎ 530-265-2692 or 800-655-6569; **www.nevadacity chamber.com.**
- **Old Sacramento Visitor Information Center** 1004 Second Street, Old Sacramento 95814; ☎ 916-442-7644; **www.oldsacramento.com.**
- **Sacramento Convention and Visitors Bureau** 1303 J Street, Suite 600, Sacramento 95814; ☎ 916-808-7777 or 800-292-2334; **www.discovergold.org.**

A **CALENDAR** *of* **FESTIVALS** *and* **EVENTS**

January

MARTIN LUTHER KING COMMUNITY CELEBRATIONS Sacramento. Parades, activities; ☎ 916-920-8655.

February

CHINESE NEW YEAR Celebration Isleton, Sacramento. Parades, music, street fair; ☎ 916-777-5880.

March

MARIPOSA STORYTELLING FESTIVAL Mariposa. ☎ 209-966-3155 or ☎ 800-903-9936; **www.arts- mariposa.org/storytelling.html.**

April

FESTIVAL DE LA FAMILIA Old Sacramento and Downtown Plaza. Held the last Sunday of each April, this is a hugely popular festival celebrating the heritage of more than two dozen Latin American countries. Puppet shows, games, storytelling, music, dancing, and food; ☎ 916-326-5520; **www.festivaldelafamilia.com.**

OPENING DAY Sacramento Rivercats Minor League Baseball. Season goes through September at brand-new Raley Field, an old-fashioned ballpark complete with children's play area; 400 Ballpark Drive; ☎ 916-371-HITS; **www.rivercats.com.**

PIONEER TRADERS' AND CRAFTS FAIR Sutter's Fort Sacramento. Modern-day craftspeople offer 1840s-era goods for sale; ☎ 916-445-4422.

May

FIREMAN'S MUSTER Columbia. Vintage hand-pumped fire engines, a parade, a kids' bucket brigade, a firefighter "shootout," and more in this weekend-long shindig; ☎ 209-532-0150; **www.columbiagazette.com/ muster.html.**

JUMPING FROG JUBILEE Angels Camp. Continuing the tradition begun by Mark Twain's story, this famed frog-jumping contest is held the third week in May as part of the Calaveras County Fair, which also boasts pig races, carnival rides, and a kids' play area; ☎ 209-736-2561; **www.frogtown.org.**

SACRAMENTO COUNTY FAIR Cal Expo, Capital City Freeway and Exposition Boulevard, Sacramento. ☎ 916-263-2975; **www.sacfair.com.**

June

CRAWDAD FESTIVAL Sacramento. ☎ 916-777-5880; **www.crawdad festival.org.**

PLACER COUNTY FAIR Highway 65, Roseville. ☎ 916-786-2023; **www.placercountyfair.org.**

July

FOURTH OF JULY PARADE AND CELEBRATION Mokelumne Hill. ☎ 209-286-1401; **www.gocalaveras.com.**

SUTTER CREEK OLD FASHION FOURTH OF JULY Minnie Provis Park, Sutter Creek. Children's parade, games, picnic; ☎ 209-267-1344; **www.amadorcountychamber.com.**

August

CALIFORNIA STATE FAIR Cal Expo, Capital City Freeway and Exposition Boulevard, Sacramento. One of the nation's largest state fairs, with rodeo riding, fireworks, and Kid's Park; ☎ 916-263-3247; **www.bigfun.org.**

September

GOLD COUNTRY FAIR Auburn. Founded in 1889, this Placer County fair has everything from thrill rides to livestock judging to juggling performances; ☎ 530-823-4533; **www.goldcountryfair.com.**

GOLD RUSH DAYS Old Sacramento. Old Sacramento is closed to cars and its streets are covered with dirt during this four-day annual Labor Day event. Period-appropriate tents and booths include blacksmith's tent, jail, and apothecary; ☎ 916-808-7777; **www.discovergold.org.**

NATIVE AMERICAN FESTIVAL Indian Grinding Rock State Park. On the weekend following the fourth Friday in September, Native American tribes gather to celebrate their heritage with food, dances, and games; ☎ 209-296-7488.

October

SPOOKOMOTIVE TRAIN RIDES Old Sacramento. Halloween season is celebrated with a pumpkin patch at the railroad museum and a train ride with ghouls and goblins on board; ☎ 916-445-6645; **www .californiastaterailroadmuseum.org.**

December

CORNISH CHRISTMAS STREET CELEBRATION Grass Valley. Held one evening a week in December, this honors the Cornish heritage of many in this former mining center and includes performances by the Grass Valley Cornish Choir and street stalls with traditional foods and crafts; ☎ 530-272-8315; **www.ncgold.com.**

LAMPLIGHT TOUR Columbia. The town re-creates a different year in its history each December, and docents lead visitors through town by lamplight to "eavesdrop" on 19th-century goings-on; ☎ 209-532-0150.

The BEST PARKS

AMERICAN RIVER PARKWAY This meandering park runs through Sacramento and its suburbs along the banks of the American River for more than 30 miles. The **Jedediah Smith Memorial Bicycle Trail** winds for 23 miles from Old Sacramento to Beals Point in the town of Folsom. It's also great for jogging, horseback riding, picnics, river rafting, fishing, and birding; ☎ 916-875-6961 or ☎ 916-875-6672; **www.sacparks.net.** To rent bikes, try **American River Bike Centers** (256 Florin Road, Sacramento; ☎ 916-427-6199; **www.americanriverbikes.com**).

DISCOVERY PARK This Sacramento County park, situated at the confluence of the Sacramento and American rivers, is near Old Sacramento and is another starting point for bike trails. Boat launching, picnic area, horseshoes, archery, restrooms, barbecues; ☎ 916-875-6672.

 STATE HISTORIC PARKS Because many state parks in Gold Country are also the region's primary historical attractions, we've placed their individual descriptions under "Attractions" in each section. We've covered **Old Sacramento State Historic Park, Sutter's Fort State Historic Park, Empire Mine State Historic Park, Indian Grinding Rock State Historic Park, Calaveras Big Trees State Park,** and **Columbia State Historic Park.** In addition, **Malakoff Diggins State Historical Park** is discussed under the listing for Chute Hill Campground in "Family Lodging" in the Northern Gold Country section. For more information, go to **www.parks.ca.gov.**

unofficial **TIP**
The best thing about Land Park is **Fairytale Town,** a wonderful amusement park for the very young.

WILLIAM LAND PARK The 15-acre **Sacramento Zoo** (Sutterville and 17th Avenue, Sacramento; ☎ 916-264-5888; **www.saczoo.com;** weekday admission: $7 adults, $5 children ages 3 to 12; weekends and holidays: $8 adults, $5.50 children) is located here, as well as a public golf course, picnic area, and amusement area. For information about the terrific **Fairytale Town,** see the listing under "Attractions" in the Sacramento section of this chapter.

FAMILY OUTDOOR ADVENTURES

BICYCLING See American River Parkway under "The Best Parks." Also, self-guided and escorted bike tours along with equipment are available at **Bike Sacramento** in Old Town next to the river trail; ☎ 916-444-0200.

CAVING Several cave systems first explored by miners in the 1850s are open to the public today. The world down under can be creepy or awesome, depending on your child's perspective. For an introduction to caves, check out **Mercer Caverns** near Murphys (☎ 209-728-2101; **www.mercercaverns.com**), which is open summers, Sunday through Thursday, 9 a.m. to 5 p.m.; Friday and Saturday, 9 a.m. to 6 p.m.; from October 1 through Memorial Day weekend, hours are daily, 10 a.m. to 4:30 p.m. Admission is $11 for adults and kids over age 12, and $6.50 for children ages 5 to 12.

An exhilarating experience for teens is to descend into **Moaning Cavern** on a 180-foot rappel (note that there are special rules for kids ages 12 to 17 that include need for parent's authorization or presence). Moaning Cavern is open year-round and also offers guided 45-minute walking tours (includes steep spiral staircase) and a three-hour Adventure Tour (reservations required) that involves climbing and narrow passages. General admission is $12.50 adults, $6.25 children ages 6 to 12. Located near Vallecito (☎ 209-736-2708; **www.caverntours.com**). The same company offers tours of **Black Chasm Cave** at 15701 Pioneer–Volcano Road near Volcano. The 50-minute family tour of Black Chasm costs $12.50 for adults and $6.25 for kids. There's also "gemstone mining" for the little ones at both Moaning Cavern and Black Chasm.

unofficial **TIP**
Even the least water-savvy family can enjoy an afternoon on a flat-bottomed patio boat or a few lazy days on a houseboat on the Sacramento River Delta.

HOUSEBOATING The Sacramento River Delta area offers about a thousand square miles of calm-water waterways. You can drive a houseboat more or less as you would, say, a 1958 Buick, while the kids fish, sunbathe, and watch for herons and other waterbirds. Tie up at a small-town marina on one of the many islands or to a tree stump and swim or picnic on shore.

Houseboats are usually offered for three to seven nights and can sleep one or two families; patio or fishing boats can be rented for a day's water play. Among the houseboat companies renting in the Delta: **Forever Resorts** (☎ 800-255-5561 or 480-998-1981; **www.forever resorts.com**) and **Seven Crown Resorts** (☎ 800-752-9669; **www.seven crown.com**). For one-day boat rentals, contact **Paradise Point Marina**

(8095 Rio Blanco Road, Stockton; ☎ 209-952-1000 or 800-752-9669; **www.sevencrown.com/lakes/california_delta**).

RIVER RAFTING With older, water-safe kids, you can up the excitement and take a white-water rafting trip, ranging in thrill level from mild to wild. There are several popular rafting areas on the American, Stanislaus, and Tuolumne rivers in Gold Country, heading out of such rendezvous points as Columa, Angels Camp, Sacramento, and Stockton. Typically ranging from two days to a week, trips are offered from April through October; the wildest rapids are found in early spring, when runoff is greatest. Some outfitters offer quickie half-day rides. In many overnight trips, you camp out in style en route, with cooking and camp chores provided by staff members; at the journey's end, a van will take you back to the starting point. Some companies have overnight packages with nearby bed-and-breakfast inns or motels.

It is generally recommended that children under age 12 go on a raft that's powered by a guide; minimum ages vary by the excursion, with age 6 being about the youngest. Fares range from $70 to $200 per person for half- or all-day excursions and include meals and transportation back to the rendezvous point.

We know several families who have had excellent white-water adventures with an outfitter called **A Whitewater Connection;** (☎ 530-622-6446 or 800-336-7238; **www.whitewaterconnection.com**). Its home base is a beautiful 40-acre private campground (complete with horseshoes, fishing, and gold panning) alongside the south fork of the American River in the heart of Gold Country, next to Marshall Gold Discovery State Park. Kids over age 6 can participate in the Class III trips, which range from a half day to two days; there's also a great discounted two-day trip for families with little kids. Mom gets to go rafting one day and Dad the other, while a parent plays at camp with the little ones. Some other rafting companies include **Whitewater Excitement** (☎ 800-750-2386; **www.whitewaterexcitement.com**); **All-Outdoors Whitewater Rafting Trips** (☎ 925-932-8993 or 800-247-2387; **www.aorafting.com**); **Arta River Trips** (☎ 209-962-7873; **www.arta.org**); and **O.A.R.S. River Trips** (☎ 209-736-4677 or 800-346-6277; **www.oars.com**).

THE SCHOOLHOUSES OF GOLD COUNTRY

NOTHING WILL BRING THE GOLD RUSH ERA ALIVE for your kids more than the sight of the wonderful one-room schoolhouses of the region. Almost every historic town has one, some fully restored and open for pretending, some shuttered and awaiting renovation, and a few turned into private homes. Each is named for its town.

ALTAVILLE SCHOOL (1858) is red brick with dainty white trim; it was used until 1950 and is open to visitors.

COLOMA SCHOOL HOUSE is part of Marshall Gold Discovery State Historic Park and can be found, like other historic buildings, by referring to the guide map available at the Gold Discovery Museum; ☎ 530-642-3470.

COLUMBIA SCHOOL HOUSE is at the north end of Columbia and makes for a nice walk through the residential blocks (imagine living in a state historic park) up the hill to the building that housed the state's first public school. Built in 1860, it's a two-story brick building outfitted with the desks, inkwells, and slates that were used by 19th-century children; the old town cemetery is located in back; ☎ 209-532-0150.

FIDDLETOWN SCHOOLHOUSE (circa 1850) is a beautiful shell of a building, waiting to be restored. It has the classic schoolhouse shape with the little bell tower.

MURPHYS GRAMMAR SCHOOL (1860) was, until it closed in 1973, California's oldest public school. It's on a hill near the corner of Main and Jones streets and awaits restoration.

OLD SACRAMENTO SCHOOLHOUSE is a yellow wood-frame building, beautifully restored and dramatically situated at the waterfront with Tower Bridge rising behind it. Kids can swing in the schoolyard (note the outhouse), and the classroom's open for exploring Monday through Saturday, 10 a.m. to 4 p.m., and Sunday, noon to 4 p.m. Admission is free; ☎ 916-483-8818.

SUTTER CREEK SCHOOL (1871), an imposing two-story stone building on a hill east of the town center, is fun to drive past.

VOLCANO SCHOOL has been impeccably restored and is now a private residence. Though the building is not open to the public, it does have a historical marker.

KID-COVETED SOUVENIRS

Hats Bonnets for the girls can be expensive but may be cherished; miners' felt floppy hats or various historically inaccurate but fun versions of coonskin and cowboy hats are popular with boys.

Minerals Everywhere, you'll find gold (and fake gold, of course). Little vials of water with microscopic gold flecks fascinate kids and are inexpensive or come from their own gold-panning efforts (for which they'll be charged a fee by a whiskered miner).

Old bottles Gold Country is dotted with antiques shops to lure the tourist, and if parents can't resist browsing, kids might have fun picking out an old glass bottle of curious shape and color (but not of great age if you want it to be affordable).

SACRAMENTO

ALTHOUGH IT SEEMS OFF THE BEATEN TRACK because of its inland location, Sacramento was once a major hub thanks to its busy riverfront (now a vital outdoor recreation area) and its position as a gateway to Gold Country, the Sierra, and the agricultural valley areas of the state. As the state capital, it's often filled with California schoolkids visiting the buildings where legislators make the laws, and its **Old Sacramento** and **Sutter's Fort state historic parks** allow kids to visit environments that bring history to life. The **DASH trolley,** linking tourist areas and hotels, is free from 11 a.m. to 3 p.m. daily; ☎ 916-321-BUSS; **www.sacrt.com.**

For vacationing families, Sacramento can be a convenient base for several days of varied activities in the region, but we don't recommend an extended stay in the city unless you're visiting friends. Accommodations, although often very competitive in price, are geared to the capital's many business visitors, and only a few hotels (see below) are located in family-friendly areas (most of the chains are in desolate, freeway-adjacent locations). Bed-and-breakfast inns are isolated in quiet residential areas throughout the city.

Instead, plan a convenient overnight at the beginning or end of a few days devoted to houseboating on the Delta or exploring Gold Country, especially if you're arriving in the area by plane.

FAMILY LODGING

Holiday Inn, Capitol Plaza
300 J Street, Sacramento; ☎ 916-446-0100; www.jqh.com; $80–$122, suites $175–$350; children under age 18 stay free

Located at Capitol Plaza, this 364-room motel is in a mixed-use area that includes an upscale shopping plaza with movie theaters, restaurants, a pedestrian walkway (under the freeway) to Old Sacramento, and pedestrian access to the city's business district. From here your teens can walk to the movies while you and the toddlers play in the pool, and then you can all stroll out to one of the lively restaurants nearby. There is a coffee shop with a kids' menu; room service has its own menu that includes kids' items.

sacramento

FAMILY LODGING
1. Holiday Inn,
   Capitol Plaza
2. Radisson Hotel

ATTRACTIONS
3. California State
   Railroad Museum
4. Discover Museum
5. Fairytale Town
6. Old Sacramento
   State Historic
   Park
7. Sacramento Zoo
8. Six Flags
   Waterworld USA
9. Sutter's Fort State
   Historic Park—
   California State
   Indian Museum

FAMILY-FRIENDLY RESTAURANTS
10. California Fats
11. Delta King
    Pilothouse
    Restaurant
12. Fat City
13. Tower Cafe
14. Willie's Burgers

Five rooms are suites with refrigerators. Babysitting is available. There are no special kids' programs.

Radisson Hotel
500 Leisure Lane, Sacramento; ☎ 916-922-2020 or 800-333-3333; www.radissonsac.com; $98–$230

One of the few resortlike lodgings in the area, this 309-room motor inn is situated on 18 acres with a small lake; some rooms have patios or decks. Kids are welcomed, and they stay free in their parents' room, with an extra charge for roll-away beds. Some suites, a pool, bike rentals, pedalboats.

ATTRACTIONS

 California State Railroad Museum

APPEAL BY AGE	PRESCHOOL ★★	GRADE SCHOOL ★★★	TEENS ★★
YOUNG ADULTS ★★		OVER 30 ★★★	SENIORS ★★★★

125 I Street, Old Sacramento; ☎ 916-445-6645 or 916-445-7387; www.californiastaterailroadmuseum.org

Hours Daily, 10 a.m.–5 p.m.; closed Thanksgiving, Christmas, and New Year's Day. **Admission** *Museum:* $4; children ages 16 and under, free. *Train ride:* $8 adults, $3 children ages 6–17, free for children age 5 and under. **Touring time** Average 3 hours; minimum 2 hours. **Rainy-day touring** Yes. **Restaurants** No. **Alcoholic beverages** No. **Disabled access** Yes. **Wheelchair rental** Yes. **Baby-stroller rental** No. **Lockers** No. **Pet kennels** No. **Rain check** No. **Private tours** No, but docents are available.

DESCRIPTION AND COMMENTS An impressive museum that grabs visitors in several ways, with movies, miniatures, and hands-on experiences. Displays include 21 restored locomotives and train cars, some of which you can walk through. Ticket allows for admission to the nearby restored Central Pacific Passenger Station, and on weekends April through September there are hourly six-mile-long steam train rides from the Central Pacific Freight Depot.

Discover Museum: The Sacramento Museum of History, Science, and Space Technology

APPEAL BY AGE	PRESCHOOL ★	GRADE SCHOOL ★★★	TEENS ★★★
YOUNG ADULTS ★★★		OVER 30 ★★	SENIORS ★★

History Center: 101 I Street, Old Sacramento; ☎ 916-264-7057
Science and Space Center: 3615 Auburn Boulevard; ☎ 916-575-3941; www.thediscovery.org

Hours *History Center:* June–August, daily, 10 a.m.–5 p.m.; September–May, Tuesday–Sunday, 10 a.m.–5 p.m. *Science and Space Center:* July–August, daily, 10 a.m.–5 p.m.; September–June, Tuesday–Friday, noon–5 p.m.; closed major holidays. **Admission** $5 adults, $4 seniors age 60 and over, $4 children ages 13–17, $3 children ages 4–12, children age 3 and under free. **Touring time** Average 1–2 hours; minimum 1 hour. **Rainy-day touring** Yes. **Restaurants** No. **Alcoholic beverages** No. **Disabled access** Yes. **Wheelchair rental** No. **Baby-stroller rental** No. **Lockers** No. **Pet kennels** No. **Rain check** No. **Private tours** No, but docents are available.

DESCRIPTION AND COMMENTS Two separate facilities—the Museum of History and the Science and Space Center—share management and a common hands-on approach. A visit to the History Center's Gold Gallery (entered through a miner's shaft) is a great way to kick off a driving tour of the Gold Country; it includes fun hands-on exhibits that allow kids to touch real gold and see a miner's cabin. In the Science Center, you'll find a planetarium, the Challenger Learning Center, and such rotating exhibits as the Bone Zone, an exploration of the human body. The Challenger Learning Center offers simulated missions on occasional Friday evenings, 5:45 to 8:30 p.m.; $20, $18 each for two people, $15 each for three or more people. Reservations: ☎ 916-485-8836.

Fairytale Town

APPEAL BY AGE	PRESCHOOL ★★★★★	GRADE SCHOOL ★★★	TEENS ★
YOUNG ADULTS ★	OVER 30 ★		SENIORS ★

3901 Land Park Drive, Sacramento; ☎ 916-265-5233; www.fairytaletown.org

Hours Summer: daily, 9 a.m.–4 p.m.; November–February: Thursday–Sunday, 10 a.m.–4 p.m. **Admission** $4, children age 2 and under free. **Touring time** Average 2 hours; minimum 1 hour. **Rainy-day touring** Yes, but you'll get wet. **Restaurants** No. **Alcoholic beverages** No. **Disabled access** Some. **Wheelchair rental** No. **Baby-stroller rental** No. **Lockers** No. **Pet kennels** No. **Rain check** No. **Private tours** No.

DESCRIPTION AND COMMENTS Located across the street from the Sacramento Zoo, Fairytale Town makes a wonderful stop for families with toddlers to kids about age 8. *Play* is the operative word here—the 2.5-acre nonprofit park comprises some 25 play sets, where kids can pretend, climb, slide, and explore. Inspired by children's literature, the fun includes the Sherwood Forest play fort, a slide down Jack's beanstalk, a race along the Crooked Mile path (actually an eighth of a mile), a slide down Alice's Rabbit Hole, and an exploration of Mr. McGregor's Garden. The petting-zoo animals include three Nigerian dwarf goats (the Three Billy Goats Gruff), Peter Rabbit and his sisters, and three Vietnamese pot-bellied pigs (the Three Little Pigs); time your visit for the afternoon if your kids want to witness feeding time.

Old Sacramento State Historic Park

APPEAL BY AGE	PRESCHOOL ★★	GRADE SCHOOL ★★★	TEENS ★★
YOUNG ADULTS ★	OVER 30 ★★		SENIORS ★★★

Four blocks bounded by Capitol Mall, I Street, Second Street, and the Sacramento River; ☎ 916-442-7644; www.oldsacramento.com

Hours Vary by area and attraction. **Admission** Free to area; some attractions charge. **Touring time** Average 4 hours; minimum 2 hours. **Rainy-day touring** Not great for enjoying the walk around district. **Restaurants** Yes, many. **Alcoholic beverages** In some cafes and clubs. **Disabled access** Yes. **Wheelchair rental** No. **Baby-stroller rental** No. **Lockers** No. **Pet kennels** No. **Rain check** No. **Private tours** No.

DESCRIPTION AND COMMENTS This restored historic district has an especially pleasurable area at the waterfront, where wooden walkways face the river. Here you'll find Tower Bridge, the unique *Delta King* paddlewheel boat hotel, and boat docks where visiting cruise ships and yachts tie up for an hour or a day. The area is home to several museums, including the California State Railroad Museum (see profile), the California Military Museum, and the Discovery Museum (see profile). But overall, there are more souvenir shops and cafes than historic points of interest, so the effect can sometimes be of a completely commercial, tourist-tacky area. We recommend a morning visit with a stroll around the waterfront, followed by a museum visit, lunch, and a bit of shop-crawling.

May through October, the River Otter Water Taxi (ticket booth near Rio City Cafe) departs several times a day on an hour-long river loop ($6 adults, $4 kids); ☎ 916-446-7704; **www.riverotter.com.**

Sacramento Zoo

APPEAL BY AGE	PRESCHOOL ★★★★	GRADE SCHOOL ★★★★	TEENS ★★
YOUNG ADULTS ★★		OVER 30 ★★	SENIORS ★★

3930 West Land Park Drive; ☎ 916-264-5888; www.saczoo.com

Hours February–October: daily, 9 a.m.–4 p.m.; November–January: daily, 10 a.m.–4 p.m.; closed Thanksgiving and Christmas Days. **Admission** $7.50 adults, $5 children ages 3–12, free for children age 2 and under. **Touring time** Average 3–4 hours; minimum 1 hour. **Rainy-day touring** Yes. **Restaurants** Snack bars. **Alcoholic beverages** No. **Disabled access** Yes. **Wheelchair rental** Yes, free. **Baby-stroller rental** Yes. **Lockers** No. **Pet kennels** No. **Rain check** No. **Private tours** No.

DESCRIPTION AND COMMENTS Zoo camps and overnight safaris are among the special kids' activities at this friendly, midsize (400 animals) zoo. There are weekend hippo, giraffe, and chimpanzee talks. Key to Adventure is a new, easy audio tour: A key activates "talking boxes" at certain exhibits, so you can hear fun facts, stories, and songs about the animals. If you have little ones, buy a combination ticket for the zoo and the neighboring Fairytale Town, a swell play place for the under-age-7 set.

Six Flags Waterworld USA

APPEAL BY AGE	PRESCHOOL ★★★★★	GRADE SCHOOL ★★★★★	TEENS ★★★★★
YOUNG ADULTS ★★★★		OVER 30 ★★★	SENIORS ★★

Cal Expo, 1600 Exposition Boulevard; ☎ 916-924-3747; www.sixflags.com

Hours Mid-June–Labor Day: daily, 10:30 a.m.–6 p.m.; hours and days vary at other times of the year. **Admission** $25 adults, $14 seniors, $20 for children under 48" tall, free for children age 2 and under; tubes $2; parking $7. **Touring time** Average 5 hours; minimum 3 hours. **Rainy-day touring** No. **Restaurants** Yes. **Alcoholic beverages** Yes. **Disabled access** Yes. **Wheelchair rental** No. **Baby-stroller rental** No. **Lockers** Yes, $5. **Pet kennels** No. **Rain check** Yes. **Private tours** No.

DESCRIPTION AND COMMENTS The summer heat here is unrelieved by ocean breezes. We love water parks for a great change from sightseeing, a chance for adults to read and talk, a safe environment for kids to splash, and a cool, summery time for all. Water-world has all the features a family looks for in a water park: a wave pool, a wading area for toddlers, a moving-water river-tubing area, an activity lagoon, and, of course, slides ranging from the modest to the terrifying. The most popular is the Hono-lulu Halfpipe, a four-story "wave" slide that's a good screamer.

*un*official **TIP**
The summer heat in this part of the state can be startling, even overwhelming—which is why a water park can make a good destination.

Sutter's Fort State Historic Park and California State Indian Museum

APPEAL BY AGE	PRESCHOOL ★★	GRADE SCHOOL ★★★	TEENS ★★
YOUNG ADULTS ★★	OVER 30 ★★		SENIORS ★★★

Sutter's Fort: 2701 L Street at 27th; ☎ **916-445-4422**
Indian Museum: 2618 K Street; ☎ **916-324-0971;**
general information: ☎ **916-324-0539; www.parks.ca.gov**

Hours Daily, 10 a.m.–5 p.m.; closed holidays. **Admission** Fort and Indian Museum separate admissions: $4 adults, $2 children ages 6–12; free children age 5 and under. **Touring time** Average 2 hours each; minimum 1 hour each. **Rainy-day touring** Yes. **Restaurants** No. **Alcoholic beverages** No. **Disabled access** Limited. **Wheelchair rental** No. **Baby-stroller rental** No. **Lockers** No. **Pet kennels** No. **Rain check** Yes. **Private tours** No.

DESCRIPTION AND COMMENTS Built by early California rancher John Sutter in 1839, this fort was aban-doned after one of Sutter's employees, James Mar-shall, found gold at a sawmill Sutter was building; within a year, everyone was looking for gold. Cos-tumed docents demonstrate spinning, weaving, and cooking in this reconstructed fort; the several buildings include a candle-making room, cooper-age, trading post, and blacksmith shop. The audio wands for a self-guided tour are free and fun.

*un*official **TIP**
Call first to find out when this state park has living-history events scheduled, because they provide kids with an engaging three-dimensional view of the past.

The California State Indian Museum is part of the complex and has exhibits that connect well with youngsters—featuring artifacts that include games, toys, feather baskets, and jewelry. It includes some hands-on exhibits.

Sutter's Fort Trade Store sells period toys, games, and clothing.

FAMILY-FRIENDLY RESTAURANTS

California Fats
1015 Front Street, Old Sacramento; ☎ 916-441-7966;
www.fatsrestaurants.com

Meals served Lunch and dinner. **Cuisine** Pacific Rim. **Entree range** Lunch, $8–$13; dinner, $10–$24. **Kids' menu** Yes. **Reservations** Accepted. **Payment** All major credit cards.

A chic spin-off of the legendary Frank Fat's, the Chinese restaurant that's fed legislators and lobbyists for years, this Old Town hot spot is more Pacific Rim than Chinese, serving things like Asian pizzas, seared ahi, and venison in cashew crust. The kids' menu includes the grilled-cheese basics, but it also offers a terrific chow mein. The restaurant is lively and handsome, decorated with photos of Sacramento's Chinese immigrants.

Delta King Pilothouse Restaurant
1000 Front Street, Old Sacramento; ☎ 916-441-4440;
www.deltaking.com

Meals served Lunch Monday–Saturday, dinner nightly, and Sunday buffet brunch. **Cuisine** American. **Entree range** Brunch, $20; lunch, $8–$10; dinner, $17–$30. **Kids' menu** $8; brunch, $10. **Reservations** Recommended, especially on weekends. **Payment** AE, MC, V.

When you see the historic landmark paddlewheeler at the dock in Old Town, your kids will clamor to go on board, but be forewarned: this is the kind of restaurant seniors select for a picturesque lunch or dinner, and noisy preschoolers will disrupt the atmosphere. With elementary-age or older kids, go ahead and give it a try, but know that the food doesn't live up to its slightly pretentious presentation—and besides, the views of the river can be had from the dock itself. On the other hand, it's a good bet for a one-grandparent, one-child brunch, lunch, or dinner that's to be a bit special.

Fat City
1001 Front Street, Old Sacramento; ☎ 916-446-6768;
www.fatsrestaurants.com

Meals served Lunch, dinner, and Sunday brunch. **Cuisine** American. **Entree range** Lunch and brunch, $8–$15; dinner, $12–$22. **Kids' menu** Yes. **Reservations** Accepted for large parties only. **Payment** AE, MC, V.

Run by the Fat family, descendants of Chinese-immigrant railroad workers and now the city's leading restaurateurs, Fat City is the best family-oriented restaurant in Old Town. It's a pretty place, with a fine view of the river and passing carriages. The straightforward California fare—salads, sandwiches, fresh fish, burgers—is quite good.

Tower Cafe

1518 Broadway, William Land Park; ☎ 916-441-0222

Meals served Breakfast, lunch, and dinner. **Cuisine** Californian. **Entree range** Breakfast, $5–$7; lunch, $4–$8; dinner, $8–$16. **Kids' menu** $5. **Reservations** Not necessary. **Payment** AE, MC, V.

One of those fun restaurants that are discovered by a new generation of hipsters every few years, the Tower Cafe is located in a landmark building that also houses a revival movie house. It serves creative, reasonably priced fusion cuisine of the Asian-burrito variety, as well as burgers, pastas, and good wine by the glass. The outdoor tables are wonderful in spring and early summer, and at Sunday brunch there's a mean French toast. The location is perfection, at the entrance to William Land Park.

Willie's Burgers

2415 16th Street, William Land Park; ☎ 916-444-2006

Meals served Lunch and dinner. **Cuisine** American. **Entree range** $2–$5. **Kids' menu** No. **Reservations** Not accepted. **Payment** Cash only.

Located across from Land Park, this plain but clean joint makes the best (and messiest) burger in town. The fries and chocolate shakes are also outstanding.

NORTHERN GOLD COUNTRY:
Grass Valley and Nevada City

NORTHERN GOLD COUNTRY EXTENDS INTO THE MOUNTAINS above Sacramento, but distances are greater and the driving harder between attractions, so we recommend a beginning or end at Nevada City. **Grass Valley** and **Nevada City** are small cities so close that they alternate Fourth of July celebrations between them. Both have beautiful, hilly settings with historic town centers of 19th-century buildings given over, for the most part, to such contemporary uses as shops and galleries. Grass Valley is the busier of the two, but Nevada City is best for overnighting and is great for antiquing and strolling to admire Victorian houses. We recommend a half-day visit to **Empire Mine State Historic Park.**

FAMILY LODGING

 ### Chute Hill Campground

23579 North Bloomfield Road, Nevada City; ☎ 530-265-2740; reservations through ReserveAmerica , ☎ 800-444-7275; www.reserveamerica.com; tent sites $12, cabins $20

The best family campground in Gold Country, Chute Hill is part of Malakoff Diggins State Historical Park, comprising the old mining town of North Bloomfield and the old Diggins hydraulic mining operation, which in its heyday was an environmental nightmare. Today, there are 30 excellent tent and camper sites as well as three old prospectors' cabins under huge ponderosa pines overlooking the town and Diggins. Kids will love walking to the museum town, with its general store and blacksmith; swimming in Blair Lake, which has a wooden raft in its center; and taking flashlights on a hike to Hiller Tunnel, a cool remnant from mining days. Water, flush toilets, wood for sale, picnic tables, fire rings.

Northern Queen Inn
400 Railroad Avenue, Nevada City; ☎ 530-265-5824 or 800-226-3090; www.northernqueeninn.com; $80–$125

This pleasant facility is an affordable haven. Its 70 rooms, suites, and efficiency units are adjacent to easy parking but built along a woodsy creek.

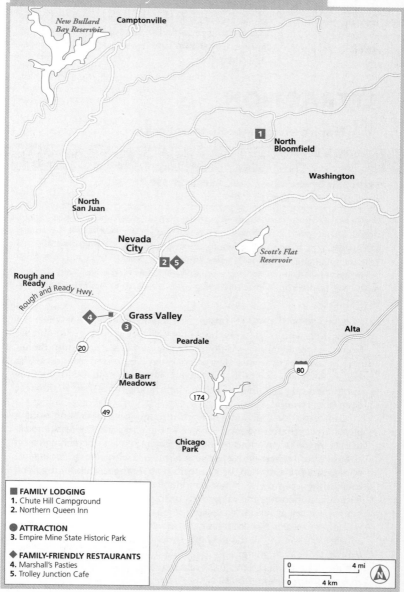

northern gold country: grass valley and nevada city

New Bullard Bay Reservoir

Camptonville

1 North Bloomfield

Washington

North San Juan

Nevada City

2 **5**

Scott's Flat Reservoir

Rough and Ready

Rough and Ready Hwy.

4 ■ Grass Valley
3

Peardale

Alta

20

La Barr Meadows

174

80

49

Chicago Park

■ **FAMILY LODGING**
1. Chute Hill Campground
2. Northern Queen Inn

● **ATTRACTION**
3. Empire Mine State Historic Park

◆ **FAMILY-FRIENDLY RESTAURANTS**
4. Marshall's Pasties
5. Trolley Junction Cafe

0   4 mi
0   4 km

Some are individual cottages with lofts, decks or terraces, kitchens, and wood-burning stoves or fireplaces; even the basic rooms have little refrigerators and coffeemakers. Our kids found blackberry vines on the hillside behind the deck. There's a picnic area, a good restaurant (see profile on facing page) that overlooks the creek's huge waterwheel, and restored train cars next door. Children under age 6 stay free.

unofficial **TIP**
If you take the time, Empire Mine takes you beyond the legends and stories.

ATTRACTION

Empire Mine State Historic Park

APPEAL BY AGE	PRESCHOOL ★	GRADE SCHOOL ★★★	TEENS ★★★
YOUNG ADULTS ★★★	OVER 30 ★★★★		SENIORS ★★★★

10791 East Empire Street, Grass Valley; ☎ 530-273-8522; www.empiremine.org

Hours May–August: daily, 9 a.m.–6 p.m.; September–April: daily, 10 a.m.–5 p.m; closed Thanksgiving, Christmas, and New Year's Day. **Admission** $3 adults, $1 children ages 16 and under, free for children under 6. **Touring time** Average 3 hours; minimum 1 hour. **Rainy-day touring** No. **Restaurants** No. **Alcoholic beverages** No. **Disabled access** Limited. **Wheelchair rental** No. **Baby-stroller rental** No. **Lockers** No. **Pet kennels** No; leashed dogs only. **Rain check** No. **Private tours** No.

DESCRIPTION AND COMMENTS This state park is quite undervisited, which is a shame. Kids who spend a few hours here will get a real sense of mining, from the individual miner's point of view (witness the Cornish dinner pails on exhibit) to an overview of how gold is extracted from rock. The Empire Mine was one of the oldest and richest mines in California. Cornish miners dug 367 miles of tunnels here, going more than 10,000 feet deep underground.

Call ahead for tour times (March through November) and bring a picnic lunch; there's no food for sale at the park, and the brisk mountain air made us ravenous in minutes. Begin in a little screening room at the visitors center with a viewing of movies with vintage footage of miners at work and then, by all means, join a ranger walk for a guided tour of the site's owner's mansion, mining offices (with period office fixtures), clubhouse, and mine-shaft entrance. Then get out your camera for a stroll around a graveyard of rusty mining equipment. If you hike, there are ten miles of trails here, too. At the end of your visit, allow a little time to browse the new gift shop. Restoration and interpretive exhibit work is ongoing, and construction has begun on the Underground Tour, an interactive tram ride into a mine shaft that is expected to open in the summer of 2007.

FAMILY-FRIENDLY RESTAURANTS

 ## Marshall's Pasties

203 Mill Street, Grass Valley; ☎ 530-272-2844

Meals served Daily, lunch and takeout. **Cuisine** Cornish. **Entree range** $3–$5. **Kids' menu** No. **Reservations** No. **Payment** No credit or debit cards.

The miners in this part of the world hailed from Cornwall, England, and their staple food was Cornish pasties, the specialty of Marshall's. Hand-rolled, these large pastries are stuffed with savory fillings such as sausage and broccoli and cheese. You can eat them at a little table upstairs or take them on a picnic.

Trolley Junction Cafe

Northern Queen Inn, 400 Railroad Avenue, Nevada City;
☎ 530-265-5259

Meals served Daily, breakfast and lunch; dinner, Thursday–Sunday. **Cuisine** American. **Entree range** Breakfast, $3–$7; lunch, $6–$7; dinner, $7–$15. **Kids' menu** Yes. **Reservations** Recommended. **Payment** All major credit cards.

There's a lot of charm and good food at this fun place overlooking the woods, creek, and waterwheel, but for kids, the biggest appeal is the train ride across the parking lot. The train runs in summer (tickets are $3 for kids and $6 for adults). From the French toast to the omelets to the ribs, the food is generous and carefully prepared, and the children's menu is extensive.

CENTRAL GOLD COUNTRY:

Jackson, Volcano, and Murphys

THIS IS THE ROAD-TRIP PART OF GOLD COUNTRY. Highway 49 leaves the more developed areas along the Sacramento-to-Tahoe thoroughfare and becomes more countrified. The highway goes through the business or historic centers of some gold-rush towns; others are a few miles off the main drag. There are too many small towns, each with a historic landmark or two, to mention here; one of the most attractive is **Sutter Creek,** a Victorian–New Englandy–looking town that's home to many artisans. **Volcano,** a town that was a highlight for our kids, is listed below as an attraction in and of itself. This is also the region for cave touring (see "Family Outdoor Adventures") and the site of **Indian Grinding Rock** and **Calaveras Big Trees state parks.**

FAMILY LODGING

El Campo Casa Resort Motel
12548 Kennedy Flat Road, Jackson; ☎ 209-223-0100; $63–$72

An older motel, not quite dating back to the gold-rush days (its restrooms have 1950s-era tile) but with some good features for families. Its 15 rooms are comfortable if not spacious, and there's a playground, a swimming pool with an extra-shallow section, and a barbecue for guest use.

Jackson Lodge
850 North Highway 49, P.O. Box 1147, Jackson; ☎ 209-223-0486; www.thejacksonlodge.com; $65–$150; children under age 16 stay free

A kitchen away from home is sometimes a blessing, and this recently renovated place has eight duplex housekeeping cottages, some with their own patios. The pool is refreshing in the summer and heated in the winter. It's right on Highway 49 but not too noisy.

Murphys Historic Hotel and Lodge
457 Main Street, Murphys; ☎ 209-728-3444; www.murphyshotel.com; $70–$120; children age 12 and under stay free

central gold country: jackson, volcano, and murphys

■ FAMILY LODGING
1. El Campo Casa Resort Motel
2. Jackson Gold Lodge
3. Murphys Historic Hotel and Lodge

● ATTRACTIONS
4. Amador County Museum
5. Calaveras Big Trees State Park

6. Indian Grinding Rock State Historic Park
7. Sutter Gold Mine
8. Volcano

◆ FAMILY-FRIENDLY RESTAURANT
9. Rosebud's Cafe

For families who will be spending time in the caves near Murphys, this well-maintained hostelry (part 1855 landmark, part new rooms) is quite serviceable, and the tree-shaded town center offers restaurants and shops. The restaurant and old saloon are popular stops for weary modern '49ers. If you're visiting in summer, be warned that the historic rooms are not air-conditioned; in the spirit of historic accuracy, they also don't have TVs or phones (but rooms in the newer annex do).

ATTRACTIONS

Amador County Museum

APPEAL BY AGE	PRESCHOOL ★★	GRADE SCHOOL ★★	TEENS ★★
YOUNG ADULTS ★★		OVER 30 ★★	SENIORS ★★★

225 Church Street, Jackson; ☎ 209-223-6386

Hours Wednesday–Sunday, 10 a.m.–4 p.m. **Admission** Donation. **Touring time** Average 1½ hours; minimum 30 minutes. **Rainy-day touring** Yes. **Restaurants** No. **Alcoholic beverages** No. **Disabled access** Limited. **Wheelchair rental** No. **Baby-stroller rental** No. **Lockers** No. **Pet kennels** No. **Rain check** No. **Private tours** No.

DESCRIPTION AND COMMENTS A small-scale museum that offers an overview of gold-rush history, at a point in the drive when kids have seen enough to be able to attach facts to sights and when they'll still be seeing more that will apply. You'll see models of mines, a gold room, and a child's period bedroom.

Calaveras Big Trees State Park

APPEAL BY AGE	PRESCHOOL ★★★	GRADE SCHOOL ★★★★	TEENS ★★★★
YOUNG ADULTS ★★★★		OVER 30 ★★★★	SENIORS ★★★★

In Arnold, 20 miles northeast of Murphys; ☎ 209-795-2334

Hours Daily, sunrise–sunset. **Admission** $6 per car, $2 per dog. **Touring time** Average 2 hours; minimum 1 hour. **Rainy-day touring** No. **Restaurants** No. **Alcoholic beverages** No. **Disabled access** Yes, except trails. **Wheelchair rental** No. **Baby-stroller rental** No. **Lockers** No. **Pet kennels** No. **Rain check** No. **Private tours** No.

DESCRIPTION AND COMMENTS Native Americans had known about and held sacred the giant sequoias of this grove for eons when it was discovered by outsiders during the gold rush. For the next 20 years, although the big tree groves of Yosemite and Sequoia were discovered, the Calaveras site was the most visited and best known. Its tourist hotels continued as popular and stylish destinations until the turn of the 19th century. Today, the park is less well known, and its South Grove remains secluded and primeval; it is home to the park's largest tree, the Louis Agassiz, which is 250 feet tall and more than 25 feet in diameter 6 feet above the ground. Creek swimming, developed campgrounds with 129 campsites, and a rustic recreation hall make it one of the most attractive Gold Country camping areas.

unofficial **TIP**
The North Grove's self-guided, one-mile trail and the "Three Senses" trails are the best for nonhiking families.

Indian Grinding Rock State Historic Park

APPEAL BY AGE	PRESCHOOL ★★★	GRADE SCHOOL ★★★	TEENS ★★★
YOUNG ADULTS ★★★		OVER 30 ★★★	SENIORS ★★★

881 Pine Grove–Volcano Road; ☎ 209-296-7488; www.parks.ca.gov

Hours Daily, sunrise–sunset. **Admission** $2 per private vehicle. **Touring time** Average 2 hours; minimum 1 hour. **Rainy-day touring** No. **Restaurants** No. **Alcoholic beverages** No. **Disabled access** Yes. **Wheelchair rental** No. **Baby-stroller rental** No. **Lockers** No. **Pet kennels** No. **Rain check** No. **Private tours** No.

DESCRIPTION AND COMMENTS You get the idea that there are rocks here, but few visitors are prepared for the sight of hundreds of feet of flat limestone outcropping spread out over the rolling countryside. A closer look reveals more than a thousand mortar cups (or *chaw'ses*) chiseled into the largest rock, which also displays 363 petroglyphs. The mortar cups were used for grinding acorns and seeds, staple foods in the Miwok people's diet. The Regional Indian Museum exhibits and slide show illuminate the hunting and gathering way of life of ten Sierra Nevada tribes, and a full-scale model roundhouse, bark conical dwelling, and football field provide further insight into daily native life a hundred years ago. Twenty-one campsites with tables and stoves; piped water and restrooms, but no showers.

 Sutter Gold Mine

APPEAL BY AGE	PRESCHOOL ★	GRADE SCHOOL ★★★	TEENS ★★★
YOUNG ADULTS ★★★		OVER 30 ★★★	SENIORS ★★★

13660 Highway 49 between Sutter Creek and Amador City;
☎ 888- 818-7462; www.caverntours.com

Hours Summer: daily, 9 a.m.–5 p.m.; winter: daily, 10 a.m.–4 p.m. **Admission** *Family tour:* $15 adult, $10 child. *Deep Mine Experience:* $99 per ticket, ages 12 and up only; gold panning, $5. **Touring time** Average 2 hours; minimum 1 hour. **Rainy-day touring** Yes. **Restaurants** Volcano General Store. **Alcoholic beverages** Bar in town. **Disabled access** Limited. **Wheelchair rental** No. **Baby-stroller rental** No. **Lockers** No. **Pet kennels** No. **Rain check** No. **Private tours** No.

DESCRIPTION AND COMMENTS It's one thing to pan for gold in a creek—it's another experience entirely to descend down into a real underground mine shaft. You and your crew will be fitted with hard hats before descending for a one-hour tour, during which you'll see lots of mining equipment (including a huge haul truck) and learn how to distinguish real gold from pyrite. Above ground, you can mine for gemstones, pan for gold, and see a film on gold mining and its history. The same outfitter operates tours into nearby Moaning Cavern, the state's largest cave chamber; the walking tour down 234 stairs is fun for the whole family, and the rappel, dropping 165 feet into the huge main chamber, is a tremendous thrill for kids 12 and up—but be advised that they'll be allowed to descend only if parents sign a waiver; if a parent isn't present, a signed and notarized waiver must accompany the child.

unofficial **TIP**
The typical 11-year-old will pronounce this underground mine-shaft adventure totally cool.

Volcano

APPEAL BY AGE	PRESCHOOL ★	GRADE SCHOOL ★★★	TEENS ★★★
YOUNG ADULTS ★★★		OVER 30 ★★★	SENIORS ★★★

Choose a loop trip from Highway 49. We took Gopher Flat Road from Sutter Creek, which turns into Shake Ridge Road and winds 13 miles to Daffodil Hill (first planted in the 1800s and bursting with 400,000 flowers in the spring). The exciting Ram's Horn Grade was a dramatic 3-mile descent to Volcano. We took Pine Grove–Volcano Road out to Indian Grinding Rock State Historic Park.

Touring time Average 1 hour; minimum 30 minutes. **Rainy-day touring** No. **Restaurants** Volcano General Store. **Alcoholic beverages** Bar in town. **Disabled access** Limited. **Wheelchair rental** No. **Baby-stroller rental** No. **Lockers** No. **Pet kennels** No. **Rain check** No. **Private tours** No.

DESCRIPTION AND COMMENTS Traveling south, you'll see Plymouth, Amador City, and Sutter Creek before you come to the turnoff for Volcano. Sutter Creek appeals to many adults because its historic buildings mix so pleasantly with its tasteful modern development. But we recommend a Volcano side trip combined with a visit to Indian Grinding Rock State Historic Park. There are four different scenic routes that converge in Volcano, where you'll find a park with grassy mounds and ruins, a few places to get refreshments, and some charming residential blocks. You can also check out the Black Chasm Cave's 50-minute Family Tour (a few restrictions apply regarding children in backpacks; ☎ 866-762-2837; **www.caverntours.com**). See this chapter's "Family Outdoor Adventures" section for more info.

unofficial **TIP**
Volcano General Store has a wonderfully atmospheric old soda-shop counter that serves kid chow like burgers and hot dogs.

█▌ FAMILY-FRIENDLY RESTAURANT

Rosebud's Cafe
26 Main Street, Jackson; ☎ 209-223-1035

Meals served Breakfast and lunch. **Cuisine** American. **Entree range** $5–$12. **Kids' menu** Yes. **Reservations** Not accepted. **Payment** MC, V.

A sweet little cafe with an Art Deco look and a wonderful children's menu, offering waffles, junior cheese omelets, even a small turkey hot plate with homemade mashed potatoes. Parents can get a proper latte and a good meal, too. Breakfast is served all day.

SOUTHERN GOLD COUNTRY:
Columbia and Sonora

IF IT'S LIVING HISTORY YOU WANT, this part of the Mother Lode is the place to get it before heading on to the scenic wonders of Yosemite, or back north or south to big-city civilization. Enjoy the oak- and pine-dotted hills and the river vistas—but be prepared for hot, hot weather in the summer.

■ FAMILY LODGING

Best Western Sonora Oaks
19551 Hess Avenue, Sonora; ☎ 209-533-4400 or 800-532-1944; www.bestwestern.com; $79 and up

This 101-room motel may be a chain, but it nevertheless has a rural feel, with an oak grove in its backyard and a pool that's a necessity in the summer. Ask for a deluxe king room, which has both a king bed and a queen sleeper sofa. There's an adjacent coffee shop with a children's menu, and children under age 12 stay free.

■ ATTRACTION

 Columbia State Historic Park

APPEAL BY AGE	PRESCHOOL ★★	GRADE SCHOOL ★★★★	TEENS ★★★★
YOUNG ADULTS ★★★		OVER 30 ★★★	SENIORS ★★★

4 miles north of Sonora on Highway 49, Columbia; ☎ 209-532-9128 (visitor services), ☎ 209-532-0150 (park office), ☎ 209-532-3120 (play info), ☎ 209-588-0808 (stagecoach and horseback riding); www.parks.ca.gov

Hours Daily, 10 a.m.–5 p.m.; tours at 11 a.m. Saturday and Sunday. **Admission** Free to park, various charges at concessions. **Touring time** Average 4 hours; minimum 2 hours. **Rainy-day touring** No. **Restaurants** City Hotel; ice-cream parlor. **Alcoholic beverages** Yes. **Disabled access** No. **Wheelchair rental** No. **Baby-stroller rental** No. **Lockers** No. **Pet kennels** No; leashed dogs only. **Rain check** No. **Private tours** No.

southern gold country: columbia and sonora

FAMILY LODGING
1. Best Western Sonora Oaks

ATTRACTION
2. Columbia State Historic Park

FAMILY-FRIENDLY RESTAURANT
3. Goldstreet Bakery and Cafe

DESCRIPTION AND COMMENTS More modest than a theme park (by far), more honky-tonk than you'd expect in something called a historic park, Columbia is actually a perfect stop for school-age kids. It's a historic landmark, a four-block area of intact 1850s and 1860s buildings (which survived because the town was rebuilt almost entirely in brick after a fire), but it's also a tourist town. There are concessions operating within the park that allow you to pan for gold, go on a tour of a working mine (☎ 209-532-9693), and go on a horseback or stagecoach ride throughout the town. You can brave the ghosts and stay in a restored historic hotel right in the park (☎ 209-532-1479; operated by hotel students at a nearby community college), attend a play at the town playhouse (though it will likely be a modern show), sip a sarsaparilla and listen to bluegrass music at the saloon, watch the blacksmith work, browse for souvenirs and knickknacks, or head for the ice-cream parlor.

FAMILY-FRIENDLY RESTAURANT

Goldstreet Bakery & Cafe
22690 South Gold Street, Columbia; ☎ 209-533-2654

Meals served Breakfast and lunch, Thursday–Monday. Cuisine American. Entree range $4–$7. Kids' menu No. Reservations Accepted. Payment No credit or debit cards.

Local products, often organic, are featured at this cheerful spot, where the baked goods are decadent and the breakfasts (French toast, egg scrambles) delicious. Good soups and salads for lunch, too. Conveniently located at the edge of the state park.

PART EIGHT

NORTHERN CALIFORNIA

SPARSELY POPULATED AND RICH IN DRAMATIC LANDSCAPES, Northern California is given over in large part to national forest land. The coastal area (roughly **Sonoma, Mendocino,** and **Humboldt** counties) begins in the south as rugged, beautiful beach country and leads to the **Redwood Coast,** home of the big trees. It's bounded on the east by the north–south chain of mountains known as the **Coast Range.** Immediately to the east of the range is a huge swath of forest. From south to north, **Mendocino National Forest** merges into **Trinity National Forest** and Trinity into **Klamath National Forest.** In northern midstate is **Lake Shasta,** a man-made lake of immense proportions and a major recreation site, and **Mount Shasta.** Directly north of San Francisco is the famous wine-producing Napa Valley, not covered in any detail here as its primary pleasures are adults-only.

Many of the small towns and cities of Northern California have neighborhoods catering to tourists and travelers, but these are sometimes simply a few motels and chain restaurants near the freeways. In this region, the fact that a town has a larger population may mean that it has more industry and jobs, not more vacation options, so we've organized this chapter around counties instead of cities. We feature only selected Northern California counties with significant family-vacation options.

These are, on the coast, the counties of Sonoma, for its agricultural producers and historic sites; Mendocino, for whale watching, the **Skunk Train,** tide pools, and picturesque shop-filled towns; and Humboldt, with three state parks of giant redwoods and the huge, primeval oasis of **Redwood National Park.** Inland we'll focus on Trinity and Shasta Counties for the **Shasta-Trinity National Recreation Area,** with Lake Shasta as its centerpiece (allow a few days for houseboating or Jet Skiing here).

A significant number of city, state, and county parks in this region have summer swimming options, so when you load up the car in the

northern california

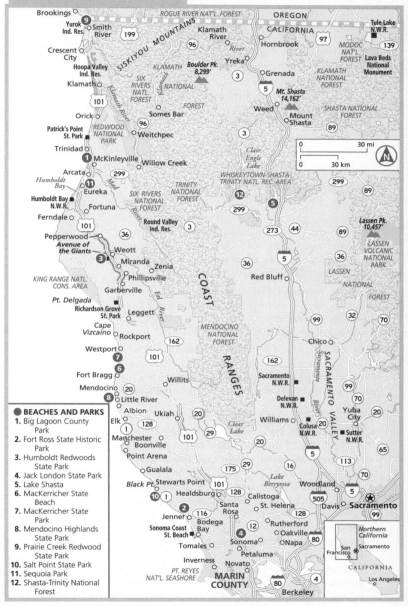

● **BEACHES AND PARKS**
1. Big Lagoon County Park
2. Fort Ross State Historic Park
3. Humboldt Redwoods State Park
4. Jack London State Park
5. Lake Shasta
6. MacKerricher State Beach
7. MacKerricher State Park
8. Mendocino Highlands State Park
9. Prairie Creek Redwood State Park
10. Salt Point State Park
11. Sequoia Park
12. Shasta-Trinity National Forest

morning, keep bathing suits and inflatable rafts within easy reach. Your midday stop can be a festive highlight at a beautiful redwood-forest recreation area, where you can swim, play a little catch, and picnic.

Because children are famously indifferent to scenery, the spectacular but challenging winding roads of the Northern California coast should be carefully reviewed before setting out on road trips. Parents of children who get motion sickness should also plan carefully.

The same is true for inland scenic routes. Although the Trinity National Forest is a beautiful region of pine-covered slopes and rocky chasms plunging to rivers far below, it took us much longer to cover the miles than we had anticipated. On one vacation, we had to change our itinerary midtrip (cutting down on the places we'd visit) to allow enough time to actually get out into the outdoors we'd spent so much time driving through.

GETTING THERE

BY PLANE If you're flying into the western United States, you can investigate connecting regional air service into one of Northern California's small-city airports and rent a car on arrival. For example, **Alaska Airlines** serves Eureka/Arcata and Redding airports from Portland, Oregon; **United Express** offers service to Eureka/Arcata and Redding from San Francisco.

BY TRAIN Amtrak's *Coast Starlight* goes from Sacramento through Chico, Redding (access Lake Shasta), and Dunsmuir (access Mount Shasta) before continuing on to Seattle. Call ☎ 800-USA-RAIL; or go to **www.amtrak.com.**

BY CAR **Highway 1** north of San Francisco takes you to the Mendocino coast. Continue on **US 101** from San Francisco to get to Sonoma and the Redwood Empire area. For a direct drive to the Shasta-Trinity area, take **Interstate 5** north from Sacramento.

HOW TO GET INFORMATION BEFORE YOU GO

- **California State Parks information** P.O. Box 942896, Sacramento 94296-0001; ☎ 800-777-0369 or 916-653-6995; **www.parks.ca.gov.**
- **Fort Bragg–Mendocino Coast Chamber of Commerce** P.O. Box 1141, Fort Bragg 95437; ☎ 866-GO MENDO or 707-961-6300; **www.mendocinocoast.com** or **www.gomendo.com.**
- **Greater Santa Rosa Conference and Visitors Bureau** 9 Fourth Street, Santa Rosa 95401; ☎ 707-577-8674 or 800-404-7673; **www.visitsantarosa.com.**
- **Humboldt County Convention and Visitors Bureau** 1034 Second Street, Eureka 95501; ☎ 707-443-5097 or 800-346-3482; **www.redwoodvisitor.org.**
- **Sonoma County Convention and Visitors Bureau** 5000 Roberts Lake Drive, Rohnert Park 94928; ☎ 800-576-6662 or 707-539-7282; **www.sonoma.county.com** or **www.sonoma.com.**

- **Sonoma Valley Visitors Bureau** 453 First Street East, Sonoma 95476; ☎ 707-996-1090; **www.sonomavalley.com.**
- **Trinidad Chamber of Commerce** P.O. Box 356, Trinidad 95570; ☎ 707-677-1610; **www.trinidadcalif.com.**

The BEST BEACHES and PARKS

NOTE: SWIMMING IS NOT PERMITTED AT SOME of Northern California's rugged beaches because of dangerous water conditions. Never leave children unattended near the ocean anywhere in this region.

BIG LAGOON COUNTY PARK Although it's a popular park, the setting here is one of splendid isolation, and although it's adjacent to the highway and thus easily accessed, the huge expanses of beach, water, and sky make it seem remote. It's a county (read: low-budget) campground, so it's more rustic than amenity laden. The site makes a nice break between the northern redwoods and Eureka. Fee for day use and camping. Boat launching, picnicking, camping, fishing, swimming, sanitary facilities, and cold running water. Reservations are not accepted; campsites are on a first-come, first-served basis. Seven miles north of Trinidad, exit Highway 101 at Big Lagoon Park Road.

HUMBOLDT REDWOODS STATE PARK The most famous part of Humboldt Redwoods State Park is the dramatic **Avenue of the Giants,** a winding bypass road, with turnouts and parking areas, that curves along the south fork of the Eel River through a magnificent forest of redwoods. You feel as if you're moving through a green undersea world as you drive for miles under the forest canopy, only occasionally coming into a sunny meadow. Slanting beams of sunlight impart that sense of sanctuary and awe so often remarked upon in connection with the big trees. You'll find picnicking, swimming, and other recreation along the drive, as well as towns about every six miles.

unofficial **TIP**
The chance to camp in the redwoods is not to be missed.

The hours spent in those awe-inspiring groves are unlike any other camping experience. See "Family Lodging" for details. The park has remarkable scenic picnic areas, and the campgrounds are near trails in the most important redwood groves. Gentle, easy, self-guiding nature trails may be found at several locations; don't miss the half-mile **Founders Tree Trail,** which leads to the massive **Founders Tree** and the **Dyerville Giant,** a 500-ton redwood that crashed to the ground several years ago. There are bike trails, and a park auto tour is available. Humboldt Redwood State Park is 45 miles south of Eureka on Highway 101; ☎ 707-946-2409; **www.humboldtredwoods.org.** The visitors center is next to Burlington Campground, 2 miles south of Weott.

MACKERRICHER STATE BEACH You won't find sunbathers and bikini-clad skaters on this stretch of rugged, often-foggy coastline, but rather hikers, bikers, and anglers, along with horseback riders and whale and seal watchers. Look for the Seal Point Trail, a short walk leading out to Seal Rocks, where you'll find loads of sunbathing seals. North of Seal Rocks is a popular spot for ocean fishing, and the whole area has great tide pooling at low tide. For a great adventure, contact **Ricochet Ridge Ranch** (☎ 707-964-7669) about its guided horseback rides on the beach or in the redwoods. There are many wheelchair-accessible areas as well as superb tent and RV campsites (for reservations, call ☎ 800-444-7275 or go to **www.reserveamerica.com**). Three miles north of Fort Bragg on Highway 1 near Cleone; ☎ 707-937-5804.

SALT POINT STATE PARK   A 6,000-acre park encompassing six miles of rugged coastline, Salt Point is a well-loved tide pooling spot. There are trails for hiking and horseback riding, but it's the hidden coves, with their secret spots and strange sandstone formations, that appeal to little ones. Good camping, too. Twenty miles north of Jenner on Highway 1; ☎ 707-847-3221 or 707-865-2391.

SEQUOIA PARK   This lovely city park in Eureka has a free zoo where you can see animals native to the area, such as bears, elk, and deer, as well as exotic species. There are also picnic areas, a playground, a duck pond, and more than 50 acres of North Coast redwoods. In the summer months, a petting zoo is open Tuesday through Sunday, 11:30 a.m. to 3:30 p.m. The zoo is closed Mondays, but the park itself is open every day. W and Glatt streets, Eureka; ☎ 530-442-3738.

FAMILY OUTDOOR ADVENTURES

BOATING ON LAKE SHASTA   One of the most memorable days of our Northern California vacation was spent on a patio boat on Lake Shasta. We donned bathing suits and sunscreen in our motel room, packed rented fishing poles and hot dogs for barbecuing, grabbed the two-person inflatable rowboat and some rope, and headed for the rental dock. Over the next idyllic hours, we took turns driving the flat-bottomed boat over calm lake waters, marveling at how close the forested mountains looked in the clear, high-elevation air. We cooked on the grill and took turns swimming off the side or floating in the inflatable rowboat tied behind the bigger boat. We tied up on shore from time to time, fished over the side, and waved to other patio boaters as they passed. Motel reservations the night before and the night after at Bridge Bay Lodging at Lake Shasta allowed us to fully enjoy the long day on the lake. Contact **Seven Crowns Resorts** (☎ 800-752-9669; **www.sevencrown.com**) for information on lodging and renting houseboats or patio boats.

HIKING   Whether it's poking along a half-mile, stroller-friendly trail in a redwood forest or negotiating a beach trail for an entire morning, you are guaranteed to spend time hiking in Northern California.

So integral is the experience that we won't even get into details here, because this chapter is loaded with descriptions of state, national, and regional parks and their trails.

HORSEBACK RIDING Although horseback riding for casual visitors is available throughout the state, in the Northern California area the trail rides lead you along routes that are really the stuff of fantasy. Picture yourself cantering along the beach? The one-and-a-half-hour ride at **Ricochet Ridge Ranch** (24201 North Highway 1, Fort Bragg; ☎ 707-964-7669; both group and private rides available) takes you to MacKerricher State Park for a good portion of the saddle time, and you'll ride right along the tideline and be able to see seals on the offshore rocks—and, in season, whales.

Thinking of a few days or a full vacation at a family-oriented ranch resort? See the listing for **Coffee Creek Ranch** under "Family Lodging" in the "Trinity and Shasta Counties" section. Do you have preteen and teen riders ready for the adventure of an overnight pack trip into the wilderness, or at least a daylong trip along the Klamath River? Combine a wilderness pack ride with a ranch stay, or try a "saddle and paddle" package that combines trail rides with rafting or mountain biking at **Marble Mountain Ranch** (see "Family Lodging" in the "Humboldt and Del Norte Counties" section).

How about a moonlight trail ride with your kids? Try the guided trail rides (children must be age 8 or older) through **Jack London State Park** with the **Sonoma Cattle Company** in Glen Ellen (☎ 707-255-2900; **www.napasonomatrailrides.com**); $75 per person for a two-hour ride. Group rates available.

RIVER RAFTING The ocean may be wilder way up north, but the rivers tend to be milder, making for excellent, not-too-scary rafting trips suitable for kids as young as 4 years old. One of the best rivers for families is the **Trinity,** which wanders along the Trinity Alps Wilderness. Companies to try include **Bigfoot Rafting** (Willow Creek; ☎ 530-629-2263 or 800-722-2223; **www.bigfootrafting.com**) or **Aurora River Adventures** (Willow Creek; ☎ 800-562-8475), which have half- to two-day trips on Class I and II stretches for families; ask about the trip to ancient Hupa Indian sites, or the one with a professional storyteller on board. Over Shasta way, the Klamath River is another gentle one that can be great for family rafting; **Turtle River Rafting** (Mount Shasta; ☎ 530-926-3223 or 800-726-3223; **www .turtleriver.com**) offers trips geared to children ages 4 to 11.

WHALE WATCHING ON THE MENDOCINO COAST If you're a winter or spring visitor to Northern California, be sure to join locals for the annual whale-watching rites. Gray whales pass this coast on their way south to Baja California between December and February and on their return home to the

unofficial **TIP**
It's not necessary to take a boat to see whales—the high bluffs along the shoreline in the Mendocino area offer ideal viewing from land.

Bering Sea from mid-March through April. There are programs and docent-led walks at **MacKerricher State Park** near Fort Bragg, **Mendocino Highlands State Park** in Mendocino, and **Point Cabrillo Light Station** near Mendocino; call ☎ 707-937-0816.

When looking from shore, it's hard to fully appreciate the size of these mammals, so many wildlife enthusiasts take a whale-watching boat trip. **Noyo Harbor** in Fort Bragg is an embarkation point for several such charters, which cost about $25 to $45 per person for a two-hour trip. For information, contact **Anchor Charters** (☎ 707-964-4550; **www.anchorcharterboats.com**); **Fort Bragg Whale Watching** (☎ 707-964-3000; **www.fortbraggwhales.com**), or **Telstar Charters** (☎ 707-964-8770; **www.gooceanfishing.com**).

SONOMA COUNTY:

Sonoma, Santa Rosa, Windsor, Forestville, and Glen Ellen

ALMOST AS FAMOUS A WINE COUNTRY NOW AS NAPA, **Sonoma County** is actually a mixed agricultural area with a variety of outstanding products, including cheese, apples, wine, and carnivorous plants. Families traveling on Highway 101 will find such rest-stop recreations as skating rinks, bumper cars, and a steam railway in the city of **Santa Rosa,** which also has one of the area's airports. The historic town center of **Sonoma** is a nice lunch stop—a stroll through the fort where the **Bear Flag Revolt** took place can be combined with a meal and a look at the cheese-making process. But although some of the wineries serve juice or soda, we don't recommend tasting-room stops for families.

Much is made of the **Jack London State Park,** but we don't think kids get it, even if they've read *White Fang* (how to explain the connection between the stories and the ruins of a dream house?); however, the outdoor activities at this park can be fun.

FAMILY LODGING

Best Western Sonoma Valley Inn
550 Second Street, West Sonoma; ☎ 707-938-9200 or 800-334-5784; www.sonomavalleyinn.com; $150–$400

A pleasant 75-room motel just a block away from Sonoma Plaza, with a pool and garden setting. Courtyard rooms have private balconies and fireplaces, all rooms have coffeemakers and refrigerators, and a continental breakfast is delivered to your room. Children under age 12 stay free. Activity packages; babysitting available.

Flamingo Resort Hotel
2777 Fourth Street, Santa Rosa; ☎ 707-545-8530 or 800-848-8300; www.flamingoresort.com; $119–$250 May–October, less in off season; children under age 12 stay free

A family-run resort with 136 rooms spread over ten acres of grounds and spa facilities, this Santa Rosa hotel boasts a playground, lawn games, pool, wading pool, tennis courts, and horseback riding. All the public areas are

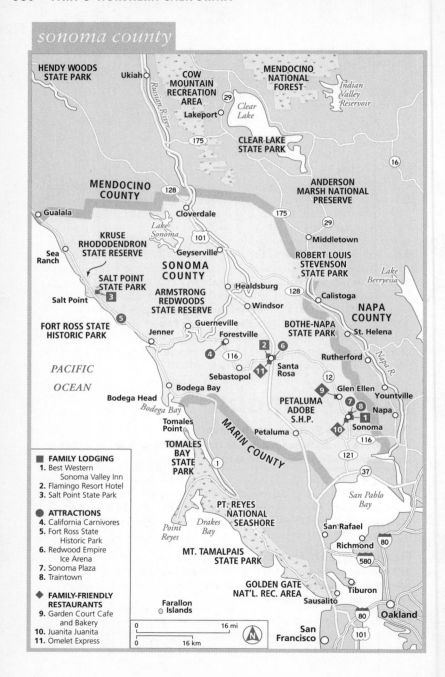

sonoma county

HENDY WOODS STATE PARK

Ukiah

COW MOUNTAIN RECREATION AREA

MENDOCINO NATIONAL FOREST

Indian Valley Reservoir

Russian River

29

Lakeport

Clear Lake

175

CLEAR LAKE STATE PARK

16

MENDOCINO COUNTY

128

ANDERSON MARSH NATIONAL PRESERVE

Gualala

Cloverdale

175

Lake Sonoma

101

Middletown

29

KRUSE RHODODENDRON STATE RESERVE

Sea Ranch

Geyserville

ROBERT LOUIS STEVENSON STATE PARK

Lake Berryessa

SALT POINT STATE PARK

SONOMA COUNTY

Salt Point

3

ARMSTRONG REDWOODS STATE RESERVE

Healdsburg

128

Calistoga

NAPA COUNTY

5

Windsor

FORT ROSS STATE HISTORIC PARK

Jenner

Guerneville

BOTHE-NAPA STATE PARK

St. Helena

Napa R.

Forestville

4

116

2

6

Rutherford

PACIFIC OCEAN

11

Sebastopol

Santa Rosa

12

Bodega Bay

9

Glen Ellen

Yountville

Bodega Head

Bodega Bay

PETALUMA ADOBE S.H.P.

7

8

Napa

Tomales Point

10

Sonoma

116

MARIN COUNTY

Petaluma

121

TOMALES BAY STATE PARK

1

37

San Pablo Bay

FAMILY LODGING
1. Best Western Sonoma Valley Inn
2. Flamingo Resort Hotel
3. Salt Point State Park

PT. REYES NATIONAL SEASHORE

Drakes Bay

San Rafael

Richmond

80

ATTRACTIONS
4. California Carnivores
5. Fort Ross State Historic Park
6. Redwood Empire Ice Arena
7. Sonoma Plaza
8. Traintown

Point Reyes

MT. TAMALPAIS STATE PARK

580

FAMILY-FRIENDLY RESTAURANTS
9. Garden Court Cafe and Bakery
10. Juanita Juanita
11. Omelet Express

GOLDEN GATE NAT'L. REC. AREA

Sausalito

Tiburon

Farallon Islands

0   16 mi
0   16 km

N

San Francisco

80

Oakland

101

completely smoke free. The hotel's spa (Montecito Heights; ☎ 707-526-0529) offers a daytime child-care program, with games, arts, and crafts, for kids from 4 months to 12 years old, for the modest fee of $5 an hour. For 4 months to 16 months, add $1.50 per hour; reservations are essential.

Salt Point State Park

Highway 1, north of Jenner; ☎ 707-847-3221; reservations: Reserve America, ☎ 800-444-7275; www.reserveamerica.com or www.parks.ca.gov; campsites $25 (less for walk-ins)

This gorgeous park on the rugged Sonoma Coast is rich with family pleasures: hiking and horseback trails, a sandy beach, a marine reserve with tide pools, and proximity to Fort Ross. Pack warm clothes, even for August, but know that warm, sunny days happen, too. Facilities include fire rings, picnic tables, water, and restrooms, but no showers.

ATTRACTIONS

California Carnivores

APPEAL BY AGES	PRESCHOOL ★★★	GRADE SCHOOL ★★★	TEENS ★★
YOUNG ADULTS ★★		OVER 30 ★★	SENIORS ★★

2833 Old Gravenstein Highway South, Sebastopol; ☎ 707-824-0433; www.californiacarnivores.com

Hours Tuesday–Thursday, 10 a.m.–4 p.m.; closed Wednesdays, Thanksgiving, Christmas Eve, Christmas, and New Year's Day. **Admission** Free. **Touring time** Average 1 hour; minimum 30 minutes. **Rainy-day touring** Yes; no problem in greenhouses. **Restaurants** No. **Alcoholic beverages** No. **Disabled access** Yes. **Wheelchair rental** No. **Baby-stroller rental** No. **Lockers** No. **Pet kennels** No pets allowed. **Rain check** No. **Private tours** No.

DESCRIPTION AND COMMENTS This nursery and farm specializes in insect-eating plants, a fact that makes it the coolest nursery in the world for a 10-year-old. Some 350 varieties are on display, and many are for sale. Picnic areas. Kids must be accompanied by adults, but there's no age limit.

 Fort Ross State Historic Park

APPEAL BY AGE	PRESCHOOL ★★★	GRADE SCHOOL ★★★★	TEENS ★★★★
YOUNG ADULTS ★★★★		OVER 30 ★★★★	SENIORS ★★★

19005 Coast Highway 1, Jenner; ☎ 707-847-3286; www.parks.ca.gov or www.fortrossstatepark.org

Hours *Park:* daily, sunrise–sunset; *fort:* daily, 10 a.m.–4:30 p.m.; closed Thanksgiving, Christmas, and New Year's Day. **Admission** $6 per private vehicle. **Touring time** Average 2 hours; minimum 1 hour. **Rainy-day touring** Not recommended. **Restaurants** Nearby. **Alcoholic beverages** No. **Disabled access** For some areas.

Wheelchair rental No. **Baby-stroller rental** No. **Lockers** No. **Pet kennels** No. **Rain check** No. **Private tours** Yes.

DESCRIPTION AND COMMENTS Its spectacular location on a high bluff above the roiling ocean would be reason enough to stop here, but Fort Ross is also a great reconstruction of the Russian-American Company's 1812 outpost. Here's one of the few places to learn about a foreign power's one-time foothold on continental America. You'll see reconstructed 12-foot-high stockades, soldiers' barracks, and an octagonal Orthodox chapel, as well as museum displays on Native American, Russian, and Yankee culture. Russian Orthodox services are held Memorial Day and Fourth of July. Try to allow time to explore either Sandy Beach or North Cove, both of which have terrific tide pools when the conditions are right. And if you visit in spring, you'll be present for harbor-seal pupping season; call ☎ 707-869-9177 for information.

Redwood Empire Ice Arena

APPEAL BY AGE	PRESCHOOL ★★★★		GRADE SCHOOL ★★★★	TEENS ★★★
YOUNG ADULTS ★★		OVER 30 ★★		SENIORS ★★

1667 West Steele Lane, Santa Rosa; ☎ 707-546-7147; www.snoopyshomeice.com

Hours Complicated because of many ice shows, but call for skate times; consider reserving for an ice show; some public hours daily, but hours vary. **Admission** $9 adults, $6 ages 11 and under; skate rental $3 per person. **Touring time** Average 3 hours to skate and shop; minimum 1 hour to see gallery and gift shop. **Rainy-day touring** Just dandy. **Restaurants** Yes. **Alcoholic beverages** No. **Disabled access** Yes. **Wheelchair rental** No. **Baby-stroller rental** No. **Lockers** Yes. **Pet kennels** No. **Rain check** No. **Private tours** No; limited private rentals possible.

DESCRIPTION AND COMMENTS Built and operated by *Peanuts* creator Charles Schulz, this rink (decorated with huge photo murals of Switzerland and life-size trees) offers rentals, public skating sessions, and ice shows. It's a great place to burn off some kid energy on rainy or cold days—or to cool off on hot days.

Sonoma Plaza

APPEAL BY AGE	PRESCHOOL ★★		GRADE SCHOOL ★★	TEENS ★★★
YOUNG ADULTS ★★★		OVER 30 ★★★★		SENIORS ★★★★

Spain and First streets, Sonoma; Sonoma Valley Visitors Center; ☎ 707-996-1090

Hours *State Historic Park:* daily, 10 a.m.–5 p.m.; closed Thanksgiving, Christmas, and New Year's Day; shops and cafe hours vary. **Admission** *Mission and Vallejo Home:* $3, $2 children ages 6–12. **Touring time** Average 2 hours; minimum 1 hour. **Rainy-day touring** Not recommended. **Restaurants** Yes. **Alcoholic beverages** At some restaurants. **Disabled access** Yes. **Wheelchair rental** No. **Baby-stroller rental** No. **Lockers** No. **Pet kennels** No. **Rain check** No. **Private tours** No.

DESCRIPTION AND COMMENTS California was proclaimed a republic when the Bear Flag was raised here in 1846; a few weeks later it became a state. The plaza itself, created in 1835, is now a National Historic Landmark. Sonoma State Historic Park is also here; it includes a hotel and barracks, a mission, and, at another location, a historic residence. The mission has exhibits of religious and ranching life, and on weekends children can help bake bread in the garden workshop area (call ☎ 707-938-1519). Historic buildings are interspersed with contemporary shops and restaurants; all surround a pleasant park square.

Traintown

APPEAL BY AGE	PRESCHOOL ★★★★★		GRADE SCHOOL ★★★★	
TEENS ★	YOUNG ADULTS ★	OVER 30 ★		SENIORS ★

20264 Broadway, Sonoma; ☎ **707-938-3912;** www.traintown.com

Hours September–May: Saturday and Sunday, 10 a.m.–5 p.m.; June–Labor Day: daily, 10 a.m.–5 p.m. **Admission** $4; carousel and Ferris wheel, $2 per ride. **Touring time** Average 1½ hours; minimum 45 minutes. **Rainy-day touring** Not recommended. **Restaurants** Snack bar. **Alcoholic beverages** No. **Disabled access** Yes. **Wheelchair rental** No. **Baby-stroller rental** No. **Lockers** No. **Pet kennels** No. **Rain check** Unused tickets can be used another time. **Private tours** No.

DESCRIPTION AND COMMENTS Take a ride on a quarter-scale railroad that replicates a steam train of the 1890s used in the mountains. The 20-minute trip winds through ten acres of forest, past lakes, and through tunnels to a miniature town. There's also a merry-go-round and petting zoo. This is heaven for your typical 4-year-old.

FAMILY-FRIENDLY RESTAURANTS

Garden Court Cafe and Bakery
13647 Arnold Drive, Glen Ellen; ☎ **707-935-1565;**
www.gardencourtcafe.com

Meals served Breakfast and lunch; dinner first and second Wednesday of month by reservation only. **Cuisine** American. **Entree range** $5–$12 (breakfast and lunch). **Kids' menu** Yes. **Reservations** Not accepted on weekends. **Payment** MC, V.

The bright, peaceful interior of this countryish cafe is perhaps the best place to sit, because sometimes the body shop next door makes the patio a bit noisy. The children's menu is cheerful, with choices ranging from Goldilocks porridge (an oatmeal that's not too hot, not too cold, but just right) to turkey sandwiches and small salads.

 ## Juanita Juanita

19114 Arnold Drive, Sonoma; ☎ **707-935-3981**

Meals served Lunch and dinner. **Cuisine** Mexican. **Entree range** $4–$10. **Kids' menu** No. **Reservations** Not accepted. **Payment** No credit cards.

A friendly local restaurant, this place puts a healthy spin on Mexican standards. Aside from the usual tacos and burritos, you can get a veggie tamale and a grilled-mushroom quesadilla. Kids love the homemade chips; parents like sampling from the roster of beers, including some locally brewed. The best Mexican food for miles around.

Omelet Express
112 Fourth Street, Railroad Square, Santa Rosa; ☎ 707-525-1690

Meals served Breakfast and lunch. **Cuisine** American. **Entree range** $6–$12. **Kids' menu** Yes. **Reservations** Not accepted. **Payment** MC, V.

This bright, cheerful diner is a good spot for breakfast or lunch en route north or south: bagels, omelets, sandwiches, burgers, and such.

MENDOCINO COUNTY:

Mendocino, Fort Bragg, Willits, and Leggett

IT'S CONSIDERED ONE OF THE MOST BEAUTIFUL AND ROMANTIC places in the world, but the **Mendocino Coast** loses some of its charm if you have a 4-year-old throwing up in the backseat. Travel time along the scenic 80-mile "Dramamine Drive" (**Coast Highway 1**) between **Bodega Bay** and **Fort Bragg** can take twice as long as you might think from looking at a mileage chart. The pace is slow due to hairpin turns—but you're grateful it's slow when you encounter the careening log trucks. It all makes for a much longer time between bathroom stops than the map might suggest.

Traveling at a leisurely pace, and with plenty of picnic supplies for tailgate lunches (and with kids capable of scrambling down a fern-covered gully for a desperation rest stop), we have had a wonderful and memorable family drive along Highway 1. But if your children are under 6 years of age or prone to car sickness, or if you want to cover a lot of miles (say, to get to the redwoods near **Eureka** or the Oregon border), we suggest the drive along 101, with its rolling agricultural landscape, instead of dramatic ocean cliffs. You can access the major Mendocino attractions using connecting roads from 101.

The towns of **Mendocino** and **Fort Bragg** make the best overnight bases for families. Fort Bragg is less picturesque, but it's the best point to board the area's major family attraction, the **Skunk Train.**

FAMILY LODGING

Emandal

16500 Hearst Post Office Road, Willits; ☎ 707-459-5439; www.emandal.com; 1-week August–September family camps, $826 adults, $203–$578 kids (varies by age); seasonal themed weekends throughout year

A laid-back family camp with few structured activities, this is a working ranch and farm complete with pigs, cows, and pickle making. Don't expect luxury—the charming little redwood cabins lack hot water, and you'll have to walk a bit to the bathrooms and showers—but do expect reasonable comfort and lots of old-fashioned farm charms, from hearty (and organic)

mendocino county

PACIFIC
OCEAN

0 ——— 12 mi
0 ——— 12 km

■ **FAMILY LODGING**
1. Emandal
2. Little River Inn
3. Pine Beach Inn
4. Russian Gulch State Park Campground
5. Stanford Inn by the Sea–Big River Lodge
6. Surf Motel

● **ATTRACTIONS**
7. Drive-Thru Tree Park (aka Chandelier Tree)
8. Fort Bragg Footlighters
9. Mendocino Coast Botanical Gardens
10. Point Arena Lighthouse and Museum

11. The Skunk Train– California Western Railroad

◆ **FAMILY-FRIENDLY RESTAURANTS**
12. Egghead Omelettes of Oz
13. Mendocino Cafe
14. North Coast Brewing Company

home-cooked meals to swimming holes (in the Eel River), hiking trails, campfire songs, berry-picking, even helping with such farm chores as feeding the chickens. It's located inland from Mendocino near Willits.

Little River Inn

7751 North Highway 1, Little River; ☎ 707-937-5942 or
☎ 888-466-5683; www.littleriverinn.com; $110–$325

Ideally located above the ocean and next to Van Damme State Park (which has an excellent beach and an easy trail through a pygmy forest of dwarf pines), this is a terrific small resort that's more welcoming than most here in the land of romantic bed-and-breakfasts. There's a good family suite in the main complex, as well as comfortable rooms, most with superb views. Extras include a nine-hole golf course, tennis, gardens, and a highly regarded restaurant with a children's menu.

Pine Beach Inn

16801 North Highway 1, south of Fort Bragg; ☎ 707-964-5603 or
888-987-8388; www.pinebeachinn.com; $89 and up

There's room to run at this moderately priced, family-friendly coastal inn four miles south of Fort Bragg. The 50 rooms (including nine two-bedroom suites, some with kitchenettes) sit on an 11-acre site that spills onto a little sandy beach cove fed by a small creek. Elsewhere on the grounds are two tennis courts, lawns, and a good Mexican restaurant (closed Sundays).

Russian Gulch State Park Campground

Off Highway 1 just north of Mendocino; ☎ 707-937-5804;
reservations: Reserve America, ☎ 800-444-7275;
www.reserveamerica.com; campsites $12

Tucked under a picturesque bridge just north of Mendocino, this is a beautiful little campground that's perfect for family tent or RV camping. There are only 30 sites, each with picnic table and fireplace, and what it lacks in isolation it makes up in beauty and convenience. The campground itself is nestled in a little canyon; just across a stream is the white-sand beach, which is warmer and more protected than most in these parts. The town of Mendocino, with shops, food, and charm galore, is an easy hike of less than a mile. You can fish, swim, explore, and cycle, as well as rent a canoe from **Catch-a-Canoe and Bicycles, Too!** (two-person canoe, $18 per hour, $54 per day; four-person, $22 per hour, $66 per day; call ahead for tide information; ☎ 707-937-0273; **www.catchacanoe.com**). You can paddle on the Big River estuary to look for seals and osprey. Showers, flush toilets, wood for sale.

Stanford Inn by the Sea–Big River Lodge

44850 Comptche–Ukiah Road, Mendocino; ☎ 707-937-5615
or 800-331-8884; www.stanfordinn.com; $275–$785; $25 children
ages 3–18; $25 pet fee

This four-diamond hotel describes itself as a "self-sustaining ecosystem." Its ten acres of landscaped grounds include a certified organic garden, nursery, and working farm, and guests can take classes in organic gardening and medicinal herbs—it's all so Mendocino here. You'll also enjoy the indoor swimming pool, complimentary full breakfast, video library, and mountain bikes. There are 33 wood-paneled rooms and suites, many with four-poster beds and wood-burning stoves or fireplaces. Babysitting, VCRs, mini-refrigerators, coffeemakers, vegetarian restaurant (breakfast and dinner only).

Surf Motel

1220 South Main Street, Fort Bragg; ☎ 707-964-5361 or 800-339-5361; $69 and up; $10 children over age 9; apartment units, $125–$135; www.surfmotelfortbragg.com

A good choice for families on a budget, this motel is well located in Fort Bragg, not far from the Skunk Train. The two apartment units sleep up to six and are a particularly good value. Outside there's a barbecue and picnic area, landscaped grounds, and fish-cleaning facilities. Refrigerators can be put in rooms for $6 extra. There's no restaurant, but the kids will be happy to spot the McDonald's right across the street.

ATTRACTIONS

Drive-Thru Tree Park (aka Chandelier Tree)

APPEAL BY AGE	PRESCHOOL ★★★	GRADE SCHOOL ★★★	TEENS ★★★
YOUNG ADULTS ★★★		OVER 30 ★★	SENIORS ★★

Highway 101 in Legget; ☎ 707-925-6464

Hours Memorial Day–mid-October: daily, 8:30 a.m.–8:30 p.m.; rest of year: daily, 9 a.m.–sunset. **Admission** $5 per vehicle. **Touring time** Average 15 minutes; minimum 5 minutes. **Rainy-day touring** Okay. **Restaurants** No. **Alcoholic beverages** No. **Disabled access** Yes. **Wheelchair rental** No. **Baby-stroller rental** No. **Lockers** No. **Pet kennels** No. **Rain check** No. **Private tours** No.

DESCRIPTION AND COMMENTS   On US 101 in Leggett, a town situated where Coast Highway veers in and meets up with US 101, you'll find the famed drive-through tree: a privately owned 315-foot-tall redwood, 21 feet in diameter, which had a car-sized tunnel carved into it in the mid-1930s. Weird but memorable. Picnic facilities are on site.

Fort Bragg Footlighters

APPEAL BY AGE	PRESCHOOL ★	GRADE SCHOOL ★★★★	TEENS ★★★
YOUNG ADULTS ★★★		OVER 30 ★★★	SENIORS ★★★★

248 East Laurel, Fort Bragg; ☎ 707-964-3806

Hours Memorial Day–Labor Day: Wednesday thru Sunday, and the Sunday before Labor Day, show starts 8 p.m. **Admission** $12 adults, $10 children and seniors. **Touring time** Average 2 hours; minimum 1½ hours. **Rainy-day touring**

Yes. **Restaurants** No. **Alcoholic beverages** No. **Disabled access** Yes. **Wheelchair rental** No. **Baby-stroller rental** No. **Lockers** No. **Pet kennels** No. **Rain check** No. **Private tours** No.

DESCRIPTION AND COMMENTS What to do for a special outing at night? This 1890s-style musical-comedy and melodrama troupe offers entertainment the kids won't see on MTV, but the show fits in nicely with the historical era they'll see in the architecture of Mendocino. This 50-year-old company has its own theater, and it performs the same show year in and year out: *The Play Must Go On, Or: We Still Got It.*

Mendocino Coast Botanical Gardens

APPEAL BY AGE	PRESCHOOL ★★	GRADE SCHOOL ★★★	TEENS ★★★
YOUNG ADULTS ★★★		OVER 30 ★★★	SENIORS ★★★★

18220 North Highway 1 (2 miles south of Fort Bragg); ☎ **707-964-4352; www.gardenbythesea.org**

Hours March–October: daily, 9 a.m.–5 p.m.; November–February: daily, 9 a.m.– 4 p.m. **Admission** $7.50 adults, $6 seniors age 60 and over, $3 teens ages 13–17, $1 children ages 6–12, free for children age 5 and under. **Touring time** Average 3 hours; minimum 1 hour. **Rainy-day touring** Not recommended. **Restaurants** Yes; garden setting. **Alcoholic beverages** No. **Disabled access** About 1 mile of paved trails. **Wheelchair rental** Electric carts. **Baby-stroller rental** No. **Lockers** No. **Pet kennels** No. **Rain check** Yes. **Private tours** Yes.

DESCRIPTION AND COMMENTS Botanical gardens, with their smooth paths and landscaped environments, can make a pleasant parklike stop for families with strollers and young children who need some safe, easy running time. This 47-acre facility is known for its rhododendrons and fuchsia gardens. Families will enjoy the easy one-mile loop trail to the ocean, and the Fern Canyon section with its six small wooden bridges over the creek. Food, gift shop, retail nursery.

Point Arena Lighthouse and Museum

APPEAL BY AGE	PRESCHOOL ★★★	GRADE SCHOOL ★★★★	TEENS ★★★★
YOUNG ADULTS ★★★★		OVER 30 ★★★★	SENIORS ★★★

Off Highway 1 just north of Point Arena; ☎ **707-882-2777; www.pointarenalighthouse.com**

Hours April–September: daily, 10 a.m.–4:30 p.m.; October–March: daily, 10 a.m.– 3:30 p.m. **Admission** $5 adults, $1 children under age 12. **Touring time** Average 1 hour; minimum 30 minutes. **Rainy-day touring** Yes. **Restaurants** No. **Alcoholic beverages** No. **Disabled access** No. **Wheelchair rental** No. **Baby-stroller rental** No. **Lockers** No. **Pet kennels** No. **Rain check** No. **Private tours** No.

DESCRIPTION AND COMMENTS The first lighthouse at this location was destroyed in the 1906 San Francisco earthquake; the current historic building, now restored, dates from 1907. It towers 115 feet over the sea, which makes for a swell view and a moderately challenging and fun climb to the top for all but the littlest kids; in spring, this is a great place to look for migrating whales. A small museum is located next to the lighthouse in the 1869 Fog Signal Building.

 ## The Skunk Train–California Western Railroad

APPEAL BY AGE	PRESCHOOL ★★★★	GRADE SCHOOL ★★★★★	TEENS ★★★
YOUNG ADULTS ★★★★		OVER 30 ★★★★★	SENIORS ★★★★★

Highway 1 and Laurel Street, Fort Bragg; ☎ 707-964-6371; www.skunktrain.com

Hours Half- and full-day trips from Fort Bragg or Willits available early June–early September; from Fort Bragg only during rest of year. **Admission** Round-trip Fort Bragg–Northspur fares: $45 and up for adults, $20 and up for kids ages 3–11. **Touring time** Average 4–5 hours for half-day trip, including boarding time and the like; minimum half-day ride is 3½ hours. **Rainy-day touring** Not recommended. **Restaurants** Snack bar at Northspur. **Alcoholic beverages** Yes. **Disabled access** Yes. **Wheelchair rental** No. **Baby-stroller rental** No. **Lockers** No. **Pet kennels** In the area. **Rain check** Yes. **Private tours** Yes.

DESCRIPTION AND COMMENTS It's a family joke that Mom liked this train ride even more than the kids did, but part of my pleasure in the excursion was of the happy-surprise variety. I was especially pleased with the go-the-extra-mile attitude of this recreational-railroad company.

We boarded the vintage passenger cars of the diesel train at the Skunk Depot in Fort Bragg and settled in to enjoy the 40-mile trip through forest and meadowland, over bridges and trestles, through tunnels and around curves. I was happy enough, and then a friendly strolling guitar player began walking through the cars, adding a festive touch with railroad-themed folk songs. At Northspur, the round-trip midpoint railroad camp, we disembarked and enjoyed a cool interlude in a shady grove where picnic tables, refreshment stands, and souvenir stands offer a country-fair feeling. The round trip from Fort Bragg to Northspur is about 3½ hours long, and reservations are advised during high season. Real buffs can inquire about riding in the cab with the engineer.

 # FAMILY-FRIENDLY RESTAURANTS

Egghead Omelettes of Oz
326 North Main Street, Fort Bragg; ☎ 707-964-5005

Meals served Breakfast and lunch. **Cuisine** American. **Entree range** $6–$13. **Kids' menu** No. **Reservations** Not accepted. **Payment** MC, V.

A fanciful place devoted to the land of Dorothy and Toto, Egghead is a great place to know about, if only for its location one block from the Skunk Train depot. Fortunately, the food is as appealing as the location: every sort of omelet imaginable, carefully prepared and happily split in two for kids, along with great pancakes and, at lunch, soups, salads, and burgers.

Mendocino Cafe

10451 Lansing Street, Mendocino; ☎ 707-937-2422

Meals served Lunch and dinner. **Cuisine** California/International. **Entree range** Lunch, $6–$10; dinner, $12–$26. **Kids' menu** Yes, $7–$8. **Reservations** Accepted. **Payment** MC, V.

Tell the kids it's Chinese or Mexican food, but know that you're settling in for some Pacific Rim–Latin–contemporary American cuisine, prepared with organic Mendocino flair: nachos with black beans, Vietnamese chicken salad, St. Louis–style ribs, Brazilian seafood stew, Thai *tom yum* soup, scampi. The menu is all over the map, and it's all tasty. Good kids' menu.

North Coast Brewing Company

455 North Main Street, Fort Bragg; ☎ 707-964-2739;
www.northcoastbrewing.com

Meals served Dinner. **Cuisine** American. **Entree range** $9–$17. **Kids' menu** No. **Reservations** Recommended. **Payment** All major credit cards.

Okay, maybe a brewpub doesn't seem like the ideal place for kids, but this one is relaxed and family friendly, and the food is terrific. Try the Route 66 chili, the shrimp and chips, the huge burger, or the Carolina-style barbecued pulled pork. Excellent local wines and a fun outdoor patio.

HUMBOLDT *and* DEL NORTE COUNTIES:
Eureka, Trinidad, and Redwoods

THE MOST NORTHERLY COAST OF CALIFORNIA is big country—big trees, big rivers, big mountains, and big distances. There are both state and national redwood parks, quaint seaport villages, and plenty of opportunities for outdoor adventures, from river rafting to rock climbing. The city of **Eureka** is the best base for exploring the area, and it's where you'll connect to the highway east to **Lake Shasta.**

Whatever you do up here, make sure to visit **Humboldt Redwoods State Park,** especially **Avenue of the Giants,** the road winding through an astounding primeval redwood forest (see listing under "Family Lodging"). If at all possible, you should camp out in the state park, one of the most beautiful family campgrounds in the country.

Eureka's renovated Victorian-era Old Town neighborhood brings the days of the free-spending lumber barons to mind, but **Old Town Eureka** also makes for a fun afternoon of dining and shopping. We don't recommend taking the kids on the historic walking tours, but look for the local children's museum with interactive exhibits, **Discovery Museum** (see profile in "Attractions"). Also see "The Best Beaches and Parks" for several important sites.

With a picturesque village perched on a promontory above a tiny harbor with a pier, a lighthouse (replica of the 1871 original), and a dozen pretty shops and cafes, **Trinidad** is home to some motels and bed-and-breakfasts, and it makes a restful overnight on the way to or from the redwoods. We hiked the **Trinidad Head Trail** to look down on the beach, had supper in the harbor, and had a fine time shopping in the crafts stores.

◾▐ FAMILY LODGING

Bishop Pine Lodge
1481 Patricks Point Drive, Trinidad; ☎ 707-677-3314; www.bishoppinelodge.com; $96 for 4 people; $120 with kitchen; $10 extra person/pet fee

A funky but utterly charming little cabin resort in the pines behind the village of Trinidad. We loved the old-fashioned playground and the chance to

humboldt and del norte counties

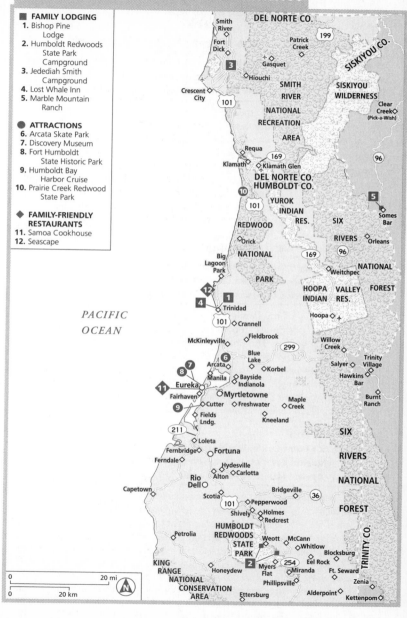

FAMILY LODGING
1. Bishop Pine Lodge
2. Humboldt Redwoods State Park Campground
3. Jedediah Smith Campground
4. Lost Whale Inn
5. Marble Mountain Ranch

ATTRACTIONS
6. Arcata Skate Park
7. Discovery Museum
8. Fort Humboldt State Historic Park
9. Humboldt Bay Harbor Cruise
10. Prairie Creek Redwood State Park

FAMILY-FRIENDLY RESTAURANTS
11. Samoa Cookhouse
12. Seascape

PACIFIC OCEAN

DEL NORTE CO.

Smith River
Fort Dick
Patrick Creek
199
Gasquet
Hiouchi
Crescent City
101
SMITH RIVER NATIONAL RECREATION AREA
SISKIYOU CO.
SISKIYOU WILDERNESS
Clear Creek (Pick-a-Wish)

Requa
169
Klamath
Klamath Glen
96
DEL NORTE CO.
HUMBOLDT CO.
YUROK INDIAN RES.
REDWOOD NATIONAL PARK
Orick
Big Lagoon Park
169
Weitchpec
HOOPA VALLEY INDIAN RES.
SIX RIVERS NATIONAL FOREST
Somes Bar
Orleans
96
Trinidad
Crannell
101
Fieldbrook
McKinleyville
299
Blue Lake
Arcata
Korbel
Manila
Bayside
Indianola
Eureka
Myrtletowne
Fairhaven
Cutter
Freshwater
Maple Creek
Kneeland
Hoopa
Willow Creek
Salyer
Hawkins Bar
Trinity Village
Burnt Ranch
Fields Lndg.
211
Loleta
Fernbridge
Fortuna
Ferndale
Hydesville
Carlotta
Alton
Rio Dell
Capetown
Scotia
101
Bridgeville
36
Pepperwood
Shively
Holmes
Redcrest
SIX RIVERS NATIONAL FOREST
Petrolia
HUMBOLDT REDWOODS STATE PARK
Weott
McCann
Whitlow
254
Miranda
Eel Rock
Blocksburg
Ft. Seward
KING RANGE NATIONAL CONSERVATION AREA
Honeydew
Myers Flat
Phillipsville
Ettersburg
Alderpoint
Zenia
Kettenpom
TRINITY CO.

0   20 mi
0   20 km
N

sit on the porch and look at those bright, bright stars in the rural sky. Twelve wooden cottages and two two-bedrooms; some have kitchens and barbecues on the decks. Outside is a barbecue area.

 ## Humboldt Redwoods State Park Campground

45 miles south of Eureka off Highway 101, Humboldt; ☎ 707-946-2409;
www.humboldtredwoods.org; reservations: Reserve America,
☎ 800-444-7275, www.reserveamerica.com; campsites $12–$22

unofficial **TIP**
The best way to help your family absorb the majesty of the giant redwoods is to live with them for a day or two at one of the park's campgrounds.

Try to spend more time in this remarkable state park than just driving through to see the incredible old-growth redwoods—although whether you camp here or not, you must take the 30-mile drive called Avenue of the Giants. The two campgrounds here are Burlington, near the park headquarters, and Hidden Springs. Each area has restrooms, hot showers, and laundry tubs, as well as evening campfire programs and interpretive programs in the summer.

 ## Jedediah Smith Campground

4241 Kings Valley Road, Crescent City; ☎ 707-464-6101;
reservations: Reserve America, ☎ 800-444-7275;
www.reserveamerica.com; campsites $12 and up

The happiest stay of my family's see-the-redwoods trip when I was a kid, Jedediah Smith continues to be a superb family campground in a setting of God-fearing beauty. The Smith River runs right through the redwood-studded campground, and kids love to splash, fish, and paddle rafts in it. This park is warmer than some of the coastal camps, because it's inland enough to avoid much fog. A footbridge over the river leads to the marvelous Simpson-Reed Discovery Trail, an educational loop that's easy even for toddlers. Flush toilets, showers, picnic tables, fireplaces.

Lost Whale Inn
3452 Patrick's Point Drive, Trinidad; ☎ 707-677-3425;
www.lostwhaleinn.com; May–October: $200–$230;
November–April: $140–$170; extra adult $25, extra child $20

Usually a bed-and-breakfast on a prime piece of coastal land like this is aimed at romancing couples, and children are as welcome as Scud missiles. Not so here. Some of the rooms and suites are great for families (ask for one with a sleeping loft), and while they're certainly charming, with wood floors and ocean views, they're not full of delicate antiques. The kids won't mind the lack of TV when they can pick berries, play in the playhouse and playground, feed ducks, and look for whales or sea lions. The rough beach is fun for (supervised) tide pooling, otter spotting, and rock climbing, but not swimming—but the kids can take a cold shower in the waterfall. While Dad's at the beach with the kids, Mom can get an in-room hot-stone massage.

Marble Mountain Ranch

92520 Highway 96, Somes Bar; ☎ 530-469-3322 or 800-552-6284; www.marblemountainranch.com; housekeeping cabins $60 for 2 people, plus $20 per extra person (kids under age 6 stay free); deluxe cabin homes $100–$200 double occupancy, plus $30 per extra person (kids under age 6 stay free); tent sites and RV hookups $15; all-inclusive family vacations offered; packages include accommodations, meals, and 1 activity per day

For the ambitious, this guest ranch at the edge of the Marble Mountain wilderness offers pack trips into the wilds. For the rest of us, it's possible to enjoy a night or a week in the company of the ranch's 18 horses and various dogs, goats, and chickens. Self-guided activities include horseback riding and, in fall, drift-boat fishing; guided excursions include rafting, mountain biking, and horseback riding (one-hour to custom multiday adventures). The lodge serves family-style meals nightly and a weekend Western barbecue, and the deli packs lunches to take along on hikes. Accommodations vary from RV hookups and tent sites to no-frills housekeeping cabins (which sleep up to six) and fancier "deluxe cabin homes." Kids (and parents) never get bored here, thanks to the games (air hockey, Ping-Pong), zip cable, swings, swimming pool, bocce ball, petting farm, casting pond, and sparkling lake for swimming and fishing.

◼️ ATTRACTIONS

Arcata Skate Park

APPEAL BY AGE	PRESCHOOL ★	GRADE SCHOOL ★★★★	TEENS ★★★★
YOUNG ADULTS ★★		OVER 30 ★	SENIORS ★

900 Sunset Avenue, Arcata; ☎ 707-822-7091

Hours Open daily in daylight hours. **Admission** Free. **Touring time** Average 2 hours; minimum 1 hour. **Rainy-day touring** No. **Restaurants** No. **Alcoholic beverages** No. **Disabled access** No. **Wheelchair rental** No. **Baby-stroller rental** No. **Lockers** No. **Pet kennels** No. **Rain check** No. **Private tours** No.

DESCRIPTION AND COMMENTS Skateboard heaven, right off Highway 101, with three bowls, good rails, a fun box, and lots of vertical edges. Helmets are required.

Discovery Museum

APPEAL BY AGE	PRESCHOOL ★★★★	GRADE SCHOOL ★★★	TEENS ★
YOUNG ADULTS ★		OVER 30 ★	SENIORS ★

Third and F streets, Eureka; ☎ 707-443-9694

Hours Tuesday–Saturday, 10 a.m.–4 p.m.; Sunday, noon–4 p.m. **Admission** $4, free for children age 3 and under. **Touring time** Average 2 hours; minimum 1 hour. **Rainy-day touring** Yes. **Restaurants** No. **Alcoholic beverages** No. **Disabled access** Some. **Wheelchair rental** No. **Baby-stroller rental** No. **Lockers** No. **Pet kennels** No. **Rain check** No. **Private tours** No.

unofficial **TIP**
The Discovery Museum is a godsend for young children on a rainy day.

DESCRIPTION AND COMMENTS The sweeping vistas, big trees, and dramatic vistas of the North Coast are best suited to older kids—so we're thankful for this friendly haven for the little ones. It's a cheerful, small-town children's museum with a dozen or so interactive, play-based exhibits that are great for preschoolers and early-elementary kids. They can play in a mini-hospital, learn about North Coast ecology, pretend to build a house, and do much more.

Fort Humboldt State Historic Park

APPEAL BY AGE	PRESCHOOL ★	GRADE SCHOOL ★★	TEENS ★★
YOUNG ADULTS ★★		OVER 30 ★★	SENIORS ★★

Fort Avenue off Highlands Avenue, Eureka; ☎ 707-445-6567 or 707-488-2041; www.parks.ca.gov

Hours Open daily in daylight hours. **Admission** Free. **Touring time** Average 1 hour; minimum 1 hour. **Rainy-day touring** Not great. **Restaurants** No. **Alcoholic beverages** No. **Disabled access** Yes. **Wheelchair rental** No. **Baby-stroller rental** No. **Lockers** No. **Pet kennels** No. **Rain check** No. **Private tours** No, docents available.

DESCRIPTION AND COMMENTS This 19th-century fort has been partly reconstructed and is a testimony to some of the grim, violent history of the area. Exhibits on gold mining, logging, and Native American history; look for junior ranger activities in summertime.

Humboldt Bay Harbor Cruise

APPEAL BY AGE	PRESCHOOL ★★★★	GRADE SCHOOL ★★★★	TEENS ★★★
YOUNG ADULTS ★★★		OVER 30 ★★★★	SENIORS ★★★★

Foot of F Street, Eureka; ☎ 707-444-9440;
www.humboldtbaymaritimemuseum.com

Hours March–October: cruises depart Monday–Saturday at 1 p.m., 2:30 p.m., and 4 p.m.; Sunday, 1 p.m. and 2:30 p.m. **Admission** $15 adults, $13 children ages 12–17, $7.50 children ages 4–11. **Touring time** Average 3 hours; minimum 2 hours (allow for boarding and the like). **Rainy-day touring** Not recommended. **Restaurants** Cocktail brunches, dinner cruises. **Alcoholic beverages** Yes. **Disabled access** Yes. **Wheelchair rental** With notice. **Baby-stroller rental** No. **Lockers** No. **Pet kennels** No; pets allowed on cruise. **Rain check** Yes. **Private tours** No.

DESCRIPTION AND COMMENTS A tiny, storybook-like 1910 ferry (which holds just 49 people) takes visitors on a 1-hour, 15-minute tour of the Humboldt Bay area, past sawmills, a former Indian village, and bird habitats. The narration will bore little ones, but the stories are interesting enough to engage older kids. Kids can watch for fishing boats, otters, and special birds, while Mom and Dad can belly up to the smallest licensed bar in the state.

 Prairie Creek Redwood State Park

APPEAL BY AGE	PRESCHOOL ★★★★	GRADE SCHOOL ★★★★	TEENS ★★★
YOUNG ADULTS ★★★★		OVER 30 ★★★★	SENIORS ★★★★

Highway 101, 6 miles north of Orick; ☎ 707-464-6101, ext. 5301

Hours Daily, 24 hours. **Admission** Day-use fee $6; $2 per dog (leashed only); limited number of day-use permits issued. **Touring time** Average a half day; minimum 2 hours. **Rainy-day touring** Not great. **Restaurants** No. **Alcoholic beverages** No. **Disabled access** Some trails. **Wheelchair rental** No. **Baby-stroller rental** No. **Lockers** No. **Pet kennels** No. **Rain check** No. **Private tours** No.

DESCRIPTION AND COMMENTS This state park also happens to be a UNESCO-designated World Heritage Site. It's particularly worth a family visit because of its daily (in summer) one-hour junior ranger programs for children ages 7 to 12. The other great reason, aside from the usual amazing forests of redwoods, is the herd of protected native Roosevelt elk roaming the 40,000 acres, often in the meadow near the highway. The 75 miles of trails include wheelchair-accessible routes. Interpretive exhibits on the elk and other flora and fauna of the region are offered. A nature walk near the visitors center takes you to Chimney Tree, where a family lived in the 1930s; little kids love the half-mile loop trail into Fern Canyon. Also consider camping here—there are 100 family campsites, including some on the beach.

 # FAMILY-FRIENDLY RESTAURANTS

Samoa Cookhouse
445 West Washington, Samoa Road, Eureka; ☎ 707-442-1659

Meals served Breakfast, lunch, and dinner. **Cuisine** Lumberjack American. **Entree range** $8–$13. **Kids' menu** $4–$6; children under age 5, free. **Reservations** Not accepted. **Payment** All major credit cards.

If you have an overeater in the family, don't stop here. It's an old lumber-camp cookhouse, and it serves meals as if we are all lumberjacks. Diners seat themselves at long tables, and family groups are brought platters heaped with chicken, ham, or fish (depending on what the cook's up to that night), vegetables, breads, and dessert—it's an all-you-can-eat feast. Equally hearty breakfasts and lunches are served. For anyone with the willpower to avoid a stomachache, it's a fun stop—the tables have checkered cloths, and there's a mini-museum of old-time kitchen and logging equipment.

Seascape
Trinidad Harbor at the foot of Bay Street, Trinidad; ☎ 707-677-3762

Meals served Breakfast, lunch, and dinner. **Cuisine** American. **Entree range** $5–$20. **Kids' menu** $3. **Reservations** Only accepted for 5 or more. **Payment** MC, V.

Right at the harbor in Trinidad, this place is notable mostly for its views of the pier, bay, and harbor seals right outside the window. The food is fine: good breakfasts (try the blackberry pancakes), basic burgers, fish and chips, omelets, and, at dinner, fresh seafood.

TRINITY *and* SHASTA COUNTIES

WE'RE TALKING AN AREA AS BIG AS SOME STATES when it comes to these two counties, and the landscapes they encompass are impressive Western mountain pine forests and big-deal rivers—the kind that inspire people to build dams.

The city of **Redding** is where the **Central Valley** meets the mountains, but it's no vacation mecca—that honor is reserved for the awkwardly named **Whiskeytown, Shasta, Trinity National Recreation Area.** Above it all towers **Mount Shasta,** a dormant volcano whose slopes are home to five living glaciers. A mountain that has figured in legends and lore of several cultures, its snow-shrouded peak is often circled with mysteriously shaped clouds.

FAMILY LODGING

Bridge Bay Resort
10300 Bridge Bay Road, Shasta Lake; ☎ 530-275-3021 or 800-752-9669; www.sevencrown.com; $89–$185

A just-okay 40-room marina motel that we nevertheless valued highly because we were just knocked out after days of fresh air and water—we simply couldn't get back in the car and cover more miles. So we extended our stay, relaxed in the air-conditioned room, and floated in the pool. You'll want to stay in this motel the night before you patio-boat or begin a house-boat vacation, or the night after you spend a day or a few days on the lake. There's a restaurant, a mini-mart, and some larger units with kitchens.

Coffee Creek Ranch

Coffee Creek Road off Highway 3, HC 2, Box 4940, Trinity Center; ☎ 530-266-3343 or 800-624-4480; www.coffeecreekranch.com; $1,045–$1,065 per week for adults, $925–$945 per week for children (children under age 3 stay free), $1,025–$1,045 per week for teens; daily rates $189–$213; riding in summer is extra

A well-regarded family dude ranch, Coffee Creek is located in the Trinity Alps at 3,100 feet elevation. Guests should be inclined to spend a lot of *trinity and shasta counties*

ACCOMMODATIONS
1. Bridge Bay Resort
2. Coffee Creek Ranch
3. Railroad Park Resort

ATTRACTIONS
4. Lake Shasta, Shasta-Trinity National Forest

5. Shasta Caverns
6. Weaverville Joss House State Historic Park

RESTAURANTS
7. Railroad Park Restaurant

0   10 mi
0   10 km

time on horseback, as that's the main activity. Other activities include volleyball, archery, canoeing, square dancing, pedalboating, basketball, and hayrides. The ranch also has a pool, rifle range, and trout pond; kid programs include the Kiddie Corral, with supervised play for toddlers; games, hikes, and pony rides for 3- to 7-year-olds; and horsemanship, roping, and hiking programs for older kids. Fifty guests a week can be accommodated in the rustic, comfortable cabins, all with fireplaces or potbellied stoves. Riders must be at least 5 years old for all rides; no one under 8 years of age is permitted on all-day trips, but lessons are available for kids age 4 and up.

Railroad Park Resort

100 Railroad Park Road, Dunsmuir; ☎ 530-235-4440; www.rrpark.com; $90–$210, plus $8 for each person over 2 people; rooms sleep up to 5; $10 pet fee; camping fees $20–$28

In the town of Dunsmuir just south of Mount Shasta and near Castle Crags State Park, a collection of old freight-train cabooses are linked together to make an atmospheric family motel. The cabooses surround a pool, spa, and deck; inside the cabooses are motel rooms, each decorated differently. Also on the property are four cabins with kitchens, a restored water tower, a huge logging steam engine, and an RV campground with a creek, swimming hole, and convenience store. The train-car restaurant is a fun place to eat.

 # ATTRACTIONS

Lake Shasta, Shasta-Trinity National Forest

APPEAL BY AGE	PRESCHOOL ★★★★		GRADE SCHOOL ★★★★	TEENS ★★★★
YOUNG ADULTS ★★★★		OVER 30 ★★★★		SENIORS ★★★★

(For patio boating or houseboating on lake)
2400 Washington Avenue, Redding; ☎ 530-275-1587; www.fs.fed.us/r5/shastatrinity

Hours Vary. **Admission** Free; fees for boat rental; camping $16–$26 per night. **Touring time** Average 1 day; minimum 4 hours. **Rainy-day touring** Not great. **Restaurants** Mostly snack bars. **Alcoholic beverages** Limited. **Disabled access** Some. **Wheelchair rental** No. **Baby-stroller rental** No. **Lockers** No. **Pet kennels** No. **Rain check** No. **Private tours** No.

DESCRIPTION AND COMMENTS This man-made lake is so large that once you chug away from the dock on your houseboat, patio boat, or water-ski boat, you'll feel as if you could get lost for days. The water is cool and exhilarating for swimming; fishermen pull up 21 varieties of fish; and the slopes surrounding the lake are covered in pine forest. See "Family Outdoor Adventures" for more on patio boating and houseboating. For camping reservations in the forest, call ☎ 800-365-CAMP.

Shasta Caverns

APPEAL BY AGE	PRESCHOOL ★★	GRADE SCHOOL ★★★★	TEENS ★★★★
YOUNG ADULTS ★★★		OVER 30 ★★★	SENIORS ★★★★

20359 Shasta Caverns Road, O'Brien; ☎ 530-238-2341 or 800-795-CAVE; www.lakeshastacaverns.com

Hours Summer: daily, 9 a.m.–4 p.m., with tours every half hour; April, May, September: daily, 9 a.m.–3 p.m., with tours every hour; winter: tours leave at 10 a.m., noon, and 2 p.m. **Admission** $20 adults, $17 seniors age 65 and older, $12 children ages 4–11, free for children age 3 and under. **Touring time** Average 2 hours; minimum 2 hours. **Rainy-day touring** No problem. **Restaurants** Snack bar. **Alcoholic beverages** No. **Disabled access** No. **Wheelchair rental** No. **Baby-stroller rental** No. **Lockers** No. **Pet kennels** Staff will care for. **Rain check** No. **Private tours** No.

DESCRIPTION AND COMMENTS We took a day off from the sun, sunburn, and water sports of Lake Shasta to descend into the cool, eerie depth of Shasta Caverns. This is not an excursion for little ones or anyone who has trouble walking—the day begins with a steep descent to a boat that takes you across Lake Shasta to board a bus that takes you, gears grinding, up a narrow steep road to the top of a mountain. In the course of visiting the cave you'll go up or down more than 600 steps. But for the energetic and hardy, it's a worthwhile look at those always-amazing underground formations, culminating in a 60-foot room of crystal-studded "draperies."

Weaverville Joss House State Historic Park

APPEAL BY AGE	PRESCHOOL ★★	GRADE SCHOOL ★★★★	TEENS ★★★★
YOUNG ADULTS ★★★		OVER 30 ★★★	SENIORS ★★★★

Main Street, Highway 299 West, Weaverville; ☎ 530-623-5284 or 530-225-2065; www.parks.ca.gov

Hours Memorial Day–August: daily, 10 a.m.–5 p.m., with tours on the hour; December–March: Saturday, with tours on the hour. **Admission** $2 adults, free for those under 16. **Touring time** Average 1 hour; minimum 30-minute walk-through tour of Temple. **Rainy-day touring** Adjustments made on the tours. **Restaurants** Nearby. **Alcoholic beverages** No. **Disabled access** With assistance. **Wheelchair rental** No. **Baby-stroller rental** No. **Lockers** No. **Pet kennels** No. **Rain check** No. **Private tours** Yes.

DESCRIPTION AND COMMENTS On the road to Shasta Lake from the North Coast is a reminder that California's ethnic diversity is no new development. The Weaverville Joss House is the oldest continuously used Chinese temple in California, named by its builders "The Temple of the Forest beneath the Clouds" (an apt description of its setting). Descendants of the gold miners who built this temple still worship here in the Taoist tradition. Art objects, mining tools, and other artifacts are on display. The temple is open to the public only for guided tours.

FAMILY-FRIENDLY RESTAURANT

Railroad Park Restaurant
100 Railroad Park Road, Dunsmuir; ☎ **530-235-4611**

Meals served Dinner. **Cuisine** American. **Entree range** $10–$19. **Kids' menu** Yes. **Reservations** Recommended. **Payment** All major credit cards.

A collection of 100-year-old train cars makes up this charming family restaurant next to the motel of the same name. Kids love the setting, and they're welcomed with a children's menu. The food is straightforward, moderately upscale dinner-house American, and there's a full bar.

FAMILY LODGING INDEX

RESTAURANTS INDEX

SUBJECT INDEX

Unofficial Guide Reader Survey

If you'd like to express your opinion about traveling in California with kids or this guidebook, complete the following survey and mail it to:

Unofficial Guide Reader Survey
P.O. Box 43673
Birmingham, AL 35243

Inclusive dates of your visit:_____

Members of your party:

	Person 1	Person 2	Person 3	Person 4	Person 5
Gender:	M F	M F	M F	M F	M F
Age:					

How many times have you been to California? _____
On your most recent trip, where did you stay? _____

Concerning your accommodations, on a scale of 100 as best and 0 as worst, how would you rate:

The quality of your room?   The value of your room?
The quietness of your room?   Check-in/checkout efficiency?
Shuttle service to the airport?   Swimming pool facilities?

Did you rent a car?_____   From whom?_____

Concerning your rental car, on a scale of 100 as best and 0 as worst, how would you rate:

Pickup-processing efficiency?_____   Return processing efficiency?___
Condition of the car?_____   Cleanliness of the car?_____
Airport shuttle efficiency?_____

Concerning your dining experiences:

Estimate your meals in restaurants per day? _____
Approximately how much did your party spend on meals per day? ____

_____

Favorite restaurants in California: _____

_____

Did you buy this guide before leaving? _____ While on your trip?_____

How did you hear about this guide? (check all that apply)

Loaned or recommended by a friend □   Radio or TV □
Newspaper or magazine □   Bookstore salesperson □
Just picked it out on my own □   Library □
Internet □

What other guidebooks did you use on this trip? _____

_____

_____

_____

On a scale of 100 as best and 0 as worst, how would you rate them?

_____

_____

_____

Using the same scale, how would you rate the *Unofficial Guide*(s)?

_____

Are *Unofficial Guides* readily available at bookstores in your area? _____

Have you used other *Unofficial Guides*? _____

Which one(s)? _____

_____

_____

Comments about your California trip or the *Unofficial Guide*(s):

_____

_____

_____

_____

_____

_____

_____

_____

_____

_____

_____

_____

_____

_____

_____

_____

_____

_____